10759973

BOSS LINCOLN

ALSO BY MATTHEW PINSKER

Lincoln's Sanctuary: Abraham Lincoln and the Soldiers' Home

Abraham Lincoln (American Presidents Reference Series)

BOSS LINCOLN

The Partisan Life of Abraham Lincoln

MATTHEW PINSKER

W. W. NORTON & COMPANY

Independent Publishers Since 1923

Printed in the United States of America
First Edition

For information about special discounts for bulk purchases, please contact W. W. Norton Special Sales at specialsales@wwnorton.com or 800-233-4830

Manufacturing by Lakeside Book Company
Production manager: Lauren Abbate

ISBN 978-0-393-24078-8

W. W. Norton & Company, Inc., 500 Fifth Avenue, New York, NY 10110
www.wwnorton.com

W. W. Norton & Company Ltd., 15 Carlisle Street, London W1D 3BS

1 0 9 8 7 6 5 4 3 2 1

For Boss Rachel—

Who rules our household with love

and maybe just a little bit of fear

A free people, in times of peace and quiet—when pressed by no common danger—naturally divide into parties. At such times, the man who is of neither party, is not, cannot be, of any consequence.

—Abraham Lincoln, age forty-three (July 6, 1852)

CONTENTS

PART III UNIONIST

BOSS LINCOLN

INTRODUCTION

ONE OF THE FIRST depictions of Abraham Lincoln in the national press mocked him as little more than a country politician. In the summer of 1847, the *Boston Courier* sent a special correspondent, Joseph H. Buckingham, to cover the Chicago River and Harbor Convention, a political gathering organized in the fast-growing city on Lake Michigan. One of Buckingham's more memorable reports detailed the aftermath of the convention, when he took a daylong stagecoach trip through the Illinois prairie with two of the state's top delegates: Robert Smith, an incumbent Democratic congressman representing an Illinois district across the river from St. Louis, and the thirty-eight-year-old Lincoln, a member of the rival Whig party and recently elected as congressman from the district around Springfield.

Buckingham found the banter of these politicians tiresome and seemed to reserve special ridicule for Lincoln, whom he did not identify by name. "We are now in the district represented by our Whig congressman," the reporter sniffed as they approached the state capital, "and he knew, or appeared to know, every body we met, the name of the tenant of every farm-house and the owner of every plat of ground." With disdain, Buckingham added, "Such a shaking of hands—such a how-d'ye-do—such a greeting of different kinds, as we saw, was never seen before; it seemed as if he knew every thing, and he had a kind word, a smile and a bow for every body on the road, even to the horses and the cattle, and the swine."[1]

This amusing account, which Buckingham included in a travel series called "Letters from the West," offers more than a rare contemporary portrait of a future president ingratiating himself with his rural constituents. The details concerning the convention and the subsequent stagecoach journey illustrate an overlooked dimension of Lincoln's improbable rise to power. That week in July 1847 marked a pivotal moment in his career as a political party leader.

The Chicago River and Harbor Convention was a major event of the 1840s. Buckingham opened his reporting by calling the gathering "great, long-talked of, and very important." He claimed nearly twenty thousand people were in attendance—more than the population of the city at the time. The estimate of Horace Greeley, editor of the country's leading Whig newspaper, the *New-York Tribune*, was a more "judicious" ten thousand delegates. Thurlow Weed, an influential Whig editor from Albany, simply concluded: "This is undoubtedly the largest deliberative body that ever assembled."[2]

Whig newspapers had been promoting the convention for months. Its purpose was to cultivate support for internal improvements along the nation's inland waterways, with a focus on better dredging for the harbors and passages along the Ohio and Mississippi rivers and around the Great Lakes. The Whigs hoped at Chicago to engage politicos across party lines, a process known as "fusion." Party leaders sensed opportunity because President James K. Polk, a Democrat, had been blocking attempts by the Democratic-controlled U.S. Congress to fund these expenditures. On August 3, 1846, the president even vetoed a river and harbor bill passed by Congress, denouncing it as unconstitutional and too costly for "comparatively unimportant objects."[3]

Polk's dismissive veto message inflamed residents of the country's western interior, regardless of party affiliation. A coterie of influential northern businessmen also considered Polk's rigid views to be shortsighted. But the president was indifferent to the criticism because his focus was elsewhere. After pressing for the annexation of Texas during his election contest in 1844, Polk was now leading a war against Mexico designed to secure the nation's southwestern border from foreign threats—by imperial Great Britain as much as by newly independent Mexico. Antislavery northerners were suspicious of the Tennessee Democrat's expansionist policies, however, fearing that his war-making was more about adding new slaveholding states than legitimate security concerns. These "free soilers" were also working across party lines to prevent the spread of slavery into the western territories.

Whig strategists believed that Polk's denunciation of federal spending was a response to the rising fusionist pressures. They thought his larger purpose was to mobilize the party of Andrew Jackson—the Democratic hero, just recently deceased, who had been a strict constructionist himself. But many Democratic leaders were unhappy with Polk and disagreed with his veto. The nation's partisan future appeared to be at a crossroads.

Lincoln was elected to Congress on the same day in August 1846 that Polk vetoed the river and harbor bill. Lincoln's victory capped a remarkable journey for an unlikely political figure who had been "raised to farm work," as he once put it, growing up with his family in the western states of Kentucky, Indiana, and Illinois. Once on his own, Lincoln became a prominent local politician and lawyer in Illinois, residing by the 1840s in the state capital of Springfield with his wife and young children. The Polk veto infuriated the congressman-elect, who had been an advocate of waterways improvements since his earliest days in politics.[4]

Lincoln's decision to attend the meeting on rivers and harbors at Chicago meant that he would miss a convention in Springfield charged with revising the state's constitution. Not many leading lawyers or politicians from central Illinois made the same choice. Lincoln went to Chicago—his first trip to the young city—mainly owing to his responsibilities as de facto leader of the Illinois Whig party. As an organized political movement, the Whigs were only about as old as Lincoln's own career in politics, which had begun, not long after his arrival in Illinois, with an unsuccessful run for the state legislature in 1832. The Whigs came together as a national party during the early 1830s under the leadership of Senator Henry Clay of Kentucky. Positioned in opposition to President Jackson's Democratic administration, the Whigs became best known for supporting a strong federal government capable of underwriting national economic development, especially through internal improvements of roads, canals, railroads, rivers, and harbors. Whigs also advocated social reforms such as restrictions on the sale of alcohol that were designed to make America more orderly and, in their view, more Christian. But on the issue of slavery's future, Whigs, like Democrats, were divided into regional factions. Both national parties had been struggling for years to contain the sectional and moral passions over slavery's place in American society.[5]

Lincoln's adopted hometown of Springfield was a Whig stronghold, but outside the state capital, their partisan landscape in Illinois appeared bleak. By 1847, Illinois Whigs controlled no statewide offices. They were in the minority in both chambers of the General Assembly. Out of the state's seven congressional districts, they held one seat—Congressman-Elect Lincoln's. He was the state's leading Whig almost by default.

This shaky distinction brought with it a precarious leadership status because partisan organizations were still relatively new and built mostly on vapors. There had always been factions or parties in the United States. In the 1780s, Federalists and Anti-Federalists had vied over the ratification of the new constitution, followed in the next decade by Jeffersonians and Hamiltonians, who battled over its implementation in the new republic. Those political contests evolved in subsequent decades, but mass party organizations—with fixed partisan labels, regular conventions, and central committees—developed only during the clashes between Jackson and Clay. And party structures and operations were still not settled. Voters did not have to register to participate in elections before the Civil War; nor did parties maintain headquarters staffed by political regulars. They raised and spent campaign money in haphazard, unreported fashion. Political parties operated through appointed committees and met in election-year conventions, but they often struggled to adopt policy platforms and nominate slates of candidates. Between elections, party leaders tried to hold everything together through networks of loyal newspapers and the implicit bonds of government jobs or "patronage." The result was a "party system" that was not very systematic.[6]

Party organization was, however, Lincoln's life's work. To understand Lincoln as a politician, we must recognize that he was not an office seeker so much as a party builder, and that his peculiar talent for party management was the driving force in his political career. We don't remember him as "Boss Lincoln," but we should. Lincoln was not a midwestern Boss Tweed running a prairie-style Tammany Hall, demanding loyalty from his minions, and lining his own pockets. He was instead a master of "men and measures," a phrase used in that era to highlight the combination of patronage and policy considered essential to successful political movements.[7]

Lincoln helped to build three party organizations in his years as a politician: Whigs, Republicans, and Unionists. This book examines

Lincoln's party-building strategies as he crafted and implemented them, mostly behind the scenes. The result is a biography of a party leader, one that focuses on his pivotal strategic choices, including those that helped save a divided nation. The more familiar public Lincoln—the orator, debater, and writer—certainly appears in these pages. But my focus is on the party boss who operated in the political shadows at private meetings, during long carriage rides and other stolen moments, and through his extensive private correspondence.

Lincoln sounded much different in private than he did in public. He offered his party colleagues little prose poetry and rarely indulged in the warm, folksy language of his popular legend. The partisan Lincoln was intense—barking out orders, providing advice, pressing others to stay on task. The famously unkempt prairie attorney was methodical about political organization. There were still flashes of humor, but as a party leader Lincoln wielded a sarcastic wit to get things done. And what he wanted done was inevitably to forge and maintain a winning partisan strategy organized around enduring principles.

The partisan strategies of the time revolved around two competing impulses: ultraism and fusionism. The "ultra" approach aimed to mobilize party organization around a core constituency or set of policies—defining what today we would term "the base." Ultraism shaped how participants viewed men, measures, or both. "Old Line" Whigs treated their party as a type of fraternity, resistant to newcomers, especially immigrants. There were ideological ultras, such as "radical" Republicans who advocated emancipation and equality for African Americans. They also pushed for a more aggressive war against the Confederates and criticized what they viewed as Lincoln's failures to purge the Federal military of its most suspect Democratic officers. The ultraist model established party tests to help purify political purpose.

Fusionism offered an outward-looking alternative to the more inner-facing ultra strategy. Fusionists sought to expand rather than intensify their movements by co-opting old political rivals or third parties into broader, more viable electoral coalitions. The organizing effort for improvements of rivers and harbors was about fusion. So, at first, was the antebellum Republican movement, as its architects sought to build an antislavery fusion between former Whigs and former Democrats across the free states. Fusionists could be pragmatic to a fault and often appeared opportunistic to contemporaries. They were not, however, bipartisan. Fusionists crossed party lines but, in most cases, only to maximize their own party advantage.

Over the trajectory of Lincoln's partisan career, he shifted from one strategy to the other before learning how to alternate between them in a more fluid fashion. The young Lincoln began in politics as an independent who tried to navigate the nascent Jacksonian parties by appealing to nearly everyone. Soon he settled on a Whig affiliation and rose quickly inside his chosen party. He admired Henry Clay, the party's founder, but became more of a Whig fusionist than a reliable Clay supporter. That was why he backed General William Henry Harrison for the Whig presidential nomination in 1840, and why he devoted much of his lone congressional term to campaigning for the nomination of General Zachary Taylor over Clay in 1848. Harrison and Taylor both won their elections—the only Whigs to do so at the national level—but their victories ultimately proved disappointing for the party and especially for Lincoln.

Lincoln's decision to become a Republican grew out of his frustration with Whig politics. By the mid-1850s, his long-standing commitment to fusion positioned him to be one of the most effective organizers for the new Republican party in Illinois as it attempted to unite old partisan enemies over antislavery principles. Once Lincoln and the Republicans started experiencing greater electoral success in the state, his partisan strategy shifted. Lincoln was never an antislavery radical, but he became an ultra Republican. During the late

1850s, he worked to purify the party's men and measures in Illinois and across the nation. Most notably, he held out against a proposed fusion with Senator Stephen Douglas and his northern Democratic followers. In 1857 and 1858, Douglas broke with President James Buchanan and other national Democrats over slavery policy in the Kansas territory. Some leading Republicans in the East wanted to capitalize on this split by getting Douglas to switch parties. Lincoln's decisive role in opposing this gambit nearly won him a seat in the U.S. Senate in 1858 and eventually helped make him the Republican presidential nominee in 1860.

Lincoln's antebellum partisan experiences also prepared him to become an effective wartime president. His officeholding experience before entering the White House was limited to four terms as a state legislator and a single term as congressman. After leaving Washington in 1849, he held no public office until his inauguration as president in 1861. But in his years as a Whig and Republican chieftain, he learned the craft of coalition building. As president, he put these skills to work leading a divided nation.

Lincoln tried at first to manage the Civil War on a dual track, supporting Republican policies and patronage as executive head of government while mobilizing partisans of all stripes for military service as commander in chief. But with Republican leaders at odds over this strategy, the balancing act soon proved untenable. Republicans such as Secretary of State William Seward believed in a broader patriotic fusion called "no party now" that aimed for a wartime bipartisanship. More radical party leaders, such as Secretary of the Treasury Salmon Chase, insisted on an "unconditional" unionism that embraced vigorous war measures and the eradication of slavery. By late 1862, the president arrived at a partisan framework largely of his own making. It put democratic principles first by making the aim of saving the union synonymous with saving democracy. And it targeted a political fusion with patriotic men of all parties under the terms of an ultraist approach to antislavery measures. This was the partisan strategy behind the Emancipation Proclamation, and it became the strategy that reoriented northern politics through the emergence of a Union party. The Unionists came together as a formal political coalition in 1862 and 1863, essentially replacing the Republican party. The story of that critical realignment is told in these pages with a focus on Gettysburg, from the politics behind the 1863 military campaign to Lincoln's indelible address at the cemetery afterward.

It was Unionists, not Republicans, who nominated Lincoln in 1864 on a national ticket with former Democrat Andrew Johnson of Tennessee. At the same time, the party endorsed a constitutional amendment to abolish slavery. Although Unionists did not win over most Northern Democrats or border state conservatives with this approach, they co-opted just enough to reelect Lincoln and secure overwhelming control of Congress. The achievement was essential for winning the war. Lincoln firmly believed that his administration could not save the union without first building a successful Union party.

Histories and biographies of Lincoln have covered the basic elements of this story but have not emphasized the significance of his evolving partisanship. Lincoln is generally portrayed in modern scholarship as a loyal Henry Clay Whig who entered a period of near political retirement after leaving Congress in the late 1840s. The consensus is that Lincoln was a reluctant Republican who clung to his moderate—even conservative—views on slavery and race well into the 1850s. Most accounts credit Lincoln with putting country above party as a wartime president, but they also tend to describe him as a Republican long after he abandoned the label. They often treat his 1864 nomination as a National Unionist as a campaign gimmick, not the major strategic shift it was.

This standard interpretation derives in part from Lincoln himself. In his public speeches and across a few scattered autobiographical sketches, Lincoln made a deliberate effort to downplay his partisan decision-making. At times he also obscured his more radical principles with pragmatic rhetoric. On the stump, Honest Abe was never Candid Abe. He recognized that the management of party factions required deft manipulation and even occasional deception. He almost never showed his strategic hand in his public remarks. That was good politics, but it has sometimes led students of Lincoln astray.[8]

Some historians also underestimate how much Lincoln kept his own counsel. Even the men and women who knew him best often understood little about his most sensitive political maneuvers. To a surprising degree, Lincoln was a loner as a party leader. He appeared friendly and eager to engage peers, but he almost never asked for advice and rarely confided in anyone. William Herndon, his longtime law partner, described Lincoln as "the most secretive, reticent, shut mouthed man that ever existed."[9] Following the president's assassination, many Lincoln insiders claimed to recall insights that he supposedly shared with them in confidence, but their self-promoting memories are suspect. For this reason, every word from Lincoln that appears in the following pages is contemporary—put in writing, as events unfolded, either by him or by someone with direct access to him, usually in private and often in haste.

Lincoln carefully marked his most secretive political directives with designations such as "Private," "Private & Confidential," "Strictly Confidential," "Very Confidential," or in some rare cases, "For your eye only." These classifications had specific meanings to him. A "private" communication could be shared but not published, while anything marked "confidential" was not supposed to be shared at all.[10] A few of Lincoln's letters were marked "Burn this," a command fortunately ignored by his less scrupulous subordinates.

Hundreds of these political letters are now available, many of them not well known and some only recently made public. Though often terse and sometimes cryptic, they provide fresh insights into Lincoln's strategic thinking and tactical behavior. In the following pages, readers will encounter dozens of confidential notes from 1849, for instance, when Lincoln engaged in a failed bid for a federal appointment after he left Congress. Though the episode was seemingly minor, the documents expose Lincoln's penchant for hardball politics and the limits of his enthusiasm for Henry Clay. The letters Lincoln wrote during his failed bid for the U.S. Senate in 1855 are also deeply revealing. It was a feverish, mainly behind-the-scenes campaign conducted at a time when state legislatures, not the general electorate, selected U.S. senators. We see Lincoln navigating the hostile territory between antislavery Whigs and Democrats and working in quiet coordination with anti-immigrant or "Know Nothing" factions as he helped bring the Republican party into existence.

During the 1858 Senate campaign against Stephen Douglas, Lincoln produced several confidential partisan letters that challenge our conceptions of him. In one recently discovered note, Lincoln, as angry as we ever see him, blasts one of his subordinates for mishandling a political communication and slanders the manhood of another. Late in that hard-fought campaign, Lincoln made a "bare suggestion" to his Republican state party chairman that now reads like a call to counteract potential Democratic voter fraud with some preventive bribery of their own. Although Lincoln's real purpose was different, it was equally tough-minded.[11]

During his 1860 presidential run—a complicated campaign with four major parties—Lincoln used his political correspondence to gather sensitive information from across party lines. In the secession crisis that followed his party's triumph, Lincoln used confidential communications to steady Republican politicians in Washington who were scrambling to save the union. And as president, he often managed wartime challenges such as emancipation policy or controversial military appointments with urgent notes that attempted to unify his fractious wartime coalition.

As late as August 1864, with his own party seemingly poised to abandon him, Lincoln's legacy and the fate of the nation appeared to be in jeopardy. That Lincoln survived this crisis of confidence in his leadership was no miracle of team loyalty; nor was it simply the result of changing fortunes on the battlefield. It was instead an astonishing political achievement that Lincoln pulled together with subtle manipulation best revealed by a secret memo that he mysteriously asked his cabinet to sign unread. What that document shows—and what his confidential correspondence over the years illustrates—is Lincoln's penchant for discretion and his willingness to realize his greatest ambitions through his party and nation, not through personal interest.[12]

One can discern key elements of Lincoln's partisan leadership in Buckingham's portrayal of their travel together on that hot, dusty road from Chicago to Springfield in the summer of 1847. Buckingham described the journey after the River and Harbor Convention as "the most fatiguing day's ride . . . I ever experienced," complaining about being crammed with a party of six—including the long-legged Lincoln—inside "a carriage built to carry but four." In his account, Buckingham noted the party affiliations of Lincoln and his Democratic colleague Robert Smith, but he did not remark on the significance other than to observe that Lincoln "badgered" and teased his "opponent" until finally everyone "laughed, in spite of the dismal circumstances."[13]

Buckingham did not register that Lincoln was pursuing Smith in an attempt at party-building outreach after a party-bending convention based on grand fusionist designs. It was no coincidence that the top Whig representative to the convention from Illinois was riding home with one of the state's most prominent Democratic delegates two days after adjournment. Lincoln and Smith had served together in the Illinois legislature during the 1830s, and they certainly knew each other, but Smith was not simply an "old personal friend," as Buckingham imagined. Rather, he was a friendly target for this latest version of western fusion.

Buckingham's reporting on the Whig congressman's overly familiar greetings to the local farmers was even more revealing of Lincoln the partisan. What Buckingham witnessed was not mere "western custom" as he thought but rather an act of calculated deference, more like a subtle partisan custom, from a political figure under pressure. The Whigs in the district, with too much ambition competing for too little political opportunity, were feuding. Other aspiring party leaders wanted the congressional seat. Lincoln himself, despite his recent victory, had become a polarizing figure. Jealous peers were whispering that he had grown haughty in the fifteen years since he had arrived among them. And there were ugly rumors during the campaign that he was a "scoffer" at Christianity.[14] That is why even before his first vote in Congress, he had made plans to serve only a single term, in a gesture of political reconciliation and coalition building.[15] Lincoln was not a typical western politician smiling and bowing to win votes that afternoon on the road to Springfield. He was instead working to unify his party.

PART I

Whig

If we do our duty we shall succeed in the congressional election, but if we relax an *iota*, we shall be beaten.

—Abraham Lincoln, age twenty-nine (July 23, 1838)

1 SELF-MADE BOSS

(1832–1847)

Abraham Lincoln sat for his first photograph probably during the summer of 1847, around the time of the River and Harbor Convention. One of Springfield's pioneering "daguerreans" composed miniature portraits of the congressman-elect and his wife Mary inside a makeshift studio. Although different from Joseph Buckingham's pen portrait of Lincoln for the *Boston Courier*, this snapshot is just as revealing. Against a dark backdrop, Lincoln poses awkwardly with his right arm across his lap and his left resting over a book on a side table, his thumb dangling enough to blur the image. He wears a dark suit with a cravat tied neatly into a bow. His hair is parted and meticulously combed, and he wears long sideburns. Mary Lincoln, ten years younger than her husband at twenty eight, wears a striped and beaded dress set off by a delicate lace shawl and a cameo brooch centered on her neckline. Her hair is also parted on the side, with tight curls set at shoulder length. Together they look like a successful nineteenth-century American couple.[1]

According to their eldest son Robert Lincoln, those daguerreotypes sat together in the parlor of the family home throughout his childhood. Lincoln was photographed more than a hundred times during his career, but the couple never again sat together for portraits. The striking images did not become public until 1895, when muckraking journalist Ida Tarbell featured them in a series of biographical articles on Lincoln for *McClure's* magazine. Tarbell believed she had stumbled onto something extraordinary. She claimed the appearance of Lincoln's first-known photograph "shattered the widely accepted tradition of his early shabbiness."[2] The image has proven less earth-shattering than Tarbell imagined. American popular culture still celebrates Lincoln's rough-hewn origins and plain prairie style, not his middle-class sensibilities or his rapid rise to political success. This latter point has been perhaps the most elusive. By 1847, Lincoln was not merely a self-made man but an imposing state party boss ready to enter the national political arena.

LINCOLN NEVER SPENT MUCH time in his Kentucky birthplace. The Lincoln family first crossed the Ohio River when he was only seven, relocating about a hundred miles from central Kentucky into southern Indiana. The Lincolns had left their small farm on Knob Creek in late 1816 seeking opportunity on the northern shore of the meandering river just as Indiana was becoming the nation's nineteenth state. This was a decision that Thomas Lincoln made "partly on account of slavery," according to his son, and also because land titles were perpetually under challenge in Kentucky courts.[3]

Thomas Lincoln was a yeoman farmer, but his true passion was carpentry. He cherished his tools and spent time training his only son in the trade. Preservationists have recently discovered a mallet with Abraham Lincoln's initials that evokes the apprentice carpentry he must have tackled as a boy under his father's supervision.[4] This unique artifact also suggests the challenges of the Lincoln family's experience. Although Thomas Lincoln produced some impressive wood pieces (still extant), he was never able to generate enough income by selling cabinets and other fine furniture. The market economy of the region was too primitive—too restricted by limitations in transporting goods to market. As the family struggled to get by with scratch farming, Abraham grew up with no illusions about backcountry life. He detested farmwork, sparred with his frustrated father, and aspired to escape into the wider world. Lincoln's mother Nancy and his older sister Sarah both died during this time in southern Indiana. Thomas Lincoln remarried, and Abraham seemed to love his stepmother, Sarah Johnston, and to get along with his stepbrother, stepsisters, and the cousins who lived in their blended household. Still, in his later description of his childhood home, he called it "as unpoetical as any spot of the earth."[5]

By age nineteen, the young man was ready to break away. With his father's grudging approval, in 1828 Lincoln and a friend undertook a small flatboat expedition down the Ohio and Mississippi rivers carrying local trading goods to the bustling port city of New Orleans. In early 1830, Lincoln helped his family migrate to the Sangamon River Valley of central Illinois. Once the extended family got settled, Lincoln and one of his cousins ventured back to New Orleans as part of an even longer trading journey. He was gone for nearly three months. Upon his return, Lincoln established himself at the small outpost of New Salem, a tiny village situated farther west along the Sangamon River from where the rest of his family had settled. Living on his own, Lincoln worked on local flatboats and then as a store clerk, while also earning money from odd jobs. After residing at New Salem for less than a year, he entered politics in the spring of 1832. At the age of twenty-three, separated from his family, with less than a year of formal schooling and no steady income, Abraham Lincoln announced his candidacy for the state house of representatives.[6]

The young candidate ran as a self-proclaimed expert on rivers. Drawing on his experiences as a flatboat man, Lincoln argued that navigational improvements to the Sangamon were "important and highly desirable" to the region's economic future. With proper dredging and clearances, he suggested, the local waterway—a relatively shallow, meandering 250-mile tributary of the Illinois River, which itself fed into the great Mississippi—could become part of a thriving national trade route from the Great Lakes to the Gulf of Mexico. Though acknowledging that roads, canals, and railroads were also highly beneficial internal improvements, he staked out a position in favor of redirecting the local river to make it more accessible for seasonal steamboat navigation, "an object much better suited to our infant resources." The young candidate even tried to play the experience card, wryly alluding to his flatboat work by claiming that he had given "as particular attention to the stage of the water in this river as any other person in the country."[7]

Support for river improvements also happened to be the position of the *Sangamo Journal*, an independent newspaper recently launched in Springfield. The *Journal* claimed that a successful steamboat run on the Sangamon "would be worth more to us than a dozen railroads."[8] Now here was a candidate promising to deliver on that goal—shrewd positioning for an aspiring legislator. Lincoln also proved adept at evading polarizing policy matters involving finance and social issues. His campaign statement endorsed a crackdown on "exorbitant rates of interest" for private lending, but to avoid offending any major creditors, Lincoln also pointed out that if such a statute ever proved too burdensome, "there could always be means found to cheat the law." He described education as "the most important subject which we as a people can be engaged in" and extolled its virtues in promoting the reading of "scriptures and other works." He stopped short, though, of backing any costly specifics, such as reviving a system of taxpayer-financed "common" or public schools, which had been abandoned in the state just a few years before. The candidate took notice of other complaints about regulations on stray animals, executing debts, and compulsory road-building duty but dealt with them by pledging to support whatever "might tend most to the advancement of justice."[9]

All in all, this was a sophisticated performance, especially coming from the pen of a barely educated young man who had been living in the area for less than a year. One might suspect that Lincoln had received coaching, perhaps by his occasional employer, New Salem merchant Denton Offutt, or by other better-educated local friends, or possibly by *Journal* editor Simeon Francis. But the text of the 1832 statement suggests that Lincoln had figured most of it out on his own.[10] Many of the words and phrases would reappear in his later political writings. Lincoln defended his honesty, something that would soon become his trademark. "I have spoken as I thought," he observed. For those who disagreed with his views, he vowed to be pragmatic, quoting the "sound maxim" that "it is better to be only sometimes right, than at all times wrong." He also offered to "renounce" any positions as "soon as I discover my opinions to be erroneous." Finally, he framed his ambitions as laudable pursuits, a conceit that would become characteristic for him. "Every man is said to have his peculiar ambition," he stated. "I have no other so great as that of being truly esteemed of my fellow men, by rendering myself worthy of their esteem." Still, the self-confident young man could not resist commenting that how far he might "succeed in gratifying this ambition" was "yet to be developed."

Nothing about this effort was ordinary for the times. Although Lincoln claimed that he offered his announcement "in accordance with an established custom" associated with "the principles of true republicanism," this was not really the case. Issuing policy statements was a relatively new practice in this emerging partisan era. By March 1832, the *Sangamo Journal* had announced five other legislative candidates for the August election without providing any party identification. None of these candidates expressed themselves in print. Two of the other contenders eventually tried to follow Lincoln's example, but neither seemed as comfortable with the unusual format.[11]

Lincoln was being innovative, reaching beyond ordinary family and community ties to attract what he termed "the independent voters of this county." As the least prominent choice before an electorate of about three thousand adult white males, he needed his long-shot campaign to focus on policy measures, not community standing. He was the youngest of the thirteen candidates, the newest resident on the ballot, and the only one without a local family network. He also lacked military service, a customary qualification for nineteenth-century office. Later that spring he joined the Illinois militia and served briefly in the Black Hawk War, the last major military conflict between the United States and Indian nations east of the Mississippi River. But when he later recalled his initial political campaign he reversed that sequence. He suggested to campaign biographers in 1860 that he had entered the 1832 legislative race *after* being elected captain by his militia peers, making his choice to enter politics seem more conventional. That was perhaps how he wanted people to remember his ambition; it was not the reality.[12]

Lincoln's political gamble fell short at the August 1832 election as he finished eighth in a field of thirteen candidates, with the top four vote-getters receiving state legislative seats. But Lincoln was only 150 votes behind the fourth-place finisher, Methodist preacher Peter Cartwright, who turned out to be the man Lincoln would defeat for Congress in 1846. When Lincoln and Cartwright faced off against each other the second time, they did so as the official candidates of the Whig and Democratic parties. In 1832 the candidates had no party organizations behind them, and that was Lincoln's chief problem; he ran like a partisan before partisanship was fully mobilized.

Parties or factions had always existed in American politics, from colonial-era cliques to the 1790s split between Jeffersonians and Hamiltonians. But the nature of these loose affiliations changed dramatically during the Jacksonian era. It was not just Andrew Jackson's feisty political style or the vitriol he provoked in his opponents that established the great departure from the past. Politics in early America had often been ugly, sometimes even violent. The critical Jacksonian-era shift in the 1820s and '30s was about issues, but more than anything else, it was about organization.

By the 1840s, political parties embodied a system of grassroots coalitions created out of patronage and policy platforms, the "men and measures" of the age. These new partisan coalitions operated with little coordination at the national level. They were held together on the local level—just barely—by standing committees and regular conventions. Party newspapers and campaign periodicals managed most of their public appeals and attacks.

This organizational revolution was just beginning to develop in Illinois in 1832. The self-identified "National Republicans," who would become known as Whigs by the end of that election cycle, held a nominating convention in Springfield to select presidential electors for their candidate, Senator Henry Clay of Kentucky. No such gatherings came together for the legislative campaigns, despite at least one aborted effort, and there was no overt partisanship in local races.[13] The state legislative contests revolved around attempts to form combinations of candidates usually bound together by pledges of mutual loyalty. John Todd Stuart, who later became Lincoln's first law partner, made conflicting promises to secure the mutual arrangements necessary to win his state representative seat, and he became the target of a bitter postelection pamphlet war accusing him of being dishonorable. In the past, such honor-bound politics had sometimes led to dueling, as in the ill-fated "interview" in 1804 between Aaron Burr and Alexander Hamilton following a New York gubernatorial contest. Lincoln's apparent indifference to such traditions and his groundbreaking use of the *Sangamo Journal* in 1832 for issuing his own platform of policy measures hinted at what was coming in the years ahead.

But at least for a few years, there was a surprising confusion of political labels across the state, a stubborn resistance to partisan organization especially among some of the emerging Whigs, and a lingering attachment to the honor code. "It is difficult to catch the hang of parties here," wrote one central Illinois resident in 1834, "for although there is considerable party feeling, there is very little party organization."[14] Lincoln did as much as anyone to help overcome these obstacles. Nobody worked harder to organize the Whig party in central Illinois during the 1830s and '40s, particularly in the state's most populous and powerful counties of Sangamon and Morgan.

Lincoln established his leadership position through his work in the legislature. Following his initial defeat, he secured a job as a local postmaster and county surveyor while also co-owning and then losing a failed general store in New Salem; then in 1834 he won a legislative seat on only his second try. Soon the first-term representative and second-youngest member was speaking on the floor, introducing bills, and playing an active role behind the scenes. Before too long, he was leading the Sangamon County delegation, known as the "Long Nine" for their collective height. That group became most notable for their efforts to secure the relocation of the state capital from Vandalia, along the Cumberland Road in southern Illinois, to Springfield, where Lincoln was living by 1837. Lincoln then became floor leader for the entire Whig caucus, receiving most of their ballots for the speakership during both his third and fourth terms.[15] He served four consecutive terms before departing voluntarily in 1841.

During this impressive rise, Lincoln often adopted a cynical air about his political experiences. At the start of his second term, he reported to a female friend that "the legislature is doing little or nothing," observing that the Jacksonian governor had "delivered an inflamitory political Message" that would soon produce "some sparring between the parties."[16] On the statehouse floor, he once observed that politicians were "taken as a mass, at least one long step removed from honest men," confessing that he could make such a claim "with greater freedom because, being a politician myself, none can regard it as personal."[17] At the time, he had been in public office for only three years.

The young Lincoln was particularly sharp whenever he felt threatened. During his 1836 legislative campaign, he became a target of gossip and last-minute handbill attacks. He responded to one slanderous innuendo by invoking the honor code and demanding "an answer" before issuing a feisty statement on the eve of the election, denouncing his anonymous assailant as "a liar and a scoundrel" while vowing "to give his proboscis a good wringing" if he ever determined the culprit.[18] He once complained that Speaker of the House and partisan rival William L. D. Ewing, a former U.S. senator, was "not worth a damn."[19] He also displayed no hesitation in berating members of his caucus when they threatened to defy the party line. Writing in 1839 to Andrew McCormick, one of the Long Nine, Lincoln sent an impassioned note about a patronage matter involving Simeon Francis, the *Sangamo Journal* editor. "All our friends are ready to cut our throats about it," warned Lincoln, before adding, "Stand by us this time, and nothing in our power to confer, shall ever be denied you."[20]

The overwhelming impression from Lincoln's early political correspondence was an abiding intensity. He pushed hard as a partisan. Nine months before the 1838 congressional election, he wrote to a local attorney sharing the news that his law partner John Todd Stuart, who had lost in 1836, was again planning to become a candidate for the U.S. House. Lincoln did not employ party labels in this letter, nor did Stuart's subsequent public announcement, but they were organizing like efficient partisans. "On receipt of this," Lincoln commanded, "write me all you *know* and all you *think*, in regard to our prospects for the race."[21] And as the contest came to a close, the tone of Lincoln's campaign directives intensified. Communicating with Jesse Fell, a young lawyer and newspaper editor from Bloomington, Lincoln warned that "if we relax an *iota*, we shall be beaten."[22] Stuart won by a handful of votes. As Lincoln reminded Stuart during their 1840 campaign, "You know I am never sanguine."[23]

The 1840 presidential contest was arguably the first modern campaign in American political history, marked by unprecedented levels of popular enthusiasm and partisan organization. Lincoln played his part with gusto. In addition to working with Stuart on his partner's reelection effort, he served as a member of the Whig presidential electoral ticket, considered an important surrogate position for the national race. His most time-consuming assignment, apart from speaking engagements, was to help produce *The Old Soldier*, a statewide campaign newspaper that promoted William Henry Harrison, the Whig nominee and renowned former Indian fighter. During this campaign season, Lincoln also managed to launch the only sustained romance of his life, with Mary Todd, a twenty-one-year-old daughter of a Whig politician and banker from Kentucky.

Todd had been living in Springfield with her sister Elizabeth and brother-in-law Ninian W. Edwards, partly to escape a hostile stepmother but mostly to find a husband. The Edwards home occupied an important station in the town's modest social scene, and Mary was regarded as a standout among the younger single women. One correspondent described her as "the very creature of excitement" who "never enjoys herself more" than when "surrounded by a company of merry friends."[24] By 1840, Lincoln had become one of those intimate friends, perhaps less out of merriment than partisanship. Todd was a devoted Whig. Although American women could not yet vote, they sometimes participated in political campaigns, and Todd was especially active. She had met Henry Clay several times as a young girl in Lexington because the great Whig leader was a friend of her father's, and even though the party had nominated Harrison, she supported the Whig ticket in any way she could. "This fall I became quite a *politician*," Todd confided to her closest friend, teasing that it was "rather an unladylike profession."[25]

If Mary Todd adopted a playful tone, her future husband spoke and acted in earnest. Lincoln began the fall campaign by delivering the longest, most important speech of his career to that point, the first to be republished in pamphlet form. The speech replied to a group of local Democratic orators led by Stephen Douglas (then spelling his name Douglass), who at the time was leading Democratic campaign efforts as an ambitious twenty-seven-year-old from Morgan County. He and Lincoln had met as young legislators and already disliked each other. In his remarks, Lincoln blasted his rival for being "stupid enough to hope" that he would ignore so many "untrue," "supremely ridiculous," and "audacious assertions."[26]

The bulk of Lincoln's speech, however, was a substantive discussion of banking policy. The "Bank War" had been a defining element of American partisanship since Andrew Jackson's 1832 veto of the recharter for the national bank. The Whigs blamed the Panic of 1837 on Jackson's controversial action. Now the Democrats, under Jackson's successor Martin Van Buren, were promoting a plan to keep federal revenues separated from the numerous unregulated state and private banks. With the shadow of severe economic decline still looming, the political arguments over this plan were testy.[27]

Illinois Whigs welcomed a debate about banking policy because they were losing ground on issues such as internal improvements. Lincoln had entered politics as a strong advocate for local river projects, and he became even more identified with transportation improvements when he helped orchestrate the state's adoption of an expensive program for railroad and canal building in 1837. That was the same year the Long Nine corralled the votes for the relocation of the state capital to Springfield, and Lincoln appeared to be on his way toward becoming a statewide power broker. But the national economic collapse of the late 1830s doomed major elements of the ambitious initiatives, leaving Illinois saddled with millions in debt. Lincoln's new focus on banking reflected a concerted Whig effort to shift the economic debate toward more favorable political terms. Lincoln sardonically explained the new Illinois realities in a letter to his absent law partner. "The Internal Improvement System will be put down in a lump, without the benefit of clergy," he predicted to Congressman Stuart, remarking that Whigs were nonetheless making progress in restoring funds to the depleted state bank, upon which everyone, regardless of party, relied.[28]

Lincoln addressed numerous policy issues in the 1840 campaign across more than two dozen political speeches and several articles he penned for *The Old Soldier*. His emerging style as a partisan was on display in his efforts to skewer incumbent President Van Buren's voting record as a New York legislator. Lincoln began the campaign by seeking evidence that Van Buren had once opposed the War of 1812—a stark and useful contrast to General Harrison's martial fame as "Old Tippecanoe." "*Be verry sure* to secure and send me the Senate Journal of New York of September 1814," Lincoln wrote to Stuart in January. "I have a newspaper article which says that that document proves that Van Buren voted against raisin[g] troops in the last war."[29] By March, Lincoln was demanding information about more explosive rumors that Van Buren once supported voting rights for free Black men.[30] When Stuart did not move fast enough on either request, Lincoln pursued the details by asking a friend visiting New York to "procure" copies of the relevant journals and get them back to Illinois as quickly as possible.[31]

By early May, Lincoln was employing this opposition research in speeches that attacked the Democratic president for "allowing Free Negroes the right of suffrage" in New York.[32] Neither Illinois nor

New York was a slave state, but voters in both showed hostility toward Black equality. Illinois had never allowed Black men to vote. The state had also enacted strict Black codes (soon to be made even tougher) that limited the legal and civil rights of African Americans. Lincoln's early willingness to engage in such targeted race-baiting underscores both the hostile climate toward Blacks in free states like Illinois and the young Whig leader's hard partisan edge, especially when he was on the attack and seeking what he called "good '*war-club*.' "[33]

Throughout the campaign, Lincoln also focused on the overriding goal of mobilizing Whig voters. "Our intention is to organize the whole State," he wrote in a confidential circular at the beginning of the contest, "so that every Whig can be brought to the polls in the coming presidential contest." Lincoln set out a ten-point "plan of organization" that included advice on how to create effective county-level committees, prepare useful voter lists, raise funds, and even preserve local harmony. He emphatically urged all Whigs "to keep a CONSTANT WATCH on the DOUBTFUL VOTERS" while holding their plans "CONCEALED FROM EVERY ONE EXCEPT OUR GOOD FRIENDS."[34] This confidential plan soon leaked out to the Democratic press. Lincoln, unabashed, offered a blunt defense for his overt partisanship. "With our own friends," he wrote, "we justify—we urge—organization on the score of necessity." Yet sensitive to the lingering antiparty sentiment of many Whigs, Lincoln tried to place the blame for this escalating partisanship on the Democrats. "*They* set us the example of organization," he wrote, "and we, in self defence, are driven into it."[35]

But in truth, Lincoln was embracing party building with unmatched enthusiasm. By the late summer of 1840, he composed a secret document that outlined voter mobilization duties for Whig captains at the county, precinct, and section levels in the fall presidential election. For each type of captain, Lincoln methodically repeated instructions about how to secure pledges of support. And for the all-important "Section Captain" who was supposed to have direct contact with at least ten of his neighbors, Lincoln was adamant about demanding "face to face" pledges from voters about how they would physically cast their ballots in November.[36] Once again, it was the sheer intensity of his partisan style that set Lincoln apart from most of his Whig peers in Illinois.

Personality may have fueled this intensity as much as politics. Lincoln's early private letters were peppered with signs of anxiety. He confessed to his friend Mary Owens, soon after arriving in Springfield in 1837, that he felt "quite as lonesome here as I ever was anywhere in my life."[37] To his closest friend and fellow Whig organizer Joshua Speed, Lincoln once acknowledged that "our *forebodings*, for which you and I are rather peculiar, are all the worst sort of nonsense."[38] He seemed to hide nothing from John Todd Stuart when he worried that he was having a mental breakdown in January 1841, after his engagement with Mary Todd temporarily fell apart. Lincoln complained that he was "making a most discreditable exhibition of myself in the way of hypochondraism" and that the "state of my mind" had become "deplorable."[39] He even called himself "the most miserable man living." When the worst of it finally seemed to pass in early February, he joked darkly, "I am neither dead nor quite crazy yet."[40]

But if these comments suggest depression or some form of deep melancholy, they do not explain Lincoln's day-to-day behavior. Although he did miss a full week of the legislative session in January 1841 (unusual for him), and his correspondence was perhaps less gossipy than usual, he still projected a methodical demeanor as a party leader. Every available document from this presumably dismal period included the usual array of sharp comments on partisan business, especially regarding patronage or political appointments, which Lincoln termed the "same everlasting subject" in one of his notes to Stuart.[41] After insisting that his fellow Whig and physician Anson G.

Henry was "necessary to my existence" because of his agitated mental state, Lincoln simply continued to lobby Stuart to get the struggling doctor appointed as postmaster at Springfield. In an otherwise anguished-sounding letter, Lincoln managed to report in calm detail on a meeting of "our friends" that he had organized only the night before to coordinate the announcement of Stuart's reelection campaign.[42] The hardworking partisan was clearly capable of pushing aside distractions when politics demanded it.

Though Lincoln wrapped up his last session with the Illinois General Assembly in 1841, he stayed active in partisan affairs even as the Whig party itself endured a kind of existential crisis. The problem was that William Henry Harrison, the first Whig president, died within a month of his inauguration, leaving his vice president, John Tyler of Virginia, to pursue a course totally independent of congressional Whigs and in opposition to several of the economic policies that many considered essential to the party's mission. Confusion prevailed at first, and then a political war erupted between President Tyler and Senator Henry Clay, leaving feuding Whigs to face a series of electoral setbacks across the country.[43] Lincoln made his allegiance clear by helping to form a Clay Club in Illinois in 1842 and by inviting the Kentucky senator to visit the state for a speaking tour.[44] He also began pressing local Whigs to get better organized and to stop resisting partisan innovations that Democrats had been using to defeat them. Finally, he tackled the challenge of sorting out a dangerous local logjam of competing Whig claims, including his own, to succeed Stuart in Congress.

Partisanship even helped stabilize Lincoln's personal life. He and Mary Todd had broken apart on what he called "that fatal first of Jany. '41."[45] What ruptured their engagement remains difficult to discern from contemporary evidence, but it was partisan bickering that helped bring them back together. When the state bank failed in February 1842, James Shields, a leading Democrat and the Illinois state auditor, began refusing to accept state banknotes as legal tender. Probank Whigs took offense and launched a counterattack, targeting Shields with several unsigned satirical pieces in the *Sangamo Journal*. The so-called Rebecca letters, which mocked the vain politician in both personal and partisan terms, were authored by various local Whigs, including Abraham Lincoln on August 27 and Mary Todd and her friend Julia Jayne on September 8. Shields chose to blame Lincoln for all the attacks and set in motion an honor code ritual complete with written demands for apologies. Lincoln had never dueled before, but he was familiar enough with the code and refused to back down. The affair went all the way to the western banks of the Mississippi River, which lay outside the reach of Illinois state law that prohibited dueling. In the end, however, the Lincoln-Shields duel was abruptly called off through mutual concessions orchestrated by the respective friends of the principals.[46]

The embarrassing incident compelled Lincoln and Todd to start interacting again, at first in conversations with *Journal* editor Simeon Francis regarding this "affair of honor" and eventually on their own. Lincoln made fun of "the dueling business [which] still rages in this city" in a witty letter to his friend Speed, who had moved to Louisville, Kentucky, but the episode clearly marked a serious turning point in his relationship with Mary. It provoked him in early October to ask an "impudent question" of his former roommate Speed: "Are you . . . glad you are married as you are?"[47] At about this time, Lincoln also presented his future wife with a curious courting document—a certified tabulation in his own hand of the Sangamon County legislative election results from 1832, 1834, and 1836, carefully designating party affiliations for all the candidates and showing how he rose from eighth place to become the county's top vote-getter.[48] The openly political couple married on Friday, November 4, 1842, at the Springfield residence of Todd's sister, Elizabeth Edwards.

By 1843, Lincoln had taken on the trappings of a new life. Besides his marriage, which he called a "matter of profound wonder," and the arrival in August of his first son, Robert Todd, named after his prominent father-in-law, Lincoln was also undergoing a professional transition.[49] No longer a legislator, he was now engaged in legal practice with Stephen Logan, one of the top lawyers in the state.[50] Logan was a senior Whig politico who had partnered during the previous few years with Edward Baker, another leading Whig. Logan & Baker had once overshadowed Stuart & Lincoln. Now there was a shake-up of the state capital's leading Whig firms, with Logan & Lincoln emerging as arguably the most politically influential in Illinois.

Logan and Lincoln helped produce a pivotal campaign circular for the state Whig central committee in the spring of 1843 prior to a series of county and congressional district nominating conventions. The two of them, along with another partisan attorney, drafted a statement of principles that defended several of the Whig party's leading policy positions, focusing heavily that year on the need for a higher protective trade tariff to benefit industrial development. The authors rejected perceptions regarding the party's bleak electoral future, although its own tone was sometimes despairing. "In almost all the States," wrote Lincoln and his co-authors, "we have fallen into the minority, and despondency seems to prevail universally among us." The document conceded the largely successful Democratic counterrevolution that had followed the Whig victories in 1840 and denounced their opponents for their "perseveringly vindictive . . . assaults upon all our men and measures."[51]

For Lincoln and other forward-looking Whigs, the smart response to continued electoral defeats was to reject the remaining antiparty traditions of the past. The 1843 circular was unabashed in urging immediate adoption of the most modern partisan innovations, including the "Convention System" for every contest except "small offices [in] no way connected with politics." Lincoln did not even bother to offer a moral defense for this shift. "Whether the system is right in itself," claimed the circular, "we do not stop to enquire," calling it "madness . . . not to defend ourselves with it." Although the circular asserted that it was not "censuring" the "many of the whigs" who had opposed such partisan tactics in the past, the implication was clear. Whigs had no choice but to become more disciplined. "That 'union is strength' is a truth that has been known," wrote Lincoln, before unleashing the great biblical affirmation of the point, namely that "a house divided against itself cannot stand."[52] He was proud of this section of the circular, informing someone a few days later, "I wrote it myself," while boasting that it was "conclusive upon this point" and "can not be reasonably answered."[53] Lincoln filed the metaphor away for use again in other contexts.

In the short term, though, the convention system "fixed" Lincoln in a bad way, to use his own mordant words. Sangamon County Whigs endured several inconclusive ballots at their local convention in March before finally nominating Edward Baker instead of Lincoln to succeed Stuart in Congress. Baker was a state senator originally from England, though raised in Indiana, and was widely regarded as the most articulate among the promising young Whig lawyer-politicians residing in Springfield. Local Whigs then magnified Lincoln's humiliation by appointing him, over his objection, as one of Baker's delegates for the upcoming district-wide convention set to take place in nearby Pekin. Lincoln immediately sought answers to explain his defeat, with results that astonished him. "I have been put down here as the candidate of pride, wealth, and aristocratic family distinction," he complained, after hearing rumors about his alleged arrogance and social-climbing marriage into the Todd-Edwards clan. Recalling that only twelve years earlier he had been a "friendless, uneducated, penniless boy, working on a flat boat," Lincoln seethed at the irony of it all.[54]

Lincoln also remarked on how "the strangest combination of church influence [had been] against me," pointing out that Baker was part of a popular breakaway Baptist sect known as Campbellites that had aided his campaign. Lincoln conceded that the dueling business must have hurt him among devout Christians and that he was generally "suspected of being a deist," a charge dating back to the late 1830s. People whispered that he had rejected Christianity.[55] These concerns illustrated some of the complexities of the Jacksonian era. Partisanship in the 1830s and '40s involved more than policy debates over banking, internal improvements, or tariffs. It was also about navigating religious antipathies and social status anxieties.

In May 1843 Baker went to the district convention in Pekin as Sangamon County's choice for Whig congressional nominee, but he ended up losing to John Hardin, a Whig member of the state house of representatives from neighboring Morgan County and a distant cousin of Mary Lincoln's. Hardin won the newly drawn seventh district at the August election, succeeding John Todd Stuart as the lone Illinois Whig in the U.S. Congress. At that time, Stuart (age thirty-five), Lincoln (age thirty-four), Hardin (age thirty-three), and Baker (age thirty-two) were all promising young Whigs cast together inside the state's only Whig-majority congressional district.[56] None had any realistic hope of winning statewide office because of the significant Democratic electoral advantages outside central Illinois. That meant they stood in one another's way if they measured their political success solely by holding public office.

Lincoln, however, was operating by a different calculus. Between 1843 and 1846, the former Whig state legislator proved to be an organization man first, even as he was positioning himself for a congressional seat. He demonstrated his self-restraint at the Pekin convention. In a series of highly confidential instructions ("Don't show or speak of this letter"), Lincoln explained to allies from tiny Menard County, which contained the now-abandoned village of New Salem, how they might "hold the ballance of power" between the established power centers of Morgan and Sangamon. It involved a strategy that might ultimately lead to supporting him as their first choice. But he insisted that they were not to "hinder" Baker until it was clear he could not succeed. "I would as soon put my head in the fire as to attempt it," Lincoln wrote.[57]

The Menard delegates did end up holding the balance of power, though in the end they threw their support to Hardin. Lincoln withdrew Baker's name from the balloting once it became clear that Hardin would prevail, but he responded by introducing a resolution—passed over the objections of Hardin's Morgan County delegates—that recommended Baker as the district's next Whig candidate for 1844. The implication was clear that local Whigs should rotate the congressional nomination to avoid a clash of frustrated egos. Lincoln, the aspiring party leader, became the architect of a nominating process that he later described as an attempt not only to "soothe Baker's feelings" but also to introduce "a spirit of mutual concession, for harmony's sake."[58]

Neither objective proved secure over the subsequent months. Almost immediately Hardin began expressing doubts about the commitment of Sangamon County Whigs to his general election canvass. Lincoln replied by offering a playful bet, vowing in the pages of the *Sangamo Journal* that the Whigs in his county would double the margin of victory secured for Hardin in Morgan County at the general election, but if they did not, they would host a "free barbecue" for their partisan neighbors. He also sent a reassuring note to Hardin, claiming that Whigs in Sangamon would prove reliable because they "love the whig cause" and because "we like you personally."[59] That latter observation was overstated: Lincoln himself disliked Hardin so much that he refused to cast his own ballot for him in August—a rare example of his cutting a party nominee.[60]

Hardin took up his congressional seat in December 1843, but Lincoln declined to write him again until the following May and did so almost entirely out of obligation. His perfunctory letter to Hardin pointed out that a couple of disgruntled Whig activists felt the congressman was ignoring them.[61] Lincoln also reported on the presidential contest, which was becoming his primary concern. Throughout 1844, Lincoln delivered numerous speeches and organized several meetings on behalf of sixty-seven-year-old Henry Clay, once again the Whigs' national nominee. Lincoln was not as prominent a leader for the statewide campaign as he had been in 1840 since Clay's interests in Illinois were largely managed by a set of Kentucky-born Whigs based in Alton. But for the second time in his career, the Springfield attorney was on the November ballot as a presidential elector.[62]

The 1844 presidential contest also featured Democrat James K. Polk of Tennessee, nearly twenty years younger than Clay, and Liberty party candidate James G. Birney of Ohio. The Liberty party, a fringe movement in the North, supported the immediate abolition of slavery, but the Liberty men, as they were called, were more pragmatic than other abolitionists. Unlike followers of William Lloyd Garrison, the polarizing New England abolitionist and editor of *The Liberator* who believed solely in the power of "moral suasion," the Liberty men embraced national politics as a more likely vehicle to achieve Black freedom. Salmon Chase, a crusading attorney from Ohio well known for representing fugitive slaves, helped draft the platform for their 1844 campaign. It endorsed measures that would separate the federal government from its complicity with slavery, including repeal of the 1793 Fugitive Slave Act. For their part, the Whigs tried to ignore the divisive slavery issue, focusing instead on the tariff and other economic policies that gave them an advantage. Democrats under Polk's leadership generally supported slavery as a legitimate institution, with some exceptions, such as an antislavery faction of the party in New York called the "Barnburners." Overall, Democrats pressed hardest in the 1844 campaign for Texas annexation and westward expansion.[63]

It was a close election, which Lincoln believed would have been Clay's had not the Liberty men drained away what he termed "the whig abolitionists of New York," costing his party the nation's biggest electoral prize.[64] Lincoln had confronted the politics of slavery occasionally in the past, such as in 1837, when the Illinois General Assembly adopted resolutions defending the rights of slaveholding states and denouncing abolitionists as extremists. Lincoln and Dan Stone, another representative from Sangamon County, had voted against those resolutions and were the only two legislators brave enough to sign a public statement against them, which Lincoln wrote.[65] But it was not until the aftermath of the 1844 election that Lincoln became more persistent in addressing the grave sectional issue.

In a private letter sent in 1845 to Williamson Durley, one of the Liberty party's main organizers in his congressional district, Lincoln tried to clarify his own position on slavery while laying the groundwork for coalition building in the future. "I hold it to be the paramount duty of us in the free states," he wrote, "due to the Union of the states, and perhaps to liberty itself (paradox though it may seem) to let the slavery of the other states alone." He was suggesting that allowing states to decide the fate of slavery within their own borders was a constitutional obligation forged in 1787 and thus essential to the overall cause of American liberty—at least for white people. Yet since Lincoln recognized that such an observation would offend the sensibilities of his abolitionist correspondent, he added, "I hold it to be equally clear, that we should never knowingly lend ourselves directly or indirectly, to prevent that slavery from dying a natural death." In other words, he opposed the efforts of slaveholders "to find new places for it to live in."[66]

To this version of his own emerging free-soil policy, Lincoln added an important caveat. "Of course," he wrote, "I am not now considering what would be our duty, in cases of insurrection among the slaves." With that remark, Lincoln appeared to affirm support for the view that the Constitution bound all states and the federal government to aid in the event of any domestic disturbances, including slave revolts. This was becoming a point of greater public debate by the mid-1840s in the wake of newspaper reports of an organized, clandestine "Underground Railroad" helping hundreds or perhaps thousands of slaves escape to the free states annually. There were reports of even more sensational freedom-seeking revolts on the high seas, such as the shipboard rebellions on the *Amistad* (1841) and the *Creole* (1842). Lincoln was probably trying to warn Durley that his personal antislavery views stopped short of overriding what he perceived as his constitutional obligations. But regardless, Lincoln's strategic intent in this postelection outreach was clear. He wanted to find common ground with northern antislavery radicals.[67]

Losing the presidential election was a bitter pill for Illinois Whigs. They appeared stalled as a political movement. The only power they held was in the seventh congressional district, where Hardin had stepped aside for Baker, who won the seat during the August elections. Otherwise, the Whigs lost the remaining six congressional districts by wide margins, and Polk carried the state easily in November. Democrats now controlled all the statewide offices and the General Assembly. Things looked bad for the Whigs almost everywhere except around the state capital.

These factors help explain why Hardin, and to a lesser degree Baker, began acting against the "spirit of mutual concession" that Lincoln had been trying to establish for their local party. Lincoln met with both Baker and Hardin in late 1845, seeking their agreement that it was finally his time to "take a turn" as a congressional candidate the next year. Baker appeared amenable, but Hardin balked and convinced Baker in a separate "interview" that neither of them should stand down. Baker even tried to talk Lincoln out of the race, since "in all probability" his Springfield colleague had no chance against the better-known Hardin.[68]

Lincoln would have none of it. He had been working harder for the party than anybody else. Ever since Stuart entered Congress in

1839, Lincoln had been sending along reports to whoever was serving in Washington. He sat on most statewide Whig committees, organized the largest campaign gatherings, and delivered the greatest number of stump speeches. He had even taken steps to address the perceptions of him as a candidate of "pride" and "wealth." Lincoln was now partnering with William Herndon, a younger lawyer with a much different profile from the sometimes-prickly Logan. Herndon was an antislavery Whig whose father Archer Herndon had been a popular local tavernkeeper and long-serving Democratic state senator, one of the Long Nine who had originally helped bring the state capital to Springfield.

The stalemate among Baker, Hardin, and Lincoln created an unofficial nomination campaign. Lincoln took full advantage of his successful law practice, which compelled him to "ride circuit" or travel from county seat to county seat along a judicial circuit that often overlapped with his congressional district. Hardin's correspondents kept noting nervously how much Lincoln used his circuit travels to promote himself in face-to-face encounters.[69] Lincoln also made regular contact with friendly newspaper editors, offering a standard message, "Turn about is fair play," which he repeated verbatim to nearly all his political correspondents that season, clearly hoping they would reprint or disseminate this key phrase.[70] The circuit-riding attorney from Springfield even encouraged a short-lived attempt to boom or promote Hardin as the Whig candidate for governor. Lincoln was cagey about this transparent maneuver, "lest it should be suspected that I was attempting to juggle Hardin out of a nomination for congress by juggleing [*sic*] him into one for Governor."[71] He told one correspondent whose allegiances were uncertain that he considered Hardin to be "talented, energetic [and] usually generous and magnanimous," but privately to a closer ally, he dismissed his rival as "a man of desparate [*sic*] energy and perseverance."[72]

Hardin was energetic and resourceful. In January 1846 he released a novel proposal to change the party's nominating system, away from the conventions that Lincoln had been advocating and toward something resembling a modern-day primary system. Hardin suggested opening polling places on the same day throughout the district so that Whig voters, not convention delegates, could select the congressional nominee. Recognizing the danger of this proposal to his own chances, since he had never been in Congress and was not as widely known, Lincoln worked hard to kill it. He pulled strings behind the scenes and then released a slick counterproposal to reapportion the proposed county-level voting precincts in a way that would have favored Sangamon. It was more of a shot across the bow than a serious plan, but it had the intended effect. While Lincoln was promising that he would "keep cool under all circumstances," Hardin exploded in anger, firing off an accusatory letter to his Springfield rival and then leaking the entire exchange through an anonymous story in the pages of the *Morgan Journal*.[73]

The now-public quarrel moved Lincoln to respond in aggressive fashion. He sent Hardin a long confidential letter, but clearly written with the expectation that it might also get leaked into the newspapers. With forceful language, Lincoln denied or parried every charge that Hardin had been making. Where Hardin found the business about Whig candidates taking "a turn a piece" in Washington to be thoroughly "anti-republican," Lincoln reiterated his line that "turn about is fair play." To Hardin's attack on the notion that "the District is a horse which each candidate may mount . . . without consulting any body but the grooms & Jockeys," Lincoln replied that his rival's view was no better since it merely suggested that "the District is a horse which, the first jockey that can mount him, may whip and spur round and round, till jockey, or horse, or both, fall dead on the track."[74]

Lincoln dissected what he considered to be Hardin's conspiratorial narrative of their "campaign." He argued that Hardin was mischaracterizing various private meetings that all three of the potential candidates (including Baker) had conducted to sort out who was running. Lincoln denied responsibility for the efforts to promote Hardin as a gubernatorial candidate. And while acknowledging partisan customs that operated mostly out of public view, he insisted that they lacked the nefarious coordination that Hardin was now implying. He specifically denied that Baker had any "part assigned him to act in the drama," but alluded to examples of how the process had been stage-managed at critical junctures, such as during the 1843 Pekin district convention when Lincoln had acted as Baker's chief negotiator.[75]

Lincoln conceded that despite his claims about "fair play," there had been no binding agreement about rotating the Whig nomination taken at the 1843 district convention in Pekin. "I desire *nothing* from the Pekin convention," he asserted. "If I am not (in services done the party, and in capacity to serve in future) near enough your equal . . . to entitle me to the nomination," he added, then "I scorn it on any and all grounds." The question of "services done the party" was central to Lincoln's view of things. He was insulted by Hardin's attempts to blame the internal squabbling on him. "It is certain that struggles between the candidates, do not strengthen a party," he admitted, "but who are most responsible for these struggles, those who are willing to live and let live, or those who are resolved, at all hazards, to take care of 'number one'?"[76]

Approaching his thirty-seventh birthday, a husband and father (soon to be of two boys), Lincoln did not see himself as someone who primarily looked after number one. In politics, he was an organization man, an aspiring party boss, who had broader interests in mind than merely his own prospects for officeholding. He had chosen to become a Whig, and he believed in the party's future. Even when he was angling for himself, he never seemed to forget this. Lincoln kept repeating several of his best digs against Hardin in notes to friendly newspaper editors. But he always warned against their publication unless it was "rather urgently necessary" because unlike Hardin, "I want to keep all points of controversy out of the papers, so far as possible."[77]

Lincoln's pragmatism and painstaking attention to detail left Hardin feeling out of options in the run for Congress. The former representative soon withdrew. Lincoln received the endorsement of the Whig party at the beginning of May, though without the usual fanfare, even from the always-supportive *Sangamo Journal.* Given the long-standing Whig advantage in the district, there was little to get excited over once Hardin dropped out. This new reality worried Lincoln. He chased down at least one delegate prior to the district convention to ensure his attendance, claiming he had become "a little more anxious . . . that the convention shall be full."[78]

The general election campaign was also muted. Not only was the congressional district considered safe for the Whigs, there were also fewer issues than usual separating the two major parties. President Polk had recently maneuvered the country into war with Mexico over the disputed Texas border. A handful of congressional Whigs voted against the declaration of war on May 13, 1846, but most Illinois Whigs supported the conflict out of patriotic devotion. Both Hardin and Baker signed up to help lead American troops into combat. Lincoln stood apart from these Whig war hawks, but he did not speak out against the conflict during his congressional campaign. He claimed afterward that he had known from the beginning that the war with Mexico was a grave mistake but chose to "remain silent" out of a sense of duty.[79]

Lincoln was anything but silent, however, when his opponent, Democratic congressional candidate and Methodist preacher Peter Cartwright, began "whispering" over the summer about his alleged religious "infidelity." Painfully aware of how such accusations had damaged him in the past, especially in 1843, Lincoln issued a handbill, intended to be reprinted across local newspapers, that denied the charges even while acknowledging some degree of religious unorthodoxy. Lincoln's statement began by conceding that he was not a church member. He also noted that "in early life" and until about the time of his marriage, he had sometimes argued for a moral philosophy grounded in fatalism that he termed the "Doctrine of Necessity." The bulk of the short document, however, reaffirmed his acceptance of religion and traditional ideas of morality. "I have never denied the truth of the Scriptures," he wrote. "I have never spoken with intentional disrespect of religion in general, or of any denomination of Christians in particular," adding, "I do not think I could myself, be brought to support a man for office, whom I knew to be an open enemy of, and scoffer at, religion."[80]

By 1846, Lincoln had been dealing with occasional partisan attacks on his faith for nearly a decade. Over time he had learned how to respond, and the handbill on infidelity proved it. There was a sectarian deftness to Lincoln's phrasing, such as when he pointed out that "several of the Christian denominations" shared his fatalistic leanings. This appeared to be a clear dig at Cartwright's "new light" or free will Methodism, a faith born out of the Second Great Awakening that rejected fatalism and irritated members of the large number of "old light" churches in the district, especially Episcopalians and Presbyterians.[81] In addition, Lincoln was sophisticated about his communication strategy. After the contest, he explained to one correspondent how he had debated the merits of responding, observing that even though "nine persons out of ten had not heard the charge at all," he decided that "it was not entirely safe to leave it unnoticed." Lincoln was concerned enough about setting the record straight that he kept pressing for dissemination of the handbill even after the votes were counted.[82]

Lincoln won the August congressional election by roughly the same margins as Hardin and Baker had before him, though overall turnout was down markedly. Some of the internal Whig tensions of the previous months were probably on display in those depressed results. Lincoln racked up larger margins than his predecessors had in Sangamon but secured only a razor-thin victory in Morgan, and turnout in that key county plummeted. This was a bad sign for Whig unity. Lincoln brooded over this problem for nearly the next sixteen months—the standard Illinois interval between an August congressional election and the start of the next Congress in December of the following year. He eventually spread the word that he would not run for reelection, though he later told Herndon privately that he would consider it if no other Whig wanted to run.[83]

During the long transition period Lincoln admitted to his old friend Joshua Speed that his victory left him "not pleased as much as I expected."[84] He seemed more reflective than usual and even started writing poetry.[85] There were no signs of depression, however. From this point forward, Lincoln banished all direct mention of depression or the "hypo" from his letters and conversations.

Instead, the family man and attorney presented a more upbeat front, punctuating his daily routine with a litany of stories and jokes. An apprentice lawyer in the Lincoln & Herndon office wrote home in autumn 1846 with a memorable depiction of the senior partner's penchant for "tales and anecdotes," of which, young Gibson Harris noted, "he has any amount." "I sometimes have to hold my sides at times, so convulsed with laughter," wrote Harris, "as to be almost unable to keep my seat." According to the young man, he had "seen a dozen or more, with their hands on their sides their heads thrown back, their mouths open, tears coursing down their cheeks, laughing as if they would die, at some of Lincoln's jokes."[86]

Lincoln appeared to be in a good mood as he prepared to leave for the July 1847 political gathering in Chicago. He joked easily about his plans with Orville Browning, an old legislative friend from Quincy, Illinois. "As to what I, Baker, and every body else are doing," Lincoln wrote, "*I* am preparing to go to the Chicago River & Harbor

Convention. *Baker* has gone to Alton, as is thought, to be Colonel of the Sixth Regiment, and *every body* is doing pretty much what every body is always doing."[87] These breezy observations made light of some major developments. Baker was finally heading off to a war that Lincoln opposed and that had just a few months earlier taken the life of Colonel Hardin at the Battle of Buena Vista.

If Lincoln had strong reactions to the death of his toughest partisan rival, there is no way to document them. He helped organize a public meeting in April 1847 to coordinate plans for Hardin's memorial service.[88] There is no record of Lincoln eulogizing Hardin at the funeral. The following summer, during a political speech in Congress, he did say, "we lost our best whig man," when referring to Hardin's death in the war.[89] And finally, a few years later, as Lincoln eulogized President Zachary Taylor, the commanding general at Buena Vista, he extolled the brave men lost at "Gen. Taylor's great battle," including "our own beloved Hardin," but those fleeting public references are about all that remains to gauge his inner feelings.[90]

Regardless of how deeply he may have felt about the loss of Hardin or the tragedies of what he considered to have been an unjust war, the politics of the conflict with Mexico transformed Lincoln's partisan landscape. At the local level, it had the effect of clearing the field. Baker and Hardin were gone—both for good. Baker survived the war but relocated to Galena in northwestern Illinois soon after he was mustered out of service. Nor was Baker's decision an isolated one. Leading Democrat Stephen Douglas, now a U.S. senator, also headed northward, moving his residence to Chicago in 1847 after he married the daughter of a wealthy southern planter. Nearly everyone seemed to be migrating toward the northern section of the state. In 1840 Morgan County had been the most populous county in Illinois, with Sangamon not too far behind. By 1850, Cook County (home to Chicago) had more residents and voters than Morgan and Sangamon combined. During those ten remarkable years of growth, the state's population nearly doubled, with the greatest influx of migrants coming from New England. The new demographics altered Illinois politics. What had once been a political culture centered in Springfield and led by ex-Kentuckians such as Stuart, Lincoln, and Hardin, was now increasingly dominated by Chicago and peopled with transplanted Yankees. Here was yet another reason why Lincoln, the new head of the Illinois Whig party, had to go to the River and Harbor Convention. Chicago was the future of political power in Illinois.

The convention opened on Monday, July 5, with fireworks and a slow-moving parade that formed around nine o'clock at Dearborn Park, featuring delegates from across the country, including more than a thousand from Illinois. The men plodded through the oppressive early-morning humidity led by Chicago Democratic congressman "Long John" Wentworth, an imposing figure, "seven feet in height" by correspondent Joseph Buckingham's stunned estimation. The convention attendees then tried to assemble under a tented pavilion that had been hastily constructed in the courthouse square, but thousands, including the forlorn Boston reporter, found themselves on the outside.[91]

The organizing session of the convention revealed a determined effort to feature independent Democrats such as Wentworth and Robert Smith of Alton, who served as the Illinois representative on the nominating committee. Like the Dartmouth-educated Wentworth, Smith was a cosmopolitan figure, originally from New Hampshire. He had migrated to Illinois over a decade earlier and had become a leading businessman and land speculator. Even more than Wentworth, Smith was a prime prospect for fusion. In 1846 he had won his second term in Congress following a rupture with the local Democratic party establishment, which had backed a respected state judge named Lyman Trumbull. Regular Democrats such as Trumbull or U.S. senator Stephen Douglas, who had just moved to the city, were nowhere to be found on July 5. Not all

Democrats at the convention were potential party bolters, but any Democrat present at the Chicago gathering was risking the wrath of the Polk administration. For this reason, the organizers were eager to cultivate them.[92]

Such aggressive outreach created its own partisan tensions. Whig delegates clamored for speeches from their party notables and soon managed to secure some impromptu remarks on that first afternoon from U.S. senator Tom Corwin of Ohio and the *New-York Tribune* editor Horace Greeley. Corwin was popular with anti-war Whigs because he had come out earlier in the year with a defiant speech against Polk's Mexico policy.[93] Corwin also dazzled the Chicago delegates that afternoon and could have been named convention president if he wanted it. Instead, however, the gavel went to St. Louis attorney and former congressman Edward Bates, a prominent Missouri Whig who was not nearly as polarizing a figure as Corwin.

The simmering partisan tensions burst out into the open on the second day. After a platform committee disappeared to conduct the main work of the gathering on Tuesday morning, July 6, the remaining delegates listened to statements from political figures who could not attend. A note from the Democratic presidential front-runner, U.S. senator Lewis Cass of Michigan, provoked such vocal and "withering scorn" from Whig delegates that it had to be read aloud twice.[94] Soon there was also a lengthy exchange between Whig congressman Andrew Stewart from Pennsylvania and Democratic attorney David Dudley Field from New York over the constitutionality of internal improvements. Greeley observed that Stewart's enthusiasm for federal funding had proven too much "for the weak stomachs of some present," provoking Field, a noted legal scholar, to offer an impassioned defense of strict constructionism and traditional Democratic doctrine about limited government. Whig delegates unleashed a verbal barrage against Field, who later complained that the scene had been "in bad temper and worse taste."[95] On that sour note, the convention recessed for a midday break.

Following the short break, Lincoln made his first entrance on the national stage. Announcing that he was speaking "for the sake of harmony," the congressman-elect reminded his audience of their purpose: "We meet here to promote and advance the cause of internal improvement." While acknowledging that partisans "have differed on that subject" in the past, he insisted, with a crisp allusion to Shakespeare, that "we meet here to break down that difference—to unite, like a band of brothers, for the welfare of the common country." He invoked biblical phrases as he warned fellow delegates against "firebrands" who might be "cast amongst us to produce discord and dissensions."[96]

Lincoln stated that Field "has a right to be heard, and should not be interrupted," expressing "hope" that the "hisses" and "jibes" would stop. He vowed that "the delegates from Illinois will keep quiet." Lincoln conceded his disagreements with Field but dismissed the importance of their argument over the Constitution. "He loves it in his way; I, in mine," Lincoln claimed, before concluding that there were "many here who entertain the same views which I do."

These were not the words of an awestruck novice eager to make a good first impression. Speaking at Chicago in July 1847, Lincoln was a commanding figure. Moreover, the curious way in which he opened his remarks, noting that he had chosen to "avail" himself of the "few minutes allowed" since nobody else seemed "desirous to do so," suggested that this was part of a coordinated effort to help settle things down. Lincoln appeared chosen for this performance, as the senior Whig elected official from Illinois and also as someone, at six foot four, tall enough to capture notice inside the pavilion. In his subsequent report, Greeley barely made mention of the speech but identified Lincoln memorably as "a tall specimen of Illinoian."[97] The first national Whig newspaper to publish any summary of Lincoln's comments was more impressed. On July 15, the *National Intelligencer* from Washington, DC, praised "Mr. Lincoln" for making "some sound and sensible remarks," and for his useful warning that "if any thing were said that the Whigs did not like they could well afford to be silent."[98]

Lincoln's speech initiated a period of greater calm. With only a few more fleeting objections, the delegates adopted sixteen resolutions submitted by the platform committee in favor of federally funded river and harbor improvements. They pledged to continue to press their case in Washington. On the following morning, convention president Edward Bates gave a rousing valedictory speech, "frequently interrupted by vehement applause," one remembered and cited for his political benefit as late as 1860, when he was briefly considered a leading candidate for the Republican nomination for president.[99]

SHORTLY AFTER RETURNING FROM Chicago, Lincoln hosted an intimate gathering for about twenty of the Whig delegates from the state constitutional convention who were in Springfield that summer. Judge David Davis of Bloomington described the private dinner at the Lincoln home in a gossipy letter to his wife Sarah. The rotund judge, who liked to eat, was unimpressed by the "bill of fare," which he dismissed as "the same as is usual in this town." A wealthy former Marylander who had studied at the Yale law school, Davis poked fun at his host, whom he was just getting to know. The two men would later become close friends, riding the judicial circuit and navigating political campaigns together. For now, Davis merely observed, "You cant [*sic*] make a gentleman in his outward appearance, out of Lincoln, to save your life."[100]

The judge might have been thinking about the contrast between his amiable host and the pair of elegant daguerreotype portraits featured in Lincoln's parlor. "Mrs. L, I am told, accompanies her husband to Washington City next winter," reported Davis before adding, "She wishes to loom largely."[101] In the years ahead, the conservative Bloomington judge and eventual Supreme Court justice would always seem to blame Mary Lincoln for meddling in her husband's career. But in 1847 she was not the only Lincoln with big plans for their future.

2

WHIG FUSIONIST

(1847–1849)

AFTER THE OFFICIAL CLOSE of the Chicago River and Harbor Convention on Wednesday morning, July 7, many delegates remained to listen through another afternoon of triumphal speeches about America's promising economic future, including a novel proposal to extend a transcontinental railroad to the Pacific coast. It was a moment of grand ambition. Even Joseph Buckingham, the acerbic Boston journalist, sounded enthralled as he informed readers that Chicago would soon become "one of the largest cities in the Union" and that he was leaving the convention "filled with the wonders and the capacities of the West." He dismissed the earlier "disaffections and the quibblings" among the delegates as little more than the "effervescence of a soda bottle."[1]

But despite the high hopes, partisan "quibblings" continued, the rise of the West came more slowly than many were predicting, and the fight for river and harbor improvements never materialized as the transformative political issue that its advocates had imagined. President James Polk responded to the political pressure of that summer's gathering by issuing yet another veto once Congress returned to session in December, this time for a minor waterways appropriation that had been tucked inside a Wisconsin territorial bill. A few days later the House of Representatives, now under the control of a slim Whig majority, responded with its own resolution, written by Chicago Democratic congressman John Wentworth, asserting in a single sentence that the "General Government" had all the power it needed to "construct such harbors and improve such rivers as are 'necessary and proper.' "[2] Freshman representative Abraham Lincoln cast one of his first congressional votes for the measure, on December 21, 1847, but despite the lopsided, bipartisan tally (138 in favor to 54 opposed), Lincoln's personal efforts at western fusion kept falling short. Robert Smith, his friendly target from the stagecoach ride, was one of the few western Democrats who skipped the vote, and he remained a regular Democrat until the Civil War. Lincoln spent most of his next two years in Congress trying to find a better approach for broadening the Whig coalition. That quest led him effectively to repudiate the man he would later remember as his "beau ideal of a statesman," none other than Whig party founder, Henry Clay.[3]

SINCE NOTHING MUCH CAME out of the Chicago convention, it has largely escaped historical notice. The episode nonetheless highlights the evolution of Lincoln's partisan career and the nation's shifting political landscape. By the summer of 1847, the party system had matured in ways that left many participants frustrated. A new generation of partisans had opened up the American political process by extending universal suffrage to most adult white males and abandoning the old-fashioned custom of oral or viva voce voting in favor of printed party ballots.[4] But there was still a nagging perception that the new era of mass political parties had failed to save American republicanism from its own elitist limitations.

The discontent was most evident in those still legally excluded from the democratic process. Led by Elizabeth Cady Stanton, women's rights advocates gathered in 1848 at Seneca Falls, New York, invoking the revolutionary framework of the Declaration of Independence to express their "Declaration of Sentiments" for gender equality. Meanwhile Black activists in the North were organizing what was essentially the nation's first civil rights movement, an aggressive network of vigilance or self-protection committees designed to help thwart slave catchers and kidnappers in the region. Abolitionist newspapers touted it as the Underground Railroad. And even as the Liberty party struggled as a political organization, a more broad-based free-soil movement was emerging, one that attracted greater support across party lines by focusing on banning slavery in the western territories. In response, slaveholding politicians threatened disunion. This was no era of good feelings. The two national political parties, Democrats and Whigs, now only about fifteen years old as organizations, appeared to be out of touch and locked in a stalemate.[5]

Adding to this climate of political discontent were signs of economic and social disruption. New technologies such as the railroad and the telegraph were accelerating an already fast-paced and often turbulent national marketplace of goods and services. New immigrants from Ireland and Germany were altering the American social complexion, especially across the urban North. By 1847, the steady movement of people was also creating an entirely new demographic landscape in the nation's interior, caused not only by free white migration westward but also by the brutal coercion of the domestic slave trade and forced Indian removal from the Southeast. With the admission of Florida (1845), Texas (1845), Iowa (1846), and Wisconsin (1848), the American nation comprised thirty states over three million square miles of territory with a population approaching 23 million, including over three million enslaved Americans by 1850.

Lincoln did not condone all these changes, but he adapted to them with impressive facility. Out of the dozens of leading Whig lawyers and politicians around Springfield—including several like him who had been born in Kentucky, participated in the Black Hawk War, served in the state legislature, and rode circuit as members of the legal bar—Lincoln was by far the most forward-looking. Old Line Whigs such as John Todd Stuart drifted out of political power during this era by resisting key aspects of the rising modern tide. Stuart had managed two successful terms in Congress earlier in the decade and served a single term as an Illinois state senator during the early 1850s but then abandoned politics until returning to the fray as a Democratic congressman during the Civil War.

By contrast, Lincoln was eager to embrace new options for his party. For the 1848 presidential contest, pragmatic, fusionist-minded Whigs wanted someone in the mold of William Henry Harrison, "Old Tippecanoe," the popular military figure who had so far been their only successful national nominee. General Zachary Taylor, a career officer and recent hero of the Mexican War, stood out in this regard. The general had been in command at Buena Vista, where John Hardin had lost his life. Taylor was respected but had feuded with Polk over management of the war. He had also never voted before nor demonstrated any commitment to Whig policy measures.[6]

Lincoln was not bothered by Taylor's apolitical background and made clear his support for the general by late August 1847. At that time, leading Whig delegates from the state constitutional convention gathered in Springfield for a private caucus to discuss the presidential question.[7] Lincoln attended and claimed afterward that enthusiasm for Taylor had been strong, but others recalled that devotees of Whig founder Henry Clay were angered at his treatment by the group.

One of the participants, James Singleton, later suggested that Lincoln "proposed to throw Henry Clay overboard," while warning his fellow Whigs that they "had fought long enough on principle and ought to begin to fight for success." When this accusation became public in the late 1850s, Lincoln never fully denied it. And in the few of his letters that remain from the 1848 campaign, the new Whig congressman did indeed sound dismissive about the longtime Whig standard-bearer. "Mr. Clay's chance for an election," he assured one correspondent, "is just no chance at all." Lincoln also never forgave Singleton, blasting the Whig-turned-Democrat as a "miracle of meanness."[8]

Lincoln left for Washington in October 1847. Mary and their two young boys went along, an unusual decision at a time when most congressmen lived at boardinghouses and left their families at home. Along the way from Springfield, the Lincolns visited the Todd family in Lexington, Kentucky, for about three weeks. It was a rare opportunity for Mary to see her family and friends and to receive some much-needed cash from her father.[9] But the stopover in Clay's hometown also presented an awkward challenge for the Taylor-supporting Lincoln.

Clay, who was in Lexington during the Lincolns' visit, delivered a widely reported speech blasting the Mexican War as "unnatural." The Whig elder statesman, who had lost one of his sons in the war, insisted that no territory should come out of the conflict with Mexico unless through "fair purchase." He did not embrace the terms of the so-called Wilmot Proviso—a controversial House resolution to prohibit slavery from any of the territories acquired by defeating Mexico—which the Senate refused to consider. But Clay went out of his way to call slavery "a great evil" and even offered compromise text for an alternative to the proviso that might secure final passage and get signed into law. It was a bold move that signaled Clay's intentions to revive his fading national party leadership and pursue the Whig presidential nomination. Lincoln should have attended such an important speech and certainly should have called at Clay's estate at Ashland at some point during the visit with his father-in-law, who was a longtime friend and associate of the Whig founder. Yet it seems that Lincoln avoided Clay entirely. There is no record of any encounter between them, nor any later reference by Lincoln to such a meeting.[10]

Clay would have welcomed a chance to promote himself, even with an ambivalent supporter. He suggested in a letter to Horace Greeley, the editor and now a freshman member of the new Congress, that his Lexington speech would "represent" him well on the national scene "as a Western Man . . . with Northern principles." Clay denied that he was seeking the presidential nomination but went out of his way to remark on the favorable prospects of Greeley ally William Henry Seward, former governor of New York, as either vice president or a cabinet officer in the next Whig administration. Finally, the Whig founder assured Greeley that "Taylorism is everywhere on the decline," claiming it had been "a burst of enthusiasm" that many would come to "regret."[11]

Lincoln showed no signs of regret, however. His support for Taylor helped open important doors as soon he arrived in Washington in late November. In a letter to Richard Yates, a younger Whig attorney from Jacksonville in Morgan County, Lincoln mentioned that he had already been in conversations about the Taylor campaign with Duff Green, one of the city's top lobbyists or "lobby members," after only his first week in the city. Green owned and frequently boarded at Mrs. Sprigg's, the Capitol Hill boardinghouse or congressional "mess" where all four of the Lincolns were staying in a single room. Known as "Abolition House" because Ann Sprigg seemed to have an affinity for antislavery guests, the conversations at the dinner table were even more intense than usual. "President making has commenced" was how fellow lodger and Ohio congressman Joshua Giddings, a Whig and an abolitionist, described the scene in mid-December. By New Year's Day, Lincoln was predicting that despite "a good deal of diversity" on the presidential question, he expected the party to unite behind Taylor. A Whig lobby member from Galena, Elihu B. Washburne, recalled that Lincoln emerged quickly as "one of the most ardent and outspoken" Taylor supporters in the new Congress.[12]

Of Taylor's several pockets of support on Capitol Hill, Lincoln found his niche with a group of junior Whig congressmen mainly from the South who called themselves "Young Indians." According to Alexander Stephens of Georgia, the Young Indians had formed the first Taylor Club in Washington, which Lincoln soon joined. Lincoln also got to know Kentucky senator John Crittenden, the senior force in Washington behind the Taylor effort.[13]

In 1848, "president making" was still an unsettled process. A national convention system was tentatively in place, but the nominating campaigns were played largely without rules. Most key decisions occurred out of the public eye, through private conversations and without either formal announcements or pre-convention events. Organizers attempted to manage the "booming" process through letter-writing campaigns and by promoting candidates in party newspapers. There were no primary elections. Even the practice of holding national party conventions for presidential nominations was not fixed. The Whigs had so far managed only two such gatherings, at Harrisburg in 1839 and Baltimore in 1844. There was talk of trying to move forward in 1848 without one.[14]

What Taylor and his key supporters had been angling for was to make him a people's or "no party" candidate who could enter the fall contest with widespread Whig support but without a formal nomination.[15] Fusion on this scale would require abandoning the Whig label, a prospect that antagonized some leaders in the party. The movement now faced a defining choice: The Whigs had either to evolve under Taylor and move away from their existing organizational identity or remain true to their original principles and structures by backing Clay.

Lincoln's support for Taylor showed where he stood. The election for him was about winning. But in Congress, Lincoln remained a loyal northern Whig who followed the party line on issues like the Mexican War. Early in his term, he introduced the so-called Spot Resolutions, which questioned Democratic claims about the conflict's origins by disputing the "spot" where American blood had first been shed. In January 1848 he also voted for a Whig-sponsored resolution that censured Polk for having "unconstitutionally and unnecessarily" launched the controversial war, and he denounced the Democratic president during a floor speech in mid-January. The young congressman clearly aligned himself with free-soil, antislavery Whigs like Giddings. Lincoln would later claim that the Wilmot Proviso "was constantly coming up in some shape or other" during this period and that he had voted for it "at least forty times."[16] That was likely an exaggeration, but there is no doubt that Lincoln was positioning himself, much like Clay, "as a Western Man . . . with Northern principles."

Some of this maneuvering made Taylorite Whigs back home uneasy. Herndon and friends like Anson Henry were adamant that Lincoln was making a mistake with his opposition to the war. The congressman bristled at this criticism. "Would you have voted what you felt you knew to be a lie?" he demanded of Herndon, instructing him to read his Mexican War speech "sentence by sentence." When the junior partner continued to press, Lincoln replied with a heated explanation of constitutional war powers, concluding that Herndon's more expansive view "destroys the whole matter, and places our President where kings have always stood." Herndon ignored Lincoln's obvious irritation and asked for more documents. "Can I send speeches that nobody has made?" replied Lincoln, before adding impatiently, "You ask how Congress came to declare that war existed by the act of Mexico. Is it possible you dont understand that yet?"[17]

Though he sometimes lost his temper with Herndon, Lincoln proved diligent and patient in office, devoting the bulk of his lone term to constituent service while almost never missing a vote. He was active on his committees and even tried to take initiative on the contentious slavery issue, pulling together a plan, near the end of his term, to promote voluntary abolition within the District of Columbia. That measure never came to a vote; nor did any of his legislative efforts win final passage. Still, Lincoln learned about the challenges of coalition building from these otherwise frustrating experiences. At one point, while complaining in a floor speech about the parochialism of the president and his supporters after they had repeatedly blocked river and harbor improvements, Lincoln observed sagely:

> There are few things *wholly* evil or wholly good. Almost every thing, especially of government policy, is an inseparable compound of the two; so that our best judgment of the preponderance between them is continually demanded.

Greeley's *New-York Tribune* praised Lincoln's pragmatic efforts on behalf of rivers and harbors undertaken across party lines with Democratic congressman John Wentworth. "Tall men come from Illinois," reported the *Tribune*. "John Wentworth and Lincoln are both men of mighty stature, and their intellectual endowments correspond with their physical."[18]

Although only a one-term member who wrote no bills into law, Lincoln's congressional service was significant for his partisan achievement. His main goal in Congress was to help elect a Whig president, and he did.

The visible campaign for the Whig nomination began in January 1848 when congressional Whigs decided to ignore the "no party" idea from the Taylor camp and set a national Whig convention in Philadelphia in June. That decision sent the Taylor and Clay forces scrambling to secure endorsements from Whig caucuses in state legislatures, briefly creating a rare public battle for the nomination. Three southern states (Kentucky, North Carolina, and Virginia) planned to hold caucus meetings on February 22 (Washington's birthday), the same day that Taylor supporters were organizing what they called a "Buena Vista Festival," celebrating Taylor in Philadelphia on the first anniversary of his major victory in Mexico.

Lincoln missed the Buena Vista Festival because of a commitment to help raise funds for the still unfinished Washington Monument, but he sent along a letter to be read at the gathering. The Illinois congressman ignored Clay, but he declared himself "decidedly in favor of General Taylor" and noted that since he was the state's "only Whig member," he would have to speak for all Illinois Whigs. Lincoln claimed that the private gathering held during the previous summer had "nominated General Taylor for the Presidency." This was bold revisionism, because as Lincoln acknowledged, the attendees in August 1847 had not been selected for any such purpose and were acting "as so many individuals expressing their own preferences."[19]

Lincoln produced a more aggressive pro-Taylor statement to be deployed at the Virginia caucus meeting. He explained that he favored General Taylor because "we can elect him . . . and we can not elect any other whig," adding that Taylor would help the party "make great inroads among the rank and file of the democrats," and he "probably" could win the state of Illinois, while "certainly" helping to elect an additional Whig to the state's congressional delegation.[20]

By the spring of 1848, Taylor's managers were focused on identifying their man as a Whig while still suggesting that he could appeal to independent-minded Democrats. It was a challenging strategy that they sometimes found difficult to defend. In April, under pressure, the general released a letter declaring himself to be "a Whig but not an ultra Whig," a formulation that satisfied no one. Lincoln was neither a Taylor insider nor a potential vice president nor a possible cabinet officer such as his future rival William Seward, but the first-term congressman tried to draft a statement on Taylor's behalf that focused on issues. The effort went nowhere.[21]

The Taylor forces may have stumbled on their way to the Philadelphia convention, but they arrived in a strong position nonetheless. The septuagenarian Clay had proven incapable of fully repositioning himself. Taylor retained solid southern Whig support and made just enough inroads among northern delegations in Democratic-majority states such as Illinois that he emerged, barely, as the front-runner at Philadelphia. Lincoln, feeling "anxiety" about the outcome, attended the convention but was not an official delegate.[22] Taylor won the nomination on the fourth ballot. Lincoln wired news of the results to the Whig newspaper in Springfield on Friday, June 9, at 11:15 p.m., likely his first use of the nation's new telegraphic system.[23] Delegates chose Millard Fillmore, a conservative New York Whig, to balance the ticket as vice president and took the unusual position of avoiding a formal platform. They adopted instead a handful of resolutions extolling Taylor's military service, claiming that he would have voted for the Whig ticket in 1844, and promising that he would govern in patriotic fashion.

Lincoln soon wrote Herndon an enthusiastic letter about how the "nomination of 'Old Rough' " would produce an "overwhelming, glorious triumph." Whig faithful such as Greeley were angry over the rejection of Clay and the blatant disregard for Whig policy measures at the convention, but Lincoln appeared unconcerned. He espoused nothing but full-throated fusionism to his partner back in Springfield. As the "unmistakable sign" of their impending success, he claimed "that all the odds and ends are with us—Barnburners, Native Americans, Tyler men, disappointed office seeking locofocos, and Lord knows what."[24] That single line captured a great deal about Lincoln's view of the partisan situation in 1848. His litany of temporary Whig allies—everyone from antislavery Democrats ("Barnburners"), anti-immigrant Protestants ("Native Americans"), and independent Whigs ("Tyler men"), to even the most corrupt, self-serving Democrats ("disappointed office seeking locofocos")—illustrated his support for a broad Whig coalition even if that meant accepting a cynical combination of men without measures.

Lincoln sent Mary a chatty letter on the same day he wrote Herndon. The couple was exchanging letters because Mary and the boys had returned to her family in Lexington. The tumult of their boisterous crew inside a small boardinghouse room had proven too distracting for the congressman. "In this troublesome world, we are never quite satisfied," Lincoln had written in April not long after their departure. "When you were here, I thought you hindered me some in attending to business; but now, having nothing but business—no variety—it has grown exceedingly tasteless to me," adding, "I hate to stay in this old room by myself." The Lincolns eventually arranged for Mary and the children to return to Washington following the convention, but they did not arrive until mid-July.[25]

The most notable new contact Lincoln made at the Whig convention was with Thaddeus Stevens, then an attorney and congressional candidate from Lancaster, Pennsylvania. Although Stevens was not yet a prominent figure, Lincoln recognized his talents. Later in the summer he wrote Stevens a short note that began, "You may possibly remember seeing me at the Philadelphia Convention, introduced to you as the lone whig star of Illinois." Lincoln claimed he was looking for the "undisguised opinion of some experienced and sagacious Pennsylvania politician" on how the state would turn out in the election. "In casting about for such a man," Lincoln wrote, "I have settled upon you."[26] The usually cantankerous Stevens proved equally charming in reply, offering guarded optimism about Pennsylvania, depending on how well the Whigs coordinated with the anti-immigrant "natives." Stevens requested insights from Lincoln about Whig prospects in the western states, since "your means of information are much better than mine."[27]

The exchange illustrated that Lincoln was becoming one of the national campaign's more valuable workhorses. In late July he delivered a partisan stump speech of nearly an hour's length from the House floor, extolling the Taylor candidacy, beating back Democratic attacks, and mocking the pretensions of their nominee, Michigan senator Lewis Cass. Lincoln almost surely sent a copy of that speech to Stevens, to whom he mentioned that he was working out of "the Whig document room" while composing his letter.

He was referring to his work for the campaign committee. Congress had been adjourned for weeks, but Lincoln was still sitting inside a sweltering Capitol Hill office, while his now-returned family waited impatiently for him back at the boardinghouse, so that he could affix his official signature to pamphlets that were being franked (or sent out with free postage) to Whig activists around the country. These pamphlets contained printed copies of political speeches by Whig members and were designed to provide what Lincoln had once called "war-club" for the coming campaign. The congressional franking privilege was not intended for partisan purposes, but it was frequently used that way and nobody used it more in this fashion in 1848 than Congressman Lincoln. During his sole term in office, he sent out at taxpayer expense more than 12,000 political documents, including 7,000 copies of his own speeches and more than 5,500 copies of speeches by other members.[28]

Most of these political pamphlets went out at the direction of an "Executive Committee" of Whig congressmen headed by Truman Smith of Connecticut. Smith was one of the original Young Indians and had become a top architect of the national campaign.[29] Lincoln was comfortable in this intense partisan environment and kept himself busy doing whatever the committee required, even when it involved staying behind and working long after the regular congressional session ended.[30]

For months, Mary Lincoln had been angling for a family "sightseeing" excursion to New York and Boston once they were ready to return home after the congressional session.[31] Lincoln agreed but wanted to make good partisan use of the trip. On the same day that he wrote to Stevens, Lincoln contacted an old Illinois Whig acquaintance who was now an attorney in Boston to help him arrange a speaking trip in Massachusetts. Lincoln suggested that he had "the elements of one speech in mind," which he hoped to deliver in "politically affected" communities.[32]

Lincoln ended up delivering nearly a dozen speeches across Massachusetts over two weeks in September 1848. He then dragged his family to Albany, New York, where he had arranged for meetings with Whig editor and power broker Thurlow Weed and vice-presidential nominee Fillmore. The Lincolns finally departed for home at the end of September, traveling along what Mary called the "lake route" so they could visit Niagara Falls.

Massachusetts was considered a pivotal Whig objective, its twelve electoral votes at risk because of widespread defections from Conscience Whigs into the new antislavery Free Soil party. Meeting in August in Buffalo, New York, the Free Soilers nominated former Democratic president Martin Van Buren to head their ticket, with Charles Francis Adams, son of recently deceased former president John Quincy Adams, their vice-presidential nominee. The Free Soilers, who tried to be more pragmatic in approach than the Liberty men, combined fervent antislavery views with fusionist planks including endorsements for "cheap postage" and river and harbor improvements. Like the political abolitionists in the Liberty party, they viewed the destruction of slavery as a process, one that would begin with "no more Slave States and no more Slave Territory." Salmon Chase of Ohio was a main organizer of the Buffalo convention and chief author of the platform. The Free Soil strength across New England was considerable. Lincoln, who was calling himself a "Western free state man" with "personal feelings . . . against the extension of slavery," was determined to help head off this third-party threat in Massachusetts.[33]

The highlight of Lincoln's trip was a September 22 speech in Boston, where he shared a stage with fellow antislavery Whig William

Seward of New York. The impressive Friday-night event drew over three thousand attendees at the imposing Tremont Temple. The *Boston Courier* praised Lincoln—by name this time—for his "most forcible and convincing speech."[34] But Seward was unhappy, complaining to his wife that the local newspapers had butchered his remarks. "Such is the fortune of political lecturers," he sighed, making no mention of any fellow lecturer from Illinois.[35]

Lincoln's initiative in organizing the Massachusetts speaking tour was an indication of his political character. He had always been willing to pay his dues, but he was also capable of self-promotion. Lincoln acknowledged this formula in the summer of 1848 when his partner Herndon complained about a lack of political opportunities for younger Whigs in Illinois. Lincoln was unmoved. "Do you suppose that I should ever have got into notice," he asked, "if I had waited to be hunted up and pushed forward by older men?"[36]

In early October, Lincoln returned to Illinois to face disappointing political news. During the August elections, Stephen Logan, his former law partner, had lost the once safe Whig congressional seat around Springfield. David Davis had been warning for months about Whig overconfidence, claiming that local party activists were "in a more disorganized state than I have ever known them to be."[37] And in the campaign's closing days, Democratic candidate Thomas Harris employed effective negative attacks.[38] Elsewhere, however, Illinois Whigs had done better than usual. Mexican War veteran Edward Baker won a congressional seat in Galena, and Whigs in fast-growing northern Illinois made other gains in legislative contests.

The local Democratic newspaper greeted Representative Lincoln's return to Springfield with sarcasm: "We are pleased to observe that his arduous duties since the adjournment of Congress in franking and loading down the mails with whig electioneering documents, have not impaired his health. He looks remarkably well."[39] As if to prove their point, Lincoln started stumping for Taylor right away. The general won Lincoln's congressional district handily in November, far outpolling Logan's disappointing results.

The national election results were closer. Taylor prevailed, but not by much, and it soon became clear that Whigs had lost their bare majority in the U.S. House. They made up for some of that disappointment by securing gains (though not a majority) in the U.S. Senate, but this new phase of divided government heralded an uncertain future for the party. The Mexican War ended with the announcement of a peace treaty in July that confirmed one of the largest territorial gains in U.S. history, but the partisan disruptions intensified by the conflict endured. The most controversial issue was whether territories acquired by the United States through the war would remain free (since Mexico had abolished slavery) or would become part of American slavery's fast-expanding southwestern empire.

The pressure of that challenge helps explain why Free Soilers did better than expected in the 1848 contest. The third party won about 10 percent of the nation's popular vote, more than 12 percent in Illinois, and finished second in both Massachusetts and New York. They were more potent than the Liberty party had ever been. In Illinois, Taylor fell only three thousand votes short out of nearly 125,000 ballots cast and might have won the state had not the Free Soilers run a third-party slate. There was hope for the Whig party's future in Illinois if they could only co-opt the antislavery radicals. For Lincoln, the problem was familiar. He had been worried about third-party antislavery votes since 1844, when he believed that Liberty men had cost Whigs the electoral votes of New York and Clay's chance at a presidential victory.

Taylor's victory created partisan work for Lincoln when he returned to Washington for his final session of Congress. No Illinois politician had ever served in a presidential cabinet, and Congressman-Elect Edward Baker, now from Galena, wanted that honor. Recently back from combat service in Mexico and still in his thirties, Baker seemed like a promising model for Taylor and his advisers, who were eager to move beyond the ultra Whigs and build what some were already calling the "Taylor Republican Party."[40]

Lincoln was ambivalent about Baker's abilities and skeptical that any Whig from a Democratic-controlled state could get selected for the cabinet, but he beat the drum on Baker's behalf for several weeks. Lincoln even brought the matter directly to Taylor's attention. The president-elect brushed him off, however, directing that he should send any endorsement letters for Baker "through the mail," which Lincoln somewhat sheepishly did.[41]

Baker's reputation in Washington was mixed. Judge Davis of Bloomington informed his wife that the war had left their friend "dissipated." Baker was also known as a bit of a blowhard. During the campaign, Lincoln joked that his friend was "a good hand to raise a breeze."[42] Joshua Speed, now living in Kentucky, reported that Senator (now Governor) John Crittenden had confided to him that Baker's career had been a little too "erratic." Lincoln shared the senator's comments with Baker, assuring his former Springfield roommate that it was no secret, that he and Baker had "talked it over frequently," and that Baker was determined to change people's minds.[43]

Although Baker never entered President Taylor's cabinet, he tried to exhibit more political leadership in early 1849. That winter he and Lincoln worked together closely in Washington, scrambling to secure for Illinois as many patronage appointments as possible and to hold the one subcabinet level post that the state currently did control—the commissionership of the General Land Office. Democrat James Shields, Lincoln's old dueling antagonist (and now recently elected to the U.S. Senate), and his party colleague Richard Young, a former U.S. senator, had both served as Land Office commissioners during the Polk administration. Originally part of the Treasury Department, the General Land Office, which managed the sale of public lands, was in the process of being moved to the newly created Interior Department. It was a lucrative post and a powerful one. A savvy commissioner could reward party friends and punish political enemies. Illinois Whigs wanted one of their own for the post.

The obvious Illinois candidate for such a critical party job was Lincoln. The outgoing congressman informed David Davis in February that he had no doubt "that I could take the Land-office if I would," admitting that the position's $3,000 annual salary "would make me more money than I can otherwise make." But Lincoln claimed that he was more interested in the law and did not want all the other disappointed job seekers "snarling at me about it." Unimpressed, Judge Davis replied, "I would take the Land Office." Lincoln trotted out similar rationalizations with Speed after his Kentucky friend passed along the welcome news that Crittenden thought highly of him for such a position. Dismissing the commissionership as a "second class" office, Lincoln boasted that he could "have" the job "by common consent," but "I fear I shall have trouble to get it for any other man in Illinois."[44]

Other Whigs were clamoring for the appointment. Cyrus Edwards, a prominent attorney from the Alton area, wrote to Lincoln "soliciting his aid."[45] Edwards was an imposing figure, nearly Lincoln's equal in height and of a distinguished political lineage. A native of Maryland, Edwards had grown up in Kentucky, where his older brother Ninian had been the commonwealth's top jurist before serving as the Illinois territorial governor and eventually as the state's first U.S. senator. Following his brother's death in the early 1830s, Cyrus launched his own political career in Illinois, spending years in the state legislature. He was an unsuccessful Whig candidate for governor and twice for U.S. senator. Most recently he had been a delegate to the state constitutional convention. It was his nephew, Ninian W. Edwards, who had hosted the Whig gathering at Springfield that endorsed Taylor for president.[46]

Cyrus Edwards also loomed large in Lincoln's social network. His nephew Ninian, the son of the former territorial governor, was a Springfield attorney and a Whig state legislator who was married to Mary Lincoln's older sister Elizabeth. It was at the Edwards home on the north side of Springfield where Lincoln had met and married Mary Todd. The Edwards residence was also where Lincoln had once encountered and apparently developed an embarrassing crush on Cyrus Edwards's teenage daughter Matilda—an episode that may have contributed in 1841 to his temporary breakup with Mary.[47]

There was a second candidate for the Land Office post whom Baker preferred. Colonel James Morrison, a lawyer from nearby Belleville known as "Don," was more than twenty years younger than Edwards but had an appealing background for the Taylor administration. Morrison had graduated from the U.S. Naval Academy and served in the navy during the 1830s before becoming a lawyer, a successful real estate investor, and a Whig legislator in Illinois. He helped raise troops for the Mexican War in 1846 and served as a regimental army officer under General Taylor. Morrison knew Lincoln as well and seemed to be full of ambition, talent, and boundless self-promoting energy. But he was not yet even thirty-three years old.[48] Throughout the early months of 1849, Baker and Lincoln seemed unable to sort out how to handle the Land Office logjam and so they focused for a time on other patronage priorities.

From the start of the appointments process, Lincoln knew that he was going to disappoint people. Over the winter, he grew particularly annoyed about the sore feelings of a young Whig activist from Springfield named Walter Davis, a carpenter who had lent him the use of his woodshop in the weeks after the election. Lincoln was trying to develop a model for a device to help boats caught in shallow water that he had invented and was seeking to patent. Davis was one of the active "mechanics" or workingmen in the local party, someone whom Lincoln described as "an always *faithful* and never *troublesome* Whig." Davis had also served in the Mexican War and got involved on the party's behalf in a scurrilous postelection attack on Major Thomas Harris, the Democrat who had defeated Logan for Congress. Relying on testimony that originated from ex-sergeant Davis, the Springfield Whig newspaper accused Harris of "skulking" or hiding during one of the battles in the Mexican campaign. Enraged, the new congressman demanded vindication, and once again Springfield was awash with talk of dueling.[49]

Davis wanted to be rewarded for his partisan services with an appointment as the town's postmaster, an important position otherwise above his party standing. He believed (wrongly, it turned out) that Lincoln was on his side. "There must be some mistake about Walter Davis saying I promised him the Post-Office," Lincoln wrote to Herndon. He explained to Davis: "I said, that if the distribution of the offices should fall into my hands, you should have *something*." According to Herndon, party regulars in town complained that Lincoln was playing favorites with his woodshop assistant, an accusation that deeply offended the experienced leader. "I have certainly not been selfish," Lincoln replied, pointing out that "in my greatest need of friends [Davis] was against me and for Baker." The congressman was referring to the 1843 Sangamon County Whig convention, when he had felt whipsawed by all the gossip about him and had lost the chance for a congressional nomination.[50]

Lincoln had once derided patronage, or the filling of public offices with party operatives, as the "same everlasting subject," but there was no longer room for such cynicism. The distribution of government jobs, from cabinet positions to local postmasters and land office agents, truly mattered. Just as Lincoln once fought to defend the convention system as essential for the modern Whig party, he was now determined to promote better Whig management of the often vilified "spoils system," the notorious term invented by Jacksonians to suggest that election "victors" were entitled to the "spoils" of government.

The problem was that nobody in the Taylor administration

seemed to care. Time and again in early 1849, Lincoln responded to requests for office by promising to try for "something" but also warning correspondents that he really had no idea what might "fall into my hands." He was routinely forced to admit that he was not even sure if the Taylor administration would proceed with "removals" on a partisan basis.[51]

Lincoln's frustrations were boiling over by the time of Taylor's inauguration on March 5, 1849. Finding little traction for any of his requests, he felt compelled to use his attendance at "the very inaugeration," as he put it glumly afterward, to press for appointments.[52] Yet the experienced party leader remained undaunted. On March 8, he informed the new secretary of state, John Clayton, that he was "*exceedingly* anxious" to get an appointment in the Minnesota territory for his old friend and Whig activist, Anson Henry. Dr. Henry was the one who had orchestrated the recent slanderous attacks on Major Harris. It was also Henry, as one of Springfield's early physicians, who had helped Lincoln through his attacks of "hypo" as a young man. Lincoln collected nearly fifty signatures from Whig congressmen endorsing Henry.[53]

Next Lincoln went in pursuit of Treasury Secretary William Meredith, reminding him, on the department head's second official day in office, that he and Baker were the "only Whig members of congress from Illinois" and that "the whigs of that state hold us responsible, to some extent," for the distribution of government positions. Lincoln asked "most respectfully" to be "heard" whenever appointments for Illinois Whigs were being contemplated within Treasury.[54]

But Lincoln's aggressive notes had little immediate impact. By the end of the administration's first week, and with only days left before he was scheduled to depart for home, Lincoln decided to ratchet up the pressure. On Sunday, March 11, he swung into a final round of action on behalf of his various patronage objectives. He began the day by sending a note to Secretary of War George Crawford, drafted for him by John Morrison, a desperate Illinois job seeker who had come to the nation's capital to press his claims in person. Morrison's handwriting is still visible on the body of the letter that a harried Lincoln merely signed. In the note, Lincoln (Morrison) observed sharply that, "There is not now a single Whig Clerk from Illinois in any of the Departments."[55]

That afternoon Lincoln and Baker also wrote a joint letter to Thomas Ewing, an experienced Ohio politician, at the new Interior Department. Alluding to a previous face-to-face conversation, the two men informed the secretary that they were renewing "in writing" their "earnest request that no appointments of citizens of Illinois not local be made (and especially that of commissioner of the land office) without the consultation with us which you were kind enough to say you thought proper."[56] The reference to the General Land Office was significant because Lincoln and Baker had just become aware that a well-known Henry Clay supporter from their state, Chicago attorney Justin Butterfield, was now seeking the job.[57]

During one of their encounters with Ewing, Baker apparently slandered Butterfield, intimating that the fifty-nine-year-old attorney had suffered some type of stroke and that his mind and body were so "impaired" that he had been unable to attend court in Springfield. Word of this exchange eventually reached Butterfield, who responded with hot indignation. By mid-April, Butterfield furnished Ewing with a series of affidavits from doctors testifying to his good health. The noted attorney dismissed his failure to attend court the previous winter, blaming the "most horrible roads" between Chicago and Springfield. Galena lobbyist Elihu Washburne, appalled, wrote that "Baker, while in Washington, backed up in a measure, I am sorry to say, by Lincoln, lied about Butterfield most outrageously to Mr. Ewing."[58]

Washburne detested Baker as a carpetbagger who had stolen into his district, but such harsh words for his friend Lincoln were especially damning. Both Lincoln and Baker felt threatened by Butterfield. By Lincoln's own reckoning, it was specifically to prevent Butterfield's appointment that he decided to show up unannounced on the evening of March 11 at the boardinghouse of William Preston, an ex–Virginia congressman who had since become the new secretary of the navy. Preston had nothing in particular to do with the General Land Office, but he was the one member of Taylor's cabinet whom Lincoln knew well. One of the Young Indians who had supported Taylor from the beginning, Preston worked with Lincoln during the campaign and was elevated into the cabinet out of deference to Whig political strength in Virginia. On March 11, Lincoln "besought" his old colleague to help ensure that "no man from Illinois should be appointed to any high office, without my being at least heard on the question." Lincoln was angry about Butterfield because the Chicago attorney had supported Clay over Taylor and then shirked, in Lincoln's opinion, any work on the general campaign. Preston agreed that Lincoln's request was "a reasonable one."[59]

Before Lincoln left town, he found time to argue his only case before the U.S. Supreme Court. He lost but it was a notable career milestone. Lincoln also filed an official patent application for his woodshop invention, which he labeled a new "method" of lifting vessels over shoals (U.S. Patent No. 6,469). But he remained mostly absorbed by patronage matters. On his fortieth birthday, just a few weeks earlier, he had complained to his friend Davis about the incessant political demands. "Out of more than three hundred letters received this session," he wrote, "yours is the second one manifesting the least interest for me personally."[60]

John Morrison, the office seeker from Tremont who had ghostwritten his own endorsement letter, saw for himself that Lincoln was longing for "*home*," especially for his oldest son, "*Dear little Bob*," now five years old. But the stakes for Whig activists like Morrison, an ex–county clerk now approaching fifty, were simply too high. Their lives and careers appeared to hang in the balance—a fact driven home by Morrison's particularly sad case. He angrily pointed out to Lincoln, before the congressman departed, that he had his own children to worry about (at least five, including a six-year-old daughter) and that he had become "a bankrupt" who could no longer "shield & protect" them. "I would cheerfully give all I possess," Morrison wrote, "if some philanthophist [*sic*] would be so charatable as to expend a dimes worth of powder & lead in blowing my brains out."[61] Lincoln must have recognized in Morrison's sad tale a dark alternative to his own story. For devoted partisans of this era, whether Whig or Democrat, politics offered one of the most open pathways for advancement in the race of life. Lincoln certainly understood the personal stakes involved. He even paused during his journey back to Springfield to file letters of recommendation for other job seekers he had encountered along the way.[62]

Lincoln avoided Cyrus Edwards, however, while passing through Alton on his return home in late March. Instead, he left a note for his "old friend" that revealed an unexpected obstacle in his quest for the Land Office appointment. According to Lincoln, he was planning to help Edwards but could not do so because Baker, his congressional colleague, was supporting Don Morrison. Lincoln suggested to Edwards that he and Morrison had to work something out between them. He claimed that Baker had agreed that after one of the applicants stepped aside, the two Whig congressmen would then "jointly recommend the other" and that only such an arrangement would keep the position in Illinois. It was galling for a would-be patrician like Edwards to be pushed into such a negotiation with a brash youngster like Morrison. To make matters worse, Lincoln's only advice to Edwards was, "Don't surrender too easily."[63]

Despite Lincoln's claims to Edwards, there is good reason to believe that he was working in tandem with Baker to defeat Butterfield.[64] The Whig congressmen had been consistent in working as a unit whenever they were discussing the Land Office position. They also appear to have shared a room together at Mrs. Sprigg's boarding-house in February 1849, and to have returned home with each other in March.[65] If they were traveling together as they passed through Alton, that would help explain why Lincoln failed to pay his respects to Edwards. Baker and Edwards hated each other.

Shortly after his return to Springfield, and after further consultations with local activists, Lincoln authorized political allies in the area—for the first time—to begin working to secure the Land Office appointment for himself. Lincoln continued to express hope that somebody from Illinois might be able to get the position, but he was now finally admitting that he would "feel complimented" by the selection. He acknowledged this was a sensitive matter. "I gave my word" to Edwards, Lincoln explained in early April, and had "stipulated" with Baker over how to handle Morrison's competing claims. "In relation to these pledges," he wrote carefully, "I must not only be chaste but above suspicion."[66]

The peculiar phrasing, and Lincoln's actions, suggest that even though he did not really want a "second class" commissionership, he was unwilling to surrender any influence as state party leader. Whether the position went to Edwards, Morrison, or himself, Lincoln was now determined to remain a key decision-maker. He could declare victory for the fusionist wing of the party with any one of those three appointments. If the position went outside the state or to a notable Clay supporter like Butterfield, then Lincoln would have to acknowledge defeat for his faction. This was not the kind of tawdry patronage fight that he wanted, but it was the leadership battle that Lincoln was now determined to win.[67]

On the same day in April that he wrote about his new position on the Land Office commissionership, Lincoln penned at least four fresh patronage letters to Washington. One of these new recommendations was for carpenter Walter Davis. Lincoln had finally decided to urge Davis's appointment as receiver of the Land Office in Springfield, replacing none other than Archer Herndon, the father of Lincoln's law partner. Lincoln had nothing bad to say about the incumbent but noted that Herndon, a Democrat, was "a very warm partizan" who had "openly & actively opposed the election of Gen. Taylor."[68]

Lincoln was also pushing for deeper changes in Whig partisan norms. In late April, he turned his attention toward a bitter local dispute over a postmastership that was erupting in Tremont, a small town situated in his former congressional district. There were Taylor men, Old Line Whigs, political abolitionists, and others fighting to seize control of the position. Claiming he was "perplexed" by the infighting, Lincoln ordered Whig activists to organize a meeting. "Let it be public, full, and fair," he instructed, with "no cliqueism or cheatery about it."[69] Lincoln had always pushed for greater transparency in the political process, and after spending so much of his time consumed and frustrated by Whig "cliqueism," he understood the opportunity that Taylor's fusionist victory provided. There was finally an opening to expand the Whig coalition.

The trouble was that impulses toward "cheatery" ran strong. William Butler, one of Lincoln's oldest political friends, tried to manipulate him into flip-flopping some of his other recommendations, including for Walter Davis, to benefit himself. When Lincoln realized that he was being played and that it was "openly avowed" around Springfield "that my supposed influence at Washington shall be broken down generally," he became furious. Lincoln drafted a statement in support of his previous patronage choices, instructing one of his key allies to copy it "in your own hand-writing" before getting "everybody" to endorse it, adding, "not three or four but three or four hundred." This was the type of leadership challenge that provoked Lincoln into full boss mode. "Dont neglect or delay in the matter," he barked. When he later explained the situation to Secretary of the Interior Thomas Ewing, he admitted that the "fault-finders" were really aiming "to stab me."[70]

Lincoln's frustrations over patronage only got worse. "I have heard nothing," he grumbled to one correspondent. To another, he was even more negative. "Not one man recommended by me has yet been appointed to any thing, little or big," he wrote on May 7, "except a few who had no opposition."[71] Lincoln received confidential word that Butterfield was "trying his best for the place" in the Land Office with quiet support from Ewing and perhaps others in the cabinet. A native of New England and with years of experience as an attorney in New York, Butterfield certainly had great "Eastern influence," according to Lincoln's friend Josiah Lucas. The clerk in the Washington office listed figures such as Daniel Webster of Massachusetts and Truman Smith of Connecticut as among the Chicago attorney's leading backers, in addition to Henry Clay. The only remaining obstacle to Butterfield's appointment was hesitation within the Taylor administration over how to avoid offending Lincoln and Baker. Lucas tried to convey the urgency of the situation to Lincoln. "Things are moved here by *personal importunity*," he advised. "And allow me to inform you, that in my humble opinion, unless something is done by *you—you*, Sir, the aforesaid Butterfield will succeed."[72]

Lincoln finally had enough. He admitted that it would "mortify me deeply if Gen. Taylors administration shall trample all my wishes in the dust merely to gratify these men." Then he let loose on William Preston, his only real friend on the inside. On May 16, he reminded the navy secretary of their conversation in mid-March and how he had expected to have input on major appointments. But, Lincoln reported, he was just now discovering that Butterfield was about to be named Land Office commissioner. After calling the noted Chicago attorney "my friend" and acknowledging that Butterfield was "well qualified" for the job, Lincoln proceeded to lodge vehement objections. What mattered to him was partisanship, and on that score, Butterfield would be disastrous. Lincoln went back to 1840, recalling "a fierce and laborious battle in Illinois" that resulted in electoral victory but "with it," according to the party leader, "the appointment of a set of drones," including Butterfield as a U.S. attorney, even though the man "had never spent a dollar or lifted a finger in the fight." He recalled that Butterfield had "played off and on" during the feud between John Tyler and Clay. And he reminded his former colleague that "when you and I were almost sweating blood to have Genl. Taylor nominated, this same man was ridiculing the idea, and going for Mr. Clay."[73]

Lincoln was so mad that for once he was not above lying. Even though he and Josiah Lucas had already discussed how Lisle Smith, another prominent Chicago Whig, was supporting Butterfield, and despite knowing that Butterfield had spent much of the spring openly collecting endorsements in Chicago, Lincoln simply pretended none of this was true.[74] "If there is one man in this state who desires B's appointment to any thing," Lincoln wrote, "I declare I have not heard of him." He warned Preston that Illinois Whigs might revolt. "Our whigs will throw down their arms, and fight no more," Lincoln predicted darkly, "if the fruit of their labor is thus disposed of."[75]

That was a big threat to make, especially in writing, but Lincoln was serious. He followed up with an urgent barrage of confidential letters to his far-flung network of state and national contacts. He asked someone to reach out to Crittenden from Kentucky. "He can control the matter," claimed Lincoln, warning that even though "Old Zach hangs fire" (or delays), the decision was all but settled. He was equally blunt with Washington insider Duff Green, calling the appointment "the only crumb of patronage which Illinois expects" and urging him to "defeat B" in "whichever [way] you can." Lincoln still hedged his bets about exactly who should become commissioner, but he was adamant that he was the one who should decide it. "I wish you to write General Taylor at once," he advised key correspondents on May 25, "saying that either *I, or the man I recommend*, should, in your opinion, be appointed to that office." A few months earlier, he and Baker were merely asking "to be heard." Now Lincoln was demanding a veto. He kept repeating that Butterfield's appointment would be "an egregious political blunder."[76]

While Lincoln was attempting to mobilize this raw display of political influence, his stepbrother John Johnston reported that Thomas Lincoln, age seventy-one, was dying from what the family believed was "Disease of the Heart." Lincoln's elderly father lived with Johnston in Coles County, less than a hundred miles from Springfield. Despite the proximity, Lincoln and his father had hardly seen each other since the headstrong son first struck out on his own about eighteen years before as a "penniless boy" in New Salem. Johnston begged Lincoln to visit, telling him that Thomas Lincoln "Craves to See you all the time" and that he had "all most Despared of see ing you." Another relative chimed in: "I am told that His cries for you for the last few days are truly Heart Rendering."[77] In late May, Lincoln finally dropped everything and rushed out to see his father, who it turned was not dying after all. The local doctor finally concluded it was not heart disease but rather an "unusual amount of matter being confined in His lungs" that had caused Thomas Lincoln's breathing problems.[78]

Nobody knows for sure what transpired during this rare father-son reunion, but it was clear that patronage issues never left Lincoln's mind. While in Coles County, he received a telegram from Anson Henry, sent on Tuesday, May 29, 1849, reporting that the administration was about to announce the appointment of Butterfield as commissioner. *"You must go on,"* Henry urged, describing how *Journal* editor Simeon Francis was wiring a special request to the president asking for a delay until Lincoln had a chance to come to Washington.[79] Lincoln decided to move quickly. On June 1, in a letter dated from Charleston in Coles County, he informed Pennsylvania congressman Moses Hampton that he had finally made up his mind. "At last I concluded to take the General Land-Office if I can get it," Lincoln wrote, "more to prevent what would be generally bad for the party here, and particularly bad for me, than a positive desire for the office." He asked Hampton to "write old Zach" what he termed "as pretty a letter for me as you think the truth will permit," specifying that it not be sent to "Mr. Ewing" and adding, "Time is important. What you do, do quickly."[80]

It was no accident that Lincoln turned to someone like Hampton at such a critical moment. Their relationship was emblematic of Lincoln's impressive networking accomplishments from his days in Washington. He had proven himself a good organization man, with a friendly demeanor and a useful ability to get things done. A few months earlier Hampton had sent Lincoln his own patronage request, reminding his "friend" of crude jokes they used to share, like one that Lincoln had told about "the old Virginian stropping his razor on a certain *member* of a young negro's body" or another about the "old womans *fish*" that got "*larger*, the more it [was] handled." This type of humor had apparently once been part of their fraternal life together in Washington. In this context, it took the edge off some obvious neediness. "I want that appointment and *must have it*," the Pennsylvania politician had written in March, promising Lincoln that anything he could do to help "shall be repaid with compound interest, if ever in my power to do so."[81] With his own sense of urgency and passing attempts at humor, Lincoln was ready to collect.

The request from Springfield editor Francis managed to secure a three-week delay from the administration, which Lincoln and his friends learned about by telegram on June 2. Taylor cabinet officer William Preston shared the news, admitting that "Lincoln is the only man in Illinois that can beat Butterfield, but that he can do it if he comes on, & his friends back him up." Lincoln later recalled that message as the turning point in his decision-making, forgetting what he had written to Hampton the day before. "I first determined to be an applicant, unconditionally, on the 2nd. of June," he later wrote, "and I did so upon being informed by a Telegraphic despach, that the question was narrowed down to Mr. B. and myself, and that the Cabinet had postponed the appointment three weeks for my benefit."[82]

The message from Washington set off a feverish letter-writing campaign. Lincoln reached out to figures such as William Seward, now a first-term U.S. senator from New York. He also circled back to old acquaintances such as Duff Green, the cagey lobbyist and boardinghouse owner who happened to be married to Cyrus Edwards's sister, and pressed him to take a final stand, which Green did, on his behalf. The hurried effort was so strenuous, crammed as it was into a matter of days and hours, that Lincoln needed help. He turned once again to Anson Henry, who penned the letter to Green and signed it for him.[83] He also relied on his wife Mary. Lincoln essentially created a series of form letters, which Mary then copied and sometimes signed for him, and which they mailed at their own expense across the country.[84]

Butterfield was busy as well. On the same day that Lincoln reached out to Seward, Butterfield wrote a blistering letter to Major David Hunter, an old friend who had once lived in Chicago between his deployments in the U.S. army. Hunter had served under Taylor in Mexico and was now stationed in Washington. Butterfield blasted what he called "the bare-faced audacity of Mr. Lincoln's friends." He denied that his appointment would be "unpopular" or that "the great majority of the whigs" in Illinois backed Lincoln. He ridiculed Baker as "a vain supercilious Englishman," and denounced both "Lincoln and Baker" for "making misrepresentations" to the administration.[85]

Butterfield was shrewd, experienced, and memorably caustic. He was old enough to have been caught up in the bitter politics surrounding the War of 1812 and had been accused by some in that era of siding with the enemy. He turned this sobering experience into a widely repeated joke about why the Whigs needed to tamp down their opposition to the Mexican War. "I opposed one War," Butterfield reportedly said. "That was enough for me. I am now perpetually in favor of war, pestilence and famine." This was a punch line that Lincoln himself enjoyed so much that he even repeated it during the Civil War while swapping tales with then Secretary of State Seward.[86] Butterfield also enjoyed widespread respect for his legal talents. Ewing described him as "the most profound lawyer in the state, especially as a land lawyer." John McLean, the only Whig then on the U.S. Supreme Court, commended Butterfield as a "gentleman of high character," calling him "studious and systematic in his habits of business." Elihu Washburne said it was "not possible to have a better appointment."[87]

All this helps explain why Butterfield's final moves in the scramble for the Land Office job turned out to be highly effective. As soon as his outburst to Hunter ended, and probably still angry over the malicious gossip concerning his alleged stroke, the Chicago attorney decided to brave the roads down to Springfield to attend court. He showed up on June 5 and found, "without any solicitation on my part," a group of fourteen local Whigs, including some officeholders, willing to endorse him. His new allies claimed that "the appointment of Mr. Butterfield would give as general, if not greater satisfaction to the whigs of this section as that of Mr. Lincoln."[88]

Now brimming with confidence, Butterfield mocked what he termed Lincoln's "little cabal here." Meanwhile Lincoln and his longtime Whig ally Stephen Logan spent their time chasing after the petition signers "in the most pathetic manner," according to the Chicago attorney. Butterfield also arranged for damning letters from former candidates Edwards and Morrison. Each acknowledged in writing that Butterfield had legitimate claims to the office, and both denied having ever agreed to withdraw in favor of Lincoln. Edwards was particularly disappointed with Lincoln's behavior, writing that he had "too much self-respect to be used as a cats-paw to promote the success of one on whom I relied to procure the appointment for myself."[89]

Under pressure, Lincoln began dissembling about his intentions, telling one of Butterfield's allies that he was not "yet" a candidate and practically hiding from his Chicago rival. "Lincoln says nothing to me," Butterfield reported smugly. The confident office seeker even dared to suggest to Lincoln that he should drop out of the contest. But Lincoln refused. Instead, on Sunday, June 10, he left for Washington by train for what was a literal scramble for office. It would be his final visit to the nation's capital until his inauguration in 1861.[90]

3 MAN OF CONSEQUENCE

(1849–1853)

When Abraham Lincoln made some autobiographical statements in preparation for the 1860 presidential campaign, he cast the period after his single term in Congress as one conducted largely out of the public eye. "From 1849 to 1854, both inclusive," Lincoln wrote with characteristic precision, "practiced law more assiduously than ever before." The candidate seemed to imply that he had essentially retired from politics until passage of the Kansas-Nebraska Act in 1854 reignited the national controversy over slavery and vaulted him back into the arena. "I was losing interest in politics" was how Lincoln put it, "when the repeal of the Missouri Compromise aroused me again."[1]

These observations contained some truth but were also calculated to help a candidate positioning himself as both an outsider and a moderate. The reality was more complicated. During the early 1850s, Lincoln was losing interest in Whig politics. And while Lincoln expanded his law practice following his return to Springfield in 1849, the most important—and most lucrative—of his legal activities involved exercising political influence as a lawyer and lobbyist for large railroad companies. Ex-congressman Lincoln was out of office in Illinois but not entirely out of power. He also continued working in politics as a party organizer. But like many pragmatic northern Whig leaders, he kept looking for ways to connect a dying Whig party with the broad antislavery movement in the North, a political and moral force that had first become fully "aroused" after the Compromise of 1850.

WHILE LINCOLN WAS SCRAMBLING to get to Washington to secure the General Land Office commissionership in June 1849, two of his more devoted Illinois supporters, Land Office clerk Josiah Lucas and visiting politico Nathaniel Wilcox, met with President Zachary Taylor to press him to honor the promised delay in the decision. Wilcox, a top Whig partisan from western Illinois, later recalled how he and Lucas sat on a sofa at the White House, sparring with Taylor himself, who seemed annoyed by their meddling. Wilcox then waited for Lincoln at the Washington railroad depot to share news about the encounter with the president. "I met you at the arrival of the cars," Wilcox wrote in an 1864 letter to Lincoln, "and informed you of his purpose to appoint Mr Butterfield—chiefly upon the grounds of his locality in the north part of the State."[2]

Hearing these details, Lincoln rushed over to Wilcox's boardinghouse to prepare a response. "You wrote in my presence & read to me," recalled Wilcox, "your able letter to the Cabinet, setting forth the '*Claims of the Center*' &c &c." In the memo, Lincoln dismissed the reported concerns about regional imbalances in the Illinois patronage appointments. "I am in the center. Is the center nothing?" he asked. "That center which alone has ever given you a Whig representative?" It was a weak argument, however, since the party had just lost Lincoln's old district in central Illinois and because fellow Whig Edward Baker was now representing the Galena district in the north.[3]

The Taylor administration announced the appointment of the new Land Office commissioner on June 21. According to Wilcox, Lincoln was eating a meal at the boardinghouse when a friend slipped into the dining room and whispered that Butterfield was appointed. Although not unexpected, the result was still upsetting. "Mr. L. ate but a mouthful or two more," recalled Wilcox, "dropped his knife and fork, and went up to his room, threw himself on the bed, and commenced telling stories & trying to sing to console himself under his defeat."[4] Lincoln remained in the city a few more days before departing for home.

No doubt Lincoln was angry and maybe even depressed by his failure to secure the Land Office post in 1849, but he did not leave Washington as a disappointed office seeker or unpopular ex-congressman with no future in politics. His standing as state party leader had been diminished by the recent feuding, but it was not destroyed. Lincoln certainly showed no sign of backing down in his commitment to the Whig fusionist movement. This is the key point. Despite everything that had occurred during that difficult spring, Lincoln remained loyal to the Taylor administration.

Immediately after the announcement, Lincoln made a point of conducting courtesy calls on various members of the cabinet, including Postmaster General Jacob Collamer that afternoon, Interior Secretary Thomas Ewing the next morning, and Secretary of State John Clayton sometime before his departure. Lincoln also kept up his usual stream of patronage recommendations, both while he was still in Washington and after his return to Springfield. There were no signs of pouting or petulance, and he took care to warn supporters against such displays themselves. "As to my Washington trip," he wrote David Davis, "you know the result," adding, "I hope my good friends every where will approve the appointment of Mr. B. in so far as they can, and be silent when they can not."[5]

But soon Lincoln discovered that somebody at the Interior Department had tampered with his file of recommendation letters, removing key endorsements. Acknowledging that he was "never disposed to wrestle with the court after the case is decided," Lincoln could not help himself from chasing after Secretary Ewing in the subsequent weeks seeking an explanation for what had happened. They exchanged curt letters, before Lincoln finally concluded on July 27 that he would drop the matter even though the cabinet officer had been "deceived."[6]

The next day Lincoln finally let loose some of his seething resentment. He crafted a note of Machiavellian advice directed to Secretary of State Clayton but aimed squarely at the president. Not wanting to go public with his grievances but no longer content to work through his old friend Secretary of the Navy William Preston, Lincoln blasted the administration for delegating too much patronage responsibility away from the president and into the departments. He complained it made Taylor look weak, "a mere man of straw," in Lincoln's memorable phrase. "The appointments need be no better than they have been," he claimed with just a hint of self-conscious irony, "but the public must be brought to understand, that they are the *President's* appointments. He must occasionally say, or seem to say," Lincoln remarked, " 'by the Eternal,' 'I take the responsibility.' " He closed with a surprising nod to their old political enemy. "Those phrases were the 'Samson's locks' of Gen. Jackson," he wrote, "and we dare not disregard the lessons of experience."[7]

One can only imagine how General Taylor reacted to such patronizing advice about the "lessons of experience" coming from a former militia captain. Whether the president saw this letter or merely discussed it with Clayton, a former senator from Delaware and close friend of Kentucky governor John Crittenden, he took Lincoln's complaints seriously.[8] The administration made a concerted effort over the next few months to placate the disgruntled Illinois party boss. By

September, several of Lincoln's top patronage recommendations had come through. Lincoln himself received offers to be named either as secretary or governor of the Oregon territory—both of which he declined.[9]

Lincoln's refusal to accept such prizes from the Taylor administration raised concerns that he was embittered and would soon be on the political warpath. Some wild rumors even circulated in Washington that the former congressman was offering "a thousand dollars" in bribes to help scuttle Butterfield's confirmation hearings. Lincoln wrote to Ewing denying the charges. "This annoys me a little," he informed the secretary in October. "I am unwilling for the administration to believe or suspect such a thing."[10] After Whig state representative Usher Linder denounced Thomas Ewing by name on the floor of the Illinois General Assembly, Lincoln also defended both Ewing and Butterfield in print while condemning Linder for his indiscretion.[11]

The Taylor administration rewarded this loyalty by keeping Lincoln allies such as Josiah Lucas in the General Land Office. Lincoln observed in November that "Mr. Ewing is keeping faith with me in regard to my friends," and he calmly assured an anxious Lucas that he had "a better opinion of Mr. Ewing than you, perhaps, suppose I have."[12]

Part of Lincoln's faith was rooted in his expectations that things would start looking better in 1850 once the focus shifted from the clashes of ambitious men toward more unifying party measures. "I think there is some reason for hoping," he wrote, "that this year has been the administration's 'darkest hour,'" adding that "appointments were it's [*sic*] most difficult task. . . . Next," he claimed, "we can get on grounds of *measures*—policy—where we can unite & rally again."[13] That turned out to be a false hope. State election results that fall proved devastating for the Whig party, setting off a frenzy of finger-pointing and recriminations. The Whigs won only 30 percent of the congressional elections held in 1849 and prevailed in just four out of fifteen gubernatorial elections, winning none outside New England.[14] The main dynamic behind those problems was sectional, but it generated contradictory prescriptions for policy solutions. Across the North, successful Democrats showed far greater facility than northern Whigs in winning back former Free Soilers after the 1848 contest. Southern Whigs also found themselves outflanked by proslavery Democrats. Both sectional factions of the Whig party were thus pulling in completely different directions.

The result was a polarized environment once Congress reassembled in December 1849, with signs of panic inside the Whig caucus. The contest over the House speakership lasted for weeks, eventually producing a Democratic victory helped along by southern Whig defections, including from the once loyal Alexander Stephens of Georgia. In his annual message, President Taylor tried to promote the usual suspects of Whig fusion, including support for river and harbor improvements, but none of those proposals turned into serious legislative activity. Instead, ordinary politics practically ground to a halt during the bitter and transformational debates over the Compromise of 1850.

Springfield's Whig newspaper first reported on the stunning compromise effort on January 30, 1850. Henry Clay, back in the nation's capital as a U.S. senator from Kentucky, had just made a dramatic presentation, promising, in the words of the newspaper's unnamed special correspondent, "to settle the whole question of slavery" with a series of far-reaching compromise resolutions.[15] Lincoln surely read that breathless piece of reporting in an anxious mood. The disjointed and partially inaccurate report for the *Illinois Journal* contained worrying details about Clay's proposals that would have struck Lincoln as ill-considered for the nation and dangerous for their struggling party. But more important on a personal level, Lincoln was facing a desperate family tragedy. His second son, Edward or Eddy, not yet four years old, was on his deathbed.[16]

Despite Eddy's painful monthslong demise from consumption (tuberculosis), Lincoln was compelled to remain busy throughout that winter both in his law practice and in politics. On the same day that Clay stood before the Senate, Lincoln was corresponding with Orville Browning, a Whig from Quincy, about a patronage matter. Three days after his son's funeral, which occurred during the week of Clay's presentation, attorney Lincoln was back in court. And Clay's challenge to Taylor's party leadership was too important for any prominent Whig to ignore.

Just a week earlier the president had sent Congress a message about the lands acquired from Mexico, declaring his preference for immediate statehood for California and an expedited process for New Mexico that dispensed with any formal territorial organization. These areas in the Southwest had been largely free of slavery under Mexican rule. The westernmost former Mexican provinces were thus almost certain to enter the union as free states unless slaveholders were allowed to gain more power during a period of extended territorial government. Quick statehood meant freedom, and for Taylor and his advisers, the reality of free soil seemed good enough. They wanted to avoid any further "unnecessary agitation" over the Wilmot Proviso and the recurring arguments about whether Congress should formally ban slavery in the western territories. Taylor warned Congress to follow his advice, or the nation would find itself overwhelmed by sectionalism or what he termed "the creation of geographical parties."[17]

Clay shared Taylor's nationalist goals but lacked confidence in his former rival's ability to handle such a major crisis. The aging senator avoided making any open rupture with his proposals but acknowledged the tension in his opening remarks. "Disposed" as he was "to defer to higher authority," he claimed, and "anxious to cooperate heartily with the other departments of the Government," Clay still considered it "a dereliction of duty" for Congress to fail to provide for territorial governments in the lands acquired from Mexico.[18]

This was not an outlook that Lincoln shared. After so recently complaining to Taylor's advisers that the president was starting to resemble "a mere man of straw," Lincoln was in no mood to counsel deference toward congressional prerogative. On this matter of territorial policy, the former congressman also had something of a personal investment. In March 1849, when he and Edward Baker had huddled in Louisville with Joshua Speed while returning home together from Washington, Lincoln endorsed a scheme of Baker's to mobilize California for immediate statehood, claiming in a private memo to Secretary of State Clayton that if it was "at all practicable," he supported the idea of sending Baker to help accomplish that purpose.[19] Baker's proposal may have been the genesis of the Taylor administration's new strategy in 1850. Regardless, after spending so much energy in supporting Taylor over Clay, there can be little doubt that Lincoln disliked Clay's maneuvering to undermine the president's message.

The content of Clay's package was also troubling. The first part included four proposals concerning the lands acquired from Mexico and was unobjectionable to Lincoln and most other leading northern Whigs. There was no clear statement of free-soil principle—no Wilmot Proviso—but that was not a fatal omission for a pragmatist like Lincoln. Clay had paired a free-soil triumph (immediate statehood for California) with plans for a neutral territorial government in greater New Mexico (later divided into New Mexico and Utah). The idea was to allow the sparsely inhabited sections of the Southwest to be organized without any "restriction or condition on the subject of slavery." Residents could decide for themselves whether to authorize slavery, presumably by some form of referendum or what was becoming known as "popular sovereignty." This was a concession to southerners and marked a clear difference with Taylor's approach, but Clay argued that it was no real "sacrifice of principle" since slavery was "not likely" to take hold in that arid climate. Lincoln could have accepted such a minor concession. Even as late as 1861, he confessed to William Seward that he did not really "care much about New-Mexico, if further extension [of slavery] were hedged against."[20]

The rest of Clay's plan was more problematic. The senator included resolutions that had nothing to do with either California or New Mexico but covered the abolition of slavery in Washington, DC, the domestic slave trade, and the federal Fugitive Slave Law. Clay mainly intended these measures as concessions to proslavery forces. Antislavery radicals objected that he was sacrificing too much. Freshman Democratic senator Salmon P. Chase of Ohio, a former Liberty man and Free Soiler, complained privately that these proposals were nothing but "sentiment for the north [and] substance for the south."[21]

Lincoln did not express himself like Chase, certainly not in writing. But he was well versed on the policies and the politics of slavery issues and had serious differences with Clay's approach. Lincoln's own proposal for DC abolition, drafted just before he left Congress in 1849, included an offer to hold a referendum on the question for the territory's residents. That was the extent of his willingness to conciliate proslavery forces in Washington, and even that had failed to win support from other antislavery Whigs. Now Clay was proposing to require both local acquiescence and approval from the neighboring slave state of Maryland before any steps could be taken toward compensated emancipation. This was an entirely different level of concession.[22]

Clay also called for Congress to refrain from regulating the interstate slave trade and to adopt a "more effectual" fugitive slave law. These were both political concessions beyond the requirements of the Constitution—always a red flag for Lincoln. He had witnessed slave coffles along the Ohio River. Recalling one encounter from 1841 in Kentucky, he later confessed to his friend Joshua Speed that the "sight" of "a dozen slaves, shackled together with irons" had been "a continual torment" for him ever since.[23] As a young attorney, Lincoln had represented both slaveholders and the enslaved in a handful of fugitive slave cases, but none after 1847, when he was involved in a wrenching case involving a Black woman and her four children. In that case, Lincoln represented a Kentucky slaveholder who was trying to take the family from Coles County, where Lincoln's father lived, back to slavery. Lincoln lost the case and later confessed to Speed that he despised the fugitive slave rendition system. "I hate to see the poor creatures hunted down, and caught, and carried back to their stripes, and unrewarded toils," he wrote, "but I bite my lip and keep quiet."[24]

What Lincoln chose not to emphasize to Speed, a slaveholder, was that he also kept quiet about escapes from enslavement. Just two weeks before Clay introduced his compromise proposals, Springfield had been rocked by a sensational "slave stampede," as the newspapers called it. A group of about a dozen runaways from St. Louis passed through Sangamon County on their way to freedom. There was violence, some arrests, and even a successful rescue effort involving some of the fugitives who were being held in custody. This dramatic Underground Railroad operation in the middle of Springfield was spearheaded by a Black wagon driver named Jameson Jenkins, who also happened to be Lincoln's neighbor on Eighth Street. Although openly identified in the newspapers, Jenkins was never arrested. Several other episodes involving runaways were reported over the years in the Springfield newspapers—none of which Lincoln ever denounced in public.[25]

Lincoln also kept surprisingly quiet during debates over the 1850 compromise. He gave no speeches and offered little public commentary on the politics of sectional compromise that year. His private papers are silent as well, containing only a handful of political pamphlets on slavery and the compromise measures that he was apparently reading while the crisis unfolded.

Yet silence can sometimes be revealing. Unlike the majority of his local Whig peers, Lincoln did nothing in Springfield to help promote Clay's compromise. This was unusual because the Senate debates over the proposals would become the stuff of American political legend.

Too sick to speak for himself, Senator John C. Calhoun, shivering and bundled in blankets, watched as Senator James Mason of Virginia, lead author of what would become the new fugitive slave bill, read his harsh denunciation of abolitionists and shared the South Carolina senator's dire warnings about looming minority status for the South. Senator Daniel Webster of Massachusetts, the most prominent Whig in the nation after Taylor and Clay, took to the Senate floor with his dramatic "Seventh of March" speech, a stirring patriotic appeal that provoked the wrath of many antislavery politicians who considered it too accommodating.[26]

William Seward, also a Whig, entered the fray with his first Senate speech. He repudiated Webster by invoking a "higher law" on the territorial question that echoed the natural rights arguments of the free-soil movement. Seward was willing to accept constitutionally mandated compromises with slavery in states where it already existed, but he refused to acknowledge either the moral legitimacy or the political expediency of extending those compromises into any new territories. He insisted that the Wilmot Proviso could not be "waived" because it was no "mere abstraction." The territories had been free and therefore must remain free.[27] Seward dismissed all southern threats of disunion as "chimerical" and vowed to "vote for the admission of California directly, without conditions, without qualifications, and without compromise."

Seward also devoted a passage in his Higher Law speech to shrewd partisan analysis. He rejected those who blamed the disunion crisis on the "violence of party spirit." On the contrary, he claimed that what "we are seeing and hearing . . . is the agony of distracted parties—a convulsion resulting from the too narrow foundations of both the great parties, and of all parties—foundations laid in compromises of natural justice and of human liberty." Seward urged a more open partisanship about slavery, one that tackled the great "moral question" of the age in the true spirit of "Progress." But what Seward cast as progressive, others heard as radicalism.[28]

Until that point, the junior senator from New York had been widely regarded as a trusted adviser to President Taylor. But Seward's invocation of a higher law for the issue of slavery in the territories began pushing him away from the more cautious Taylor. Few other leading Whigs seemed prepared to join Seward on the strong antislavery grounds of his March 11 speech, and he soon became a lightning rod for Democratic criticism.

Lincoln would also later distance himself from the rhetoric of Seward's Higher Law doctrine, but in 1850 he seemed more worried about the partisan fusion that Clay and conservative Whigs were promoting. Clay's compromise measures aimed to push conservative Whigs and conservative Democrats together on a unionist basis. This was patriotic in sentiment but untenable as partisan strategy. When conservative Whigs and Democrats in Springfield organized a "Union Meeting" in mid-June to endorse the Committee of Thirteen report—Clay's vehicle for his so-called omnibus package of compromise measures—Lincoln declined to participate. John Todd Stuart, Lincoln's first law partner and political mentor, along with dozens of other prominent local figures from both parties, publicly joined this effort, but Lincoln did not.[29]

The Springfield attorney was not alone in his distaste for omnibus compromise. President Taylor was skeptical, too. After months of wrangling, and following an open break between Taylor and Clay, all hopes of accommodation appeared lost by that summer. Then, on July 9, the president died unexpectedly from a severe stomach infection. Taylor's death elevated Vice President and conservative Whig Millard Fillmore into power, briefly restoring hopes for a deal.

Lincoln used that occasion to offer rare public commentary on the political situation. In a eulogy delivered for Taylor in Chicago, Lincoln confessed his "apprehensions" that "the one *great* question of the day" would not be resolved without the old general. "The Presidency, even to the most experienced politicians, is no bed of roses," he observed, noting that Taylor had "found thorns within it." By Lincoln's reckoning, however, only an elected president, one who had fully earned the "confidence and devotion of the people," could expect to rally the political willpower necessary to settle the dangerous sectional crisis. Lincoln refused to "despair" but expressed doubt that "any successor" could achieve national unity under such circumstances.[30]

Lincoln was not far off the mark. Even with backing from the new president, Clay could not deliver on his omnibus approach. By the end of July, his compromise package was dead, and the aging statesman left for the summer recess without any plans for how to proceed. The job of marshaling the necessary political forces for a cross-sectional arrangement fell to the Democratic Illinois senator. Stephen Douglas, age thirty-seven, broke apart and subtly altered the compromise measures, finally managing in September 1850 to pass a series of separate bills with majority coalitions that shifted, depending on the specific element of the package being considered.[31]

Whether it was true sectional compromise or an example of crafty partisan co-option, Douglas's legislative triumph was a profound blow to Whig fusionists. The entire year had been a dismal one for them. President Taylor failed to change the terms of the national debate, struggled to outmaneuver the always wily Clay, and then succumbed to acute gastroenteritis, leaving the Taylor Whigs adrift. Fillmore dismissed the entire Taylor cabinet, largely replacing them with conservatives known as "Silver Grays." He also moved quickly to align the Whig party with the Clay-inspired compromise, now under the management of the Democrat senator from Illinois. For northern antislavery Whigs, these developments were painful to endure.

From Lincoln's perspective, it was difficult to imagine a worse scenario. The union had ostensibly been saved from sectional extremists but only temporarily, and the price appeared to be Whig party suicide in the North. But what was he willing to do about it? There is one indirect clue about his state of mind.

Historians have long known that Lincoln was a frequent ghost-writer; throughout his career, he produced materials for other legislators, candidates, and party newspapers. In the late summer of 1850, he almost certainly drafted a speech for Richard Yates, a young Whig congressional candidate from Morgan County and close friend of William Herndon. Yates was trying to regain the congressional seat for the Whigs following Stephen Logan's unexpected defeat in 1848. This was an important partisan goal, especially for Lincoln, who tried to help support and guide the Yates campaign.[32]

Sometime after Taylor's death and following the defeat of the omnibus package in late July, but before Douglas took over the legislation in September, Lincoln drafted a statement for Yates on the stalled compromise.[33] Lincoln (as Yates) began by suggesting that there was "good reason" to believe that "the whole will be settled before my service will commence." He then offered a ringing endorsement for the Wilmot Proviso, claiming that Yates was "inflexible" on the question of maintaining his "opposition to the extention of slavery into territories now free." He did admit something that Seward had not appeared to acknowledge in his Higher Law speech: He would "abandon" the proviso if it truly appeared to "endanger" the nation, because "the preservation of the Union stands number one with me."

But Lincoln, writing as Yates, agreed that the disunion threats were exaggerated, if not quite as "chimerical" as Seward claimed. "I have not at any time supposed the Union to be in so much danger as some others have," he observed, claiming that not one congressional district in the country had a majority in favor of "dissolution." Still, unlike Seward's speech, this draft labeled it "arrogant" and even "silly" to ignore "the opinions of the very many great and good men who think there is real danger." Lincoln (as Yates) suggested in the spirit of "reasonable deference to the opinions of the author of the late compromise bill," meaning Clay, that "I *some what regretted* the defeat of that measure" (emphasis added). Despite this lukewarm endorsement, the draft speech closed by acknowledging that had the omnibus measure "passed the Senate, and I been a member of the lower House I think I should have voted for it, unless my district had otherwise directed me."[34]

That final halting admission stands out because nearly all northern Whigs in the Senate had just voted to kill the omnibus. But Lincoln's statement for Yates did not project him into those July 31 Senate votes, which were complicated by procedural issues. It framed the question as a true "up or down" proposition, following Senate passage and with the fate of the country presumably in the balance. Even then, Lincoln (as Yates) still hedged by invoking the nineteenth-century doctrine of instruction, which asserted that state legislatures could instruct their federal representatives on how to vote on important measures by passing nonbinding resolutions.

It was clear that Lincoln the speechwriter did not like Clay's compromise. He was willing to encourage Whigs to support it under certain circumstances, but he considered the compromise to be a bad deal for the nation and the wrong direction for his party. When Stuart organized a second "Union" endorsement meeting in October, after Douglas secured final passage of the separate compromise measures, Lincoln was once again nowhere to be found.

Nothing provoked more anger in the North than the final version of the 1850 Fugitive Slave Act. This new law, which revised the federal statute from 1793, created an unprecedented federal enforcement system for catching runaway slaves. The statute envisioned U.S. commissioners operating from their own hearing rooms across the free states, without the necessity of holding jury trials, to order fugitive slave renditions. Penalties for those caught aiding such freedom seekers now included fines of up to $1,000 and prison sentences for up to six months. The statute authorized U.S. commissioners and their marshals to deputize northern citizens as slave catchers and seemed to deny even the most basic habeas corpus or personal liberty rights to accused Blacks. This draconian measure clearly aimed to destroy the Underground Railroad of Black-led vigilance committees that had recently been growing in their defiance. But to many northerners—not just abolitionists—these stark changes to the federal criminal code appeared as a gross overreaction and unwarranted assault on traditional American liberties. In October, the Chicago City Council adopted a resolution condemning the "cruel and unjust law," proclaiming that any "Senators and Representatives in Congress from the free states, who aided and assisted" in its passage, deserved "to be ranked with the traitors Benedict Arnold and Judas Iscariot."[35]

In 1850 Illinois began holding its elections in early November (and not August as had been custom), but Whigs were unable to take advantage of the outrage from Chicago or elsewhere because of their national party's support for the compromise. Yates regained control of the seventh district around Springfield, but Democrats won back the Galena district in the northwest. There was still only a "lone Whig star" from Illinois. In other contests, the Whigs continued to fare poorly, stuck in the minority in both chambers of the legislature with no statewide officeholders. In Sangamon County, the legislative delegation was now led by conservative Whigs such as state senator John Todd Stuart and Representative Ninian W. Edwards, both of whom rejected free soilism. The Whig future in Illinois looked even bleaker than usual.

Meanwhile a feud was developing between President Fillmore's Silver Gray conservative faction and northern antislavery Whigs led by William Seward. This schism was painfully reminiscent of the existential crisis that had engulfed the party during John Tyler's troubled time in the White House. Once again a conservative Whig vice president had been elevated to national power after the death of a former military hero and was battling with key figures in his party's congressional caucus to the detriment of the movement at large.

By contrast, the Democrats appeared more unified and forward-looking. The emergence of Stephen Douglas during the compromise crisis proved to be one of the most significant developments of the entire political era. Despite his relative youth, the "Little Giant" was already being considered as a serious candidate for the next Democratic presidential nomination. Lincoln's longtime opponent was well on his way to becoming one of the most powerful men in American politics.

Douglas's new influence came as much from his genius at promoting railroads as from his ability to manage sectional compromise. The same month in which he engineered the bipartisan deal over California's admission to the union, he also secured a groundbreaking federal land grant for the Illinois Central railroad line—the first direct federal subsidy to a railroad in American history. It was a remarkable achievement for a self-identified Jacksonian Democrat, signaling the potential for a new era of partisan cooperation on internal improvements. The next few years in Illinois were dominated by a frenzy of activity for railroad charters, road grading, and increased freight tonnage. Whigs, Democrats, and a multitude of political opportunists scrambled into Springfield to help organize what became for a time the longest railroad line in America, more than seven hundred miles from Cairo, Illinois, to Galena, including a branch line that went to fast-growing Chicago. By early 1851, Springfield was awash with money from investors vying to secure their share of the windfall. Douglas, with his tactical genius, had launched this process from Washington, but it was ex-congressman Lincoln, with his own finely honed set of political skills, who was present in the state capital to help reap many of the benefits.[36]

Lincoln first served as a corporate attorney and railroad lobbyist for the Alton & Sangamon Railroad, one of the smaller lines that opened for business in 1851, founded by Robert Smith, Lincoln's traveling partner from the River and Harbor Convention. The Alton & Sangamon eventually connected St. Louis to Chicago and later, following the Civil War, became a major part of E. H. Harriman's national railroad syndicate. But in 1851 the company was facing a knotty legal problem and turned to Lincoln for help. Several stock subscribers were attempting to renege on their commitments because alterations in the road plan had devalued their real estate holdings. The question was whether the company could enforce the original contracts in state courts. Failure to do so might threaten the highly speculative and entrepreneurial railroad enterprise.

That is what Lincoln argued in court. He tackled this case with the same intensity that he had previously reserved for political campaigns. In a series of confidential business letters and urgent telegrams to company officials in Alton and New York, he demonstrated his characteristic attention to detail and relentless work ethic.[37]

Writing to a company official in February 1851, Lincoln observed without apology that he had "at last" found the "time to attend to the business you left with me," because the legislature had finally "got out of the way."[38] He was alluding to his extensive lobbying work that had preoccupied him during the legislative session. The 1851 session was the one marked by the fierce contest to secure the Illinois Central charter—arguably the most combative and corrupt General Assembly of the period.

Lincoln was so overwhelmed with lobbying work in early 1851 that he also felt compelled to disappoint his family in Coles County. They had once again started sending him a flurry of anxious letters warning that Thomas Lincoln was dying, though this time it was for real. The busy lobbyist stayed put and at first did not even respond to their appeals. Finally, in mid-January, he explained in an awkward note why he was not planning to come. "My business is such that I could hardly leave home now," he wrote, suggesting only that they "should use my name, if necessary, to procure a doctor, or any thing for Father in his present sickness." In fairness, Lincoln was a new father himself. Mary had delivered their third child, William or Willie, in December, less than a year following Eddy's death, and as Lincoln noted to his family, she was in bed, too, with "baby-sickness."[39]

But there was more to Lincoln's reluctance than mere demands on his time and energy. He claimed he had not responded sooner because "it appeared to me I could write nothing which could do any good," and he worried that a final deathbed meeting "would be more painful than pleasant." He ended by counseling faith in "our great, and good, and merciful Maker" but otherwise provided little more, even after Thomas Lincoln died less than a week later. Lincoln did not attend the funeral, nor purchase a tombstone for his father, surely signs of their long-standing alienation.[40]

The rest of that year was quiet politically, but several Whig leaders in Illinois made a point of rallying together in November. They issued a public call for "a more thorough organization of the Whig party at an early day" in advance of the next year's state and national elections.[41] The appeal demonstrated a renewed sense of purpose, borne out of desperation. The state Whigs were powerless and mostly adrift. If they were to regain any influence, they would need to send a strong delegation to the 1852 national convention in Baltimore. Lincoln's name was the first on this call for a much-needed planning session. Stuart's was second. The rest of the nearly two dozen or so prominent Whigs featured in that announcement came from across the state party's ideological and regional spectrum.

But the obstacles they faced were just too daunting. Only about thirty men attended the December meeting, which accomplished little. The attendees decided it was "inexpedient" to nominate candidates for state office and merely set up a "provisional" state central committee that was supposed to make further plans for a statewide convention in July. The men nominated a slate of delegates to the Baltimore convention, but the group was younger and less prominent than previous state delegations. Lincoln served on the selection committee but declined to go as a delegate himself. Instead, Elihu Washburne of Galena emerged as the leader of the antislavery delegates.

The December gathering offered no instructions on either policy matters or candidate endorsements. Democratic newspapers picked up on the hollow nature of this Whig session almost immediately, labeling the effort "a failure," while explaining that the absence of endorsements was a deliberate strategy, "deemed more prudent by the wire-workers of Seward," who were angling for the nomination of General Winfield Scott at Baltimore, another apolitical military hero from the Mexican War in the Taylor mold.[42]

There was some truth to this Democratic analysis. Seward came to the June 1852 convention determined to move the Whig party out of the control of Millard Fillmore by uniting behind Scott, who was "available" and could serve as a blank political slate useful for fusionist efforts at coalition building. Seward's forces wielded influence at Baltimore, but it still took them fifty-three ballots to secure General Scott's nomination. They also struggled to control the platform process. Resolutions about the 1850 compromise measures attempted awkwardly to address the complaints about the package, proclaiming that the party had "acquiesced" in the "series of acts" from 1850, which the delegates declined to label a "compromise."[43]

The Whig platform in 1852 did not go as far as President Fillmore had gone in his earlier presidential messages when he declared the compromise to be a "final settlement" of the slavery controversy. Instead, the Whig convention asserted that the measures represented "a settlement in principle and substance, of the dangerous and exciting question which they embrace," vowing that they would "maintain them" until "experience shall demonstrate the necessity of further legislation."[44] The caveat about "further legislation" was an obvious gesture toward antislavery voters in the North who were inflamed more than ever by the Fugitive Slave Law.[45]

Illinois delegates were divided over all this, voting as a unit for Scott's nomination but against the Seward faction on key procedural votes. They also split 6–5 on the main platform questions.[46] And in a rare public showdown just prior to the national convention, Whigs in Sangamon County removed state representative Ninian W. Edwards from the party and the legislature. Local Whigs had goaded Lincoln's brother-in-law into resigning his statehouse seat and submitting himself to a June special election after the conservative had effectively switched parties and was voting with Democrats on most matters. Edwards had even helped engineer a repeal of the earlier state house of representatives endorsement for the Wilmot Proviso. Lincoln was "deeply mortified" by the spectacle of this betrayal, according to David Davis, and relieved by his brother-in-law's defeat in June 1852. Conservative Whigs were appalled, however. John Todd Stuart chose this moment to withdraw from public life, declining to run for reelection as state senator later that year.[47]

Whig power in Illinois was clearly shifting northward and away from central Illinois conservatives like Edwards and Stuart. Lincoln had once bridged those gaps but no more. Now it was Washburne, the Galena politician, who was trying to play the role of state party chieftain, though his influence was mostly limited to northern Illinois. Washburne was a practical man and antislavery, but the Maine native was not quite as deft as Lincoln had been, with a Yankee sharpness about his style that seemed to alienate many of his downstate contemporaries.[48]

Following his return home from the Baltimore convention, Washburne engineered a coalition of Whig and antislavery forces across the state's northern counties. Coordinating that summer with figures such as abolitionist editor Zebina Eastman of Chicago, Washburne persuaded many former Liberty men and Free Soilers (now also calling themselves Free Democrats) to throw their support toward selected antislavery Whig candidates for Congress. Some of the abolitionists, such as Ichabod Codding, a prominent Congregationalist minister, initially resisted this fusion as too Whiggish in nature, but that was largely how candidates Washburne in the First District, Jesse O. Norton in the Third District, and James Knox in the Fourth District managed to position themselves successfully for the fall congressional campaign. Though he remained within the Democratic party, Chicago newspaper editor and former congressman John Wentworth also benefited from the growing antislavery fusion.

Richard Yates was the only antislavery Whig congressional candidate seeking reelection in 1852, but he was outside Washburne's northern orbit and faced a more challenging political environment in the more conservative central region of the state. In addition, the latest federal reapportionment had carved out a new district for Yates, covering Morgan, Sangamon, and some surrounding counties but no longer including the more northern counties that had once provided the old Lincoln district with significant Liberty party votes. Yates kept his distance from Washburne and the emerging antislavery coalition.[49]

This was the political landscape facing Abraham Lincoln when he heard the news that Henry Clay had died on June 29, 1852. The passing of the Whig founder was yet another sign of the changing times, and the confluence of events appeared to motivate Lincoln to break the public silence he had largely maintained on the issues of the day.

Springfield essentially closed for a day in mid-July to memorialize Clay. Lincoln helped organize the arrangements and was invited to deliver the main eulogy from the state capitol building. He later said it was difficult for him to find enough material for an extended address. Years later in the White House, reminiscing with Seward about this challenge, Lincoln noted that Clay himself avoided giving eulogies. Seward blamed that habit on Clay's ego, commenting that the Kentuckian rarely spoke "in laudatory terms of a contemporary." Both men said they considered Whig founders Clay and Daniel Webster "to have been hard and selfish leaders, whose private personal ambition had contributed to the ruin of their party."[50]

In 1852 Lincoln still managed to deliver an eloquent memorial that extolled Clay's "fortunate combination" of virtues and his "predominant sentiment" that—in Lincoln's estimation—embraced "a deep devotion to the cause of human liberty."[51] Nevertheless, the eulogy was more notable for its omissions. Lincoln did not once invoke the word "Whig." He did not claim to have met Clay or to have heard him speak. There was nothing of any substance in the speech covering the last years of Clay's life, including what Clay and other moderates had defended as the union-saving Compromise of 1850. Instead, Lincoln praised Clay's antislavery views and gave him credit for acknowledging the "human right" of Black people (despite enslaving some of them). Lincoln tried to invoke Clay's memory against the "increasing number of men," such as the late John C. Calhoun and other proslavery extremists, who were "beginning to assail and to ridicule the white-man's charter of freedom," the Declaration of Independence, which he surprisingly misquoted as, "all men are created free and equal."[52]

Lincoln made one telling observation that seemed more about himself than Clay. "The man who is of neither party," he stated, "is not—cannot be, of any consequence." Lincoln had always aspired to be a man of consequence by channeling his personal ambitions into the larger Whig party. By the summer of 1852, those aspirations appeared to be in considerable jeopardy. Nineteenth-century partisan organizations were about men and measures, and the Whigs just did not have enough men. That was what the Whig fusion project had always been about—finding ways to broaden the coalition and attract more voters. But western issues such as river and harbor improvements had failed to ignite any sustained realignment of partisan forces. And Lincoln's disappointing experience with the Taylor administration demonstrated that a more cynical "men without measures" approach was no solution either.

Antislavery was the obvious next step for Whig fusionists, but that was a high-risk strategy. To oppose slavery was to make political battle over moral principle, not mere public policy. It also meant ending the Whig party in the South and maybe even abandoning the Whig label in the North. Some northern party leaders seemed unconcerned by these prospects, but others were worried about the rise of the "geographical" or sectional parties that Taylor had once warned against. Moderates feared that sectional partisanship would lead to disunion. But if Lincoln feared this, it did not stop him from publicly acknowledging the wrongs of slavery or lead him into an embrace of the recent compromise. As he reflected on the meaning of Clay's life, Lincoln was obviously grappling with these political dilemmas. With his eulogy, he seemed to be burying both a man and a party. The very next day other Whig leaders gathered in Springfield for what turned out to be their final statewide convention. Lincoln did not even bother to attend.[53]

Lincoln later explained his unusual partisan behavior in 1852 by claiming that while he did "something in the way of canvassing" for the Whig national ticket, he participated less than in the past "owing to the hopelessness of the cause in Illinois." The situation was not truly hopeless for Whigs in either the state or the nation, but they were fighting uphill on both levels. Democrats had nominated Franklin Pierce of New Hampshire, a young, little-known figure, to contest the race against General Scott. A coalition of political abolitionists and antislavery radicals, calling themselves Free Soilers or Free Democrats, put forward as their candidate Senator John P. Hale, also of New Hampshire and a bitter rival of Pierce's. The Pierce ticket seemed to have a decisive edge from the outset. Many antislavery Democrats or Barnburners from the 1848 campaign were migrating back to their regular party. And Scott's candidacy inspired little enthusiasm in the North. Recognizing these challenges, Lincoln looked southward. In August, he asked one southern acquaintance from his congressional days whether "we can carry North Carolina for Scott?" joking mysteriously that he would "relinquish" the "affections of Miss L.K." if the answer was satisfactory.[54]

In Democratic-dominated Illinois, there was considerable uncertainty about the direction of the Whig presidential campaign. The official Whig elector from Lincoln's congressional district reported to Rep. Richard Yates that he was confused as to how to represent the party's ticket. "I don't know where to begin," the elector complained, "I have not yet been able to discover what are the issues to be tried."[55] For once Lincoln was not a Whig elector, but he appeared more confident about how to proceed. In August he delivered a hard-hitting campaign speech to the Scott Club of Springfield, one that he framed as a rebuttal to a recent speech delivered by Stephen Douglas in Richmond, Virginia.[56]

Commenting that responding to Douglas "reminded [him of] old times," Lincoln dismissed the "shirks and quirks" of Douglas's pugnacious personality and offered a lively rebuttal of the senator's claims for the Democratic ticket.[57] In Lincoln's analysis, the heart of the presidential contest concerned slavery—and particularly the politics of antislavery in the state of New York. He identified "Raw Head and Bloody Bones" Seward as the target of Democratic ire. "That they really do hate him there is no mistake," Lincoln observed, before claiming that Democrats were hiding the "true ground" of their "insane malice" for the New York senator. It was not about Seward's Higher Law doctrine. What Lincoln called the "real secret" of their attacks was that "whoever does not get the State of New York will not be elected president." With Seward's help, Scott threatened to draw enough antislavery vote in New York to secure a Whig victory.

According to Lincoln, the need to win New York without losing the South also explained why Democrats had nominated the little-known Pierce. Even though the New Hampshire attorney and politician had reportedly "declared his loathing for the Fugitive Slave Law" as recently as January 1852, he was such a blank slate on the national scene that he could still be useful to southern party activists. The Democrats were trying to have it both ways. Lincoln charged that Pierce's "southern allies . . . pretend to disbelieve the report" about their nominee's criticism of the Fugitive Slave Law despite knowing full well that it was true. "Mark me," Lincoln stated emphatically, "*he will not contradict it*." From his perspective, this was simply "the necessity of the party."[58]

Lincoln declined to admit that Whigs had their own contradictions to navigate. In his stump speech, he appeared restrained by the national Whig party's recent straddles over slavery. The former Whig congressman no longer offered the strong support for northern free soilism that he had articulated in 1848 or even in his speechwriting for candidate Yates in 1850. There was no endorsement, or apparently even mention of, the Wilmot Proviso in his remarks. But Lincoln's main partisan challenge in 1852 concerned how to navigate the growing fugitive slave crisis.

Militant abolitionists and Underground Railroad operatives were openly resisting the new Fugitive Slave Law. In 1851 there had been several defiant rescue episodes spearheaded by Black vigilance committees in Massachusetts, Pennsylvania, and New York. One Maryland slaveholder was killed on September 11 in southeastern Pennsylvania during what authorities labeled a "riot." The incident was considered so grave that thirty-eight men were tried in Philadelphia for treason, but the federal jury acquitted the first defendant within about fifteen minutes and the rest were soon released. The 1852 Whig national platform, however ambiguous in some respects, was explicit about responding to this explosive climate by including the hated statute by name in the "series of acts" to which the party had "acquiesced."[59]

Though he had been quick to condemn mob violence in the past, Lincoln declined to do so now. He was no advocate of violent resistance to the rule of law, but his 1852 remarks tried to neutralize the issue by not even mentioning the fugitive crisis or the new law, except to point out Pierce's hostility toward it. Lincoln also said practically nothing of substance about the compromise itself other than to push the issue aside by claiming "the compromise measures were not party measures." He asserted that he had read only "once hastily" Douglas's public defense of the compromise, offered in Chicago on October 23, 1850, following the city council's fiery resolution against his role in securing passage for the "cruel and unjust" fugitive law. Lincoln pronounced himself satisfied, calling the senator's defense, with just a hint of condescension, "a very able production." But whether the compromise itself deserved "praise or blame," Lincoln still declined to say.[60]

Part of Lincoln's reticence was a reflection that antislavery sentiment held the balance of power in the northern region of his state. There were pivotal congressional races in play, and Lincoln wanted to avoid undermining antislavery Whig candidates. He did campaign in the northern congressional contests and seemed to make a difference. Party newspapers suggested that his biggest impact came in the fourth congressional district, where the Whig antislavery candidate was James Knox, a Yale graduate and fellow attorney. Near the end of October, Lincoln also engaged Stephen Douglas at an event in Springfield attended by orators from both major parties. Despite the firecrackers set off by local Democrats while Lincoln was speaking, he still managed to "put in a few good licks," proving himself to be, in the words of the *Illinois* (formerly *Sangamo*) *Journal*, a "skillful operator."[61]

During the final days of the campaign, Lincoln also displayed the harder edge of his partisan skills by drafting an election eve statement on illegal voting. Among central Illinois Whigs, especially those of a conservative bent, there was widespread anxiety that illegal ballots cast by foreign-born residents, such as Germans or Irish Catholics, would hurt the party on Election Day. Lincoln helped secure a nonpartisan statement signed by Whig attorneys and a Democratic state supreme court justice, asserting that foreign-born voters in Illinois should be prepared to show naturalization papers at the polling places. The statement represented a thinly veiled threat, one that signaled to Whig party workers in the region that they should be aggressive about challenging any foreign-looking or foreign-sounding voters.[62]

The statement on Illinois election law also suggested uneasiness over the Scott campaign strategy toward immigrants. From the beginning, the Whig presidential candidate had been aggressive and notoriously clumsy about trying to cultivate foreign-born and Catholic voters who were viewed as Democratic in their orientation. The Illinois Whigs had attempted to follow suit, nominating Francis Arenz, a German immigrant, for state treasurer, and Don Morrison, who had a Catholic wife, for lieutenant governor. Washburne strongly backed these outreach efforts. He even wrote to Seward at one point requesting assistance in securing a political endorsement from Catholic Archbishop John Hughes of New York. "I am quite sure," the senator sputtered in reply, "that Arch Bishop Hughes has never done any such thing."[63]

Conservative Whigs felt embarrassed by such opportunistic contortions. By taking a harder line on naturalization papers, Lincoln was addressing some of their discomfort. The immigrant issue was looming larger than ever and not just for the Whigs. An influx of European settlers since the mid-1840s was altering the demographics of the North, even affecting the politics of rural communities in central Illinois. Congressman Yates, for one, had started to receive multiple warnings from his political correspondents that a rising population of German settlers migrating eastward from St. Louis would eventually hold the "balance of power" in his district.[64] These concerns were beginning to spark an angry nativist backlash. In the future, several leading conservative Illinois Whigs such as attorney Benjamin Edwards, who co-authored the election eve statement with Lincoln, would find themselves drifting toward open affiliation with the nascent anti-immigrant "American" or "Know Nothing" movement.

For now, however, the defining issue in several of the Illinois contests concerned the future of slavery. That is why 1852 ultimately turned out to be a banner year for Illinois Whigs. Though the party came up short in the presidential election, and as always, in other statewide races and in the forlorn effort to gain control of the General Assembly, antislavery Whig candidates managed to win an unprecedented four out of the state's nine congressional seats. This was a remarkable, unexpected triumph, impossible to explain without recognizing the genius of the Washburne-led antislavery fusion effort in the northern districts. The hard work since the national convention had seemingly paid off, but not everyone was happy. To many observers, it was unclear to what extent those winning congressional tickets deserved the "Whig" label or whether they were better understood as the beginnings of a new northern antislavery party.

The congressional victories depended heavily on antislavery fusion. John Hale, the Free Soil or Free Democratic presidential candidate, received some ten thousand ballots in Illinois, nearly all from those four northern congressional districts. But in the same districts, Free Soil candidates for Congress received fewer than 7,500 votes. The roughly 2,500-vote difference explains why Washburne was able to win his close race by fewer than three hundred votes, and why Whig candidates Jesse Norton and James Knox prevailed in their contests by fewer than two hundred votes each. They owed their slim margins of victory to abolitionist-minded voters willing to cross party lines. Yates's success was also a close-run affair, but there was no third-party antislavery candidate on the ballot in his part of the state. Wentworth was the only antislavery candidate in northern Illinois who won with a comfortable margin, but he was unique because he was a Democrat representing Chicago.

All this helps explain why Illinois Whigs appeared demoralized in the aftermath of the 1852 elections and why Lincoln later commented on the "hopelessness" of their party's cause. There was no obvious way to reconcile fusionist-minded antislavery voters in the northern part of the state with central Illinois Whig conservatives. Nor was anyone exhibiting much in the way of effective statewide leadership on these or other challenges. The statewide candidates were weak. The central committee was even weaker. There was never another statewide Whig convention, aside from the one that followed the memorial for Henry Clay. And then the other great founder of their national party, Daniel Webster, died in October 1852 at the age of seventy. The signs of a passing partisan era were practically everywhere. Facing the political future without state leadership or patronage, absent national icons and bereft of mobilizing issues, the Illinois Whigs were in a precarious position by 1853.

Illinois Democrats were in a much stronger position than their Whig counterparts, but they were by no means immune to shifting partisan pressures. By early 1853, even though Senator Douglas had cruised to a landslide reelection victory courtesy of the Democratic-controlled legislature, he was facing mounting challenges as a state party leader. As always, national patronage was proving to be source of distraction and widespread disappointment for westerners. There were always more job seekers than jobs, and whether under a Whig or Democratic administration, Illinois partisans consistently felt ignored by Washington. Much to Douglas's dismay, former congressman John McClernand soon emerged to play the role of Edward Baker—yet another ambitious and ultimately unsuccessful Illinois candidate for a place inside President Pierce's cabinet. Douglas himself, the most obvious choice for a cabinet position, was notably excluded from the administration's inner circle and had to content himself with reappointment as chairman of the Senate Committee on Territories. With comparatively few electoral votes, the state of Illinois kept coming up short in the national contest for power. The state would not place any of its leading political figures inside a presidential cabinet or on the U.S. Supreme Court until the Civil War.

Sorting out Democratic measures in 1853 proved no easier than placating the organization's men. The Age of Jackson was over in Illinois. The state's recently elected governor, Joel Matteson, a forty-four-year-old businessman from Joliet, had made a name for himself as a pro-bank Democratic state senator. He was a vocal supporter both of railroads and of river and harbor improvements. He had also backed the Wilmot Proviso when it was first debated in the state legislature, though he later claimed to have done so only because of instructions from his constituents.[65] There was strong cross-party support in Illinois for legislation known as the "Maine Law," modeled after that state's measure prohibiting the sale of intoxicating beverages. In 1853 alone, Illinois legislators received petitions with over 27,000 signatures supporting such an anti-liquor proposal, including many from leading Democrats.

In 1853 there was also significant cross-party debate over a new addition to the Illinois "Black Laws." The amendment tackled the growing fugitive slave crisis by prohibiting out-of-state Blacks from remaining within the state's borders for more than ten days, on penalty of the forced "sale" of their labor, as if they were slaves. John A. Logan, a young Democratic legislator from southern Illinois, authored the legislation, but its draconian punishments produced discord within the generally anti-Black Democratic coalition. The Springfield-based *Illinois Journal* reported that views on this issue came "without reference to party predilections."[66] Unlike temperance, which stalled in the Illinois General Assembly, the anti-Black measure became law on February 12. From Rochester, New York, the noted abolitionist Frederick Douglass was appalled. "What kind of people are the people of Illinois?" he asked in disgust, wondering in the editorial pages of his newspaper if they were "the offspring of wolves and tigers."[67]

Lincoln, who had just turned forty-four, was busy at home and in the law office, focused more than ever on generating income. Little Eddy was gone, but there were two more young boys in the household besides eldest son Robert; Willie, born just ten months after Eddy's death in 1850, and Thomas or Tad, who arrived in April 1853. In addition to his lucrative corporate lobbying, the father of three children was busy riding circuit, handling hundreds of civil and criminal client cases each year. Since leaving Congress, Lincoln had developed thriving practices in the state's appellate courts and in the federal courts. By the mid-1850s, Lincoln the lawyer appeared to be almost everywhere, averaging more than 150 days per year on the road.[68]

In 1853 Lincoln got involved in a groundbreaking legal battle on behalf of the Illinois Central Railroad (ICRR) with millions of dollars at stake. Upon receiving its charter in 1851, the Illinois Central had agreed to pay the state an unprecedented annual tax on its gross receipts in exchange for limitations against other state and local taxes or fees. Yet as the company began building its great railroad line in 1852, several Illinois counties tried to impose their own taxes on the company. The ICRR planned to sue and wanted to retain Lincoln as its courtroom attorney, expecting the landmark case to reach the state supreme court.

But Lincoln was worried about a potential conflict of interest because he might be viewed as having already been retained by one of the smaller counties through an earlier arrangement. The prominent attorney wrote the county in September, calling the fight "the largest law question that can now be got up in the State" and asking for clarification about their arrangement. Admitting that the railroad company was pursuing him, Lincoln suggested that he should either be released from any previous understanding or be hired immediately by a consortium of the several counties, adding, "I can not afford, if I can help it, to miss a fee altogether." He was released, and Lincoln signed with the ICRR. The company became his most lucrative client, generating more income by the end of the 1850s than his local circuit-riding cases combined.[69]

By 1853, Lincoln had built a substantial postcongressional career in Illinois working at the intersection of law and politics. He was a man of consequence, important enough even to have a town named after him. That year Lincoln represented a group of investors connected to the Chicago & Mississippi Railroad, which was busy extending some Alton & Sangamon railroad lines throughout north-central Illinois. The speculators approached the state legislature during the 1853 session with plans to incorporate a new town and railroad junction in Logan County along one of their extensions. Lincoln quickly helped them secure the charter, and the group decided to name the new place "Lincoln" in honor of their skilled lobbyist.

The town of Lincoln, Illinois, was born in August 1853. "At present it contains but few houses," reported the *Illinois State Register*, "but a few weeks will show how western villages can be manufactured to order, and flourish in spite of extreme infancy."[70] According to one resident, Abraham Lincoln himself joined the naming celebration and playfully helped "christen" the small community by splitting open a large watermelon.[71] Today Lincoln, Illinois, is a town of about thirteen thousand people, and one of more than seventy other places in the country named after the great president. But few people realize that five years before the Lincoln-Douglas debates, a decade before the Emancipation Proclamation, and about a dozen years before his apotheosis as a national martyr, Lincoln received his very first American namesake in gratitude for his lobbying acumen on behalf of the railroad industry.

4

STANDING WITH ANYBODY

(1854)

WHILE THE LINCOLN NAMESAKE was being added to the Illinois state map, Stephen Douglas, as chairman of the U.S. Senate Committee on Territories, was devising a controversial scheme to organize the Nebraska territory of the former Louisiana Purchase. Drawing from "popular sovereignty" measures that had been included for the New Mexico and Utah territories in the final compromise legislation of 1850, Douglas proposed allowing Nebraska residents to decide for themselves, by some form of referendum, whether to create a territorial government "with or without slavery." Douglas reported the first version of his Nebraska bill to the Senate on January 4, 1854, but after some intense negotiations with southern senators, including leading Whigs, Douglas altered the measure on January 23 to separate the region into two territories—Kansas and Nebraska—and to clarify that by establishing the doctrine of popular sovereignty in these territories, the 1820 Missouri Compromise—which had prohibited slavery in the region—was now "inoperative."[1]

The political reaction to this move was immediate. While Douglas was still rewriting the bill in January, Ohio senator Salmon Chase organized antislavery radicals from both houses of Congress and across party backgrounds to issue a joint pamphlet opposing the new measure. *Appeal of the Independent Democrats in Congress, to the People of the United States* made clear that its goal was to mobilize a fusion of antislavery forces against Douglas's plan for overturning the "sacred pledge" regarding the western territorial limits of slavery. Declaring that "the cause of human freedom is the cause of God," the self-proclaimed independents vowed that they would "go home to our constituents [and] erect anew the standard of freedom." Chase was a nominal Democrat, one of the Free Soilers from 1848 who had since returned uneasily to their regular party, but he and fellow antislavery radicals such as Senator Charles Sumner of Massachusetts and Rep. Joshua Giddings of Ohio were determined to use this new sectional agitation to finally bury the Jacksonian-era party system. They saw Douglas's Nebraska maneuver as a gross overreach and jumped at the chance to appeal across party lines for the sake of opposing slavery.[2] Abraham Lincoln was also ready for such an opportunity, but he differed from Chase and his crew of independents over the tactics of managing such a delicate antislavery fusion operation. From Illinois, Lincoln proceeded to navigate the altered 1854 political landscape in a more deliberate manner. Behind the scenes, however, he was clearly heading in their direction.

IN DECEMBER 1851, DOUGLAS had vowed "never to make another speech upon the slavery question." He suggested that the nation was moving past what seemed like endless sectional controversy.[3] But the Compromise of 1850 had settled nothing regarding slavery, as most astute party leaders soon realized, including Douglas himself. Several factors ultimately convinced the Illinois senator to support repeal of the Missouri Compromise—legislation that he had once claimed "no ruthless hand would ever be so reckless to disturb." One of the main purposes of his about-face in 1854 was to reassert his party leadership.[4] The Nebraska territorial plan represented one facet of Douglas's multilayered effort to reframe Democratic party strategy along an east–west axis. Douglas had approached the December 1853 congressional session with a flurry of ideas on how to promote popular western issues, including establishing Pacific railroad routes, funding subsidies for homestead farmers, and using state-imposed tonnage duties as an alternative method for financing long-delayed river and harbor improvements.[5]

But the intense public reaction to the Nebraska bill overwhelmed these other priorities. By early February, there were "Anti-Nebraska" public meetings in northern cities like Chicago, and the outpouring of hostile editorial comment spread across party lines. In state capitals such as Springfield, there were battles over legislative instructions to guide the upcoming votes on the repeal effort. A frustrated Douglas vented his anger at this unexpected backlash in a series of urgent letters to Charles Lanphier, one of his top political advisers and a Democratic newspaper editor from Springfield. "I have been told," Douglas wrote in February, "that a Plot has been formed between the Whigs, Abolitionists, & some disappointed office-seekers, professing to be Democrats to endeavor to get our Legislature to instruct me on the Nebraska Bill & Tonnage Duties." Douglas saw nothing but base partisan motivations from such cross-party opposition. "The object of the Whigs & Abolitionists is apparent," he observed. "They wish to divide the Democratic Party, & thus elect a Whig Senator."[6]

Lincoln, the most likely candidate for this alleged "Whig Senator," was present in Springfield as the legislature debated a resolution on Douglas's shocking moves. Lincoln was not involved in any plot to promote himself for office, but he believed that he was watching nefarious conspiracies play out in the state legislature. He later described how he had heard from a "bolting democratic member" that only three out of seventy Illinois Democratic state representatives or senators initially supported the Nebraska plan during their caucus meetings, but once Douglas's "orders" arrived through Lanphier, the endorsement of popular sovereignty passed with hardly any defections. Lincoln called it "perfectly astonishing" and blasted the entire process as illegitimate, claiming the law had been "conceived in violence."[7]

As the Nebraska controversy unfolded that spring, however, Lincoln declined to offer public commentary. The reason for his caution was professional as much as political. Early that year Lincoln was consumed by the needs of his railroad clients. A conglomerate of smaller companies—spearheaded by Robert Smith's operation out of Alton and including the investors behind the town of Lincoln—were pushing for what they called "state policy," a plan for local Illinois companies to reap the benefits of transporting trade and passengers between Chicago and St. Louis. They were struggling to overcome powerful out-of-state interests that seemed to have persuaded—or perhaps bribed—key legislators to oppose their efforts. Lincoln, a chief lobbyist in this corporate warfare, warned in mid-February that "Springfield" was "preparing to stab us," suggesting with grim determination that "all we can do is to take care of ourselves as we best may."[8]

As important as this time-consuming power struggle over "state policy" was for Lincoln as a lobbyist, it was still secondary to the demands of his biggest client, the Illinois Central Railroad. In 1853 Lincoln had signed on to represent the ICRR in its landmark tax case that was scheduled for appeal in late February to the state supreme court. This was the biggest case of Lincoln's legal career, and he must have spent dozens of hours preparing for the oral arguments. The case ended up getting continued—ultimately for two years—but Lincoln also had several major ICRR cases in circuit court to deal with that spring.

Lincoln was busy, but he did not ignore the swirling political controversy. When William Seward first spoke out against the Nebraska bill in the U.S. Senate, Lincoln offered him praise through his partner William Herndon. Seward had initially declined to join Chase and other independents in their antislavery fusionist endeavors, but he agreed with them that the repeal of the Missouri Compromise was launching a sectional realignment of the parties—something he had been predicting since the debates over the Compromise of 1850. "I tell you now, as I told you in 1850, you buried the Wilmot Proviso . . . [but] here it is again," Seward crowed on February 17, "striking through these halls in complete steel, as before." The New Yorker's point was that "slavery agitation" was their future, and no amount of "conservatism" could stop the escalating battle between "right and wrong." In Springfield, Herndon was thrilled and wrote an admiring letter to Seward while sharing that Lincoln—"your friend"—considered the speech "most excellent."[9]

Both Lincoln and Herndon also penned several unsigned editorials for the *Illinois Journal* throughout the spring of 1854, while editor Simeon Francis suffered from an illness. Lincoln probably provided his most important editorial assistance in March and April, just as the national political debate over Nebraska policy reached a fever pitch.[10]

Douglas secured comparatively easy Senate approval for the legislation on March 4. But House members faced voters sooner in the fall midterm elections, and they proved a much tougher hurdle for passage. Illinois Democratic congressman William "Dick" Richardson spearheaded the effort for Douglas as chair of the House Committee on Territories, but it took him until late May to finally secure passage of the bill and then only by a thin margin. At Douglas's urging, President Franklin Pierce made the measure a test of party loyalty, threatening retribution from the administration for any Democratic bolters.

Nevertheless, there were still two defections from within the Illinois Democratic delegation: John Wentworth of Chicago and William Bissell, a Democrat from southwestern Illinois and a Mexican War hero. Both opposed Douglas's legislation but struggled with what seemed like a potentially career-ending decision.[11]

The Illinois Whigs in Congress had an easier political calculation. All four members were antislavery, and three of them—James Knox, Jesse Norton, and Elihu Washburne—had been elected in 1852 as part of an antislavery coalition that was a clear precursor to the broad "standard of freedom" that Chase and independent-minded Democrats were now trying to establish across the North. Richard Yates, representing central Illinois, also earnestly opposed the Nebraska bill. Jonathan Baldwin Turner, the president of Illinois College in Jacksonville (which both Yates and Herndon had attended), wrote the Whig congressman an effusive letter in April, praising him for his opposition to the bill but also urging him to think about the future with an open partisan mind. "Whig, Democrat, and Free Soil are now all 'obsolete ideas' and all bygones are gone forever," wrote Turner. "And what shall we do next? What but unite on *principle* instead of *party*?" Yates, in reply, was friendly but noncommittal about how opposition forces might best unite in the upcoming elections.[12]

On May 30, when President Pierce signed the Kansas-Nebraska Act into law, a violent confrontation over a fugitive slave in Boston heightened the sectional drama. Anthony Burns, a runaway from Virginia, had been recaptured recently—a rare occurrence in New England. The Boston vigilance committee immediately mobilized to rescue him, but they failed, killing a federal officer in the process. As the rendition hearing in Boston proceeded under heavy police guard, senators were offering their closing commentary on the Nebraska legislation. With his customary bluster, Douglas pointed to what was happening around the country and warned Whigs against getting drawn into any "great northern party" willing to have "the black flag of abolition floating over it." The Illinois senator dared them to try it—"preach your war on the Constitution," he announced. "We will be ready."[13]

In response, Seward offered some threats of his own. The next day the New Yorker warned that the way the southerners had orchestrated the repeal of the Missouri Compromise was teaching northerners a dangerous lesson about how to exercise raw sectional power. "The Free States are not dull scholars, even in practical political strategy," he observed, claiming that they finally understood the "secret" strength of their emerging northern majority—"that a law permitting or establishing slavery can be repealed, and the Union nevertheless remain firm." This was a clear warning, and Washington was soon awash with gossip about whether Seward had suddenly become "too much of an antislavery man" for the party of Webster and Clay or remained "too much a Whig" to lead any independent antislavery political movement.[14]

It was Congressman Washburne, not Lincoln, who initially played the role of a Chase or a Seward as the antislavery leader in Illinois. For months, the Whig congressman worked quietly across party lines, with figures such as Dr. Charles H. Ray, the editor of the Democratic newspaper in Galena. Ray came out early against the Nebraska bill despite the pressure from Douglas, Lanphier, and others. "Great God!" he had written Washburne privately in February, "How I hate and despise the movers of that infamous scheme," vowing that he would "defy the whole tribe of milk-sops and doughfaces" within the Democratic party. "I am fighting on my own hook," he wrote to Washburne, who represented his district.[15]

Washburne was also working hard outside his district, especially with the goal of cultivating Free Soilers and former Liberty men. He communicated regularly with Zebina Eastman, the editor of the Chicago *Free West*, the state's leading antislavery newspaper. Washburne came back to Illinois briefly in June and tried to meet face-to-face with Eastman, but they missed each other. "I had many things to communicate with you in regard to future policy," Washburne suggested. The congressman was interested in regional coordination across party lines but had special concerns about his own district. Washburne wanted Eastman's help in convincing the most ultra of the antislavery radicals to abandon any plans to run a separate "free-soil candidate" against him. Eastman needed no convincing. He eagerly supported Washburne's antislavery fusion efforts in 1854, just as he had done two years earlier.

In July, Washburne made plans with Eastman to coordinate a statewide antislavery planning session in Chicago. "The whigs in Congress from Illinois have talked over the very thing you suggest," Washburne wrote on July 5, "and we all agree with you that in our State we should discard all party names for the occasion and unite all the elements and make a straight-out fight against Nebraska and slavery extension." It was a turning point, marking an unprecedented level of cross-party fusion around the antislavery principle, involving not just northern Illinois Whigs like Washburne, Knox, and Norton but apparently Yates, too. "We expect to be in Chicago, all at the same time, about the first of August," the Galena congressman informed Eastman, "and hope then and there to be able to consult all friends in regard to a general state movement against Nebraska."[16]

The U.S. House of Representatives ended its legislative work slightly later than Washburne had anticipated, on Saturday, August 5. Most of the Illinois Whig representatives started home that weekend before Congress officially adjourned for its summer recess on Monday. Richard Yates made it to Jacksonville, by way of Chicago and Springfield, on Wednesday evening, August 9. Sometime earlier that week, antislavery members of the state's congressional delegation appear to have gathered in Chicago with former partisan opponents to plan an antislavery fusion for the upcoming elections.

Lincoln might have attended such a meeting. It was around this time in 1854 that Lincoln's second known photograph was taken. The sitting was instigated by George Schneider, editor of the German-language *Illinois Staats-Zeitung* and one of Chicago's earliest and most vocal opponents of the Nebraska bill. Schneider later claimed that he and Lincoln were dining in Chicago with Isaac Arnold, a leading antislavery radical—just the type who would have been meeting with Washburne, Eastman, and the others—when the editor convinced Lincoln to sit for a political portrait at a nearby photographic studio. The portrait shows the future president seated alone, wearing a dark suit against a dark backdrop, with his hair looking practically uncombed. The long, fashionable sideburns from Lincoln's first portrait have been shortened, and his tie—with Mary Lincoln not around—is loosely done. He is holding a newspaper folded awkwardly between his lap and a fabric-covered side table. Schneider later remembered that newspaper as John Wentworth's *Chicago Democrat*. The image was designed to show the possibility of antislavery fusion in Illinois—with a leading former Whig clutching the most important anti-Nebraska Democratic newspaper in the state.

Schneider later insisted that the photograph was taken in his "presence" on August 9, 1854.[17] If true, the story provides evidence for Lincoln's attendance at the fusion meeting in Chicago, for which no other records exist. But even if the image was not taken until later in the fall, when Lincoln was publicly campaigning in Chicago, he clearly knew the details of Yates's summer travel plans. On August 9, they met at the railroad depot in Springfield, where they tried to further the coordination of the local fusion effort. We know this because Lincoln wrote about it himself. "I am disappointed at not having seen or heard from you since I met you more than a week ago at the railroad depot here," he complained in a note to Yates on August 18, adding firmly, "I wish to have the matter we spoke of settled and working to its consummation."

Lincoln explained in this follow-up note that he was eager to announce Yates's renomination for Congress in the *Illinois Journal*, Springfield's traditionally Whig newspaper. He wished to do so without any formal Whig convention, observing cryptically, "I understand our friend B. S. Edwards is entirely satisfied now." Lincoln was apparently concerned because Benjamin Edwards, the prominent Whig attorney, was in the process of organizing an anti-immigrant nativist party in Sangamon County.[18]

Anti-immigrant sentiment had been building for several years, especially in the North, but 1854 marked a new era for nativist political aspirations. In the spring, secret fraternal organizations such as the Order of the Star-Spangled Banner used stealth turnout tactics to score unexpected victories in various state and local elections in Massachusetts, Pennsylvania, and elsewhere across the East. In an era without official government-printed ballots, the Know Nothings, as they were called, excelled at turning out voters without their opponents even realizing that a covert campaign was underway.[19]

By the summer, there were signs that Know Nothings were organizing in Illinois. William W. Danenhower, a Philadelphia bookseller who had moved to Chicago in the aftermath of the 1847 River and Harbor Convention, took notice of this development in June, writing in his newspaper, "Some folks think pretty loud that there is a body of men somewhere around who are rather more than sum pumpkins. The name of Know-Nothing is attached to them, but nobody knows anything about such an organization."[20] This was not mere gossip. The thirty-four-year-old Danenhower would later become the principal organizer of the Illinois nativists and a particular ally of Lincoln's. By the late summer of 1854, there was also a brand-new nativist newspaper in Springfield, the *Capital Enterprise*, which claimed around five hundred subscribers and featured the firm of Stuart & Edwards—managed by former Whig leaders John Todd Stuart and Benjamin Edwards—as one of its leading patrons. That is why Lincoln was warning Yates that they had to clear his unusual renomination plans through Edwards.[21]

Consider how difficult it must have been for Lincoln to oppose holding a district convention. The former congressman had always been among the most ardent Whig advocates for convention organizing. He had first invoked the "house divided" line in 1843 when defending the necessity of party conventions to achieve movement unity. Yet when he showed Yates a draft for his reelection announcement in the summer of 1854 as the "Whig candidate for this congressional district," it was under the pretext that it would appear in the local newspapers "without consultation" ("May I do this?" Lincoln asked slyly in his letter to Yates) and in hopes that it would produce "unanimous acquiescence without a convention." This was apparently the bargain they were making with Edwards. The nativist organizer would be "entirely satisfied" with the Yates renomination so long as it did not hinder his efforts to build a separate Know Nothing party.[22]

The published version of Yates's renomination notice made Lincoln's fusionist purpose even clearer, because it omitted the word *Whig* altogether, offering the incumbent simply as "a candidate for re-election to Congress, subject to the decision of a convention should one be held." Two weeks later the *Illinois Journal* followed the same format in announcing both attorney Stephen Logan and Lincoln as candidates for state representative in Sangamon County, framing their announcement once again without any party label, "subject to the decision of a Convention, should one be held."[23] It was highly unusual for an ex-congressman like Lincoln to run for the state legislature and to do so without a party label, but the anti-Nebraska forces were trying to avoid division by dispensing with public conventions and rallying around prominent candidates.

All this was fusion code, and it produced scorn from local Democrats. Newspapers such as the *Illinois State Register* of Springfield hurled insults at the former Sangamon County Whigs, blasting them for being "abolitionized." The *Illinois Journal* denied the charges, but the accusations had some merit. There were no Whig conventions or committee meetings in Sangamon or most other counties across the state. The Whig identity was still alive in people's hearts, but the party itself—at least as an organization—was dead across most of Illinois. Greeley's *New-York Tribune* even acknowledged this startling development within its national "Political Intelligence" section, labeling Yates as "the People's Anti-Nebraska candidate" and identifying Lincoln and Logan specifically as "Republicans."[24] "So Sangamon Whiggery is sold to the abolition-fusion *republicans*!" the *Illinois State Register* howled in response. "The faithful are expected to walk up and endorse, and know whiggery no more."[25]

Lincoln recognized that the Whig "faithful" might balk at joining such bold fusionism. He spent most of his efforts during the fall campaign cultivating Whig voters, trying to ensure that any transition toward a new anti-Nebraska or antislavery coalition would be a smooth one. His first speech in the contest was to a small band of Scott County Whigs, one of the few groups in the state who had managed to pull together a local convention under their old party name. Lincoln attended that gathering in late August and spoke at length about the Nebraska controversy even though Winchester was on the western edge of the Yates congressional district and far removed from his own state legislative campaign in Sangamon County.

Lincoln also ignored state issues in his 1854 campaign and focused his attention on the repeal of the Missouri Compromise. Despite identifying himself on occasion in public as "an old Whig," he discarded everything that had once been the basis of the Whig party's appeal. There was no more talk of tariffs, banking, or internal improvements. He clearly viewed the repeal of the Missouri Compromise as the only viable rallying point for the campaign, one that allowed him to frame his effort as a conservative call to antislavery action. Lincoln also avoided disruptive issues such as nativism or the Fugitive Slave Law and just hammered away at the ideas of restoring the old sectional compromises and keeping slavery out of the western territories.[26]

Local Democrats responded with mockery. "The whole tenor of his discussion," observed the *Register* in early September, "was to satisfy the whig portion of his audience that affiliation with abolitionism was the only salvation of their party." The local Democrats were especially disdainful of how Lincoln seemed to be ducking the growing Know Nothing controversy, noting how he denied the movement's "existence." "Of course he did," smirked the newspaper. "He 'Knows Nothing' about it."[27]

Lincoln shrugged off attacks from Douglas Democrats and focused his attention on the handful of leading anti-Nebraska Democrats, like John Palmer, who resided in the southwestern edge of the Yates congressional district and along the Chicago & Alton Railroad line. Lincoln assured the state senator, whom he had gotten to know while lobbying in Springfield, that he had "deserved" the Democratic congressional nomination in the sixth district—which had gone to Douglas loyalist Thomas Harris instead—and would have received it if only "your party omitted to make Nebraska a test of party fidelity." If Palmer had been nominated, Lincoln claimed, he would have "voted for the whig candidate" but would have "made no speeches" and "written no letters . . . happy that Nebraska was to be rebuked at all events." On the same day, Lincoln wrote to another leading politico in the district, urging him to "press Palmer hard" about the need to challenge Harris on the Nebraska question.[28]

The next day Lincoln made an even more delicate intervention on Yates's behalf. Calling himself "anxious" for Yates's reelection, he warned Richard Oglesby, a former officer in the Mexican War, that the candidate's political "enemies are getting up a charge against him . . . that he is in the habit of drinking secretly—and that they calculate on proving an instance of the charge by you." This was an explosive accusation against Yates in an era when anti-alcohol sentiment was so strong. By the summer of 1854, several state legislatures had adopted a version of the "Maine Law" that prohibited the sale of alcohol—though not yet in Illinois. Lincoln was concerned about the allegations and determined to protect Yates. Acknowledging that he preferred "a temperate man, to an intemperate one," he remarked, "still I do not make my vote depend absolutely upon the question of whether a candidate does or does not *taste* liquor."[29]

He suggested that if the rumor was true about Oglesby witnessing Yates drunk, then the young man must have been confused. "Thousands and thousands of us," wrote Lincoln, "have known Yates for more than twenty years," yet nobody had ever accused him of such behavior before. It turned out, however, that Yates was a heavy drinker, a fact that later nearly destroyed his career.[30] Perhaps Lincoln was unaware of this problem, or more likely, he chose not to be aware of it. In either case, he asked for a written reply from Oglesby denying the allegation, promising that if such a favor came, he would "reciprocate at any time."[31]

The day after his confidential exchange with Oglesby, Lincoln participated in a public debate on the Nebraska question with local Democrat John Calhoun, the former county surveyor and one of his employers from New Salem days. Observers found Lincoln's performance impressive. Even the *Illinois State Register* offered some faint-hearted praise, acknowledging that Lincoln had "made the best of a bad position."[32] Lincoln was scheduled to leave town for a busy couple of weeks of circuit court in Bloomington, but before he departed, he composed an unsigned editorial for the *Illinois Journal* summarizing one of his key claims from that argument with Calhoun about how the Nebraska bill had repealed the "sacred" Missouri Compromise.[33]

Here was Lincoln in full motion as a mature party leader—capable of deft manipulation, blunt intimidation, or thoughtful argument as the circumstances required. Lincoln also arrived in Bloomington early, before his court cases began, so that he could attend antislavery fusion meetings taking place that week. Lincoln first addressed the German "Anti-Nebraska" meeting on Tuesday,

September 12. The same evening there was also a secret "Republican" gathering for the third congressional district, which included most of the counties between Bloomington and Chicago. Several of these northern and heavily antislavery counties had been part of Lincoln's congressional district in the 1840s. By 1852, they had been reapportioned and proved to be a keystone in the alliance that elected antislavery attorney Jesse Norton, a native New Englander, to Congress. But a fierce debate erupted over how to label Norton's reelection campaign, with the Chase-friendly forces trying to rally the district under a new Republican label. Whether Lincoln attended the Republican meeting in Bloomington is unclear, but it seems unlikely that he would have stayed away.[34]

Local Democrats suspected Lincoln of involvement in every fusionist effort. One Democratic newspaper accused him of aspiring to become the "Goliath of the anti-Nebraska black republican fusionists," claiming they had seen him "nosing for weeks in the state library" as part of his determined effort to research the Nebraska controversy.[35] His speaking requests multiplied. By mid-September, former Whigs from Quincy practically begged Lincoln to come and help their congressional candidate Archibald Williams when the Little Giant was scheduled to arrive. "It is believed by all who know you, that a reply from you," pleaded resident Abraham Jonas, "would be more effective, than from any other."[36] Lincoln made it to Quincy, for the first time in his life, in early November, but he demonstrated his effectiveness against Douglas earlier, in a kind of indirect debate with the senator on September 26 at Bloomington. Douglas spoke first during the day, and Lincoln replied that evening.

Objecting to the way Douglas had belittled the "new party" as "Black Republicans," Lincoln retorted that he would not "pander to prejudice" or "bandy such language." Douglas had claimed that the 1854 campaign marked a "swallowing up of the whigs" by "abolitionists." Pointing to recent state election results across the North showing declining Democratic majorities since the eruption of the Nebraska controversy, Lincoln asked, "What right had Judge Douglas to intimate that none but abolitionists and tender-footed whigs were embraced in the 'fusion,' and that whigs were the only ones 'swallowed up'?" To Lincoln it seemed that both parties were being "swallowed up" by the slavery controversy, a development that he did not consider either "very serious or alarming."[37]

There was no doubt that former congressman Lincoln was emerging as a leader—if not quite the "Goliath"—of the central Illinois antislavery fusion effort, just as his Democratic critics had been asserting. His leadership stature was on full display during the Illinois state agricultural fair held in Springfield at the beginning of October. The opening day of the annual gathering included a welcoming speech by Douglas that was originally planned for outdoors before heavy rains forced everyone inside the crowded, steamy statehouse.

Douglas dispensed with the usual paeans to farming that one might expect at an agricultural fair and launched into a vigorous defense of his Nebraska policy. Acknowledging some hastily printed handbills indicating that Lincoln would "answer" the U.S. senator, as he had done earlier at Bloomington, Douglas demanded to know if his nemesis would "step forward" so they could "arrange some plan upon which to carry out this discussion."[38] Lincoln was not initially present, but he soon appeared within the capitol rotunda, declaring to the hostile crowd that either he or Lyman Trumbull would respond the next afternoon for the anti-Nebraska forces, and that they would welcome any rebuttal from Douglas if he should choose to offer one.[39]

By promoting Trumbull, Lincoln was acting as an organizer, focused on the larger strategic objective of drawing antislavery Democrats into the fusion movement. Judge Trumbull was the independent, anti-Nebraska Democratic candidate for Congress from Alton, a town situated along the Mississippi River. Just as Lincoln had pursued state senator John Palmer a few weeks before, now he was after even bigger game in Trumbull. Both targets were Democrats in open rebellion against Douglas. And neither figure had anything to do with Lincoln's own contest for state representative. This was about a broader antislavery fusion strategy, one that had started across northern Illinois congressional districts in 1852 and was finally arriving in the central region—with Lincoln as its main architect.

Trumbull did not appear the next day, as Lincoln had seemed to anticipate, and so the former Whig congressman was left to debate Douglas himself. He rose to the occasion, delivering the most important speech of his career to date, which he had spent weeks preparing. At two o'clock on Wednesday, October 4, Lincoln offered an eloquent three-hour address inside the stifling house chamber to a crowd of several hundred, including a restless Douglas, who kept interrupting. The speech was lawyerly in its attack on the Nebraska bill and the territorial policy of popular sovereignty, but at its core, Lincoln's rhetoric contained a profound moral repudiation of slavery and a stirring affirmation for the natural rights doctrine of the Declaration of Independence.[40] Lincoln expressed disgust that a Democratic U.S. senator from Indiana had recently derided the phrase "all men are created equal" as "a self-evident lie" and that Douglas had not denounced him. "Let no one be deceived," Lincoln stated with his rival seated nearby, "the spirit of seventy-six and the spirit of Nebraska, are utter antagonisms."[41]

After Lincoln concluded, the abolitionist Owen Lovejoy stepped forward to invite members of the audience to join him at what one skeptical reporter termed "the Fusion Republican Anti-Nebraska Convention," in the nearby senate chamber.[42] Lincoln and most of the crowd remained to listen, however, as Douglas provided two hours of rebuttal.

Lovejoy was a respected minister and the younger brother of Elijah Lovejoy, who had been murdered in 1837 by a proslavery mob at Alton. He was also a candidate for the state legislature. But more important, Lovejoy—along with antislavery lecturer Ichabod Codding, *Free West* editor Eastman, and several other veterans of the 1852 congressional antislavery coalition—had been organizing "Republicans" across northern Illinois for the fall campaign through a series of county conventions. These Republicans wanted to capitalize on the Nebraska ferment by transforming their regional efforts into a statewide political party. Eastman had been advertising in his newspaper for such a gathering at Springfield since early September.[43]

But the Republicans were out of their element in central Illinois, where antislavery fusion had been proceeding in a quieter, more ad hoc fashion. When Republican organizers arrived during the state fair, they were dismayed to find that no handbills had been printed and no rooms reserved for their "convention." Anxious about attendance and perhaps carried away by the sensation surrounding Lincoln's dramatic confrontation with Douglas, Lovejoy mistakenly thought he could seize that moment and overcome some of their disorganization. But turnout that Wednesday evening for the rump convention proved to be an embarrassment. Most observers stayed to hear Douglas. The delegates regrouped the next morning, however, and did better in conducting their official business. Local fusionists mostly ignored their efforts, and pro-Douglas newspapers like the *Illinois State Register* mocked them.

Although the modest Republican gathering on October 5 was dominated by former Liberty men from northern counties, they were experienced as antislavery fusionists. The group named Amos Throop, the most recent Maine Law candidate for Chicago mayor, as their convention president. They also adopted a set of carefully phrased resolutions that denounced the Nebraska bill and the extension of slavery into the western territories but offered little else that might offend traditional Whig sensibilities. They invoked Massachusetts senator Charles Sumner's slogan, "Freedom national, slavery sectional," and demanded personal liberty protections for accused runaways. They stopped short, however, of calling for a repeal of the Fugitive Slave Law, the abolition of slavery in Washington, DC, or making any pledge of "no more slave states" that might undermine the Compromise of 1850. They also denied harboring any "hostility" toward southerners and highlighted various northern states where anti-Nebraska fusionists had created successful cross-party coalitions. Their pragmatic platform even included an endorsement for western river and harbor improvements.[44]

The Republican convention had only one statewide nomination to make—for state treasurer—but it was a contest with special meaning for these radicals. The previous July, when Kentucky abolitionist Cassius Clay came to speak in Springfield, incumbent treasurer and Democrat John Moore had been responsible for denying him access to the statehouse. To defeat Moore, the Republicans endorsed a moderate, anti-Nebraska Whig candidate to replace him. They also showered praise on Lincoln for his speech against Douglas and included him—without asking permission—as a charter member of their newly formed Republican state central committee.[45]

Several days later, when news of his appointment reached the public, Lincoln did nothing about it. The *Illinois State Register* announced the development on October 14 under the headline "Lincoln Completely Fused—His Abolitionism Avowed." Democratic editors feigned astonishment. "We supposed at first that there must be some error in this," they wrote, suggesting they were shocked at Lincoln's refusal to disclaim the appointment. "All disguise is thrown off, and he now openly proclaims himself in full brotherhood with [William Lloyd] Garrison, Fred. Douglas [*sic*], Lovejoy, Codding & Co."[46] The *Register* also reprinted what it claimed was the October 5 platform of the "Black Republican Convention," but it was a mash-up of radical antislavery resolutions voted upon earlier in the campaign at various county conventions in the northern region of the state.[47]

This mistake by the *Illinois State Register* was no doubt malicious in its intent, designed to embarrass Lincoln and other former Whigs with whatever political fiction was convenient. But Lincoln was unmoved. "Stand with anybody that stands RIGHT," he told an audience in Peoria two days after the inflammatory article appeared, dismissing it as "silly" that any former Whigs would consider staying away from a political movement to oppose the Nebraska bill "lest they be thrown in company with the abolitionist."[48] Yet he also made no mention of Lovejoy or Codding and offered no statement on his own party affiliation. Lincoln took a full six weeks—until long after the fall elections—to even acknowledge his placement on the new Republican committee, and when he did so, he did it quietly and with considerable caution to avoid offending his new allies.

What triggered Lincoln's delayed response to the Republican invitation was that he missed the first central committee meeting and felt compelled to explain why. Lincoln told Ichabod Codding in a private letter that he had been "perplexed" by his selection. He claimed that he had discovered the news of his appointment only "by accident two or three weeks afterward," a subtle reference to the *Illinois State Register*'s misleading report. "I suppose my opposition to the principle of slavery is as strong as that of any member of the Republican party," Lincoln wrote in late November, before suggesting that he had been led to believe that "the *extent*" to which he felt "authorized to carry that position, practically," was "not at all satisfactory to that party." Here Lincoln was referring to the phony resolutions printed in Democratic newspapers that he must have known were being challenged as fake. Noting that the Republicans had already heard him speak, Lincoln observed that they should have "had full opportunity to not misunderstand my position," before adding: "Do I misunderstand theirs?"[49]

That suggestive closing question revealed that in the fall of 1854 Lincoln was less interested in distancing himself from the Republicans than in clarifying the basis for their common strategy. They all agreed that slavery was wrong and that opposing it would be the basis for their emerging movement. Their underlying fusion was on the antislavery principle, and their common strategy in 1854 was to focus on restoring the Missouri Compromise. When it came to other antislavery policy measures, there were serious divisions of opinion that would take time to sort out. That was why Lincoln believed the attempts to organize a statewide Republican organization were premature. What he really wanted from his cagey postelection exchange with Codding was confirmation that the purported Republican platform had been doctored and that Republicans from northern Illinois were still prepared to move forward with anti-Nebraska forces from central Illinois in a principled but pragmatic manner.

During the final weeks of the 1854 campaign, Lincoln himself was nothing if not pragmatic. He was standing "with anybody" who was willing to call slavery wrong, including conservative Sangamon nativists, Maine Law temperance advocates, antislavery German and English immigrants, and the stray political abolitionists who lived in and around Springfield. His only demand was that they focus on their mutual desire to restore the Missouri Compromise and repudiate "Nebraskaism."

Nobody was busier in this wide-ranging effort. Between the state fair in early October and Election Day on November 7, Lincoln was on the road almost every night.[50] He was traveling ostensibly for his legal work, but along the way delivered political speeches as far north as Chicago and as far west as Quincy. More important, he was consulting regularly with candidates and operatives across several key districts. Jane Johns, the wife of one anti-Nebraska legislative candidate from Decatur, distinctly remembered Lincoln's advice to her husband about the need to stay focused as he passed through their town in late October.[51]

That memory is true to Lincoln's approach in 1854. From the beginning of the canvass, he had warned his peers about the importance of avoiding distractions. Near the end of the fall contest, he directed a flurry of last-minute appeals to Richard Yates urging the incumbent congressman to deflect a controversy in their district over his alleged ties to nativism. Lincoln was worried about this problem because late in the campaign Yates accepted an endorsement from the *Capital Enterprise*, the local nativist newspaper, something Lincoln had been counseling against. Lincoln had no problem coordinating operations with Benjamin Edwards and other Know Nothings in Sangamon, but he wanted these efforts kept out of public view.[52]

The reason for this caution became apparent on October 30, when Lincoln reported learning that "the English" immigrants in Yates's own county of Morgan had become "dissatisfied" about "No-Nothingism." Despite his campaign travels, Lincoln fired off two separate warnings and even provided a draft public statement for Yates to release, denying that he had ever been a Know Nothing. There were about eight thousand English immigrants in Illinois, the third-largest foreign-born group in the state after the Irish and Germans. Jacksonville, the county seat of Morgan, was home to many of them.[53]

But Jacksonville was also where Yates lived. This was not the kind of political intelligence that he should have needed to hear from someone else. Clearly perturbed, Lincoln shared the unwelcome news along with a set of instructions about how to head it off. "The day before election will do," Lincoln concluded. Yates later admitted he never bothered to take care of this matter, attributing what turned out to be his close defeat to this failure. That was how Lincoln saw it, too. After the contest, he observed that "the turning of about 200 english whigs" was the primary cause of Yates's loss.[54]

LINCOLN WATCHED IN FRUSTRATION on November 7 as Yates and Archibald Williams, the anti-Nebraska candidate whom he had helped in Quincy, both lost their congressional races, apparently tripped up by their open associations with nativism. The situation was not much better on the eastern side of the state, where Lincoln had campaigned for anti-Nebraska candidate and former Whig William Archer. His hotly contested seat remained vacant because of vote-counting disputes until 1856. The anti-Nebraska candidate also fell short in the balloting for state treasurer. But Republican or antislavery fusionist forces held the four northernmost congressional districts, which they had first captured in 1852 (by electing one of their own in Chicago for Democrat John Wentworth, who had temporarily retired). They also claimed credit for the victory of Lyman Trumbull, the anti-Nebraska Democrat, in the eighth congressional district around Alton. Regular Democrats maintained their control in "Egypt," the southernmost region of Illinois and the closest thing to a proslavery section within the state. Though not quite the landslide racked up by anti-Nebraska forces in other northern states, these victories were impressive.

More stunning in Illinois were the results of the 1854 legislative contests. Within days, it became clear that despite a proliferation of partisan labels—one respected source listed more than a dozen different self-described affiliations—there appeared to be emerging an anti-Nebraska or antislavery fusionist majority in the state house of representatives and perhaps in the state senate as well.[55] This meant that new legislators might select an antislavery U.S. senator. James Shields, the incumbent, had voted for the Nebraska bill, helped Douglas enforce the measure as a test of party loyalty, and also happened to be a naturalized citizen from Ireland. On the surface, there could hardly have been a more tempting target for the fusionists.[56]

Senator Shields was also an especially tantalizing opponent for Lincoln. The Springfield attorney had a long, painful history with the bombastic former state auditor. The two had nearly dueled in 1842, at bottom a political spat but one that also involved Lincoln's then former fiancée, Mary Todd. The whole sordid episode still seemed to embarrass Lincoln, who refused to talk about it. But now he was the man best positioned to defeat Shields.

PART II

Republican

I have a bare suggestion. When there is a known body of these voters, could not a true man, of the *"detective"* class, be introduced among them in disguise, who could, at the nick of time, control their votes?

—Abraham Lincoln, age forty-nine (October 20, 1858)

5 REPUBLICAN ORGANIZATION

(1854–1856)

ABRAHAM LINCOLN BEGAN CAMPAIGNING for the U.S. Senate seat held by Democrat James Shields almost as soon as the 1854 election contests had ended. Since state legislatures still selected federal senators, however, it was not a public campaign. Lincoln's efforts over the winter mainly involved reaching out to friends of anti-Nebraska legislators, mostly by letter, before the joint balloting expected in January. On Friday, November 10, while on the road for legal business and with his local newspaper still reporting that returns from the General Assembly were not "sufficient to determine its character," Lincoln launched a letter-writing effort on his own behalf.[1] "Some friends are really for me, for the U.S. Senate," he wrote to an acquaintance in northern Illinois, "and I should be very grateful if you could make a mark for me among your members." Charles Hoyt was a longtime client, an old Whig, and a leading merchant in Aurora, a bustling trading town west of Chicago. "Please write me at all events," Lincoln demanded, "giving me the names, post-offices, and '*political position*' of members round about you."[2]

The acerbic Hoyt appreciated this need for urgency and replied with candid perspectives on the legislators from his district. Hoyt still considered himself a Whig but recognized that Lincoln was operating in a new partisan environment. He belittled one local figure as a Whig "Bull Head," dismissed another for having once been part of the "free soil Humbug in 48," and identified a third as a former "Loco" or Democrat.[3] But all of them, according to Hoyt, were part of the same "fusion ticket." For most Illinois politicos, the bewildering partisan situation seemed almost paralyzing. Nobody else moved as quickly as Lincoln to solicit support in the upcoming U.S. Senate balloting. Shields himself did not even begin evaluating the complexion of the incoming legislators until two weeks after Lincoln had begun his canvassing.[4]

William Herndon regarded his law partner's eagerness as a measure of his restless political aspirations. He later described Lincoln's ambition as "a little engine that knew no rest" and claimed that during this period, Lincoln "slept, like Napoleon, with one eye open."[5] That was not how Lincoln saw himself, but he was open about his senatorial aspirations, telling one correspondent that he had "the chance of being the man" and acknowledging to another that he had "got it into [his] head to try to be U.S. Senator."[6] Yet regardless of what Lincoln wanted for himself, he needed a more unified party apparatus to achieve it. The upcoming ballot for U.S. senator only underscored the need to perfect the statewide antislavery fusion that had developed during the 1854 fall campaign but was still essentially unorganized. Lincoln had always been careful about using party labels during the general election, but he recognized that the time had come to embrace new terms for new allies. Lincoln did not launch his solicitations for support as a Republican, but his senatorial contest quickly evolved into a turning point for the emerging Republican party of Illinois.

In mid-November, when Rep. Elihu Washburne received Lincoln's request for information, he observed, "Every single Senator and representative" in his district "belongs to the Republican Party." Washburne regarded this development as no obstacle to Lincoln's success, claiming that "if the Anti-Nebraska men or republicans have a majority in both branches you ought to be able to go through."[7]

Lincoln sometimes used the Whig label during his senatorial canvassing but just as often did not. And sometimes he left his affiliation intentionally vague. On the same day that he reached out to Hoyt and Washburne, he penned an appeal to Chicago attorney and banker Jonathan Young Scammon. The two men had known each other from a distance for years, sharing clients and occasional legal business. Scammon was a former Whig and prominent enough to be talked about as a possible Senate candidate himself, but his affiliation in this new landscape was uncertain. He seemed like the kind of Benjamin Edwards–style conservative who might just be migrating into the nativist camp. Lincoln took no chances as he rushed out a short note asking Scammon to "make a mark for me with the members" around Chicago, adding, "If you know nothing, and feel nothing to the contrary." The partisan pun was clearly designed to tease out where Scammon stood. Scammon responded that he would discuss the matter with Lincoln in person.[8]

Many of Lincoln's peers would have assumed that he and Scammon were Know Nothings. Despite his attempts at keeping public distance from the nativists, there were signs that they were trying to embrace Lincoln. His vote totals in the November legislative election in Sangamon County were almost identical to fellow fusionists Stephen Logan's and Richard Yates's. This suggests that all three men were beneficiaries of a coordinated Election Day effort between local Whig antislavery fusionists and nativists, even though, unlike the others, Lincoln had declined a formal Know Nothing endorsement in his legislative campaign. Several newspapers across the state, such as Zebina Eastman's *Free West*, did not hesitate during this period to connect Lincoln to nativism. "Mr. Lincoln is a Know Nothing," declared the abolitionist journal, "and expects the full vote of the Republicans as well as the influence of the Know Nothings." Don Morrison, an ex-Whig state senator who had once battled for the Land Office commissionership, made the same assumption in a private letter indicating that he was planning to "give the Know Nothings a blow" after the fall elections, which he believed would "throw me entirely out of the Lincoln ranks." Within those Lincoln ranks, several figures, such as attorney Leonard Swett of Bloomington, a close friend of Judge David Davis, took note of Know Nothing support for Lincoln whenever they were counting senatorial votes on his behalf. Swett assured Lincoln in December that one former Whig editor was "without doubt a know nothing and for you."[9]

Lincoln also appeared to take his Know Nothing support in the Senate contest for granted and seemed more worried about the challenges of cultivating antislavery radicals. The key question about the newly organized Republican men from northern Illinois was what type of measures or policies they would insist upon in exchange for their endorsement. "Things look reasonably well," Lincoln wrote near the end of November, "but I fear some will insist on a platform, which I can not stand upon."[10]

Lincoln expressed this concern on the same day that he questioned Ichabod Codding about his appointment to the new Republican central committee. Lincoln suspected that Democratic claims about Republican antislavery extremism were bogus—especially regarding alleged party "tests" for the repeal of the Fugitive Slave Law, pledges for no more slave states, or calls for the abolition of slavery itself—but he needed more reassurance that the spirit of broad antislavery fusion from the fall was still holding. Northern Republicans were wary of Lincoln in this regard, too, fearing that he was capable of backsliding in his previous commitments to the antislavery cause. After his delicate exchange with Codding declining his appointment to the central committee, some Chicago-area antislavery newspapers became openly hostile. "We could not advise the republicans to support for this station [of U.S. senator], Lincoln, or any moderate men of this stamp," Eastman wrote in *Free West* at the very end of November. "He is only a Whig, and this people's movement is no whig triumph."[11]

The criticism stung Lincoln. "There must be something wrong about U.S. Senator, at Chicago," he warned Washburne in mid-December, questioning his old Whig ally about whether he had been premature in predicting radical support. Lincoln was full of advice about how to turn the tide. "Wentworth has a knack of knowing things better than most men," he wrote of Long John, the departing Democratic congressman from Chicago. "I wish you would pump him, and write me what you get from him," Lincoln wrote, adding, "Please do this as soon as you can, as the time is growing short." Lincoln was also adamant about the need for secrecy: "Don't let *any one* know I have written you this." The Galena congressman mostly did as he was told but reached out to Eastman to pressure him about tamping down the antislavery resistance to Lincoln. He reminded the skeptical editor that Lincoln had to appear moderate to hold support from the center of the state. "I know he is with us in sentiment," Washburne assured Eastman.[12]

Washburne was making some headway with his lobbying, but a special election in December 1854 nearly derailed Lincoln's efforts with the radicals. Early on Lincoln had been informed that he should resign his seat in the legislature since the Illinois state constitution barred members of the General Assembly (who were the actual voters for the Senate seat) from being considered as candidates for U.S. senator. The U.S. Supreme Court later threw out this type of suspect state limitation as a violation of requirements that could be established only by the U.S. Constitution, but at this critical stage Lincoln was taking no chances. He declined to accept his recent election as state representative, and the special election to fill the vacancy occurred on the Saturday before Christmas. The Democrats won a surprise victory after pretending to concede the seat and catching local Whig fusionists by surprise—a tactic they seem to have borrowed from the Know Nothings. The stunning result even made national news. The *Boston Post*, recalling the former Illinois Whig congressman who had campaigned so aggressively in Massachusetts for Zachary Taylor in 1848, mocked Lincoln's pretensions. "Abe appears to have resigned for nothing," claimed the Democratic newspaper, "as he will now be neither in the state nor U.S. legislature," adding in a biting couplet:

Honorable Abram Lincoln,
How much you have to think on![13]

Lincoln's allies were more sympathetic, but according to Galena editor Charles Ray, the setback raised new questions about Lincoln's commitment to antislavery fusion. "The election of that Nebraska man in the county of Sangamon to fill the vacancy occasioned by Abe's resignation," he wrote to Washburne, "has done more than anything else to damage him with the Abolitionists."[14]

Ray, who would soon become the editor of the *Chicago Tribune*, knew what he was talking about. This was an embarrassing moment, reflecting unexpected weakness, even though Lincoln tried to convince Washburne that the result was "not of the least consequence" since antislavery fusionists would still hold the balance of power in the state house of representatives. Lincoln blamed the setback on a combination of bad weather and stealth tactics by Democrats.[15] But for most observers, the defeat suggested that central Illinois remained hostile terrain for the antislavery movement. This was a political reality that Lincoln would face for the rest of his career. He won his legislative race in 1854 as an avowed opponent of slavery, but he would never again prevail in an election in his home county, not in 1858 during the Lincoln-Douglas campaign, not in 1860 in the presidential contest, and not even in 1864, when he ran for reelection as president during the Civil War. Sangamon County was Lincoln's adopted home, but after December 1854, it would never again represent his partisan home base.

Perhaps for that reason, the aftermath of that disappointing special election provided some useful clarity for Lincoln. He no longer seemed as beholden to the state's conservative center. He started thinking and acting more as a Republican and less as a Whig. Sometime after Christmas, for example, he compiled a set of notebooks that alphabetized the incoming one hundred state representatives and senators, meticulously identifying their home counties and partisan affiliations. Like everyone else during this confused period, he employed an array of party labels to accomplish this task, but what was most remarkable was that he was acknowledging how a "great many" of the "Whigs" and "Anti-Nebraska Democrats" had gone into what he was willing to term in his notebooks the "Republican organization." What he meant by that reference was a legislative caucus that he hoped was preparing to endorse him as its candidate for U.S. Senate. At the end of 1854, just over two months after he skipped the Republican convention at the state fair and less than one month after he questioned Codding about the Republican platform, Lincoln was embracing—at least in private—the Republican label.[16]

The new General Assembly was supposed to begin its organization on Monday, January 1, 1855, but the process was delayed because of all the disruptions to the traditional party caucus system. The Democrats were able to put together a regular slate of officer nominations (for house speaker, secretary, clerk, and so on), but the antislavery or anti-Nebraska fusionists were not capable of achieving ordinary legislative organization under the Republican or any other label, especially in the closely divided state senate. The Independent or Anti-Nebraska Democrats in the state senate, led by Norman Judd of Cook County and John Palmer of Macoupin County, held the balance of power and avoided caucusing with any former Whigs. Still, by Wednesday afternoon, the anti-Nebraska forces were able to organize both the house and the senate by negotiating with a few former Democrats with antislavery leanings. But regular Democrats held a hidden advantage. They retained just enough strength in the state senate to delay the call for a joint session, necessary for the U.S. Senate ballot. The Democratic strategy was to hold off any election until they had gained (or perhaps bought) the necessary votes from among the doubtful legislators who were willing to bargain, those Lincoln privately called, in disgust, "the rotten material."[17]

With that objective in mind, Democrats in Springfield began plotting to find a candidate they could more easily sell to their members than the pro-Nebraska incumbent, James Shields. This did not please Douglas. The stubborn party leader had been promoting Shields since the November elections. Douglas saw the Irish immigrant as a useful vehicle for changing the political calculus. "At all events our friends should stand by Shields," he urged from Washington, "and throw the responsibility of the whigs of beating him *because he was born in Ireland.*" Ever the opportunist, Douglas wanted a political landscape shaped more by immigration than by slavery. "The Nebraska fight is over," he wrote, "and Know Nothingism has taken its place as the chief issue of the future."[18] Shields had doubts about this ambitious pivot and suspected that his Democratic "friends" were preparing to abandon him. "There is a snake in the grass," he wrote in mid-January. "They are holding back to bring out a new man."[19]

Just as Shields was expressing these anxieties, Lincoln warned outgoing congressman Richard Yates that Democratic legislators were preparing to support William Bissell as a "pretext" for corralling back some of the less "sincere" antislavery Democrats.[20] Bissell was finishing up his third and final term in Congress from the district that had just elected Judge Lyman Trumbull, an avowed anti-Nebraska Democrat. Bissell was a Democrat who had opposed the Nebraska bill but was absent for the final vote because of illness and had not run for reelection. He was best known for nearly dueling with Mississippi senator Jefferson Davis during the Compromise of 1850 debates. But Lincoln did not trust Bissell on the slavery question, calling his potential candidacy "as dangerous a card as we have to play against."[21]

Lincoln himself was playing a complicated hand during this period. The day after the legislature organized, he gave a speech to the state colonization society that had ramifications for the fusion effort. Lincoln would not join the society until 1856, but he had spoken to the group once before and had been scheduled to do so again the previous year but canceled because of family illness.[22] A haven for conservatives who claimed to oppose slavery, the colonization society supported sending freed slaves to live in Africa as the only way to secure voluntary abolition in the southern states. The national organization tried to demonstrate the effectiveness of its emancipation strategy by purchasing and manumitting enslaved people and then establishing them on the west coast of Africa in Liberia. Most antislavery radicals considered colonization to be a dangerous distraction. Lincoln was taking a risk by agreeing to return to speak to the group in the midst of his senatorial bid.

He tried to navigate this dilemma by devoting the bulk of his speech to the history of the African slave trade, and by attempting to show how the Nebraska bill had opened the door for its revival. Lincoln even claimed that the suppression of the illicit African slave trade was one of the "collateral objects" of the colonization movement.[23] His rhetoric fell flat. The Chicago *Democratic Press*, an independent journal, suggested that despite laboring "very ingeniously against occupying a position obnoxious to the favor of anybody," Lincoln had "lost a point or two which he held in his hand before this playout." The regular Democratic press was more caustic, chuckling over how Lincoln had become "lost in the mazes of fusion."[24] Antislavery papers ignored the episode.

Despite this stumble, Lincoln kept up his outreach efforts throughout January, making direct contact with new legislators and firing off confidential reports to allies. One Springfield lobbyist recalled how persistent Lincoln was about buttonholing legislative members even as he tried hard to appear "delicate."[25] The result was that nobody in town had a better political intelligence or whip count than Lincoln, and he knew it. In a revealing letter to Washburne, he even mocked another would-be candidate for overestimating his commitments based on what he dryly called "insufficient evidence."[26] Some found Lincoln's aggressiveness distasteful. The *Aurora Guardian* criticized his "over-weaning anxiety" for the office.[27] When Yates wrote from Washington to ask for help in promoting himself for the Senate seat, however, Lincoln shared his latest information, acknowledging only somewhat grudgingly that if the contest turned into a "general scramble," then "*your chance* will be as good as that of *any other* I suppose."[28]

The U.S. Senate contest was becoming more of a scramble. The antislavery fusionists met to discuss the contest as a caucus on January 10 but could not reach a consensus about their senatorial nominee.[29] The independent Democrats, led by Judd and Palmer, also continued to decline to caucus with them. Lincoln's chief problem as a candidate remained lingering resistance from northern Republicans. Working in part through Washburne, he secured a pivotal endorsement from Joshua Giddings, his old congressional messmate who had become one of the leading Republicans in Ohio. At their joint request, Giddings sent a letter to Owen Lovejoy, the abolitionist who now held a seat in the statehouse. Representative Lovejoy was by far the most active antislavery radical in the entire legislature. He introduced a small blizzard of controversial measures, including ones to repeal the state's Black Laws and to integrate the public schools. He also defiantly presented a petition from African Americans against colonization.

But ultimately Lovejoy and the more radical antislavery bloc were not going to stand in the way of general antislavery fusion. The independent anti-Nebraska Democrats represented a much greater obstacle. There were signs throughout January that some of these men were more Democratic than independent in their outlook. The party regulars had finally found a candidate who seemed to have just enough appeal with these wavering antislavery forces, but it was not William Bissell. Instead, Governor Joel Matteson emerged as the "snake in the grass" whom Shields had been warning about. Lincoln claimed afterward that the ostensible surprise had been rigged for months, and that Matteson had "been secretly a candidate ever since (before even) the fall election." Around Springfield, rumors flew about vote buying. According to Lincoln, the governor and his men did not reveal their plans to the "Nebraska democrats" until they could demonstrate before "their greedy eyes" that they had been "tampering" successfully with enough of the fusionists to secure victory.[30] Once they did so, the regular Democratic party leadership agreed to enter a senatorial ballot by joint session, scheduled initially for January 31. A crippling snowstorm delayed that plan, however, and for a brief period in early February, the fate of the contest appeared to be in limbo.

By that point, almost everybody in town had become aware of Matteson's scheming. Before the storm, Mary Stuart, wife of John Todd Stuart, told their daughter that the governor appeared to have a "better chance of success than any of the other numerous candidates." Some of the more experienced newspaper correspondents began predicting his success. Even John Palmer, the leader of the anti-Nebraska Democrats, was impressed, informing his wife that the governor was "anti-slavery in all his antecedents and is a decided anti-Douglas man," which he called "the real point involved in the controversy." Under those conditions, Palmer seemed ready to return to the party fold. "The chances are that both wings of the democracy will unite on him," the state senator wrote. "I think Gov. Matteson will be elected Senator."[31]

Still, the somewhat shaky "Republican organization" kept up a brave front. Once the snow cleared, the caucus had the joint ballot postponed by another few days, until February 8, so they could try to counteract the sudden Matteson boom. To that end, pro-Lincoln legislators introduced a series of resolutions about problems with the state finances in a transparent attempt to embarrass the governor. Lincoln also continued with his lobbying efforts, though he complained afterward about being unable to get "sufficient access" to any of the "old democrats."[32] Finally, the fusionist leadership pushed forward policy measures designed to placate key elements of their coalition. The legislature adopted a compromise Maine Law bill, introduced by new Sangamon County representative Stephen Logan, that promised to submit the issue of prohibiting the sale of alcohol to a statewide referendum in the spring. Northern Republicans also got a public hearing on some of their policy priorities. Lovejoy was able to introduce several resolutions of instruction for the state's federal officeholders (including, of course, Senator Stephen Douglas), calling for them not only to restore the Missouri Compromise but also to oppose the admission of any more slave states and to support revisions to the federal Fugitive Slave Law.

Lovejoy held the house floor for nearly two hours with an impassioned defense of the era's most radical antislavery positions. He was even espousing views, on the federal fugitive code, that Northern Republicans had been downplaying as recently as October at their convention during the state fair. Following Lovejoy's lengthy plea, and after a brief rejoinder from some regular Democrats, a majority did approve the antislavery preamble and the first resolution against the Kansas-Nebraska Act. This was the ground on which all fusionists agreed. The other resolutions failed by wide margins.[33] But the radicals had been heard, and that seemed to be the point.

These were the types of concessions that succeeded in solidifying support for Lincoln as the nominee of a Republican caucus. Conservatives got the promise of a ballot initiative on temperance. Radicals got a floor debate on slavery. Everybody in the coalition received a timely reminder that Democrats had found their compromise candidate and might well succeed. Lincoln seemed relieved to have made the necessary headway with the antislavery radicals. "Through the untiring efforts of friends," he told Rep. Jesse Norton afterward, "among whom yourself and Washburne were chief, I finally surmounted the difficulty with the extreme Anti-Slavery men, and got all their votes."[34] But nobody really thought it was enough without the handful of anti-Nebraska Democrats who stubbornly refused to join the caucus. Lincoln stated it plainly afterward: "So we stood, and so went into the fight yesterday; the Nebraska men very confident of the election of Matteson, though denying he was a candidate; and we very much believing also, that they would elect him."[35]

On the first ballot, Lincoln was the top vote getter with 45. Shields followed with 41. Trumbull received 5 votes, while the remaining handful of ballots (out of 99 legislators participating) were scattered. The Democrats had decided to lead with Shields in deference to the wishes of Douglas. But the plan all along was to switch in the later rounds to Matteson after allowing what Lincoln called "our secret Matteson men" time to demonstrate some "good faith" to their constituents by voting for a few credible antislavery candidates. Lincoln was convinced that the Matteson forces had bribed some members of the Republican caucus and had the ability to control their votes.[36]

Two more rounds did little to change the complexion of things. Shields held his regular Democratic support. Lincoln lost some stray votes. Trumbull's totals barely moved. Nobody else was really emerging as a serious alternative. Then, after the third round, Stephen Logan, acting as Lincoln's floor manager, tried to buy more time by moving for an adjournment. But the combined Democratic strength, and some stray fusionist votes, defeated the motion.

During the next three rounds, nothing much changed. Lincoln's totals dipped but made a recovery. Shields picked up one vote but dropped back again. Trumbull gained ground but only pulled together about ten supporters. Finally, in the seventh round, Democrats made the long-anticipated switch to Matteson. This scare helped Lincoln briefly, but his support collapsed over the next couple of ballots. Nearly all northern Republicans left him for Trumbull. By the end of the ninth round, only fifteen legislators remained with Lincoln, all former Whigs elected on fusion tickets, mostly from the center of the state.[37]

Jane Johns, the wife of one of those stalwart Lincoln supporters, later claimed that back in her hotel room during a recess, she overhead two members discussing a "contract" that they had arranged with Matteson in exchange for their votes. Realizing that these men were describing the worst kind of corruption, she rushed over to the capitol to give the news to her husband, Dr. Harvey Johns. He immediately conveyed the gist of the story to Lincoln. Bribery was not that shocking—they had all suspected Matteson's corruption beforehand—but the revelation about which legislators were involved was jarring. One leading fusionist "whose name came near the head of the roll call," according to Mrs. Johns, was supposed to switch his vote to the governor in the next round. Years later she could not recall the name of that traitor, but Lincoln essentially did it for her when he explained to Norton afterward that they had received "strong signs" that Matteson had been "tampering" with Frederick Day of LaSalle County, who had otherwise been outwardly loyal to the antislavery camp.[38]

Lincoln suddenly realized what he had to do. He conferred with State Senator Palmer, one of Trumbull's chief supporters. But to Palmer's surprise, Lincoln did not try to use the new information about Day to browbeat him into giving up on Trumbull. Lincoln instead explained how he intended to secure victory for Trumbull and stave off the "*imminent* danger of Matteson's election." He directed

Dr. Johns and his other remaining supporters, including a distraught Stephen Logan, to vote for Trumbull on the tenth round. "I gave the direction," Lincoln claimed afterward, "simultaneously with forming the resolution to do it." They moved just fast enough to secure Trumbull's election before the unholy "contract" for Matteson could be fulfilled.[39]

It was high drama in Springfield. Regular Democrats were furious. "Every ism, every faction, every disconcerted demagogue," complained Jacksonville's *Illinois Sentinel*, "have concentrated their efforts for the only purpose they ever can unite, 'to beat the democrats.'"[40] Trumbull confided to Lincoln that his former Democratic colleagues were truly enraged and would "do anything to give vent to their malice." On the other hand, Trumbull and the anti-Nebraska Democrats were overjoyed, not only by their unexpected victory but also by the depth of Lincoln's partisan sacrifice. Palmer later claimed that he and other members of the Trumbull inner circle vowed that night to stand by Lincoln in any future campaign. Trumbull soon assured his defeated rival that they would work together to overcome the "Slavery expansionists in Illinois." And for some years afterward, the notoriously cold, bespectacled politician kept up with what seemed to be sincere expressions of gratitude to Lincoln.[41]

Former Whigs were less satisfied. David Davis, who had not been in Springfield that day, expressed outrage that forty-five men had been forced to yield to a coterie of five. Logan blamed the antislavery radicals, who in his opinion had "rode to death" the rest of the coalition with their policy demands. Mary Lincoln took the results personally and for a time stopped speaking with Julia (Jayne) Trumbull, the senator-elect's wife, a woman who had been her bridesmaid and one of her oldest friends in Springfield.[42]

No such bitterness came from Lincoln. "I regret my defeat moderately," he reported on the day after the balloting, "but I am not nervous about it." If anything, Lincoln seemed defiant. "I could have headed off every combination and been elected," he claimed, "had it not been for Matteson's double game—and his defeat now gives me more pleasure than my own gives me pain." A week later he assured Jesse Norton that he was "quite convalescent." Lincoln realized that his decision to anoint Trumbull had achieved what had been eluding him for months—a successful antislavery fusion that included the core anti-Nebraska Democrats. It was worth an individual defeat to achieve such a party milestone. As Lincoln told one correspondent, he simply could not "let the whole political result go to ruin, on a point merely personal" to himself.[43]

This achievement represented the first statewide victory for Illinois Republicans. They were not yet a fully organized political party, but they were in power. That was why, just a week after the contest, Lincoln hosted a raucous celebration at his home for "anti-Nebraska" members of the legislature. According to a local newspaper, Lincoln's gracious "liberality" produced "good eating," "good speeches," and "excellent sentiments."[44] But it was also an obvious sign that he was still determined to lead, even if he was no longer a candidate or an officeholder.

Lincoln and Trumbull corresponded in the months ahead, clearly trying to establish parameters for an effective partnership. Lincoln attempted to be charming, offering a sardonic report about Democratic plans to challenge the judge's eligibility. The Democrats were going after him on state constitutional grounds not too dissimilar from the ones Lincoln had confronted earlier in his own campaign, regarding potential eligibility restrictions. Trumbull also made sure to be solicitous, consulting with Lincoln about rumors that Robert Smith of Alton would be vying to fill his vacant U.S. House seat as a pro-Nebraska Democrat.[45] Both men headed into what was supposed to be an off political year determined to try to work together.

Yet the task of building a new political party was daunting, something none of the coalition leaders in Illinois, apart from a few Liberty men and Free Soilers, had even attempted in nearly two decades. The emerging Republicans would have to reorient a network of partisan newspapers while establishing new committees for calling nominating conventions. There were letters to write and days to be spent on the road, encouraging former partisan enemies to work together in counties across the state. Lincoln had to return to his legal work, however, picking up what he described as the "lost crumbs" of his circuit-riding business.[46] So did most of the other lawyers involved in the previous year's political efforts. But abolitionist minister Ichabod Codding was available. Funded by Republicans in northern Illinois, he launched a statewide antislavery speaking tour and organizational drive in 1855, though it was almost immediately undermined by the surprising tenacity of the state's Know Nothings.[47]

During the legislative session, the nativist forces had offered no rhetorical fireworks like the antislavery radicals and did not present much of a legislative agenda other than holding a brief debate in the state senate about naturalization laws and supporting the referendum on prohibition. But in early March 1855, they scored their biggest political victory in Illinois to date, sweeping city elections in Chicago as part of an anti-immigrant "Law & Order" coalition. After feigning no interest in the contests, the Know Nothings gained control of the city council and helped elect a new mayor. They immediately moved to end the sale of alcohol on Sundays, sparking what was called a "lager beer riot" in April that pitted an expanded and mostly native-born local police force against hundreds of disgruntled German immigrants.[48]

The violence in Chicago subsided, but the political repercussions were felt widely. Newspapers from across the state were suddenly full of renewed speculation about the shadowy nativist forces. There was talk that Know Nothings were angling to control other cities and statewide contests, including an election for state supreme court occurring in June. For that race, Lincoln promoted his former law partner Stephen Logan and may have been compelled to work with Know Nothings to help him. Lincoln signed a public statement of support for his friend along with nativist Benjamin Edwards and die-hard Whig conservative John Todd Stuart. On the surface, it looked like an endorsement from Springfield's legal elite, but in the context of the times, it was intended as a unity message reflecting a coalition of distinct political constituencies across central Illinois.[49]

The nativists might have come to dominate this coalition if they had handled themselves better. Instead, a bitter personal feud erupted in May between rival Chicago-based Know Nothing leaders Amos Throop and William Danenhower. The fight was ostensibly over slavery, with one faction led by Throop arguing for a broad fusionist approach that could embrace antislavery and perhaps co-opt the emerging Republicans, while the other more ultraist faction led by Danenhower was demanding that Know Nothings keep their focus strictly on anti-immigrant and anti-Catholic measures. This kind of debate was roiling nativist organizations across the country in 1855, but it had a particularly devastating impact in Illinois.[50] The feud influenced the June balloting, helping to send statewide prohibition down to a narrow defeat amid a record-breaking turnout. Logan also lost in the judicial race, by a much wider margin. Gossiping about it afterward, Lincoln was unforgiving, remarking that his former law partner had been "worse beaten than any other man ever was since elections were invented."[51]

The dismal results allowed Danenhower to take control, as an embittered Throop abandoned nativism altogether. Once his main rival was gone, the ambitious Danenhower pivoted again. In July the Know Nothings gathered in Springfield under his direction to organize for the upcoming 1856 elections. For their first official statewide convention, they discarded their habitual secrecy, adopted the name American party, and endorsed a platform containing discussion of the slavery crisis as much as any nativist measures. Following a national trend among northern Know Nothings, Danenhower and his followers essentially downplayed their anti-immigrant roots and tried to present themselves as an alternative for conservatives of either party who were uncomfortable with the heated rhetoric and growing radicalism of the sectional debate.[52]

Danenhower's opportunism was a worrying development for antislavery fusionist leaders like Lincoln. Simeon Francis, the longtime editor of the *Illinois Journal*, felt particularly victimized by the "American" maneuvering. In the summer of 1855, two newspaper men from Alton with nativist connections suddenly announced their intentions to challenge the *Journal* with their own publication in the state capital. Francis wanted Lincoln to step up and defend him, but he declined to do so. Feeling abandoned, the longtime Whig editor sold his interests to the outsiders and left journalism.[53] He had published Lincoln's first campaign statement in 1832 and had been a local Whig leader for over twenty years. In 1855 he was a casualty of changing partisan times.

Watching Danenhower and the Illinois Know Nothings get organized for the upcoming 1856 election, Owen Lovejoy decided that Republicans could wait no longer. In early August he reached out to Trumbull, Lincoln, and others from the state's antislavery coalition to propose holding a Republican state convention in the fall.[54] The abolitionist was careful to sound as moderate as possible. Admitting that a statewide platform might seem "rather tame" to his old abolitionist allies, Lovejoy expressed confidence that "they will all see & acknowledge the necessity of not loading the Middle & Southern portion of the State with too heavy a load." Lovejoy tried to sound reassuring. "I feel willing & anxious to unite on ground where *all can unite*," he insisted.[55]

These words were music to pragmatic ears, but the gist of the proposal was worrying to both Lincoln and Trumbull. Lovejoy was still trying to build a statewide Illinois Republican party from the northern end of the state, with old Liberty men and Free Soilers in charge. He was taking advantage of his own newfound prominence in the state legislature and Codding's recent labors in the field. Neither Trumbull nor Lincoln wished to encourage the northern antislavery radicals in this way, and so they deflected Lovejoy's outreach effort. Trumbull claimed that around Alton, where he lived, "there is so much party feeling, so great aversion to what is called *fusion*, that very few democrats would be likely to unite in a Convention composed of all parties." Trumbull wrote that he was uneasy about committing to a statewide gathering until after he reached Washington and understood better the lay of the land. "I should feel disinclined at this time to enter into a political convention of any kind," the senator-elect replied to Lovejoy's overture.[56]

Lincoln tried to sound more agreeable. "Not even *you* are more anxious to prevent the extension of slavery than I," he wrote on August 11, "and yet the political atmosphere is such, just now, that I fear to do any thing, lest I do wrong." He was thinking about recent local problems like the ones with Francis and the *Illinois Journal.* "Know-nothingism has not yet entirely tumbled to pieces," he observed, suggesting this was an impediment for organizing their party. "I have no objection to 'fuse' with any body provided I can fuse on ground which I think is right," he wrote, "and I believe the opponents of slavery extension could now do this, if it were not for this K.N.ism." He claimed that around Springfield, the Know Nothings were "mostly my old political and personal friends," and even though he thought "little" of their "principles," which "degrade a class of white men," he was still hoping to avoid "the painful necessity" of "taking an open stand against them."[57]

Perhaps these sentiments were truly felt, but they sounded like excuses. Lincoln was surely less bothered about losing old friends than he was about losing ground to new allies. He had been at odds with the Springfield Whig conservatives and the local Know Nothings for years. They were friends but no longer allies. Yet he was wary of Lovejoy and other abolitionists as polarizing figures who might drive away moderates. Conventions were unpredictable if not properly managed. That was why Lincoln made sure to highlight for Lovejoy a recent "Anti-Nebraska meeting" held in Quincy that he considered a model for statewide antislavery fusion. Describing the resolutions adopted there, Lincoln claimed that although "I saw them but once," they embodied "the ground I should be willing to 'fuse' upon."[58]

Lincoln was almost surely consulted in the making of the Quincy resolutions. Just days before the Quincy meeting, he had tried an important case in U.S. district court with their author, former Whig congressional candidate Archibald Williams, while other national antislavery figures were in town.[59] And by referencing the fusion work at Quincy, Lincoln was suggesting an important connection with Codding, the Republican field organizer and main speaker at the meeting.

It was equally revealing that Lincoln pointed to the Quincy platform as a ground for fusion and not to one of his earlier 1854 speeches. Much had changed in less than a year. The first territorial elections in Kansas in March 1855 had been a disaster, with suspicious proslavery results that the Free Staters, as they were called, immediately denounced as fraudulent. By the summer, both sides were arming for battle in what soon became known as Bleeding Kansas. The crisis over runaway slaves was also worsening. Since the bloody rendition of Anthony Burns in May 1854, when a deputy federal marshal in Boston had been killed, no fugitives had been returned from any of the New England states or from most northern states. In late 1854 another "stampede" of more than two dozen slaves from St. Louis had made it all the way to Chicago, before some of them were identified. Local vigilance committee resistance quickly mobilized, however, and the U.S. commissioner backed down from enforcing the Fugitive Slave Law in fear. None of the runaways were recaptured, and St. Louis newspapers blasted the "nullification" of federal law.[60]

The meeting at Quincy was a by-product of this tense period, which the organizers aptly described as "the universal commotion upon the subject of Slavery." Their resolutions illustrated how the moderate antislavery position was becoming radicalized. The preamble adopted at Quincy began by offering the usual assurances about federal obligations to slaveholders, specifically "disclaiming any intention of interference either directly or indirectly with the institution of slavery in the States where it exists," but it did so within an antislavery framework.[61] Describing "Freedom as the rule, and Slavery as the exception," the Quincy platform underscored the key free-soil point that the Constitution "no where sanctions the idea of *property in man* as one of its principles." This was the "freedom national" doctrine espoused over the past few years by Senator Charles Sumner, a leading political abolitionist. Sumner might well have pressed this point himself on Williams and Lincoln earlier in July 1855—he was in Chicago while they were trying their case together.[62]

Even more surprising was the hard-line sectional view taken in the actual resolutions, which dismissed most of the "rights" claimed by slaveholders as illegitimate. These "oppressive" southern claims "must be resisted," asserted the Quincy gathering, not only through restoration of the Missouri Compromise but also with a candid recognition that "the restriction of Slavery" was "paramount" and that it was their "duty" as "freemen" to "unite for the purpose of giving [their views] practical effect." In a letter to the *Chicago Tribune*, Codding cheered the work at Quincy as the "inauguration of the Republican movement in Middle & Southern Illinois."[63] Now Lincoln was telling Lovejoy that he agreed—that this was ground that he was willing to "fuse upon."

Lincoln's embrace of the new Republican framework was even more apparent in a letter that he sent a few days later to George Robertson, a noted conservative from Kentucky. Robertson was an aging former congressman and judge who had been involved in the original

Missouri Compromise. He had passed through Springfield in July but had missed seeing Lincoln and left behind a copy of his memoir that extolled the virtues of moderation in the battle against slavery. Lincoln expressed gratitude for the gift but derided what he called the "signal failure of Henry Clay and other great and good men" to achieve gradual abolition in Kentucky. Lincoln bemoaned the rise of proslaveryism in America, remarking that the Russian "Autocrat" would sooner "resign his crown" than "will our American masters voluntarily give up their slaves." For Lincoln, this hypocrisy was eroding the national faith everywhere. "The fourth of July has not quite dwindled away," he observed with bitter sarcasm, "it is still a great day—*for burning fire-crackers!!!*"[64]

On the matter of how to solve the problem of slavery, Lincoln was more uncertain. He closed his letter to Judge Robertson with a startling question. "Our political problem now is 'Can we, as a nation, continue together *permanently—forever*—half slave, and half free?' " That challenge "was too mighty for me," he wrote at the time, but merely by framing the question—which he would eventually answer in his "House Divided" speech in 1858—Lincoln was indicating how much his views had changed since his days as a loyal Whig.[65]

Lincoln continued to consider how best to justify and defend his newfound antislavery commitment in terms that would not seem dangerously sectional. Responding later that month to a letter from Joshua Speed, a once-close friend who had been living in Louisville, Kentucky, for the past fourteen years, Lincoln revealed that he felt victimized by some elements of the Compromise of 1850 and by what he considered the gross betrayals of 1854. Ignoring Speed's complaints about violations of the Fugitive Slave Law, he remarked instead that the "great body" of northerners had been compelled to "crucify their feelings" on that volatile issue. But when it came to the Kansas-Nebraska Act, Lincoln found no such legal or moral obligations to control himself. "I look upon the enactment not as a *law*, but as *vio-*

lence from the beginning," he asserted. "It was conceived in violence, passed in violence, is maintained in violence, and is being executed in violence."[66]

Lincoln remained cagey about his current partisan status with his old Whig ally. Speed had asked where he stood in relation to their former party. "That is a disputed point," Lincoln wrote, after waiting over three months to reply to Speed's initial query. "I think I am a whig, but others say there are no whigs, and that I am an abolitionist." This was just a form of wordplay, however, no different from saying to an old friend, *I think I am the same man.*[67] Lincoln was not yet consistent in embracing the Republican label, but he was committed to the Republican strategy of unifying northern antislavery forces around the principle that slavery was wrong and around policies to contain its spread. This was partisan sectionalism, but as Lincoln blithely assured Speed, "if we succeed, there will be enough of us to take care of the Union."[68]

In August 1855, with cross-party fusion still developing, Lincoln was more worried about political divisions within the North. The previous year had opened his eyes to the "rotten material" within the northern political parties. He confided to Speed that if southerners merely continued to stand "as a unit among yourselves, you can, directly, and indirectly, bribe enough of our men to carry the day." There was no doubt Lincoln had a demagogue like Douglas in mind. "Get hold of some man in the North, whose position and ability is such, that he can make the support of your measure—whatever it may be—a *democratic party necessity*," Lincoln wrote, "and the thing is done." For Lincoln, the lesson of the 1854 Kansas-Nebraska political controversy was to fight for every political inch. He expected setbacks along the way, even admitting to Speed that it was "probable" that "we shall be beaten" on the question of the future of Kansas.[69]

Lincoln was trying to sound deliberate, maddeningly so for figures like Lovejoy, shockingly so for some old friends like Speed. He was also growing more independent in his decision-making, consulting with almost everybody but confiding fully in nobody. This had become his way. He had friends and allies during this period but no mentors or intimate advisers. And he urged such independent ways on others. That autumn, when an aspiring law student asked to "read" with him, as was the custom, Lincoln turned him down. "I did not read with any one," he replied. "Get the books and read and study them . . . that is the main thing," adding, "Always bear in mind, that your own resolution to succeed is more important than any other one thing."[70]

Lincoln spent the rest of 1855 mainly attending to his law practice, riding the circuits in Illinois, and traveling to Cincinnati for a major patent case. Then in December the *Morgan Journal* called for a meeting of Free State newspaper editors who were opposed to slavery in Kansas. Lincoln supported this effort. He apparently also attended an informal caucus of leading antislavery fusionists in Springfield. That gathering, held quietly during a session of the state supreme court, focused on the possibility of finding a consensus antislavery candidate for governor. This was a nomination that Lincoln might have coveted for himself, but instead he was persuaded to support former Democratic congressman William Bissell.[71]

THE CALL FOR AN 1856 convention of editors in Illinois came at the right political time. Several newspapers endorsed the proposal, and the Anti-Nebraska Editors, as they called themselves, met in Decatur on February 22. A snowstorm reduced their anticipated numbers, but more than a dozen top antislavery fusionist editors still attended (although not John Wentworth from Chicago). Joining them was Lincoln, who in early February informed the organizer of the gathering that he would also "try and have some business at Decatur at the time of the convention."[72] Democratic newspapers noticed that Lincoln was the only noneditor in attendance, one commenting that he "seems to be ready, at the tap of the fusion drum, on all occasions."[73] The purpose of the gathering was to establish a common antislavery platform and help organize a call for a mass nominating convention in the spring.

Lincoln was at the center of all of it. The Decatur editors took a copy of the Quincy platform that he had recommended to Lovejoy and adapted it as their own. Repeating whole passages from that earlier public statement, they proclaimed once again, "freedom as the rule and slavery as the exception," while still conceding various obligations to their "sister states." Most important, they pledged antislavery unity "regardless of differences of opinion upon other issues," vowing that all attempts to expand slavery "must be resisted." During the platform discussion, according to George Schneider, the German newspaper editor who had helped arrange Lincoln's fusionist photograph in Chicago in 1854, the only real argument came over what to say about nativism. Schneider believed that Lincoln was the decisive voice in favor of resolutions distancing the antislavery fusionists from the more "proscriptive doctrines" of the Know Nothing movement.[74] At the banquet that followed, it was Lincoln who offered the evening's key unifying toast touting Bissell as their preferred standard-bearer.[75]

Owen Lovejoy was not at the Decatur meeting. He was in Pittsburgh, along with Ichabod Codding and other Illinois antislavery radicals, at the organizing session of the national Republican party. Just as in Illinois, the tone of the gathering in Pennsylvania was almost defiantly sectional. Francis Preston Blair, a former Jacksonian Democrat from Maryland, the president of the session, announced in his remarks that the new party was not organized to promote the "abolition of Slavery" but rather that its "real design" was "to prevent the nullification of the rights of the North." There was argument about policy matters, but the climate of the meeting was businesslike and unified.[76] Republicans agreed to hold their first national convention in Philadelphia in June 1856.

The Republican name was still not entirely accepted in Illinois, however. The Decatur editors were cautious as to how to label their efforts. So were key figures like Lincoln and Trumbull. But there was no doubt that behind the scenes they were embracing the Republican strategy. Illinois antislavery fusionists were working hard to rally former Whig and Democratic men around a set of antislavery measures. There was no turning back the partisan clock in their state. The Whig party in Illinois had vanished as an organization. The future for opponents of Douglas and the Democratic party lay with either the Republicans or the Know Nothings. Lincoln had already made his choice and knew that he had done more than anyone else in Illinois to spearhead the birth of a "Republican organization." He had sacrificed personal ambition for movement unity. The only question was whether his efforts and those by others would prove enough to sustain their coalition as the crisis over slavery's future intensified.

6 UNDER HOT FIRE

(1856–1857)

As Abraham Lincoln and Owen Lovejoy sparred with each other in August 1855 over how to organize an antislavery political party in Illinois, abolitionist John Brown began a long trek from North Elba, New York, to join several of his sons in the Kansas territory. The men of the Brown family were part of an influx of antislavery migrants, Free Staters who were determined to prevent Missouri proslavery settlers, the "border ruffians," from seizing power in Kansas. Both sides had been propelled into this collision by Stephen Douglas's doctrine of popular sovereignty, a policy that soon generated more violence than democracy.

Brown and his sons welcomed the fight. John Brown's commitment to wage war against slavery dated back to the murder of Owen Lovejoy's brother in 1837, when a proslavery mob in Alton, Illinois, lynched abolitionist editor Elijah Lovejoy. Brown subsequently stood up at a memorial service in Ohio, where he was then living, raised his hand before a church full of witnesses, and vowed to "consecrate" his life "to the destruction of slavery."[1] For the next two decades, Brown aided escaping slaves on what he termed the "Subterranean Pass Way" and organized his own version of a vigilance or anti-kidnapping committee that he called the League of Gileadites.

After passing through Chicago carrying supplies and weapons, Brown arrived in Kansas in October 1855. He sent his wife Mary promising news about the territory, assuring her that the "free staters" had "a decided majority" and should be able to "get a Constitution adopted making *Kansas Free.*"[2] But the view from the Brown encampment near Osawatomie quickly turned grim. There was sporadic violence in the region that soon came to be known as the Wakarusa War. Once that fighting started, Brown saw himself and his sons as revolutionary combatants. They were in Kansas to build an army, he decided, not a political party.

Lincoln had always opposed political violence. Not long after Elijah Lovejoy was murdered, he argued that every American should respond to assaults like the one at Alton with restraint, remembering "that to violate the law, is to trample on the blood of his father, and to tear the charter of his own, and his children's liberty."[3]

That was in 1838, when Lincoln was still a young Whig leader. Now in 1856 the situation seemed more troubling. Lincoln had not abandoned politics—unlike Brown, he was building a political party, not an army—but it was a new, more confrontational type of partisan movement that might have shocked the younger, Whiggish Lincoln. Since the Republicans were willing to fight over the principle of slavery, and not merely men and measures, their party upended old political norms in disruptive, uncertain ways. "Of *strange*, *discordant*, and even *hostile* elements, we gathered from the four winds," Lincoln recalled, "and *formed* and fought the battle through, under the constant hot fire of a disciplined, proud, and pampered enemy."[4] Politicians always fall back on metaphors of warfare to describe their "campaigns." But in 1856, those descriptions became less metaphorical, as American politicians increasingly battled with the moral fervor of holy warriors.

IN FEBRUARY 1856, JUST as the Republicans were concluding their initial national organizing effort at Pittsburgh, the new anti-immigrant American party nominated Millard Fillmore for president in Philadelphia. Fillmore was a popular choice in central Illinois, one who appealed to conservative ex-Whigs. Under the leadership of William Danenhower, the Chicago bookseller who had organized the Know Nothings in their state a year before, the Illinois Americans made a serious push in 1856 to win over the disaffected former Whigs. State senator Joseph Gillespie agreed to chair their state convention in early May because—as he later confessed to Lincoln—he had become frustrated with the constant concessions that Republicans were making to former Democrats. He resented antislavery Democrats, "who would rather see the Country go to the Devil than vote for a whig."[5] The Americans nominated William Archer, a respected ex-Whig from eastern Illinois, as their choice for governor. Archer had no intention of leading the nativist ticket, however. He was in Washington at the time, angling for a verdict in his undecided congressional race from 1854, but he worried that a flat refusal might offend Know Nothing congressmen whose support he needed. He asked Lincoln to manage the issue for him at home, and together they left the matter deliberately unsettled for weeks.[6]

The Americans' disarray on their gubernatorial nomination was good news for the emerging Illinois Republicans, who also benefited politically from the growing unease over the fate of Kansas. A congressional report had just documented the extent of the fraud in the recent territorial elections, and the sporadic violence over the past year made antislavery fusionists seem almost prophetic in their earlier warnings about the dangers of repealing the Missouri Compromise. The timing finally seemed right for a statewide convention of opposition forces. U.S. Rep. Elihu Washburne wrote his former colleague Richard Yates in early April that he had consulted with the antislavery members of the state's congressional delegation, including Senator Lyman Trumbull, and all agreed to support the upcoming Bloomington gathering that the Decatur editors had announced. "It can be and should be the most imposing convention ever," Washburne assured him.[7] On May 20, William Herndon told Trumbull, who seemed to be wavering about it, that Lincoln was fully confident in the Republican efforts. "I have never seen him so sanguine of success," claimed his officemate, "*he is warm*." According to Herndon, Lincoln had been finding a "dogged determination" among ordinary Illinois voters about the slavery question, and that only "a few corrupt old line whigs" would betray them, as Herndon crudely put it, for the "nigger driving gentlemen" of the southern-dominated Democratic party.[8]

The Decatur editorial meeting had named May 29 as the date for a statewide "Anti-Nebraska" convention. That also happened to be the week in 1856 when all hell broke loose over Kansas. Just days after Herndon wrote to Trumbull, reports reached Springfield that proslavery forces had sacked the free state enclave of Lawrence and that Senator Charles Sumner of Massachusetts, the great advocate for "freedom national," had been caned nearly to death on the floor of the U.S. Senate. The political climate was intense as hundreds of delegates headed toward Major's Hall, a nondescript three-story brick building in Bloomington, for their unprecedented party gathering.[9]

The meeting was not an official Republican party convention. The delegates at Bloomington continued to label themselves "Anti-Nebraska" instead of "Republican." For the rest of the 1856 campaign, in fact, Illinois newspapers routinely identified their statewide electoral ticket as Anti-Nebraska or People's but rarely as Republican.[10] Sometimes the naming customs were different for the national ticket, but they were never consistent. And in private comments, the participants were even less fastidious.[11]

Yet the Bloomington convention built on the partisan strategy of Republican or antislavery fusion that Lincoln and others had been framing for well over a year. The emerging Illinois Republicans were largely willing to give antislavery Democrats the "men" and antislavery Whigs the "measures," while fusing everyone around the principle that slavery was a moral and political wrong. The delegates at Bloomington followed this formula by nominating ex-Democratic congressman William Bissell for governor, allowing Browning, a former Whig, to spearhead the platform committee, and by hearing from a litany of speakers, including notable radicals, regarding the evils of slavery in Kansas and elsewhere.[12] Lincoln gave the capstone address at Bloomington, which Herndon later called "the grand effort of his life." Although no transcript exists for the speech, Lincoln reportedly said "he was ready to fuse with anyone who would unite with him to oppose slave power," called the threat of disunion a "bugbear," and urged his wildly cheering audience to remember that "the *Union must be preserved in the purity of its principles as well as in the integrity of its territorial parts*" (italics in original).[13]

Lincoln was supposed to go to Philadelphia in June 1856 as a Republican delegate but declined to undertake the long journey. He warned Trumbull from Springfield that the national Republicans had to find a way to "divert" what he termed "a good many whigs, of conservative feelings," with a sensible choice for president, someone like U.S. Supreme Court justice John McLean of Ohio, a former Whig who was antislavery. By Lincoln's estimation, such a pick would hold wavering ex-Whigs like John Todd Stuart, but he denied that it would matter to him personally. "I am *in*," Lincoln assured his former rival, "and shall go for any one nominated unless he be '*platformed*' expressly, or impliedly, on some ground which I may think wrong." Lincoln was indicating that like most former Illinois Whigs, he cared more about the measures than the men, but he was not above making a pointed dig about the inequities of the fusion process. Noting that even though nearly all votes for antislavery fusion had come so far from "old whigs," they had been "totally disregard[ed]" when the party was "setting stakes." "I need not point out the instances," he observed to the man he had recently helped elect.[14]

The national Republicans passed over the aging Ohio justice, however, and when powerful antislavery leaders like Salmon Chase of Ohio and William Seward of New York decided against trying for the nomination, they chose John Frémont, a fifty-three-year-old former military man and celebrated western explorer with no political experience. The party also adopted a strongly antislavery platform that managed to include popular economic measures such as support for a Pacific railroad and for western river and harbor improvements. The vice-presidential nomination was not as straightforward. The Illinois delegation caucused back at their hotel with Trumbull. Delegates William Archer and Nathaniel Wilcox both pushed hard for Lincoln, and the group eventually came around to supporting him. The next morning John Palmer, the state senator and Trumbull supporter, nominated Lincoln for vice president, extolling him as "a good man and a hard worker in the field."[15] In the balloting, Lincoln came in second to U.S. senator William Dayton of New Jersey, receiving 110 votes from Illinois, Indiana, and California and a scattering of delegates in northeastern states.

According to Wilcox, who had also helped Lincoln during the Land Office episode in 1849, not every member of the Illinois delegation had been enthusiastic at first about promoting his friend. Yet the balloting for the vice president, combined with Lincoln's selection as one of Frémont's at-large state electors, signaled his status as a top party leader.[16] For the rest of the year, Lincoln was undoubtedly the most active Republican organizer in Illinois. During the 1856 campaign he gave dozens of speeches across the state, ranging as far north as Galena, on the Wisconsin border, and as far south as Olney, approaching Kentucky. Nobody else traveled as widely.[17] He was frequently invited to speak outside the state as well, declining most such invitations, however, because, as he put it, "I can hardly spare the time," and he was "plagued" by being so "superstitious." "I have scarcely known a party, preceding an election," he wrote, "to call in help from the neighboring states, but they lost the state." Still, for the first time since 1844, when he spoke in his home state of Indiana for Henry Clay, Lincoln left Illinois and campaigned in Kalamazoo, Michigan, on behalf of the Frémont ticket.[18]

The bulk of Lincoln's campaign duties occurred out of public view. He was charged principally with trying to manage the conservative ex-Whigs. In early July, in the third congressional district, Owen Lovejoy won the Republican nomination for Congress over incumbent Jesse Norton and close Lincoln ally Leonard Swett, from Bloomington. Lincoln admitted to David Davis and other conservative friends in the district that Swett's defeat had "turned me blind," but he also warned them against bolting from the party. Noting the "great enthusiasm for Lovejoy" among the antislavery voters in the district, and "considering the activity they will carry into the contest with him," Lincoln urged party unity. "I really think it best to let the matter stand," he wrote. They reluctantly agreed.[19]

Lincoln had more trouble with conservatives on the presidential question. "It would have been easier for us, I think, had we got McLean," he told Trumbull after the Republican national convention, "but as it is, I am not without high hopes for the state." He suggested he was feeling optimistic about governor because Archer had finally declined the American party nomination, leaving the Know Nothing movement temporarily without a gubernatorial candidate. "I think we shall elect Bissell, at all events," Lincoln concluded, "and, if we can get rid of the Fillmore ticket, we shall carry the state for Fremont also."[20]

Getting rid of the Fillmore ticket was the project that occupied

Lincoln for most of the 1856 contest. His campaign speeches were often focused on areas where Fillmore support was strongest. Then in September and October, he developed an innovative campaign technique that directly targeted Fillmore's supporters. He had multiple photographic prints made of a persuasive letter that he had written, which he then personalized by filling in the names of the recipients by hand. There had never been anything quite like it in Illinois politics.[21] Lincoln's mass mailing technique may have been pioneering, but his object was simple: convince as many Fillmore supporters as possible not to waste their votes. "I understand you are a Fillmore man," each letter began. "Let me prove to you that every vote withheld from Fremont, and given to Fillmore, *in this state*, actually lessens Fillmore's chances of being President."[22] Lincoln was trying to convince supporters of the American party that since the only real chance their candidate had was if no candidate achieved an Electoral College majority, then they should be eager to see once-reliably Democratic Illinois fall into the Republican column.

Lincoln worked hard to make a difference in this regard, but it was an uphill battle. "Your speech did us good here," claimed Richard Yates in September, even as he acknowledged that it did not seem to be enough. Though they were "constantly gaining some," Yates glumly concluded that "the Filmore Organization" remained "formidable."[23] Republican organizers also accused Democrats of underwriting the American party effort in Illinois to divide the opposition vote. The national Democrats had nominated James Buchanan of Pennsylvania, choosing the experienced diplomat over both incumbent Franklin Pierce and Stephen Douglas, each of whom had been badly damaged by the Nebraska uproar. Although disappointed, Douglas continued with his usual partisan work during the fall canvass. Aside from his extensive speaking tour, Douglas cultivated a close relationship with the former Know Nothing coordinator William Danenhower, apparently through illicit means. Lincoln told Herndon that

Illinois Democrats were paying American party leaders to help prop up the Fillmore vote.[24]

The Republicans managed to win the 1856 statewide races in Illinois, including the governor's contest, but they narrowly lost the state for Frémont. If Frémont had won Illinois, along with Pennsylvania, he would have become president. Yet the national future seemed bright for Republicans, who won sweeping victories in the presidential balloting across the rest of the North. In those two lower northern states, and in Indiana and New Jersey as well, it was clearly the Fillmore candidacy, which netted only eight electoral votes total, that split the popular vote and deprived Republicans of a presidential victory. Republicans knew that if they could find a way to eliminate the third-party drain on their northern vote totals, they could attain national power in future elections.

That was the message Lincoln took to a Republican banquet in Chicago that he headlined in early December. "All of us who did not vote for Mr. Buchanan, taken together," he told cheering party activists, "are a majority of four hundred thousand." He urged them to fuse together with the Americans, whose national party seemed poised to collapse. "Let past differences, as nothing be," he advised, "and with steady eye on the real issue, let us reinaugurate the good old 'central ideas' of the Republic." Lincoln was in an ebullient mood. "We *can* do it," he assured them. One reason for Lincoln's confidence was that he had seen it done. The organizer of this event was Jonathan Scammon, a conservative ex-Whig whom he had once suspected of having Know Nothing ties. Lincoln's remarks followed a rousing toast from the influential Chicago attorney, now wholly committed to the Republican cause. Scammon raised his glass to "THE UNION" but added a sectional twist: "The North will maintain it—the South will not depart therefrom."[25]

For Lincoln, the struggle was also about democracy. The "central idea" of the American republic, Lincoln explained to those celebrating in Chicago, was "the equality of men." For him, American politics in the 1850s had become about persuading a majority of people to expand that principle, not to "discard" it as the Democrats had done in the late election. "Our government rests in public opinion," he said that night. "Whoever can change public opinion, can change the government, practically just so much." By "public opinion," Lincoln meant the voting electorate and the transformative power of democratic elections.[26]

Lincoln approached 1857 determined to build on the previous year's successes by improving Republican coordination and organization. While in Chicago, attending to federal court and celebrating with fellow activists, he also consulted with Cook County legislators on what he considered to be pressing state political matters. Despite William Bissell's gubernatorial victory and other statewide party wins, the Republicans had failed to gain control of the new legislature. Lincoln was agitated by this setback and wanted action. With the state overdue for reapportionment, Democrats were threatening to gerrymander Republicans even further out of legislative power. Such a power play would only smooth the path to Douglas's reelection in 1859.[27]

Incoming governor Bissell was also in contact with Lincoln at this time. Bissell asked his fellow Republican to "write out, as hastily as you please," his views on the Kansas issue, so that Bissell might "make such use of it as I deem proper" for his upcoming message to the General Assembly.[28] Lincoln never drew a salary from the Bissell administration, but he became one of its most influential political strategists.

Lincoln's top priority for Republicans in 1857 was reorganizing the state committee. He supported Cook County state senator Norman Judd for state party chairman and promoted the idea of establishing a party "headquarters" at the Chenery House hotel in Springfield. Lincoln also pushed Republicans to hire full-time field organizers like John O. Johnson, a seasoned operative from New York. Illinois Whigs had never been so focused and professional in their partisan endeavors. Johnson became an important but shadowy figure in Illinois politics for the next couple of years, serving ostensibly as secretary of the Republican state central committee but mainly acting as Lincoln's top political aide.

Lincoln confided to Richard Yates later that year that although Johnson was "a new-comer," he was working "in concert" with him, because the field coordinator "can devote more time to getting up an organization, than any one I know."[29] To another political contact in Bloomington, Lincoln called Johnson "my friend," explaining that "I gave your name to him" because he was "doing the work of trying to get up a republican organization" and they should "quietly cooperate."[30] Lincoln was never the head of the Republican party committee, but his letters on Johnson's behalf show him wielding party power out of the public view.

Johnson's organizing tactics were straightforward. A bachelor who worked long hours, he developed a bulging black book of important Republican contacts, with names alphabetized by county, stretching across the state. Johnson was also shrewd in his handling of Lincoln, maintaining good relations not only with the man who was in effect his boss but also with the boss's law partner (William Herndon) and his wife.[31] The latter relationship was especially important, because in the midst of all her husband's political and legal activities, Mary Lincoln was starting to feel ignored.

The tensions at home manifested in a rare difference of political opinion. Mary Lincoln had supported Fillmore in the 1856 election, breaking with her husband's party affiliation for the first time in their marriage. She had come to this position, she told her half-sister who lived in Kentucky, because she considered Fillmore to have been a "good" president, a "just" man, and perhaps most important, a leader who "feels the necessity of keeping foreigners, within bounds." Mary was no fan of what she termed "the wild Irish." She was also careful to identify her husband as a "*Fremont* man," though no "*Abolitionist*," insisting, "In principle he is far from it," and suggesting that Lincoln desired merely "that slavery, shall not be extended, let it remain, where it is."[32]

For Mary, even more frustrating than their political disagreements was the time her husband spent out of town. In one of her letters, she noted that "Mr. L is not at home," observing that "this makes the fourth week he has been in Chicago." For a mother of three young boys (ages fourteen, six, and four), the frequent absences of her husband and their father were challenging. The Lincolns were on stable enough financial footing to afford some expensive renovations to their home—they added a second story in 1856—and to keep a variety of domestic servants on occasional hire, but Mary Lincoln still felt needy. She commented about money in various letters, noting that former governor Matteson's new mansion in Springfield had reportedly cost him $100,000. The Lincoln home improvements had cost only about $1,300. In the summer of 1857, the Lincolns did travel together to New York City during a business trip for the Illinois Central Railroad, stopping along the way at Niagara Falls, but afterward Mary appeared more focused on their inability to experience even greater adventure, such as journeying together on one of the "large steamers" that she had seen headed for Europe. Sighing playfully over her "poverty," she reported to her half-sister, "I often laugh & tell Mr. L that I am determined my next Husband *shall be rich*."[33]

Following the end of the legislative session in February 1857, the Lincolns hosted a large party, entertaining a few hundred guests in their newly renovated home.[34] At the time Lincoln was preparing to sue the Illinois Central Railroad for a fee they had never paid him on the groundbreaking McLean County tax case, which had lasted from 1854 to 1856, when his victorious appeal was finally rendered. Lincoln was expecting to be dropped as a corporate counsel because of this contentious litigation, and despite his steady income as a lawyer and lobbyist, the couple must have been feeling the strain of that possibility in the aftermath of their social extravagance.[35]

Lincoln acknowledged tension later that month in a minor spat with Mary about his political expenditures. Early in 1857, there was an attempt to launch a new Republican newspaper in Springfield. When an issue arrived at their home, Mary refused to accept delivery. The newspaper responded by making tart mention of it in one of its columns. John Rosette, a local attorney and key supporter of the project, apologized to Lincoln for the unwanted publicity. In his reply, Lincoln dismissed the episode as a "mistake" and tried to explain away Mary's behavior with a lame joke. "When the paper was brought to my house," he wrote, "my wife said to me, 'Now are you going to take another worthless little paper?'" Lincoln confessed he had answered her "*evasively*" by saying, "I have not directed the paper to be left." Lincoln's suggestion to Rosette was that he had ducked a dispute with his wife about money.[36]

Lincoln also seemed to be avoiding further confrontations with Mary over politics. His wife's description of his political position, as having differences "in principle" from the abolitionists, was not the way he was presenting it to others. Lincoln had told Ichabod Codding that his "opposition to the principle of slavery" was "as strong" as that of any political abolitionist.[37] His disagreements with antislavery radicals concerned men and measures, not principles. Lincoln clearly wanted Illinois abolitionists like Codding and Owen Lovejoy working with him inside the new Republican party. Mary Lincoln did not seem as comfortable with that idea, nor with her husband's willingness to support Frémont over Fillmore.

Mary Lincoln was surely hoping, along with other conservatives, that in 1857 the sectional turmoil of the past several years was finally starting to recede. But in March the controversial Supreme Court decision in the *Dred Scott* case prevented any such return to normalcy. Dred and Harriet Scott had both filed freedom suits in Missouri in

1846, claiming that they had been held illegally as slaves in a free state (Illinois, in Dred's case) and a free territory (then Wisconsin, now present-day Minnesota, in both cases) by their former slaveholder, a U.S. army surgeon, who had died. The Scotts won in some of the early rounds of state litigation against his widow, but on appeal their case ended up in the federal court system as *Dred Scott v. Sandford*. After a series of delays and multiple rearguments, the Supreme Court prepared a relatively narrow opinion on the doctrine of comity—how states should enforce each other's laws—written by Justice Samuel Nelson of New York. But when two moderate antislavery justices, John McLean of Ohio and Benjamin Curtis of Massachusetts, drafted vigorous dissents, it annoyed Chief Justice Roger Taney, who decided there should be a more sweeping proslavery ruling on this "troublesome question."[38]

That was at least how Justice Robert Grier described the surprising development to fellow Pennsylvanian, President-Elect James Buchanan, in a confidential letter dated February 23, 1857. Grier told Buchanan that he was joining with Taney and other southern members of the Court because he was "anxious" about any appearance that "the line of latitude should mark the line of division in the court." But Taney's proslavery opinion was reckless and did far more than try to settle a question of comity. The majority declared that Blacks had "no rights" as federal citizens, and that Congress had no constitutional authority to prohibit slavery in any of the nation's territories.[39]

Grier warned Buchanan that a revised majority opinion, written by Taney himself, might come as early as Friday, March 6, two days following the presidential inauguration. Buchanan used this confidential information to help frame his inaugural address. Referring to the problems in Kansas, the new president acknowledged that there had been some "difference of opinion" as to "when the people of a Territory shall decide this question for themselves," but he dismissed the controversy as "a judicial question, which legitimately belongs to the Supreme Court of the United States." He claimed that whatever "their decision" was, he would "cheerfully submit." Two days later, just as Grier had indicated, Taney read his stunning fifty-four-page opinion from the bench, followed by written statements from each of the eight other justices—an extraordinary outpouring of judicial review.[40]

Republicans were stunned. The decision seemed to be a direct attack on their partisan existence. Since 1854 they had been fighting as a matter of policy to restore the Missouri Compromise. Now the Taney Court had essentially ruled that the compromise was unconstitutional. Lincoln called the verdict "a burlesque upon judicial decisions," vowing it "must be overruled, and expunged from the books of authority." Seward complained that the Court "had forgot its own dignity" by committing such an act of "judicial usurpation." Republicans knew nothing of Grier's secret communication with Buchanan, but they suspected the worst. Within a year, Seward was openly speculating that the "whisperings" he had noticed on inauguration day between the president and the chief justice were in retrospect a telling precursor to the "judicial battery" that Buchanan had been orchestrating.[41]

Lincoln was equally suspicious. He later explained that the ruling had finally compelled him to "run [his] mind over the string of historical facts" since 1854, making "several things" seem far "less *dark* and *mysterious* than they did when they were transpiring." By 1858 he was offering a litany of conspiratorial conjectures to Illinois audiences that connected the Kansas-Nebraska Act with the *Dred Scott* decision and almost everything in between, culminating with a stark question about Buchanan: "Why the incoming President's *advance* exhortation in favor of the decision?"[42]

Experienced politicos like Seward and Lincoln thought they understood what had happened in March 1857. They considered themselves victims of a devious partisan strategy employed by Democratic leaders such as "Stephen, Franklin, Roger and James" (as Lincoln put it, blaming Douglas, Pierce, Taney, and Buchanan) to defuse growing northern outrage against the nation's proslavery policies.[43] The *Dred Scott* ruling undermined Republican claims to the conservative high ground and focused public attention on the issue of Black people and their rights. This had always been the great political vulnerability for antislavery fusion. Many northerners held slaveholding in contempt but still did not support interracial equality. Color prejudice was simply too strong. That was why Democrats had denounced fusionists from the beginning as "Black Republicans."

Douglas made sure to frame the impact of the *Dred Scott* decision in terms of Black rights. He needed such a diversion because the Taney ruling was just as dangerous to the doctrine of popular sovereignty as it was to Republican containment policy. How could territorial residents decide for themselves whether to prohibit slavery if the constitution protected slaveholders' rights to their human property? Douglas tried to shrug off this conundrum at a speech in Springfield in mid-June 1857, when he was invited to comment on the case before the Illinois judges and lawyers who were then attending federal court. With Lincoln listening in the distinguished audience, Douglas shifted quickly toward the more fruitful political terrain of Black citizenship. Orville Browning, who was also there, observed with disdain that Douglas was trying to prove that "the only issue now before the people was that of negro equality."[44]

Douglas expressed complete support for Taney's position that the descendants of slaves did not qualify for American citizenship. He mocked unnamed Republicans for invoking natural rights philosophy in opposition to Taney's opinion, as if "to prove that the Almighty created a negro equal to a white man." Taking a swipe at Seward, Douglas predicted that under national Republican rule, "all human laws in conflict with that divine right," including the Illinois Black codes (which he defended), "must yield and give place to the 'higher law.' " With obvious disgust, and to what the Democratic newspaper described as "immense cheering," Douglas warned that such a revolution would ultimately "authorize negroes to marry white women on an equality with white men." As Lincoln and Browning sat there in silence, Douglas asserted that even though "the leaders of the republican party in this state" had not deemed it "prudent" to "make a frank and honest confession of faith," everyone knew "what they intend to do so soon as they get the power."[45]

Unwilling to let such a challenge stand, Lincoln replied two weeks later from the same platform with his own blistering statement of partisan principle and policy. After dispensing with the recent outbreak of violence in the Utah territory, a new round of fraudulent elections in Kansas, and the legal debate that had developed over whether the precedent set by the *Dred Scott* decision had "settled" all the issues regarding the future of slavery in the territories, Lincoln turned to some "frank" observations about the Declaration of Independence and the question of equality. He asserted his view that "the authors of that notable instrument" meant "to include *all* men" in their claims for natural equality, even without intending "to declare them equal *in all respects.*" He cast the nation's founding as a promise. "They meant to set up a standard maxim for free society," he argued, something "constantly looked to, constantly labored for, and even though never perfectly attained . . . [something] augmenting the happiness and value of life to all people of all colors everywhere." He also claimed the natural rights philosophy of the Declaration was "proving itself" to be an invaluable "stumbling block" ("thank God," he added) "to those who would turn a free people back into the hateful paths of despotism."[46]

Lincoln had been invoking the Declaration with greater frequency since his eulogy for Clay in 1852, but this was his most sweeping affirmation of natural rights yet. He was essentially speaking in the idiom of the political abolitionists. But with conservative constituents also weighing on his mind, the Republican leader did not leave the matter there. Acknowledging the "drumming and repeating" about race, he accused Douglas of "basing his chief hope" for political survival on the "natural disgust in the minds of nearly all white people" for race mixing. Without apology, Lincoln blasted the "counterfeit logic" that "because I do not want a black woman for a *slave* I must necessarily want her for a *wife*." Lincoln was turning the tables on proslavery forces. He observed that Dred and Harriet Scott, and their daughters, Eliza and Lizzie, "were all involved in the suit," then noted that if Republicans "had our way," then "the chances of these black girls, ever mixing their blood with that of white people, would have been diminished." Lincoln's grim insight was that "nine tenths of all the mulattoes" in the nation were the result not of freedom but of slavery, the outcome of a rape culture that he termed the "forced concubinage of their masters."[47]

Lincoln followed this observation with an ambivalent endorsement for colonization. Calling the "separation of the races" the "only perfect preventative of amalgamation," Lincoln conceded that such efforts looked "impossible" at present, and "if ever effected at all," they would be at best "difficult" to organize over the long haul. He did not specify how the removal of American Blacks might occur, but he seemed to rule out the possibility of coerced deportation by emphasizing that "the negro is a man" and "that the field of his oppression ought not to be enlarged." Lincoln also pointed out that removal was not part of the Republican "platform" and that neither major party was "now doing anything directly for colonization."[48]

The strategic calculation was obvious. With Douglas playing the race card for Democrats, Lincoln countered that Republicans might hold a few of their own. Lincoln had a clear-eyed view of his electorate and its racial prejudices. As a state party leader, he was trying to uphold core principles while offering a strategic roadmap for the near-term electoral future. The debate offered an ugly glimpse of what lay ahead, especially for African Americans and their allies. Here was a top Republican in Illinois speaking eloquently to the "central idea" of American equality but still advocating for the separation of the races. In the context of the debate at Springfield, Lincoln seemed to be using colonization as a political tactic, but the ambiguity was real enough that some of his more radical peers could see it only as hypocrisy.

Lincoln's response that night in Springfield was part of a coordinated Republican effort. Speaking from the same location three evenings later, Lyman Trumbull provided his own sharp perspective on "the points at issue between [the] parties." But unlike Lincoln, Trumbull framed his remarks for former Democrats. He focused on events in Kansas, the fallacies in the doctrine of popular sovereignty, and the false claims from what he airily dismissed as "the self-styled Democracy." He quoted from the Declaration and went so far as to describe the Republican "creed" as emanating from the "principles of Washington and Jefferson," but he also made clear his solidarity with "white people" and dismissed all talk of race "amalgamation" as "repulsive."[49] Illinois Republicans soon mass-produced the two Springfield speeches by Lincoln and Trumbull as a popular pamphlet, which they distributed at the cost of a dollar per hundred.[50]

That summer Lincoln fielded requests for these pamphlets from across the state, including one from B. C. Lundy of Putnam County, in north-central Illinois. Lundy was the son of the late Benjamin Lundy, a pioneering Quaker abolitionist who had been a mentor to the abolitionist editor William Lloyd Garrison.[51] In July, the younger Lundy told Lincoln how anxious he was to get his region organized for the Republicans. All antislavery eyes were already focused on the 1858 legislative contests and the subsequent U.S senatorial balloting for Douglas's seat. Trumbull had called for Republicans to use these contests to repudiate "the author of all these evils," and by that he did not mean Chief Justice Taney. Lincoln did not mention the upcoming elections in his Springfield remarks, but he agreed that Lundy was "perfectly right" to want to get an early start on the campaign and pushed him to open correspondence with party chairman Norman Judd. Soon afterward Lincoln also urged Lundy to start pulling together and regularly updating alphabetized voter lists culled from the poll books held in the county clerk's office. "This will not be a heavy job," the experienced party organizer assured him, "and you [will] see how, like a map, it lays the whole field before you," adding that it would demonstrate "at once, *how*, and with *whom* to work."[52]

This was Lincoln at his partisan best. He was just as devoted to the mechanics of targeting voters as he was to the defense of America's founding principles. He was more skilled at either task than any other Illinois Republican—a more adept organizer than John Johnson and a more inspiring orator than Senator Trumbull. But the exchange with Lundy had deeper personal meaning for Lincoln. Lundy was part of a cohort of former Liberty men—the Durley brothers of nearby Hennepin were others—who had been the objects of his antislavery outreach since the mid-1840s. When Lincoln wrote to Williamson Durley following Henry Clay's defeat in the 1844 election, he failed to draw the abolitionist toward greater electoral pragmatism. Now men like this were relying on him for political guidance. But who had really changed? In 1856 Lincoln had advised Lundy, "Stand by the *cause*, and the cause will carry you through."[53] For some, it seemed that Lincoln had adopted their antislavery cause as his own, helping to make it the organizing principle of the Republican party. They reciprocated by embracing him as a worthy leader.

Earlier in the year, Herndon had described his senior partner to Boston abolitionist Wendell Phillips as a true western-style "hoss" or boss, despite his propensity for being a "joker" and a "funny man."[54] Executives from the Illinois Central Railroad also recognized Lincoln's leadership qualities that summer. They confided to each other in August that they still needed Lincoln, despite his lawsuit, because he was "not only the most prominent of his political party, but the acknowledged special adviser of the Bissell administration." Claiming they had made a "narrow escape" from potential trouble by having "settled with Lincoln," the railroad officers congratulated themselves for continuing to engage the shrewd operator "in our interests."[55]

The company had been forced to pay Lincoln nearly $5,000. He gave half of the windfall to Norman Judd as a loan for a land investment scheme in Iowa. Lincoln had loaned out money before, but never on such a scale. Judd was a shrewd operator himself up in Cook County and appeared to be a relatively safe risk for default, but Lincoln surely had more than annual interest in mind when he gave his new party chairman (and former die-hard Trumbull ally) those funds.[56]

Lincoln was using political money more than ever before. In July he organized an exclusive network of Republican officeholders and donors, including himself and Trumbull, to provide $500 each to help promote the circulation of a Republican newspaper from St. Louis throughout the counties of "Southern and Middle Illinois."[57] This expensive undertaking was necessary to keep the flagging party organization afloat in areas still dominated by regular Democrats. Lincoln had the money delivered to John Nicolay, an industrious twenty-five-year-old newspaper editor and German immigrant from Pike County. Nicolay had first been impressed by Lincoln at the Anti-Nebraska convention in Bloomington in 1856. He was being hired to supplement the work of organizer Johnson; later he would become known in Washington as Lincoln's most doggedly loyal aide, the "grim Cerberus of Teutonic descent."[58]

In August 1857 a speculative railroad bubble burst, causing a "panic" in the United States followed by a severe worldwide economic depression. Lincoln himself did not suffer notably from the downturn, kept up his political activities, and never apologized for his allegiance to the rapacious railroad industry. His railroad work only deepened during the autumn of 1857, when Judd helped him obtain a landmark case representing a railroad bridge company being sued by a steamboat operator because of an accident on the Mississippi River. In the Rock Island Bridge or *Effie Afton* case, tried in federal courts in Chicago, Lincoln argued successfully on behalf of the first railroad bridge across the Mississippi, defending its public necessity even if it had created new hazards for waterway travel. The case set an important legal precedent and signaled the beginning of the end of a water-dominated transportation era. During the 1850s, there were still battles in Washington over federal river and harbor funding—various measures drew vetoes from both presidents Pierce and Buchanan—but most western partisans, like Lincoln, had moved on to locomotives and the need to cultivate railroad investment.[59]

The economic crisis of 1857 did not alter the nation's political dynamic. There was little talk of realigning parties around banking or monetary reform. Temperance had faded as a political force, especially in Illinois, where there was no attempt to revive the Maine Law after the failed 1855 referendum. The American party also essentially collapsed following Fillmore's defeat, and although the shadow of nativism remained a factor in many northern states, including Illinois, the Know Nothings no longer represented a serious organizational rival for the emerging Republicans. Still the Republican label was not entirely fixed, at least not in places like central Illinois. In October, Lincoln's name led a call for a local Sangamon County nominating convention that deliberately avoided the term *Republican* and instead identified itself only as a movement open to any voter "opposed to the policy of the present National Administration."[60]

That flicker of organizational weakness mattered, because in the months ahead, shocking political events in Kansas tested how Republicans felt toward fusion with opponents of the Buchanan administration. From September to November, a collection of proslavery delegates held meetings in Lecompton, Kansas, aimed at drafting a constitution for statehood. The worst of the Bleeding Kansas violence had subsided, but political chaos was on the rise. Free State forces boycotted the Lecompton constitutional process and were holding their own territorial elections for legislature. As a result, there was little democratic legitimacy to the actions taking place in Lecompton, which worried Senator Douglas. He spent much of 1857 seeking to coordinate with President Buchanan on a political solution in Kansas that might placate southern Democrats while also upholding the doctrine of popular sovereignty. It was a near impossible task, one that soon set Douglas in stark opposition to a Buchanan administration that was more inclined to placate than to uphold. Adding to the combustible mix, John Brown was back in the territory after spending most of 1857 in New England raising funds fueled by outrage at the *Dred Scott* decision. Brown largely ignored the political developments in Kansas, however; he was now contemplating raids into slave states themselves.[61]

The president of the Lecompton convention, John Calhoun, was a Douglas ally and an old acquaintance of Lincoln's—his surveying boss from New Salem days and a Democrat who had debated him during the 1854 campaign. Calhoun managed to convince the Lecompton delegates, reportedly with Douglas's covert help, that instead of simply adopting a proslavery constitution for Kansas statehood, they should appear more conciliatory by submitting the question of slavery's future to territorial voters in a manner stacked in their party's favor. This was called at the time "partial submission" and involved procedural maneuvers designed to ensure that whether voters cast their ballots for a state constitution "with" or "without" slavery, the property rights of existing slaveholders would be preserved. There were few actual slaveholders in Kansas, but the operation reeked of partisan manipulation.[62]

The Lecompton convention adjourned on November 7, 1857. By mid-November, Republican newspapers were pushing reports of a "swindle" with headlines like one in the *Chicago Tribune* that announced "ASTOUNDING DISCLOSURES."[63] Douglas made no public comment at first but soon began writing letters expressing his concern, even disgust, at the news from Lecompton. "I fear he has made a fatal mistake," the senator wrote about Calhoun, "and got us all into trouble."[64] Pro-Douglas newspapers, like the *Chicago Times* and the *Illinois State Register*, signaled that the senator might not be able to accept the Lecompton proposal as a legitimate expression of popular sovereignty. But pro-Buchanan Democratic newspapers in Washington and elsewhere pushed hard for party consensus. The word, apparently coming from the president himself, was that it was time for the country to move beyond its obsession with Kansas.[65]

SIGNS OF A DEMOCRATIC split worried Lincoln. In late November he asked Trumbull what he was thinking about this "probable '*rumpus*' among the democracy," warning that they should "stand clear of it." Lincoln seemed most bothered by confidential reports that Douglas was trying to "draw off some Republicans" through the "dodge" of appearing to stand against proslavery forces in his own party. Douglas returned to Washington in early December and consulted with Buchanan in what was rumored to be a tense meeting just prior to the convening of the new Congress. Many Republican newspapers celebrated signs of Democratic disagreement over Kansas policy, even in ways that seemed to glorify Douglas. Claiming each man had been "absolute in his position," the *Chicago Tribune* asked: "Has Douglas at last rebelled? Has he mustered the courage to brave the lion in his lair?"[66]

Democratic newspapers were more circumspect. "Judge Douglas denies that he has broken ground with the administration on the Kansas question," claimed the *New York Herald*. "He says he disapproves much that has been done, but will wait until he sees the Message and hears all sides before determining definitely upon his course of action. He hopes all differences will be healed."[67] Buchanan's lengthy presidential message devoted nearly one-fifth of its content to the subject of Kansas, despite his grumbling that the troubled territory had "for some years occupied too much of the public attention." Buchanan then endorsed the results of the Lecompton convention. The next day, in a fiery speech from the Senate floor, Douglas denounced the president's willingness to go ahead with the rigged Lecompton balloting, scheduled for later in December.[68]

Back in Springfield, Lincoln pored over newspapers from across the country, seeking insight into how the rupture was affecting Republican views outside Illinois. He was not pleased. Horace Greeley's influential *New-York Tribune* appeared to be encouraging the idea of turning the prodigal Douglas into a Republican. Lincoln angrily asked Trumbull what the "constant eulogizing, and admiring, and magnifying [of] Douglas" really meant. He wanted to know if party leaders in the East had "concluded" to sacrifice Illinois Republicans, suggesting that it would be good to know "soon" since it would "save us a great deal of labor to surrender at once."[69] In his reply, Trumbull conceded that "some of our friends here act like fools in running after & flattering Douglas," but he assured Lincoln it was "preposterous" to imagine that Republicans would even consider making a "leader" out of a political demagogue whose failures had brought "the country to the verge of civil war."[70] To Lincoln's dismay, this was exactly what was about to happen.

7 AN ULTRA STRATEGY

(1858)

FACING HIS BUSIEST DOCKET of cases yet in the upcoming January 1858 session of Springfield's federal court, Lincoln still carved out time that winter to draft a hard-hitting speech on the volatile national political situation. Warning fellow Republicans not to "fall into rank behind" Stephen Douglas, he recalled the senator's history of slanderous attacks against them. He wondered what Douglas's "present opinion" might be "as to the inclination of Republicans to marry with negroes." He suggested that they should discover for themselves what "a great free-State Democratic party" under Douglas leadership might say about the charges of "Sectionalism" that he had once lobbed so furiously against antislavery fusionists. Lincoln closed by noting that slavery was "morally wrong" and represented a "deadly poison" in an American system "based on the equality of men." Calling this point his "radical difference of opinion" with Douglas and the ground upon which "the Republican party was organized," he vowed to continue the fight for the sake of the country. "I think the true magnitude of the slavery element in this nation," he wrote, "is scarcely appreciated by any one."[1]

Any antislavery radical might have expressed similar sentiments in 1858. After years of heated arguments about the future of slavery, and after watching violence break out sporadically around the country, mainstream politicians north and south were becoming radicalized. Although Lincoln did not intend to declare himself a radical in the speech he was drafting (he would not deliver it in public until June 1858), his phrasing indicated an important shift in partisan strategy. The escalating feud between Democrats James Buchanan and Stephen Douglas would soon prove Lyman Trumbull wrong and force Lincoln to confront what he considered the gravest threat to Illinois Republicans—pressure by his own party elite to make an alliance of convenience with Douglas. In the past Lincoln had favored fusion strategies, but he could not accept this prescription with Douglas. In 1858, Lincoln became an ultra Republican, determined to rally the party's loyalists against any coalition with Douglas Democrats.

LINCOLN BEGAN THE YEAR pushing hard for greater Republican unity. In Chicago, he stepped into a minefield of party feuds involving former Democratic congressman John Wentworth, the city's new Republican mayor. Lincoln made it known that he wanted the "unrelenting warfare" against his former colleague to cease. "We can not afford to lose the services of 'Long John,'" Lincoln told the city's top Republican editors.[2] He also offered help to abolitionist Owen Lovejoy, the first-term Republican congressman from a district near Chicago. Early in the spring, Lincoln sent Lovejoy a "strictly confidential" warning, offering what he termed an "inside view that few will have" regarding the "danger" from Democrats in Lovejoy's district who were secretly trying to "wheedle" some conservative Republican to run against the noted radical. Lincoln reported that he had "seen the strong men" in the region (Leonard Swett and David Davis) to ensure they "will not consent to be so used." Still, he wanted Lovejoy to remain vigilant.[3]

The hard feelings in that district ran deep. A few months later Lincoln even felt compelled to rebuke the *Chicago Tribune* over its handling of the Lovejoy renomination battle. In early June the newspaper had published a report claiming that Judge Davis was scheming to unseat his fellow Republican. At first Lincoln communicated only in private to *Tribune* editor Charles Ray. Describing Davis as "my intimate friend for more than twenty years," he denounced the report as a fabrication and expressed regret that Ray had allowed it to be published.[4] The editor agreed to publish an edited version of Lincoln's comments to help calm conservatives. "Judge Davis is my friend," Lincoln wrote under the pseudonym "A Republican," adding, "That charge that he has no sympathy for the vitalizing principle of Republicanism is based on your own radical and progressive views, as advanced in the editorials of the TRIBUNE."[5] This rare public letter to the editor provided assurances that Davis was prepared to support the incumbent. Davis and other conservatives did ultimately help secure Lovejoy's renomination and reelection.[6]

But in the 1858 election cycle, congressional races were almost secondary to Republican organizers. Lincoln's abiding interest lay with the state legislative races and their potential impact on Douglas's reelection, which was to occur by vote of the joint General Assembly in early 1859. Lincoln had long been concerned about state apportionment, and he especially worried about the effects of gerrymandering because the Republicans had lost control of the General Assembly in 1856. A stupefying error by Governor Bissell made matters worse. During a single week in February 1857, when he was putting his signature on nearly 350 different bills, Bissell somehow signed an apportionment measure that he had meant to veto, apparently thinking it was an appropriations bill. His aides rushed the botched document back to the governor's mansion, and Bissell tried to undo the damage, but Democrats howled in protest and took the matter to court. The legal dispute came to a head in January 1858. That was Lincoln's busy month of federal litigation, but he also took charge of this case, which he won for the governor before the state supreme court.[7]

Despite the legal victory, Illinois Republicans were still stuck with an outdated set of district lines that heavily favored the Democrats. Lincoln redoubled his efforts to recruit strong candidates.[8] "The adversary has his eye upon that district," he warned a Republican leader in eastern Illinois, "and will beat us, unless we are wide awake." Calling himself "most anxious to know that you will not neglect the matter," Lincoln urged consultation with former "Fillmore men" to help identify the most "expedient" legislative candidates.[9] Lincoln was adamant about identifying the right men for each race. Republicans had to hold their ground on key measures, especially in the aftermath of the *Dred Scott* decision, but they also had to be smart in choosing their nominees across the conservative-leaning districts of southern and central Illinois. He explained himself most fully in an exchange with Richard Yates that addressed the complexities of finding a suitable candidate for their own congressional district. "The leading Fillmore men have wish to act with us," Lincoln assured him, but pointed out that "they want a name upon which they can bring up their rank and file." "Don't you see?" he asked with some exasperation. "We must have some one who will reach the Fillmore men, both for the *direct* and the *incidental* effect."[10]

Lincoln's steady and effective party leadership in the spring of 1858 contrasted starkly with Douglas's combative approach. The Illinois Democrat seemed to be spoiling for an intraparty fight over slavery that had no visible resolution. Buchanan was willing to try to conciliate, at least at first, but Douglas never could bring himself to hammer out a final deal among Democrats on Kansas policy. That spring on Capitol Hill, several viable compromise measures were under debate, including the English bill—sponsored by Rep. William English (D–IN)—which ultimately was passed over Douglas's objections. This measure tied an agreement for a second vote on the original Lecompton constitution for Kansas with a revised package of economic incentives for statehood. But nothing proved good enough to satisfy Douglas. Lincoln wrote to one associate that Illinois Democrats were particularly "annoyed" that Douglas "did not go for the English contrivance" and were beginning to suspect, according to Lincoln's rough colloquialism, that there was a "negro in the fence" or that something bad was being hidden from them, because "Douglas really wants to have a fuss with the President."[11]

The final maneuvering over the compromise proposals gave birth to mythmaking about the Little Giant. In late March 1858, *New York Times* editor Henry Raymond reported from Washington that nobody in town "talks or thinks of anything else" besides "the fate of Lecompton." Raymond suggested that "at the bottom of most of it" were competing Democratic stratagems for "*party* divisions, or *party* supremacy." The *Times* was a Republican newspaper, and like Greeley's *Tribune*, it had been busy "magnifying" Douglas since the feud with Buchanan had first erupted over the winter. Raymond concluded that the president was committing a fatal error by insisting on Lecompton as a test of party loyalty and that Douglas's continued defiance would be "a death-blow to his Administration."[12]

To help dramatize this point, Raymond provided his readers with a vivid account of the December meeting between Buchanan and Douglas. According to unnamed sources—presumably Douglas—the president had tried to bully the senator into standing with him in supporting the contrived Lecompton constitution. Buchanan reportedly attempted to end their argument by invoking a story about Andrew Jackson's legendary bile against party bolters. The threat to Douglas and his career was plain, but the senator remained defiant.

"Permit me, Mr. President," he had apparently replied, "permit me to remind you *that General Jackson is dead.*"[13] The tale became an instant political classic, repeated and embellished across the country as an example of Douglas's pugnacious style and Buchanan's hapless nature. Republicans were thrilled.

The continued eagerness of eastern Republicans to celebrate Douglas and his alleged stand on principle bothered Lincoln and his allies back home. The problem was more than the mythologizing of Douglas in partisan newspapers. Leading Republican elected officials, such as Senator William Seward of New York and Rep. Anson Burlingame of Massachusetts, were also drawn to the idea of convincing Douglas to switch parties. They wanted him to become a Republican and seemed willing to make accommodations to enable it. Lincoln was convinced that they were being manipulated. "My judgment is that we must never sell old friends to buy old enemies" was his advice.[14]

This was a departure for the inveterate fusionist. In the past, Lincoln had been willing to find common ground with "old enemies." So why not now? Few leading Republicans in Illinois trusted Douglas or even liked him—though Herndon claimed to understand his soul because they had "drank 'bouts' together."[15] Lincoln had always despised Douglas, especially since 1854, but what he really feared were the looming risks to Republican unity from fusion with Douglas Democrats. The Republicans had come together and won electoral majorities as an antislavery party. But they could not remain a true antislavery party by joining forces with advocates for popular sovereignty in the territories. Lincoln delivered his warning about not buying "old enemies" after hearing reports that Douglas had secretly promised that he would be willing to "go into private life for a brief period" to work with the Republicans. Lincoln dismissed this improbable news and decided it was time to stamp out the whispering campaigns. "Let us have a State convention," he insisted, adding that in the meantime "let us all stand firm, making no committals as to strange and new combinations."[16]

Lincoln's steadiness was reassuring, but top Republicans in Illinois held off making any public announcements about a state convention until after the Democrats held theirs in mid-April. Their patience was rewarded. On April 21 at Springfield, Illinois Democrats broke apart into rival gatherings, a larger contingent remaining with Douglas and his followers, but a smaller faction bolting to show support for the national administration. Peter Cartwright, Lincoln's former congressional opponent, now seventy-three, was there to back Douglas and denounced Buchanan in a fiery speech.[17] Lincoln reported that the signs of their opponents' disarray made other Republican leaders feel in "high spirits."[18]

The next day the Republican central committee issued a call for its own statewide convention, to be held in Springfield on June 16, 1858. Over the next several weeks, with Lincoln's active support, Republican organizers laid the groundwork for a series of county conventions to select delegates and propose platform resolutions for this all-important meeting. For the first time in the party realignment that followed the repeal of the Missouri Compromise, Illinois antislavery fusionists were organizing across the southern and central counties explicitly under the Republican banner.

"If we do not win," Lincoln observed after the Democratic crack-up at Springfield, "it will be our own fault."[19] But Republicans in Illinois could not seem to help themselves. The stakes were too high, and the pressure from national party leaders to meddle in the Democratic feud was unrelenting. Uncertainty about the prospects for coalition with Douglas Democrats lingered. In the weeks before the June convention, Lincoln nervously described the situation as having "a very *mixed* and *incongruous* aspect."[20]

Lincoln tried his best to calm the waters. By late April, there were reports that Rep. Elihu Washburne was urging Republicans in Illinois to support Douglas for reelection. Lincoln tried to quash that rumor. He addressed it directly with Washburne, explaining that he just wanted to set the record straight as a "hedge against bad feeling."[21] But Washburne was furious and blamed Chicago mayor Wentworth for trying to embarrass him. "It was a lie, made out of whole cloth," he angrily told Lincoln.[22] Wentworth was considered a strong Lincoln ally, though some in Illinois suspected his loyalty had come at a steep price. Douglas Democrats encouraged speculation that Wentworth was angling for something—probably the U.S. Senate seat or perhaps to replace the ailing Bissell as the state's next governor. Some of Wentworth's Republican rivals took the bait.

In a reply to an angry letter from a Republican editor in Chicago, Lincoln rejected the gossip and offered stern advice: "I believe we need nothing so much as to get rid of unjust suspicions of one another." He admitted having "many free conversations with John Wentworth" but claimed that Long John had "never hinted at any condition" for his support.[23]

Most important, Lincoln tried to clear the air over Douglas's future. With unusual candor, he suggested that he understood why leading national figures such as Greeley and Seward believed that Douglas's "superior position, reputation, experience, and *ability*" made him a better choice in Illinois for their party than other "undistinguished pure republicans," such as himself. He called this an obvious mistake, "a drag upon us," but went out of his way to sound magnanimous, observing that he considered Greeley for one to be "incapable of corruption or falsehood."[24]

Lincoln's handling of the Douglas matter "with patience," as he told one friend, did not mean that he was being passive. Although he never confronted Greeley or any other eastern party figure himself, Lincoln kept up a steady stream of correspondence with his Illinois contacts in Washington—Trumbull, Washburne, and more obscure friends such as Josiah Lucas, who had been so helpful to him during the Land Office episode.[25] Lincoln also relied on surrogates. On a rare trip east in March, Herndon met with several leading political figures, including Douglas. And in early May, party organizer John Johnson warned Greeley on behalf of the party's central committee to stay out of the fray. Responding to a private letter from Greeley, an old acquaintance, Johnson assured him that "if an attempt is made to any extent, to get up sympathy for Mr Douglas, in his present position, it will *inevitably result in our defeat.*"[26]

Despite the encouragement of Norman Judd and other state party leaders, Lincoln did not attempt to promote himself that spring as a Senate candidate and the clear alternative to Douglas. A number of county Republican conventions had begun adopting resolutions that proclaimed Lincoln to be their "first" or "only" choice for U.S. senator (and sometimes even as the "first, last, and only choice"), but he demurred whenever local organizers asked if they should push for such public statements at their conventions.[27] In this era before popular elections for U.S. senators, Lincoln understood that such open campaigning struck many contemporaries as unseemly. And he had no need to challenge political custom now. He was in such a commanding position within the state party that pushing too hard for his own sake might have backfired.

Lincoln's major objective in any case was not to get into the Senate; it was to keep Douglas out of the party. Lincoln's maneuvers in 1858 were designed to establish a clear limit on the Republican party's coalition. No matter what antislavery measures he might embrace for expediency's sake during the Lecompton struggle, Douglas rejected the movement's organizing principle, which to Lincoln, as he indicated in repeated statements since 1854, demanded a public recognition that slavery was wrong.

The first official state convention of the Illinois Republican party began in Springfield on June 16, 1858. Richard Yates, as president pro tem, made a few opening remarks. "Our party, beyond all controversy, at this very day and hour," Yates said, "is the most powerful party on the continent of North America." Platform chairman Orville Browning from Quincy and party chair Norman Judd then moved the body through several procedural matters, before the delegates recessed for lunch.

In the afternoon, German immigrant Gustave Koerner replaced Yates as the presiding officer and delivered an attack on the Buchanan administration. A former Democrat and old friend of Stephen Douglas, Koerner declined to criticize the senator and promised that if his supporters wanted to leave the Democratic party, "we will welcome them into our ranks."[28] Over five hundred assembled delegates from nearly all the state's counties then adopted a relatively muted antislavery platform drafted by Browning and with a voice vote approved an unprecedented resolution endorsing Abraham Lincoln as their "first and only choice" to compete against Douglas in the U.S. Senate contest. Lincoln appeared that evening in the Hall of Representatives, the second-floor room where he had spoken against Douglas during the state fair in 1854 and where he had responded to the senator's race baiting after the *Dred Scott* decision. On this night, he delivered a shorter but more powerful address, soon to become known as his House Divided speech.[29]

Lincoln startled his audience that evening by predicting the end of slavery in America. "A house divided against itself cannot stand. I believe this government cannot endure, permanently half slave and half free," he said. "I do not expect the Union to be *dissolved*—I do not expect the house to *fall*—but I *do* expect it will cease to be divided." This was the radical speech he had been tinkering with since the winter. It was radical in that Lincoln finally connected his customary natural rights arguments against slavery with a call to end the institution over time. Prior to this moment, Lincoln had been cautious about invoking the demise of slavery. Moderate Republicans had always focused on measures such as restoring the Missouri Compromise or fighting the extension of slavery into the territories. They left principled abolition talk to the abolitionists. But the party's de facto senatorial nominee now offered a vision of the nation's future that promised gradual abolition everywhere—including in the southern states—with a call for the "ultimate extinction" of slavery, as Lincoln termed it in his speech.[30] His willingness to risk offending moderates or conservatives at this moment was a deliberate strategy essential to warding off the lingering siren calls of fusion with Douglas Democrats.

In crafting the address, Lincoln drew upon insights and even some phrases from his long partisan career. It seemed as if he were trying to make sense of his improbable transformation from promoting river and harbor improvements to embracing what struck many as antislavery radicalism. His invocation of the biblical wisdom "A house divided against itself cannot stand" indirectly recalled his days as a Whig, when in 1843 he had promoted acceptance of political conventions with the same proverb. His comments about the consequences of the nation's divisions over slavery derived from his anguished 1855 letter to Kentucky jurist George Robertson. Then he had suggested that the question of whether the nation could "continue together *permanently—forever*—half slave, and half free" was "too mighty" for him. Now he was willing to answer the same question in public without qualification. Also in 1855 he had complained to Joshua Speed that if southerners succeeded in bribing a few key northern men to make slavery extension "a democratic party necessity . . . the thing is done." In his House Divided speech, Lincoln expanded on this cynical insight, laying out in public how such deceitful Democratic "workmen" had been attempting to frame the "timbers" of their corrupt partisan strategy.[31]

Lincoln drew his speech to a close by mocking Douglas as "a *caged* and *toothless*" lion and by asserting that the Republican movement should be represented on the campaign trail only by those "whose hands are free" and "whose hearts are in the work." After effectively demolishing the fusionist position of his party's national leaders, Lincoln offered something of an olive branch. "Whenever, *if ever*, he and we can come together on *principle* so that *our great cause* may have assistance from *his great ability*," Lincoln pledged that he would present no "adventitious obstacle."[32] But his presentation that evening left no doubt that Lincoln was asserting himself as the "first and only" Republican leader in Illinois.

Lincoln was obviously rallying his troops in an expression of western defiance—a kind of backcountry revolt against the corrupt centers of eastern political power. But the moment was also about Lincoln's own independence within Illinois. Connected to nearly all the party's factions, he was indebted to none. Although Lincoln had been preparing this polished speech for months, he consulted with almost no one.[33] And those few insiders with whom he did share his plans on the eve of the convention objected unsuccessfully to his newfound radicalism.[34]

Signs of trouble over Lincoln's bold strategy began to appear within a few days of the convention. Chicago newspaper editor John Locke Scripps sent Lincoln a confidential critique of the House Divided remarks that challenged the new positioning. Scripps observed that although the candidate's expression of "truth" had given him "infinite satisfaction," its "ultraism" on the future of slavery had bothered some of the Republican editor's unnamed "Kentucky friends who want to be Republicans." Urging Lincoln to keep such conservative views in mind, Scripps implored him to seize an early opportunity to reiterate "the policy of the Republican party, as a National political organization," specifically its opposition to any congressional "meddling" with the institution of slavery in the southern states themselves. Lincoln responded impatiently, asserting that he had already "declared a thousand times" that the "General Government" could not "constitutionally or rightfully interfere with slaves or slavery where it already exists." Lincoln was frustrated that he could not reconcile everyone with his new balancing act of stronger principles and flexible policies but agreed to clarify the point during the campaign.[35]

Lincoln exhibited less concern when he heard that Democrats in Chicago were accusing him of having voted as a congressman against supplies for the army in protest of the Mexican War. Lincoln received letters from three correspondents on the same day in mid-June, urging a quick response to this scurrilous attack by the *Chicago Times*. One suggested that they ask party organizer John Johnson to "collate all the statistics."[36] Lincoln urged everyone to calm down. "There is not a word of truth in the charge," he assured his advisers, before providing a detailed explanation of what had occurred. He speculated that the source of the "vile" confusion was a controversial vote by another Whig congressman from Illinois (John Henry) who had preceded him in office. Lincoln described the relevant roll call votes from memory. "I can not be mistaken," he wrote categorically, "for I had my eye always upon it."[37]

At the outset of the campaign, Lincoln was more worried that his allies in Chicago were losing their focus. Just two days after setting the record straight on his congressional votes, he let loose an uncharacteristically nasty note to *Chicago Tribune* co-editor Charles Ray. The blistering message may well be the angriest document in all of Lincoln's writings. Lincoln sent the short letter on June 27, 1858, along with a clipping or "cut" from the previous day's paper that touted a potential alliance in Terre Haute between Indiana Republicans and Douglas Democrats. Lincoln began with a series of stinging questions. "How in God's name do you let such paragraphs into the Tribune, as the enclosed cut from that paper of yesterday?" The sarcasm was unbridled and unrelenting. "Does Sheahan write them?" Lincoln asked, referring to James Sheahan, the editor of the *Chicago Times*, the city's Democratic organ that had assailed him earlier in the week for his alleged Mexican War votes. "How can you have failed to perceive that in this short paragraph you have completely answered all your own well put complaints of Greely and Sister Burlingame?" In his controlled fury, the candidate was indulging in a rare bit of name-calling. "Sister Burlingame" was his sneering reference to the manhood of Massachusetts Republican Anson Burlingame, one of the many establishment party leaders who, along with Horace Greeley, William Seward, and Henry Raymond of the *New York Times*, had been so persistent over the past several months in their encouragement of Douglas as a potential convert to the Republican cause.[38]

This seven-sentence outburst concerned nothing more than some overly enthusiastic coverage of a fusion effort with Douglas Democrats in a neighboring state. Personal attacks from political enemies Lincoln handled calmly, but inconsistency from leading Republican newspapers like the *Chicago Tribune* truly bothered Boss Lincoln. His sharp criticism had little impact, however. Ray did not respond until mid-July, and his reply was nonchalant. "It was done in my absence," he informed Lincoln, noting coolly, "sometimes somethings go wrong." He even tried to pin the blame on one of his co-editors. "I think [Joseph] Medill did it," he concluded.[39]

Lincoln decided to let it go, but the painful episode was indicative of his priorities. He was focused on the party's strategic challenges as a whole, not on his own interests.[40] During this same period, Ray and the other *Tribune* editors had been after him for autobiographical material they could use to promote him in their columns as a self-made success story. Lincoln refused their entreaties, preferring that attention remain on the antislavery cause and the party's most unifying measures.[41]

The candidate also preferred to describe his de facto nomination by the Republicans as a matter of party unity. He told Lyman Trumbull, who had been unable to attend the state convention, that he considered the "first and only" resolution to have been more significant for "closing down" the "everlasting croaking about Wentworth" and his divisive personal ambitions than for "anything else."[42]

Lincoln's hesitation about promoting himself also came in part from his own measured expectations regarding the contest to replace Douglas. This was not a direct contest for popular votes but rather an indirect campaign to influence legislative elections. Republicans had to overcome serious inequities in the state apportionment and Democratic holdover seats in the state senate. Republicans had a growing demographic edge in Illinois, but the prospect of controlling the General Assembly remained distant for them. Lincoln admitted as much to Trumbull. He predicted that Republicans would be able to elect their statewide candidates in the fall once again "without much difficulty" but because of Democratic "advantages" across the legislative districts "we shall be very hard run to carry the Legislature."[43]

Still, in the weeks after the Republican state convention, Lincoln worked with characteristic intensity to pull the operation together. He began by producing a comprehensive eight-page chart of the Illinois electoral landscape that was based on calculations from the state's 1856 election results. Using a set of optimistic projections, Lincoln depicted Republicans as holding a potential edge in 48 of the 75 state house of representatives seats (all up for reelection), and in 13 of the 25 state senate seats (including the various holdovers who were not up for reelection but would still be voting in the next General Assembly). Yet that potential majority depended heavily on securing what Lincoln termed the "joint vote of Fremont and Fillmore," especially in those "doubtful" districts where everything was "to be struggled for."[44] Most of these swing or doubtful areas lay across the central part of the state where the implicit concern was that former Whigs who had identified as "Fillmore men" in 1856 might hold out against the Republicans, especially now that Douglas was positioning himself as an independent partisan force in opposition to the Buchanan administration.

Out of concern for winning over these central Illinois conservatives, Lincoln made the risky decision to approach Senator John Crittenden of Kentucky. Crittenden had once been full of praise for Lincoln, when they were both pragmatic Whig fusionists supporting President Zachary Taylor, but the aging senator had migrated into the American or nativist movement with Fillmore. He identified with an amalgamation of old Know Nothings and former Whigs in the Upper South who called themselves the Southern Opposition and who had been working closely with Douglas to try to resolve the Lecompton crisis.[45] Lincoln confessed in a private letter to Crittenden that he had become uneasy about "a story being whispered about here" that the Kentucky senator was planning to draft a public statement of support for Douglas. Lincoln assured Crittenden that "ninety-nine hundredths" of his "warmer friends" in the state would be "mortified exceedingly" by such a bold cross-party endorsement. Lincoln denied that he was "fishing for a letter on the other side" but suggested to his old ally that "you would better be hands off!"[46]

Crittenden responded with a mixture of flattery and contempt. "You are entitled to be frank with me," he agreed, acknowledging a long-standing "personal regard" for Lincoln before delivering his own blunt assessment. Douglas had acted "like a Man" during the Lecompton battle, Crittenden asserted, which meant that the Illinois senator's reelection was "necessary as a rebuke to the Administration." The Kentuckian dismissed Lincoln's concerns about his potential "intermeddling" but refused to promise "any restriction upon my conduct."[47] The unyielding response from an influential conservative did not bode well for the effort to win over other skeptical former Whigs.

Lincoln was also busy putting electoral calculations to work on the ground. He connected with local candidates in the doubtful districts, sharing numbers from his chart and prodding them into action. Lincoln urged Joseph Gillespie, a Republican state senator in Madison County and a former Whig conservative with strong Know Nothing ties, to be especially "wide awake" about the Fillmore vote. He had heard rumors that Democrats were making inroads with that critical segment. "Dont neglect it," he commanded. But Gillespie was downcast, admitting that Douglas and his men might carry over half of the former Fillmore men in his area—more than enough to defeat him. Lincoln mocked this "doleful" report and replied, "We must not lose that district." Always a believer in studying every crevice of the political landscape, Lincoln pushed Gillespie to conduct what he called "a little test," directing him to take the first one hundred names of the American party voters from the local 1856 poll books and "quietly ascertain" how many were defecting to Douglas. Only then, Lincoln observed, could they know the real situation and which "other agencies" might have to be activated to help "compensate" for the loss of those essential voters.[48]

Also active in fundraising, Lincoln asked for $500 from one longtime backer, even though he conceded that "times are tighter" in the aftermath of the Panic of 1857.[49] "I am now in need of money," he confessed to another supporter in July, seeking to track down $50 that had been promised to him.[50] He started spending more campaign funds, too, suggesting to Gustave Koerner in the middle of the month that the party should hire a German-speaking surrogate to help stump for them among the immigrant communities in the central counties.[51] Lincoln was quietly proposing this investment ("for your private eye") almost as a hedge against his difficulties in cultivating the Old Line Whigs. He told Koerner that Gillespie had been warning him of trouble in Madison County but observed that "this fact itself, would make it, at least no harder for us to get accessions from the Germans." Calling it a "special job," Lincoln urged the former lieutenant governor to help ensure that none of the immigrants got "cheated" at their polling places in the fall. "Others of us must find the way to save as many Americans as possible," Lincoln explained. "Still others must do other things. Nothing must be left undone."[52]

There was also the prospect of stoking further divisions among the Democrats. Even after passage of the English bill and its plan for a party compromise on the Lecompton crisis, Buchanan seemed determined to punish Douglas for his resistance. In early June, pro-Buchanan Democrats in Illinois, the ones who had bolted from the Douglas faction in April, held their own statewide nominating convention. They seemed eager to make trouble for the Douglas Democrats, even at the risk of a Republican victory in the Senate contest.[53] Earlier in the summer Lincoln had denied to Trumbull that he would authorize any Republican "alliance" with the Buchanan forces, certainly nothing involving "concession of principle," "partition of offices," or the "swopping of votes." Yet by July Lincoln had agreed to meet privately with the pro-Buchanan candidate for state treasurer and learned from him that the Democratic bolters were planning to run candidates "for each and every office" across the state, including the legislative seats. According to Herndon, Lincoln was thrilled by this news of the impending split in the Democratic vote, observing, "If you do this [then] the thing is settled."[54]

Lincoln made sure to keep his sensitive lines of communication both open and secret. He asked state auditor Jesse Dubois to meet with another unnamed contact in the Buchanan camp. Afterward Dubois explained that he had met with "your man according to your desire" but reported that "they did not agree upon any thing further than to canvass the Doubtful counties."[55] In addition, a pro-Buchanan editor wrote to a Republican state official who had been working closely with Dubois, claiming that Lincoln had promised but failed to deliver $500 for his work in publishing anti-Douglas articles.[56] This covert outreach to Buchanan's Illinois men may not have constituted a formal alliance, but it was an important back channel cultivated by Lincoln himself.

Not everyone agreed with this approach. Wentworth's *Chicago Democrat* had been urging Republicans to blast all Democrats with equal vigor and to keep lumping Douglas and Buchanan together despite their ongoing feud. "In defeating Douglas, we kill Buchanan, too," crowed Wentworth's organ.[57] Back in New York, Greeley was still embittered over what he considered a badly missed opportunity. "You have repelled Douglas, who might have been conciliated," he wrote to Medill of the *Chicago Tribune* in July, "and, instead of helping us in other states, you have thrown a load upon us that may probably break us down." Greeley was also annoyed that he was receiving complaints about his paper's coverage of the Illinois contest. He declared himself to be "neutral . . . hereafter." Medill shared this angry note with Lincoln, who copied it out by hand and filed it away.[58]

In the midst of these frenetic organizing activities, Lincoln decided to shadow Senator Douglas wherever he had major speaking engagements. In Chicago on July 10 and in Springfield on July 17, he sat in the audience for Douglas's initial campaign speeches and afterward offered impromptu rebuttals. The candidates traded charges on sectional questions, discussed *Dred Scott* and Lecompton, and made some ugly detours into matters of race mixing and colonization. The two men had debated informally like this in the past, but the spectacle of these latest exchanges under campaign conditions drew a great deal of attention and some criticism. The *New York Times* sniffed that Lincoln had occupied "the strictest party grounds" in his foray at Chicago but in doing so he had disappointed "political friends at the East" who were hoping for a more conciliatory tone.[59] A leading abolitionist from Jacksonville, Illinois, took Lincoln to task for not being aggressive enough. "All debators know that it is much easier to <u>assail</u> than to <u>defend</u>," he wrote. Lincoln replied to this reprimand, conceding the wisdom of "placing one's self on the offensive." He claimed he had done just that in Springfield. "I am already improving," the candidate observed.[60]

A few days later an emboldened Lincoln approached Douglas about transforming their ad hoc debates into a series of jointly scheduled appearances. He drafted a proposal suggesting an "arrangement" for the ostensible U.S. Senate candidates to "divide time" as equals and had Republican chairman Norman Judd deliver it in person. Douglas balked at first, blaming his already overcrowded schedule while also noting a suspicion that the plan was merely a ruse by Lincoln to inflame Democratic divisions. Douglas accused the Republicans of trying to create conditions that would encourage a third senatorial candidate from the Buchanan faction to join them on the debate platform. Still, he suggested a cautious willingness to meet Lincoln alone in each of the seven congressional districts where they had not yet spoken together. Lincoln quickly accepted this counterproposal. The first "joint discussion" in the Lincoln-Douglas debates was scheduled for Ottawa, in northern Illinois, on Saturday, August 21, 1858.[61]

Ottawa was a Democratic-majority town, but it was situated within the third congressional district represented by Republican and prominent abolitionist Owen Lovejoy. For Douglas, it was the near perfect setting to launch an attack on Lincoln and his new sectional party for what he considered to be their radical departure from the tradition of fully national parties. The terms of the joint discussions gave each speaker ninety minutes, with the opening speaker taking his first hour and reserving his final thirty minutes for a closing rebuttal after the second speaker had delivered his full oration of an hour and a half. That schedule yielded three hours of concentrated speechifying in seven locations spread across the state, over the span of about two months between mid-August and mid-October. Douglas opened at Ottawa and used his hour-long inaugural slot to make an extended attack on Republicans as abolitionists in disguise.

It was not a surprising strategy, but the incumbent senator seized the offensive in a startling manner. Douglas began the debates with a series of lies. He repeated charges from the 1856 campaign, long since repudiated, that Lincoln and Trumbull had made a corrupt "arrangement" in 1854 to "dissolve" their old Whig and Democratic ties, so that they could "abolitionize" their followers to help make each other U.S. senator. Then, claiming to read directly from the platform of the "Black Republican Party" adopted at the state fair in Springfield in October 1854, Douglas cited planks calling for the unconditional repeal of the Fugitive Slave Law and an outright prohibition against the admission of any more slave states. He tried taunting Lincoln by asking if he still believed in such radical ideas, before pivoting to a series of ugly questions about race. Claiming somehow that the slavery issue had been "settled," Douglas asserted that the real problem before the nation was "what shall be done with the free negro?" It was quite a performance—about sixty minutes of mostly baseless innuendo, name-calling, and overt race-baiting before an audience of thousands.[62]

Lincoln knew it was unwise to appear defensive in political debates, but in responding to this bewildering array of false and misleading charges, he stumbled. He surely recalled that the 1854 resolutions that Douglas read aloud had been doctored when they first appeared in the local Democratic newspaper, but he seemed unprepared or unwilling to dispute it on the spot. Instead, he lamely invoked the presence of Lovejoy on the speaker's stand in Ottawa to help underscore his political distance from the radicals. He claimed, with Lovejoy nodding along, that the abolitionist had "tried to get me into it," meaning the so-called Republican party of 1854, but "I would not go in." Lincoln could use Lovejoy as a foil with the abolitionist's assent because they were no longer worried about that dimension of antislavery fusion. Partisan calculations had changed a great deal since the aftermath of the Kansas-Nebraska Act. Lincoln's recent "house divided" line had reassured most radicals about his long-term purpose. The current Republican strategy was more focused on targeting the few remaining ex-Whigs, those "Kentucky friends who want to be Republicans," as Scripps had termed them, who were still holding out against joining the antislavery coalition. For this reason, Lincoln closed his remarks at Ottawa by extolling the memory of Henry Clay, calling him for the first time in public "my beau ideal of a statesman" and claiming—presumably with fingers crossed—that Clay was "the man for whom I fought all my humble life."[63]

Once each candidate sized up the other's positions, the quality of the debates improved. Despite some repetition, embarrassing patches of low demagoguery, and dreary asides into policy minutiae, each figure managed moments of enduring eloquence. A tired Douglas defended his doctrine of "popular sovereignty" and the inherent virtues of self-government with bracing defiance. A steadier Lincoln responded with stirring appeals to natural rights philosophy. But Lincoln never ignored the appeal of popular sovereignty as an American principle. "Public sentiment is everything," he conceded in 1858. "Whoever moulds public sentiment, goes deeper than he who enacts statutes, or pronounces judicial decisions."[64] At their finest, the Lincoln-Douglas debates offered an extended, lively argument about the direction of American constitutional democracy in the age of slavery.

But the actual campaign was far more about party strategy than about democratic principles. In the contest to shape the race for the legislature, Lincoln and Douglas both had the state's partisan landscape in mind, each trying to outmaneuver the other for advantage with targeted segments of the Illinois electorate. Lincoln was particularly focused on the public presentation of his party's antislavery policies. Without alienating Whiggish conservatives, he tried to emphasize the moral clarity of Republican positions against what he mocked as the Douglas "don't care" policies about the future of slavery. This delicate balancing act rested in part on the question of whether Republicans were opposed to the extension of slavery in the territories or pledged against the admission of any more slave states. Northern conservatives generally understood opposition to slavery's expansion and even sympathized with it, but they regarded unconditional pledges as too extreme and out of line with previous compromises.

Lincoln was careful to rebut the charge that Republicans were *pledged* against any more slave states. He denied it repeatedly on the stump and addressed the matter with precision in private correspondence. "I do not understand the Republican party to be committed to the proposition 'No more slave States,'" Lincoln wrote to one party activist. "I know there are many of them who think we are under obligation to admit slave states from Texas, if such be presented for admission."[65] He was referring to the 1845 joint congressional resolution authorizing Texas annexation. Both the Texas annexation measure and the Compromise of 1850 had detailed special conditions for potential slave state applications—up to four to be carved out of the Texas territory, and two more from the New Mexico and Utah territories, but only if their residents voted for it. Lincoln recognized in 1858 that any pledge to the contrary would undercut Republican efforts to frame their party's antislavery principles as moderate and grounded in the rule of law.

This mattered so much to Lincoln that when Douglas invoked Rep. Elihu Washburne as an example of a Republican who backed the idea of no more slave states, Lincoln sent his old Galena ally an urgent letter. "If his allegation be true," he wrote in mid-September, "burn this without answering it." The matter was sensitive enough that Lincoln wanted no paper trail of his query if, for once, Douglas had accurate information. Lincoln suspected, however, that it was just another in a long line of false charges, so he told Washburne, "If it be untrue, write me such a letter as I may make public with which to contradict him." Washburne did not burn the note, but neither did he reply in writing. Douglas's accusations were mangled from a Democratic newspaper account of Washburne's local party newspaper—his "mouthpiece"—having endorsed the "no more slave states" pledge, but the story was complicated enough that it made no sense for Republicans to argue it. With great reluctance, Lincoln declined to challenge Douglas on the matter in public.[66]

The 1858 Illinois legislative elections also raised controversial questions about illegal voting. Since 1848, voters in Illinois had to be legal citizens over the age of twenty-one and voting in the district of their permanent residence. Lincoln and other leading Republicans were convinced that Douglas Democrats were intentionally sending loyal Irish immigrants from Chicago into the state's "doubtful" districts to sway the results. Republican party newspapers reported a steady stream of rumors about such "colonization" schemes involving hordes of immigrant railroad workers being mysteriously dispatched to central Illinois counties as the election approached on the pretext of working on new railroad construction. Near the end of August, Herndon complained about it to Boston abolitionist Theodore Parker. Lincoln's law partner dismissed Irish Catholic immigrants as "voting Buffalo," predicting "they will be run down here *on pretence of getting a job*, and so in the closely contested fight, they will carry *we fear*, the uncertain Counties."[67]

Lincoln worried that Norman Judd, the state party chairman, was not taking this danger seriously enough. On September 23, he predicted to Judd that winning a Republican majority in the state legislature was within their grasp, "unless they overcome us by fraudulent voting." "Men imported from other states and men not naturalized can be fought out," he wrote, expressing confidence in the Republican poll watchers of the day, but the real threat in his opinion came from the "qualified Irish voters of Chicago" who would swear falsely to residence in "a doubtful district." Lincoln urged the chairman to take the matter "into anxious consideration at once." Then, most certainly to goad Judd, who had long despised fellow Chicagoan John Wentworth as an undeserving rival, Lincoln asked with seeming innocence: "Is 'Long John' at hand? His genius should be employed on this question."[68]

Judd at first tried to tamp down the rising paranoia about the alleged voter colonization schemes of the Douglas Democrats. One close ally informed Lincoln that he had been attempting to warn the state chairman about the Irish voter problem but had been unable to convince him to act. Lincoln's friend warned that "the majority of the illegal voting of that kind will be carried on in the *out of the way* precincts where our people are not up to matters of that kind & do not know well how to resist them."[69]

Less than a week later, while traveling through some of those "out of the way precincts" in the western part of the state and just days after his final debate with Douglas at Alton on October 15, Lincoln sent party chairman Judd another, more urgent warning about fraudulent Irish voters. The candidate began by reporting that he had just encountered "fifteen Celtic gentlemen, with black carpet-sacks," while passing through the railroad junction at Naples. Lincoln decided to follow them around himself. He spied the men "hanging about" the "doggeries" or saloons. Soon he ascertained where the group had come from and found out that possibly four hundred more "of the same sort" were coming soon to join them. He conceded, however, that local Republican party boss John Bagby considered such reports as little more than nervous gossip.[70]

"What I most dread," Lincoln confessed after relaying his startling new information, was that these "Celtic gentlemen" might be "legal voters in all respects except residence" and that Douglas forces were introducing them into districts where the final vote was sure to be close because they knew that under Illinois election law "it is next to impossible to convict them of Perjury" for lying about where they resided or intended to reside. "Now," according to Lincoln, "the great remaining part of the campaign, is finding a way to head this thing off. Can it be done at all?"

Lincoln's answer to this loaded question was something he called "a bare suggestion" that sounded suspiciously like a scheme to bribe or intimidate the immigrants. "When there is a known body of these voters," he explained to Judd, "could not a true man, of the '*detective*' class, be introduced among them in disguise, who could, at the nick of time, control their votes?" Lincoln's mention of an undercover detective was a reference to Allan Pinkerton, the Scottish immigrant whom the *Chicago Tribune* was hailing as "the celebrated detective of this city." Pinkerton had won celebrity for his work as an undercover agent fighting a crime spree in Chicago, then for his agency's role in helping to ferret out fraud and theft on the Illinois railroads. Judd was one of Pinkerton's most enthusiastic advocates. Acknowledging that his plan to employ a detective was extremely sensitive, Lincoln added, "I have talked, more fully than I can write, to Mr. Scripps, and he will talk to you."[71]

Was Lincoln making "a bare suggestion" or an illegal one? By the end of the tense 1858 campaign, he might well have been anxious enough to rationalize fighting one form of political cheating with another. Herndon claimed around this time that Lincoln "does not know the details of how we get along."[72] But the confidential communications from this campaign suggest otherwise. Lincoln seemed to know every dirty detail, even more than the loose-lipped Herndon did.

Yet something else in the confidential October 20, 1858, letter to Judd indicates that with his request for a "true man" of the " '*detective*' class" Lincoln was not contemplating bribery or violence. He concluded by dismissing the whole Democratic voter colonization operation as little more than a "trick." "Think this over," he wrote about his suggestion. "It would be a great thing, when this trick is attempted upon us, to have the saddle come up on the other horse." If the Douglas Democrats were willing to skirt loosely written state election laws by moving immigrant voters around to maximize their impact, why couldn't the Republicans justify a little trickery of their own to minimize such gamesmanship? Lincoln's "detective" could lead the unsuspecting "Celtic gentlemen" to a less doubtful district, where their fraudulent ballots for Douglas would not actually change the outcome. The Irish immigrants from Chicago would hardly notice the difference in these rural counties so unfamiliar to them. Moreover, the whole operation might be easy to accomplish after the visitors spent even more time in the "doggeries."[73]

That was surely what Lincoln wanted Scripps, one of the *Chicago Tribune*'s trio of editors, to explain in person to Judd, but the plan never materialized. On October 19—the night before Lincoln outlined his delicate scheme—a prominent former Whig named T. Lyle Dickey dropped a political bombshell that reshaped the final days of the contest. During a widely reported speech in Decatur, Illinois, Dickey read a fulsome letter from Senator Crittenden of Kentucky praising the virtues and manliness of Stephen Douglas.[74] It was the endorsement that Lincoln had been trying to head off since July, and it proved devastating. Dickey was part of a coterie of former Whigs, including Benjamin Edwards, James Singleton, and John Todd Stuart, who had gone public with their support for the Democratic incumbent. Now they were using words that Crittenden had written in August (after he had corresponded with Lincoln) to inflict maximum political damage on their former Whig friend and colleague. Within days there were also reports in leading St. Louis newspapers about Crittenden's private correspondence with Lincoln. David Davis complained to Lincoln afterward that it was "perfectly outrageous" and "shameful," but the last-minute attack was effective.[75]

The unexpected Crittenden endorsement gave the party's central committee bigger problems to overcome than Irish colonization. Still, chairman Judd dutifully sent around a confidential circular on October 22 detailing how local party organizers might thwart the "imported hordes" on Election Day through better preparation. The instructions explained how to frame more effective poll watching questions and urged Republicans to post friendly constables near polling places to make any necessary arrests. "One or two such arrests in the morning," the circular predicted, "will be very likely to deter others from attempting so hazardous a game." Lincoln drafted a similar document of his own advising poll watchers how to challenge suspected nonresident voters. And on Election Day, Republican partisans in the central counties did in fact make several efforts to expose fraudulent ballots, but it was too little, too late, just as Lincoln had anticipated.[76]

Republicans lost every contested district in that crucial central region of the state, maintaining only a lone holdover state senator.[77] Back in July, Lincoln had envisioned the possibility of his party controlling about 61 out of 100 representative and senatorial seats. But this projection hinged on a new round of successful fusion in the state's center, and Republicans could never win over enough of the old Fillmore vote to accomplish that. Lincoln later recalled that Illinois Know Nothing founder William Danenhower was "the only marked representative of the American organization" who "co-operated with us in 1858."[78] Instead, pushed and prodded by Crittenden, Dickey, and other notable Whig conservatives, Fillmore voters broke decisively for the Douglas Democrats where it mattered most, presumably providing their margin of victory. The incumbent senator's forces ended up with a solid majority of 54 in the General Assembly. The Republicans won the statewide popular vote and came close to controlling some key counties across the central belt, but they narrowly lost their chance to remove the hated Douglas.[79]

Lincoln appears to have sensed this outcome. In the final days of the campaign, he looked beyond his own fading prospects and attempted to situate the overall Illinois Republican effort in a broader context. "I have never failed [and] do not now fail," he wrote, "to remember that in the republican cause there is a higher aim than that of mere office." He compared their struggles as antislavery Republicans to the heroic British abolitionists of the eighteenth century, who had fought by his reckoning for nearly a century before bringing an end to the notorious African slave trade. "I can not but regard it as possible that the higher object of this contest may not be completely attained within the term of my natural life," he concluded.[80]

Lincoln also tried to put his personal struggles into perspective. "With *me*, the race of ambition has been a failure—a flat failure," he stated in what are apparently notes for a speech, conceding that for Douglas it had been "a splendid success."[81] Lincoln claimed to "affect no contempt for the high eminence" that his opponent had reached, but he observed that he would rather share his own "elevation" in life with "the oppressed of my species" than "wear the richest crown that ever pressed a monarch's brow." This was posturing, but it was also insightful. Lincoln had always been more disciplined and less selfish as a party leader than Douglas, who was a brilliant tactician but not always a successful strategist. Describing their recent campaign as often "painful," Lincoln observed that he had been "bespattered with every imaginable odious epithet." But still, he noted with pride, "I have cultivated patience, and made no attempt at a retort." The reason for this restraint, according to Lincoln, was his commitment to a larger cause and a longer horizon than a mere Senate race. "Ambition has been ascribed to me," he wrote. "God knows how sincerely I prayed from the first that this field of ambition might not be opened." He suggested that if only the Missouri Compromise could be restored, or if there were "unyielding hostility to the spread" of slavery "on principle," then he would be happy to see that "Judge Douglas should never be *out*, and I never *in*, an office, so long as we both or either, live."[82]

Once the election passed, Lincoln took pains to appear steadfast. Two days after the balloting, he assured Senator Crittenden that "despite the emotions of defeat . . . to which the use of your name contributed largely," he was unwilling to accuse him of "anything dishonorable."[83] He called himself "convalescent" in a note to Norman

Judd, vowing that "the fight must go on," though he did hesitate to provide the forlorn party chairman with any additional funds from his own pocket until after "you and I settle the private matter between us."[84] Lincoln was referring to the $2,500 he had lent Judd in the previous year for land investments in Iowa. The state Republicans also owed $2,500 to their creditors after the hard-fought fall campaign.

Lincoln kept repeating that line about "the fight must go on" to other correspondents, but the more he did so, the more defiant he seemed to become. "The cause of civil liberty must not be surrendered at the end of *one*, or even one *hundred* defeats," he asserted. To another supporter, he confessed, "I am glad I made the late race."[85] "The question is not half-settled," he vowed, "we shall have fun again."[86]

The Illinois results in 1858 were promising for Republicans. They had demonstrated their statewide appeal despite ongoing problems with central Illinois conservatives, whom Lincoln now dismissed as little better than remnants of "the old exclusive silk-stocking whiggery."[87] He was satisfied that Republicans could win in the future without them. "We have some hundred and twenty thousand clear Republican votes," he noted, adding, "That *'pile'* is worth keeping together."[88] As always, his attention was on details. Lincoln wanted Judd to get to work right away on drafting a new apportionment bill, warning that without changes in the makeup of the legislative districts, Trumbull would face likely defeat in his reelection effort in 1860. Lincoln was also quick to capitalize on the value of the campaign's intensive media coverage. He had been keeping a scrapbook of his campaign with Douglas, which he now set out to preserve "in some permanent form." It eventually became the first book-length publication of his speeches.[89]

LINCOLN UNDERSTOOD THAT HIS 1858 Illinois campaign against Douglas had exposed a fatal flaw in the national Democratic party. Its internal divisions were crippling not only because of clashing party leadership in Buchanan and Douglas but also owing to contradictory policies over slavery's future within a party coalition that stretched across all geographic sections, free and slave. "There will be another 'blow up' in the democracy," Lincoln predicted to B. C. Lundy, his old abolitionist ally from Putnam County. "Douglas managed to be supported both as the best instrument to *break down*, and to *uphold* the slave power," Lincoln observed. "No ingenuity can keep this deception—this double position—up a great while."[90]

The inevitable Democratic implosion came with its own risks for Republicans, however. Lincoln reported to Trumbull in December that Douglas had just left the state for a fence-mending tour of the South, "seeking to re-instate himself in that section," as he put it with obvious disdain. By Lincoln's estimation, the shrewdest move for national Democratic party leaders, a majority of whom wanted to "kill" Douglas, was simply to "let him into the Charleston Convention" in 1860 and "outvote him," so that they could deny him a "pretext for bolting." But Lincoln warned that if extremist southern Democrats succeeded in pushing through a territorial "Slave code" in the aftermath of the *Dred Scott* decision—rules that would officially authorize and regulate slavery across the federal territories—then once again Douglas would "turn upon us, as in the case of Lecompton," seeking terms for the cross-party support of Republicans. The anticipated final breakup of the national Democratic party would thus represent a golden opportunity, and a grave danger, transforming "the struggle in the whole North . . . as it was in Illinois . . . whether the Republican party can maintain it's [*sic*] identity, or be broken up to form the tail of Douglas' new kite."[91]

With heavy sarcasm, Lincoln noted the irony of this predicament. Seward, Greeley, and other Republican bosses, he pointed out, would surely hate to make room for the bombastic and unreliable Douglas within their own partisan domain despite having pushed such medicine on Illinois Republicans during the past year. "Some of our great Republican doctors will then have a splendid chance to swallow the pills they so eagerly prescribed for us last Spring," he wrote. "I do not feel that I owe the said doctors much," he added, but "I will help them, to the best of my ability, to reject the said pills." The Senate campaign was over, but the fight to maintain the unity of the Republican cause was not. Lincoln entered 1859 determined to extend his ultraist strategy to the national Republican party. Some in Washington were already discussing Lincoln's presidential prospects, according to the ever-faithful Josiah Lucas, still a clerk hidden away in the General Land Office.[92] But for now, Lincoln's emphasis remained on the party as a whole and his role within it as an organizer.

8 REPRESENTATIVE MAN

(1859–1860)

AFTER THE 1858 CAMPAIGN, Abraham Lincoln began expanding his party leadership to the national level. In March 1859, in his first public remarks since the contest, Lincoln admitted to a group of Chicago Republicans that his House Divided speech had created some "dissatisfaction" among "good men," but he reiterated his view that framing their movement around a "great principle" was essential to their ultimate success. He claimed that Republicans must "in every way resist [slavery] as a wrong, treating it as a wrong, with the fixed idea that it must and will come to an end." He conceded that it might take quite "a length of time" to abolish slavery "peaceably," but he insisted that it had to be destroyed. "Stand by your principles," the party leader concluded, "stand by your guns; and victory complete and permanent is sure at the last."[1]

A month later Lincoln leaned on principle in tough comments about the sectional crisis to Massachusetts Republicans. Declining an invitation to join them in Boston for a "Festival" on the anniversary of Thomas Jefferson's birthday, he sent a letter to the organizing committee that noted the irony in Republicans' holding such a celebration. "The principles of Jefferson are the definitions and axioms of free society," he observed, before accusing Democrats as Jefferson's self-identified heirs with "plotting against the people" by ignoring "unalienable" rights. Lincoln claimed that the decline of Democratic party faith in the ideals of Jefferson's Declaration was a dismal sign of "returning despotism" in America. "We must repulse them," he stated, "or they will subjugate us."[2] It was an ominous reflection of hardening partisan attitudes as the nation approached the 1860 election.

LINCOLN'S HARD LINE ON slavery and human rights raised expectations for principled stands on other policy fronts. In April, when the Republican state central committee met in Bloomington, the members tabled a resolution from Lincoln that criticized a recent anti-immigrant measure in Massachusetts. That state's Republican-controlled and Know Nothing–influenced legislature had approved and submitted for ratification a constitutional amendment designed to curtail the political rights of naturalized citizens.[3] On his return to Springfield, Lincoln found an angry letter from Gustave Koerner demanding to know why Illinois Republicans had declined to denounce nativism. "It is time that we should quit the absurd hope of gaining converts from the Knownothings by a tenderfooted course," complained the German-born party leader.[4]

Lincoln bristled at such criticism. He blamed Lyman Trumbull for the party's failure to act, describing how the senator had convinced others that "it would be better" to lodge a protest against nativism through "some act of our adversaries rather than of our own friends." In a public letter written in May, however, Lincoln adopted Trumbull's approach and conceded that it was "no privilege of mine to scold [Massachusetts] for what she does." He claimed only that he would oppose similar anti-immigrant provisions for his own state. "I have some little notoriety for commiserating [with] the oppressed condition of the negro," he added, admitting it would be "strangely inconsistent" if he somehow favored "curtailing the existing rights of *white men*."[5]

In the past, Lincoln had kept his observations about the hypocrisy of antislavery nativists private. The widely reprinted letter to German-born editor Theodore Canisius served notice that he was willing to become more vocal in a shifting political landscape. By the spring of 1859, almost everybody recognized that Republicans constituted the main northern opposition to the Democratic party. With the Whig party gone and the Know Nothings and their American party in disarray, Republicans had new opportunities to cultivate support from foreign-born antislavery voters. That was the point Koerner had been trying to make. He criticized Republican backing for anti-immigrant measures anywhere as hurting the party with German American voters everywhere. Framing the argument in practical terms, Koerner claimed that the Republicans had lost the doubtful districts in central Illinois in 1858 because too many estranged immigrants had stayed away from the polls, disgusted by the state party's indifference to prejudice against them.[6]

Though he disagreed with Koerner's analysis of the 1858 defeat, Lincoln acted anyway. The party leader had already authorized spending party money on German-language pamphlets and speakers, but now Lincoln also began investing his personal funds to back a new German-language Republican newspaper in Springfield. Canisius agreed to become the editor, though Norman Judd objected, calling him "a leech."[7]

Lincoln saw value in Canisius despite the complaints about him. His public correspondence with the journalist not only put him on the record about the nativist controversy in Massachusetts but also allowed him to comment on the party's evolving fusion prospects. In response to a question about the wisdom of widening their coalition, Lincoln replied: "As to the matter of fusion, I am for it, if it can be had on republican grounds," adding that "any other terms, would be as foolish as unprincipled." On the matter of the antislavery principle, he was adamant. "I am against letting down the republican standard a hair's breadth," he concluded. But Lincoln tried to distinguish men from measures. "The question of *men* is a different one," he noted. "There are good patriotic men, and able statesmen, in the South whom I would cheerfully support," he claimed, "if they would now place themselves on republican ground."[8]

The week before, Lincoln had counseled a longtime supporter that they should never "lower the Republican standard" regarding antislavery principles either for "Douglasism" or for the "Southern opposition element." Nor should they delude themselves into thinking that fusion could be "attempted on the basis of ignoring the Slavery question."[9] He was even tougher in an exchange with a well-known conservative journalist, insisting that the party's only way forward was to focus on "preventing the spread and nationalization of Slavery" even if such a platform would ruin Republicans in slaveholding states. "If the rotten democracy shall be beaten in 1860," he wrote, "it has to be done by the North; no human invention can deprive them of the South."[10]

Lincoln's concern was sustaining Republican unity in the North. In early June, when Ohio Republicans issued a call to repeal the 1850 federal Fugitive Slave Law at their state convention, he took quick action.[11] Lincoln considered the Ohio platform a strategic mistake because it would allow Democrats to stoke Republican divisions elsewhere. He wrote to Governor Salmon Chase (whom he had not yet met in person) imploring him to ensure that no such measure would get introduced at the party's 1860 national convention. He claimed that the Ohio action was "already damaging us here" in Illinois and warned it would be worse at a national party gathering, where the antagonistic factions would only "quarrel irreconcilably."[12]

Unimpressed by this prediction, Chase assured Lincoln that any pragmatists would simply have to be "educated up to" the necessity of repealing a law that the governor considered "unnecessarily harsh & severe" and yet "almost absolutely useless as a practical measure of reclamation." That latter point represented a burst of candor from a great antislavery lawyer known as the "Attorney General for Fugitive Slaves." But it was true. The fugitive slave rendition system in the North was broken. Northern personal liberty laws, hostile local juries, and an aggressive army of Black-led vigilance committees had largely succeeded in overwhelming the shaky federal reclamation or recapture process. Chase could admit as much to Lincoln, even while acknowledging that he was essentially agreeing with "all the minds of the South" who had been complaining for years that the notorious statute had become "next to worthless as a practical measure."[13]

The numbers told the story. So far that year, fewer than a dozen fugitive rendition cases had been reported across the entire North. Nationwide, over the nine years since passage of the Fugitive Slave Law, U.S. commissioners had conducted only about a hundred formal hearings. In Illinois, there had been a mere handful of official renditions involving only about half a dozen captured runaways. William Herndon had represented one of those unlucky defendants, Frederick Clements, in the summer of 1857, while Lincoln was traveling in New York with his wife. There were kidnappings of free Blacks and examples of recaption (the seizure of runaways without due process), but the fierce backlash against the federal law had diminished those threats as well.[14]

For Chase, who was in the middle of a heated controversy in Oberlin, Ohio, involving dozens of accused Underground Railroad agents, the situation illustrated why Republicans should push even harder to repeal the broken statute. But from his perch in Springfield, Lincoln saw the crisis differently. Why risk internal division over a measure that was draconian in spirit but "next to worthless" in practice? He had always avoided the topic in public, biting his lip and keeping quiet, as he once explained to Joshua Speed. In the 1858 debates, when Douglas pressed him about abolitionist calls to repeal the Fugitive Slave Law, Lincoln seemed almost mute. "I have had nothing to say in regard to the existing Fugitive Slave Law," he sputtered during the second debate at Freeport.[15] Later in that campaign, he adopted a stronger stance but still offered few specifics. "We profess to have no taste for running and catching niggers," he blurted out at the final Lincoln-Douglas debate on October 15—"at least I profess no taste for that job at all." He asked, "Why then do I yield support to a fugitive slave law? Because I do not understand that the Constitution, which guarantees that right, can be supported without it."[16]

On that constitutional point, Chase agreed with Lincoln. They both accepted the fugitive slave clause in Article IV of the Constitution, which required that enslaved people should "be delivered up" whenever they fled between states, regardless of whether a state was slave or free. In his 1859 letter to Lincoln, the Ohio governor conceded that Congress had "an obligation" to provide "a fair law" concerning runaway slaves. Lincoln also favored that type of evasive construction, always claiming that he supported *a* fugitive law, not necessarily *the* 1850 fugitive law.[17] But Chase insisted to Lincoln that the constitutional responsibilities for enforcing the federal law rested exclusively with the states.[18] In reply, Lincoln explained why he favored federal enforcement, but he considered this legal digression secondary to the main political point. "I did not write you on this subject, with any view of discussing the constitutional question," he noted, claiming that his "only object" was to warn against a policy debate that would "explode the convention and the party."[19]

Lincoln continued his unity campaign in 1859 by reaching out to other Republican leaders around the country. He sent Schuyler Colfax, a congressman from Indiana, a "for your eye only" note, urging him to stand "against divisions in the Republican ranks . . . particularly for the contest of 1860." To Colfax, who had been affiliated with the Know Nothings, Lincoln mentioned the Massachusetts "movement against foreigners" as well as the Ohio effort to repeal the fugitive law as two of the approaches most liable to provoke "discord." Lincoln urged greater discipline from everyone. "In every locality we should look beyond our noses," he wrote to Colfax, "and at least say *nothing* on points where it is probable we shall disagree."[20] Colfax agreed but expressed doubt that such unity was possible within a party that contained "men of all shades & gradations of opinion." Anyone who could shape such a "mass of mind" into "a victorious phalanx in 1860," he wrote, would be "worthier of fame than Napoleon."

Colfax was clearly teasing Lincoln even as he flattered him. "The 'lions in the way' are numerous indeed," the future Speaker of the House observed, "but to them who, like yourself, are not slothful, difficulties are half surmounted." Colfax promised Lincoln (falsely, it turned out) that "if you will lead in this work, you will find me a faithful follower." Yet the notoriously slippery "Smiler" ended up backing Edward Bates of Missouri at the outset of the 1860 convention.[21]

Some Republican activists were promoting Lincoln as a potential national nominee, but he preferred to deflect such candidate-booming talk at this early stage. In 1859 he was not campaigning for himself so much as working to help build a national Republican majority. He kept claiming in letters that he did not consider himself "fit for the Presidency," discouraging any "concerted effort" on his behalf.[22]

Throughout the late summer and fall, Lincoln gave major political speeches at Republican campaign events in Iowa, Ohio, and Wisconsin. He also spoke to Republicans in the Kansas territory in December and accepted an invitation to give an antislavery "political" speech in New York in February. The Ohio campaign—a heated contest to succeed Governor Chase—featured speeches from Stephen Douglas with responses from Lincoln, reminders of their famous debates. Lincoln used his remarks to make Republicans aware that despite their sectional appeal, they represented an emerging national majority and could soon wield enough power to overturn the political and legal mistakes of the previous decade. "The people—the people," he proclaimed, "are the rightful masters of both congresses, and courts—not to overthrow the constitution, but to overthrow the *men* who pervert it." As always for Lincoln the party leader, the key to success was hard work. "We must hold conventions, adopt platforms, select candidates, and carry elections," he said.[23]

Lincoln also remained consistent in expressing strong opposition to the "steady debauching of public opinion" masterminded by Douglas in his ongoing campaign for popular sovereignty. And to Salmon Chase—who did not find the time to meet with him while he was campaigning in Ohio—he offered advice about the necessity of defeating the Douglas Democrats. Claiming that "Douglasism" was the only "ism" that stood in their way across the North, Lincoln implored Chase to push harder for victory. "You must, one and all, put yours [*sic*] souls into the effort," he wrote following his return to Springfield.[24]

The 1859 contests found Lincoln more strident than ever regarding the threats from southern Democrats. "Will you make war upon us and kill us all?" he asked rhetorically during a speech in Cincinnati.[25] What sounded like hyperbole in September, however, appeared far more ominous by the end of October. That month, abolitionist John Brown led his sons and other die-hard supporters on a raid of the federal arsenal at Harpers Ferry in western Virginia. They were hoping to steal guns and liberate slaves, essentially bringing the Underground Railroad—and perhaps even a Haiti-style revolution—to the South. It was a wild scheme that Brown had been plotting for months from the Kansas territory and elsewhere. Speaking in Kansas in December, on the day after the Commonwealth of Virginia executed Brown for his crimes, Lincoln remained defiant and warned that if southerners would "undertake to destroy the Union" following a Republican victory in 1860, "it will be our duty to deal with you as Old John Brown has been dealt with."[26]

The flashes of tough talk were expressions of Lincoln's ultraist strategy. He was determined to keep national Republicans from fusion either with Douglas Democrats or with southern conservatives. On returning from his visit to Ohio, he had responded to a gloomy note from Rep. Tom Corwin with a confidential outburst against political compromise. Corwin, the former Whig sensation from the 1847 River and Harbor Convention, was now an Ohio Republican anxious about growing sectional extremism. After hearing Lincoln speak at Cincinnati, Corwin expressed concern that the Illinois politician had claimed that "a Moderate" candidate would doom their party in 1860. An annoyed Lincoln wrote Corwin that he was "tired" of so-called moderates attempting to distract attention from the slavery debate with secondary issues like the tariff or political corruption in Washington. Lincoln mocked this fusionist "pretense" as a formula for "which the whig party was beat out of existence." He was adamant: "Slavery" was "the living issue of the day," and it was "idiotic to think otherwise."[27]

Republicans prevailed in the Ohio state election as they did across most of the free states in 1859.[28] The party was in the ascendant, although in Illinois lingering organizational problems consumed a great deal of Lincoln's time. It was a period of embarrassing scandal in state politics for both parties. Former governor Joel Matteson, a Democrat, was exposed as a crook, and current governor William Bissell, a Republican, faced allegations of financial misfeasance. Neither man endured a criminal trial (though in Bissell's case, perhaps only because he died in early 1860), but Illinois newspapers spent months exposing the corruption in Springfield. Throughout the year, Lincoln seemed almost desperate to protect Bissell's reputation.[29]

Lincoln was also preoccupied with brawling Chicago politicians. State chairman Norman Judd had long despised Chicago mayor John Wentworth, a fellow Republican. But in 1859, when Wentworth's newspaper helped lead a public assault against Judd and a few other Republicans for the alleged mismanagement of their party and the state government, Judd determined to ruin Long John for good. He filed a libel suit against Wentworth on December 1 and wrote Lincoln on the same day, demanding his help. "Does not your position in the party require you to right these things?" Judd asked, adding, "My job [as state committee chairman] is heavy—yours is simple."[30]

Lincoln, in Kansas at the time, responded as soon as he returned. Knowing that Judd was preparing to seek the Republican nomination for governor in the spring of 1860, Lincoln arranged for a group of "old whig friends" to query him in writing about the charges that Wentworth had unleashed, so Judd could deny them without seeming "to come before the public as a volunteer." After explaining the plan to Judd, Lincoln pushed him to focus on getting the Republican national convention for Chicago. One week later Judd did just that, securing approval for his city as the site of the Republican presidential nominating convention, scheduled for May 1860. Judd later recalled his role in that decision as one of the "great political feats" of his career.[31]

Lincoln's hand in bringing the convention to Chicago was a sign that the party leader was interested in a potential presidential candidacy. In December he had come to terms with an Ohio firm for publication of the text of the Lincoln-Douglas debates. Lincoln had written hundreds of newspaper articles and even anonymous poems in the past, and some of his campaign speeches had been reprinted as popular pamphlets, but he had never attempted to produce a book.

Even more revealing, the day after he made this deal, he submitted an autobiographical sketch to a Pennsylvania newspaper that was preparing a series of profiles on leading Republican contenders for president.

Jesse Fell of Bloomington, formerly of Pennsylvania, was the one who had arranged for the "little sketch," as Lincoln put it, on behalf of the *Chester County Times*, a Republican newspaper from outside Philadelphia. Fell was serving as the secretary of the Illinois Republican state central committee and handled the request. Lincoln put together about six hundred words to provide the essentials of his life story.

The compressed autobiography was calculating, despite Lincoln's strained attempts at humility. "I suppose there is not much of it," wrote the prospective candidate, because "there is not much of me." The opening described Lincoln's "undistinguished" family background and the "wild region" where he grew up but made no mention of his wife or children. Lincoln highlighted his connections to almost every region of the country except the Deep South and the Far West. He also identified himself with most of the era's leading occupations: farming, retail trades, the law, and even soldiering. He recalled that his election as a captain of volunteers in the Black Hawk War had provided him "more pleasure than any I have had since." He was terse about his extensive political career, noting only his former Whig affiliation, his years of service in the state legislature and Congress, and his "aroused" reaction to the repeal of the Missouri Compromise in 1854. There was no description of his current policy views, nor any mention of his work in the Republican party. He ended with a curious physical description that included his height (six foot four), weight (about 180 pounds, "on an average"), his "dark complexion, with coarse black hair, and grey eyes," and that said he had "no other marks or brands recollected"—a self-deprecating reference to newspaper ads for stray animals. In his cover note to Fell, he reminded his friend that no matter how "modest" the profile, "it must not appear to have been written by myself."[32]

Lincoln surely wanted to appear modest in deference to political custom, but the sketch marked a turning point. From now on, among friends and allies, he acknowledged that he was a contender—though not a front-runner—for the presidential nomination at Chicago. Lincoln mentioned his change of heart in a letter to John Wentworth in early February. The embattled Chicago mayor responded by sharing with Lincoln advice that he claimed to have offered Douglas and that would have elected him in 1852 if he had followed it. "When it is ascertained that no one of the prominent candidates can be nominated," Wentworth wrote, with only the slightest condescension, "then <u>ought</u> to be your time."[33]

Lincoln was unfazed by such skepticism. In a letter to Norman Judd, he cast his presidential ambition squarely in terms of state leadership. "I am not in a position where it would hurt much for me to not be nominated on the national ticket," he wrote before departing for his speaking tour in New York, "but I am where it would hurt some for me to not get the Illinois delegates." He used this insight to press Judd about the feud with Wentworth, pointing out that his "favorite son" campaign for the presidential nomination was becoming collateral damage of their state saga. "Your discomfited assailants are most bitter against me," Lincoln wrote, and would "for revenge" be willing to "lay to the Bates egg in the South [of Illinois], and to the Seward egg in the North, and go far towards squeezing me out in the middle with nothing."[34]

This fallout worried Lincoln enough that he wrote to Wentworth on the same day, assuring him that he would convince Judd to delay the libel suit "til after the Presidential election," if the Chicago mayor would agree to clarify an earlier statement he had made about the "political" nature of his attacks. Lincoln suggested that he was willing to serve as the final arbitrator of the libel claim—which he would ultimately dismiss—if the rivals would just agree to stand down for the rest of the campaign.[35]

Lincoln was playing a high-level game with these Chicago politicians. To Judd, he had emphasized his help for the party chairman's floundering gubernatorial campaign and asked for some reciprocal assistance at Judd's "end of the vineyard." This direct request for a favor had the immediate effect of producing an endorsement from the *Chicago Tribune.* Some of the more radical-leaning figures at the newspaper had long favored Chase for president, but once Judd conveyed the word, the *Tribune* mobilized for Lincoln. In mid-February, Joseph Medill wrote an editorial extolling Lincoln's "unimpeachable purity" and "acuteness of intellect," noting that he was "Right on the record" regarding slavery. The endorsement highlighted Lincoln's "executive capacity." "Never garrulous, never promising what he cannot perform, never doing anything for show or effect," the newspaper touted how Lincoln was "laboriously attentive to detail" and "industrious," qualities it suggested were sorely needed in Washington. Wentworth was impressed, telling Lincoln, "These men are all afraid of you."[36]

Right before the *Tribune* endorsement appeared in Chicago, the *New York Evening Post* offered comparable praise, labeling Lincoln as one of the nation's "representative men." In a thoughtful editorial on "Our Presidential Candidates," editor and noted poet William Cullen Bryant urged fellow Republicans to guard against the siren call of fusion with the old Fillmore Whig conservative element. He called instead for their party to rally around a "real Republican" who could "unite and consolidate our own ranks." "With such men as Seward and Chase, [Nathaniel] Banks [of Massachusetts] and Lincoln," he wrote, "and others in plenty, let us have two Republicans, representative men, to vote for."[37]

Bryant's use of the term *representative men* was no accident. Earlier in the decade Ralph Waldo Emerson had used it as the title for his collection of short biographical profiles of great men, and journalists had since used the phrase to describe accomplished political leaders who helped shape public opinion.[38] The term stood in contrast to politicians who were "available" or electable across party lines. An available nineteenth-century candidate was a blank political slate, a war hero like Zachary Taylor or a military explorer like John Frémont, someone popular and free of controversy who would make fusion efforts easier to manage. Lincoln was not a candidate because of his availability, even though some people referred to him that way. Most of Lincoln's allies framed his preconvention appeal in terms of experienced party leadership, as the *Tribune* and the *Post* had done. One longtime friend from Kansas described Lincoln as "the Representative man of the West."[39]

The "eminent citizen of the West" was how *Post* editor Bryant introduced Lincoln on February 27, 1860, in the Great Hall of Cooper Union, a new school offering an adult education "open and free to all." Lincoln enthralled the audience of nearly fifteen hundred people with sledgehammer logic against what he portrayed as the false conservatism of proslavery and pro-Douglas forces. He denied that Republican positions were sectional, insisting that the party's antislavery platform embraced the views of most of the nation's founders. And with wavering northern Democrats and conservatives squarely in mind, he was especially tough on those who had devised "contrivances" that involved "groping for some middle ground between the right and the wrong." Lincoln denounced both the "don't care" posture of Douglas's "popular sovereignty" doctrine "on a question about which all true men do care," as well as the weak-kneed patriotism of those "beseeching true Union men to yield to Disunionists."[40] It was a radical speech cloaked in conservative garb and one that impressed most Republicans. Lincoln continued his successful speaking tour across the New England states, finding time along the way to visit his oldest son Robert, who was attending Phillips Exeter Academy in New Hampshire. In his letter home to Mary, Lincoln complained mildly about the "toil" involved in the tour but admitted that things "went off passably well."[41]

Republican newspapers showed more enthusiasm, but Lincoln was still no front-runner for the party's nomination. His name did not appear in a leading journalist's 1860 campaign book, *Our Living Representative Men*, which featured profiles of nearly three dozen prospective presidential candidates from all parties.[42] That spring, when promoting himself, Lincoln was conscious of his modest national standing, explaining to one supporter that since his name was "new to the field," the "policy" of his campaign was "to give no offence to others—leave them in a mood to come to us."[43]

There was plenty of preconvention talk even among Illinois Republicans of other candidates besides Lincoln. Senator Seward remained the most formidable of the Republican contenders, but some moderates had concerns about his appeal in the key doubtful states of Illinois, Indiana, New Jersey, and Pennsylvania. Seward and his erstwhile manager, Thurlow Weed, had also made enemies in New York, especially among former Democrats like Bryant but also with their former Whig ally, Horace Greeley. On the eve of the Chicago convention, Medill's *Tribune* raised the "question of availability" in connection with Seward but focused its praise of Lincoln on his status as "a representative man." Lincoln occupied "a happy mean," in the newspaper's judgment, between the party's radical and conservative factions.[44]

Not everybody saw it that way. Trumbull warned Lincoln in April that his House Divided speech had damaged him among some leading moderates. "When urging your claims," he told Lincoln, "I am almost always met with the remark, 'if you are going to nominate a man of that stamp, why not take Seward.'" According to Trumbull, too many Republican insiders "associate you together" because "you have both given expression to a similar sentiment in regard to the ultimate extinction of slavery."[45]

As the May convention approached, Lincoln admitted to Lyman Trumbull, "The taste *is* in my mouth a little."[46] The month began with Democrats in total collapse. They were forced to adjourn their national nominating convention in Charleston after more than a week of bitter infighting, including a dramatic walkout by southern delegates, and nearly sixty inconclusive ballots for president. In Springfield, Lincoln was growing ever more confident about the "lay of the land" for his own prospects. He told one correspondent that he was heading into the convention with "unanimous" support from Illinois delegates and that the Indiana delegation would "not be difficult to get." Elsewhere, he claimed, "one or another is preferred to me," but hardly anyone had a "positive objection" to him as the party's nominee.[47]

Although Illinois Republicans were more divided than Lincoln indicated, they gave him their hearty endorsement at their state convention in Decatur on May 9, 1860. On that day, Lincoln was introduced to the nation for the first time as "The Rail-splitter." His cousin John Hanks had brought two wooden rails or split logs to the gathering, claiming that they were among thousands that Lincoln had split as a young frontier farmer. When asked, Lincoln demurred on whether he had split the rails but claimed playfully that if not, he was still certain "he had mauled many and many better ones since he had grown to manhood." The biggest fireworks at the convention involved the gubernatorial race, where Norman Judd, Leonard Swett, and Richard Yates battled for the party's support, with Yates emerging as the nominee.[48]

Afterward Lincoln remained focused. "Be careful to give no offence," he advised supporters, "and keep cool under all circumstances." Though he had gone to Decatur, he chose not to attend the national convention in Chicago out of deference to partisan custom. Instead, he worked to coordinate what he could from Springfield. Lincoln used some of his own money to help underwrite travel expenses for supportive delegates but parried most requests for campaign funds. He told one supporter, "I can not enter the ring on the money basis," and to another, even more emphatically, he stated, "I could not raise ten thousand dollars if it would save me from the fate of John Brown."[49]

Just before the Chicago convention was set to begin, Judge David Davis commandeered a hotel suite where Illinois supporters such as Jesse Dubois, Norman Judd, John Palmer, Leonard Swett, and a handful of others coordinated their campaign efforts and entertained delegates. Lincoln started receiving daily and at times almost hourly updates by letter and telegram. Dubois reported at first that there was "great confusion," but that Lincoln had surprising strength and that he had never seen Davis "work so hard and so quick." Lincoln told Wentworth that he kept "no secrets" from Davis, but the judge was not Lincoln's campaign manager in any modern sense. Davis was helpful with his money and a small network of national contacts. And he was certainly friendly with Lincoln, but he did not pretend to manage him. Davis himself had told Lincoln that it was "the wonderful power of John Wentworth" that he should rely upon for his campaign efforts. "You ought to have got him long ago to 'run you,'" Davis concluded. Lincoln knew better. On the eve of the convention, rumors flew that Wentworth, still embittered over his feud with Judd, was lobbying against Lincoln.[50]

On May 14, *Tribune* editor Charles Ray sent Lincoln a "Profoundly Private" note that expressed optimism about the "great success" they were finding with delegates but also warned that "a pledge or two may be necessary when the pinch comes." He urged the candidate to empower "a few trusty friends" (like Davis, Judd, or himself) to make the necessary bargains.[51] But Lincoln authorized no deals and remained at Springfield.

Lincoln's self-appointed operatives in Chicago worked instead to create favorable conditions for a bandwagon effect. They tried to line up early support from friendly delegations like Indiana's while pursuing the second ballot option with delegates from more doubtful states.

The local organizers also manipulated the daily agenda and even the seating arrangements at the convention hall (called the "Wigwam") to aid their favorite-son candidate however they could. They tried to isolate Seward's forces amid large pockets of prominent support for Lincoln. Judd later boasted that the strategic rearrangement of the seating chart was another great feat of his political career.[52]

As the convention opened on Wednesday, May 16, Judd felt confident about Lincoln's chances. He wired the candidate a hasty but positive update: "Dont be frighten[e]d Keep cool things is working."[53] David Wilmot of Pennsylvania served as president pro tem of the gathering. On May 17, the Republican platform committee secured approval for seventeen resolutions that embraced the "permanent" organization of the party, quoted approvingly from the Declaration of Independence, and set out a tough line against the extension of slavery in the western territories while acknowledging the "rights" of existing states to manage their "domestic institutions." The platform included popular but still unrealized regional economic positions, including endorsements for river and harbor improvements, a Pacific railroad, homestead land grants, and a "sound" tariff. It condemned any new or additional restrictions on naturalized citizens and made no direct mention of the Fugitive Slave Law.[54] It was exactly the type of platform that Lincoln had been recommending for months.

The presidential balloting began on the morning of May 18. Working until the last minute, Lincoln's cadre of Illinois backers secured enough support to allow him to finish second to William Seward, the front-runner, in the first round of balloting. Lincoln's forces had originally considered Edward Bates the most formidable anti-Seward candidate. Key figures such as Horace Greeley and Schuyler Colfax supported the Missouri conservative. But during the second round, the pivotal Pennsylvania delegation switched from their own favorite-son candidate—Senator Simon Cameron—to Lincoln, creating a sensation in the Wigwam. The move by Pennsylvania

These daguerreotype portraits of Abraham Lincoln, age thirty-nine, and Mary Todd Lincoln, age twenty-eight, were probably made in the summer of 1847, when he was statewide leader of the Illinois Whig party and they were about to leave for Washington for his only term in Congress. Their oldest son, Robert Lincoln, later recalled that the portraits were kept on display in the parlor of their Springfield, Illinois, home until the family left again for Washington in 1861. Their residence on Eighth and Jackson streets, pictured here in 1860, when Lincoln (outside with two of his younger sons) was a Republican presidential candidate, was the site of several partisan meetings and private receptions that proved critical to his pre-presidential political career. *(Unless otherwise noted, all illustrations are from Library of Congress, Prints & Photographs Division.)*

Lincoln admired Whig founder Henry Clay (top left) but did not support him for their party's presidential nomination in 1848. The cartoon entitled "The Assassination of the Sage of Ashland" depicts Clay's defeat at the Whig convention that year as a political murder orchestrated by conspirators such as Kentucky politician John Crittenden, New York editor Thurlow Weed, and southern abolitionist Cassius Clay (the three men depicted on the far right of the group). Congressman Lincoln was not yet prominent enough to be included. During their famous senatorial debates ten years later, however, Stephen Douglas, a Democrat (top right), blasted Lincoln for having betrayed the Whig party founder in that 1848 contest. Lincoln did not deny the charge but responded by labeling Clay, somewhat defensively, as his "beau ideal of a statesman."

Trapp, A. H. A.N.D. St. Clair
Turner, T. J. A.N.D. Stephenson
Walker, George Do. Hancock
Wheeler, Alonzo K. W. Kendall
Democrats 30
Whigs 28
A.N.D. 14

Abn 1 Of the three last classes, a great many have gone into the Republican Organization
Nebraska Whig 1.
Vacancy 1

During the 1854 elections, Lincoln helped lead an antislavery fusion effort in Illinois composed of former Whigs, Democrats, abolitionists, and nativists. The coalition ultimately became the foundation of the state's Republican party. The photograph above, taken in Chicago during the campaign, shows Lincoln, a former Whig, holding an antislavery Democratic newspaper as a symbol of their unprecedented partisan coordination. Over the winter, Lincoln prepared notebooks detailing the party affiliations of the new state legislators (including 28 "Whigs," 14 "A.N.D." or Anti-Nebraska Democrats, and 1 "Abn" or Abolitionist) who were now caucusing with what he privately labeled near the bottom of the page the "Republican organization." (Left: *Abraham Lincoln Presidential Library and Museum;* right: *Virginius H. Chase Special Collections Center and Bradley University Archives)*

Private & confidential

Springfield, Ills. Dec. 10. 1860
Hon. L. Trumbull.

My dear Sir,

Let there be no compromise on the question of extending slavery— If there be, all our labor is lost, and, ere long, must be done again— The dangerous ground—that into which some of our friends have a hankering to run—is Pop. Sov. Have none of it— Stand firm. The tug has to come, & better now, than any time hereafter—

Yours as ever
A. Lincoln.

As a politician and party leader, Lincoln often communicated with his partisan allies through short, confidential notes that he coded with varying degrees of urgency and confidentiality—including occasionally the phrase "burn this," which at least some of his peers ignored. In this letter from the president-elect to Senator Lyman Trumbull of Illinois, written during the secession crisis of December 1860 and marked "Private & confidential," Lincoln commands his fellow Republicans to accept "no compromise." "The tug has to come," he concluded, "and better now, than any time hereafter." *(Huntington Library, San Marino, California)*

SOME OF LINCOLN'S KEY ILLINOIS ALLIES

David Davis was a conservative Whig from Bloomington who helped Lincoln win the 1860 Republican nomination and served as a U.S. Supreme Court justice during the Civil War.

Norman Judd, a former Chicago Democrat, became chairman of the Illinois Republican party during the 1850s and later a U.S. diplomat in Europe and a key Lincoln administration ally. *(House Divided Project at Dickinson College)*

Owen Lovejoy, a leading northern Illinois abolitionist, served as a Republican and Unionist congressman during the Civil War era.

Elihu Washburne, a former Whig from Galena who helped Lincoln organize both the Republican and Unionist parties, was one of the most senior members of Congress during the Civil War.

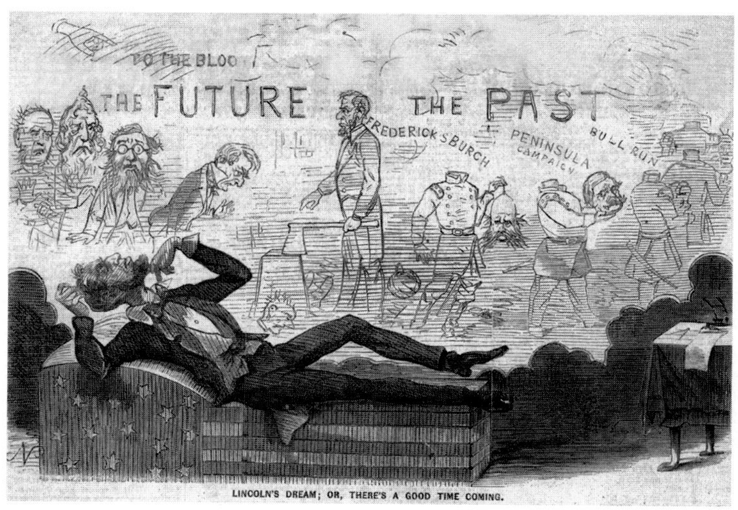

LINCOLN'S DREAM; OR, THERE'S A GOOD TIME COMING.

The 1863 political cartoon "Lincoln's Dream," from the pro-administration *Frank Leslie's Illustrated Newspaper*, depicts the dream of retribution of a president experiencing personnel crises in both his cabinet and the army over the winter of 1862–63. Lincoln survived in part by committing to building a Union party. The dismissed (beheaded) generals are (from left to right) Ambrose Burnside, George McClellan, and Irvin McDowell. The cowering advisers (from left to right) are Henry Halleck, Gideon Welles, Edwin Stanton, and William Seward. *(House Divided Project at Dickinson College)*

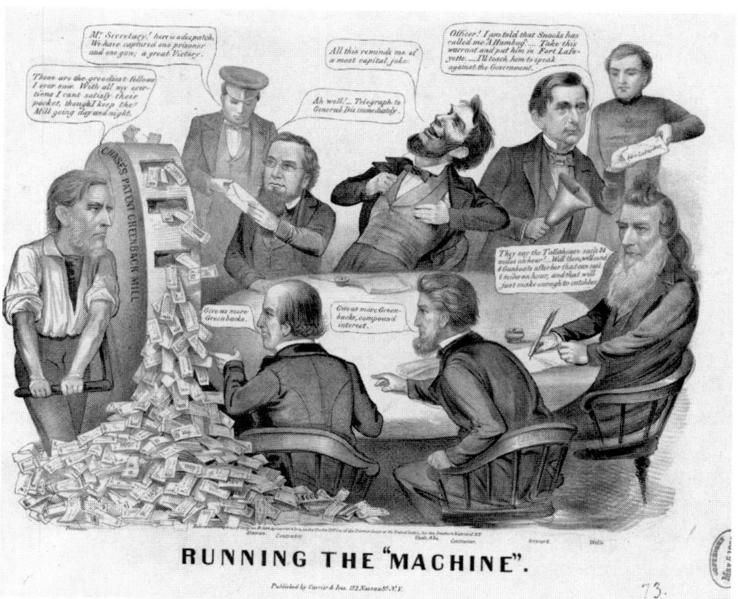

RUNNING THE "MACHINE".

This 1864 cartoon, reflecting a Democratic perspective, depicts Lincoln's administration as corrupt partisan hacks who were unable to win the war because they were too busy enriching themselves and their allies by "Running the Machine."

The dedication of the cemetery at Gettysburg on November 19, 1863, was both a somber occasion and a partisan moment—the only time during the war when so many leading Unionist politicians from across the North gathered together. Some of the key but partially obscured figures surrounding the hatless Lincoln (encircled) likely include Pennsylvania Union party chairman Wayne MacVeagh (labeled 1), White House aides John Hay (2) and John Nicolay (3), Secretary of State William Seward (4), and main orator and former Constitutional Unionist vice-presidential candidate Edward Everett (5).

Samuel Wilkeson, a noted radical and leading war correspondent for the *New York Times*, was not present at the commemoration on November 19, but he had lost a son at the battle of Gettysburg. The resonant closing phrase of Lincoln's dedication address ("a new birth of freedom") evoked a well-known line from Wilkeson's stirring report on the battle ("a second birth of Freedom in America"). *(Smithsonian American Art Museum)*

Executive Mansion
Washington, Aug. 23, 1864.

This morning, as for some days past, it seems exceedingly probable that this Administration will not be re-elected. Then it will be my duty to so co-operate with the President elect, as to save the Union between the election and the inauguration; as he will have secured his election on such ground that he can not possibly save it afterwards.

A. Lincoln

William H. Seward
W. P. Fessenden
Edwin M. Stanton
Gideon Welles
Edw. Bates
M. Blair
J. P. Usher
August 23. 1864.

Lincoln wrote a secret memorandum on August 23, 1864, when he decided not to yield to mounting political pressure but to stay the course with his reelection effort and the larger Unionist party strategy. In case of electoral defeat, however, Lincoln's plan was to show this document to his Democratic opponent—the next president—and try to persuade him to form a bipartisan patriotic coalition "to save the Union between the election and the inauguration," because he did not believe it could be saved otherwise. The image at left shows the memorandum's reverse side, with the signatures of the cabinet officers and the date of their signing, essentially date-stamping a document that they had not read.

made clear that Lincoln, not Bates, was the best-positioned alternative to the Seward machine. Rumors flew that Lincoln's men made illicit deals with Cameron's advisers, but there was nothing that Lincoln's men could have offered Cameron that Seward or Weed would not have matched. And afterward Davis and Swett flatly denied that there had been any corrupt deals. Judd assured Lincoln that no "committals" had been made at Chicago, scoffing at the idea that Davis or any of the other men could have been "secretive" enough to keep such information from him.[55]

The final verdict came quickly on the morning of May 18, after only three rounds of balloting. By afternoon, Lincoln of Illinois and Hannibal Hamlin of Maine were the faces of the Republican party's second national ticket. Word about the balloting results reached Lincoln in Springfield by telegram around noon on the eighteenth. The delegation of party elders came bearing his official nomination the next day, a beautiful Saturday afternoon, where they reportedly enjoyed nothing more than glasses of cold water at the bustling Lincoln home at Eighth and Jackson streets. The candidate and his wife made pleasant conversation with the delegation, and Lincoln accepted the nomination. Just thirteen years before, Judge Davis had been in the same parlor, staring at the daguerreotype portraits of the Lincolns, quietly mocking his new friend's rumpled demeanor, and musing about Mary Lincoln's desire to "loom largely" in Washington.[56]

To many, the news of Lincoln's selection was startling. An attorney from Springfield, Illinois, was about to become the nation's chief executive. On this point, most political insiders agreed. Following the Democratic implosion in Charleston in May, the Republican party had moved into a commanding political position. The Democratic rupture did not become final until June 1860, but the rift between northern and southern Democrats had appeared both irreparable and fatal even before the Republicans met at Chicago. Northern Democrats soon formed their own party and nominated Stephen Douglas as their candidate, with former Georgia governor Herschel Johnson as his running mate. Southern Democrats chose Buchanan's vice president, thirty-nine-year-old John Breckinridge of Kentucky, along with Senator Joseph Lane of Oregon, as their ticket. Neither Democratic ticket seemed to have a viable path toward national victory.

Among the nation's conservative elites there was chatter about the need to rally a patriotic alternative to what they viewed as the dangerously sectional partisan choices, but such appeals gained little popular traction. Only in Kentucky, Virginia, and a few other Upper South states where the so-called Southern Opposition or former Whig forces had been active during the late 1850s, was there any discernible energy behind what became known as the Constitutional Union party. This new pro-compromise coalition did succeed in pulling together a national ticket composed of sixty-four-year-old Senator John Bell of Tennessee and noted orator and former Whig politician Edward Everett of Massachusetts, who was even older than Bell. But the Constitutional Unionists were formidable in only a handful of southern states.[57]

The result was a messy four-way race. There was always uncertainty in such a complicated contest, but heading into the summer, expectations for the Republicans were sky high. Lincoln's friends often expressed astonishment at his sudden prominence. "You can hardly imagine, and I am sure I can not describe my feelings," wrote Joshua Speed, Lincoln's best friend from his bachelor days, "when I saw by the papers this morning that you were a Candidate for the Presidency."[58]

"Cant you come & see us?" Speed asked Lincoln wistfully from his plantation in Kentucky. But however heartfelt, it was still an empty gesture from an old Whig ally and future Bell supporter who considered himself a "political opponent" of his former roommate.[59] A journey to the slaveholding South would have been a grave mistake. Lincoln could not risk traveling outside Sangamon County, let alone to Kentucky, mainly out of political calculation. As the Republican standard-bearer, Lincoln was expected to stay put and keep quiet. There was plenty of campaign work to be done, but the candidate was discouraged from participating—at least openly—in any of it. Shortly after the national convention, Republican organizers began blitzing Springfield with photographers, portrait artists, and campaign biographers. All were rushing in to help polish the candidate's image at the outset of a busy general election campaign. Lincoln himself was supposed to project the dignity of a man who was standing—not running—for the mantle of General Washington. Such feigned reticence was no longer required for other political contests, as Lincoln and Douglas had recently proven in their groundbreaking U.S. Senate race, but it was still the norm for presidential candidates. Some candidates had challenged elements of this lingering eighteenth-century custom, most notably losing Whig candidates Henry Clay and Winfield Scott, but the perception was that they suffered for it.[60]

Lincoln's closest friends took the lead in promoting or "booming" his virtues. At the end of May, Rep. Elihu Washburne helped launch the campaign for "Old Abe" with a fulsome biographical speech delivered on the House floor. Republicans turned those remarks into a popular campaign pamphlet. Calling Lincoln "emphatically a representative man," Washburne emphasized his friend's sound political views and sharp oratorical skills over biographical details. "He has doctrines, not hatreds," Washburne concluded, "and is without ambition, except to do good, and serve his country."[61]

For his part, Lincoln stopped practicing law, delivered no formal speeches, and did not venture beyond Springfield for the rest of the 1860 contest. But he remained full of leadership ambitions. Almost nothing proved too trivial for the candidate's attention. Lincoln even disputed an expensive hotel bill not long after the convention, announcing, "I do not wish to be 'diddled'!"[62] Nervous about avoiding mistakes, Lincoln spent significant time supervising the most minor projects. He could be finicky, even arguing points of grammar with a Republican lawyer from New York who was trying to publish Lincoln's well-received Cooper Union speech from February 1860. In other cases, however, the candidate intervened with a larger strategic purpose. In June, Lincoln drafted his longest autobiographical statement yet for John Locke Scripps of the *Chicago Press and Tribune.* One of the main goals of this effort was to help smooth over the details of Lincoln's shift from Whig to Republican.[63]

The need to reassure former Whig conservatives preoccupied the new Republican candidate. "Like yourself I belonged to the whig party from it's origin to it's close," Lincoln wrote to Samuel Haycraft of Kentucky, an aging local politician who had known his father and stepmother and who had written to the nominee. The problem was that Haycraft had been a true Henry Clay Whig, far more like conservative John Todd Stuart than the fusionist-minded Lincoln had ever been. The two men differed over slavery, though neither was inclined to admit it. Lincoln avoided the subject until Haycraft encouraged him (as Speed had done) to visit his birthplace. To this offer, the "Black Republican" joked grimly, "Would not the people Lynch me?" Haycraft indicated a clear animus for the "Ultra abolitionists of the North" but politely held them apart from the son of his former neighbors.[64]

For most of the summer, such outreach seemed to be working well. Lincoln even joked with reporters about deflecting requests to visit Kentucky—until a damaging version of his comments appeared in the *New York Herald.* In August a correspondent for the nation's leading Democratic newspaper reported as fact that "Judge Lynch" had threatened the Republican nominee, and that Lincoln and his advisers were afraid any invitation to journey southward was "a trap laid by some designing person." Concerned and embarrassed, Lincoln apologized to Haycraft in private and then tried to get a correction placed in the *Herald*, but editor James Gordon Bennett refused to do so without identifying Lincoln himself as the source. This was a price that neither the candidate nor his handlers were willing to pay. "I prefer letting it run it's course," Lincoln seethed to his advisers, "[than] to getting into the papers over my own name."[65]

Lincoln expected his political activities to be kept quiet and grew angry with any violations of that unwritten rule. He provided confidential interviews for a campaign biography being prepared by William Dean Howells, a young magazine writer fast growing in national acclaim. But when the Ohio firm behind the project started marketing the volume as an "authorized" edition, Lincoln grew noticeably perturbed. "I *authorized nothing*," the candidate wrote in an "Especially Confidential" note to his longtime Ohio supporter Samuel Galloway. Why should he lend official credence to "a volume of a hundred pages, for adversaries to make points upon without end," asked Lincoln, "when, by the lessons of the past, and the united voice of all discreet friends, I am neither [to] write or speak a word for the public"?[66]

During the summer of 1860, William Herndon reported that his longtime law partner had become "bored—*bored* badly" by his muted public role as a presidential candidate. That may have been true, but Lincoln remained busy. With the help of John Nicolay, the full-time campaign aide who had replaced organizer John Johnson, now returned to New York, he spent most of his summer days powering through the campaign's vast and growing national correspondence. By Herndon's own account, Lincoln was also conducting a steady stream of personal meetings with "many visitors," practically "Every hour" and "from all sections."[67] The majority of these face-to-face encounters were little more than staged performances, but they could be draining. Lincoln described one such episode to his Bloomington ally David Davis, observing dryly how Thurlow Weed, William Seward's designated emissary, had come to Springfield in late May, seeming "merely to desire a chance of looking at me, keeping up a show of talk while he was at it," before departing, according to Lincoln, "satisfied."[68]

Republican organizers like Weed were hard to keep satisfied, though. An undercurrent of grousing came from nearly every faction, especially those in vital electoral prizes like New York and Pennsylvania. The toughest challenges involved winning over former Whigs and Americans who seemed uncertain about where to affiliate within the fractured political order. In Pennsylvania, party regulars were so concerned about scaring away such conservatives that they even rejected the Republican label and billed themselves as a more fusionist-oriented People's party. David Davis and Leonard Swett typically got dispatched to placate any anxious conservatives. Swett had joined the earlier meeting with Weed and kept Lincoln aware of the subsequent contacts he was making with old Fillmore loyalists in upstate New York. The candidate reviewed Swett's draft communications and occasionally provided comments, often emphasizing his intention to rely on "*fairness* and fairness only" in the perennial quest for Republican unity. He urged the Bloomington lawyer to "keep up a correspondence" with Weed and others but also wanted his interest in this delicate intraparty business to remain quiet, noting in one exchange, "Burn this, not that there is anything wrong in it; but because it is best not to be known that I write at all."[69]

"Burn this" was also the way Lincoln closed a private note to Richard Thompson, a nativist and former American party organizer from Indiana. During that summer, Thompson was supposedly aligned with the Constitutional Unionists and their nominee John Bell, but since late May the Indiana politician had also been conducting a secret correspondence with Lincoln at the Republican candidate's initiative. By midsummer, Thompson was offering to help Republicans co-opt the emerging Bell movement within his state, but he did not want his role exposed to the public. Thompson had served with Lincoln in Congress and had once supported him for the Land

Office position. "I have to manage the matter with exceeding delicacy & could do nothing," Thompson wrote, "if I were to avow openly my ulterior object." The Springfield party boss understood the need for such discretion. He even allowed Thompson to convey to Indiana Constitutional Unionists that he would never be "led into ultraism by Radical men," as Thompson framed it, and that his administration would remain firmly "national." This was not the message of the House Divided speech or even the 1860 Republican platform, but Lincoln seemed to consider it a useful strategic prescription for the moment.[70]

Thompson grew nervous about their covert scheming and eventually insisted that Lincoln start addressing his letters to someone else in Terre Haute to avoid a snooping postmaster. He also asked to meet in person "to talk about some things you ought not to write about." By mid-July, Lincoln decided to send Nicolay to Indiana to communicate with Thompson directly. He was adamant that he wanted his twenty-eight-year-old assistant to proceed with such a high-stakes negotiation. He dictated a set of conditions that, in Nicolay's tightly composed notes, appear almost as a pair of elegant haikus on nineteenth-century power politics:

> Ascertain what he wants.
> On what subjects he would converse with me.
> And the particulars if he will give them.
>
> Is an interview indispensable?
> Tell him my motto is "Fairness to all,"
> But commit me to nothing.[71]

Lincoln sent Nicolay to deal with ex–Know Nothings in Indiana just before he held an equally important private encounter of his own with Carl Schurz, a leading German-born Republican from Wisconsin. Schurz had gone to the Chicago convention as a Seward delegate, but he was also friendly with Lincoln and sent him a polite note afterward explaining away his initial preference for the New Yorker, whom he respectfully labeled the "old chieftain of the Anti-slavery movement." Schurz appeared eager to gain Lincoln's approval for a plan he was developing to help Republican mobilization efforts among immigrant voters. The convention delegates had named the thirty-one-year-old as a member of the party's national committee, charged with organizing a "foreign department." After the convention, Schurz approached Lincoln for guidance about this mission because, as he put it, "you are now the natural center towards which everything converges and from which everything radiates."[72]

Somehow that important request had gone unanswered among the "multitudes" of communications that had inundated Lincoln following his nomination. When Illinois Republican and German-born leader Gustave Koerner reproached Lincoln for such an inexcusable oversight, the candidate apologized profusely. Lincoln then assured Schurz in writing that previous support for other Republican contenders was "not even remembered by me for any practical purpose."[73] But near the end of July, when Schurz finally arrived in Springfield to speak at a bilingual campaign rally, Lincoln made sure to cultivate him in person. Schurz described their impromptu meeting in a letter written in German to his wife, Margarethe. He expressed himself as amazed that the nominee had shown up at his hotel room unannounced. The two men ended up talking for almost two hours that afternoon. Their conversation represents one of the best snapshots of Lincoln as a candidate and party leader.[74]

During their discussion, Lincoln appeared "calm and easy," according to Schurz, almost "as if the matter under concern were a potato crop." The candidate admitted he was already "overwhelmed" by patronage requests but suggested that such "clamorous" grasping for spoils disgusted him. Lincoln vowed to be "a tough customer" for "those who do nothing." "Men like you," he assured Schurz, "who have real merit and do the work, are always too proud to ask for anything." This was not so true of Schurz, whom most of his peers regarded as a chronic self-promoter, but it was surely an effective way to forestall premature job requests. "I shall know how to distinguish deserving men from the drones," Lincoln warned darkly. This term *drones* was apparently a favorite of his, one that he had employed in similar discussions over patronage matters in the past. Schurz came away impressed by all the bravado. As he confided to his wife, he immediately thought: "All right, Old Abe."[75]

That night Schurz dined with the Lincoln family at their home. The men then joined a boisterous contingent of militia-style supporters known as "Wide Awakes" and marched over to the torchlit state capitol, where Schurz gave a passionate campaign address in both German and English. It was a memorable experience for Schurz, who later recounted an embellished version of the story in his memoirs. He might have been even more impressed with Lincoln and his hard-edged professionalism if he had been aware that, at nearly the same time, one of the candidate's top aides was secretly cultivating a prominent nativist in neighboring Indiana.

On top of his work as an organizer of German immigrant voters, Schurz was a rising leader among antislavery radicals. Both groups needed careful tending that summer for Republicans to succeed. Lincoln's law partner Herndon tried to address radical concerns about the candidate. When the Boston abolitionist Wendell Phillips attacked Lincoln in the columns of *The Liberator* as "the slave hound of Illinois," over his alleged support for fugitive slave rendition, Herndon moved to quash the criticism. In August he wrote to Sydney Howard Gay, a former Garrisonian abolitionist then working for Greeley's *Tribune*, with a detailed explanation of Lincoln's positions on slavery, including the fugitive slave provision that he had written into his own failed Washington, DC, emancipation bill from 1849. Herndon offered Gay an unqualified endorsement of Lincoln's "radical heart," claiming his partner had been "a strong Anti-Slavery man" in Congress "and is now the same." Pointing to the inevitable compromises of the political process, Herndon wrote memorably, "His heart is better than his platform."[76] During the 1860 contest, most Garrisonian abolitionists remained skeptical about such claims. Some antislavery radicals even continued to support remnants of the Liberty party, which was still limping along in a handful of northern states with New Yorker Gerrit Smith as their official presidential nominee.

Any unity challenges Republicans might have been facing that summer paled, however, in comparison to the organizational catastrophe looming before the Democrats. Not only had the southern bolters ruined the attempted Douglas nomination at Charleston, but by early July, incumbent President Buchanan had decided to cast his lot with the party's rebels, effectively endorsing Vice President Breckinridge as the true Democratic nominee.[77] This decision extended Democratic party divisions deep into the North, as Buchanan loyalists began dutifully organizing Breckinridge electoral tickets across several key northern states. The multiplying challenges compelled Douglas to blast both Republicans and Southern Democrats as like-minded extremists, while trying to promote a fusion between Northern Democrats and Constitutional Unionists. If successful, the strategy might have prevented Lincoln and the Republicans from securing an electoral majority, creating opportunities for Douglas in the subsequent state-by-state congressional balloting required by constitutional rules. "We should treat the Bell & Everett men friendly and cultivate good relations with them, for they are Union men," the senator wrote to his Springfield confidant, editor Charles Lanphier. "If the election goes to the Ho[use] of Reps, Lincoln, Bell and myself will be the *three* highest."[78] But the odds against achieving such a fusion were daunting, impelling Douglas to become the first American presidential candidate to stump openly for office.

Douglas took to the campaign trail in his usual no-holds-barred style, despite the traditions tilting against such partisan combat from presidential nominees. He repeatedly attacked "Black Republicans," just as he had done during the 1858 senatorial campaign, but also directed venom at the incumbent president who had abandoned him. Recalling their last face-to-face meeting at the White House in December 1857, Douglas claimed in July that the president had threatened, "if I did not obey him and vote to force that Lecompton Constitution on the people of Kansas against their will, that he would take off the head of every friend that I had in office."[79] Douglas said he had dismissed such an outrageous bullying tactic by announcing, "if I had a friend who was not willing to lose his office rather than to degrade me into a tool of the Executive power, he did not deserve to be my friend."[80]

Buchanan was offended by this grandstanding. "I never held any such conversation with Judge Douglas," the president wrote in an August letter that was leaked to friendly Democratic newspapers, claiming it was "not in my nature to address such threatening and insulting language to any gentleman." In private, however, the thin-skinned president assailed his party rival, observing archly to several colleagues that the senator's father-in-law and brother-in-law both held "lucrative offices" in his administration.[81] American politicians feuded all the time in this turbulent era, but there was something wildly unprecedented about the public spectacle of this intraparty brawl. Even Buchanan conceded as much. "I have transgressed a rule," he admitted sheepishly, before explaining how "the present case [was] a proper exception," because Douglas's extraordinary statement had come "with such force."[82]

In Springfield, Lincoln felt uneasy about the growing boldness of the Douglas strategy. He came to believe that his longtime Democratic rival was playing a false and yet potentially effective game. "Douglas is managing the Bell-element with great adroitness," Lincoln confided to Thurlow Weed in August. He expressed concern that Douglas Democrats were secretly propping up Constitutional Unionist candidates in places like Kentucky to damage the Breckinridge forces and to give the sectional moderates false hope. He suspected it was part of a design to manipulate the Bell men toward fusion in more critical electoral states like New York.[83]

Lincoln still retained an underlying confidence. "The thing starts well everywhere," he observed in May, warning his supporters only that they should expect some kind of "back-set yet."[84] By mid-July, he was boasting to old friend Dr. Anson Henry, now an Oregon resident, that "it looks as if the Chicago ticket will be elected."[85] A few weeks later he described the anticipated Republican triumph as "inevitable" in a friendly, though private, exchange with the formerly disgruntled *Illinois Journal* editor Simeon Francis, who had also settled in Oregon.[86]

Lincoln never grew complacent, however. He had been warning Seward's man Weed from the outset that Democrats were going to "require close watching," and he maintained this stance throughout the campaign. That summer he quietly beat back several false charges made regarding his record.[87] He also repeatedly pestered Republican organizers across the country to stay focused on turnout, demanding to know, for example, if People's party chairman Alexander McClure in Pennsylvania was being diligent enough about mobilization efforts. "When you say you are organizing every election district," the nominee queried the state party leader, "do you mean to include the idea that you are 'canvassing'—'counting noses?' "[88]

Lincoln focused on the Republican party's success as well as his own election. In July, he contacted his vice-presidential nominee Hannibal Hamlin, a man whom he had never actually met before, about apparent problems in Maine's congressional campaigns. Informing the Maine senator that he was "annoyed" by such unexpectedly grim news from Republican-dominated New England, Lincoln remarked simply, "You must not allow it."[89] The next month the busy presidential candidate took the time to chase down a Republican organizer from Vermilion County in eastern Illinois, to spur him to deal with reported "trouble" in a state legislative contest there, lest it adversely affect U.S. senator Lyman Trumbull's reelection contest in 1861.[90]

Republican overconfidence was one of the party's main challenges in 1860, according to U.S. senator Henry Wilson of Massachusetts. The New Englander tried to convey a wake-up call to Springfield in late August, not long after he finished delivering almost two dozen major campaign speeches across the North. Wilson noted that while Republican popular enthusiasm seemed high, party organization appeared to be falling into a state of "neglect." "Do not trust to these mass meetings entirely," the senator urged. "Press action upon our National Committee." Lincoln had recently attended what he called one of those "monster meetings" at the Springfield fairground on August 9 (his first such public event since watching Schurz speak in July), but he agreed with the necessity of maintaining "thorough organization." Lincoln complained to Wilson that far too many of their friends found this essential political work "dry" and "irksome labor." "I do what I can in my position, for organization," Lincoln assured him, "but it does not amount to so much as it should."[91]

Concerned by these scattered reports of trouble, Lincoln decided in September that he needed to gather better information. He began a secret and politically risky correspondence with John Pettit, a federal judge in the Kansas territory and an estranged former ally of Douglas. Pettit shared that he was hearing how Douglas's attempts to build an anti-Republican "fusion" in New York were falling short. Intrigued, Lincoln asked the noted Breckinridge supporter to "name the sources of your information." Lincoln admitted he was worried, despite receiving "a good deal of news" predicting his party's success in that critical state. Pettit declined to identify his informants but assured the Republican nominee that "the fusion is not & cannot be made perfect." What made this brief written exchange so noteworthy was that in the mid-1850s Lincoln had vilified Pettit, then a Democratic U.S. senator from Indiana, for having declared on the Senate floor that the phrase "all men are created equal" was "a self-evident lie." Despite his disdain for Pettit's indifference to the principles of natural rights, Lincoln was willing to engage a leading Democrat to secure vital information about the high-stakes political landscape.[92]

Another sign of Lincoln's last-minute anxiety came early in October, when William Seward passed through Springfield. The New York senator had just launched a long-delayed western speaking tour for the Republican ticket but was planning to skip a visit with his party's nominee until rumors of lingering tension between the former rivals compelled a show of unity. It was not much of a show. Seward never left the railroad depot when he arrived in town on October 1, 1860. Their meeting lasted only minutes, but Lincoln had an important point to convey. The Republican candidate wanted Seward to alter his stump speech, to reiterate their party's long-standing principle of noninterference with slavery in the existing slave states. Seward reported a few days later, somewhat defensively, that he had tried to accomplish this shift during a subsequent speech at Chicago by addressing the point "which had given you uneasiness," but he admitted that he was unsure "how successfully I met your wishes."[93]

Lincoln's worries diminished after October 9, when Republicans won sweeping victories in state and congressional contests across Indiana, Iowa, Minnesota, Ohio, and Pennsylvania. The lopsided results in Indiana and Pennsylvania were especially noteworthy, because Republicans had lost both states in the 1856 presidential contest. "It now really looks as if the Government is about to fall into our hands," Lincoln reported almost gleefully to Seward. Most Republican leaders agreed with this assessment. There was still the dim prospect that an anti-Republican fusion in New York could deprive Republicans of the all-important state and throw a stalemated presidential election in November over to the House of Representatives. But for all practical purposes, Lincoln became a president-in-waiting in mid-October.[94]

This meant that Stephen Douglas was facing his first defeat as a general election candidate since 1838, when he had lost a congressional race to John Todd Stuart at the age of twenty-five. A younger Lincoln had had a hand in that outcome, whipping up support for his senior law partner by warning everyone not to "relax an *iota*." It had taken over two decades, but Douglas was finally being outworked and outmaneuvered once again. The senator had been campaigning vigorously since July, despite signs of the failing health that would kill him in June 1861. Douglas had traveled across the New England states, through the Great Lakes region, and into a handful of states in the Upper South, but it had not been enough to overcome the crippling divisions within his own party.[95]

After he died, Douglas loyalists claimed that once the Democratic candidate had learned about the disappointing results from the October states, he altered his speaking schedule in the campaign's closing weeks to devote his efforts toward preventing secession. "Mr. Lincoln is the next President," he reportedly told his private secretary, James Sheridan. "We must try to save the Union. I will go South."[96] But that is not quite what Douglas did. The Democrat spent most of the rest of the month in the North so that he could exact some revenge on the partisan rival whom he had come to despise more than anyone else—President James Buchanan.

Douglas began his final assault on the troubled Democratic incumbent on October 13 at an outdoor rally in Milwaukee, Wisconsin, where he gave one of the more dramatic speeches in nineteenth-century American political history. The combative senator was in a foul mood. He began by acknowledging that he had received a copy of the previous day's *Chicago Tribune*, which he dismissed as an "Abolitionist newspaper," and announced that he would depart from his prepared remarks to address the newspaper's allegations that he was the mastermind behind the 1857 Lecompton swindle.[97]

This was a recycled accusation from December 1857, when the Buchanan-Douglas feud over Kansas territorial policy had originally erupted. Now, however, former Lecompton convention delegates were willing to put their allegations into print for the Breckinridge campaign.[98] Labeling the charge "false in every particular," Douglas unleashed an angry account of his "personal history" with the Kansas territory and its Lecompton controversy. He also provided new first-hand details of his now-legendary confrontation with Buchanan at the White House in December 1857. Douglas assured his audience that he had responded to Buchanan's attempt at bullying by coolly reminding him, "General Jackson is dead, sir."[99]

The cascade of last-minute charges concerning the Democratic feuds over Kansas policy revealed the surprisingly durable impact of the Lecompton crisis on the politics of the 1860 campaign. The Kansas-Nebraska Act of 1854 and its divisive repeal of the Missouri Compromise had been the great partisan turning point for most former Whigs like Lincoln and Seward. But it was the Buchanan-Douglas rupture over the Kansas territory during the winter of 1857–58 that had proved to be the main force behind the Democratic party's collapse. Douglas knew it better than anyone. That is why he felt compelled to deliver a heroic version of the story for posterity, both at Milwaukee and again a week later, at a speech in Springfield, Illinois. He clearly wanted to get his partisan record straight before he ventured down south to save the union.[100]

At a reception following the senator's campaign speech in Springfield, the organizers "expected *hundreds*," gossiped Mary Lincoln afterward, but instead found their turnout "only numbered thirty." She observed tartly that for the Little Giant, it was "as if his greatness had passed away."[101]

While Douglas flailed about in his bitter party feud, Lincoln was engaging in a whimsical correspondence with a young girl from New York. Grace Bedell, an eleven-year-old from upstate New York, had written to "Hon A.B. Lincoln" on October 15, 1860, just after her father, a loyal Republican businessman, brought home a popular lithograph depicting the Lincoln-Hamlin ticket. In her letter, Grace called this campaign image "very pretty," framed as it was by an ornate rail fence, but she suggested to the candidate that "if you will let your whiskers grow . . . you would look a great deal better" because, as she frankly noted, "your face is so thin." Amused, Lincoln replied to Grace on October 19, the day after Douglas's Springfield speech, answering the young girl's questions about his family ("I regret the necessity of saying I have no daughters") and adding, "As to the whiskers, having never worn any, do you not think people would call it a piece of silly affectation if I were to begin it now?"[102]

For most of their careers, Lincoln had been chasing after Douglas, scrambling from a position of perennial partisan disadvantage. With less than three weeks remaining before the election, their roles were reversed. The turnabout reflected the state of their respective parties. Lincoln had spent much of the previous decade cultivating organizational unity among the Republican party's contentious antislavery politicians. The labor was often tedious, but his relentless efforts proved successful. "Work, work, work, is the main thing" was Lincoln's motto.[103] Douglas was quite driven himself, but too often he seemed to lack his rival's steadiness. Time and again the pugnacious Democrat had proved to be an unpredictable opportunist with a vindictive streak and a painfully thin skin. Under his leadership during the 1850s, the Democratic party had imploded multiple times. By 1860, it was clear that the strategic choices of the previous decade had made all the difference for these two talented Illinois politicians.

The impending Republican victory, however, came with its own set of dangers. By mid-October, Lincoln was facing renewed pressure from northern conservatives to conciliate the South for the sake of avoiding sectional war. He appeared unwilling to consider it. Ever since his national speaking tours in 1859 and 1860, he had viewed calls for conciliation with suspicion, considering them signs of weakness rather than real efforts at compromise. The prospect of Republican national victory changed nothing for Lincoln. In the final days of the presidential campaign, the candidate dismissed the value of expressing "conservative views and intentions" to the "good men of the South." It would do absolutely no good, he claimed. "I have also *bad* men to deal with, both North and South," he confided, noting ominously, "I intend keeping my eye on upon these gentlemen." This was not mere bluster. Just days earlier Lincoln had written to General David Hunter, a former Chicago resident stationed at Fort Leavenworth, asking the military man to keep him "apprize[d]" of any suspicious movement by southern officers in the army.[104]

One of the most persistent voices in Lincoln's ear urging conciliation was Truman Smith of Connecticut, the once-influential Whig organizer with whom he had worked on behalf of Zachary Taylor in 1848. On the eve of the 1860 presidential balloting, Smith sent an urgent message to Springfield warning of financial catastrophe in the East without some clear postelection statement by Lincoln endorsing the cause of national unity and compromise. The Republican nominee listened but agreed to nothing. "If I should be elected," Lincoln stated without equivocation, "[my] first duty to the Country would be to stand by the men who elected me."[105]

Lincoln was not alone in holding on to such feelings of grim determination. Across the country, millions of white men—and also some thousands of eligible Black voters—walked into their polling places on Tuesday, November 6, 1860, with a hardened sense of purpose, casting their ballots openly, in the custom of the day, cut straight from partisan newspapers.[106] On the main issue of the contest, Republicans stood for declaring slavery wrong and for containing it, in the hope that southern states would eventually abolish the institution on their own as northern states had done. Southern Democrats endorsed slavery as a social good and a constitutionally protected property right, arguing for its expansion and continued influence over national affairs. Northern Democrats responded to this collision of principles by promoting Douglas's "popular sovereignty" as the only practical path forward, while otherwise trying to deflect attention from the slavery problem with full-throated appeals to white supremacy. Constitutional Unionists seemed the most committed to achieving a compromise over slavery's future, wrapping their campaign around sweeping patriotic appeals—and also some nativist slurs. Even if most loyal Americans still hoped for and perhaps expected a peaceful arrangement over the fate of slavery, anyone could foresee the potential for political catastrophe and escalating violence.

In response to these high stakes, turnout among the six million eligible voters in 1860 exceeded 80 percent, the highest popular participation ever recorded to that time. Lincoln achieved a clear victory of 180 votes in the Electoral College, or 59 percent of the total. He won across the North and in nearly all the doubtful states that Republicans had lost in 1856—Illinois, Indiana, and Pennsylvania—while splitting New Jersey with the Northern Democrats. The triumph was so sweeping that Lincoln would have prevailed even if all three of his opponents had been able to combine in perfect fusion. Despite his electoral majority, the Republican standard-bearer secured just under 40 percent of the national popular vote, about 1.9 million ballots out of roughly 4.7 million cast. Almost all that support came from the northern and western free states. The Republican ticket received only some 26,000 ballots scattered across five Upper South slave states. Douglas came in second in the national popular vote, with over one million supporters, but he failed miserably in the Electoral College, netting only 12 electoral votes from a single state (Missouri), which he had won by just 140 popular votes. The rest of the contests across the Upper South had also been extremely close, pitting Breckinridge's

Southern Democratic supporters against Bell's Constitutional Unionists. In an ominous sign, Breckinridge and the fire-eating Southern Democrats won eleven of the nation's fifteen slave states, with landslides across most of the Deep or cotton South.[107]

In Illinois, Lincoln won in Springfield but did not carry Sangamon, his home county, losing by a narrow margin to Douglas and the Northern Democrats. Nor did it seem at first that Republicans had won enough districts to overturn likely Democratic majorities in the U.S. House and Senate. The new administration was facing the prospect of divided government. Even worse, the same proslavery Taney Court that had ruled against Dred Scott (1857) was still holding sway over the federal judiciary. The country appeared hopelessly fractured.

In Columbia, South Carolina, as the national results came in on election night, one of the state's leading congressmen, William Boyce, speaking to a boisterous crowd in front of the state capitol, offered a scathing assessment of the long-anticipated Republican victory. Calling the "Black Republicans" a "*party which hates us*" because it was so thoroughly "sectional" and was "founded upon a principle destructive to our social system," Boyce called on white southerners to prepare to "resist." "The way to create a revolution," he snarled, "is to start it." Although once regarded as a sectional moderate, Boyce had been making angry statements since the summer. In August, the *New York Times* highlighted his warning about secession under the headline "ANOTHER DISUNION BLAST." "The vital principle of this [Republican] party is negro equality," he charged during a pro-Breckinridge speech, adding, "the only logical finale of which is emancipation." Boyce admitted that he had once been a cooperationist, someone who supported regional unity and had for years been urging "consummate prudence" on southern states, but now he claimed that the situation had changed. "If the Republican Party triumph in the Presidential election," he warned during the campaign, "our State has no choice but to immediately withdraw from the Union." On election night, he repeated that admonition with greater gusto. Urging his listeners "to dare! to dare!! to dare!!!" an enraged Boyce thrilled the crowd by announcing that "to submit to Lincoln's election, is to consent to a lingering death."[108]

For a respected South Carolinian such as Boyce to frame the nation's partisan war as being unresolved after an election marked an ominous departure from political custom. Conservatives regarded such sectional radicalism as a disunion threat of a different magnitude than what had come before. They began practically begging for national conciliation. The question was whether Lincoln, who often presented himself as a conservative, might in this moment of crisis for American democracy finally start to listen to them.

PART III

UNIONIST

What I *cannot* do, of course I *will* not do; but it may as well be understood, once [and] for all, that I shall not surrender this game leaving any available card unplayed.

—Abraham Lincoln, age fifty-three (July 26, 1862)

9 LINCOLN'S UNION

(1860–1861)

Abraham Lincoln never responded to the angry election night threats from South Carolina, but the president-elect was himself in an unyielding mood. Writing to former congressman Truman Smith of Connecticut after his victory, Lincoln observed that Republicans had done more than enough to prove their moderate intentions, and that anything else would appear "wanting in self-respect." "I am not at liberty to shift my ground," he wrote to another correspondent, predicting that if southern fire-eaters ever came to believe that he was "alarmed," they would simply "clamor all the louder." In face-to-face encounters, Lincoln also conveyed calm resolve. He liked to deflect anxious visitors by saying, "Ah! You have not read my speeches. Let me make you a present of my speeches."[1]

But Lincoln was less settled about men than measures. He later recalled that, unable to sleep on election night, he tinkered with potential lineups for his prospective cabinet. On a small card, he penciled in two columns with eight leading Republican names. The first column contained former Whigs: Lincoln, William Seward, Edward Bates, and William Dayton. The second column featured former Democrats: Norman Judd, Salmon Chase, Montgomery Blair, and Gideon Welles. It was a slate designed to highlight party balance, and it was a pretty good prediction. Five of the seven cabinet appointments eventually came from this late-night list.[2]

Within the two weeks following the November election, Lincoln broke his self-imposed isolation and ventured up to Chicago for a series of meetings about personnel matters. It was his first trip outside Springfield since his nomination in May. Mary Lincoln came along so the couple could finally meet Vice President–Elect Hannibal Hamlin and his wife. The Lincolns also toured the Wigwam building where the Republicans had nominated the Lincoln-Hamlin ticket and enjoyed a series of public receptions. Lincoln's longtime Kentucky friend Joshua Speed and his wife Fanny joined the excursion. Although there were several private meetings during the trip with Senator Lyman Trumbull and other top Republicans, nothing got resolved at Chicago.[3] The final makeup of the cabinet remained unsettled over the next three months of transition and escalating crisis.

WHILE IN THE CITY, Lincoln sat for a photographic portrait that captured the president-elect with a growing beard, neatly trimmed and just beginning to sprawl upward on his cheeks, a hint of the iconic image to come.[4] Lincoln had teased the young Grace Bedell when she first suggested "whiskers" during the campaign, but he clearly understood the power of personal image as he prepared to enter the White House. As president, he would sit for numerous photographers, producing dozens of portraits that made him the nation's first photography president. Until his death in 1865, the nation's first subject also spent dozens of hours working with artists and sculptors. More than once he even dipped his face and hands into plaster to assist with precise casts. As a rising politician, he had never been indifferent to image making, but once he became a national party leader, he helped transform a minor campaign practice into a presidential norm.[5]

But image making was secondary to prosaic matters such as how to achieve party unity by balancing contending factions in the new administration. Just days following the Electoral College balloting that confirmed his victory, Lincoln began the coalition-building process by attempting to name former rival Seward as his nominee for secretary of state. On December 8, 1860, he reached out to senators Hamlin and Trumbull so they could help arrange the formal offer to their colleague. It was a delicate operation, because the president-elect correctly guessed that his rival might try to decline. Both Seward, an inveterate politician with his "perpetual cigar," in the words of New England intellectual Henry Adams, and Thurlow Weed, Seward's moody political fixer, had been loyal to the party during the campaign, but they now appeared alienated, concerned that their influence was waning.[6] Lincoln was diplomatic in his overtures, extolling Seward's "integrity, ability, learning, and great experience," but he conceded nothing about other cabinet appointments, only reiterating his "maxim" about "Justice to all."[7] Unimpressed by such apparent even-handedness, Seward asked for more time to consider the offer, and his decision dragged out for weeks.[8]

Seward's thinking was complicated by uncertainty about the fate of the party's other leading men, such as Governor Salmon Chase of Ohio and Senator Simon Cameron of Pennsylvania. Both were gifted but controversial politicians. Chase could be rigid and cold, almost haughty, as Lincoln had experienced during their tense correspondence about the Fugitive Slave Law. Like Seward, the Ohioan also had enemies within his own state party. Cameron, too, provoked "fierce opposition," as Lincoln described it, mainly because so many Republicans regarded the savvy operator as the worst kind of political crook. Lincoln left him out of his original lineup on election night. But pressure from leading organizers in Pennsylvania was unrelenting. Lincoln listened to them and tried to sort through the charges against Cameron. At the end of December, he even crafted a secret memo outlining the senator's history of alleged bribes as he struggled to make up his mind about what to do.[9]

Lincoln later told Trumbull that he would have preferred to keep Cameron in the U.S. Senate but came to believe that "Gen. C." provided a counterweight to Chase, a leading antislavery radical and the most prominent former Democrat among the cabinet contenders. In a "Very Confidential" letter written to Trumbull, who was himself a former Democrat, Lincoln was blunt about his desire to use Cameron's Whiggish economic views to help appease the former Whig "protectionists" in Pennsylvania and elsewhere. "Gen. C. must be brought to co-operate," Lincoln wrote, acknowledging that the price of such cooperation would be steep if it involved putting the tainted Cameron himself into the cabinet. Yet Lincoln considered it "a *necessity*" that the former Democrat Chase take control of the Treasury Department, less because of his "ability, firmness, and purity of character," which he recognized, than owing to the governor's partisan utility. Lincoln claimed that Chase "alone" would reconcile influential *New York Evening Post* editor William Cullen Bryant "and his class"—meaning former Democrats in the nation's financial capital—to the appointment of Seward, a former Whig whom they despised. The conflict over Cameron created a stalemate. For several weeks, no nominations were announced. "I can only say I shall have a great deal of trouble," Lincoln admitted to Bryant in late December, vowing to "do the best I can."[10]

A different kind of partisan calculation was at play with lesser cabinet posts such as secretary of the navy, attorney general, postmaster general, and secretary of the interior. For these lower-profile appointments, Lincoln focused on balancing regional interests. He felt that he needed "representative men" from outside the big states of New York, Ohio, and Pennsylvania. But doing so with fairness to the other fourteen solid Republican states proved difficult. Lincoln confessed to Seward in January that he was delaying these cabinet announcements "as long as possible . . . to avoid being teased to insanity to make changes."[11] One thing was clear: The president-elect devoted precious little time to ascertaining the expertise of his potential cabinet appointees. He approached these governmental choices as purely political decisions. Such partisan priorities were typical for cabinet making in that era. The only exception to this approach by Lincoln and his Republican allies was their interest in filling a token cabinet post with a southerner from outside their party. For conservatives and more fusionist-minded Republicans, this provided the most available means for gesturing toward sectional conciliation.[12]

Lincoln's one caveat to the proposed appointment was that he wanted nobody in his cabinet who would challenge his party's core antislavery principles. "Do they come to me? or I go to them?" Lincoln asked warily of potential southern selections, noting the obvious problem, "or are we to lead off in open hostility to each other?"[13] This dilemma propelled the president-elect and his advisers to narrow their consideration to a handful of relative moderates from the Upper South, men who had been affiliated with the Southern Opposition or Constitutional Unionists but who might be persuaded to tone down their support for slavery. At first Lincoln favored Rep. John Gilmer of North Carolina as the only prospect with a "*living* position," since he had been a recent and viable candidate for House Speaker. That idea went nowhere, however, because Lincoln could not even convince Gilmer to come to Springfield to talk with him.[14] In the end, the Lincoln cabinet contained only two slave-state Republicans—Edward Bates of Missouri and Montgomery Blair of Maryland—both long affiliated with the antislavery cause and neither representing real outreach toward white southern unionists.

Nor was Lincoln willing to conciliate the South on any important antislavery measures. After the election, he wrote a single, somewhat conciliatory statement on the noninterference principle for Trumbull to use in a speech. He had Trumbull try to clarify the party's long-standing "freedom national" doctrine by reiterating that Republicans, despite their opposition to the extension of slavery across the western territories, had no intention of interfering with slavery where it already existed. The message assured white southerners that they would be able to retain (in Lincoln's phrasing) "complete control of their own affairs." The disheartening reaction to this slim olive branch only confirmed for Lincoln the wisdom of his otherwise tight-lipped approach. He complained to Henry Raymond at the *New York Times* that while southern and Democratic newspapers had basically ignored Trumbull's comments, antislavery journals were paying angry attention to them. He was struck that the *Boston Courier* (which had once mocked him as an overeager Whig congressman) was blasting him for "an abandonment of Republican ground" in what it viewed as appeasement orchestrated out of Springfield.[15]

Once again, however, eastern journalists were underestimating Lincoln. Behind the scenes, he was aggressive in holding "Republican ground" and at the same time trying to persuade leading southerners to hold their fire. He reached out to his former congressional colleague Alexander Stephens of Georgia, for example, but offered nothing of substance to win him over. "You think slavery is *right* and ought to be extended," Lincoln wrote in a "*For your own eye only*" message to the future Confederate vice president, "while we think it is *wrong* and ought to be restricted."[16]

To northern allies, Lincoln was even more explicit. "Let there be no compromise on the question of *extending* slavery," he informed Trumbull in private on December 10, 1860, a week after Congress had returned for its second session and just after he had decided on Seward as head of the State Department. "The tug has to come &

better now, than any time hereafter." The next day Lincoln repeated that memorable directive in a confidential letter aimed at wavering House Republicans. And despite a rising chorus of voices calling for greater northern unity, the president-elect remained adamant about keeping political distance from Douglas Democrats. "Douglas is sure to be again trying to bring in his 'Pop. Sov.,'" Lincoln wrote. "Have none of it." To longtime friend Rep. Elihu Washburne, he preached grim resolve about the "territorial question." "On that point," he urged, "hold firm as with a chain of steel." Moreover, when it came to the compromise schemes then being discussed on Capitol Hill, Lincoln sounded almost dismissive. "I am sorry any republican inclines to dally with Pop. Sov. of any sort," he wrote, adding in words the *Courier* would have loved, "It acknowledges that slavery has equal rights with liberty, and surrenders all we have contended for." To Trumbull, he was blunter: "If any of our friends do prove false, and fix up a compromise on the territorial question," he wrote on December 17, "I am for fighting again—that is all."[17]

During this period, Lincoln provided direct guidance over how Republicans should handle the ongoing fugitive slave controversy. "You know I think the fugitive slave clause of the constitution ought to be enforced," he wrote to his congressional contacts in mid-December, "to put it in the mildest form, ought not to be resisted." This sounded conciliatory on its face, but it was merely a restatement of his long-standing and evasive approach of acknowledging the legitimacy of the constitutional clause without endorsing the current abysmal law. The key challenge, as Lincoln well knew, was deciding how far northern states should be allowed to go in securing habeas corpus or personal liberty rights for Black people accused of being runaways under the law.

Lincoln had firm views on personal liberty, but he was not inclined to share them in public. Gilmer of North Carolina wrote Lincoln on December 10 to ask if he was prepared to repudiate the northern states' personal liberty laws, which most white southerners regarded as nothing less than state nullification. In a remarkable response, the president-elect feigned ignorance. "I really know very little of them," he claimed, despite a recent Supreme Court decision, *Ableman v. Booth* (1859), that denounced them. Although Illinois had never adopted an anti-kidnapping statute for its own free Black residents, Lincoln as an attorney had encountered these state laws and the Supreme Court debates over their constitutionality on multiple occasions.[18]

With the election over, Lincoln's strategy on the territorial question and the fugitive issue was to maintain Republican unity, which he considered the key to governing through the current crisis. He was firm on the policy of containing slavery, the foundation of the antislavery fusion that had first drawn Republicans together in 1854 "from the four winds," as Lincoln once put it. And he carefully parsed his words on the process of fugitive rendition, which was so divisive, as he had explained to Governor Chase the previous year, not only to the opposing sections of the country but within the Republican movement itself.[19]

That winter the fugitive issue proved to be one of the main obstacles to any union-saving compromises. In December, even before the secession crisis fully erupted, both House and Senate formed special committees to explore an all-inclusive deal that could avert disunion. Congressional warhorses such as Senator John Crittenden of Kentucky and Rep. Thomas Corwin of Ohio proposed various ways the nation might amend the Constitution to quell the growing political unrest. Some newspapers, led by Horace Greeley's influential *New-York Tribune*, also floated creative and sometimes wildly unrealistic solutions to the crisis. None of them stuck. It was left to Virginia and a handful of other border states to promote a peace conference, organized to meet in Washington in February, aimed at staving off disaster before the transfer of national political power in March. Each of these efforts faltered over the contentious fugitive problem.

On December 20, 1860, the same day that South Carolina seceded, Thurlow Weed met with the president-elect in Springfield to discuss the stalled compromise negotiations. Lincoln sent the renowned fixer back to Washington with a set of draft resolutions on fugitive policy for Senate Republicans to review. This marked one of his more aggressive behind-the-scenes interventions during the transition period. Lincoln's proposals accepted the constitutional obligation for rendition and endorsed changes to the 1850 law but made no explicit call for repeal. He also suggested some ambiguous language guaranteeing accused runaways "the usual safeguards to liberty," though conceding that state personal liberty statutes might be repealed, "if there be such, really, or apparantly [*sic*]" obstructing the federal code on slave rendition. Seward informed Lincoln that Senate Republicans discussed his recommendations but held off on a vote, deciding it would merely "divide our friends."[20]

As the new year began, Republican leaders generally agreed with Lincoln's intuition that the "tug" had finally come, but they were at odds over strategy. On the question of how to form a patriotic fusion that might stifle the escalating rebellion—whether with Douglas Democrats or Upper South conservatives or both—there was deep internal division. Antislavery radicals were skeptical of almost any outreach effort. Chase warned that their "watchword" should be "Inauguration first—adjustment afterwards."[21] But plenty of Republicans viewed the secession crisis as an opportunity to expand the party's base while pursuing patriotic goals. Some Republican moderates—such as Seward, Bates, or Cameron—would have moved the party away from the ultraist strategy that Lincoln was holding on to "like a chain of steel."[22]

Lincoln, however, felt an obligation to convince "the *bad* men" of the country that they could not undermine popular balloting with sectional bluster. In early January, writing to a Pennsylvania congressman who was attempting to pull together a variation on Crittenden's plan for national compromise through constitutional amendments, Lincoln offered a concise reiteration of his hard-edged analysis. "We have just carried an election on principles fairly stated to the people," Lincoln wrote. "Now we are told in advance, the government shall be broken up, unless we surrender to those we have beaten, before we take the offices." This "surrender," he assured his correspondent, would be "the end of us, and of the government."[23]

From inside the Lincoln operation at Springfield, that kind of bold, plain-spoken defiance was thrilling for a veteran antislavery radical like William Herndon. Continuing in his self-appointed role as Lincoln's chief liaison to eastern abolitionists, Herndon began writing to Wendell Phillips and other skeptical Garrisonians, assuring them that the Lincoln administration would offer no concessions to the Slave Power. Calling his longtime law partner "Jackson redivivus" (reborn), Herndon vowed that the incoming president would "make a grave yard of the South" if "rebellion or treason lifts its head," and he insisted that he was "firm as a rock" on matters of "Justice, Right, Liberty, Man & God."[24]

Yet Herndon also intimated that he was the driving force behind most of Lincoln's "brave acts" and "brave words." This was clearly an exaggeration. The two men had been officemates and law partners since the mid-1840s. Nobody except Mary Lincoln knew the incoming president on a more intimate, everyday basis. But the political distance between the two men was palpable. Herndon had contributed to Republican party efforts throughout the 1850s and even served briefly as mayor of Springfield, but he never emerged as an influential political adviser to Lincoln. His role in the presidential campaign had been peripheral. He had not even attended the 1860 convention in Chicago. His partial irrelevance may have been the result of what his contemporaries considered personal failings. Like newly elected Illinois governor Richard Yates, who was a close friend, Herndon appears to have suffered bouts of alcoholism that only grew worse over time. Although we don't know what Lincoln really thought of him, after the president-elect left Springfield in 1861, the two men hardly corresponded and barely saw each other again. Herndon played no role in the Lincoln administration.[25]

A number of Lincoln's Illinois friends were starting to feel abandoned. During the transition period, Norman Judd, well known even outside Illinois as an effective state party chairman and as a leading member of the Republican national committee, had legitimate expectations that he might be considered for the new cabinet. But after what Judd had gone through during his feud with John Wentworth, and amid the lingering disappointment over his failed bid for the 1860 gubernatorial nomination, the cigar-chewing party boss from Chicago was in a dark mood about his Washington prospects. "E.B. Washburne, [Schuyler] Colfax and others are trying to make a combination against me and influence Mr. Lincoln," he warned colleagues as early as December.[26]

Washburne himself was also downbeat about Lincoln's cabinet-making plans. As the new year began, the congressman warned *Tribune* editor Charles Ray that reports of Cameron's likely appointment to the cabinet were creating "a most painful impression" among their friends "that our victory has turned to ashes, and that Lincoln is a failure." Joseph Medill from the *Tribune* tried to convince some of his fellow editors that they did not have to put up with either the elevation of the notoriously corrupt Cameron or the likely snub of their favorite, Judd. "We made Abe and by God we can unmake him," he commented. From Washington, the usually taciturn Trumbull also appeared agitated. "I think Mr. Lincoln is making a grave mistake by not taking [Judd]," the senator wrote that same week. "He is just such a man as Mr. L. needs near him."[27]

Every Republican faction placed a premium on getting their own men near the new president and thereby presumably controlling him. None however seemed to have confidence in their success. Cameron's camp was just as anxious as the *Tribune* crowd. On January 22, 1861, Joseph Casey, a former Whig congressman from Pennsylvania, warned David Davis, "I have never seen our people in such a ferment." Casey, who had helped spearhead the talks with Lincoln's forces at Chicago, claimed there was a nefarious radical "Cabal" making "desperate efforts to capture the Administration." The conflict appeared to Casey a battle of egos as much as ideology. "Greely [*sic*] hates Seward most intensely," he wrote, "but is too great a Coward to attack him openly." Casey predicted that Greeley's plan was to surround the new president with men whom Seward detested and thus drive the New Yorker out of the incoming administration. "Does not Mr. Lincoln see through his purpose?" Casey asked.[28]

Indeed, Lincoln's experience enabled him to see through such schemes. Party organization was one subject he understood completely. Behind his bland credo of "fairness to all" was a determination that no faction would dominate. Lincoln intended to be his own man. Nor did he have any intention of cobbling together a kitchen cabinet of old friends or personal loyalists. Other than John Nicolay, the taciturn former newspaperman and state party staffer who came along to Washington as a private secretary, the only other local figure who joined the transition was a promising young attorney and aspiring writer named John Hay. This was a frustrating, unexpected reality for many Illinois Republican leaders. "I know Mr. L. to be honest & well meaning and I appreciate his difficulties," Trumbull wrote in near despair, "but I think it not the way to get through them to cast off his home-friends."[29] But Trumbull and the others failed to appreciate that Lincoln, despite his genial manner, relied on an independent approach to party leadership that reflected his supreme self-confidence.

Lincoln also began to distance himself from the compromise talks in Washington. On February 1, when Texas became the seventh southern state to secede, he sent a confidential note to Seward that signaled he had run out of patience. "I say now, however, as I have all the while said, that on the territorial question . . . I am inflexible." On the rest of the compromise measures, he had no more instructions to give—at least not from Springfield. "As to fugitive slaves, District of Columbia, slave trade among the slave states, and whatever springs of necessity from the fact that the institution is amongst us," he wrote, "I care but little, so that what is done is comely, and not altogether outrageous."[30]

Lincoln concluded this confidential guidance to Seward by observing, "Nor do I care much about New-Mexico, if further extension were hedged against." His minor concession mostly underscored the long-standing willingness of free soilers to make an exception of the arid, sparsely populated region, permitting popular sovereignty there to be carved into the Compromise of 1850. But it was still notable that Lincoln decided to float this idea even though Chase had urged him not to do so just days before.[31]

Early on the morning of his departure from Springfield on February 11, 1861, Lincoln withdrew $400 of traveling money from his local bank and met with a crowd of supporters at the town railroad depot. In poignant farewell remarks, he expressed sadness at leaving the small community where he had "passed from a young to an old man" and where one of his four sons was buried. But his remarks also contained some self-pitying candor, owing perhaps to the complaints of his closest friends about his apparent ingratitude toward them, coupled with his real anxiety over the growing secession movement. "I now leave," he observed, "not knowing when, or whether ever, I may return, with a task before me greater than that which rested upon Washington."[32] In private, Lincoln told Herndon that he still expected to prevail. "I am decided—my course is fixed—my path is blazed," he said. "I expect the People to sustain me," he added. "They have never yet forsaken any true man."[33]

There was one detail, however, that Lincoln kept from both his neighbors and his law partner. He had finally decided to make a return visit to Kentucky, which remained, precariously, in the national union. While readying for his departure, Lincoln drafted remarks on lined notepaper that he pasted inside one of the first printed versions of his inaugural address. As with his farewell statement in Springfield, the planned remarks betrayed sensitivity to the avalanche of criticism being leveled at him. "No man can be elected President without some opponents," he wrote, while noting that ever since November he had been urged "by many patriotic men . . . to shift the ground upon which I had been elected." "This I steadily refused," he explained, "not from any party wantonness, nor from any indifference to the troubles of the country," but rather because he would not allow himself to break his pledges, nor betray "his friends" simply to take his constitutional oath. "Demands for such surrender," he claimed, "once recognized, are without limit, as to nature, extent and repetition. They break" what he called "the only bond of faith between the public and public servant" and would "set the minority over the majority." Echoing words that he had written earlier in private, he added "that such surrender would not be merely the ruin of a man, or a party; but, as a precedent, would be the ruin of government itself."[34]

Those powerful democratic sentiments remained private. With seven of the nation's fifteen slave states, all from the cotton-growing regions of the Deep South, trying to dissolve their national ties, there was no margin for political error. And with the prospect of political violence looming as never before, the president-elect's train route to Washington avoided Kentucky and the slaveholding South until the very end of the trip.

Lincoln's preinaugural journey in February 1861 took him through nearly a hundred whistle-stops. At a series of hastily improvised rallies, the president-elect delivered brief remarks designed to stoke patriotic sentiments while avoiding controversy. Republican organizers brought Grace Bedell to the stop at Westfield, New York, after the president-elect's train passed through nearby Cleveland, Ohio. Lincoln gamely showed off his new "whiskers" to Bedell—who had written to him during the campaign suggesting a beard—then planted a kiss on her cheek.[35]

On February 21, the eve of George Washington's birthday, Lincoln spent the bulk of the day in New Jersey, the only free state that his party had not won outright in the presidential election. In Trenton, the state capital, the national Republican leader addressed the house and senate chambers, both controlled by Democrats. The delicacy of cultivating patriotic sentiment amid a hostile partisan environment seemed to encourage Lincoln to offer some fresh reflections on the nation's past and his own.

The fifty-one-year-old recalled "away back in my childhood" having read the popular Parson Weems biography of George Washington. Out of the many struggles during the Revolutionary War that the book describes, Lincoln observed, the one that "fixed" in his memory was the story of the Battle of Trenton and how General Washington and his men crossed the Delaware River on Christmas Eve 1776 against desperate odds. "I recollect thinking then, boy even though I was," he explained, "that there must be something more than common that those men struggled for." Their objective was greater than mere "National Independence," according to Lincoln; it was about the "liberties" of the "almost chosen people." This universal principle still offered, in Lincoln's opinion, "a great promise to all the people of the world."[36]

As he invoked patriotic themes that might resonate with skeptical New Jersey Democrats, Lincoln tried to cast his appearance before them in the most unifying way possible. Calling himself a "humble instrument in the hands of Almighty God," he acknowledged that while most of his audience "did not think I was the man" during the presidential balloting, he was nonetheless about to become "the representative man of the nation." He seemed to intend this statement as a conciliatory gesture.[37]

But the tug had come. Lincoln drew loud cheers in Trenton when he warned that "it may be necessary to put the foot down firmly" against the challenge of secession. The reaction must have confirmed for Lincoln what he knew to be his party's crucial advantage in the fast-escalating crisis. It was now protecting the people's government, not just its own partisan interests. Whatever southern politicians might argue about slavery, "state rights," or the alleged nefarious schemes of "Black Republicans," they lacked the authority of a national election behind them. Only Lincoln and his victorious party held such unifying power. Yet the canny Illinois party boss also realized that when it came to Northern Democrats, his main task was to find ways to neutralize them, not to fuse with them. As he prepared to swear an oath to the Constitution, Lincoln remained convinced that restoring the nation must begin with sustaining his own party's unity.

At his next stop, in Philadelphia, word reached the president-elect from multiple sources that there was a credible plot to assassinate him. Insurrectionists were reportedly planning an attack in a couple of days at his scheduled change of trains in Baltimore. Wary of appearing intimidated, Lincoln decided to proceed with his public schedule. Early on Friday morning, February 22, he appeared at Independence Hall to help raise the new thirty-four-star national flag, reflecting the addition of Kansas, which had finally been admitted to the union as a free state the previous month.

The entourage continued to Harrisburg, the Pennsylvania state capital, where a friendly Republican legislature awaited a patriotic speech. However, later that afternoon, Illinois party chairman Judd and Chicago detective Allan Pinkerton finally convinced Lincoln to alter his travel plans to Washington. After speaking to the assembled legislators, he agreed to take an unscheduled series of overnight trains to avoid potential danger from the secessionist mobs expected in Baltimore. Accompanied by Pinkerton and Bloomington lawyer

Ward Hill Lamon, the president-elect made the secret late-night journey, arriving without public ceremony at the B&O railroad depot on New Jersey Avenue in Washington by 6 o'clock on Saturday morning. Waiting for the anxious trio with a handy carriage was Illinois congressman Washburne.[38]

The irony was almost too perfect. One of the first figures to witness Lincoln's unceremonious arrival in Washington had also been one of the last men to see him leave the city nearly a dozen years earlier. Back in March 1849, Washburne had been one of Congressman Lincoln's closest associates, a young lobbyist who often boarded with him at Mrs. Sprigg's mess. The two Whig politicos had devoted themselves to electing Zachary Taylor as president, but by the time Lincoln was ready to depart following the general's inauguration, he and Washburne had already fallen out over the possible appointment of Justin Butterfield to the coveted Land Office job. Now tension was brewing between them again. Washburne had helped lead the public booming of candidate Lincoln in 1860, but he since felt betrayed by the messy postelection cabinet-making process. Like several Illinois cronies of the incoming president, the congressman was annoyed by all the attempts at balancing the party's competing factions. But the stakes were just too high for any further intraparty pettiness. Washburne was one of the few men privy to the president-elect's secret arrival information. Lincoln still trusted him.

That first day in Washington on Saturday, February 23, was a whirlwind. Washburne's carriage went straight to Willard's Hotel, near the White House, where Lincoln was to occupy a second-floor suite of rooms. The president-elect breakfasted with Senator Seward, who had just been announced to the public as the nominee for secretary of state.[39] After a private discussion, the New Yorker escorted Lincoln across Lafayette Square to meet with President Buchanan and his cabinet. For the rest of the day, Lincoln kept up a near-constant stream of meetings, mostly at the hotel, with General Winfield Scott, Senator Stephen Douglas, and other Washington insiders. Mary Lincoln and the boys did not arrive until late in the afternoon—after passing through the streets of Baltimore almost on their own. But Lincoln's political work continued until well after nine o'clock at night, when former Ohio governor (and now senator-elect) Chase came over to his suite to introduce some friendly Republican delegates from the Washington peace conference. That last-ditch compromise gathering, promoted by a cohort of Upper South moderates, had been in session at Willard's since the beginning of February, though without much progress. Radicals were participating to ensure that northerners were contemplating no real concessions. Chase himself had not yet been announced as a member of Lincoln's cabinet, but he was already vying with Seward for prominence in the new administration.

But Lincoln was more comfortable in his dealings with Seward, a fellow former Whig and a natural politician. At their breakfast together, Lincoln shared the draft of his inaugural address for Seward's review—a rare sign of respect and trust. The address offered a firm statement against secession that ended with the startling question: "Shall it be peace, or a sword?"[40]

Seward managed to talk Lincoln out of that provocative closing line. On February 24, the senator sent over a heavily marked-up copy of the draft. To his editorial suggestions, Seward added some blunt advice. He warned that such a tough-sounding speech would only drive Maryland and Virginia into the secessionist camp. He also dismissed the views of their more radical "party friends" as dangerously uninformed. Seward obviously wanted nothing to do with hard-line strategies such as Chase's "Inauguration first—adjustment afterwards" approach.[41] Instead, he highlighted his own repeated attempts at accommodation during recent Senate debates. "Only the soothing words which I have spoken, have saved us and carried us along thus far," he assured Lincoln with tone-deaf vanity.[42]

Seward also tried to inspire Lincoln toward greater conciliation by comparing their moment of crisis to 1801, when "Partisan as he was," Thomas Jefferson "sank the partisan in the patriot in his inaugural address." He urged Lincoln to adopt the "magnanimity of a victor" as Jefferson had done when he declared, "We are all Federalists, all Republicans." Seward did not mention that his advice on conciliation included a paraphrase of Stephen Douglas, who in early January had punctuated an impassioned pro-union speech on the Senate floor by expressing the hope "that Mr. Lincoln would have sunk the partisan in the patriot, and abandoned the ultra principles of the Republican party."[43] Seward's suggestion appealed to Lincoln, but only on a rhetorical level. He agreed to moderate the tone of his address and remove the stark concluding question.

But Lincoln refused to propose any real compromise. In his confidential note, Seward had emphasized the need to offer serious "concessions" that must come "at the cost of the winning, the triumphant party." "I do not fear their displeasure," Seward remarked about their fellow Republicans. "They will be loyal, whatever is said." "Not so," he added, "the defeated, irritated, angered, frenzied party."[44]

Seward was suggesting that the inaugural address might provide a framework for patriotic fusion. Over the past several weeks—and without Lincoln's approval—he had been working with Douglas and a handful of others to try to forge a temporary unionist coalition, something most Washington insiders considered essential for avoiding national catastrophe. This patriotic strategy aimed to find a bipartisan arrangement just strong enough to suffocate the fire-eating contingent in the South. The "irritated" and "angered" targets of Seward's outreach were not the self-declared Confederates but those still-loyal fellow citizens who distrusted a new Republican administration. The incoming cabinet officer aspired to bring together Douglas Democrats and willing southern conservatives with triumphant Republicans in a show of patriotic force that would avoid the outbreak of general war. In late January, at a dinner party Douglas hosted for the French minister, Seward and other compromise advocates such as Senator Crittenden and Supreme Court justice John Campbell of Virginia were able to talk in private. According to Campbell's notes, Seward offered a toast that seemed to reveal his intentions and those of his Democratic host. "Away with all parties, all platforms, all previous committals," the Republican leader said with glasses raised, "and whatever else will stand in the way of restoration of the American union."[45]

Not long afterward, Confederate agents in the capital claimed to hear that same "tenor" from Seward in a series of unauthorized discussions with him. "I have built up the Republican party" and "brought it to triumph," Seward allegedly boasted in early March, "but its advent to power is accompanied by great difficulties and perils." "I must save the party and the government in its hands," Seward asserted. "To do this, war must be averted; the negro question must be dropped; the 'irrepressible conflict' ignored; and a Union party to embrace the border states inaugurated."[46] Whatever his exact language might have been, Seward was not repudiating his earlier antislavery views but rather was adapting to the increasingly dangerous political landscape. The senior Republican leader seemed to intend his patriotic talk as a means of buying valuable time for the new administration. Seward explained this "singular" strategic outlook to Lincoln a few weeks later: "We must *Change the question before the Public from one upon Slavery, or about Slavery* for a question *upon Union or Disunion*. In other words, from what would be regarded as a Party question to one of Patriotism or Union" (emphasis in the original).[47]

For savvy political operatives like Seward, patriotism was a necessary strategy for the moment, but for a larger swath of northerners, it was a visceral reaction to the unprecedented crisis. In late February 1861, the *New York Times* featured a beseeching letter from a "National Union Man" urging Seward, not Lincoln, as "the chief and foremost representative of the policy to be inaugurated on the 4th of March," to set about organizing a governing coalition grounded only in patriotic devotion. "We want no party now but one for the Union," wrote the anonymous author, who was perhaps noted author Francis Lieber.[48] One of Lincoln's more eloquent correspondents from Boston also pleaded with him to select a bipartisan cabinet that would draw upon the loyal elements of the country. "In the appointment of your Cabinet you have performed your duty to your party," the man complained, based on press leaks suggesting the composition of Lincoln's likely team, "but what is a party without a country? or a country deluged with fraternal blood?" This man wanted Seward, Douglas, and others to participate in a true coalition government.[49]

Lincoln's daily pace remained frenetic from his arrival in the city straight through to Inauguration Day on March 4. Besides dealing with the pressure of cabinet making, tensions over the failing compromise efforts, and anxieties concerning last-minute revisions to his inaugural address, he also had to endure an embarrassing report of his covert entrance to the nation's capital. On February 25, the *New York Times* published an explosive dispatch about the secret travel operation, containing a sensationalized mix of fact and fiction from correspondent Joseph Howard, including the memorable but entirely invented detail that while switching trains at Baltimore, the president-elect had tried to disguise himself with "a Scotch plaid cap and a very long military cloak." Democrats pounced on this false information to portray a timid Lincoln as practically sneaking into the city, while some illustrated magazines, such as *Vanity Fair*, skewered him with a series of blistering cartoons mocking his lack of manhood.[50] It was a deflating presidential launch, one made even more awkward because Lincoln was still trying to sort out his cabinet lineup until Sunday evening, March 3, when he was finally able to host a private dinner for his seven prospective cabinet secretaries. Yet even that show of unity proved illusory.[51]

A clash of egos erupted just before the March 4 inauguration ceremony, threatening a full cabinet breakup. Apparently in a fit of pique over his perceived lack of influence, Seward announced he was changing his mind and wanted out. That afternoon Lincoln felt compelled to send his former rival a terse note from the White House, urging him to "countermand the withdrawal," which the New Yorker grudgingly did.[52] The drama set off a chain reaction, and within a couple of days Chase was indicating his own preference for serving in the Senate. Lincoln somehow managed to strong-arm him back into the fold as well.[53] It was only the opening week, but the tone had been set. One shrewd observer believed the instability was an inherent product of Lincoln's "fairness" policy, which favored no faction. "This Cabinet as it stands is not a fusion of various shadowings of a party," explained Adam Gurowski, a State Department translator, in his gossipy diary, "but it is a violent mixing or putting together of inimical and repulsive forces, which, if they do not devour, at the best will neutralize each other." Most political contemporaries seemed to agree with Gurowski's biting assessment.[54] But it appeared to be the price Lincoln was willing to pay to be his own man.

The best evidence of this determination came across in the final version of his inaugural address. Speaking early on Monday afternoon, March 4, 1861, from the east portico of the recently expanded U.S. Capitol, with a crane and scaffolding still in view before the unfinished center dome, the new president dispensed with the usual inaugural pleasantries and jumped headlong into what he termed the "special anxiety" of the moment, namely the "accession of a Republican Administration" and the consequent fears felt among the "people of the Southern states." Lincoln repeated his party's standard noninterference pledge, assuring everyone that "I have no purpose, directly or indirectly, to interfere with the institution of slavery in the States where it exists. I believe I have no lawful right to do so, and I have no inclination to do so."[55] For good measure, Lincoln also quoted from the 1860 Republican platform affirming the "rights of the States" to control their "domestic institutions," and denouncing any "lawless invasion" of them, a reference to John Brown's raid at Harpers Ferry. But by that point, such claims were not truly conciliatory. No prominent Republican was proposing to abolish slavery by federal action—especially not by violence. Everybody knew that. The question was whether it was the party's hidden agenda, as southern fire-eaters and bombastic Northern Democrats had been claiming all along.

If Lincoln really wanted to conciliate the South, he would have followed his bland statements of conservative principle with a framework for sectional compromise, as Seward and others were promoting. No Republican could have endorsed the sweeping compromise proposals made by Kentucky senator John Crittenden—which included constitutional amendments permanently protecting slavery—but there were other ways to approach conciliation or to lower the temperature of the crisis.[56] Instead, Lincoln declined to endorse any of the compromise packages circulating around Capitol Hill, and he even claimed that he had "not seen" the most recent effort, which proposed making the standard Republican pledge of federal noninterference with slavery in the slaveholding states an "irrevocable" constitutional amendment. This idea had been bouncing around for months, but the latest version, by Rep. Thomas Corwin of Ohio, passed the House and Senate with two-thirds approval only hours before the inauguration. Lincoln offered that if he understood the text correctly, he had "no objection" to it.[57]

In his inaugural address, Lincoln did briefly engage with the controversy over fugitive slaves, but here too the president conveyed almost nothing conciliatory. As he had done for the past decade, Lincoln focused on the constitutional clause on fugitives, not the hated law of 1850. He acknowledged the long-standing argument about whether delivering up runaways should be considered a state or a federal matter, but he dismissed this debate as unimportant in a manner that must have infuriated Chase and other leading antislavery radicals. Lincoln declined to call for repeal of the current statute, but neither did he promise to do anything extraordinary to enforce it. Instead, he suggested that any resolution of the nation's fugitive crisis would require the equivalent of federal personal liberty protections for accused Black runaways.[58] This was almost a taunt to white southerners, who had been complaining for years about northern state personal liberty laws and their "nullification" of the federal fugitive code.

With the prospect of disunion and civil war looming, the only inaugural statements that really mattered were Lincoln's rejection of secession as "the essence of anarchy" and his stern promise to "hold, occupy, and possess" all federal property in the South. These shots across the bow, which everyone was watching for in March 1861, set into motion a frenzy of editorial activity and congressional speechmaking gauging the depth of Lincoln's commitment to crush secession.[59]

A spirit of conciliation did register at the end of the inaugural address. Seward had provided Lincoln with an alternative to the stark choice he had posed in his draft between peace and a sword. Carefully revised by Lincoln in his own voice, the majestic finale of the inaugural invoked the "mystic chords of memory" and the "better angels of our nature" to urge Americans to hold fast to their "bonds of affection."[60]

"NO PARTY NOW" HAD become a rallying cry across the North, but this was not the president's political strategy in his inaugural address. Lincoln remained firm about his sectional positions on everything from personal liberty protections to excluding slavery from the territories to reiterating the basic Republican view on the immorality of slavery. Some northern newspapers touted the story of how Senator Douglas sat on the inaugural stage, graciously holding Lincoln's stovepipe hat while the new president spoke. But allowing an opponent a place on the speaker's platform was not nearly the same as including him in the cabinet, as both party leaders well understood.[61]

Still, Douglas's presence on the inaugural stage was a useful symbol for the peaceful transfer of power, a process that Lincoln made sure to highlight in his speech. Immediately after declaring that "the central idea of secession is the essence of anarchy," he pivoted to define its opposite, which, by his reckoning, was American democracy itself. "A majority held in restraint by constitutional checks and limitations, and always changing easily with deliberate changes of popular opinions and sentiments," he asserted, "is the only true sovereign of a free people." He then added, "Whoever rejects it does of necessity fly to anarchy or to despotism. Unanimity is impossible."[62] This was the underlying message of Lincoln's inaugural address, and it represented nothing less than his definition of the national union. For him, the sacred abstraction of "union" signified neither a mere compact of states, nor some platitude about the people at large, but rather the specific bond between electoral majorities and minorities. This was the essential union that had to be reframed after every election and consecrated with every inaugural oath. In 1861 these words also represented Lincoln's only significant promise to those patriotic "enemies" who were still willing to listen to their unwanted representative man: American democracy was not merely about majority rule but was also fundamentally about minority rights.

The genius behind Lincoln's commitment to an electoral union was its partisan utility. He aimed his elegant words at those who felt angered by the escalating secession crisis but sidelined by the Republican victory. Disaffected Northern Democrats and anxious Constitutional Unionists were the obvious targets of his inaugural appeal. Though he closed by addressing "my dissatisfied fellow-countrymen," beseeching would-be secessionists to take their time with "the momentous issue of civil war," he was refusing to engage or negotiate with representatives from the seceded states. In the address, the secessionists served as Lincoln's rhetorical foil, not his intended audience. His crisis strategy, unlike that of Seward or Douglas, was about neither abstract patriotism nor the abandonment of parties but almost the reverse. He wanted everyone still clinging to the nation to recognize that ordinary partisanship could save them. He was essentially asking citizens in the loyal states to sink the patriot into the partisan, trusting that representative democracy, with all its sharp elbows, was their best formula for achieving national unity. Keep believing in the power of elections, he was suggesting to his political opponents, and we can always resolve our problems with ballots, not bullets. From his perspective, any other conciliatory strategy would have fractured the Republicans and ultimately ruined their efforts. It was a risky gambit, and a singular one, but this was the central lesson about partisanship that Lincoln had absorbed over his long years in the rough-and-tumble of Illinois politics. The crucible of the secession crisis finally sharpened these experiences into a powerful expression of the American democratic creed.

10 MAKE HASTE SLOWLY

(1861–1862)

"WHILE THE INAUGERAL [*sic*] address was being delivered from this place, devoted altogether to saving the Union without war," Abraham Lincoln recalled about his first presidential oath taking, "insurgent agents were in the city seeking to destroy it without war." He blamed these men—and by implication those willing to treat with them—for "seeking to dissolve the Union, and divide effects, by negotiation."[1]

Lincoln's hard line in March 1861—and his willingness to defy conventional Washington wisdom about the need for conciliation—was no surprise to anyone who understood his track record. During nearly two decades as a state party leader, Lincoln had developed a habit of self-confident command. He understood how important it was to stand up to pressure from friends as well as enemies. And he continued to keep his own counsel as the crisis escalated into war. He was not always right, but he was consistent about forming his own judgments and setting his own priorities. He proved methodical in mobilizing the nation's armed forces and in shaping a grand strategy that would help end the rebellion.

After assuming office on March 4, 1861, Lincoln told his Illinois friend Orville Browning that "the very first thing placed in his hands after his inauguration was a letter from Majr Anderson announcing the impossibility of defending or relieving Sumter."[2] This news was grim but not entirely unexpected. The potential for trouble in the Charleston harbor had been looming since early January, when a civilian ship contracted to bring supplies to Fort Sumter had been fired upon by overeager South Carolina secessionists. The Buchanan administration ignored this provocation—which might have been considered the war's first shot—leaving artillery officer Robert Anderson from Kentucky, newly installed as commander of the U.S. garrison, to await further instruction. Major Anderson and his small contingent of troops subsequently dug in, but by March they could wait no longer.

Lincoln described the six weeks after receiving the details of Anderson's dilemma as the worst "troubles and anxieties of his life."[3] At first the president tried to rely on his general-in-chief, Winfield Scott. But Scott, a Virginian by birth and a Constitutional Unionist by choice, shied away from the prospect of provoking sectional war. On the evening of March 5, Lincoln sent Secretary of State William Seward over to Scott's residence seeking an opinion about the dire report from Anderson. Scott hastily scribbled a reply, blaming Buchanan for his ill-advised pursuit of "some thing like a truce" during the months prior to the inauguration. The result of this inaction, Scott complained, made evacuation "almost inevitable." Stunned, Lincoln pressed his chief military adviser to answer more deliberately, directing him to reply in writing to a set of questions about the status of a potential relief operation. In the coming days, Scott did so twice, but his bottom line never wavered. It was "merely a question of time," he argued on March 12, before they would have to surrender the fort.[4]

This gloomy conclusion by the nation's senior military figure unnerved most of the new cabinet members. When the president asked for their opinions in writing, the majority indicated that any attempt to reinforce Anderson's forces would be either unwise or impractical. Only Montgomery Blair, the postmaster general, favored taking bold action. Even Treasury Secretary Salmon Chase, the supposed hard-liner, offered just tepid support for a resupply effort. The rest, led by Seward, opposed any last-minute attempt to save Sumter.[5]

That was not what Lincoln wanted to hear. He spent the next few weeks working with Blair's brother-in-law, Gustavus Fox, a Massachusetts businessman and former naval officer, who was pushing an innovative plan to rescue the besieged fort. Lincoln asked Fox to present his ideas to the cabinet, before sending him to Charleston to gather more information. The president also authorized additional intelligence-gathering missions to South Carolina by two of his Illinois friends with southern ties: Stephen Hurlbut, originally from Charleston, and Ward Hill Lamon, who was Virginian-born. Hurlbut's report was grim. He wrote on March 27 that the "unanimity of sentiment" that he was encountering was "astonishing," and that there was "no attachment to the Union" left anywhere in Charleston. He warned that an attempt to resupply Sumter, even with provisions alone, would be resisted by force.[6]

As the cabinet debated their limited options, they worried about the partisan effects. During one discussion in mid-March, the president—or someone on his behalf—outlined the various pros and cons of withdrawing from Sumter. There were eight reasons listed in favor and only two against, but the first "con" was all-important: "The danger of demoralizing the Republican Party by a measure which might seem to many to indicate timidity, or in common parlance, 'want of pluck.'"[7]

Lincoln certainly did not want to be perceived as wanting in pluck. But by rejecting expert advice without settling on a firm alternative, he was starting to look weak. The second-guessing became intense by the end of his first month in office. Hard-liners demanded immediate action while moderates preached caution, but many establishment figures seemed more concerned about the rumors of vacillation inside the White House, spurred on by leaks from the warring cabinet officers, including Seward and Blair, who were lobbying aggressively for their respective positions.[8]

Adding to fears of a leadership vacuum was Lincoln's insistence on reviewing even the most routine political appointments. It had taken him nearly four months to sort out a cabinet of seven men. Now he was facing decisions involving over fifteen hundred presidential appointees.[9] He seemed determined to control virtually all of them. Norman Judd, the Illinois party chairman, became U.S. minister to Prussia. John Johnson, the former top field organizer in Illinois, secured a comfortable post at the New York Custom House. William Danenhower, the bookseller and former Illinois Know Nothing leader, got a clerkship in the Treasury Department. Each received direct attention from the overworked president. This was one of the central "lessons of experience" that Lincoln thought he had learned from watching President Zachary Taylor's inept leadership in 1849. Men were just as important as measures, and party loyalty had to be rewarded. By the end of his first term, Lincoln succeeded in replacing nearly 80 percent of the existing Democratic officeholders with Republican appointees largely of his own choosing. But the effort came at the cost of precious time and energy in early 1861.[10]

A devotion to patronage also threatened some important relationships. In March, Lincoln began doling out diplomatic appointments with a degree of abandon that irritated Seward. There was not even consultation about some, including Judd's. There was also a sloppy breach of confidentiality involving Carl Schurz. During the transition, Lincoln had promised the young German-born Republican that his valuable campaign efforts would be rewarded with a good posting in Europe. But Seward objected, and Lincoln made the mistake of telling Schurz about it. The former Seward delegate then took it upon himself to confront the secretary directly, revealing what Lincoln had told him. Seward was furious that his advice had been exposed in such a casual manner. Lincoln tried to slough off the tension by treating their discussions of what he called their diplomatic "card" like negotiations over any electoral slate. He offered to defend Seward's top choices but still wanted Schurz satisfied. "And then what about Carl Schurz?" he asked, "or, in other words, what about our german friends?" They eventually agreed to send the campaign organizer to Spain, which Schurz assured his wife was "the most important diplomatic post" after Mexico—an appointment that went to Ohio power broker Tom Corwin.[11]

Some Washington insiders, such as Republican congressman Charles Francis Adams, found these developments embarrassing. Adams complained in his diary that the president had "no conception of the situation" and yet "has undertaken to manage the whole thing as if he knew all about it." He gossiped with Senator Charles Sumner, head of the Foreign Relations Committee, and with Seward about what he considered Lincoln's appalling unfamiliarity with affairs of state. Adams, the son of one American president and the grandson of another, was offended by the instances of blatant partisanship, calling Lincoln "more blind and unsettled . . . as to men . . . than as to measures." The future U.S. minister to Britain declared, "He is ignorant, and must have help."[12] Edwin Stanton, the widely respected lawyer who had served as attorney general under Buchanan, also perceived signs that Lincoln lacked "settled principle." "Bluster & Bravado alternate with timidity & despair—recklessness, and helplessness by turns rule the hour," he wrote sourly in mid-March. "What but disgrace & disaster can happen?"[13]

Disgrace did nearly arrive at the end of the first month, when General Scott dropped another bombshell on the cabinet. In a memorandum dated March 28, Scott recommended withdrawing both from Fort Sumter in Charleston and from Fort Pickens outside Pensacola, Florida. Federal troops held several smaller forts along the Florida coast, but Pickens and Sumter were clearly the most significant military installations remaining under U.S. control inside the seceded states. Such a move would have represented a total abandonment of Lincoln's inaugural pledge and destroyed any prospect of Republican unity. There had been some hope that abandoning Sumter on grounds of military necessity might be explained away to party hard-liners if the government also retained control over Pickens, where Federal forces were in a much stronger position. Scott proposed a double withdrawal as a way to contain secession to the Deep South and keep a majority of the fifteen slave states in the union. Showing his colors as a Constitutional Unionist, Scott argued that "evacuation of both the forts would instantly soothe and give confidence to the eight remaining slaveholding States and render their cordial adherence to this Union perpetual."[14]

The general's naïve political advice proved to be a turning point in the crisis. Faced with the prospect of appearing cowardly to their fellow partisans, and convinced that Scott was playing politics himself, most of the cabinet rallied around the president's commitment to his inaugural vow to hold all the remaining U.S. forts. The one notable dissent came from Seward, who argued that Lincoln and his "party friends" were the ones being dangerously naïve.[15]

On the morning of April 1, Seward went over to the White House, along with his son and top aide, Frederick Seward, to deliver a document the secretary called "Some thoughts for the President's consideration." The blistering confidential memo began, "We are at the end of a month's administration and yet without a policy either domestic or foreign." Acknowledging that some of their problems had been "unavoidable" because pressing "patronage" concerns had overwhelmed "more grand matters," Seward urged the president to refocus on the secession crisis by announcing a delay of any further appointments. Here the New Yorker tried to explain his "singular" views about how best to reframe the national debate from a "Slavery" or "Party question" to a more patriotic issue of "Union or Disunion." But what Seward had in mind was even more shocking to Lincoln than Scott's suggestion of abandoning Sumter: He wanted the president to rally the nation around a confrontation with European imperialists. Seward outlined an elaborate scheme "to rouse a vigorous continental *spirit of independence* . . . against European intervention," suggesting that the sectional crisis might end with a request for Congress to "declare war" against Spain and France for recent incursions into the hemisphere.[16] This was a patriotic fusion strategy of sorts, but of a different dimension than anything either party leader had attempted before.

Seward concluded his startling proposal with thinly veiled personal criticism. "But whatever policy we adopt," he wrote, "there must be an energetic prosecution of it." He warned Lincoln that "it must be somebody's business to pursue and direct it incessantly," suggesting that if the president could not manage things while being "all the while active in it," then he should "Devolve it on some member of his Cabinet." On this point, Seward had a suggestion in mind. "It is not in my especial province," he wrote. "But I neither seek to evade nor assume responsibility."[17]

Lincoln recognized the assault on his own leadership for what it was. He drafted a reply but appears to have decided it would be better to discuss it in person with his former rival, which they did the next day. In his response, Lincoln asserted that his inaugural address had already outlined their official policy. They were going to try to hold all remaining federal property and military forts in the seceded states, even "Sumpter," as Lincoln called it. Seward supported reinforcing Pickens despite Scott's advice because he considered only Sumter to have become an unnecessary test of party loyalty. Lincoln flatly rejected this argument. "I do not perceive how the re-inforcement of Fort Sumpter would be done on a slavery, or party issue," he pointed out, "while that of Fort Pickens would be on a more national, and patriotic one." The president admitted to concerns about an attempted Spanish annexation of Santo Domingo in the Caribbean, but chose to ignore the rest of Seward's risky plan for ratcheting up enforcement of the Monroe Doctrine. He closed their revealing exchange by observing that there should be no questions about who would direct administration policy. "I must do it," Lincoln concluded.[18]

Seward came away from this confrontation unfazed. If anything, he turned even more Machiavellian in his efforts to avoid war. First, he apparently decided to leak his complaints to Henry Raymond at the *New York Times*. "WANTED—A POLICY" was the newspaper's searing headline on the day after their encounter. The *Times* made no mention of dealing with European threats, but it hit the rest of Seward's talking points with full force. "The Union is weaker now than it was a month ago," Raymond wrote, blaming Lincoln for squandering much of his "time and strength in feeding rapacious and selfish partisans." The editorial urged the president either to call Congress back into session to mobilize immediately for war and thereby scare the rebels straight, or to pursue a patient peace strategy by building "a Union Party in every Southern State."[19]

In early April, Lincoln ordered the resupply of Sumter and the reinforcement of Pickens with a contingent of regular army troops. But within days a series of botched orders, amateurish miscommunications, and other suspicious logistical failures—almost all involving Seward—guaranteed that neither of these expeditions would succeed fast enough.[20] In desperation, Lincoln tried to buy time by informing the South Carolina governor about the limited relief effort—only food and supplies—sailing toward Charleston. The Confederates, however, having advance notice of what they considered a blatant violation of the previous "truce," launched their bombardment of Sumter on April 12. Less than two days later Anderson surrendered, and the Civil War began in earnest.

Lincoln had tried hard to avert war, but he took solace in how the eruption of fighting unified the North. Later that summer he assured Browning, "The plan succeeded. They attacked Sumter—it fell and thus, did more service than it otherwise could."[21] This was candor, not cynicism. The "service" that Lincoln had in mind involved more than shifting blame for the outbreak of hostilities. The way the Sumter crisis had unfolded managed to preserve Republican party unity by proving the administration's determination to keep its promises. And it provided Northern Democrats and southern unionists with a clear rationale for remaining patriotic. The resulting split of slave states was also a partial victory for the Lincoln strategy. Virginia seceded, and three more Upper South states (Arkansas, North Carolina, and Tennessee) followed during the next two months. But four critical border slave states—Maryland, Delaware, Kentucky, and Missouri—remained loyal.

Most northerners, regardless of partisan affiliation, responded to the attack on Sumter with patriotic fervor. Starting in mid-April, the president issued a series of directives that declared an insurrection, called up state militias, ordered Congress back into special session on July 4, 1861, established a blockade of southern ports, and suspended civil liberties around the nation's vulnerable capital.[22] The public reaction to these initial steps appeared supportive and overwhelmingly nonpartisan. "I am not deceived in my faith in the North," exclaimed the shrewd Polish exile Adam Gurowski after Sumter. "Party lines burn, dissolved by excitement." He considered Northern politics to have been cast almost overnight "in fusion as bronze."[23]

Inside the White House, however, partisan business continued. On April 15—the day he issued his first military proclamation—Lincoln hosted a meeting about parceling out New York City patronage. Chase had pushed for the session, informing Lincoln that Manhattan attorney David Dudley Field was in town and reminding him that "each wing" of the party had been promised a fair share of appointments in New York. Field was a former Democrat who had clashed with Lincoln in 1847 at the River and Harbor Convention in Chicago and had since become a leading Republican in New York.

The key patronage position in the city was the collectorship of the U.S. Custom House in Manhattan, which had already been turned over to antislavery radical Hiram Barney, a favorite of both Chase and Field. Now Seward and Thurlow Weed were bearing down with their own slate of candidates for other lucrative posts within the massive port operation and elsewhere across Manhattan, Brooklyn, and beyond. The arguments over these appointments represented a continuation of the bitter intraparty Republican battles that had plagued the cabinet selections. They mainly pitted former Democrats and antislavery radicals against former Whigs and leading moderates—a factional rivalry personified by the emerging power struggle between Chase and Seward. Preston King, the strong-willed U.S. senator from New York who straddled both factions, joined the White House meeting, along with a few other cabinet officers. Lincoln took detailed notes as the group struggled to find a compromise. The president annotated a list of potential appointees in his own peculiar shorthand, indicating "S.W." presumably for former Seward Whigs, "R.D." for those Republicans with radical and Democratic antecedents, and even one "Am" designating a former American party figure, for the ex–Know Nothings whom they intended to placate. Most of the figures discussed on April 15 eventually received their appointments.[24]

If news of a secret patronage discussion had leaked out as a civil war was just getting started, Lincoln would have faced intense public criticism. That same morning the *Philadelphia Inquirer*, a major Democratic newspaper, declared its readiness to embrace the "no party now" sentiment rising in the North. "All party lines cease," the editors wrote on April 15, "all merge into one of two parties—Patriots or Traitors."[25] Even before Sumter fell, the *New York Times* had been using the ugliness at the Custom House to call for a more high-minded approach from the president. "We are Republicans—but above and beyond all that, we are Americans," Raymond had written, vowing to deliver the "truth" to Lincoln about the necessity of appointing good men regardless of partisanship. "We love our party," the editor stated, "but we love our country better."[26]

At the outset of the war, nobody expressed this country-first sentiment with greater zeal than Stephen Douglas. The principal Northern Democratic leader gave a series of rousing patriotic speeches in Illinois designed to help raise troops. On April 25, he told the state legislature that even though he had once been "a very good partisan fighter," those days were over. He predicted that a civil war would become both "Bloody" and "calamitous." On May 1 at Chicago, inside the massive building that had been the Wigwam of the 1860 Republican convention (since renamed National Hall), Douglas laid blame for the outbreak of violence directly on Southern Democrats. "Are we to tolerate the idea that a defeated party in a national election may resort to the sword when defeated by the popular will?" To the cheering crowd, he exclaimed, "Every man must be on the side of the United States or against it. There can be no neutrals in this war. There can be none but patriots and traitors." He closed with a warning: "Whoever is not prepared to sacrifice party organizations and platforms on the altar of his country does not deserve the support and countenance of honest people."[27]

Lincoln, however, was proceeding with a more complicated dual track of his own making. As a new president assembling his administration, he remained loyal to the Republican party, rewarding its men and promoting its measures. But as the commander in chief of armed forces engaged in combat, he encouraged patriotic support from all parties through the strategic use of military appointments and promotions. His approach to mobilization took partisan factors into consideration but was decidedly multipartisan. And Lincoln proved just as aggressive in asserting himself into military personnel decisions as he had been in managing political patronage.

The initial April 15 militia call-up of 75,000 men was limited by law to only three months, so the War Department quickly began planning for a longer mobilization. The strategy was to supplement the regular army, which at the time numbered only about 1,100 officers and 16,000 enlisted men, with hundreds of thousands of state-recruited volunteers serving for up to three years and a number of new field commanders.[28] Northern governors and other political leaders worked furiously to raise the necessary regiments. In May and June, even before Congress was set to reassemble, Lincoln began appointing the highest-ranking major generals and other senior officers to help supervise the influx of volunteers.

Benjamin Butler, a prominent Democratic state legislator from Massachusetts, was an initial beneficiary of Lincoln's multiparty outreach. Despite his New England roots, Butler had been a supporter of Southern Democrats during the 1860 campaign. However, he had also opposed secession and helped organize the Massachusetts militia troops sent down to Washington by Republican governor John Andrew in the immediate aftermath of the firing on Sumter. In mid-May, Lincoln named the fifty-two-year-old Butler, who had no previous combat experience, as a major general of volunteers.

The president also promoted John Dix, another leading Breckinridge supporter, to the same high rank, after Dix came out vigorously against the rebellion. The aging Dix, a New Yorker, had some relevant military experience, but it was in the War of 1812. Of the several prominent Douglas Democrats who received early appointments, the most notable was Illinois Central Railroad executive and West Point graduate George McClellan, who reentered the nation's military service in the spring of 1861 as a general charged with leading Ohio volunteers. Lincoln balanced high-profile Democratic officers by naming Republican political figures such as former presidential candidate John Frémont, ex–Speaker of the U.S. House Nathaniel Banks, and New York senator E. D. Morgan to other key commands in the fast-expanding U.S. military.

The president's attention extended beyond the highest ranks. In early June, he wanted regular army officer Montgomery Meigs designated as a quartermaster general owing partly to Seward's lobbying, but mainly because he was so impressed by the younger officer's "masculine intellect." But the appointment faced unexpected opposition from Secretary of War Simon Cameron. Lincoln wrote a private note to General Scott requesting "influence" to help "remove Gen. Cameron's objection." Scott complied but pressed for a return favor, asking Lincoln to promote William Rosecrans, one of his protégés, to brigadier general within the regular army. A distracted president pushed through a new rank for "Rosencrantz" while also acting on behalf of his Illinois political acquaintances. These included southern-born informant Stephen Hurlbut as well as West Point graduate John Pope, son of a federal judge in Springfield, who were among the first brigadier generals appointed in the new U.S. Volunteer forces.[29]

Lincoln was by no means alone in mixing political influence with military mobilization. Partisan leaders of all stripes lobbied aggressively for their respective favorites. Republican senator John Sherman from Ohio (who had replaced Chase when the radical leader joined the cabinet) helped secure a series of appointments—and some occasional reprieves—for his older brother, William Sherman, an experienced ex-military man who was plagued, in those difficult early months of the war, with severe bouts of depression and anxiety. Even more notably, Galena congressman Elihu Washburne helped get a colonel's commission with the Illinois volunteers for a struggling constituent of his own, a Douglas Democrat and former regular army officer named Ulysses Grant.

The one Douglas Democrat who never received a military appointment was Douglas himself, who fell seriously ill not long after his return to Chicago in May 1861. He initially tried to dismiss his weakened condition as a bout of rheumatism, but he died in early June, probably from the cumulative effects of alcohol abuse. The Democratic leader's stirring patriotic appeal at the former Republican Wigwam was his last public appearance. To replace him, Governor Richard Yates announced the selection of one of Lincoln's oldest political friends, Republican Orville Browning from Quincy. With Browning's appointment, Lyman Trumbull became the state's senior U.S. senator, and Republicans seemed poised to dominate the once doubtful state of Illinois. The loss of influence frustrated Northern Democrats. One newspaper complained, "The hopes of many that the Governor of Illinois would make good the Republican boast that there is 'no party now,' by appointing a Douglas Democrat to succeed Douglas, have been disappointed."[30] Adding to the frustration among Democrats, Douglas apparently told confidants before he fell ill that he was about to take a major command in the army.[31]

That story seems unlikely. Behind the patriotic talk, tension persisted between Lincoln and Douglas and their respective followers. In his final public statements, Douglas made clear that he considered noninterference with slavery to be a red line for any successful patriotic fusion. "I will never sanction nor acquiesce in any warfare whatever, upon the constitutional rights or domestic institutions of the people of the Southern States," he promised his fellow Democrats. This was a direct warning to Lincoln. The inaugural address had committed to noninterference as a peacetime principle, but now that the shooting had started, Northern Democrats were concerned. Although the Republican president had been careful not to threaten extreme antislavery action, such as wartime emancipation (something already being touted by radicals as a possibility), he had vowed in his inaugural that "fugitive slaves, now only partially surrendered, would not be surrendered at all" in the event of any national "separation."[32]

Near the end of his life, Douglas seemed to acknowledge that Lincoln might strike more radical blows against slavery in the name of military necessity. Admitting that he could not answer questions from fellow Democrats "in regard to the policy of Mr. Lincoln and Cabinet," he confessed in a letter dictated from his deathbed, "I am not in their confidence." With apparent disdain, he added, "I am neither the supporter of the partisan policy nor the apologist of the errors of the Administration." Still, Douglas urged Northern Democrats to rally around the union and the Constitution as they understood it. On the topic of his potential role in the Republican-led war effort, he merely concluded that his relationship with the administration was "unchanged."[33]

Even if Douglas had somehow recovered his health and been able to lead men into combat, Lincoln was unlikely to have trusted such an unpredictable rival. He set no antislavery litmus test for military appointees in 1861, but from the beginning of the conflict, it was clear that the newly reorganized Federal army would be confronting the institution of slavery in a multitude of ways as it worked to suppress what many were already calling the slaveholders' rebellion. Lincoln wanted Democrats and conservatives to serve within the military, but he needed them to put aside their views on slavery or any other partisan issue whenever ordered to do so. From years of firsthand observation, he understood that yielding in such manner was not Douglas's style.

Individuals can surprise, however. The most ardent antislavery general at the outset of the war proved to be Ben Butler, the erstwhile New England supporter of the Southern Democrats, who tackled the knotty problem of how to handle runaway slaves in late May from his posting at Fortress Monroe, on the Virginia peninsula. Even before

Douglas's death, Butler took actions, inspired by Lincoln's inaugural threat and supported by the War Department, that effectively declared fugitive slaves who came behind U.S. lines to be "contraband of war" and hence not liable for return under the ordinary operations of the federal fugitive slave code. Butler, a former lawyer, was applying traditional European laws of war on "contraband" property to American freedom seekers. Most U.S. officers did not follow this antislavery practice during the early period of the conflict, but Butler's actions set in motion a chain of precedents that by 1863 would evolve into a full-fledged wartime emancipation policy.[34]

From the outset, leading radicals recognized that the necessities of war might afford such opportunities. In late April, Massachusetts senator Charles Sumner commented to fellow abolitionist Joshua Giddings that "this generous and mighty uprising of the North seems to menace defeat to the rebels, and the extinction of slavery in blood." Writing from a diplomatic post in Montreal, former congressman Giddings agreed, noting with almost cold calculation that "never were the political heavens more bright or auspicious." He added, "The first gun fired at Fort Sumter rang out the death-knell of slavery."[35]

The opening of the war also radicalized some once-cautious moderates. In a series of letters from his home near the banks of the Mississippi River, Orville Browning, still working as an attorney in Quincy, eagerly informed Lincoln about the aroused state of public opinion around Illinois and Missouri. He reported on the overwhelming support for the president's vigorous war measures and joined Giddings in predicting "doom" for the slaveholders. By the end of April, he was also suggesting a scheme for a separate Black protectorate or reservation to be carved out of the soon-to-be conquered rebel region. "Whenever our armies march into the Southern states, the negroes will, of course, flock to our standards," he wrote on April 30. "They will rise in rebellion, and strike a blow for emancipation from servitude, and to avenge the wrongs of ages." The Kentucky-born Browning called this "inevitable" before asking Lincoln, "What is to be done with them?" Browning himself thought the answer obvious: They would need their own land. Although a long-standing advocate of colonization for freed slaves, he was no longer looking to Africa as the site for such settlements. Calling it the "one thing, and one thing only that we can do," Browning urged the president to grant formerly enslaved people a semiautonomous state of their own by breaking up the old southern plantations. "Let them have the soil upon which they were born," he concluded.[36]

On May 7, John Hay, one of Lincoln's new White House assistants, burst into the president's office to relay the gist of this letter to Lincoln and fellow aide John Nicolay. During those early months of the administration, the twenty-two-year-old Hay handled the president's correspondence, while Nicolay, a former Illinois journalist and party field organizer who was a slightly more grizzled twenty-nine, managed visitors and served as de facto chief of staff. The two bachelors lived together in the White House and represented the extent of the president's full-time political operation during his first year in office. That morning, in sardonic tones, Hay described Browning's plan as one proposing "to subjugate the South" while allowing freed Black people to live under "a protectorate" as "they raised our cotton." The president responded dryly, "Some of our northerners seem bewildered and dazzled by the excitement of the hour." Lincoln mentioned other radical ideas he had received, some from surprising corners. Wisconsin senator James Doolittle, a noted moderate, had told the president that the war would result in "the entire abolition of slavery." Lincoln noted that Alexander Hamilton's seventy-three-year-old son James, a respected former Jacksonian Democrat, had been pressing for "enlisting the slaves in our army." Hay assured the president that his official correspondence was also "thickly interspersed by such suggestions."[37]

The shifting political landscape seemed to provoke an unusual burst of candor from Lincoln. "For my own part," he confessed, "I consider the central idea pervading this struggle is the necessity that is upon us, of proving that popular government is not an absurdity." He claimed that "the real question . . . was whether a free and representative government had the right and power to protect and maintain itself." He explained to his aides that he was thinking more deeply about these ideas in preparation for his upcoming message to the special session of Congress scheduled to convene on July 4. He seemed willing—almost eager—to provide a glimpse inside his strategic calculations. This was unusual for the "Tycoon," as Nicolay and Hay were starting to label him, in an ironic allusion to the Japanese shogunate ruler. Until this point, under the crush of endless patronage meetings and through the intensity of the Sumter crisis, the young aides had little time for candid talk with the boss, especially on weightier political matters.[38]

Lincoln's comments about the importance of maintaining faith in democratic self-government were not new, but he did share something explosive that morning. Addressing the recent onslaught of unsolicited advice, he insisted that antislavery ideas must be taken seriously, though "not for us to use in advance." He then invoked a phrase from his 1858 debates with Douglas, referring to slavery as "a vast and far reaching disturbing element." He observed that his administration might well have to try to destroy the institution during the war, but only to avoid a "final judgment," meaning defeat on the battlefield. "That however is not for us to say at present," he added. "Taking the government as we found it we will see if the majority can preserve it."[39] His aides seemed surprised that the president was holding on to such radical cards. Later that day Hay put down a verbatim account of the conversation in his diary, and Nicolay made a rare memorandum of the exchange for his file as well.[40]

Few in Washington appreciated what Lincoln was contemplating. The conventional wisdom held that the president was being too cautious in the opening months of the conflict. "The war is ostensibly prosecuted with vigor," Seward wrote his wife in early June. "But you have no idea how incessant my labors are to keep up the conduct of it up to the line of necessity and public expectation." Noting that "executive skill and rigor are rare qualities," Seward observed that Lincoln was "the best of us." But his letter made clear that he meant "best" as a measure of human decency, or what he sometimes called Lincoln's "magnanimity," a trait that Seward described, tongue in cheek, as "superhuman." When it came to leadership qualities, the secretary remained more skeptical, assuring his wife that Lincoln needed "constant and assiduous cooperation." "I have said too much already," Seward sighed as he closed his letter with a warning that Frances Seward ignored: "Burn this."[41]

Lincoln seemed to be hoping that his message to Congress might win over such skeptics. By mid-June, according to Nicolay, the president was "engaged almost constantly" on the special message, cutting back on his stream of patronage meetings and practically isolating himself in the White House. Only at the end of the process did Lincoln share copies with Seward and John Defrees, an experienced Indiana journalist who was managing the Government Printing Office. The two men offered minor suggestions, most of which the president accepted. But the July 4 message was almost entirely Lincoln's work, even more so than his inaugural address.[42]

The final version, read aloud by a congressional clerk on July 5, 1861, began with a gripping but also self-serving narrative of the Sumter crisis, culminating in a charge that by firing on the Federal fort, the "so-called" Confederates had "forced upon the country the distinct issue, 'Immediate dissolution or blood.' " For the president, this choice of words represented a kind of vindication. He had wanted to end his inaugural address with a stark question ("Shall it be peace, or a sword?") but pulled back at Seward's urging. The time for conciliation had passed.[43]

Lincoln also laid out his vision of the war's political framework. Claiming that the rebellion "presents to the whole family of man, the question, whether a constitutional republic, or a democracy—a government of the people, by the same people—can, or cannot, maintain its territorial integrity, against its own domestic foes," the president went on to ask: "Must a government, of necessity, be too *strong* for the liberties of its own people, or too *weak* to maintain its own existence?" He attacked what he termed the "sophism" of the secession argument that somehow state withdrawal from the union was constitutional, and he denounced the "insidious debauching" and "drugging the public mind" that had over the years "sugar-coated" this movement toward insurrection, making treason appear almost reasonable to most white southerners. Defrees tried to talk Lincoln out of using the term "sugar-coated" since it was "not exactly diplomatic," but the president was adamant. "No, let it stand," he said, "it is a word the people use; they will know what it means." The president closed this section of the message by describing the conflict as a "people's contest" designed to "elevate the condition of men."[44]

Lincoln was making the case that Congress should support waging civil war, even at an immense cost in expenditures and possible loss of life. But his message also addressed his invocation of the "war power" in his initial suspension of civil liberties. Chief Justice Roger Taney of the Supreme Court had opposed the administration's use of preventive arrests, in a stinging ex parte opinion written from the Maryland circuit. On this murky constitutional question, however, Lincoln appeared less certain. He defended himself on practical grounds, asking, "Are all the laws but one to go unexecuted and the government itself go to pieces lest that one be violated?"[45]

The president closed with powerful affirmations of representative democracy and the need for strong leadership. Claiming the crisis would yield "a great lesson," he observed that it should teach Americans "that what they can not take by an election neither can they take it by a war." As president, he stated, he "had no moral right to shrink, nor even to count the chances of his own life in what might follow," and he urged fellow citizens to "trust in God, and go forward without fear, and with manly hearts."[46]

Lincoln's invocation of "manly hearts" was more than a platitude. Earlier that spring, when a delegation from Baltimore beseeched him to avoid escalation, Lincoln practically mocked them. "You express great horror of bloodshed," he said, "yet have no word of condemnation for those who are making war on us." He stated, "There is no Washington in that—no Jackson in that—no manhood nor honor in that."[47] In private, he could be even rougher. After receiving an impertinent letter in late April from Isham Harris, the secessionist governor of Tennessee, warning against the use of "coercion" or military force against southern states, Lincoln was overheard muttering angrily to himself, "He be damned."[48]

The special session of Congress opened against the backdrop of reports that the provisional congress of the Confederacy planned to meet in Richmond on July 20. Starting at the end of June, Horace Greeley's *New-York Tribune* emblazoned its daily masthead with the stark call, "Forward to Richmond! Forward to Richmond!" Trumbull of Illinois pushed his fellow Republican senators to embrace Greeley's message, urging them to adopt a resolution calling for the immediate movement of the Federal army and an occupation of Richmond by July 20. Lincoln told newly arrived Senator Browning that he was also in favor of "the most vigorous and active measures to bring the war to a speedy close" and was "totally opposed to any compromise of any kind or character."[49]

The monthlong special session focused on securing appropriations for the fast-growing military and on the debates over how to proceed with the war, but it also addressed—as always—government patronage. Lincoln found himself besieged by legislators demanding his attention to their recommendations. The president complained to

Treasury Secretary Chase that he was quickly becoming entrapped in the "unpleasantness" developing between the new House Speaker, Galusha Grow of Pennsylvania, and influential New York senator Preston King. Both were lobbying him about auditor appointments in the Treasury Department. Lincoln was also pushing for his own favorites, such as abolitionist Zebina Eastman for a minor appointment in Great Britain, or former Democratic congressman Robert Smith of Alton, whom Lincoln labeled "always a clever man," for a midlevel military appointment.[50]

But most of Lincoln's Illinois supporters remained agitated by signs of the president's ingratitude. State auditor Jesse Dubois complained to Lincoln that he had not "appointed a single man from Illinois that was originally your friend" but had been tricked into promoting a bunch of "soreheads and Grumblers."[51] Exasperated at not being heard, David Davis accused the young White House aides of failing to show Lincoln his recommendation letters. Nicolay eventually responded to this finger-pointing with indignation, assuring Davis that Lincoln himself had authorized him to say the claim was not true.[52]

Meanwhile, as the pressure for an early military offensive mounted in Washington, General Scott proved to be the only serious holdout. In a series of meetings with the president and his cabinet, the aging general advocated for what newspapers were labeling his "Anaconda Plan," a patient strategy designed to blockade the major ports of the South and cripple its cotton-trading economy by advancing down the Mississippi and capturing New Orleans. Scott warned against premature frontal movements in Virginia, claiming that raw U.S. troops would be prone to panic. In mid-July, Lincoln convened a special council of war composed of senior military and cabinet advisers who overruled Scott and approved a plan submitted by the general's subordinate and protégé, Irvin McDowell, to launch an immediate attack through nearby Manassas Junction in northern Virginia. When

McDowell then hesitated, expressing concerns that his troops were "green," Scott ordered him to move anyway, since all the troops on both sides were "green alike."[53]

The battle at Manassas or Bull Run on July 21 was a disaster for Federal forces, who suffered hundreds of casualties amid a demoralizing retreat. In the grim aftermath of the defeat, and with leaders of the Confederacy successfully meeting in Richmond, Lincoln tried to project resilience. He traveled with Seward around the forts of Washington to rally the troops, and he drew up a memorandum outlining policy changes to help shore up the U.S. military effort. He ordered General George McClellan to come east from his position in western Virginia, where he had been achieving some success, to take command of the military forces around the capital. McClellan spent the rest of the summer organizing the Army of the Potomac, made up of tens of thousands of the new three-year enlisted men authorized during the recent special session of Congress.[54]

Congress also responded to the U.S. defeat at Bull Run by passing a resolution sponsored in the House by the aging John Crittenden of Kentucky, elected in June on a special unionist slate, and in the Senate by Andrew Johnson of Tennessee, a Democrat who had refused to join his state's secessionist majority. The Crittenden-Johnson resolution affirmed that the "object" of the current war was "to defend and maintain the supremacy of the Constitution and to preserve the Union, with all the dignity, equality, and rights of the several States unimpaired." This was intended to reassure border state unionists that the conflict—which was obviously not ending anytime soon—would not become a political crusade to abolish slavery. Republicans on Capitol Hill supported this conservative-sounding sentiment as a continuation of their traditional noninterference pledge. They did not consider it a limitation on their other antislavery ambitions.[55]

Indeed, even as the Crittenden-Johnson framework was being negotiated, Senator Lyman Trumbull reported out a "confiscation" bill from the Judiciary Committee to punish rebels by authorizing the seizure of their property and the liberation of any enslaved people who were employed to support the Confederate war effort. The final version of the statute, adopted at the end of the special session on August 6, did not include specific freedom language but instead held that those who owned enslaved people working for the Confederate military would be required to "forfeit" their claims to such labor. Antislavery legislators nevertheless conceived of the law as an emancipation measure especially useful to liberate "contrabands" who fled to Federal lines, and that was essentially how the War Department explained its implementation to commanders in the field.[56]

From his posting in St. Louis, where he headed up the Department of the West, General John Frémont decided to test the limits of the new confiscation policy. Frémont was struggling with a multitude of challenges in the border state of Missouri. On August 10, Confederates had won a decisive victory at Wilson's Creek in the state's southwestern corner, killing hundreds of outnumbered Federal troops, including Nathaniel Lyon, the first U.S. general to die in the Civil War. The resulting ferment was especially bad in St. Louis, where radical antislavery advisers around Frémont were trying to wrest control in Missouri away from a coalition of conservative and moderate civilian politicians. Rep. Frank Blair, Jr., started writing anxious reports to his brother, Montgomery Blair, the postmaster general, calling "affairs" in the state "quite alarming." Frémont declared martial law on August 30, vowing to shoot anyone found guilty of treason and proclaiming freedom for all enslaved people held by disloyal masters and not just those employed by the Confederate army.[57]

Lincoln recognized that Frémont's order could have a damaging political impact beyond Missouri's borders, particularly in neighboring Kentucky. On September 2, he sent the general a note by special messenger warning Frémont to refrain from executing anyone without his approval and urging him to modify the emancipation edict "as of your own motion" so that it would "conform" to the recent Confiscation Act. Lincoln assured Frémont that he wrote "in a spirit of caution, and not of censure."[58]

A defiant Frémont drafted a reply that he sent back to Washington with his wife, Jessie Benton Frémont, the daughter of Missouri's late senator Thomas Hart Benton. She arrived on September 10 and met with Lincoln late that evening at the White House. Their encounter was memorable. The president later said that Jessie Frémont "taxed me so violently with many things that I had to exercise all the awkward tact I have to avoid quarelling with her." From her perspective, Benton Frémont found Lincoln more patronizing than tactful. She claimed that at one point he dismissed her as "quite a female politician."[59]

The message carried by Benton Frémont challenged the president to "openly" direct his general to "make the correction" to the emancipation order if that was what he desired. According to Lincoln, Mrs. Frémont added to the tension by "more than once" intimating that her husband could "set up for himself" if necessary.[60]

Lincoln did not back down. The next day he made General Frémont's request public, announcing that he was "very cheerfully" directing a modification of the emancipation order "to conform to, and not to transcend," the recent confiscation law. A few days later Frémont escalated the crisis by ordering the arrest of Frank Blair. With charges and countercharges flying around St. Louis, the president and his cabinet debated how to regain control over the delicate situation. Within a month, Lincoln removed Frémont from his command, reassigning him to a lesser post in Virginia. Blair was released from custody.[61]

By the late summer of 1861, the pressures of the war seemed to be affecting nearly everyone. Both Nicolay and Hay fell ill, and each took significant time away from the White House. Fearing the sickness pervading Washington, Mary Lincoln took the boys on an extended vacation to New Jersey. President Lincoln remained behind in the White House. His friend District Marshal Ward Hill Lamon wrote him nervously from New York expressing concern that there were "eavesdroppers and traitors lurking about the White House" and that he should start ordering all visitors to be kept downstairs.[62] Lincoln ignored him.

Orville Browning worried that the strain was beginning to show on the president, who had seemed, in his opinion, "a little despondent" at their final meeting before the congressional recess. "You have your future in your own hands," the senator wrote after his return to Illinois, "but you must be firm, earnest, and, if need be, even inexorable."[63] Over the next several weeks, Browning continued to offer brotherly guidance on a wide range of political and military matters, from the alleged drunkenness of General Stephen Hurlbut, who was now stationed out west, to what he considered Lincoln's wrongheaded decision on Frémont's emancipation edict. "There has been too much tenderness towards traitors and rebels," Browning observed sternly. "We must strike them terrible blows, and strike them hard and quick, or the government will go hopelessly to pieces."[64]

The president responded by lecturing Browning to "give up your restlessness for new positions." He told his friend that if he would only "back me manfully on the grounds upon which you and other kind friends gave me the election . . . we shall go through triumphantly." Dismissing Frémont's order regarding "the liberation of slaves" as "purely political" and representing nothing less than "dictatorship" without the "savor" of "military necessity" to justify it, Lincoln observed how "odd" it seemed to him that a Republican senator like Browning could be indifferent to the weighty matters of "principle" in the new confiscation law that he himself had helped create. The president acknowledged that Frémont's order was "popular in some quarters" but observed it was highly detrimental in Kentucky. "I think to lose Kentucky is nearly the same as to lose the whole game," Lincoln asserted, suggesting that such a catastrophe would make the "job" of restoring the union "too large for us." Browning responded but could not change Lincoln's mind.[65]

Browning at least had the president's ear. Other Republicans, especially those most committed to achieving emancipation, felt ignored and even betrayed. The ultras had not been satisfied either with the irregular contraband policy initiated by General Butler at Fortress Monroe or with the limited August 1861 confiscation law, and they were distressed by the modification of Frémont's emancipation order. In late September 1861, Black abolitionist Frederick Douglass started attacking the administration in public, complaining in his Rochester-based newspaper, *Douglass' Monthly*, that Lincoln's unwillingness to cast off the "mill-stone" of slavery was encouraging nothing but "Weakness, faint heartedness and inefficiency." From his post in Spain, Carl Schurz expressed deep frustration, arguing that the only way to effect "a decided change of trend" would be for the president "to proclaim the freedom of all slaves." But he was not optimistic. "Application of such means demands more spirit and decision than the government possesses," he wrote glumly.[66]

The crisis of confidence among radicals worsened following another Federal military disaster, on October 21, at Ball's Bluff in Loudoun County, Virginia. This encounter was more a skirmish than a battle, but reports of U.S. army incompetence soon led to the creation of a special Joint Congressional Committee on the Conduct of the War. Radical Republicans in Congress subsequently used this joint committee as a vehicle for pressing the administration and high-ranking officers such as McClellan to adopt more aggressive war-making measures. Lincoln suffered a personal loss at Ball's Bluff when his longtime friend (and namesake of his deceased second son, Eddy) Edward Baker was killed while leading his regiment in the chaotic combat. Baker, who had moved to the West coast in the 1850s following his congressional service as a Whig representing Galena, eventually became a Republican U.S. senator from Oregon. While still in the Senate, he served as colonel of an army regiment. When he died at age fifty, he left behind a wife and four children.[67]

The president's once-loyal law partner William Herndon felt agitated by the tide of events. From Springfield, he wrote angrily to Lyman Trumbull: "What is Lincoln doing?" "Does he suppose he can Crush—squelch out this huge rebellion by pop guns filled with rose water[?]" Like many northerners, Herndon wanted blood. He claimed the president "ought to hang somebody, and get up a name for will or decisiveness of character," proposing that Lincoln could even execute a "Child or woman, if he has not Courage to hang a *man*." Herndon, who had praised Lincoln's "radical heart" during the presidential contest, now questioned his friend's commitment to freedom. "Good God!" he exclaimed. "If I were Lincoln I would have my name deeply Empressed on the worlds great [Minds] and to do this I would declare that all slaves shall be free and stand Emancipated. *I would be this ages [great] hero.*"[68]

Attorney General Edward Bates, a conservative on the slavery question, also complained in his diary about Lincoln. The administration had "no system—no unity—no accountability," according to Bates, and what he termed dismissively "no subordination." Like Herndon, the Missouri politician was fed up with what he considered Lincoln's "impotent indecision."[69]

Lincoln responded to the escalating complaints by citing the challenges he faced. "We are doing the very best we can," he explained to one agitated northern governor. "I am compelled to watch all points."[70] When Illinois Democrat John McClernand, a brigadier general in the western theater, griped to Elihu Washburne that his forces lacked supplies, Lincoln sent what he termed a "social letter," not an "official" one, to his former partisan rival. He thanked McClernand and his men for their sacrifices and apologized for what they were facing in the field. "Much, very much, goes undone," the president admitted, "but it is because we have not the power to do it faster than we do." Lincoln tried to put a patriotic spin on the logistical nightmares. "The plain matter-of-fact is," he wrote, "our good people have rushed to the rescue of the Government, faster than the government can find arms to put into their hands."[71]

Just a few days later, Lincoln took Seward and Hay on an unannounced evening visit to McClellan's home to discuss the various problems. McClellan had been promoted to chief military adviser, replacing General Scott, who had finally retired under pressure from Lincoln and his cabinet. McClellan, who retained his field command with the Army of the Potomac, assured Lincoln, "I can do it all." But apparently he meant that he preferred to do it alone.[72]

The general was not at home when Lincoln and his party arrived on November 13, so they waited for him in a parlor. But when McClellan appeared, he went upstairs, ignoring them. Confused by the delay, the guests asked a servant to remind the general they were waiting. Word came back that McClellan had gone to bed. Hay was flabbergasted at the open contempt for the president, but Lincoln said it was no time "to be making points of etiquette & personal dignity." Hay was not convinced, noting in his diary that it looked to him like "a dreadful portent of evil to come."[73]

Not long after McClellan's slight, a diplomatic crisis erupted with Great Britain that was not resolved until Christmas. In mid-November, a headstrong U.S. naval officer seized a British ship carrying Confederate envoys to Europe. One of these diplomats was former U.S. senator James Mason, author of the 1850 Fugitive Slave Act. The Republican press hailed the irony of the capture, but the British government threatened war over what it perceived as a deliberate violation of international law. The Lincoln administration eventually backed down from a military confrontation, but not before enduring weeks of wrangling.

The Thirty-Seventh Congress, which came back into session in early December, was an unexpectedly ambitious one. Republican-led committees put their expanded postsecession majority to use by enacting sweeping domestic legislation, including a homestead bill and funding for a transcontinental railroad. Lincoln engaged the Congress most directly on slavery policy and military affairs. In his annual message, drafted over several days and read on December 3, the president reminded legislators about what he regarded as the war's purpose, deriding the "insurrection" as "largely, if not exclusively, a war upon the first principle of popular government—the rights of the people."[74] Behind the scenes, Lincoln began working with Senator Browning, Rep. George Fisher of Delaware, and others to craft proposals designed to win approval for gradual, compensated abolition in the loyal border states. The president worked intensely that winter to parry efforts by the new joint war committee, which seemed determined either to goad McClellan into launching a major offensive action against the Confederates or to have him replaced.[75]

Lincoln himself was eager for combat movement, especially in Virginia and eastern Tennessee. "Consumption of time is killing us," he complained to one general.[76] But he found it nearly impossible to control or even shape the military situation. Stubbornly self-confident, McClellan was determined not to be stampeded into what he regarded as reckless action by his civilian superiors, and he had little respect for Lincoln, whom he derided in private as the "original gorilla."[77] McClellan held even greater contempt for the would-be Napoleons in Congress who kept second-guessing his field army's inactivity during this long winter period of "all quiet along the Potomac." Matters got worse when communication from McClellan essentially ceased late in December after he fell ill with typhoid fever. By the end of the year, the nation appeared on the brink of a civil-military crisis. On December 31, Attorney General Bates reported in his diary that he had confronted Lincoln, pleading with him that "he *must* command" because "the Nation requires it, and History will hold him responsible."[78]

Lincoln did begin taking more aggressive steps on December 31. He began that day by drafting a letter to a disgruntled General David Hunter, who had been reassigned from a command at St. Louis to a posting in Kansas. Hunter had blasted this "banishment" in a searing note to the president. Lincoln responded in kind, warning his old acquaintance that "you are adopting the best possible way to ruin yourself." Lincoln's advice was to stop complaining: "He who does something at the head of one Regiment, will eclipse him who does nothing at the head of a hundred." Hunter privately dismissed the president as little more than a typical politician, "anxious for approval."[79]

That evening Lincoln also met with agitated members of the joint committee and answered their questions for over ninety minutes. The president suggested afterward to McClellan that the men had left "in a perfectly good mood" once they understood the "facts" of the situation.[80] In truth, the committee was not satisfied by the president's rationalizations for McClellan, and some members began pushing to have Irvin McDowell take over field leadership of the Army of the Potomac.

Also on the thirty-first, the president began communicating directly with McClellan's subordinates in the field, using the general's illness as an excuse. In a series of separate but identical messages, he urged Generals Henry Halleck and Don Buell to launch a coordinated attack against Confederate forces in eastern Tennessee—a strategy he thought McClellan had already authorized. Within days, however, it became apparent that no such offensive had been planned. "Delay is ruining us," Lincoln remarked again in early January. "I have no arms," Halleck replied, prompting Lincoln to borrow a textbook on military strategy that Halleck, a former professor at West Point, had written. He also directed McClellan to stop avoiding the committee, "to-day, if possible." And that week he began collecting information directly from McClellan's bewildered subordinates in Washington. The president met privately with Quartermaster General Montgomery Meigs, who helped him organize a council of war meeting for Friday night, with cabinet officers Seward and Chase and divisional commanders McDowell and William Franklin.[81]

In his notes from the January 10 meeting, McDowell described the president as "greatly disturbed at the state of affairs." At one point, Lincoln tartly informed the men that "if General McClellan did not want to use the army, he would like to *borrow* it." But the conversation wandered in confused fashion, and even after a follow-up meeting two days later, the president was unable to ascertain the details of McClellan's plans for offensive action.[82] Yet by pressuring the general's subordinates so bluntly, the president sent a clear message to McClellan. His patience had run out.

On Saturday, January 11, Lincoln punctuated his displeasure over stalled military affairs by upending his cabinet and pushing the largely ineffective Secretary of War Simon Cameron out to a diplomatic post in Russia. In his place, Lincoln appointed Edwin Stanton, a former attorney general in the Buchanan administration. Stanton was no military man, but he knew Washington well. And he had ingratiated himself with Lincoln's team. He was soundly antislavery, supportive of the war effort, and had a reputation as being tough-minded and competent. Seward described him as someone "of great force—full of expedients and thoroughly loyal."[83] Republican newspapers generally cheered the appointment.

If Lincoln intended for these actions to help "hive" McClellan, as he liked to say, the plan worked when his ailing military adviser finally resurfaced. McClellan met first with the president and then with the council of war on January 13, but insisted he would not reveal his plans "unless ordered to do so." Lincoln decided against forcing the issue any further. In a letter to General Buell later that day, the president explained the strategy he thought they needed to implement. He had come to believe that "menacing" the enemy "with superior forces at *different points*, at the *same* time," was the best way of "making our advantage an over-match for *his*."[84]

Lincoln's practice as a party chief and politician had always been to gather information from multiple sources but consult almost no one when it came time to render final decisions. According to John Hay, this was how the commander in chief came to issue his first major strategic directive two weeks later. General War Order No. 1 commanded a "general movement" of Federal military forces on February 22. Hay noted that Lincoln wrote this order "without any consultation," presenting it to his cabinet "not for their sanction but for their information." The president's statement was brief—only four sentences—and listed six of the major Federal field armies scattered across the Virginia and western theaters where he expected "prompt execution" of his command.[85]

The results of the sweeping directive were disappointing, however, with few generals responding quickly and none moving in concert. McClellan did finally reveal his plans for an ambitious flanking maneuver in Virginia, in which water transport would carry the Army of the Potomac south of the Confederate field forces. But the plan was slow to unfold. In the aftermath of the president's general directive, only the recently promoted General Ulysses Grant and his men achieved any signal success. They captured Forts Henry and Donelson along the Tennessee and Cumberland rivers and launched what would become Grant's eighteen-month campaign to secure the Mississippi Valley.

In early March 1862, when the Army of the Potomac was finally ready to begin its offensive in Virginia, the president made the decision to relieve McClellan as general-in-chief. Since McClellan, who retained his field command, planned to sail the bulk of his forces down the coast and then fight northward toward Richmond, Lincoln's top cabinet advisers argued that the complicated movement of troops and supplies offered a convenient excuse for ordering the long-overdue demotion. Still, they worried it would be controversial, especially among Northern Democrats. Seward counseled issuing the directive in Stanton's name, suggesting it would help improve "public confidence" in the new war secretary and former Democrat. But Stanton was reluctant, afraid it might appear too "personal" coming from him. Hay noted that it was Lincoln who finally "decided to take the responsibility" for announcing the decision on March 11.[86]

A week later McClellan launched what became known as his Peninsula campaign, transporting the bulk of his field army toward Fortress Monroe on the Virginia coast. The massive troop movement excited Virginia unionists who had been working in the western region of the state to establish a provisional government—what they called the Restored Government of Virginia. These men had great faith in McClellan. He had helped drive out Confederate forces in the western counties around Wheeling during the first months of the war, when he was still commanding the Department of the Ohio. Now he was leading an assault near Richmond that they expected would soon topple Jefferson Davis.

Francis Pierpont, governor of Restored Virginia, wrote Lincoln in mid-March, announcing his plans to issue a "circular letter" in preparation for "the certainty" of the rebellion's collapse in the remaining part of his state. Pierpont told Lincoln that he was planning to warn traitors that they would be regarded "as Murdere[r]s" and "treated accordingly." "Some declaration should be made in regard to slaves," Pierpont added, though he was not intending an emancipation edict like Frémont's. Instead, the governor was willing to threaten "that protection to slave property should be made to depend on the co-operation of its owners in restoring the Government."[87]

Lincoln was not impressed by such bluster. He replied by reminding Pierpont of the adage "Make haste slowly," advice that reflected his own deliberate methods as a leader. "Draw up your proclamation carefully," he warned, adding, "and, if you please, let me see it before issuing."[88]

From the War Department telegraph office, situated adjacent to the White House, Lincoln followed the troop movements across Virginia. When Confederate general Thomas "Stonewall" Jackson and his "foot cavalry" emerged as a fast-moving infantry threat in the Shenandoah Valley, Lincoln increased the frequency of his telegraphic directions and admonitions to field commanders (including an annoyed John Frémont). And he visited the Virginia front three times in April and May—his first presidential excursions outside Washington—to consult with his field officers and mingle with their troops.[89]

When Grant's progress along the Mississippi River slowed following a bloody counterattack at Shiloh in early April, Lincoln decided to do even more to recalibrate the military campaigns. In particular, he sought fresh ways to support the Peninsula movement without depleting the Federal defenses around Washington. Toward the end of June, he formulated a plan with Stanton to consolidate the U.S. field armies in northern Virginia under a new commander. They decided to call upon John Pope, a young and successful combat leader from Illinois who had been serving out west under Grant. Lincoln and Stanton wanted Pope's new army to open a second line of attack through the ninety-mile land corridor between Washington and Richmond to relieve some pressure on the Peninsula operation.[90]

Lincoln believed that an endorsement from General Winfield Scott, who had recently retired to West Point, might help to overcome skepticism about the prospect of yet another costly overland attack against Richmond. The president decided to seek that endorsement in person. Late in the afternoon on June 23, ignoring the gossip that a sudden consultation with Scott might generate, Lincoln departed from Washington by train and arrived at West Point at around three the next morning. Scott, who found out about the impending visit only hours before Lincoln's arrival, was concerned. "Can McClellan be dead," the general had asked, according to a story relayed in the *Times*, "has there been trouble in the Cabinet?" "Are we in danger of defeat?" The seventy-five-year-old Scott waited for the president inside a darkened ferry across the Hudson River from West

Point. "I have only come up to see and talk with you," Lincoln assured him when he finally arrived.[91]

A few hours later the two men breakfasted together at a local hotel and continued in private conversation for "several hours" that morning with an array of maps in hand. According to Scott, Lincoln laid out the status of forces in "quite full & most distinct & lucid" fashion. The president said he wanted the general's views on whether it was a good idea to support McClellan's efforts along the peninsula with a second line of attack, perhaps from a concentration of U.S. forces near Manassas. Lincoln did not mention Pope. But he did seem worried about the defenses around Washington and asked Scott to put his opinions into writing. The general rewarded the president's solicitation with a few cautious suggestions and his assent that a successful multipronged assault against Richmond "would be a virtual end of the rebellion."[92]

Once the conversation concluded, the president toured the nearby U.S. military academy, which so many of the current generals had attended and where Robert E. Lee had once been superintendent. After meeting with some of the young cadets whom he had recently appointed, he toured a local foundry, where the amateur inventor and technology enthusiast was able to witness the test-firing of some newly developed and highly touted Parrott guns or rifled artillery pieces. He closed the long day by attending two social gatherings, including an evening reception sponsored by local ladies, where he was reportedly "full of joke and anacdote [*sic*]." Early the next morning the presidential party—now swollen by a gaggle of correspondents from New York City—departed by train, arriving in Washington that evening.[93]

MUCH ABOUT THIS WHIRLWIND journey was characteristic of the president. He made the West Point trip almost entirely on his own. The only figure who accompanied him was William Johnson, a free Black man who occasionally served as his travel valet. Lincoln displayed his habitual attention to detail as he rattled off precise troop numbers and positions by memory for General Scott. And the president was regularly updated on news from the front, relayed by telegram from the secretary of war.[94] Throughout the visit, Lincoln remained friendly, accessible, and energetic.

During a brief stop along his return journey, Lincoln delivered public remarks in Jersey City to a small crowd that had gathered near the railroad depot. He tried to sound reassuring. "I can only say that my visit to West Point did not have the importance which has been attached to it," he said, denying it had anything "whatever to do with making or unmaking any General in the country."[95] The rumors were already rampant that McClellan was being replaced. It had been sixteen months since Lincoln had last spoken in the politically divided state of New Jersey, and partisan tensions remained high. The president urged his listeners at the train depot not to regard the current crisis "through a fog" but to see the state of the war as it really was.[96] To Lincoln, who had always considered himself clear-eyed and focused, the tough, grinding work of mobilizing the military and organizing logistical support for its combat campaigns seemed to be paying off. Arriving back in Washington with the endorsement he sought and a new strategy coming together, he hoped that they were finally on the verge of crushing the rebellion.

11

BRINK OF DESTRUCTION

(1862–1863)

Even before Abraham Lincoln returned from West Point on the evening of June 25, John Pope had arrived in Washington, called east from his command with the Army of the Mississippi. Some newspapers, confused by sightings of the forty-year-old general passing through New York City, mistakenly reported that he had participated in the consultations with Winfield Scott.[1] The northern press was familiar with Pope because his field army had recently captured the railroad junction at Corinth, a key objective in the Mississippi Valley campaign. Pope reported to the War Department on the morning of June 25 and was immediately struck by the fierce scowl of Edwin Stanton, peering out from behind his standing desk, surrounded by soldiers and contractors, projecting what Pope recalled as a "shaggy, belligerent sort of look." In their initial discussion, the secretary held off providing Pope with specifics about his new assignment, claiming that he needed to consult further with the soon-to-be returning president.[2]

The next morning Stanton unveiled the strategy of consolidating armies across northern Virginia under Pope's command with the objective of launching a second line of attack against Richmond. The elevation of a junior figure like Pope was sure to provoke a backlash, which was probably why the president had not disclosed that element of the plan to General Winfield Scott during his West Point visit. The new Army of Virginia was to consist of three corps commanders—Nathaniel Banks, John Frémont, and Irvin McDowell—all senior in rank to their superior officer. Pope tried declining the promotion, but Lincoln ordered him to accept. Frémont angrily resigned in response; the others accepted their subordinate roles.

Lincoln had gone to West Point with more in mind than a reshuffle of commanders. He also wanted more men. The president was planning to ask northern governors to raise a new round of troops for the final two-pronged push against Richmond. Scott's assurance that the campaign would mean the "virtual end of the rebellion" was useful for this purpose.[3] But before Lincoln could make a formal mobilization request, the Confederate field army in Virginia—under the new command of Robert E. Lee—went on the offensive. The Seven Days' Battles, begun on June 25, the day of Pope's arrival and Lincoln's return, became the bloodiest combat of the war to that point.

The Seven Days was also the most consequential series of engagements of the war's first year. The rebel offensive ultimately fell short, but it still removed the immediate pressure on Richmond and nearly succeeded in dislodging McClellan's Army of the Potomac from the Virginia Peninsula. Despite several recent Federal successes across the western theater—at Corinth, New Orleans, and elsewhere—the bloody stalemate in Virginia sparked a crisis in northern morale. As Lincoln struggled to maintain his composure in the difficult months ahead, he continued to work to find more men and new measures in a relentless effort to win the war.

THE DAY AFTER FRÉMONT resigned, McClellan also imploded. Lee's newly reorganized Army of Northern Virginia had just won a major victory at Gaines' Mill, about ten miles outside Richmond, and was threatening to cut off Federal supply lines on the peninsula. McClellan panicked and ordered a retreat of his forces, despite holding a clear advantage in numbers. After what he called "the most desperate battle of the war," McClellan cast blame directly on the administration for failing to heed his earlier requests for more soldiers. "I know that a few thousand more men would have changed this battle from a defeat to a victory," McClellan informed Stanton on June 28 in a coded "cipher" dispatch. "As it is, the Government must not and cannot hold me responsible for the result." He closed in fury: "If I save this army now, I tell you plainly that I owe no thanks to you or to any other persons in Washington."[4]

Lincoln may not have seen this bitter closing line (a telegraph operator later claimed that he refused to transmit it), but the president responded to the obvious anguish in the message. "Save your Army at all events," he wrote to McClellan, promising to send reinforcements "as fast as we can." William Seward left for New York later that day to help organize an urgent meeting of loyal governors—some already planning to join the secretary in Manhattan and others by telegraph—so they could discuss how to mobilize new enlistments for the forthcoming second line of attack. In a letter Lincoln drafted for Seward to share with the governors, he echoed Scott's assessment from West Point, claiming that "a hundred thousand new troops in the shortest possible time" would "substantially end the war." Behind the bravado, however, was a recognition of political weakness. Lincoln wanted the governors to volunteer the soldiers on their own. "I would publicly appeal to the country for this new force," Lincoln explained, "were it not that I fear a general panic and stampede would follow—so hard is it to have a thing understood as it really is."[5]

Some of the governors expressed skepticism that such a convoluted plan to shift political responsibility for the volunteer call-up would work. On June 30, eighteen of the participating governors and Lincoln and his team spent hours haggling by telegraph over the size and potential wording for this risky public call. The governors agreed on the necessity for "prompt and vigorous measures" but there was no consensus on details, especially regarding the number of troops, with some advocating for as many as 150,000 new men. Lincoln finally left the War Department telegraph office without a resolution. "The president has gone to the country very tired," Stanton wired the other participants around 9 p.m., suggesting that they would have to reconvene the next day.[6]

Lincoln's "country" retreat was a military retirement complex owned by the federal government about three miles from the White House. The Soldiers' Home, as it was called, was situated on bucolic elevated ground. James Buchanan had used one of its cottages as a summer residence and recommended it to Lincoln during the inauguration. For the Lincoln family, the place offered more than a vacation spot. They were still grieving over twelve-year-old Willie Lincoln, who had died unexpectedly in February. Robert Lincoln, home from his second year at Harvard College, joined his parents and younger brother Tad in mid-June, when they relocated to the Soldiers' Home. Throughout the family's initial stay, which lasted until early November 1862, the president traveled back and forth to the White House almost every day.[7]

On the evening of June 30, Orville Browning was waiting for the president at the Soldiers' Home, along with other guests he had brought along. A tired and frustrated Lincoln took Browning out to the cottage porch to discuss the dire situation on the peninsula. To Browning's surprise, the president pulled out a slim volume of comic poetry, read a few stanzas aloud to his friend, and laughed with him before they went inside to rejoin the others.[8]

Once his visitors departed, Lincoln sat alone contemplating his next moves. He was still hoping to salvage a victory around Richmond but recognized that he must prepare the nation for the prospect of a longer struggle. He decided to issue a public statement calling for 300,000 more three-year volunteers. The next day, July 1, the administration released this massive call for troops, along with a backdated appeal from northern governors (drafted by Seward) claiming that they were ready to furnish "all re-enforcements that you may deem needful to sustain our Government." Some of the governors were surprised by the scale of Lincoln's final request, which essentially doubled the highest numbers mentioned in previous discussions. "It was thought safest to mark high enough," Lincoln explained to Governor E. D. Morgan of New York.[9]

The night of June 30, Lincoln also reflected on the slavery question and its potential impact on the war effort. Earlier, he had told the governors, "I expect to maintain this contest until successful, or till I die, or am conquered, or my term expires, or Congress or the country forsakes me." Lincoln was worried not only about the country forsaking a new call for troops but also about Congress challenging him over slavery policy. His concerns became apparent on July 1 at the White House, when he read a memo to Browning on that subject, one that he said he had "sketched hastily" the night before.[10]

Lincoln's new memo focused on congressional plans to revise the 1861 confiscation law. That statute had authorized several ways to punish southern treason, including the seizure of real and personal property of targeted Confederate officials and the liberation of any enslaved labor employed on behalf of the Confederate military. The 1861 law had not specified emancipation for individual slaves—just the forfeiture of the "claim to such labor"—but the practical result had been freedom for thousands of Black people. Now the Thirty-

Seventh Congress was debating a set of proposals drafted originally in the Senate Judiciary Committee, chaired by Lyman Trumbull, to enact a more sweeping form of emancipation into federal law. The new legislation would also provide for permanent forfeitures of real and personal property and authorize the enlistment of Black men in the U.S. military, all as part of an effort to suppress the insurrection, punish treason, and encourage the end of slavery.

Lincoln was wary of such radical measures. He considered them dangerous to the stability of the unionist political coalition and likely to be ruled unconstitutional by the Taney-led Supreme Court. The president's July 1 memo stipulated that while no contrabands or wartime freedom seekers should "ever to be returned to slavery," he did not want legislative "inducements" for runaways, since they could overwhelm Federal lines and become "an embarrassment to the government." For now, Lincoln also opposed arming Black men, expressing concern that it might "do more injury than good." And he reiterated the standard Republican line—and longtime Washington consensus—that "Congress has no power over slavery in the states."[11]

But a sizable faction on Capitol Hill was growing tired of Lincoln's "make haste slowly" approach and wanted new ways to press the war and slavery. The Thirty-Seventh Congress had achieved monumental results in its legislative activity, not only by adopting critical mobilization measures during its July 1861 special session, but also by passing a host of groundbreaking economic and domestic reforms throughout the spring and early summer of 1862. While Lincoln was discussing confiscation with Browning on July 1, Congress created the nation's first federal income tax and adopted the Pacific Railway Act. The next day it passed the Morrill Land Grant College Act, organizing a new system of public universities. Earlier in the session, Republicans had rammed through other major reforms establishing paper currency, the Department of Agriculture, and homestead land grants for farmers. They had revised the Articles of War to prohibit military personnel from returning fugitive slaves, abolished slavery in the District of Columbia, extended diplomatic recognition to the Black-led nations of Haiti and Liberia, and passed into law the provisions of the former Wilmot Proviso, prohibiting slavery in the western territories.[12]

As president, Lincoln supported these measures but rarely had to lobby for them. With Southern Democrats almost entirely absent from Capitol Hill, Republicans controlled both the House and the Senate with ironclad authority. During his first year in office, Lincoln was able to focus on military affairs and patronage matters, practically ignoring domestic reform. But he always made sure to hold the explosive emancipation card for himself. He corrected Frémont in August 1861, when he acted precipitously in Missouri, then partially rescinded a similar edict from David Hunter in May 1862, when the general, assigned then to the Atlantic coastal department, ordered the emancipation of all slaves in Florida, Georgia, and South Carolina.

A confrontation with Congress over emancipation was therefore a potentially ominous development for the president. But as July began, Lincoln appeared hopeful that an open break could be avoided. Despite McClellan's panicky outbursts near the end of June, the results of the Seven Days' Battles still appeared uncertain. Lincoln believed that a major victory outside Richmond was possible and would "substantially" end the rebellion. He wrote the governors on July 3, urging them to send whatever men they could as fast as possible, claiming that "*time is every-thing.*" On Friday, July 4, a correspondent for the *New-York Tribune* captured the president's intense mood, describing an encounter between Lincoln and a wagon train of wounded soldiers. The president, who was on horseback traveling along his daily commute to the Soldiers' Home, "rode beside them for a considerable distance, conversing freely with the men," clearly anxious to ascertain "the real condition of affairs on the Peninsula."[13]

The sight of so many recently wounded men must have been jarring. Mary Lincoln confessed to a friend that her husband was suddenly having many "sleepless nights." The agitated president decided that he had to go see the situation for himself, undertaking what aide John Nicolay called "a flying visit" to the peninsula. Lincoln was gone from Monday to Thursday, meeting with McClellan on Tuesday, July 8, to discuss military strategy. The former Douglas Democrat did not hold back. "Neither confiscation of property, political executions of persons, territorial organization of States, or forcible abolition of slavery," McClellan insisted, "should be contemplated for a moment." Nicolay claimed that Lincoln, unfazed by this clumsy political challenge, returned from the front "in better spirits than he went in."[14]

The day after his return to Washington, Lincoln promoted Henry Halleck to general-in-chief, a post that had been vacant since the launch of the Peninsula campaign in March. Lincoln also met with congressmen from loyal slave states, urging them to support a resolution providing federal support for gradual, compensated abolition in their states. Long a proponent of the policy, Lincoln claimed that if they had embraced it earlier, "the war would now be substantially ended." Lincoln also warned the southern unionist politicians that it was not enough to "Beat [the secessionists] at elections" once or twice in their state or congressional contests. As long as slavery existed, Lincoln observed, traitors would always retain "the lever of their power" in the politics of the South. Moreover, he suggested that there was "pressure" from other regions of the country to emancipate slaves by any means, and that it was "increasing."[15]

As Lincoln made his appeal for gradual, compensated abolition on July 12, the Senate passed a compromise version of the new confiscation bill after weeks of back-and-forth with the House. The expanded confiscation measure incorporated many of the provisions that radicals had been pushing, most notably one threatening to liberate rebel-owned slaves held anywhere, including within loyal slave states by masters who had joined the Confederacy. Nearly all Republican senators voted for the final bill, except for Orville Browning and one other moderate. Earlier in the war Browning had advised Lincoln to break up plantations in the conquered regions of the South and deliver the land to freed Black people. He had also backed Frémont's emancipation order in Missouri in 1861. But the Illinois senator was now more cautious as to how the government should go about liberating the enslaved. He also believed that the new confiscation legislation was unconstitutional in its forfeiture provisions for real and personal property. Browning felt confident that the president agreed with him.[16]

But Lincoln was having second thoughts. On July 13, there was a funeral for Edwin Stanton's infant son, who had died of illness. Lincoln rode to and from the somber ceremony in a carriage with Seward, Gideon Welles, and Seward's daughter-in-law, Anna. Along the way, the president talked about the politics of the confiscation bill and mentioned that he was considering vetoing the measure. Welles agreed that "Congress was clothed with no authority on this subject." The navy secretary later claimed that this discussion represented the first time Lincoln had ever revealed his plan to emancipate slaves. But the president was not yet settled on an emancipation strategy, and the contemporary evidence undermines Welles's self-serving recollection. In a letter sent that evening to his wife, with whom he often confided on political matters, Welles only mentioned his surprise that Lincoln and Seward had bothered to include him in the outing to the funeral—there was no hint of any discussion of presidential emancipation.[17]

That week everyone in Washington was focused on congressional confiscation and whether it was constitutional or prudent for Congress to authorize seizing more property and liberating more slaves during a midterm election year. There were also legal questions about the plans for punishing treason by permanently disposing of rebel assets through judicial hearings without the defendants present, known as in rem proceedings. On July 16, Lincoln started drafting a veto message. He suggested that although he supported "much" in the legislation, he was skeptical about the "unfortunate form of expression" used to announce the freedom of rebel-owned slaves. It seemed to him a raw and unprecedented assertion of federal power to interfere with slavery in states where it existed.[18] He also objected to a lack of detail in the promise to liberate different "classes" of enslaved refugees, runaways, or "contrabands" who had found safety behind Federal lines.

But Lincoln claimed that his chief objection to the new law was that the permanent seizure of either real or personal property might violate constitutional prohibitions against any "attainder of treason" that extended a "corruption of blood" or punishment beyond the life of the guilty. Despite these concerns, he was reluctant to veto such an important Republican measure. On Tuesday, he asked leading officers of the House and Senate to delay their adjournment, scheduled for the next day, so that he could negotiate further with them. When some Republican senators questioned the need for this delay, he got annoyed. "I am sorry Senators could not so far trust me," Lincoln snapped, "as to believe I had some real cause for wishing them to remain."

That afternoon Lincoln ordered his White House aides to ban visitors so that he could finish his veto message. But Browning was allowed to see the president and found him in the second-floor library looking "weary, care-worn and troubled." As they shook hands, the senator expressed concern about his friend's health. Gripping tightly for emphasis, the president replied, "Browning I must die sometime."[19]

The melodrama reflected the gravity of the situation. A political rupture between the president and Republicans on Capitol Hill over slavery policy might well jeopardize the entire unionist coalition. Fortunately for Lincoln, on July 15 Senator William Pitt Fessenden of Maine emerged from behind the scenes to help arrange a short delay in adjournment. He also helped secure from Republican congressional leaders a joint resolution—passed over the objections of some of the party's most radical members—that clarified their legislative intent regarding what moderates and constitutional purists considered the proper limitations on rebel asset forfeiture. The president agreed to sign the bill. Fessenden, after helping to forge the agreement, privately skewered Lincoln. "Well, we have what we bargained for," he commented, "a Splitter of rails."[20]

Lincoln went to the Capitol on July 17 and signed the law, though he appended his veto message to it. That unusual decision—an early example of a presidential signing statement—further inflamed many Republican legislators. The same day Lincoln also signed into law a revision of the Militia Act that authorized the enlistment of Black soldiers. Rep. George Julian of Indiana recalled that several of his colleagues speculated that the president had no intention of enforcing either measure and that he was nothing more than "a deliberate betrayer of freedmen and poor whites."[21]

Republican congressmen did not realize that Lincoln was preparing a multipronged political attack against slavery that would exceed their limitations as legislators. On Sunday, July 20, he began drafting a series of executive orders designed to implement the new laws. Aide John Hay helped the president prepare language for rules regarding the seizure of real and personal property, authorization for the employment of Black "laborers" in the military, mandatory record-keeping for seized property and liberated Black families (to help compensate any loyal owners punished by mistake), plans for overseas colonization of former slaves (which the confiscation statute had also recommended), and finally, a general proclamation about emancipation.

Lincoln's brief statement on emancipation extended beyond what Congress had envisioned. It began with a sixty-day warning that was part of the revised confiscation law, even though that provision was ostensibly about asset forfeiture and not emancipation. In its first four sections, the new statute outlined specific punishments for those convicted of treason or insurrection, including possible execution, permanent disqualifications against holding public office, and liberation of "all" their slaves. The fifth section detailed rules for seizing real or personal property from various categories of Confederate military and government officials, including those originally from "any loyal State or Territory." The sixth section went further, though in a vague manner. It warned supporters of the Confederacy "other than those named" that after a presidential notice they would have two months to "cease" their rebellious activities or face seizure of real and personal property. According to Lincoln, this warning was designed to provide "misguided men" with "some motive for returning to the Union." The statute listed several types of personal assets vulnerable to seizure, including stocks, but offered nothing about slaves. By including this targeted threat at the beginning of his sweeping emancipation order, Lincoln seemed to imply that anyone who continued in their disloyal activities would also lose their human property.[22]

The draft proclamation was certainly meant to be aggressive. Its next sentence announced the president's intentions to introduce at the December congressional session a plan for compensated "gradual abolishment of slavery" within the loyal slave states, something Congress had so far declined to address in any formal manner. But the third and final sentence was the critical one. "As a fit and necessary military measure," Lincoln proclaimed January 1, 1863, as the date when "all persons held as slaves" within any region of the South still in rebellion "shall then, thenceforward, and forever, be free."[23]

With this three-sentence draft, Lincoln thus outlined a trio of attack lines against slavery: congressional confiscation, state abolition, and military emancipation. His sixty-day confiscation warning began the process by targeting "misguided" supporters of the Confederacy from loyal areas who might succumb to the economic pressure of risking their human property. Some U.S. commanders in the field did later invoke this confiscation warning to liberate small groups of enslaved people not covered by the final emancipation decree, especially in occupied portions of the former Confederacy but also occasionally in loyal slave states. Second, and perhaps more important, the president's willingness to reiterate his support for abolition in the border slave states sent a clear message about his intensifying commitment to secure the "ultimate extinction" of slavery throughout the nation. But if there was any doubt on that score, Lincoln's sweeping military decree provided a resounding response.

In the ninth section of the confiscation statute, Congress held that enslaved people "coming under the control of the government of the United States"—principally refugees and runaways or the so-called contrabands from the Confederate South—should be treated as "captives of war" and made "forever free." But because the legislation was designed to punish treason or insurrection, its statutory language limited its applicability to those enslaved people who were owned by Confederates or disloyal masters. Lincoln's new decree vowed to erase that distinction. By his proposed order, every Black family across a vast swath of the American South would be liberated whenever U.S. forces reached them. A true moderate who was concerned about electoral politics and constitutional law but was unwilling to veto the confiscation bill would have approached the measure differently—likely by applying due process standards to rebel areas and using in rem proceedings in military courts to liberate only the human property of disloyal masters, and not from anyone who could prove their loyalty. Such a process would have surely delayed freedom by many months and years for thousands of Black families. Lincoln's draft military order demonstrated that his political and legal prudence did not extend this far.[24]

John Hay was so thrilled and surprised by the president's decisive shift in antislavery strategy that he all but leaked the news to a young woman he was trying to impress. On July 20, while fetching books and documents from the White House library for Lincoln's use in preparing the executive orders, he wrote a revealing letter to Mary Jay, a friend and the sixteen-year-old daughter of a well-known New York abolitionist. "The President himself has been, out of pure devotion to what he considers the best interest of humanity," Hay explained, "the bulwark of the institution he abhors, for a year. But he will not conserve slavery much longer." With authority, Hay added, "When next he speaks to this defiant and ungrateful villainy it will be with no uncertain sound. Even now he speaks more boldly and sternly to slaveholders than to the world." Hay concluded by touting his own radical bent. "If I have sometimes been impatient of his delay," he wrote, "I am so no longer."[25]

Lincoln called in his cabinet for a discussion of the new orders on the morning of July 21. Chase confided to his diary that it had been so long since they had been consulted as a body that he considered the session "a novelty." The president opened the meeting by announcing that he was "determined to take some definitive steps in respect to military action and slavery." He suggested that he was sharing his plans, not seeking advice. Yet the cabinet members proceeded to review the orders and debate them, though they soon got sidetracked by an argument over whether to enlist Black men not merely as laborers but as soldiers. Lincoln "expressed himself as averse to arming negroes" but was not prepared to decide the issue. As the discussion wandered even further afield, the men agreed to postpone additional consultation until the next day.[26]

Resuming their deliberations on July 22, the cabinet members indicated assent for each of the orders they had discussed the day before except for the one on colonization, which everyone, including the president, agreed to drop for the time being. Chase, however, continued to advocate "warmly" for enlistment of Blacks in combat, until Lincoln shifted the focus by reading his draft Emancipation Proclamation, "on the basis of the Confiscation Bill." Nobody in the cabinet seemed opposed at first, but some offered suggestions. Edward Bates wanted the measure paired with colonization for freed slaves. Chase proposed that emancipation would be easier to implement through individual military proclamations by commanders in the field. Stanton supported Lincoln and urged immediate dissemination. Only Montgomery Blair, who had arrived late, spoke out in opposition, predicting that such a radical measure would result in electoral disaster.[27]

Seward made the only suggestion that stuck. He urged a delay on any announcement about emancipation until after a major battlefield victory. With McClellan's operations essentially suspended on the peninsula, and with Halleck and Pope just getting started in organizing a second line of attack against Richmond, there was reason to be cautious. But Seward's practical advice about timing—which Lincoln soon adopted—also exposed the weakness of the claims of military necessity. Such necessity arose from losing battles, not from winning them. It was clearly political necessity that shaped the decision about when to make emancipation public.[28]

On July 25, Lincoln issued the sixty-day confiscation notice on its own, without mentioning emancipation, and the War Department promulgated the other minor orders that the cabinet had approved.[29] The president held back the explosive final order of his Emancipation Proclamation in hope that sometime later in the summer, General Pope and his men would secure a victory that could transform the announcement into a triumphal turning point.

In the short term, however, the absence of a presidential decree about the emancipating provisions of the new confiscation law only exacerbated tensions in Washington. About a week after adjournment, Browning ran into Chicago congressman Isaac Arnold, who seemed "eager" for Lincoln to clarify the issue. Arnold, a noted abolitionist, claimed it would "fire the public heart" if the government finally "set all the slaves of rebels free." Browning was more skeptical.

"I have no faith in proclamations or laws," he confided, "unless we follow them by force and actually do the thing."[30]

Charles Sumner, the Massachusetts senator and leading radical, claimed to his friends later that autumn that he had pressed Lincoln for action on emancipation on "five successive days," before returning to Boston for the summer recess in frustration at the president's lack of response. Yet Sumner recalled that an exasperated Lincoln had confided to him, "*We mustn't issue it till after a victory.*"[31]

In a conversation at the White House before Browning departed for Illinois, Lincoln apparently came even closer to revealing his full plans to the senator. He brought out a special map showing the enslaved population by county across the cotton-producing areas of the South. Then he announced that he was "determined" to open the Mississippi River, even if it meant taking "all these negroes to open it." But Seward then entered the office, interrupting their discussion.

Realizing that his old friend was being pulled in radical new directions, Browning offered what he termed "a piece of advice" after Seward departed. Browning urged Lincoln to hold steady. Nobody had "a more comprehensive and more minute view," the senator pointed out, and if the president would only "get all the facts he could" and then "adhere firmly to his own opinions," everything should work out. Lincoln responded that "he had done so to a greater extent than was generally supposed," recalling how he had ignored his cabinet's anxieties during the Sumter crisis, yet "all now admitted that he was right."[32] Still he decided to keep quiet about his plans on emancipation.

As Congress concluded its work in July, the administration dispatched Reverdy Johnson, a former Douglas Democrat and senator-elect from Maryland, to Louisiana, charged with investigating complaints about the Federal army's occupation of the state. Johnson determined that the problems in Louisiana resulted mainly from aggressive antislavery activities by General John W. Phelps. The New England officer was openly encouraging runaway slaves to find refuge at his camp.[33] Johnson warned in mid-July that Phelps was creating the "impression that it is the purpose of the Govt [to force the] Emancipation of the slaves."[34]

On July 26, Lincoln responded to Johnson that any slaveholders upset about Phelps's actions were guilty of holding on to "a false pretense." It was their "own fault," he asserted, for having "forced a necessity upon me to send armies among them." Lincoln was even more dismissive about Johnson's claims in a conversation with Browning, assuring him that there was "but little union sentiment" among Louisiana planters. In his letter to Johnson, Lincoln employed language framed to shock. "I distrust the *wisdom* if not the *sincerity* of friends, who would hold my hands while my enemies stab me," he wrote. He closed by calling himself "a patient man" but noted that he had to "save this government." "What I *cannot* do, of course, I *will* not do," he concluded, "but it may as well be understood, once [and] for all, that I shall not surrender this game leaving any available card unplayed."[35]

Three days later the president sounded no less adamant when he sent a similar message to Cuthbert Bullitt, a New Orleans attorney whom he had known in Illinois and who had recently shared his own alarming reports about Phelps. "The paralysis—the dead palsy—of the government in this whole struggle," Lincoln wrote to Bullitt, derived from southern unionists who remained "passive," even with the protection of the Federal army at their disposal, doing "nothing" for the nation, according to the president, "except demanding that the government shall not strike its open enemies, lest they be struck by accident!" Lincoln refused to hide his disgust. "What would you do in my position?" he demanded of Bullitt. "Would you deal lighter blows rather than heavier ones? Would you give up the contest, leaving any available means unapplied?"[36]

Lincoln was angry, but he remained disciplined, trying to refine his phrases in anticipation of the impending emancipation announcement and the arguments required to defend it. This testing-the-waters process was most apparent in his correspondence with August Belmont, the nation's leading Democratic party organizer and a major financier in New York. In July, Belmont forwarded comments from a disgruntled Louisiana planter residing in New Orleans. "The time has arrived when Mr. Lincoln must take a decisive course," the unidentified slaveholder had written. "Trying to please everybody, he will satisfy nobody." The southern correspondent thought the solution was simple: "Why will not the North say officially that it wishes for the restoration of the Union as it was?"

Lincoln was exasperated by this claim, wondering why "the writer thinks I have no policy," adding, "Why will he not read and understand what I have said?" "Broken eggs cannot be mended," he observed in a reply to Belmont, "but Louisiana has nothing to do now but to take her place in the Union as it was, barring the already broken eggs." By "broken eggs" Lincoln referred to the slaves and runaways liberated during the war who would not be returned to their masters. He also reiterated the implicit threat of a wider emancipation, which he had shared earlier with others. "This government cannot much longer play a game in which it stakes all," he wrote, "and its enemies stake nothing." Lincoln closed by mocking the planter for hiding away "in a closet writing complaining letters northward!"[37]

Threats of a military draft in the northern states only added to the political pressure on the president. Lincoln's call at the end of June for 300,000 volunteers to serve three-year terms had produced some patriotic songs ("We are coming, Father Abraham, Three Hundred Thousand More") but not enough enlistments.[38] On August 4, 1862, the War Department announced mandatory conscription of militia troops, to serve up to ninety days, for any state that had not met its quota of three-year volunteers by mid-August. More ominously, on

August 8, Secretary of War Stanton issued an order threatening to suspend civil liberties across the North in cases of resistance to the new draft.[39]

Lincoln responded to these political challenges by getting more involved in shaping the campaign message for the fall elections. On August 6, he attended a mass "war meeting" held on the east portico of the U.S. Capitol, organized by Edward Jordan, a close ally of Treasury Secretary Chase. The meeting, both partisan and patriotic in purpose, was designed to show the possibility of wartime fusion among Republicans, Northern Democrats, and any conservatives willing to support the administration and its policies. Jordan read a series of "pointed resolutions" culminating with a call to crush the rebellion. "Let the Union be preserved, or the country made a desert," Jordan proclaimed, to widespread applause. One resolution endorsed the recent confiscation statute "declaring free" the rebel-owned slaves and urged Lincoln "to give prompt effect" to the measure.[40]

Lincoln had arrived late, but he was on the platform as Jordan read the statement about Black freedom. He responded to the "clamoring" of the people by unexpectedly offering to speak himself. "Hadn't I better say a few words and get rid of myself?" was Lincoln's excuse to Chase.[41] The president acknowledged that there was "no precedent" for an incumbent appearing at a political rally like this, and he kept his remarks limited. He focused on denying reports about a rupture between Stanton and McClellan over the failures of the Peninsula campaign, claiming that both men wanted battlefield victories, as he himself did, since he was "for the time being the master of them both."[42]

Benjamin French, commissioner of public buildings, reported that the immense crowd—as large as any inaugural crowd, in his opinion—showed overwhelming "enthusiasm" for the embattled president. French, a former Jacksonian Democrat turned Republican who now identified as "an ultra Union man," gushed in his diary that

Lincoln was "one of the best men God ever created."[43] French was a model for the type of political transformation that the Capitol rally organizers had in mind for their new outreach effort. Across the North, Republican campaign committees began embracing labels like Unionist, Unconditional Unionist, or Union Republican, to help secure the political backing of Northern Democratic supporters of the war effort—known as War Democrats—and patriotic conservatives from the former Bell and Breckinridge camps.[44]

With midterm election contests fast approaching in more than a dozen critical states, Lincoln also seemed to recognize that the impending announcement of emancipation not only required careful framing but also some deception. In early August, he dodged pressure on the subject from an abolitionist-leaning sergeant in his cavalry escort, reportedly complaining that he was tired of requests about "the damned or Eternal niggar."[45] He also misled Leonard Swett, one of his "most trusted" friends from Illinois. Swett visited the White House in early August to push the claims for Judge David Davis to be nominated to a vacancy on the Supreme Court. The old friends talked "frankly" on several occasions while Swett was in town, yet the conservative lawyer and Unionist congressional candidate came away convinced that the rumors about emancipation were baseless. "He will issue no proclamation emancipating negroes," Swett assured his wife. "Neither will he accept negro regiments in the war."[46]

A few days later, the president allowed a stenographic reporter into a private meeting he had scheduled with a delegation of five Black civic and cultural leaders from Washington, led by Edward Thomas, a noted art collector. The subject was colonization of African Americans. The stenographer, James Clephane, was present to document Lincoln's support for the voluntary relocation of former slaves and other willing Blacks to Central America. The transcript of that meeting, which was quickly published across the country, suggests that Lincoln was trying to soften the political blow of his impending emancipation announcement.[47] In his comments, the president conceded that Black people had been "suffering . . . the greatest wrong inflicted on any people." But he reminded his visitors—none ever enslaved as far as we know—that freedom would not necessarily bring "equality" and that he did not have the power to change what he termed the "fact" of color prejudice. "I cannot alter it if I would," he said, urging the delegation to support colonization for their people outside the United States.[48] Lincoln's dismissal of Black aspirations for equality infuriated Frederick Douglass and other leading radicals and led to a cascade of criticism in the abolitionist press. But they were not the primary target of the president's remarks.

The president's messaging to racist Northern Democrats and conservatives complicated his equally pressing need to sustain support from Republican regulars and antislavery radicals. The party's ultraist leaders were increasingly upset about the stillborn nature of the confiscation law adopted on July 17. That measure had authorized the president to emancipate rebel-owned slaves, but no announcement from the White House was yet forthcoming. The August 6 war meeting urged "prompt" execution of the law's freedom provisions, but most antislavery radicals were far less restrained in their calls for presidential action. In his newspaper, Frederick Douglass skewered Lincoln for making "silly and ridiculous" comments both at the Capitol rally and in his White House meeting with Black leaders, while denouncing Lincoln's hesitation over the new law.[49]

"When Congress passed the Confiscation Bill, made the Emancipation of the slaves of rebels the law of the land, [and] authorized the President to arm the slaves," wrote Douglass, Lincoln had "evaded his obvious duty." Such hesitation infuriated the abolitionist editor, who recalled that the president had been "elected as an anti-slavery man by Republican and Abolition voters" but now appeared before the northern electorate as "a genuine representative of American prejudice and Negro hatred and far more concerned for the preservation of slavery, and the favor of the Border Slave States, than for any sentiment of magnanimity or principle of justice and humanity."[50]

As a former slave himself, Douglass's bile was understandable, but a blast from Horace Greeley at the influential *New-York Tribune* was even more politically damaging. On August 19, the mercurial Republican editor let loose in a stinging public letter attacking Lincoln's sluggish response to the July legislation. "I do not intrude to tell you," Greeley began, "for you must know already—that a great proportion of those who triumphed in your election, and of all who desire the unqualified suppression of the Rebellion now desolating our country, are sorely disappointed and deeply pained by the policy you seem to be pursuing with regard to the slaves of Rebels." Demanding that the president "EXECUTE THE LAWS," Greeley complained that Lincoln had been "strangely and disastrously remiss in the discharge of your official and imperative duty with regard to the emancipating provisions of the new Confiscation Act." Greeley also called for the immediate enlistment of Black men into the U.S. military as combat soldiers.[51]

Lincoln was annoyed by this public attack and decided to respond in kind. The opening of his reply to Greeley dripped with sarcasm. "I have just read yours of the 19th," he wrote on August 22, "addressed to myself through the New-York Tribune." To underscore his frustration with Greeley's gimmicky use of an open letter, he had his reply published in the *National Intelligencer*, a rival newspaper that had been sparring with the *Tribune* over confiscation policy.[52] Lincoln announced at the outset of his letter that he would "waive" objections to "erroneous" and "falsely drawn" statements from his "old friend," even those offered with "an impatient and dictatorial tone." He then pivoted to their current dispute. "As to the policy I 'seem to be pursuing,' as you say," the president wrote, "I have not meant to leave anyone in doubt."[53]

Lincoln informed Greeley that his "policy" was to "save the Union" and to do so in "the shortest way under the Constitution." His next sentence, however, revealed how he saw this objective in partisan terms. "The sooner the national authority can be restored, the nearer the Union will be 'the Union as it was,'" he wrote.

Lincoln had recently seen the phrase "the Union as it was" in a letter from a disgruntled Louisiana planter that Democrat August Belmont had passed along in July. But the dismissive quotation marks around the phrase referenced not their private exchange but what had become a leading slogan of anti-war Democrats—"The Constitution as it is, the Union as it was." Ohio congressman Clement Vallandigham had first employed the phrase in a speech to the Democratic congressional caucus in May. In the aftermath of Stephen Douglas's death in 1861, Vallandigham had been gaining influence among Democrats by warning his colleagues against further cooperation with Republicans, claiming that the administration's partisanship "in all civil acts and appointments" had demonstrated "the necessity of party organization" by Northern Democrats. He had insisted in May that "to restore the Union," the Democrats had to organize a national campaign to "KILL ABOLITION," and by the summer many Democratic newspapers were endorsing this strategy.[54]

Lincoln followed his reference to Vallandigham's campaign slogan with an evocative prediction about Black freedom. "Broken eggs can never be mended," Lincoln stated in the next sentence, "and the longer the breaking proceeds the more will be broken." He had used that metaphor a few weeks before in his private reply to Belmont, the Democratic committee chairman. But it was edited out of the published version of his response to Greeley because the editor of the *National Intelligencer* in Washington, where it first appeared, felt uncomfortable with Lincoln's supposedly unpresidential language.[55]

For Lincoln, the growing strength of the divisive anti-war and anti-Black faction of the Democratic party represented both a threat and an opportunity. The shift by Republicans toward Unionist labels in the summer of 1862 was mainly about patriotic fusion, but for the president it was also the surest way to stoke divisions among Northern Democrats. In that regard, Lincoln's August 22 letter was just as much a response to Vallandigham as to Greeley. Confronting the implicit challenge from anti-war Democrats, the president was making the case to patriotic segments of the northern electorate that regardless of their previous party affiliation it was time to accept emancipation as a military necessity. Those who agreed could fuse with Republicans in the fall as fellow Unionists.

The heart of Lincoln's published reply to Greeley was a powerful summary of this position from his perspective as commander in chief. "My paramount object in this struggle is to save the Union," Lincoln wrote, "and is not either to save or to destroy slavery." This framework sounded conservative, but it was not intended as a rationale for inaction on slavery. "If I could save the Union without freeing any slave I would do it," he explained, "and if I could save it by freeing all the slaves I would do it," before adding, "and if I could save it by freeing some and leaving others alone I would also do that." What his audience did not know was that the president had already decided to free "some" slaves and leave "others alone." For Lincoln, the rebellion had transformed the nature of the electoral union that he had extolled in his inaugural address as the nation's essential democratic creed. Once they resorted to violence, Southern Democrats and other willing Confederates had forfeited their constitutional "rights" and were facing the consequences in the form of occupying armies and the "broken eggs" of liberated slaves, with more to come. The president ended his letter by highlighting his "official" pragmatism—promising to adopt "new views" as soon as they appeared to be "true views"—and his "personal" principles—reiterating his long-standing "wish that all men every where could be free."[56]

Left unstated was that Lincoln had just reframed unionism as a partisan appeal. Vallandigham and the Copperheads were arguing that the only way to "restore the Union" was to "kill" abolition. Lincoln's suggestion to War Democrats and other conservatives was that the opposite might be true; that abolition might become the only way to save the union. He was framing a hard partisan choice for them on the eve of his long-awaited emancipation announcement and just prior to a set of critical elections. Lincoln's public response to Greeley was, in effect, a draft platform for an emerging Union party. That is why he made no mention of Republicans or the Republican party in the document.[57]

Thurlow Weed, for one, was impressed by Lincoln's effort. The next day he told Seward that the president's letter "clear[s] the atmosphere." "The ultras were undermining" their coalition and "getting the Administration into false position," Weed complained. "But it is all right now."[58]

All was not so good, however, on the military front. Lincoln and his cabinet had been hoping that Pope's Army of Virginia would provide the breakthrough they wanted before they unveiled emancipation to the public. But on August 29 and 30, Pope's forces suffered a devastating defeat at the hands of Lee's army near Manassas during the Battle of Second Bull Run. There was widespread panic in Washington, but Lincoln remained in a "singularly defiant tone of mind," according to Hay. The president quickly charged McClellan and his forces with defending the nation's capital. Most of the cabinet objected to this decision, but Lincoln told Hay that "we must use what tools we have."[59] McClellan and the Army of the Potomac shielded Washington until they finally managed to stop Lee's army on September 17, near Antietam Creek in Maryland, in the bloodiest day in American military history.

Following the victory at Antietam, on September 22, Lincoln issued a revised version of his Emancipation Proclamation. The new first sentence began by proclaiming that the war was being fought solely for "the object of practically restoring" the national union. The second sentence promised to recommend measures to Congress for gradual abolition in the border states and voluntary colonization of freed Black people outside the United States. The rest of the proclamation, which was longer than the original July 22 draft, declared that January 1, 1863, would be liberation day for all those enslaved and living in areas under rebellion, and it explained in some detail how the president would designate such areas in the final version of the order. The president added excerpts from recent acts of Congress: an Article of War adopted in March prohibiting military officials from enforcing the Fugitive Slave Law, and sections from the July 1862 confiscation statute confirming his support for the liberation of refugees and runaways currently protected by the U.S. army.[60]

Before releasing this initial emancipation decree, Lincoln discussed it with his cabinet. According to Welles, the president informed his advisers that after "ascertaining" their views on emancipation policy during and since their July meeting, he had "formed his own conclusions, and made his own decisions." He also claimed to have relied on divine inspiration, citing the recent victory as evidence that "God had decided this question in favor of the slaves."[61]

On September 24, the president issued another controversial proclamation subjecting those who resisted the draft or discouraged enlistments anywhere in the country to military arrest and martial law. This measure extended the War Department's decree on civil liberties from August.[62]

That night there was a serenade at the White House to celebrate the long-delayed announcement of the administration's general emancipation plans. Hay offered to help prepare remarks for the president based on the editorial reaction so far, but Lincoln waved him off, saying "he had studied the matter so long that he knew more about it than they did."[63] Several of the "old fogies," as Hay called them, gathered that evening at Chase's home, where they drank wine and reflected on the astounding turn of events. Most were Republican veterans of the partisan wars of the 1850s and recognized how improbable such a development would have seemed only a few years earlier. Chase remarked on the "insanity" of the slaveholders, who "might have kept the life in their institution for many years to come" if they had avoided secession. Slaveholders had put their hateful power "in the very path of destruction," he observed, a result that "no party and no public feeling in the North" could have accomplished on its own.[64]

Seward was not so optimistic. He confessed to his daughter Fanny his worry that the emancipation announcement was going to damage Republicans in the upcoming elections. He claimed that he was "fearful of prematurely giving to a people prone to divide, occasion for organizing parties, in a crisis which demands union and harmony, in order to save the country from destruction."[65]

The president's impromptu serenade remarks on September 24 looked toward the elections. Thanking the jubilant crowd for their support, he said, "I can only trust in God I have made no mistake." His main message, however, was about the need for the public to support emancipation at the polls. "It is now for the country and the world to pass judgment on it," Lincoln said, "and, may be, take action upon it." He added that he would "say no more upon this subject." A few days later Lincoln sounded more pessimistic with Vice President Hannibal Hamlin. "The North responds to the proclamation sufficiently in breath," he wrote in a "Strictly Private" letter, "but breath alone kills no rebels."[66]

Fourteen states held elections that fall. Lincoln followed presidential campaign custom and generally remained mute, but he nudged events along wherever he could. In mid-October 1862, the president's friends in Illinois became worried about the administration's contraband policy and its potential effect on the state's upcoming electoral contests. U.S. army officials had recently decided to transfer Black families from an overcrowded contraband camp in Cairo, Illinois, to other areas of the state. Robert Smith, who had traveled home with Lincoln from the 1847 River and Harbor Convention, sent an urgent letter to Illinois governor Richard Yates warning about the "great fuss" being raised "on account of Negroes coming into our State." Smith had remained a Douglas Democrat throughout the 1850s but was attempting to return to Congress in 1862 under the Union party label as a candidate supporting the administration. David Davis later explained to Lincoln that he had also consulted with Yates, and they agreed that the "spreading of negroes from Cairo . . . will work great harm in the coming election." On October 13, Yates telegraphed Lincoln requesting an end to the policy and instantly got the response he wanted. The anxious governor then forwarded the president's answer to the military commander at Cairo at one o'clock in the morning on October 14. The movement of the contrabands was suspended.[67]

It was not nearly enough. Robert Smith lost his race in Alton. Leonard Swett, also a Union party candidate, went down to defeat in Lincoln's old congressional district at the hands of John Todd Stuart, the president's first law partner and Whig mentor but now a War Democrat. The Democrats in Illinois—including many opposed to the war—gained control of the state legislature. Democrats also won control of the legislature in Indiana. Republicans or Unionists lost ground in most of the October and November elections, giving up nearly two dozen seats in the U.S. House and the governorship in New York. Galusha Grow of Pennsylvania, the Speaker of the House, suffered a stunning defeat. But there were some bright spots. Republicans dominated in a few states like Massachusetts and managed to drive Vallandigham out of Congress—with the help of some redistricting magic. The fate of Republican control in both the House and the Senate looked promising enough with more elections to come before the new Thirty-Eighth Congress organized in December 1863. But most Republican leaders viewed the 1862 results as a terrible public rebuke that demanded a response.

Carl Schurz, the German-born Republican who had left his diplomatic post and was serving as a brigadier general with the Army of the Potomac, sent a blunt message for the president through his wife, Margarethe. He was convinced that the entire U.S. military command needed to be purged of disloyal Democratic officers. "The defeat of the administration," he concluded, "is the administration's own fault." Coming from a man who had helped organize the successful 1860 presidential campaign, this was especially damning.[68]

"Yours of the 8th. Was, to-day, read to me by Mrs. S," Lincoln wrote on November 10. "We have lost the elections," he acknowledged, before disputing aspects of Schurz's angry postmortem. The president suggested that "ill-success" in the war was underlying the party's problems and pinned specific blame on turnout obstacles. He claimed that more Republicans than Democrats were serving in the military, and that the Democratic organizations in the North had taken advantage of that fact. He dismissed talk of his conciliating Democrats with military appointments as "mere nonsense," remarking that he had delivered "nearly all the civil patronage" to their "friends."[69]

Nor did the president back down from his position that the nation needed Democrats and all willing partisans to serve in the military. Proud of this multipartisan approach, he claimed to one Democratic officer from Illinois that "in considering military merit, it seems to me the world has abundant evidence that I discard politics."[70] Yet most professional military men were complaining about how much partisan politics was affecting their ranks. Even General-in-Chief Halleck, a friend of the administration, called it "hopeless" to think one could contain the damage of "political wire-pulling in military appointments" within the Federal army.[71]

Schurz, one of those "wire-pulling" political generals, continued to berate his commander in chief, claiming in a second letter that he needed to clarify his "honest convictions," which were only "a mild and timid repetition of what many men say." Schurz insisted that Lincoln was entertaining "too favorable a view of the causes of our defeat," and that his mistake was believing he was a Republican who had to placate Democrats. Once the rebellion erupted, Schurz argued, Lincoln became the effective head of an "Administration-party" that "would have cheerfully sustained you in anything and everything that might have served to put down the rebellion," including an "emancipation manifesto" and the removal of incompetent Democratic generals, "long before you did it." "All they wanted," Schurz asserted about the mass of loyal citizens, "was merciless energy and speedy success." He ended with a stinging personal rebuke: "I do not know, whether you have ever seen a battlefield. I assure you, Mr. President, it is a terrible sight."[72]

In a measured response, Lincoln reflected on the difficulties of wartime leadership. "I certainly know that if the war fails, the administration fails," he replied, "and that I *will* be blamed for it, whether I deserve it or not." And, he observed, with every critic offering different advice, "If I must discard my own judgment, and take yours, I must also take that of others; and by the time I should reject all I should be advised to reject, I should have none left, republicans or others—not even yourself." To Schurz's comments about the question of "heart," Lincoln responded that only he could be the final "judge of hearts"; nor was he shaken by this sobering realization. "I need success more than sympathy," he stated.[73]

There is no doubt that Lincoln's confidence in his own judgment was carrying him through these difficult days approaching the winter of 1862. For every blast he took from younger or more radical voices like Schurz's, he also felt heat from conservatives like George Robertson of Kentucky. Judge Robertson wired Lincoln around the time of the president's exchange with Schurz to complain that Federal military officials in Kentucky were declining to return fugitive slaves to loyal masters. One of Robertson's own slaves was being shielded by

Federal troops, and he wanted him released. Lincoln bristled at the request. "Do you not know that I may as well surrender this contest, directly," he wrote, "as to make any order, the obvious purpose of which would be to return fugitive slaves?" Lincoln recalled an anecdote from Patrick Henry, who had mocked the selfishness of a Tory sympathizer during the Revolutionary War for "totally disregarding all questions of country" while complaining about the seizure of his cattle, crying out, in Henry's words, "beef! beef!! beef!!!"[74]

It was a powerful rebuke, but Lincoln decided not to share it. He had known Robertson for a long time. He filed away his sharp reply and sent a more tactful note offering to pay $500 from his own pocket to help settle the matter. The Kentucky judge sniffed indignantly that his concern was about the rule of law and not about money, but this was mere posturing. After the war, a still-resentful Robertson sued the Wisconsin army officer responsible for freeing his slave, and Congress authorized over $900 in reimbursement to the aging unionist for having experienced the inconvenience of losing his human property during the war.[75]

The exchange with Robertson illustrated how complicated it was to implement confiscation in a border state like Kentucky. Robertson's runaway slave was one of several being protected by U.S. army officials; the others were from disloyal masters. Trying to navigate such policy nuances in loyal slave states was nearly impossible. But Lincoln pressed on with the multipronged antislavery strategy he had devised in July, always trying to remain firm in strategy while flexible in tactics.

On December 1, 1862, the president released his annual message to Congress, including a proposal for three constitutional amendments on the future of slavery. The first authorized federal bonds to underwrite gradual abolition in loyal border states if undertaken before 1900. The second provided that no enslaved people who "enjoyed actual freedom" during the war would ever be returned to slavery, though loyal masters might be compensated. The third outlined a vision for "colonizing free colored persons, with their own consent," somewhere outside the United States.[76]

With these proposals, Lincoln made clear that his administration was still serious about attacking slavery along multiple fronts. It continued to enforce congressional confiscation policies, however difficult in practice. It was openly promoting abolition in the loyal slave states, although on a timeline too long to satisfy most radicals. And military emancipation was coming for the rebel areas on January 1, as everyone knew. Most important to Lincoln, the general assault on slavery was being conducted solely in the name of union. "Without slavery the rebellion could never have existed," he commented in his message, "without slavery it could not continue."[77]

Tragic events on the military front soon overshadowed the major shift in national antislavery policy. In early November, the president had dismissed Generals McClellan and Buell, both notable Democrats, from their field commands. This was what radicals had long been demanding. But as Lincoln had warned Schurz, it became obvious that "the difficulty is in our case, rather than particular generals."[78] Under the more aggressive leadership of Ambrose Burnside, the Army of the Potomac suffered a catastrophic setback in mid-December after crossing the Rappahannock River near Fredericksburg, Virginia. The horrific casualties, coming so soon after the disappointing midterm elections, unnerved the Republican leadership on Capitol Hill.

The news about the retreat of the Army of the Potomac from the south shore of the Rappahannock reached Washington on the evening of December 15. By the next afternoon, Republican senators were holding a contentious private meeting to discuss it. Unable to remove the president himself, they seemed determined to change the men around him. Trumbull of Illinois was among those most agitated by recent events and most willing to blame Seward, the cabinet's strongest personality. Despite Seward's antebellum notoriety as a "higher law" radical, he was being portrayed as a dangerous wartime fusionist who was overly conciliatory toward War Democrats and border state conservatives. One senator accused the New Yorker of having "controlled the President and thwarted the other members of the Cabinet." Others attacked Seward for backing McClellan and undermining a more rigorous prosecution of the war. There was talk of the need for a cabinet shake-up. Another voice called for the creation of a new military rank, one armed "with absolute and despotic powers." There was even a motion of no confidence in the administration.[79]

At this point, Illinois senator Browning finally spoke up. Like Trumbull, he was angry at the recent tide of affairs, but for different reasons. For months he had complained in his diary about the radical shift in administration policies. On his return to Washington in late November, he told Lincoln that his proclamations on emancipation and martial law had proven "disastrous" for the idea of a unionist coalition because they had "revived old party issues." Lincoln listened politely, but remained noncommittal, acknowledging only that the "Republican party could not put down the rebellion" by itself.[80] At the senatorial caucus, Browning urged caution on his colleagues. He convinced them, over Trumbull's heated objection, that they should delay any no-confidence vote until they could meet with the president himself and "learn the true state of the case," especially regarding the explosive charges against Seward.[81]

The Republican senators met again on December 17. This time Trumbull offered more favorable comments about Lincoln but continued to cast blame on Seward and various generals. According to Browning, everyone who spoke expressed a "want of confidence" in the administration—some even called for Lincoln's resignation. In the end the caucus agreed to urge the president to make a significant "change in men and measures." They adopted resolutions demanding such changes (without naming Seward himself) and designated nine senators to speak to Lincoln the next day.[82]

Although Browning was not part of this delegation, he made sure to get over to the White House before the others were to arrive.[83] The doorkeeper informed him that the president was resting in his bedroom but ushered the old friend upstairs anyway. "What do these men want?" Lincoln asked him. Browning conceded that his colleagues were in a foul mood but suggested it was principally Seward who was in their crosshairs. But he also blamed Lincoln for having enabled the radicals in the first place. "You ought to have crushed the ultra, impracticable men last summer," he grumbled. The president became agitated. "We are now on the brink of destruction," Lincoln said.

But Lincoln was not revealing his full hand. He declined to inform Browning that Seward had already offered his resignation. Maryland senator Reverdy Johnson shared that startling fact with his colleague later on the Senate floor. And the next afternoon, when the president ran into Browning outside the War Department, he declined to talk about his previous night's encounter with the senatorial committee, other than to report that "he was trying to keep things along." Browning, stunned, thought, "He cant 'keep them along.' The cabinet will go to pieces."[84]

Lincoln had been smart to delay. On December 18, he listened to the senators for over three hours, according to a report cobbled together by Henry Raymond of the *New York Times*. The president was attentive but refused to kowtow. "What the country wanted, was military success," he asserted in the face of repeated complaints about Seward. "Without that nothing could go right—with that, nothing could go wrong." He claimed he could not see much "remedy" for this problem in a cabinet shake-up, noting that even "a Cabinet of angels . . . could not give the country military successes."[85]

Lincoln knew that the charges of malign influence attributed to Seward were distortions, stoked to a degree by Chase, who was a jealous rival. He also understood that this "Senate raid on Seward," as he called it, was really a test of his own leadership—that the secretary of state was being used as a scapegoat. Lincoln later explained to Hay "how he thought deeply on the matter" and realized that he would have to "work it out by himself" and "could have no adviser" on such a party leadership problem.[86]

By the next morning, the president felt he had found a solution. He arranged for senior aide John Nicolay to call a special meeting of the cabinet for 10:30 a.m. When the men gathered in his office—minus Seward—the president demanded total secrecy and announced that the secretary of state had submitted his resignation because Republican senators were on the warpath. Lincoln described his meeting with the senatorial delegation as "earnest and sad," concluding that the "point and pith of their complaint" was that Seward had been controlling him to catastrophic ends. He asked the cabinet advisers to come back in the evening for further discussion.[87]

When the men arrived later, they were surprised to discover most of the senatorial delegation waiting for them. Lincoln realized he needed some direct accountability. Anybody could say almost anything out of view and behind closed doors. Chase, the source of the rumors, felt particularly ill at ease with this confrontational strategy, complaining that "he wouldn't have come if he had expected to be arraigned here." But otherwise the Treasury secretary kept silent as Lincoln explained to the senators that while the cabinet met only on occasion and without formal order, they were a functional body.[88]

The president also made clear that he was the one who made the final decisions. Days later, when Browning found out about the tense meeting, he asked Senator Jacob Collamer of Vermont, the chairman of the delegation, how Chase could have avoided admitting that he had been the source of the malicious gossip about Seward. "He lied" was Collamer's caustic reply.[89]

That Friday night meeting lasted for hours, with the cabinet officers not departing until after midnight. The Republican senators stayed even longer. Lincoln told John Dahlgren, who ran the Washington Naval Yard and visited with him later that week, that "it was very well to talk of remodeling the Cabinet," but he was convinced that the senators "had thought more of *their* plans than of *his* benefit, and he had told them so."[90]

On Saturday, Chase returned to Lincoln's office to announce that he had prepared his own letter of resignation. "Where is it?" the president asked, his eyes "lighting up," according to Gideon Welles, who was also in the room. Stanton was there as well, and the three cabinet officers stared at each other while Lincoln pored over Chase's letter "with an air of satisfaction" that the navy secretary claimed he had not seen from the president "for some time." Later that day Lincoln sent a joint note to Seward and Chase, announcing that he was rejecting both of their resignations because in his "deliberate judgment" they were both essential to the "public interest."[91]

Not realizing that Lincoln had two resignations in his pocket, neither of which he intended to accept, Browning subsequently urged the president to consider remaking his entire cabinet. Unlike most of the other senators, Browning wanted Lincoln to move even further in a fusionist or moderate direction. His advice was to find more War Democrats to bring into the fold. "We must have the united support of all loyal men of all parties," lectured Browning. But Lincoln would have none of it. The president claimed that a truly bipartisan cabinet "would give him trouble," noting that it would "be in his way on the negro question." Browning warned that the radical "game" was to make Chase the "Premier" and to build "a cabinet of ultra men around him." Lincoln replied, "with a good deal of emphasis," that it would never happen because "he was the master."[92]

Lincoln had not mastered the cabinet crisis of December 1862, but he did survive it, as he had every other disaster of that difficult year. Seward and Chase remained in their positions. The only change in leading men occurred within the Interior Department, as an ill and exhausted Caleb Smith resigned to accept a judgeship in Indiana, while his assistant secretary, John Usher, replaced him. Edward Bates remarked acidly that the political crisis had "dribbled out."[93]

As the year ended, almost nobody seemed happy. John Forney, the Pennsylvania newspaperman and secretary of the Senate, tried to convince Lincoln that he should have allowed publication of the joint committee report on the defeat at Fredericksburg because "the people were excited." Disgusted, Lincoln replied "that he did not like to swear, but why will people be such damned fools?"[94] Postmaster General Blair accused Stanton and Halleck of being "heartless scoundrels" guilty of "ruining" both Lincoln and the country. Thomas Ewing, the former secretary of the interior in the Taylor administration, called Lincoln's government "very weak" and predicted that it could be "utterly overthrown" in the upcoming months.[95] McClellan told friends that the president might be forced to recall him and that he would be able to "*dictate* his own terms."[96]

General Burnside, McClellan's replacement, was struggling to overcome the aftermath of his catastrophic defeat at Fredericksburg. Despite the onset of winter conditions, Burnside contemplated another offensive action, driving the corps commanders of the Army of the Potomac into near panic. Demonstrating little loyalty to the chain of command, some of these officers went behind his back and convinced Lincoln to intervene. "You must not make a general movement of the army without letting me know," Lincoln wrote to Burnside on December 30. The next day they met briefly and arranged to hold an emergency consultation at the White House on New Year's Day.[97]

January 1, 1863, was also the date for the administration's new emancipation policy to take effect. Preparations for that moment had preoccupied Lincoln and his cabinet throughout the final days of December, as they reviewed multiple drafts of the final proclamation.

The cabinet also debated plans to form a new state out of the union-occupied western counties of Virginia. Some of the cabinet officers, including Attorney General Bates, argued that West Virginia statehood—carving a state out of another state—was unconstitutional and vehemently opposed the plan. That measure was entangled in the administration's new multipronged antislavery strategy, since the plan was to require gradual abolition in this new state to help showcase the process for other border states. Lincoln ultimately sided with those in favor of statehood.[98]

On New Year's Day, Burnside arrived early at the White House for his strategy meeting with Lincoln. Stanton and Halleck also attended. Burnside came with a resignation letter but defended his plans for the new offensive. Lincoln tried to solicit a second opinion from his general-in-chief, but Halleck refused to interfere with the discretion of a commander in the field. Following a lengthy discussion, Burnside offered his resignation. Lincoln then broke up the meeting to attend to his duties greeting foreign diplomats and the public as part of the traditional New Year's Day reception at the White House. But stealing moments away from the reception, the frustrated president hastily penned an order (which he sarcastically termed "a wish") for Halleck to go to Burnside's camp and form "a judgment of your own" about the proposed offensive. "Your military skill is useless to me," Lincoln concluded, "if you will not do this."

Halleck, a former West Point professor, reacted badly to that outburst and offered his own resignation in writing. Feeling trapped, Lincoln backed down. At around 2:30 p.m., he called Burnside and Halleck back to the White House, announcing that nobody was resigning and that he was rescinding his earlier "wish" to the general-in-chief. Lincoln buried the combative letter in his own files, writing on the reverse, "Withdrawn, because considered harsh by Gen. Halleck. Jan. 1, 1862 [*sic*]."[99]

During the historic day, Lincoln was thus consumed by stress over military matters. The final Emancipation Proclamation—a legal document and an executive military order—of course betrayed none of this. The usually self-effacing Lincoln sounded almost magisterial as he invoked his full powers as commander in chief—"Now, therefore, I, Abraham Lincoln"—to declare that millions of "persons held as slaves" across most of the rebellious southern states "henceforward shall be free." The January 1 order excluded most of the content of previous drafts—it made no mention of Congress, colonization, contrabands, or border states—and instead focused on its main task of designating specific areas in the southern states where the sweeping edict would or would not apply. The final sentence—suggested by Salmon Chase and borrowed in part from a comment made by Senator Charles Sumner during the legislative debates over confiscation—offered the only rhetorical flourish as it elegantly described the measure as "an act of justice."[100]

The challenge of enforcing such a vast paper promise in the face of a resilient Confederate military and against the judgment of a potentially hostile Supreme Court was still considerable. Just a few months earlier Lincoln had dismissed a proclamation of freedom as likely to be ineffective, nothing better than "the Pope's bull against the comet."[101] Nor was there much grandeur in announcing a divisive political measure during such a dismal period, when northern factions were at odds and the army was enduring an existential crisis. The day after the proclamation was issued, Browning complained about these ominous signs to Seward, who shrugged and asked sarcastically, "What . . . is war without a proclamation?"[102]

Emancipation had been a contentious process, long in the making, and infused with partisan calculations and unknown consequences. Even if Lincoln was distracted and worried as he placed his signature on the great proclamation, many others were totally enthralled by this new era in national policy. The true center of gravity for that inspiring moment was not on the lonely second floor of the White House anyway, but rather on the grounds of the Smith plantation near Beaufort, South Carolina.

On the morning of January 1, a joyous ceremony at that location heralded emancipation for hundreds of contraband families and dozens of abolitionist allies who joined them. The coastal district of South Carolina had been occupied by U.S. forces since late 1861, and although the final proclamation exempted certain union-controlled areas from its terms of liberation, no part of South Carolina was excluded from the decree, nor any section of Mississippi. If there had been doubts before about their legal status, none remained. Black people in places like Beaufort and Corinth were freed. Those gathered at the Smith plantation near Beaufort had created the underlying "necessity" for this policy, whether it was military, political, or—as most of them saw it—moral, and for that reason they wanted to celebrate.[103]

The president's proclamation asked the new citizens to "labor faithfully for reasonable wages" and offered those "in suitable condition" a place in the U.S. military, to "garrison forts" and "man vessels" and not only to serve as laborers. After months of hesitation, Lincoln was finally embracing the concept that the "men and measures" of the unionist coalition had to be multiracial. The Beaufort ceremony included the presentation of colors to a new regiment of Black soldiers: the First South Carolina Volunteers of African Descent, commanded by Thomas Wentworth Higginson, a bearded, thirty-nine-year-old Unitarian minister who had once been part of John Brown's secret network that helped finance the raid at Harpers Ferry in 1859. Some notable New York abolitionists also attended and brought hand-sewn flags for the occasion.

Isolated as they were from Washington, without any telegraphic connections, the Beaufort participants had to improvise by reading from the text of the September proclamation instead of the final one—with silent prayers that the president had not changed his mind. The program included several speeches by white and Black figures. With the crowd growing restless, Higginson noted that there was an "electric" interruption as a lone voice rose, singing, "My country 'tis of thee / Sweet land of liberty." Everyone soon joined in, disrupting the program with a burst of spontaneous, joyous patriotism. Some of the organizers tried to reestablish order. Higginson demurred, saying, "Leave it to them," acknowledging what all knew to be true: There were many great emancipators, not just one.[104]

For months, Lincoln had managed the nation's wartime affairs on a dual track, fusing pro-war and multiparty elements within the military while separately maintaining a Republican political administration. Now there was essentially one track. The president was committed to balancing a broader fusion of men with a more radical set of war measures. The threat of national destruction had created this improbable convergence. Boss Lincoln had plenty of experience managing difficult coalitions, but he had never faced such a complex challenge.

12 PARTISAN IN CHIEF

(1863–1864)

EDWARD ROSEWATER, A YOUNG clerk in the War Department telegraph office, often wrote home during the Civil War. His letters provide some vivid snapshots of Abraham Lincoln. "The President comes in every morning about eight o'clock to read dispatches," the nineteen-year-old explained to his parents in late 1862. "With his white satin slippers, common black suit and spectacles on, he looks funny." Rosewater reported that Lincoln "asks operators all kinds of questions" and liked to share folksy anecdotes.[1] But one morning in early 1863, he noticed that the president appeared transfixed by a political cartoon.

Lying on a table was a copy of *Frank Leslie's Illustrated Newspaper*, with a sketch titled "Lincoln's Dream; or, There's a Good Time Coming." The drawing, produced by English-born illustrator William Newman, depicted a disheveled president sprawled across a flag-covered sofa, dozing and twisting his beard. Above this pleasant scene, however, a much sterner, ghostly Lincoln wields a bloody hatchet. The upper right-hand corner, captioned "The Past," features a line of dismissed generals led by Irvin McDowell and George McClellan, holding their own severed heads. In the left corner, labeled "The Future," a gaggle of frightened advisers huddles behind a beak-nosed William Seward, who is facing imminent execution as the ax-wielding Lincoln gestures him toward the chopping block.[2]

The striking image made the point that the wartime president was no simple rail-splitter but at times a cold-blooded hatchet man. A more precise metaphor for Lincoln's position in 1863 might have depicted him with a carpenter's mallet. The prairie politician was framing not a piece of furniture—as his father had once taught him—but a political party. After enduring so much dissension over the past several months, Lincoln seemed determined to build northern unity through actions, not platitudes; more "new party now" than "no party now." Emancipation was the key for this more partisan unionism. The proclamation signaled a fresh commitment to additional men through Black enlistment and bolder measures through Black freedom. By this point, Republicans were routinely calling themselves Unionists, eager to fuse with patriotic Democrats and conservatives. But to navigate such a risky party realignment demanded more aggressive leadership from President Lincoln, both in public and behind the scenes.

On New Year's Eve 1862, most members of the Supreme Court and other leading figures in the nation's capital gathered for a private dinner. The aging Chief Justice Roger Taney was a no-show, and Lincoln was not present, but the guests included cabinet secretaries Edward Bates and Seward, Lincoln's longtime friend and newly appointed Associate Justice David Davis, as well as Illinois allies Senator Orville Browning and District Marshal Ward Hill Lamon. The political challenges Lincoln faced quickly surfaced in the conversations of these notable moderates. Some attendees complained that he appeared "fatally bent" on emancipation. One guest reported that the president had warned him that a reversal on the proclamation would spark "a rebellion in the north, and that a dictator would be placed over his head within a week."[3] A few weeks later Davis decided to try to change the president's mind, but their conversation did not go well. Lincoln dismissed Davis's concerns, remarking that emancipation was "a fixed thing." Davis complained to Browning afterward that "our cause is hopeless."[4]

For his part, the president was trying hard to breathe life into the new policy. He began by corresponding with Democratic generals to help calm their nerves. "Broken eggs can not be mended," he assured an agitated John McClernand, the former Democratic congressman from Illinois serving in the Mississippi department under Ulysses Grant. Lincoln invoked what he called this "coarse" metaphor for slavery's destruction (which had been edited out of his public letter to Horace Greeley) after McClernand's suggestion that he knew some western Confederates who might surrender if only emancipation was not enforced against their states. Lincoln countered that formerly rebellious states would not be "hurt" by the proclamation if they adopted "approved plans" for gradual abolition "at once."[5]

Lincoln conceded to McClernand that loyal slave states could retain "their rights in the Union as of old," meaning their interest in slaves, but the next day he began lobbying Republican senators John Hale of New Hampshire and Browning of Illinois to support a federal aid package to promote gradual abolition in Missouri. Lincoln warned his party colleagues that Missouri slaves had been "stampeding" to freedom since the first announcement of emancipation in September, creating fresh opportunities for political "mischief" by the now Democratic-controlled legislatures of Illinois and Indiana. His point was that only by ending slavery in Missouri would Republicans alleviate their escalating political disadvantages elsewhere in the region. But Lincoln also cast the measure in moral terms. Speaking to the former Liberty party presidential candidate, Lincoln said, "Hale, you and I must die, but it will be enough for us to have done in our lives if we make Missouri free."[6]

The president was also pushing to expand the use of Black men in the military. He huddled with Hale and Browning on a Friday night, and early the next morning he called Edwin Stanton and Gideon Welles into his office and pressed them to employ more contrabands as military laborers.[7] Lincoln went even further in an exchange with General John Dix, a leading War Democrat occupying the command in Virginia once held by Benjamin Butler. The president urged Dix to put new Black soldiers to work garrisoning forts so that more white men would be available for combat. Dix appeared annoyed by Lincoln's request, even though it reiterated a key term of the proclamation. "You do not ask my opinion in regard to the policy of employing colored troops," the general replied, "and [yet] I infer that this is a question, which has been decided." Dix's feigned confusion over the administration's new policy underscored why Lincoln felt his intense lobbying effort was essential for transforming a paper promise into a practical reality.[8]

Even then, however, Lincoln's desires were not easily realized. To help motivate McClernand, Lincoln had dangled the prospect of an independent field command, but Grant and Henry Halleck torpedoed that idea. And despite the president's intervention with Dix, Black troops did not arrive at Fortress Monroe until July. The federal bill bankrolling Missouri emancipation never passed, and the state proved unable to achieve abolition on its own for two more years because of factional disputes over how to get it done.

Such arguments over tactics and strategy felt almost crippling during this period. Lincoln complained to McClernand that his time was being consumed by too many "*family* controversies."[9] The divisions within Missouri were among the most vexing for the president. Since Frémont's turbulent reign in 1861, the state's military department had become a den of political intrigue. David Hunter and Halleck had both endured brief tenures in the military command at St. Louis following Frémont's reassignment, before giving way in autumn 1862 to Samuel Curtis, a Republican from Iowa.

By early 1863, there was an open feud between General Curtis, who aligned with radicals, and the state's provisional governor, Hamilton Gamble, a conservative who also happened to be Edward Bates's brother-in-law. Lincoln repeatedly urged Curtis to be more accommodating with Gamble. "As usual in such cases," the president observed, "each questions the other's motives" despite knowing "something which the other does not, and that, acting together, you could about double your stock of pertinent information." Curtis proved more pliable than Frémont, but he also ignored many of the president's insights and was gone by summer. Lincoln complained afterward that the contentious Missouri factions "ought to have their heads knocked together."[10]

The situation in Missouri was frustrating, but none of the internal spats proved tougher to resolve in 1863 than those involving the high command within the Army of the Potomac. After the tense New Year's Day meetings at the White House, Burnside had proceeded with his plans for a second winter offensive. Disgruntled corps commanders, led by Joseph Hooker of Massachusetts, practically erupted in revolt. During the third week of January, when a soaking rain forced the army to abort its so-called mud march near Fredericksburg, morale hit a new low. Burnside asked Lincoln to dismiss Hooker, but the president deflected the request by claiming that he needed to speak with his advisers. "If you consult with anybody you will not do it," Burnside grumbled.[11]

That evening during a public White House reception, Henry Raymond of the *New York Times* cornered the president on Burnside's behalf. The general had confided in the editor, who passed along to Lincoln tales of Hooker's defiance and his "habitual conversation" with reporters, misbehavior that seemed to occur mainly when he was drunk. The president whispered in response, "That is all true, Hooker does talk badly." Lincoln explained, though, that "Fighting Joe" was too popular to remove. Raymond asked what people would think if they knew the truth. "The country," Lincoln answered, "would not believe it; they would say it is all a lie."[12] The next day, January 25, Lincoln made the shocking decision to relieve Burnside and replace him with Hooker. The move looked panicky, but Lincoln believed it was his only option under the difficult circumstances.

"I have placed you at the head of the Army of the Potomac," Lincoln wrote in a confidential letter to his new field commander. "And yet I think it best for you to know that there are some things in regard to which, I am not quite satisfied with you." The president decided to read his criticisms aloud to Hooker at the White House—rather than risk sending them out over the telegraph—noting that the general had "done a great wrong to the country" by thwarting Burnside out of spite and ambition. Lincoln pointed out some of Hooker's more outlandish remarks, such as suggesting "that both the Army and the Government needed a Dictator." But the president appeared more dismissive than enraged by the loose talk. "Only those generals who gain successes, can set up [as] dictators," Lincoln observed. "What I now ask of you is military success, and I will risk the dictatorship."[13]

Hooker responded positively to Lincoln's unusual pressure tactics. The general launched an energetic overhaul of the Army of the Potomac and soon became wildly popular in the northern press. But Hooker's most important contribution came behind the scenes. He changed the field army's intelligence-gathering system, a perennial weakness and always a subject of keen importance to the president. Hooker established a Bureau of Military Information under the leadership of Colonel George Sharpe, a lawyer from Manhattan. Sharpe organized a small team to coordinate the Army of the Potomac's disparate espionage efforts, including cavalry, signal operations, paid informants, and the balloon corps. Sharpe's men even gathered vital information from enslaved people, a key segment of the southern population whose loyalty and knowledge of local conditions had been mostly underutilized by the U.S. military to that stage in the war.[14]

While Hooker reorganized his combat forces and their support units, the president was preparing for important spring political campaigns. The congressional election cycle had not yet finished, with a cluster of New England states holding contests in March and April. These were followed by border states, including Kentucky, Maryland, and the new state of West Virginia, all undertaking midterm congressional balloting and other contests throughout the summer and fall. A total of eight states were preparing to elect thirty-three members of the new Congress in 1863—just enough possibly to determine party control at the opening session in December. Key statewide contests were also to be held that year, such as gubernatorial races in Connecticut, Ohio, and Pennsylvania, where anti-war Democrats might well prevail.[15]

The White House was determined to reverse its fall electoral setbacks. Following the disappointing 1862 campaign, John Nicolay produced an anonymous article for the *Washington Chronicle* outlining the policy choices as the Lincoln forces saw them. "The people are for the war," Nicolay argued in late November, and to "sustain the war" patriotic leaders from all parties must "sustain the President in his war measures and war policy." Nicolay highlighted several "essential" items that he presented as beyond partisan debate, including the draft, taxes, martial law, and emancipation.[16] Nobody could have expected Northern Democratic leaders to accept such sweeping political terms, but that was the point. The administration was not cooperating with its partisan opponents so much as trying to co-opt enough of them to sustain their governing majority, and on terms that might neutralize the rest.

In this tough landscape, campaign funds were critical. In February Lincoln met with editor and political fixer Thurlow Weed to discuss fundraising efforts for the remaining New England contests, especially the tight gubernatorial race in Connecticut. Secretary of the Navy Gideon Welles, a Connecticut native, dismissed the money operation as "a scheme of Seward," but Lincoln was the one pestering Weed about it. "The matters I spoke to you about are important," the president wrote, "& I hope you will not neglect them." Weed later claimed that Lincoln allowed the use of his name for a direct appeal that raised $1,000 each from fifteen leading New York businessmen. Weed reported in March that things were back under control. "The Secession 'Patard,' in Connecticut, has probably 'hoisted' its own Engineer," Weed wrote to the president.[17] Union Republican candidate William Buckingham triumphed in April.

But Weed had misgivings about the party's national strategy. After the response to Greeley was released in 1862, he had praised Lincoln, but that was when he thought the president was preparing to abandon the antislavery ultras. Now he knew better. "Democrats will prefer Party to Country if Abolition is thrust forward [as] a reason for Prosecuting the War," he warned Lincoln in March. "The President is not strong enough to shoulder that burthen."[18] The warning from an aggrieved moderate was clear: The president had to be careful about framing his emancipation policy, or he would suffer political consequences.

Lincoln took such advice seriously but was unmoved about his new party strategy. During an exchange with Henry Winter Davis of Maryland, who was organizing the congressional campaigns in his state, Lincoln offered a decidedly radical view of the new landscape. "I give it that the supporters of the war should send no man to congress who will not go into caucus with the unconditional supporters of the war," he wrote.[19]

The message seemed clear to Winter Davis, who was far more radical than his cousin, Justice David Davis. Nobody qualified anymore as "supporters of the war" unless they accepted emancipation. A few weeks later, when Rep. Elihu Washburne shared projections for party division in the new House with Lincoln, he relied on only two categories to describe the emerging landscape: Union and Copperhead.[20] This was the divide-and-conquer strategy that Nicolay had unveiled earlier in his anonymous editorial, and that he described in even blunter terms privately to his fiancée. "Under the subterfuge of opposing the Emancipation Proclamation," he wrote, Northern Democrats "are really organizing to oppose the War."[21]

Nicolay recognized that the upcoming political campaigns were contingent on military ones. "So much depends upon the success or failure of our arms," he admitted.[22] In that regard, military setbacks during the spring of 1863 created new opportunities for anti-war agitation in the North and possible Democratic success at the polls. Across the western theater, the combat was costly and inconclusive. Grant's troops maneuvered unsuccessfully for months to capture Vicksburg, one of the last remaining enemy strongholds on the Mississippi, and there appeared to be nothing but stalemate in Tennessee. The news from the East was equally disappointing. In April, the most significant naval operation of the war to that point had failed to capture Charleston. Northern discontent intensified in early May, when the Army of the Potomac suffered another devastating defeat at Chancellorsville, Virginia, following the long-delayed launch of its spring offensive under General Hooker.

The week after his stunning victory at Chancellorsville, Robert E. Lee met in Richmond with Confederate president Jefferson Davis, seeking approval for an invasion of Pennsylvania—a military gamble built on several political considerations. The southern home front was under grave strain. Confederates felt an increasing sense of urgency about their own plunging morale. But Lee also perceived opportunities in the rising northern political divisions. "If successful this year," he wrote to his wife Mary about his combat plans, "next Fall there will be a great change in public opinion at the North." The general's calculations were openly partisan. "The Republicans will be destroyed," he predicted, "& I think the friends of peace will become so strong as that the next administration will go in on that basis."[23]

Davis agreed that Lincoln's emancipation policy threatened northern unity, but he saw greater prospects for Confederate success in the west. In an effort to save Vicksburg, he had been preparing to transfer whole divisions from Lee's Army of Northern Virginia to the western theater to help dislodge Grant. But Lee's confidence in his invasion plans—and his skepticism about the Confederate western command—changed Davis's mind at their May 15 meeting. By early June, tens of thousands of Confederate troops were marching northward under Lee's command.

Lee's surprise offensive seemed to unnerve "Fighting Joe" Hooker. The Federal commander started sending the War Department ideas for counterattacking at Richmond instead of engaging Lee. Lincoln was unimpressed, responding, "I think *Lee's Army*, and not *Richmond*, is your true objective point." Hooker began complaining about his lack of authority and what he perceived as a shortage of manpower. Regarding such excuses as defeatist—and sadly familiar—Lincoln took action. With Lee's army already having crossed the Mason-Dixon Line, on June 28 the president replaced Hooker with George Meade, a respected corps commander in the Army of the Potomac.[24]

Throughout June, there were signs of panic along the Pennsylvania-Maryland border. Newspapers reported on the "Rebel Invasion," and smaller towns began emptying out. Many Black families fled in fear of being seized as fugitive slaves. Both Governor Andrew Curtin of Pennsylvania and Lincoln issued emergency calls for short-term militia volunteers. Curtin appeared agitated, reportedly telling a *New York Herald* correspondent on June 17 that he "had pleaded" for more help from the administration "to no avail." The New York journalist was in Harrisburg to cover the Democratic state convention, which nominated anti-war candidate George Woodward, chief justice of the Pennsylvania supreme court, to face Curtin in the October gubernatorial contest. Lee's political gambit already appeared to be working.[25]

Lincoln tried to project confidence. He reassured his wife, who was traveling through Philadelphia, that everything was under control. "I do not think the raid into Pennsylvania amounts to anything at all," he wrote. On June 30, he informed the New Jersey governor—a Democrat lobbying to bring McClellan back in command—that Lee's invasion represented "the best opportunity we have had since the war began."[26]

Events ultimately proved Lincoln correct, but success at Gettysburg, where the two field armies collided, was not immediately apparent as the war's largest battle unfolded in early July. Meade even considered retreating after a tough second day of fighting, but a timely report from George Sharpe's new intelligence unit helped convince him to hold the army's position. On the third day, Meade's forces repelled the Confederate assault, and Lee's battered troops began a slow retreat toward Virginia. The total human cost was horrific, with over fifty thousand casualties across both armies.

One young Federal officer who was fatally wounded on the first day was a nineteen-year-old lieutenant from Buffalo, New York, commanding an artillery battery. Bayard Wilkeson had his lower leg shattered by a shell and died later that evening after retreating U.S. forces had to abandon him as a prisoner. The sad story might have been lost in the mass of tragedy, but the officer's father was Sam Wilkeson, a leading war correspondent covering the battle for the *New York Times*. The journalist found his son's lifeless body on July 4 and opened his account of Gettysburg with one of the war's most memorable reports. "Who can write the history of a battle," he reflected, "whose eyes are immovably fastened upon a central figure of transcendingly absorbing interest—the dead body of an oldest born, crushed by a shell in a position where a battery should never have been sent, and abandoned to death in a building where surgeons dared not stay?"[27]

Wilkeson was infuriated with the Federal army's inept divisional commanders, but the rest of his dispatch praised American combat valor and closed with a stirring vindication for the sacrifices made to achieve the hard-fought victory, including the loss of his son. On July 6, when the dramatic account appeared, the president also grew agitated by army incompetence. That evening Lincoln sent a blunt note to Halleck complaining that he was "a good deal dissatisfied" with Meade's failure to chase after Lee's retreating army more aggressively.[28]

The next day, when news reached Washington that Grant's siege of Vicksburg had finally succeeded, Lincoln grew even more adamant. "We have certain information that Vicksburg surrendered to General Grant on the 4th of July," he wrote. "Now, if General Made can complete his work, so gloriously prosecuted thus far, by the literal or substantial destruction of Lee's army, the rebellion will be over." Lincoln's prodding must have been intense because Halleck abandoned his customary deference to field commanders and wired Meade a direct warning. "The opportunity to attack [Lee's] divided forces should not be lost," he wrote. "The President is urgent and anxious that your army should move against him by forced marches."[29]

To the public, Lincoln tried to appear more grateful about the recent military successes. Serenaded at the White House on the evening of July 7, the president offered heartfelt thanks for the good news. "How long ago is it?" he asked, "eighty odd years—since on the Fourth of July for the first time in the history of the world a nation by its representatives, assembled and declared as a self-evident truth that 'all men are created equal.' " Calling the juxtaposition of the national anniversary and the country's potential salvation on the battlefield "a glorious theme," he declined to go much further, claiming that he was not ready to make a speech "worthy of the occasion."[30]

The hopeful mood collapsed, however, as Lee's army took more than ten days to retreat across the Potomac River, practically unmolested by Federal forces. Northern newspapers reported every excruciating detail of the slow retreat, with multiple leaks from Meade's contentious subordinates. In desperation, Lincoln sent Vice President Hamlin to pressure the general into greater urgency. Hamlin, however, made no impact and only annoyed Lincoln by requesting a patronage favor in return.[31]

Meanwhile Halleck kept prodding Meade, invoking the president's "great dissatisfaction" after Lee's return to Virginia on July 14. Meade offered to resign, but Lincoln declined the offer and drafted a reply explaining that he was "very—*very*—grateful" for the victory at Gettysburg and did not intend "a prossecution [*sic*], or persecution of yourself." But he could not hide his disappointment. "I do not believe you appreciate the magnitude of the misfortune involved in Lee's escape," Lincoln wrote. "He was within your easy grasp, and to have closed upon him would, in connection with our other late successes, have ended the war."[32]

Lincoln decided against sending this rebuke, but his displeasure was clear to everyone. "We had them within our grasp," he remarked to Hay. "If I had gone up there," he told Robert Lincoln, "I could have whipped them myself." To Welles, Lincoln expressed fears of a conspiracy. "There is bad faith somewhere," he said darkly. Lincoln even wrote to one of Meade's subordinates, using phrases from the unsent note. "I was deeply mortified by the escape of Lee across the Potomac," Lincoln admitted to General Oliver O. Howard on July 21, "because the substantial destruction of his army would have ended the war, and because I believed such destruction was perfectly easy."[33]

The pall cast by Gettysburg's aftermath was only worsened by the political upheaval over the new military draft. In March the outgoing Congress adopted a series of controversial measures: a national conscription law, a habeas corpus act that extended and institutionalized Lincoln's wartime suspension of civil liberties in select areas, and a judicial reorganization that effectively packed the Supreme Court by adding a tenth justice. When ex–Democratic congressman Clement Vallandigham made opposition to the national draft and the administration's other alleged tyrannies a centerpiece of his nascent campaign for governor of Ohio, General Burnside (transferred from the East) had him arrested in May for sedition.[34]

Lincoln ordered Vallandigham banished to the Confederacy instead of prison, but defiant Ohio Democrats nominated him for governor anyway. Democratic organizations across the North protested a dangerous erosion of national liberty. The president responded in June—in the midst of the Gettysburg campaign—with artful public letters aimed at justifying the unpopular wartime measures. But as draft riots engulfed New York in July, Lincoln abandoned persuasion and dispatched regiments fresh from Gettysburg to help quell the uprising.

Much of the mob violence in New York targeted Black residents. Rage against the draft combined with racial prejudice and partisanship to unleash an unprecedented fury.[35] Even as this toxic brew was boiling over, Black soldiers were providing essential manpower for the exhausted Federal military and demonstrating notable valor in combat. The United States Colored Troops (USCT) had begun enrolling Black-only regiments in the spring. By summer, Black soldiers were proving invaluable in the Mississippi Valley campaign and as part of the failed assaults outside Charleston.

Many white Unionists rallied around such displays of patriotism by Black Americans. Abolitionist newspapers touted the story of Peter, an escaped slave from the sugar plantations in Louisiana, whose back had been "scourged" with dozens of whippings by his enslavers. The resilient man had presented himself to Federal troops near Baton Rouge in April, volunteering to serve. A photographer soon captured stark images of his bare, whip-scarred back and transformed them into a popular *carte de visite*, offering powerful visual propaganda for the war effort. "This card-photograph should be multiplied by the hundred thousand, and scattered over the States," wrote one antislavery editor. On July 4, 1863, *Harper's Weekly* drew even greater attention to the story by publishing an article with illustrations showing the scarred back of the enslaved man and his subsequent transformation into a proud soldier.[36]

Lincoln was familiar with the "Sugar Coast," which he had traveled as a young flatboat man. During the 1860 campaign, he described how fugitive slaves from Louisiana had once attacked him and a companion during their Mississippi River trip, looking to steal their food and supplies. Now the region was a focal point of the war effort, and the enslaved population stood as a key to national victory. A year after Lincoln's vow to his friend Browning that he would "open" the Mississippi and "keep it open" with Black help, U.S. forces controlled the river from its headwaters to New Orleans, with support from Black soldiers. Jefferson Davis's plantation had been liberated. Tens of thousands of Black men were in uniform and carrying arms. Even more than Gettysburg, this development in the summer of 1863 seemed to mark a turning point in the conflict.[37]

The president suggested as much to Grant after the *Harper's* article appeared, urging him to provide more help with the "raising of colored troops." Grant was serving as commander of the Department of the Mississippi, the area with the greatest number of available contrabands. Lincoln made the point that enlisting freed Black men "works doubly, weakening the enemy and strengthening us," and insisted that Black enlistment, "if vigorously applied now, will soon close the contest."[38] The president had made similar predictions in the past, but he was clearly pressing on all fronts.

"The Tycoon is in fine whack," Hay reported to "Nico" in August while his fellow aide Nicolay was away on a vacation. "I have rarely seen him more serene & busy." Hay wrote that Lincoln was "managing this war, the draft, foreign relations, and planning a reconstruction of the union, all at once," adding, "I never knew with what tyrannous authority he rules the Cabinet, till now. The most important things he decides & there is no cavil." Hay was perhaps too much in awe of his boss, but he was not wrong about Lincoln's approach. The president's cabinet had never been a happy team of loyal advisers. The same day that Hay offered his praise, Edward Bates was complaining in his diary that there was "in fact, *no Cabinet*" and that their consultations were "getting more and more, a mere show."[39]

Charles Dana, a prominent journalist who worked for Stanton in the War Department, also believed that despite Lincoln's outward deference toward his peers in Washington, there was never much doubt that he "was the master and they the subordinates." Dana marveled that the president always seemed "pleasant and cordial" yet conveyed an "impression of authority" or "reserve force." He concluded that "there was no flabby philanthropy about Abraham Lincoln."[40]

Despite Lincoln's commanding ways, many of his contemporaries continued to harbor doubts about his political backbone. Radicals griped that there were still too many Democrats in the nation's military command. They expressed concern over what might happen if slavery were not entirely destroyed before the rebellion ended. In mid-August, when Frederick Douglass met with Lincoln for the first time at the White House, he pressed him on such issues and urged more clarity about the rights and opportunities for the new Black troops. The president parried most of Douglass's requests and defended himself against charges that he was "vacillating" over Black freedom by emphasizing his political steadiness. "No man can say that having once taken a position," Lincoln stated, "I have contradicted it or retreated from it."[41]

Lincoln made a similar point while arguing with Salmon Chase over the wisdom of expanding emancipation. In the interest of moving faster toward the national abolition of slavery, Chase asked Lincoln to remove the exemptions from the 1863 proclamation that applied to union-occupied areas in Louisiana and Virginia. The president declined, suggesting he could not do so without appearing opportunistic. He posed a series of skeptical questions to his cabinet officer, culminating with a starkly partisan one. "Would it not lose us the elections," he asked, "and with them, the very cause we seek to advance?"[42]

Lincoln was speaking of the fall gubernatorial races in Ohio and Pennsylvania, among others, but he was not oblivious to his own electoral future. Many insiders were already looking ahead to the 1864 campaign. Hay confessed to Nicolay in early August that he was finally realizing how imperative it was to keep Lincoln at the head of their administration. No incumbent had been reelected since Andrew Jackson in 1832 (the very year Lincoln entered politics in Sangamon County), and many "unconditional" Unionist politicians preferred Treasury Secretary Chase as a more radical successor to Lincoln. In mid-August Chase invited Gideon Welles for a carriage ride, ostensibly to talk about the challenges of southern reconstruction but really to cultivate his personal support. The navy secretary (and fellow former Democrat) quickly concluded that Chase's political views were "warped" by "partyism" and by a transparent ambition for "the coming presidential election."[43]

Just days later, Lincoln received an invitation to address a mass rally for "unconditional union men of all parties," to be held in early September in Springfield, Illinois. James Conkling, the organizer, tried dangling the prospect of electioneering to help convince Lincoln to deliver his remarks in person. "The Presidential campaign for your successor (if any) has already commenced in Illinois," Conkling wrote, warning that "the most vigorous efforts are being made to increase party strength and influence." William Herndon chimed in with a rare letter to his former law partner, predicting that the crowd would be massive and speculating that Democrats were "organizing for evil."[44]

Lincoln considered making the journey home, less to aid his reelection effort than to address a political crisis in Illinois. His home state had become a major theater of northern partisan combat. Throughout early 1863 the new Democratic-controlled legislature had clashed with Governor Richard Yates. Desperately concerned for the war effort, Yates responded by suspending the General Assembly. Protests followed in the spring, along with sporadic violence and a series of controversial arrests. In June, General Burnside crystallized the ferment by attempting to shut down a Democratic newspaper in Chicago, an order that Lincoln soon reversed. At the end of that month, Democrats held a mass gathering at Springfield where tens of thousands denounced the "misrule and anarchy" of the president and his administration.[45]

Unionists planned the September 3 rally as their public response. Lincoln concluded that he could not attend but drafted a public letter to Conkling, correcting and altering it right up until the event.[46] The president aimed his remarks at Northern Democrats "who are dissatisfied with me." At Lincoln's direction, Conkling had the president's statement read "very slowly" to an immense crowd that included General McClernand, one of the more notable pro-war Democratic speakers on the program.[47]

The president opened his letter by assuring "old political friends" (former Republicans) that they should tender "the nation's gratitude to those other noble men" (War Democrats) "whom no partizan malice, or partizan hope, can make false to the nation's life." His reticence about using prewar party labels was no accident. The word *Republican* appears just once in the statement, and then only to refer to the past party "affinity" of some antislavery generals. He had last used the party name in public in his inaugural address, and he would not use it again in any public statements. Lincoln's goal in the Conkling letter was to explain how the men and measures of the Union party had evolved since the 1862 campaign.

The president began his comments by dismissing the rising calls for peace talks. "I do not believe any compromise, embracing the maintenance of the Union is now possible," he stated. Ending the war required defeating Confederate armies. He offered a series of pointed questions designed to drive a wedge between War Democrats and Copperheads, between leaders such as McClernand and the Ohio gubernatorial candidate Vallandigham, who was "campaigning" from Canada. But Lincoln also boldly pivoted to what he labeled as the main cause of northern division: "the negro."

"I certainly wish that all men could be free," Lincoln wrote, echoing his now-famous public letter to Greeley. In this August 1863 document, however, he defended the reality of emancipation—and not merely its promise—with an array of legal and military arguments. While focusing on the proclamation's constitutionality under the "law of war" and its value to military commanders—the "heaviest blow yet dealt to the rebellion"—he took shots at the disdain of many Northern Democrats for the recent Black contributions to the war effort. "You say you will not fight to free negroes," he observed. "Some of them seem willing to fight for you; but no matter." Lincoln closed with praise for the opening of the Mississippi, or "The Father of Waters," and expressed hope that victory "does not appear so distant as it did," though reminding everyone to "not be over-sanguine of a speedy final triumph."[48]

This was the plainspoken president at his most effective. Lincoln's slick reply to Greeley had essentially reframed the 1862 midterm campaign. In January he had written some eloquent statements for British audiences on the universal meaning of emancipation. In June he produced strong and widely disseminated responses to Democratic critics of the draft in New York and Ohio.[49] But the Conkling letter in August was his most persuasive defense yet for the aggressive Union partisanship of 1863, which embraced both emancipation and the enlistment of Black soldiers as essential war measures.

The radical-leaning *Chicago Tribune* lavished praise on Lincoln's effort, concluding that despite the president's "seeming tardiness" on emancipation and his questionable "choice of agents" (meaning Seward and other moderates), his intentions were clear: "He will stand by the Proclamation!" Editor Joseph Medill admitted that many "professed Republicans" had been worried that as the president maneuvered "for a candidacy of his party for a second term," he might "grow faint-hearted," but this new statement "dispels all doubts and silences all croakers."[50]

Governor Yates, who was present at the Springfield rally, expressed some doubts when he spoke to the crowd, saying Lincoln had "made many mistakes." But he quickly denied that he was wavering in his support for Lincoln and claimed it was simply the wrong time to "make Presidents." In a rare public clarification sent after the rally to the *Tribune*, Yates suggested that all the political talk was premature and that the demands of the war required what he awkwardly termed a "not men now" approach to presidential nominations in 1863.[51]

It was true that Lincoln faced more immediate political challenges than securing renomination. Factional strife in Missouri was growing worse. In May, Lincoln had complained about being "tormented with it beyond endurance for months, by both sides." Over the summer, after Congress failed to pass a Missouri emancipation aid bill and the state legislature put off action against slavery, the president blamed radicals and their refusal to compromise for delaying abolition in Missouri. He then changed the departmental command, replacing Curtis with General John Schofield, a noted moderate. But the situation continued to degenerate. At the end of September, a delegation of radicals from Missouri and Kansas came to Washington, determined to persuade Lincoln to remove Schofield and transform his emancipation policy into "a national test question" for all Unionists.[52]

A sense of high drama surrounded that meeting. One leading figure confided to Hay that "the most momentous political issues depend upon the manner in which the President receives this delegation." Hay tried to prepare Lincoln, warning that he had canvassed the situation and nearly everyone agreed that the "Union Conservatives" were "too small to reckon" and that "it would be well not to alienate" the western radicals since "their principles were in fact ours and their objects substantially the same as ours." Lincoln brushed aside these concerns, saying, "John, I think I understand this matter perfectly and I cannot do anything contrary to my convictions to please these men, earnest and powerful as they may be."[53]

Lincoln's rigid posture worried Hay, but the September 30 encounter went better than he expected. The president avoided a major confrontation, suggesting to his visitors that their arguments against Schofield needed more evidence and that their advice on controversial war measures like emancipation or the suspension of civil liberties appeared inconsistent. "Your ideas of justice," he remarked wryly, "seem to depend upon the application of it." He also revealed his opposition to making emancipation a "dividing line" within a loyal slave state like Missouri—where the Emancipation Proclamation did not technically apply—observing that the challenge was too grave for any ultra litmus test or what he termed a "pocket Inquisition." Hay came away impressed, remarking that Lincoln "crushed them with his candid logic."[54]

Attorney General Edward Bates also felt relieved that the president had turned away this "Jacobin delegation" without yielding to their demands. The St. Louis attorney had been complaining for months about the "extreme leaders" in Missouri who had "subordinated every thing to the negro—Law, justice, policy" and even "the War itself, to their mania for abolition." Still, when Bates pressed Lincoln for details about the encounter, the president would say only that "some" of the radicals "were not as bad as he supposed."[55]

Fellow conservative and cabinet officer Montgomery Blair went public with his doubts about the radical faction, however, blasting them at an October 3 meeting of Unconditional Unionists in Rockville, Maryland. Claiming to speak in defense of the president, Blair argued that the administration was being "menaced by the ambition of the ultra-Abolitionists" whose vision was more about "amalgamating the black element with the free white labor of our land" than about restoring the national union. Blair criticized the recent talk of turning the conquered Confederate states into territories under the control of Congress—a proposal for southern reconstruction that Chase had been pushing with Welles and that Sumner had written about for *The Atlantic Monthly*. Blair rejected the idea that rebellious states had committed "suicide" or that their "restoration" should be delayed in the interests of an antislavery revolution that, in his view, would only end up "treating those loyal men of the South worse than slaves."[56]

When Lincoln chose to ignore Blair's outburst at Rockville, radicals got agitated and began to coalesce even further around Chase as an alternative for the presidency in 1864. "If such men are to be retained in Mr. Lincoln's cabinet," the powerful congressman Thaddeus Stevens grumbled about Blair, "it is time we were consulting about his successor." The ambitious Chase needed no further prodding. In mid-October, he returned to Ohio and gave a series of speeches for the gubernatorial campaign, casting his efforts as part of a singular "duty" to "vote for the Union Ticket." Bates commented privately that his colleague's electioneering was "generally understood as Mr. Chase's opening campaign for the Presidency." On his return, Chase presented his new stump speech at a Unionist rally in Baltimore. He considered it a pivotal moment. "My speech was intended as a sort of announcement of the existence of a great unconditional Union Party," Chase wrote to Horace Greeley, "with *Emancipation as a Cardinal principle.*"[57]

For Chase, the landscape clearly resembled that of 1854, when he had drafted *Appeal of the Independent Democrats* and rallied antislavery forces around a new "standard of freedom." His 1863 speech illustrated how this standard was evolving during the conflict—how a war for union was becoming a war for freedom, a turn reflected in the radical credo of "Unconditional Unionism." By contrast, Lincoln's statements and actions indicated that he did not consider such an unyielding approach to be durable enough for a successful Union party. Lincoln always contended that they were waging a war for national union, even though it was sparked and sustained by sectional fights over slavery and freedom. Their guiding principle must be to win the war and thereby preserve democracy; any actions against slavery, such as military emancipation or state abolition, had to be framed as war measures, no matter how essential. The president rejected the hostility toward radicals that was so evident in conservatives like Bates and Blair but agreed that it was no time for ultraist tests on abolition.

To Seward, the debate over framing appeared unnecessary. He wanted to blur antebellum partisan differences, not to sharpen them. "Slavery is dead," he assured former Republicans while mocking the Northern Democratic party for "devoting itself to guarding the corpse." Yet beaten down by the previous year's attempt to remove him, and older than either Lincoln or Chase by nearly a decade, Seward was no longer an aspiring president or national party leader. He remained convinced by his original "no party now" advice from April 1861, when he had urged the president to move the "question" away from slavery and toward one of "Union or Disunion." Late into 1863, Seward was even expressing doubts about the timing of the Emancipation Proclamation. "Purposes can usually better be accomplished without proclamations," Seward quietly told Hay. "And failures are less signal when not preceded by sounding promises."[58]

Despite such strategic differences among their party leaders, Unionists prevailed in most of the fall elections, cementing their control of Congress and winning the gubernatorial contests in Ohio and Pennsylvania. They also gained ground in legislative battles in New York and elsewhere. Shrewd observers credited many of these electoral victories to an increase in soldier voting, achieved by rules changes in several states. In Ohio, the most critical of the states now allowing absentee ballots from military personnel, reports suggested that men in uniform had cast nearly 100 percent of their votes against Vallandigham. The gubernatorial contest was closer in Pennsylvania, where absentee voting was still blocked because of a decision from Chief Justice Woodward, the Democratic candidate for governor. By the next year, Pennsylvania and most other northern states would also change absentee voting rules, but to deal with the challenges in 1863, the War Department authorized furloughs for many Pennsylvania soldiers so they could vote at home.[59]

On the eve of the balloting in Ohio and Pennsylvania, longtime ally Elihu Washburne told Lincoln it was time for him to "confront the question of our next presidential candidate." Without mentioning party labels, the Illinois congressman described an old Democratic acquaintance of theirs who had become a Union legislator in California and was eager to organize the 1864 campaign in his state. "I think you ought to let some of your confidential friends know your wishes and feelings in that regard," Washburne wrote. Lincoln's reply was clear despite the customary deference to presidential campaign norms: "A second term would be a great honor and a great labor, which together, perhaps I would not decline, if tendered."[60]

But first the Unionists had to retain control of Congress. Rumors began circulating in Washington that some border state conservatives and Northern Democrats had concocted a scheme to take over the incoming House of Representatives. The plan involved a corrupt House clerk willing to deploy a recently revised federal statute to invalidate certificates of election from pro-administration congressional delegations. It was a long shot technical maneuver but perhaps enough to overcome the slim Union party majority. In late October, Lincoln sent out letters warning his allies about the plot, urging them to "quietly" prepare contingencies to help overcome any potential objections to incorrectly worded certificates.[61]

At the same time, the president was dealing with Chase's challenge to his leadership of the party. Since the fall elections, the Treasury secretary had intensified his efforts to stir up trouble and to secure patronage appointments that might benefit his 1864 campaign effort. Even as Lincoln ridiculed Chase as a "blue bottle fly" intent on laying eggs "in every rotten spot he can find," he was careful to avoid any open rupture. Just days before the ceremony dedicating the Soldiers' National Cemetery at Gettysburg, Lincoln attended the wedding reception for Kate Chase, who had married William Sprague, a U.S. senator from Rhode Island and leading Unionist. Less forgiving than her husband, Mary Lincoln declined to attend.[62]

In mid-November, following his daughter's wedding, Chase decided against joining the president and other cabinet members on their journey to Gettysburg. Various newspapers cast this decision in electioneering terms, quoting one of Chase's loyalists as mocking the conservativism of the president and his rump delegation. "Let the dead bury the dead," reportedly smirked Francis Spinner, a former congressman and U.S. treasurer.[63]

Lincoln may have appeared politically dead to Chase's allies, but he never missed an opportunity for face-to-face politicking. The president even rearranged his official travel plans to ensure arrival in Gettysburg on the evening before the ceremony. The extra time was useful not only to avoid "a mere breathless running of the gauntlet," as Lincoln put it, but also because so much of the northern political class would be in attendance.[64] The cemetery ground was hallowed, but the gathering felt like a national party convention.

The partisan elements at Gettysburg were apparent from the beginning. Wayne MacVeagh, the young chairman of the Union central committee of Pennsylvania, came down to Washington on Wednesday morning, November 18, to join the presidential entourage. During the daylong journey, MacVeagh and the president got into a heated "little talk" about the political problems in Missouri. After their arrival in the small Pennsylvania town, a chastened president declined to oblige a boisterous crowd that serenaded him for a speech, claiming, "In my position it is somewhat important that I should not say any foolish things." Instead, Seward jumped in, though he appeared confused at first about their location, addressing the audience as Marylanders.[65]

Seward soon recognized his mistake and spoke of the importance of rejecting secession and defending the results of the 1860 election. But he was facing a skeptical crowd. Adams County was a Democratic-leaning region whose voters had supported Woodward over Curtin in the recent gubernatorial contest. The president's aides understood such complicated political realities. Nicolay and Hay spent the evening talking politics, drinking whiskey, and eating oysters with Pennsylvania figures such as MacVeagh and newspaper editor John Forney, a former Buchanan Democrat and now an administration loyalist serving as secretary of the U.S. Senate. The aides encouraged Forney to speak to the townspeople that night so he could detail his own political conversion. The obviously inebriated editor began by "blackguarding the crowd for their apathy," then closed with praise for Lincoln as a "great, wonderful mysterious inexplicable man . . . who keeps his own counsels" and "does his own purpose in his own way no matter what temporizing minister in his cabinet sets himself up in opposition." The tired White House aides ended the evening by singing "John Brown's Body" with their group and stumbling off to bed.[66]

They reassembled the next morning, November 19, in a more somber setting, the new military cemetery at Gettysburg. The solemn occasion nonetheless included some subtle political elements. The chaplain of the U.S. House gave a lengthy invocation that Hay mocked as "a prayer which thought it was an oration." Edward Everett, the main speaker, followed by offering a full narrative of the battle in a speech that extended over two hours. The former 1860 vice-presidential nominee for the Constitutional Union party closed with some surprisingly sharp comments on wartime politics. Everett dismissed Democratic charges that emancipation had become too polarizing and even apologized for some of his own choices during the sectional crisis, conceding that he had "taken perhaps too long to tread in the path of hopeless compromise."[67]

With a burst of gratitude, Hay called Everett's oration "perfect." Lincoln's aide was less effusive about the president's remarks but still praised him for delivering a compact statement with "more grace than is his wont." The president's well-crafted opening featured revisions to the serenade speech he had delivered in July, with its slightly awkward reference to the period since the Declaration of Independence: "How long ago is it?" Lincoln now transformed this impromptu query into the resonant biblical phrase "Four score and seven years ago." The rest of the ten-sentence tribute was elegiac in tone though unyielding on the necessity of tackling the war's "unfinished work." Lincoln concluded by emphasizing that the purpose of the tragic conflict was to ensure that democracy itself "shall not perish from the earth."[68]

To the Unionist politicians in the audience, Lincoln's inspiring statement contained a powerful message about partisanship. When the president described American democracy as "government of the people, by the people, for the people," he was offering an organizing principle for his new party and his reelection campaign. Their fight for the union was being waged on the battlefield and in the polling place. Lincoln's resonant words came from his July 1861 war message ("a government of the people, by the same people"), which itself had drawn from similar statements by a range of figures, from conservatives like Daniel Webster to abolitionists like Theodore Parker. The implicit message was about the need for northern unity.

Lincoln's deft use of allusion was apparent also in his evocative nod to Sam Wilkeson's famous battle dispatch for the *New York*

Times. After losing his son at Gettysburg on the first day of the battle, Wilkeson had ended his report by extolling dead U.S. soldiers for having "baptized with your blood the second birth of Freedom in America." In his closing, Lincoln reworked Wilkeson's familiar phrase into his own memorable appeal for "a new birth of freedom."[69]

The discerning political audience would have recognized the echo of Wilkeson in Lincoln's elegant reference to emancipation. Wilkeson had worked for years with Horace Greeley at the *New-York Tribune*, where he was one of the leading radical voices hounding the administration. As late as March 1863, Lincoln complained that the reporter was guilty of "constantly attacking" the administration for its setbacks in the war and delays in implementing Black freedom.[70] But circumstances changed after the great battle. The current Washington bureau chief for the *Times*, Wilkeson had become a committed Lincoln supporter. In November, the journalist was working behind the scenes for the president's reelection effort. Just before the ceremony, Wilkeson informed Hay that at "a formal conference of political people" that he had helped organize in the city, the "unanimous conclusion" was that "the Union nominee for the next Presidency must be Abraham Lincoln."[71] Wilkeson probably did not attend the cemetery dedication in Gettysburg (his son was buried in Buffalo), but he represented one of the key northern factions that Lincoln was cultivating with his partisan poetry.

After returning from Pennsylvania, Lincoln delivered an even more forthright expression of his purpose to an angry fellow partisan, Senator Zachariah Chandler of Michigan. Several weeks earlier, Lincoln had written Chandler, a leading radical, about the brewing border state plot to deny pro-administration (and pro-emancipation) forces control of the new House of Representatives. This upset Chandler, who grew even angrier after hearing rumors that conservatives were exerting influence on the president's upcoming annual message. He sent a blistering note to the White House.

"How are these men to be of service to You in any way," the senator demanded. Asserting that the 1863 elections had been carried with widespread enthusiasm for antislavery measures, such as "Your Glorious Proclamation," Chandler pleaded for greater political toughness from the president. "You are today master of the Situation *if You stand firm*," he urged, suggesting that "Conservatives and traitors" must be "buried together."[72]

Lincoln responded with self-assurance, remarking on how "very glad" he was that Chandler did not believe he had done anything "by native depravity, or under evil influences" to undermine Unionist success in the recent elections. The president then offered up a line that he liked so much, he read it aloud to Hay. "I hope to 'stand firm' enough to not go backward," he observed, "and yet not go forward fast enough to wreck the country's cause."[73] In that political context, this was not merely a pragmatic platitude but a description of an active program for fusion.

As the new Congress assembled in early December, Lincoln became aggressive in implementing this coalition-building agenda. His friend Washburne, the longest-serving member of the House, wanted to become the new Speaker but faced stiff competition from Schuyler Colfax of Indiana, a favorite of the Chase camp. On his return from Gettysburg, Lincoln met with the Indiana congressman several times until the two men finally reached an understanding. Presumably at Lincoln's request, Washburne withdrew from the speakership contest for the sake of party unity.[74]

Once Colfax secured his nomination from the Unionist caucus on Saturday, December 5, the focus shifted to the other major challenge in organizing the House. Emerson Etheridge of Tennessee was the chief clerk whom the Unionists suspected of orchestrating the plot to decertify certain pro-administration delegations. Lincoln's top congressional supporters gathered at the White House on Sunday to strategize a response. Their mood was defiant. Rep. Owen Lovejoy, the abolitionist from Illinois, vowed that "if it comes to a question of muscle," he would "whip Etheridge" himself. Even Lincoln engaged in some bluster, warning Colfax that if Etheridge attempted any "revolutionary proceedings" he should "be carried out on a chip" or stretcher and that a contingent of "Invalids" or wounded reserve soldiers could happily "take care of him."[75]

At midday on December 8, when the new Congress began its official business, Etheridge tried to omit some state delegations from the House roll call. Thaddeus Stevens immediately objected, and Rep. Henry Dawes of Massachusetts moved to have the chamber accept certificates of election from the new Maryland delegation, which was dominated by Unconditional Unionists such as Winter Davis. Whitelaw Reid, a correspondent writing for the *Cincinnati Gazette*, called the Unionist maneuver "a bomb" and noted that Etheridge seemed to pause as "several burly Administration men" began "sauntering" over toward the clerk's desk. Dawes's motion was technically out of order since the House had not yet organized, but Etheridge's courage wavered, and he allowed the vote to proceed. Unionists won handily, and the erstwhile political coup collapsed amid jeers. Etheridge tried to reestablish order, remarking that he would do so if given the power. Lovejoy was then overheard muttering, "Yes, the Clerk would like to disorganize the House if he could, but as he has no power, he can not."[76] After the remaining delegations were certified and seated, Colfax won his election as Speaker.

The Unionist sense of triumph grew even stronger the next day as a new House clerk read Lincoln's 1863 annual message, in which the president finally appeared to cut the Gordian knot that had been dividing his party over slavery. Lincoln made a point of avoiding the growing controversies connected to reconstruction policy, especially regarding the legal status of the former rebellious states, but he offered an amnesty proclamation, to take effect immediately, that captured rebels could swear to as individuals. The pardon offer demanded future loyalty to the Constitution and notably insisted that recipients accept "all proclamations of the President made during the existing rebellion having reference to slaves," unless they were overturned by a decision from the Supreme Court. By these terms, a successful war effort would accelerate the destruction of slavery in the former Confederate states. A year that had begun with emancipation for Blacks was ending with amnesty for whites, measures that together might finally undermine the rebellion and transform southern society.[77] Lincoln was still offering greater flexibility in the border slave states, such as Maryland and Missouri. He was not threatening a "pocket Inquisition" against patriotic conservatives who were slaveholders, as he had indicated in his earlier meeting with western radicals. But this new ironclad promise of Black freedom in the vanquished South thrilled radicals.

"I have never seen such an effect produced by a public document," Hay confided in his diary. "Men acted as if the Millennium had come." Michigan senator Chandler was reportedly "beaming." Forney pledged to endorse Lincoln's reelection in his newspapers. "We only wanted a leader to speak the bold word," he gushed. "It is done and all can follow." Even perpetual critic Horace Greeley called the president's deft policy solutions "Devilish good!" Norman Judd, Lincoln's old ally from Chicago, was in town and "watching with his glittering eyes," according to Hay. Judd and Lovejoy then reminisced at the White House about the rise of the Republican party in Illinois and what had once seemed such a reckless prediction from Lincoln in 1858: "A house divided against itself cannot stand." "In five years he is vindicated," Judd remarked with awe.[78]

That evening the president joined his old friends and young aides for some freewheeling political talk. They shared stories about the Blair family and the factional troubles in Missouri. They also took notice of a new threat from the Chase camp. In conjunction with the organization of the Thirty-Eighth Congress, there was a national gathering of "Union League" representatives in Washington. During the previous year, patriotic clubs, typically called Union or Loyal Leagues, had proliferated across the North. The movement started in Illinois in 1862 as a reaction against fears of Copperhead treason, but Union Leagues were multifaceted and sometimes idiosyncratic to localities. In larger cities such as Philadelphia, the patriotic association was almost like a social fraternity for conservative elites. But in other places, such as New York, the clubs were more political and often dominated by Unconditional Unionists who had a reputation for radicalism and were thoroughly identified with support for the emancipation policy.[79]

Lincoln's men worried that a grand council of Union Leagues might become a launching pad for a Chase presidential campaign. Seward and Weed were telling everyone that the operation represented another one of Chase's "swindles." Lincoln and his aides watched the national gathering in December closely and made sure that the elected officers were "Lincoln men." The national Union League chairman, James Edmunds of Michigan, served loyally as General Land Office commissioner—the job that Congressman Lincoln had once coveted.[80]

Lincoln's relentless coalition building during the weeks after his return from Gettysburg—pursued despite a mild bout of smallpox that sidelined him for days—represented a turning point in his "contest" with Chase. The president accumulated an array of key endorsements from leading newspapers, state legislative caucuses, and even radicals such as Wilkeson and Anna Dickinson, a young abolitionist orator. The twenty-one-year-old from Philadelphia had become a political celebrity the previous spring for speaking appearances she made in the New England midterm contests.

On January 16, 1864, Dickinson created an even greater sensation when she delivered the first political speech by a woman to a joint session of Congress, addressing what she termed "The Perils of the

Hour." The main peril she saw for northerners was a failure to recognize that their conflict with the South required an uncompromising commitment to ending slavery everywhere. She offered a fierce critique of the early "mismanagement of the war," largely blaming Democratic generals, but rallied her audience by observing that they were finally making progress in the war and that "the man of the people" who had led them so far must be allowed "to complete the grand and glorious work." The president, who was in attendance, seemed pleased by the unexpected endorsement. Nicolay wrote to Hay, who was out of town, that "Miss Dickinson made a telling harangue" and that her support for Lincoln produced "continued and repeated rounds of applause," signaling "the strength of the tide here."[81]

During the same week that Dickinson enthralled the Unionist men of the capital, Elizabeth Cady Stanton and Susan B. Anthony hosted a meeting of their Women's Loyal National League at the Cooper Union in New York, site of Lincoln's famous 1860 speech. The featured speaker in the Great Hall was Frederick Douglass, who offered an agenda more radical than anything Lincoln had articulated. "No war but an abolition war," Douglass thundered. "No peace but an abolition peace." Stanton and Anthony were eager to share this clarion call in support of their petition drive, already boasting hundreds of thousands of signatures on behalf of an abolition amendment to the U.S. Constitution. But neither Douglass nor the loyal feminists offered endorsements for Chase. They remained neutral in the contest.[82]

With Lincoln's political fortunes generally on the rise, the Chase forces sought to revive his fading presidential aspirations with a set of privately circulating pamphlets fiercely critical of the president. The documents blasted Lincoln's "want of intellectual grasp" and called his reelection "practically impossible." Soon these attacks became public, and the circulars created such a furor that Chase was forced to disown them. On Washington's Birthday (February 22), a Union party organizing committee announced plans for a national nominating convention in June at Baltimore. The Grand Council of Union Leagues soon followed, scheduling a convention of their own for the same time and place. The quick consolidation of pro-administration political forces and a relatively early convention date stacked the deck even further in Lincoln's favor. By early March, Chase was so beaten down that he publicly withdrew from the contest.[83]

That same day Lincoln elevated Ulysses Grant to general-in-chief. By the end of 1863, Grant had won important victories in the Mississippi Valley and Tennessee. Now he was coming east to coordinate all the Federal field armies with a plan for multipronged offensives. The strategy was reminiscent of the one Lincoln had pressed unsuccessfully with his General War Order No. 1 in early 1862. Grant's approach was to leave headquarters and ride with the Army of the Potomac, providing stronger leadership and firmer command over the often-contentious field army. For once, the political and military situation looked promising simultaneously. Union confidence skyrocketed.

But continuing political difficulties in the border states forced the president to negotiate with proslavery interests in Kentucky and elsewhere. In early 1864, the president made a deal with newly elected congressman Brutus Clay that troubled radicals. Clay was the older brother of Kentucky abolitionist Cassius Clay, the U.S. minister to Russia. Brutus Clay had received the Union Democratic nomination for Congress in the summer of 1863, replacing the late John Crittenden. As a candidate, Clay presented himself as a slaveholder loyal to the nation but opposed to emancipation and Black enlistment. On his arrival in Washington in December, Clay voted with Unionists to organize the new House and elect Speaker Colfax. In January, the Kentucky congressman presented Lincoln with a list of special requests, seeking to benefit from his "conditional" loyalty.[84]

Most of Clay's wish list aimed at securing the release of Confederate prisoners from Kentucky under the amnesty terms now in effect, but some of his requests involved other types of prisoners. Clay was concerned about the fate of U.S. officer William Yocum, who had been convicted of returning a freedom seeker to his Kentucky enslaver while stationed at the contraband camp in Cairo, Illinois. The president agreed to issue a pardon for Yocum, who had already been imprisoned for months, claiming the man had "suffered enough."[85]

But when Yocum's pardon passed to Edwin Stanton for review, the secretary of war blocked the action. A weeks-long bureaucratic struggle ensued. Lincoln directed Attorney General Bates to move forward despite the resistance, but even Seward joined Stanton in fighting the release. Stanton wrote to the president that he "could commit no greater mistake" than to pardon Yocum, since he "gave a colored man under his command into the hands of a slave dealer to be sold & held in bondage."[86]

There was clearly more at stake in this argument than Yocum's fate. Lincoln tried responding with an appeal to pragmatism. "While we must, by all available means, prevent the overthrow of the government," he argued on March 18, "we should avoid planting and cultivating too many thorns in the bosom of society." Lincoln proceeded to list his reasons for releasing the Kentucky prisoners and for showing leniency to Yocum and others in related cases, but he changed his mind and instead sent Stanton a single paragraph asking solely for help in facilitating the Confederate prisoner releases. The War Department immediately started expediting amnesty to POWs from Kentucky and Missouri. But Yocum was excluded from this leniency and in the spring of 1864 began serving a five-year sentence in a New York penitentiary.[87]

While Yocum was being transferred to Albany, Frank Wolford, a respected Kentucky cavalry officer in the U.S. army, was arrested for criticizing Black enlistment and thus violating the recently enacted civil liberties restrictions. The fallout from this controversy was so intense that in late March it propelled Kentucky's Democratic governor, Thomas Bramlette, to race to Washington for a meeting with Lincoln and Stanton, along with Frankfort editor Albert Hodges and former U.S. senator from Kentucky Archibald Dixon.

Lincoln assured his concerned visitors that while he was "naturally anti-slavery," he had done nothing about emancipation or Black enlistment that was not justified on the grounds of military necessity. But he also offered some concessions on how to handle the military procedure in the Wolford case. The response was encouraging. He soon told Edward Bates that he had "an arrangement" with the Kentuckians that was "satisfactory all around." A week later he boasted about this success to Orville Browning, claiming that everything had been "amicably adjusted" and that his visitors were "satisfied" and left "much pleased."[88]

Hodges requested a copy of the president's "little speech" to their group, intending to publish it for the reelection effort. Lincoln obliged in the form of a public letter to Hodges that represented another powerful example of the president's persuasive skills. In this document, Lincoln created a compact narrative of his most controversial wartime policies concerning slavery, always grounding them in what he termed "palpable facts." He ended on a note of characteristic humility. "I claim not to have controlled events," the president observed, "but confess plainly that events have controlled me."[89]

That closing observation was probably too clever by half. Nobody controlled events, especially during the Civil War, but Lincoln had always controlled his reactions to wartime events—a key to his success as a leader. On the day that he completed editing his supposedly impromptu remarks to the Kentucky delegation, the president also took aggressive steps to head off further challenges to his renomination. Between rounds of revisions, he met with one of his 1860 campaign biographers, Joseph Barrett, then serving as a U.S. pension commissioner. Lincoln wanted him to find out about a recent movement to delay the Union nominating convention. Greeley's *Tribune* had endorsed the notion as prudent. The president suspected a trap designed to help radicals regroup and challenge him with Chase or another stalking horse. Barrett later recalled that Lincoln was especially adamant about wanting "this scheme defeated," and it was.[90]

Lincoln's public letter to Hodges did not persuade most Kentucky voters (the state remained Democratic in the upcoming election), but it became Lincoln's most important communication of the 1864 campaign. Even Greeley's *Tribune* acknowledged the president's mastery at explaining himself to the public at large, conceding that moderates would "accept his letter as a vindication not less of their own course than of his." But Greeley dismissed the president's admission about not controlling events as "ingeniously loyal to truth," though not in the way intended. "Had he only been a little more docile to their teaching and prompt to apprehend their bearing," the editor snarled, "we should have been saved many disasters and precious rivers of blood."[91]

Shortly after the release of the Hodges letter, aide John Nicolay returned from a confidential trip to New York with an ominous message from Carl Schurz, a leading radical. Schurz claimed that while he was finally satisfied with the administration's policies, other German-born ultras were getting ready to bolt to a third party. With Chase gone from the contest, western radicals and antislavery German immigrants from St. Louis and elsewhere tried to convince John Frémont to offer an independent presidential challenge. Schurz "is under [the] impression," Nicolay reported to Lincoln, "that the German movement for Fremont is earnest and will be pretty strong, and that they seriously intend to run him as a third candidate—that Pomeroy, Brown & Co have transferred their strength from the Chase movement to this and are bent upon defeating you at all events."[92]

The near miss of the abolition amendment in April added fuel to the radical fire. After the Senate adopted the measure at the beginning of the month, the House fell only a dozen or so votes shy of the required two-thirds threshold for passage. Even without the amendment—and there were hopes of introducing it again after the fall elections—the first congressional session closed on a strong anti-slavery note with the repeal of the Fugitive Slave Law. The end of slavery was coming into view, but radicals were growing ever more concerned about what might come afterward for the freedpeople in the reconstructed southern states.

In late May, a newly organized Radical Democracy party nominated Frémont for president at a convention in Cleveland on a platform calling for an abolition amendment and equality for Black citizens. And while such a radical alternative was not capable of winning a national contest in 1864, the movement threatened to deprive Unionists of an electoral majority by denying them a key state such as New York. Lincoln, who had seen a result like this in 1844 when Henry Clay lost because of the intervention by "Liberty men," was determined not to fall victim to the same collision of principles and pragmatism. He kept a wary eye on the new third party as the presidential campaign began in earnest.

SENATOR E. D. MORGAN of New York called the National Union party convention to order in Baltimore on June 7, 1864. Morgan, who had been chairman of the Republican national committee, made no effort to explain the shift in party name that had occurred since the 1860 Chicago convention but simply proceeded with business as usual. The Baltimore gathering named Robert Breckinridge of Kentucky to serve as its temporary president until a formal body could be organized. The noted conservative and Presbyterian minister was no Republican, however, as he readily acknowledged. "As a Union party I will follow you to the ends of the earth and the gates of death," he offered to applause. "But as an Abolition party—as a Republican party—as a Whig party—as a Democratic party—as an American party, I will not follow you one foot."[93] For the rest of the day, the convention bickered over rules and credentials, with the main fight concerning rival delegate slates vying to represent Missouri (the radicals prevailed over the conservatives) and the question of whether to recognize delegates from southern states undergoing reconstruction, which they decided not to do.

In the evening, the convention elected a permanent chairman, former Ohio governor William Dennison, who went even further than Breckinridge in repudiating antebellum partisanship. "In no sense do we meet as members or representatives of either of the old political parties which bound to the people," he claimed, "or as the champions of any principle or doctrine peculiar to either." The only "test of membership" for their new party, he suggested, "was unconditional loyalty to the Government and the Union."[94]

On the convention's second day, the platform committee, led by Henry Raymond of the *New York Times*, defined what that loyalty meant in practice. The Unionists not only endorsed Lincoln's Emancipation Proclamation and his decision to employ Black soldiers but also stood in favor of a constitutional amendment to abolish slavery everywhere in the United States "forever." There was no debate.

On the presidential question, there was only minor quibbling. At first, some delegations supported a single vote to nominate the Lincoln-Hamlin ticket, but after some confusion that effort got derailed. The delegates proceeded with separate roll call votes for president and vice president. The Missouri radical delegation initially refused to support Lincoln and backed Ulysses Grant as a protest before yielding and allowing the convention to declare Lincoln their unanimously chosen nominee.

Things went harder for Hamlin, who got dumped from the ticket to showcase fusionist appeal with either a War Democrat or a border state conservative as the vice-presidential nominee. Behind the scenes, this had always been the primary question: Who would run with Lincoln in 1864? Unionists of all stripes had tried for months to engage the president in sorting out the second spot, but Lincoln had determined before the convention that he wanted to appear "absolutely impartial." As Hay explained it to Nicolay, who was on the ground in Baltimore, their boss had vowed he would not "interfere" even by "confidential suggestion." But by not interfering to defend Hamlin, once the clamor for a replacement grew loud at the convention, Lincoln was making his preference for a new understudy obvious to everyone.[95]

Union delegates chose Andrew Johnson of Tennessee as the party's vice-presidential nominee. Johnson had been the only U.S. senator from a Confederate state to remain loyal in 1861. The next year, he became the war governor in union-occupied Tennessee, but what made him an overwhelming favorite at Baltimore was his evolution on Black freedom. Johnson, a slaveholder, had originally convinced Lincoln to exempt Tennessee from the Emancipation Proclamation. But in the months since, he had liberated his own slaves and became a supporter of abolition. He told Lincoln, "Now is the time for settlement of this question. Hence I am for immediate emancipation." Johnson's brave political decisions against secession and his evolution on slavery made him an ideal Union party candidate.[96]

The party's adoption of the Union banner at Baltimore was a strategic choice with deep roots. Ever since the August 1862 war rally at the Capitol and Lincoln's deft public letter to Greeley, pro-administration forces had been moving their supporters toward a broad patriotic fusion of willing men from any party, but one based on strong war measures that included emancipation, Black enlistment, and now the promise of national abolition by constitutional amendment. Lincoln's contribution had been to steer the fusion movement away from more shortsighted options—avoiding the platitudes and phony consensus seeking of "no party now," while also delaying or downplaying the polarizing demands of "Unconditional Unionism." With decisive behind-the-scenes leadership and persuasive public statements, Lincoln had helped the new party develop into a stable and dynamic coalition.

The Unionist name itself reflected this new combination of men and measures. After 1862, Lincoln and his inner circle had been careful to avoid the Republican label, except as part of an amalgamation such as "Union Republican." Out of habit they sometimes slipped in private conversations or letters, but their party newspapers and state central committees consistently called themselves Unionist. Only Northern Democrats kept referring to them as Republicans—for obvious strategic reasons of their own. But as Lincoln and his supporters well understood, building a successful Union party was an essential political step toward saving their national union.[97]

EPILOGUE

(1864–1865)

ABRAHAM LINCOLN RESPONDED TO the official news of his second presidential nomination with characteristic humility, claiming he was grateful "the Union people" had decided he was "not unworthy to remain in my present position." To a delegation from the Grand Council of Union Leagues, which had also endorsed him at Baltimore, Lincoln was more playful, suggesting that while he would never dare call himself "the best man in the country," he understood why Unionists were willing to accept the wisdom of the "old Dutch farmer" who said "it was not best to swap horses when crossing streams."[1]

Behind the folksy facade, the president recognized that he was still in some political jeopardy. On June 9, when he informed the Union party delegation that he wanted time to read the platform before making a formal acceptance of their nomination, he made sure to express immediate approval of the plank on abolition, to forestall any doubts about his antislavery beliefs. He added that all "unconditional

Union men, North and South" appreciated the need to secure slavery's demise. And that evening, when an Ohio group serenaded him at the White House with a brass band, Lincoln offered a frank assessment about the limits of his victory. "What we want still more than Baltimore conventions or presidential elections," he stated, "is success under Gen. Grant."[2]

Lincoln understood that progress in the war effort would remain critical to sustaining the Union coalition. Following the convention, when reports of a bloody defeat suffered at Cold Harbor in Virginia on June 3 finally reached northern newspapers, the good mood dissipated quickly. Over the next several weeks, additional setbacks in the military campaigns around Richmond and Atlanta, and embarrassing Confederate raids into Maryland and Pennsylvania, intensified public frustration. Complaints came from the usual Democratic critics, but some Unionists also started to question the administration. By the end of summer, Lincoln was facing loud calls to change his key policies. There was even a serious threat to dump him as the Union nominee. If the Baltimore convention had been delayed to August, as editor Horace Greeley and others had wanted, Unionists might well have been willing to "swap horses."

At first, however, Lincoln's renomination provided him much-needed political leverage. Near the end of June, when Secretary of the Treasury Salmon Chase threatened resignation over a patronage battle, Lincoln surprised him by accepting. The president privately mocked his rival for a botched political maneuver that in effect asserted, "Unless you say you are sorry & ask me to stay & agree that I shall be absolute and that you shall have nothing, no matter how you beg for it, I will go." There was alarm in Washington at Chase's unexpected ouster, even among Lincoln's closest allies. Elihu Washburne called the move "a great disaster." John Hay, who was blindsided by the decision, worried that such an upheaval during a period of military stalemate was "little less than a crime." But Lincoln, undaunted, elevated William Pitt Fessenden of Maine, chairman of the Senate Finance Committee, to head the Treasury Department.[3]

Radicals had other reasons for unease with Lincoln beyond the Chase debacle. Their long-standing suspicions about the influence of Democratic and proslavery officers within the military were heightened by the return of bad news from the front. Even Sam Wilkeson, who was back with the radical-leaning *Tribune* after his stint with the *Times*, complained in print about the rash of military miscues.[4] Wilkeson did not abandon his support for Lincoln—forged after his son's tragic death—but his criticisms stung. On the political front, John Frémont and his third-party movement kept up their agitation for a bolder antislavery alternative to the administration. And radicals on Capitol Hill renewed their challenge to the president over slavery policy as part of the debate over how to reconstruct the conquered Confederate states. Senator Benjamin Wade of Ohio and Rep. Henry Winter Davis of Maryland won support for an ambitious bill with a tougher, and much slower, plan for reconstituting seceded states into the federal system than Lincoln had envisioned in his 1863 annual message and amnesty proclamation. The measure also promised to accelerate and expand the president's wartime emancipation order by declaring that "Involuntary servitude" in the former Confederate states was to be "forever prohibited." The political tension erupting around this proposed legislation—approved on July 2 at the very end of the session—recalled earlier battles over the 1862 Confiscation Act. This time, however, Lincoln had no secret proclamation hidden in his desk to reconnect the competing factions. He instead issued a pocket veto, explaining that he was "unprepared" to commit to any single plan for reconstruction and remained convinced that Congress could not abolish slavery in any state without a constitutional amendment.[5]

Not all the ultra antislavery leaders backed Wade and Davis. William Lloyd Garrison endorsed the president early in 1864, attended the National Union convention, and stuck with him throughout the campaign. Others such as *Tribune* editor Greeley seemed ready to move past arguments over how to achieve abolition and were now more concerned about finding ways to stop the bloodshed. In July, Greeley pressed Lincoln to negotiate peace terms with Confederate emissaries who were in Canada seeking a ceasefire conference with the president. In a private letter to Lincoln, Greeley wrote that "our bleeding, bankrupt, almost dying country also longs for peace." The mercurial editor who once demanded "Forward to Richmond!" had been secretly working toward this diplomatic solution for over a year. Henry Raymond of the *New York Times* recorded in his diary in early 1863 that Greeley told him the conflict must be "ended on any terms" and admitted that he was engaged in schemes to encourage "foreign mediation."[6]

Lincoln responded to the prospect of diplomatic overtures with disdain, but he did not reject them outright. He informed Greeley that he could serve as a presidential envoy for potential negotiations at Niagara Falls, but that the precondition for any talks would have to include a Confederate agreement to end the war and restore the union, and "the abandonment of slavery." Greeley sensed that he was being used and declined to go, but Lincoln persisted. Greeley went to Canada with White House aide John Hay at the end of July, but nothing came of the effort other than unwanted publicity after the details of Lincoln's dead-on-arrival ceasefire terms leaked to the press.[7]

The president assured Abram Wakeman, the postmaster in New York and a political ally, that the peace talks had been a ruse and that Confederates were merely trying to influence the selection of an anti-war nominee at the Democratic party's upcoming national convention in Chicago. Lincoln was adamant that "the present presidential contest will almost certainly be no other than a contest between a

Union and a Disunion candidate, disunion certainly following the success of the latter." He offered an explicit promise (and implicit threat) for Wakeman to convey to others: "Whoever aids the right, will be appreciated and remembered."[8]

But Lincoln's handling of his political opponents, whether Northern Democrats or border state conservatives, was more nuanced than this blunt exchange suggests. The most revealing political decision that Lincoln made that summer was to refrain from ordering the arrest of Clement Vallandigham when the Ohio politician crossed back into the United States in defiance of his banishment to the Confederacy. The president was not reluctant to act against the notorious Copperhead, but he observed privately that Vallandigham's presence would only hurt the Democrats on the eve of their convention, because having "so violent and indiscreet a man go to Chicago as a firebrand to his own party" benefited "the Union cause."[9]

Lincoln also made attempts over the summer to placate conservatives in the loyal slave states. He offered a pardon to Frank Wolford—the Kentucky cavalry officer whose arrest had prompted Lincoln's public letter to Albert Hodges in April—in exchange for a pledge by Wolford to stop complaining about the recruitment of Black soldiers in Kentucky. Wolford rejected this deal in late July, arguing that too much had changed since the war's initial multi-partisan mobilization, "composed of Democrats, Republicans, Old Line Whigs, Abolitionist[s] and men of no party." Wolford borrowed Stephen Douglas's line from 1861 to accuse the president of failing to "sink the partisan in the patriot" with his misguided antislavery policies.[10]

Lincoln shrugged off that outburst and eventually permitted the release of Wolford, who went on to serve as a Democratic elector in Kentucky for the 1864 presidential contest. Lincoln's indifference to such open hostility reflected his view that Democratic resistance to Union war measures was often self-defeating. His caution with border state politicians also reflected the increasingly dismal military news.

Ever since the defeat at Cold Harbor in early June, the Army of the Potomac had been held in check as General Robert E. Lee's men maintained their position outside Richmond. Throughout July, the U.S. army appeared almost inept as Confederates managed multiple raids into the North. In mid-July Lincoln himself came under enemy fire at a fort on the outskirts of Washington as he viewed an assault by rebel forces under General Jubal Early. The raid was unsuccessful, but the Confederates set fire to cabinet officer Montgomery Blair's home in Maryland, embarrassing the government.[11]

The public confidence in Lincoln that had helped secure him the nomination just a month earlier was starting to collapse. Attorney General Edward Bates complained to former senator Orville Browning that the nation's "great want" was "a competent leader" at "the head of affairs." Browning agreed, telling another confidant that "I have never been able to persuade myself that [Lincoln] was big enough for his position."[12] At the end of the month, the Confederate burning of Chambersburg, Pennsylvania, on the orders of Jubal Early, came as yet another shock, prompting Thurlow Weed to warn a fellow insider, "Lincoln is gone, I suppose you know as well as I."[13]

Lincoln was not gone, though. On August 3, while in the War Department telegraph office, he noticed a dispatch from General Ulysses Grant attempting to organize a response to Confederate troop movements across western Virginia. Worried about another demoralizing rebel raid, Grant ordered that General Phil Sheridan and his cavalry move "south of the enemy and follow him to the death." The bluster concerned Lincoln, who sent a coded message to Grant urging more persistence in communications with his subordinates. Lincoln closed with stern advice: "I repeat to you it will neither be done nor attempted unless you watch it every day, and hour, and force it."[14] The second-guessing marked a departure for the president, who had become less involved in military affairs since elevating Grant to general-in-chief in March. Lincoln was still watching, however, not with "an evil eye," as he explained to another officer, but with a vigilant one.[15]

The day after Lincoln intervened over the telegraph wires with Grant, Senator Wade and Congressman Davis issued a "manifesto" in Unionist newspapers denouncing the president's rejection of their recent reconstruction bill and blaming the disagreement on his "personal ambition." Reconstruction had become a topic of urgent political concern by the summer of 1864. Although much of the South remained in rebellion, U.S. forces had been occupying sections of Virginia and various ports along the Atlantic coast (including in South Carolina) since 1861; large areas of Louisiana since 1862; and nearly all of Arkansas, Tennessee, and Mississippi since the end of 1863. General William Sherman and his troops were on the march in Georgia, and Federal forces threatened the remaining Confederate field armies in Florida, Texas, and Virginia. Radicals worried that Lincoln's amnesty policy was too easy, even if tied to the acceptance of emancipation by southerners. Wade and Davis argued that Unionists should slow the process of state-by-state reconstruction and insist on tougher loyalty oaths for white southerners or risk the future of Black freedom and civil equality.[16]

Wade and Davis also backed up their policy manifesto by organizing an effort to find a new presidential nominee for the Union party. A clique around General Benjamin Butler—now stationed back in Virginia—took the lead in August by convincing disaffected Unionists that the former Democrat and originator of the contraband policy might better serve the party's cause in the fall elections. Butler's supporters argued that he could reenergize Unionists while also attracting the antislavery supporters of third-party candidate Frémont. On August 18, at a secret meeting in New York City hosted by Mayor George Opdyke, the radical opposition to the president seemed to crystallize, though without anointing a replacement candidate.[17]

Lincoln swung into action the next day. He had been thinking about issuing a public letter to defend the administration's policies, as he had done with letters to Greeley in 1862, James Conkling in 1863, and Albert Hodges in April, but the escalation of his troubles made him opt for more direct, private persuasion. On August 19, at a meeting in the White House with Frederick Douglass, he showed Douglass the draft of what he described as a potential public response to complaints from Charles Robinson, a leading War Democrat in Wisconsin. Robinson, who had served in the army and was a newspaper editor, claimed to support the administration's military measures, including emancipation. But he felt that rigid preconditions for peace talks, only recently made public from Lincoln's Niagara Falls correspondence with Greeley, left figures like him with "no ground to stand upon" in the election contest. There was an important difference, in his mind, between threatening emancipation as a military necessity and demanding the end of slavery as a condition for peace. Lincoln's draft response opened with a surprising concession: "To me it seems plain that saying re-union and abandonment of slavery would be considered, if offered, is not saying that nothing *else* or *less* would be considered, if offered."[18]

Lincoln said he was trying to prove to War Democrats like Robinson that Jefferson Davis would not even consider this more flexible offer, but Douglass was appalled by the evasive opening line. He urged Lincoln not to release the letter at all, warning it would be "a complete surrender of your anti-slavery policy and do you serious damage." Lincoln doubtless understood that even appearing to concede so much would damage him with radicals just as they were moving against him. But the president was being strategic with Douglass, not candid. He wanted to remind Douglass of the pressure he was under and the stakes of the political contest. To drive that point home, he also asked the antislavery leader—who was still not yet committed to either Lincoln or Frémont—to prepare a contingency plan in case the administration lost in November. Lincoln said he needed Douglass to organize a corps of Black agents who would infiltrate Confederate territory and help as many slaves as possible escape behind Federal lines before the war ended, as it certainly would with the inauguration of a Democratic president in March.[19] Douglass left the encounter fearing that Lincoln was considering negotiating an end to the conflict himself without destroying slavery.

But Lincoln's message was clearly designed to scare Douglass and other radicals straight about the consequences of their third-party flirtation with Frémont. He wanted to convince them that without greater political unity in the fall campaign, they were facing a catastrophic defeat that would have dire consequences for the enslaved. One thing is certain: The president never released the Robinson letter.[20]

Lincoln's commitment to his unyielding peace terms became more obvious on the evening of August 19, just hours after his discussion with Douglass, when the president met at the Soldiers' Home with a group of moderates from Wisconsin. Unlike Douglass, these men supported the president's reelection. They also appreciated the pragmatism of the opening line in his letter to Robinson (which he shared with them) because they thought it would help in their fusion efforts with War Democrats. During their conversation, however, Lincoln pushed them to recognize the danger of undertaking such a gamble in negotiations with the Confederacy and the reason peace talks would never really work. "You cannot conciliate the South," he said, assuring his visitors that if he ever retracted the promise of Black freedom, "I should be damned in time & in eternity."[21]

The politicos from Wisconsin went away impressed by this performance, but Lincoln's problems with other moderates remained. "The people are wild for peace," Thurlow Weed warned William Seward a few days later. Weed, Justice David Davis, and other moderate fusionists were almost as agitated as the radicals. Weed was openly threatening to support a War Democrat for president; Lincoln and Davis had not talked since April. The justice blamed Lincoln for having conceded too much on policy grounds to Chase and his radical supporters. By mid-August, a host of figures, such as *New York Times* editor Henry Raymond, now serving as the Union party executive committee chairman, and longtime Illinois ally Leonard Swett, now shuttling back and forth between Washington and New York, were pressing Lincoln to appear more conciliatory. On August 22, Raymond wrote, "The tide is strongly against us." He argued it was time to offer peace "on the sole condition" of national reunion. Raymond conceded that Jefferson Davis would probably reject such an offer but thought it might help restore northern morale. John Nicolay grumbled that this "stampede" of "N.Y. politicians" felt like "a sort of political Bull Run."[22]

Lincoln was unmoved by this growing opposition. On the same afternoon that Raymond sounded the alarm, the president spoke to a group of Ohio soldiers who had just completed their military service. Calm and reflective, he put the national crisis into broad context. "I happen temporarily to occupy this big White House," he said, calling himself "a living witness that any of your children may look to come here as my father's child has." He reminded the men that their shared "birthright" and "struggle" as Americans was to guarantee that "all have equal privileges in the race of life." Such a nation, he concluded, was "worth fighting for."[23]

Yet even as Lincoln seemed at peace with his underlying political strategy, he deemed it prudent to prepare a secret contingency plan in case of defeat. The next day he wrote out two sentences that he shared with no one. "This morning, as for some days past," he scratched out in pen, "it seems exceedingly probable that this Administration will not be re-elected. Then it will be my duty to so co-operate with the President elect, as to save the Union between the election and the inauguration," he wrote, "as he will have secured his election on such ground that he can not possibly save it afterwards."[24]

The potentially explosive document had no heading or salutation other than "Executive Mansion" and "Washington, Aug. 23, 1864," and closed with his usual signature, "A. Lincoln." The president folded the memo into a small rectangle and sealed it with glue. At the cabinet meeting later that day, he asked his seven department heads to sign their names over the outside crease, before putting the date underneath their list of names and filing it in his desk without explanation.[25]

No one in the cabinet read the memo or had any idea what it contained. In the days afterward, none of them mentioned the episode in their letters or diaries. They had not registered the dramatic moment because their role was only to certify the creation of the document. They were not joining the president in a pledge of loyalty.

Lincoln wanted proof of the document's date of origin, though. He understood that the audience for this contingency memo—the Democrat who might defeat him in the election—would be hostile to him and suspicious of his intentions. Democrats viewed Lincoln as a tyrant capable of ordering the imprisonment or even the execution of his political opponents. Under such conditions, he understood that for his proposal for cooperation to be taken seriously, it was crucial to demonstrate that he had known for weeks that his defeat was possible, perhaps even likely, but had never wavered in his commitment to a peaceful transfer of power.

In turn, Lincoln wanted something from his victorious Democratic opponent. A defeated president would need help to keep Federal troops in the field and available for a final push toward victory. Lincoln knew that with an incoming government pledged to peace on practically any terms, too many soldiers would be tempted to quit the fight. There was also a tangible benefit in reminding his victorious opponent, almost sure to be General George McClellan, that the last thing an incoming Democratic administration needed was to negotiate in the face of a military stalemate. That would make securing reunion with the Confederates almost impossible. If he did lose the election, Lincoln seemed convinced that true bipartisan cooperation represented his last, best way to "save the Union." Although an eleventh-hour patriotic fusion of this sort was highly improbable, it represented only a final contingency. Lincoln still believed that military and political victories were within reach. On August 23, he was not confessing his deepest fears; he was planning for every possible scenario.[26]

Lincoln's more confident assessment of the political situation became apparent over the next few days. On August 24, he drafted a letter framed as a proposal for peace talks based on nothing more than the "restoration of the Union." Henry Raymond was supposedly to take this letter to Richmond, but Lincoln had no intention of sending it. When Raymond arrived the next day to talk over the mission, Lincoln expressed his opposition to the entire plan. "The Tycoon sees and says it would be utter ruination," Nicolay scribbled to Hay (who was out of town), while Raymond was in the office arguing about its merits with Lincoln.[27] "If the President can infect R. and his committee with some of his own patience and pluck," Nicolay wrote, "we are saved." And backed by what Nicolay described as the "strongest half of the cabinet" (Seward, Stanton, and Fessenden), Lincoln finally managed to convince Raymond that to abandon the demand for the end of slavery "would be worse than losing the Presidential contest—it would be ignominiously surrendering it in advance."[28] There was no last-minute mission to Richmond.

By the end of August, it was clear that Lincoln was not stepping aside for another nominee, as the ultras or radicals had been trying to arrange. Nor was he retreating on the promise of Black freedom for the sake of peace talks, as the pragmatic fusionists were urging. Despite these competing pressures, the president was staying the course. And in keeping with his lifelong habit, he made the decision himself. He always listened, always sought out "the real condition of affairs," as the *New-York Tribune* once put it. But he had ignored advice from eastern party leaders in 1858, when many of these same men—especially Raymond—sought to make Stephen Douglas a Republican. He had defied most of them again during the secession crisis and throughout repeated wartime battles over military personnel and slavery policy. And in August 1864, with the stakes as high as they had ever been, he once again demonstrated his independence as a decision-maker.[29]

Staying the course turned out to be the right decision for several reasons, starting with the implosion of the Democratic party. At the end of the month, when Democrats met in Chicago for their national convention, Lincoln's strategy of allowing Vallandigham to return to the country unmolested paid off. Led by the Ohio politician, anti-war Democrats seized control of the platform process, producing a plank that blasted the war effort as "four years of failure." War Democrats countered by securing the nomination for McClellan, but the damage was done. The open divisions proved crippling for Democrats in the fall.[30]

Just days after McClellan's nomination, at the beginning of September, Federal troops secured a major battlefield victory, their first in months, when Sherman's forces captured Atlanta. In the coming weeks, this triumph, combined with progress in U.S. naval operations along the Gulf Coast and in army combat across the Virginia theater, contributed to a rejuvenation of northern morale.

The fall campaign was full of the usual sound and fury. Democratic operatives engaged in their standard race-baiting attacks, while Unionists responded with a flood of pamphlets and speeches praising the administration and offering up conspiracy theories of Copperhead treason. Following the lingering customs of the era, candidate Lincoln delivered no speeches, engaged in no debates, and issued no public letters. McClellan kept quiet as well, although his awkward acceptance letter, in which he tried to navigate the party's peace and war factions, only underscored the deep Democratic divisions and their inability to fuse with other northern partisans alienated from the administration.[31]

Lincoln proved more adept at tackling the tensions within the Union coalition. He agreed to overhaul the New York Custom House, rewarding the disgruntled Seward-Weed faction, which had been agitating for control of the operation since the fall of Sumter in April 1861. Mary Lincoln even got involved in this patronage battle by writing in mid-September to her friend and former postmaster Abram Wakeman, now elevated to surveyor of the port. She urged him to employ his newfound influence to cultivate some of the city's leading War Democrats, and to assist in mollifying Thurlow Weed with a mysterious "contract" that they had apparently discussed apart from her husband.[32]

At this time, the president also delivered an important reward to Frederick Douglass, who had complied with Lincoln's request to formulate a plan for an escape network for slaves remaining in the South after the election. In his message to Lincoln, which included his details for the operation, Douglass added that he needed a "great favor" for his son Charles, a soldier in the army, who was seriously ill and wanted to get home. "Let this boy be discharged," Lincoln instructed the War Department.[33]

And in mid-September, Lincoln succeeded in getting Frémont and his Radical Democracy party out of the race. With help from Senator Zachariah Chandler, the president negotiated a deal that included the removal of conservative Montgomery Blair from the cabinet in exchange for Frémont's withdrawal. When the terms became final after weeks of haggling, Lincoln coolly informed Blair, "The time has come."[34]

Frémont's removal from the race convinced most of the remaining radical holdouts to return to the Unionist fold. Leaving nothing to chance, however, Lincoln invited Salmon Chase to the Soldiers' Home for a private discussion that resulted in the ex–cabinet officer's venturing out west in October to give speeches for the campaign. Insiders gossiped that it was part of a "contract" over a future nomination for the chief justiceship of the Supreme Court.[35] And near the end of the campaign, Lincoln sent his loyal aide Nicolay to St. Louis to quiet the factional fighting in Missouri. Nothing was left undone.[36]

There was no public polling in 1864, but campaigns did occasionally solicit informal "surveys" of likely voters on railroads and streetcars. These showed the Unionists doing well. Pro-administration electoral trends also became apparent after the state and congressional contests that took place in mid-October, most notably in doubtful states such as Indiana, Maryland, and Pennsylvania. Lincoln watched those returns carefully. He was pleased that Maryland voted to abolish slavery. Unionist candidates won sweeping victories almost everywhere, practically guaranteeing success in the presidential contest, though Lincoln refused to acknowledge it at first. On the night of October 13, while reading the returns at the War Department telegraph office, the president scratched out a projected electoral count between the "Supposed Copperhead Vote" and his "Union Vote" that put the margin at only 117 to 114 in his favor. The actual result would be much larger.[37]

Lincoln spent most of Election Day, November 8, holed up in the White House with John Hay as a steady rain drenched Washington. The city seemed practically "deserted," according to the aide, and the president appeared to feel sorry for himself. He commented glumly that although he was not "a vindictive man," he had a penchant for getting mixed up in campaigns "marked with great rancor." The only contest that struck him as "a quiet time" was his 1846 race for Congress. But that had been ugly too, from the clash of egos with fellow Whig John Hardin through the last-minute charges of religious infidelity. There had always been rancor.[38]

That night, Lincoln and Hay waited for the returns at the War Department. When Thomas Eckert, chief of the telegraph office, showed up wet and muddy after falling on the rainy streets outside, it reminded Lincoln of 1858, when his party had battled Douglas Democrats in the Illinois legislative contests. Lincoln recalled that it had been raining on that election night as well, and that he had said to himself after a similar tumble: "It's a slip and not a fall." For those gathered around the telegraph sounders, the president drew the obvious lesson. "I am pretty sure-footed," he remarked.[39]

Gideon Welles and his deputy Gustavus Fox arrived late, gloating about recent defeats suffered by the ultras. The main target of their rancor was Winter Davis, who had not even been renominated for Congress by Maryland Unionists following his bitter break with the president. Lincoln gently scolded them. "You have more of that feeling of personal resentment than I," he claimed, adding, "I never thought it paid." Hay considered this to be standard fare coming from Lincoln, whose "favorite expression," according to the aide, was "I am in favor of short statutes of limitations in politics."[40]

With favorable returns coming in, Lincoln appeared "most agreeable and genial all evening." By midnight, the men were swapping tales, drinking hot coffee and other beverages, and eating fried oysters, which the president himself was happily "shovelling out." At around two in the morning, an enthusiastic crowd gathered outside the War Department building to serenade for a presidential speech. Lincoln appeared and spoke just long enough to assure the audience that "the consequence of this day's work . . . will be to the lasting advantage, if not to the very salvation, of the country."[41]

Lincoln then retired to the White House with Hay and his old friend Ward Hill Lamon, but while he slept, the other two stayed up, drinking whiskey and talking. They argued over potential replacements for Chief Justice Roger Taney, who had died in mid-October. Hay eventually suggested that Lamon could have Nicolay's place in their shared White House bed, but the district marshal decided on this night to provide extra security for the president. Taking a blanket, he lay down outside Lincoln's bedroom door, "with a small arsenal of pistols & bowie knives around him," determined to scare away anyone who might attempt to overcome ballots with bullets.[42]

The final election results showed that about four million men cast presidential ballots in 1864, only slightly fewer than in 1860 despite the absence of voters from eleven seceded states. The president did exceptionally well, securing about 55 percent of the popular vote and racking up margins closer to 70 percent in several key states. He ended up splitting the border states, winning majorities in Maryland, Missouri, and West Virginia, while losing in Delaware and Kentucky. There were some disappointments. The president prevailed in Pennsylvania, but only through the newly authorized absentee votes of soldiers in the field. And he won Illinois despite losing in Sangamon, the county where he had lived for most of his adult life.

Prewar Democratic and Republican voting patterns generally persisted, though Unionists secured solid cross-party support in some states. The fusion effect was most striking in Massachusetts, where the president gained more than twenty thousand votes over his 1860 totals and increased his winning percentage by 10 points. He received ballots from former Constitutional Unionists like Edward Everett and from old abolitionists like William Lloyd Garrison. The most celebrated party-switching story in Massachusetts involved a 104-year-old man named John Phillips, a self-described "Jeffersonian Democrat" from Sturbridge. Phillips had voted in every presidential election since George Washington's reelection, except for 1860, when he was too ill to participate. Determined to vote in 1864, Phillips arrived at the town hall with help from his seventy-nine-year-old son. Carried inside by a platoon of soldiers, he was presented with a choice of two party ballots, one for Lincoln, another for McClellan. "I shall take the one for Abraham Lincoln," Phillips said to cheers. The grateful president later thanked him with a personal note.[43]

By the evening of November 10, Lincoln was ready to put the election into a broader perspective. In prepared remarks to a serenade of local Unionist clubs gathered outside the White House, he focused on the challenge of sustaining democracy during a crisis. "It has long been a grave question whether any government, not *too* strong for the liberties of its people, can be strong *enough* to maintain its own existence in great emergencies," he said.[44] He had used the same question to frame his special written message to Congress on July 4, 1861, which sounded then, at the outset of a rebellion, like a call to action. By 1864, the point also applied to his most controversial wartime decisions, which he conceded had been divisive.

Lincoln was unequivocal that "we can not have free government without elections" and their inevitable partisan "strife." No matter the "strain" that the "political war" had imposed on their "divided, and partially paralized" nation, he emphasized that "the election was a necessity." He urged everyone to take lessons from the recent contest, observing, "Human-nature will not change." "In any future great national trial," he added, "compared with the men of this, we shall have as weak, and as strong, as silly and as wise; as bad and good. Let us, therefore, study the incidents of this, as philosophy to learn wisdom from, and none of them as wrongs to be revenged."[45]

Democracy was the animating principle both of Lincoln's union and of his Unionist party. Even during the toughest moments in August, when he had been devising multiple contingencies in the event of defeat, he never seemed to contemplate canceling or delaying the election. For Lincoln, the electoral triumphs of 1864 validated this democratic faith. As he put it in his evening remarks, "even among candidates of the same party, he who is most devoted to the Union, and most opposed to treason, can receive most of the people's votes." It was a blunt but honest assessment. "Not very graceful" was how Lincoln later described his remarks, "but I am growing old enough not to care much for the manner of doing things."[46]

The next day, the cabinet assembled for their weekly meeting. Nicolay was still in Missouri wrapping up his partisan fence-mending, but Hay was in the room, assisting the president and taking notes. Lincoln began by pulling out a mysterious piece of folded and sealed paper from his desk. "Gentlemen," he said, "do you remember last summer I asked you all to sign your names to the back of a paper of which I did not show you the inside?" Only William Dennison, who had replaced Blair as postmaster general, might have declined to nod. "This is it," Lincoln remarked with a flourish. Hay cut open the document with some difficulty, and Lincoln read the contents of the August 23 memo.[47]

When he finished reciting the two-sentence bombshell about his proposal to "cooperate" with the Democrat who might have defeated him, he recalled that he had drafted this secret offer "when as yet we had no adversary and seemed to have no friends." He said he had known McClellan was going to be his opponent, and he described how he had "solemnly resolved" to confront his former subordinate if he won, apparently even rehearsing the encounter: "I would say, 'General, the election has demonstrated that you are stronger, have more influence with the American people than I. Now let us together, you with your influence and I with all the executive power of the Government, try to save the country. You raise as many troops as you possibly can for this final trial, and I will devote all my energies to assisting and finishing the war.' "

Hay recounted this extraordinary scene in his diary without commentary, though he noted a withering response from Seward. "And the General would answer you 'Yes, Yes,' " replied the secretary of state with obvious scorn, "and the next day when you saw him again & pressed these views upon him he would say 'Yes—yes' & so on forever and would have done nothing at all."[48]

Lincoln had once asserted to Maryland senator Reverdy Johnson that "I shall not surrender this game leaving any available card unplayed." Here was one of the most dramatic "unplayed" presidential cards of the war, but in the happy haze of their electoral victory, the cabinet officers did not seem eager to rehash this past. They did not ask what Lincoln had intended by requesting their signatures on the document, nor why he had refused to confide his desperate plan to them. They simply let Seward mock McClellan and indirectly the president. Lincoln chose not to belabor the point. "At least I should have done my duty and have stood clear before my own conscience" was how he left the matter. Except for Hay, none of the men wrote about the revelation in their contemporary letters or diaries. Lincoln was offering a rare seminar on party leadership, but his young aide was the only one who even bothered to take notes.[49]

A more public glimpse of the partisan Lincoln came as he began drafting his annual message for the December meeting of Congress. He returned to an old habit of compiling a state-by-state chart of election returns. He had been making these tabulations since the start of his career and even made a gift of one to his future wife. For his upcoming message, he turned to a comparison of the 1864 results with those from 1860. He wanted to show with turnout figures that the country was not "bleeding, bankrupt [and] almost dying," as Greeley had concluded bitterly in July, when he was lobbying for peace talks. The president's table showed that loyal states had gained more than 150,000 new voters over the course of the rebellion. Observing that "we are not exhausted nor in process of exhaustion," he claimed it was possible to "maintain the contest indefinitely."[50]

Lincoln's 1864 message sounded buoyant in places. He noted that "our arms have steadily advanced," especially in the "most remarkable feature in the military operations of the year," the three-hundred-mile march through Georgia by Sherman's forces, soon to yield the "Christmas gift" of Savannah. Lincoln seemed happiest, however, with the progress of Black freedom. He noted the "complete success" of the Maryland abolition referendum and pointed with pride to the spread of "free state constitutions" across the union-occupied South. And he appeared confident about the fate of the stalled abolition amendment. Calling it "only a question of time" before the amendment won congressional approval, he asked, "may we not agree that the sooner the better?"[51]

With Lincoln's unexpected endorsement of action during the remaining lame-duck session of Congress, the amendment returned to center stage. Rep. James Ashley of Ohio and Rep. Augustus Frank of New York launched a "systematic canvass" to push the abolition measure over the required two-thirds threshold in the House. The House clerks kept a secret "tally sheet" tracking the progress of the effort, which targeted Democratic members from New York and Pennsylvania along with some wavering border state conservatives. "Probably Mr. Ashley, Mr. Frank, Mr. [Richard] Shearman, [a clerk] and myself were the only persons who ever saw that tally sheet," recalled clerk Edward Barber.[52]

Ashley reintroduced the measure in early January. After some intense lobbying and a few last-minute delays, the amendment passed on January 31. Although Democrats spread rumors about corruption and even outright bribes, none of the members who switched their votes received special patronage favors. The occasion was momentous, but the final process was predictable. Lincoln's confidence regarding the amendment never faltered. "*I knew the bill would pass*," he told a Massachusetts woman, "the day [Ashley] introduced it."[53]

Sending the abolition amendment to the states for ratification was a monumental achievement for the Union party. Unionists were also bolstered by combat victories that started coming in bunches. Amid the signs of progress, however, some party divisions lingered at Lincoln's second inauguration on March 4. John Forney, the secretary of the Senate, fired off a sharp reminder to Andrew Johnson about the challenges of sustaining their coalition when the vice president–elect suggested that he might skip the inaugural ceremonies owing to illness. Warning that "our friends will be greatly disappointed," Forney pointed out that Johnson was "the representative of the Democratic element without which neither Abraham Lincoln nor yourself could have been chosen." He warned Johnson that he was needed to "assist in shaping a generous, magnanimous and national policy," referring clearly to postwar reconstruction policy, and predicted, "If this is not done, my dear sir, the great Union party will be a failure."[54]

Johnson attended on March 4, but some observers believed he was drunk, perhaps from an attempt at self-medication. The president's brief address was majestic, remembered for its gracious closing ("with malice toward none") and its stern pledge to prevail in the conflict at any cost. Lincoln vowed that "if God wills . . . every drop of blood drawn with the lash shall be paid by another drawn with the sword," then "this terrible war" must continue. The language could have come from John Brown.[55]

As the fighting drew closer to an end, Lincoln sounded more determined than ever. "Let the *thing* be pressed," he wired to Grant in Virginia, just two days before Lee's defeat on April 9 at Appomattox.[56] The following day, Lincoln thrilled a crowd of supporters by having "Dixie" played outside the White House during a victory serenade, observing with wry pride that "yesterday we fairly captured it."[57]

Even with other Confederate armies still operating in the field after Appomattox, Lincoln felt ready to focus on the demands of peacetime politics. On April 11 he offered a speech on reconstruction policy that was designed to heal rifts in his coalition that had been festering since 1863. Speaking in the evening from the White House portico, he offered a new vision for the future of the South and the Union party.[58]

Lincoln first acknowledged the "embarrassment" of disagreements among "the loyal people" over how to proceed, and the censure of some fellow Unionists for what they considered his mistakes in setting up a restored government in Louisiana. He was referring to the political battles that had erupted after conservative forces in the occupied territory had proceeded with elections in early 1864. Some twelve thousand eligible voters—mostly white men who had signed Lincoln's amnesty pledge—produced a loyal civilian government for Louisiana. The newly installed government agreed to abolish slavery in the state, but it did not provide voting rights, social equality, or other essential personal liberty protections to freed Blacks. Despite his misgivings about this controversial effort, Lincoln had been working quietly with the state's new governor, Michael Hahn, to improve the situation. Meanwhile radicals were complaining that the entire effort was dangerously premature.[59]

The president emphasized in his April speech that his 1863 annual message had presented "*a* plan of re-construction," not "the only plan," and he implied that what was happening in Louisiana did not necessarily have to be repeated or followed as a model by other southern states. Though Lincoln did not mention Wade, Davis, or any other party critic by name, he described some of his disagreements with then–cabinet secretary Salmon Chase, without identifying the current chief justice. These were differences over the details for securing the end of slavery in the rebellious South, including the legitimacy of removing the exemptions in the Emancipation Proclamation that had left slavery intact, at least in theory, across sections of Louisiana and Virginia, and throughout Tennessee. Lincoln had refused to do what Chase wanted in 1863, and now he felt vindicated by events.

The president declined to take up the question of "whether the seceded States, so called, are in the Union or out of it," which he dismissed as "a merely pernicious abstraction . . . good for nothing at all."[60] His contempt for this abstract argument hid an even deeper truth. He believed the radical position—that the Confederate states had in effect committed political suicide—was a direct contradiction of the constitutional arguments against secession that he and other Unionists had been making since 1861. During a private conversation with Senator Chandler in the heat of the debate over the Wade-Davis bill, he called the acknowledgment that states could somehow have left the national union a "fatal admission." "If that be true," he said in July 1864, "I am not President, these gentlemen are not Congress."[61]

Now in April 1865, Lincoln urged his fellow Unionists to keep an open mind and be pragmatic about the progress of reconstruction. Speaking of the "colored man" and his "desire" for the right to vote, the president employed the same logic he had once pressed on the radical Chandler following his Gettysburg Address, asking whether full equality would be more easily achieved "by saving the already advanced steps toward it" or "by running backward over them?" Recalling earlier battles with Horace Greeley and his favored broken-egg metaphor, Lincoln asked whether to promote loyal government in Louisiana, "we shall sooner have the fowl by hatching the egg than by smashing it?" In keeping with the vow that he had made at the start of his political career in 1832 to "renounce" positions as "soon as I discover my opinions to be erroneous," he now suggested that since "bad promises are better broken than kept," he would "break" his pledge of support for Louisiana's new civilian leadership if they proved themselves unworthy. He also promised to remain "inflexible" about "Important principles" without getting distracted by "details and colatterals." This partisan refrain had long been one of Lincoln's favorites, ever since he had first appeared on the national stage with his speech at the Chicago River and Harbor Convention in 1847. "Let us avoid collateral remarks," he had urged the delegates, and "unite, like a band of brothers, for the welfare of the common country."[62]

In 1847 Lincoln had promoted fusion between Whigs and Democrats through support for western internal improvements. In 1865, he envisioned a process for building patriotic fusion across the South, a process he knew was "fraught with great difficulty" during the near anarchy that would follow the war and the end of slavery. "No man has the authority to give up the rebellion for any other man," he observed. In describing the challenges of rebuilding the loyal southern political fabric, Lincoln also added, "We simply must begin with, and mould from, disorganized and discordant elements." The last time he had used the word *discordant* in a speech was in the House Divided address from 1858, when he had described the Republican party as having been "gathered from the four winds" out of "*strange, discordant*, and even, *hostile* elements." But Lincoln's plans for southern political reconstruction were more ambitious than any of his earlier experiences with northern antislavery fusion. His aim now was to unify loyal southern whites with liberated Blacks to help build and sustain multiracial majorities capable of restoring the federal union, a truly revolutionary goal.

In offering his vision of patriotic fusion across the South, Lincoln conceded that the twelve thousand or so loyal voters in Louisiana represented a shaky start. A figure like "fifty, thirty, or even twenty thousand" would have been "more satisfactory," the habitual vote counter admitted. But Lincoln also announced himself in favor of counting Black votes along with white ones to get the job done. Acknowledging that many in his party thought all Black men should have the "elective franchise," Lincoln stated for the first time in public, "I would myself prefer that it were now conferred on the very intelligent, and on those who serve our cause as soldiers."

In a rousing close, Lincoln claimed that by standing with the restored Louisiana government, national Unionists had it within their power to "encourage the hearts" of the "twelve thousand" loyal whites in the state, so they would "adhere to their work, and argue for it, and proselyte for it, and fight for it, and feed it, and grow it, and ripen it to a complete success," while also inspiring free Blacks in the region, "with vigilance, and energy, and daring, to the same end." Lincoln was describing a reconstruction process that would begin with building a Union party in the South and presumably culminate with the birth of multiracial democracy across the nation. He did not lay out all those details, however, ending his speech by underscoring the need for more reconstituted southern states to help secure ratification of the Thirteenth Amendment. In his last lines, he suggested that he might soon have "some new announcement" on that front once he was "satisfied" that the time was "proper."[63]

Reading Lincoln's words in a Baltimore newspaper, Chief Justice Chase had his doubts. To Chase, the president appeared too hesitant about supporting civil rights for southern Blacks. He was unsatisfied by Lincoln's gesture toward enfranchising only select classes of Black men. Like a growing number of radicals, he wanted Black and white men treated alike—especially at the ballot box, where they could exercise real power in building a successful Union party in the South. "I am now convinced that universal suffrage is demanded, by both sound policy and impartial justice alike," Chase wrote in a quick letter to Lincoln the day after the speech. He mentioned that he would soon be back in Washington and hoped that they might be able to meet to "have the whole subject talked over."[64] Just two days later, Lincoln was killed by John Wilkes Booth, who had been in the crowd outside the White House on April 11 listening to the president's remarks.[65]

In early 1864, when he was battling with Chase for the presidential nomination, Lincoln had responded to an endorsement from the Union League of Philadelphia with remarks that a reporter transcribed but never published. "It is easy to say I am in the field openly for the Presidency," Lincoln admitted to the delegation that brought him the good news. He sounded almost ambivalent about a renomination, confessing that his White House experience had been "one of painful anxiety and toil far beyond anything I had ever before conceived of." He insisted, however, that he would never "shrink" from any outcome, whether "from another man's nomination for the Presidency" or from his own, if it would "advance the great cause of saving our country."[66]

Politicians always claim to act on an interest greater than their own ambition. But in Lincoln's case, the assertion was true, if more complicated than he wished to acknowledge. Throughout his political career, he acted as if saving the country required building a party, not merely winning office. He always appreciated the strategic value of securing broad coalitions around enduring principles. It separated him from so many of his rivals. He was not always a better politician than figures like Chase or Seward, but he was a more successful party leader.

Lincoln also understood that American democracy was inherently partisan, even in wartime, and that "We the people" were a divided lot, split into ever-shifting majorities and minorities. Even partisan allies often had deep disagreements about men and measures and where to draw the line over principles. Politics could be exhausting. But Lincoln never seemed to tire of heated conversations like the one Chase wanted to have over reconstruction. He always appeared to relish communicating with voters, whether through speeches on the campaign trail or by greeting them and their farm animals along dusty country roads. He enjoyed preparing charts and counting votes. Nor did he ever shy away from sending blunt reminders in confidential notes. Boss Lincoln may on occasion have lost his temper but never his focus. That is also what helped make him such a successful party leader. He was persuasive because he was so persistent.

It has always seemed an insult to call someone "partisan." The term feels like shorthand for petty combativeness. Lincoln's partisanship was more dynamic and honorable. He fought with his opponents and endured their attacks but also learned how to bring people together to save a democratic nation. As he shifted in his party allegiances from Whig fusionist to ultra Republican to partisan Unionist, he discovered the means for saving his broken country. He made mistakes along the way, and he nearly failed, but Lincoln's achievements materialized from his relentless devotion to pursuing ever more perfect unions. And that is a lesson for every generation of citizens and partisans.

ACKNOWLEDGMENTS

I WANT TO BEGIN BY thanking Michael Burlingame, Eric Foner, and James Oakes for reading the manuscript and offering their keen insights and thoughtful suggestions. They are a true all-star panel of reviewers. I have long admired each of them for their incredible body of work on Lincoln and nineteenth-century American history and feel proud to count them as friends. Jim deserves extra thanks because he was the one present at the creation of this project and stood by me through the end. Beyond that distinguished trio, however, there are also dozens of other scholarly friends of mine in this wildly competitive field who have been generous and helpful. I want to highlight two of them: Gabor Boritt, one of my mentors and role models, and Harold Holzer, who seems to know everything and everyone, not only in history but in "real politics."

This project has been a long time in development, so it's fair to say that I owe other debts from as far back as college days at Harvard University. Richard Neustadt and I talked about Truman more than Lincoln, but his ideas on presidential power have influenced me enormously. And nobody has had a bigger impact on my career than the great biographer David Donald. In many ways, the concept for this book began as a paper about the 1855 senatorial contest in his graduate seminar on Lincoln. That seminar—Donald's final class before retirement—was truly a career-defining experience for me. I was the only undergrad in an intense room at Robinson Hall where the philosopher John Rawls sat in with us as an auditor. I left there feeling like a real historian. Afterward, I served as one of Donald's research assistants and produced an honors thesis on Lincoln's role in organizing the Republican party, under the deft supervision of Gil Troy. I then expanded on that work in graduate school at Oxford University, where Daniel Walker Howe and Lawrence Goldman supervised my dissertation on Lincoln's pre-presidential political career. They further helped me develop the seed material for this book.

Working on this project naturally required assistance from numerous archivists and librarians. Michelle Krowl at the Library of Congress was invaluable in her aid. So, too, were the staff members at the Abraham Lincoln Presidential Library and Museum in Springfield, Illinois. I want to highlight the efforts of those both past and present who assisted me over the years, especially Rick Beard, James Cornelius, Tom Schwartz, Christian McWhirter, Sam Wheeler, and Daniel Worthington. At the Dickinson College Archives, I owe gratitude to Jim Gerencser and Malinda Triller Doran. And appreciation to Ching Zedric at the Bradley University Special Collections Center. I also want to offer special thanks to Craig Caba of the J. Howard Wert Collection for his deep knowledge and unflagging support.

My work on the project included time spent on fellowships at the Strategic Studies Institute of the U.S. Army War College and at the New America Foundation in Washington, DC. I want to offer personal thanks to Doug Lovelace in Carlisle and to Andrés Martinez, Fuzz Hogan, and Becky Shafer from my think-tank days in the nation's capital.

At Dickinson College in Carlisle, I am blessed to be surrounded by many wonderful students, especially my always-bustling crew of interns over at the House Divided Project. For this book project, I owe special thanks to several colleagues, past and present: Chris Bombaro, Brenda Bretz, Madeline Brown, Ryan Burke, David Commins, Karen Farynyiak, John Jones, Cheryl Kremer, Todd Mealy, Elaine Mellen, Greg Moyer, John Osborne, Glen Peterman, Steve Weinberger, and Neil Weissman. Also, I want to highlight a few alums who have been important friends to the House Divided Project: the late Brian Pohanka and his family, Eric Wittenberg, and Greg Zimmerman.

Much of the material for this book has been tested and refined at various types of training sessions. I especially want to thank Steve Wiley of the Lincoln Leadership Institute and Jeff McCausland of Diamond6 Leadership for the numerous opportunities they have afforded me to discuss "Boss Lincoln" with corporate, government, and school district groups. Over the years, I have also presented material from this project in many K–12 teacher training sessions sponsored by multiple organizations. From the Gilder Lehrman Institute of American History, I would like to personally thank Jim Basker, Lesley Herrmann, Lew Lehrman, Anthony Napoli, and Lance Warren. For support over the years at the National Constitution Center, I am grateful to Steve Frank, Kerry Sautner, Joe Torsella, and Jeff Rosen. At the History Channel, I owe a deep debt of gratitude to Kim Gilmore. Recently I have also been sharing sneak previews of the book with groups of some highly engaged high school students. At the National History Academy, I want to thank Bill Sellers for such opportunities. And from the Teagle Foundation, which sponsors the inspiring Knowledge for Freedom seminar, I want to express my sincere appreciation to Andy Delbanco and Tamara Tweel.

At W. W. Norton, a great publishing house, I want to offer special thanks to Janet Biehl, my copyeditor. She is an author herself and amazingly thorough. But my deepest gratitude goes to Steve Forman, my editor. He is a true throwback to the golden age of high standards. My students would have loved to watch him challenge my lazy word choices, imprecise analysis, and sometimes-mangled storytelling. I will always be grateful for his gracious support and help but mainly for his unyielding professionalism.

Finally, I want to thank my friends and family. I have been lucky enough to sustain contact with a network of friends from childhood, college, and graduate school. They always seem to call, text, or email whenever Lincoln appears in the news. We're an irreverent group, no doubt, but tight-knit. The best example of this kind of lifelong friend might be James DeBord. We've known each other since we were nine years old playing basketball together in the Lancaster YMCA rec league (he came off the bench). James eventually grew to six foot five and had an impressive varsity hoops career at our alma mater, J. P. McCaskey High School in Lancaster. Let's just say that I became more of a scholar. But we've always bonded over politics, working together on campaigns and in our own consulting business. He will appreciate this book. My family will respect the effort as well, though nobody in our unruly crew will ever admit it too easily. I have a big extended clan on both sides (Pinsker + Getson) that includes aunts, uncles, cousins, nieces, and nephews, full of love and even more teasing. Everyone is now scattered across the country, but our touchstone memories always return to summers at Ventnor and Margate on the Jersey Shore.

On the most immediate level, I want to thank my in-laws, Ellen and Bruce Haynes, Robyn and Darren Spiegel, and their boys, Dylan and Ronen. I want to thank my sister, Beth Pinsker, a great journalist and author herself, and Brian Cohen, and the kids (soon to be grownups), Eli and Abigail. My own parents, Ann and Sandy Pinsker, both died while I was writing this book. Nobody would have appreciated or promoted it more. They, too, were distinguished authors and teachers. It's a Jewish custom to say "May their memory be a blessing." But even more than a blessing, their memory for me has been a lesson on how to lead a good life. I miss them now more than ever.

I dedicated this book to my wife Rachel because I dedicate all my books to her. It's simple really. Without Rachel, nothing would be possible for me. But to be honest, when I was struggling to finish, it wasn't Boss Rachel who got me through so much as our two boys, Gabe and Aiden. When I began this project, they were little. We shared the basement: I tapped away at my laptop surrounded by my books and papers, and they stayed in the alcove playing with their Thomas the Tank Engine set. Now I've been pushed to the alcove, and many of my books and files are in storage, while they command the basement space with their pool table, Xbox, work desk, and their own meticulously curated books. They are young men full of promise. Gabe even helped me prepare images for the final publication, far more adept at the technology than his old man.

In my history methods classes, I teach a letter from Machiavelli that he wrote while in exile in 1513, describing to a friend how grateful he was at the end of the day to enter his study and "put on garments regal and courtly" so that he could read about "the ancient courts of ancient men" and hear from them "the reason for their actions." I am no Machiavelli, and my half-zip from Costco is certainly not regal, but I felt a kinship with those emotions as I studied Lincoln alongside my children during an era when democracy felt under siege. Today we need a president, not a prince, who can build coalitions and exercise power in ways that bring people together. I want my sons to be voters, not soldiers. That is what everyone wants for their children and for their children's children. And it is what we always need to remember most from Lincoln—how to ensure that our democracy does not perish from the earth.

NOTES

INTRODUCTION

1. J. H. Buckingham, "Illinois as Lincoln Knew It: A Boston Reporter's Record of a Trip in 1847," ed. Harry Pratt, in *Papers in Illinois History and Transactions for the Year 1937* (Springfield, IL: Abraham Lincoln Association, 1938), 139–40.
2. Buckingham, "Illinois," 110; Transcripts from Greeley's *New York Semi-Weekly Tribune* (July 17, 1847) and Weed's *Albany Evening Journal* (July 14, 1847) appear in Robert Fergus, ed., *Chicago River-and-Harbor Convention: An Account of Its Origins and Proceedings* (Chicago: Fergus, 1882), 139, 151. See also Mentor L. Williams, "The Chicago River and Harbor Convention, 1847," *Mississippi Valley Historical Review* 35 (March 1949): 607–26.
3. James K. Polk, "Veto Message," August 3, 1846, in Benjamin Perley Poore, ed., *Veto Messages of the Presidents of the United States with the Actions of Congress Thereon* (Washington, DC: Government Printing Office, 1886), 191.
4. AL to Jesse Fell ("Enclosing Autobiography"), December 20, 1859, in *Collected Works of Abraham Lincoln*, ed. Roy P. Basler, 8 vols. (New Brunswick, NJ: Rutgers University Press, 1953), 3:511–12 (hereafter cited as *CW*). For back-

ground and context on Lincoln's early years, see Kenneth J. Winkle, *The Young Eagle: The Rise of Abraham Lincoln* (Dallas: Taylor Trade, 2001).

5. See Gabor S. Boritt, *Lincoln and the Economics of the American Dream* (Memphis, TN: Memphis State University Press, 1978); Daniel Walker Howe, *The Political Culture of the American Whigs* (Chicago: University of Chicago Press, 1979); and Michael F. Holt, *The Rise and Fall of the American Whig Party* (New York: Oxford University Press, 1999).
6. The concept of a party system in American politics was introduced by James Bryce, *The American Commonwealth*, 3 vols. (London: Macmillan, 1888), and matured with Richard Hofstadter, *The Idea of a Party System: The Rise of Legitimate Opposition in the United States, 1780–1840* (Berkeley: University of California Press, 1969); William Nesbit Chambers and Walter Dean Burnham, eds., *The American Party Systems: Stages of Political Development* (New York: Oxford University Press, 1967); and James L. Sundquist, *Dynamics of the Party System: Alignment and Realignment in the United States* (Washington, DC: Brookings, 1973). For more recent historical analysis, including pushback against the party system paradigm, see Sean Wilentz, *The Rise of American Democracy: Jefferson to Lincoln* (New York: W. W. Norton, 2005); and Rachel A. Shelden and Erik B. Alexander, "Dismantling the Party System: Party Fluidity and the Mechanisms of Nineteenth-Century U.S. Politics," *Journal of American History* 110 (December 2023): 419–48.
7. See Marvin Meyers, *The Jacksonian Persuasion: Politics and Belief* (1957; reprint Stanford, CA: Stanford University Press, 1960).
8. For extended historiographical discussions of these points, see Matthew Pinsker, "Not Always Such a Whig: Lincoln's Partisan Realignment in the 1850s," *Journal of the Abraham Lincoln Association* 29 (Summer 2008): 27–46; and Matthew Pinsker, "Lincoln Theme 2.0," *Journal of American History* 96 (September 2009): 417–40.
9. William Herndon to [J. E.] Remsburg, September 10, 1887, in Alfred Whital Stern Collection of Lincolniana, Library of Congress. The quotation was later popularized in Richard N. Current, *The Lincoln Nobody Knows* (New York: McGraw-Hill, 1958).
10. Some of the nuances of this classification system were discussed with Lincoln in Samuel Haycraft to AL, August 19, 1860, Abraham Lincoln Papers, Library of Congress (hereafter cited as Lincoln Papers, LC).
11. AL to Norman Judd ("I have talked, more fully than I can write"), October 20, 1858, *CW*, 3:329–30.
12. AL, Memorandum Concerning His Probable Failure of Re-Election, August 23, 1864, *CW*, 7:514–15.
13. Buckingham, "Illinois," 136, 139–40.

14. AL to Martin Morris ("show this letter to Short; but to no one else"), March 26, 1843, *CW*, 1:320; and AL, Handbill Replying to Charges of Infidelity, July 31, 1846, *CW*, 1:382.
15. AL to William Herndon, January 8, 1848, *CW*, 1:431.

CHAPTER 1: SELF-MADE BOSS

1. The background for these images, including even the identity of the photographer, is surprisingly difficult to reconstruct. And their traditional date, 1846, seems mistaken. Mary Lincoln gave birth to their second son Edward or Eddy in mid-March 1846. She would surely not have felt ready to sit for her first formal photographic portrait with her husband for months afterward. That insight, combined with some special clothing purchases made by Lincoln in June 1847 and a few other circumstantial details, make it probable that these images were taken sometime in the summer of 1847, either just before or right after the Chicago River and Harbor Convention. See Gibson W. Harris, "My Recollections of Abraham Lincoln," *Leisure Hour* (1904): 443–51, for background on the likely photographer (Nicholas Shepherd); and Harold Holzer, "'I Look Too Stern': Mary Lincoln and Her Image in the Graphic Arts," in *The Mary Lincoln Enigma: Historians on America's Most Controversial First Lady*, ed. Frank J. Williams and Michael Burkhimer (Carbondale: Southern Illinois University Press, 2012), 308–11, for subtle analysis of the composition.
2. For Robert Lincoln's recollections of the photographic portraits, see Robert T. Lincoln to Editors of *McClure's*, November 21, 1896, quoted in *Lincoln Lore* no. 1382, October 3, 1955. Tarbell is quoted in Keith A. Erekson, *Everybody's History: Indiana's Lincoln Inquiry and the Quest to Reclaim a President's Past* (Amherst: University of Massachusetts Press, 2012), 142.
3. AL, Autobiography Written for John L. Scripps [c. June, 1860], *CW*, 4:61.
4. Rick Callahan, "Indiana Museum Unveils Mallet Lincoln Used as Young Man," *Springfield (IL) Journal Register*, February 9, 2016.
5. AL to Andrew Johnston, April 18, 1846, *CW*, 1:378.
6. Kenneth J. Winkle, *The Young Eagle: The Rise of Abraham Lincoln* (Dallas: Taylor Trade, 2001), 10–85.
7. AL, Communication to the People of Sangamo County, March 9, 1832, *CW*, 1:5–9.
8. *Sangamo Journal*, January 19, 1832, quoted in Richard Lawrence Miller, *The Early Years: Birth to Illinois Legislature*, vol. 1 of *Lincoln and His World* (Mechanicsburg, PA: Stackpole Books, 2006), 128.

9. AL, Communication to the People of Sangamo County, March 9, 1832, *CW,* 1:5–9.
10. Michael Burlingame identifies New Salem resident John McNamar as one of Lincoln's possible editors in 1832. Burlingame, *Abraham Lincoln: A Life*, 2 vols. (Baltimore: Johns Hopkins University Press, 2008), 1:71. An expanded online version of this two-volume biography, available from the Lincoln Studies Center at Knox College, will be cited hereafter.
11. AL, Communication to the People of Sangamo County, March 9, 1832, *CW,* 1:5–9.
12. AL, Autobiography, December 20, 1859, *CW,* 3:512.
13. "Sangamo County Meeting," *Sangamo Journal*, August 25, 1832; Lincoln later described parties at that time as being either "Jackson" or "anti-Jackson." William D. Howells, *Life of Abraham Lincoln* (1860; reprint Bloomington: Indiana University Press, 1960), 40.
14. James Finley to Joseph Duncan, May 27, 1834, excerpted in Elizabeth Duncan Putnam, "The Life and Services of Joseph Duncan, Governor of Illinois, 1834–1838," *Transactions of the Illinois State Historical Society* (1919): 150.
15. Burlingame highlights the partisan fluidity of this period in Illinois by noting that Lincoln lost the 1838 speakership contest to Democrat William L. D. Ewing despite the fact that his party ostensibly held a thin majority in the statehouse. Three members of the Whig caucus missed the vote, and two switched sides. Burlingame, *Lincoln: A Life*, 1:143.
16. AL to Mary Owens, December 13, 1836, *CW,* 1:54.
17. AL, Speech in the Illinois Legislature Concerning the State Bank, January 11, 1837, *CW,* 1:66.
18. AL to Robert Allen ("you are at liberty to publish"), June 21, 1836, *CW,* 1:48–49; AL to the People of Sangamo County, undated, *CW,* 8:429. *Proboscis* means "nose."
19. AL to John Stuart, February 14, 1839, *CW,* 1:143.
20. AL to Andrew McCormick, c. January 1839, in Lincoln, *Collected Works of Abraham Lincoln: First Supplement, 1832–1865*, ed. Roy P. Basler (New Brunswick, NJ: Rutgers University Press, 1974), 5–6 (hereafter cited as *CWS*). Note that in *CWS* this document has been misdated as January 1841, but a reexamination by James Cornelius, formerly of the Abraham Lincoln Presidential Library and Museum, and further research by the staff at Papers of Abraham Lincoln, have confirmed that Lincoln sent this note almost certainly on or around January 16, 1839. The shift in dating has consequences for ascertaining whether Lincoln suffered from depression as a young man and might have had a nervous breakdown in January 1841. See Joshua Wolf Shenk, *Lincoln's Melancholy* (New York: Mariner Books, 2005), 46.
21. AL to William Minshall, December 7, 1837, *CW,* 1:107.

22. AL to Jesse Fell [July 23, 1838], *CW*, 1:120.
23. AL to John Stuart, January 20, 1840, *CW*, 1:184.
24. James Conkling to Mercy Levering, September 21, 1840, quoted in Ruth Painter Randall, *Mary Lincoln: Biography of a Marriage* (Boston: Little, Brown, 1953), 5.
25. Mary Todd to Mercy Ann Levering, December [15?], 1840, in Mary Todd Lincoln, *Mary Todd Lincoln: Her Life and Letters*, ed. Justin G. Turner and Linda Levitt Turner (New York: Knopf, 1972), 21.
26. AL, Speech on the Sub-Treasury, December 26, 1839, republished in pamphlet form in January 1840, *CW*, 1:177. See also AL to John Stuart, January 20, 1840, *CW*, 1:184.
27. Boritt, *Lincoln and Economics*, 65.
28. AL to John Stuart, January 20, 1840, *CW*, 1:184.
29. AL to John Stuart, January 20, 1840, *CW*, 1:184.
30. AL to John Stuart, March 1, 1840, *CW*, 1:206.
31. AL to Richard Barrett, April 17, 1840, *CW*, 1:209.
32. AL, Speech at Tremont, May 2, 1840, *CW*, 1:210.
33. AL to John Stuart, January 20, 1840, *CW*, 1:184.
34. AL, Campaign Circular from Whig Committee, January [31?], 1840, *CW*, 1:201–3.
35. AL, Communication to the Readers of *The Old Soldier*, February 28, 1840, *CW*, 1:205.
36. AL, Lincoln's Plan of Campaign in 1840 [c. January 1840], *CW*, 1:180–81. The *CW* editors appear to have mistakenly identified this undated document as having been created in January even though the document spells out how to cull voter lists from all those "who voted the Whig ticket in August." There were local elections in August 1839, but the more relevant elections for the state's General Assembly occurred in August 1840.
37. AL to Mary Owens, May 7, 1837, *CW*, 1:78–79.
38. AL to Joshua Speed, February 25, 1842, *CW*, 1:280.
39. AL to John Stuart, January 20, 23, 1841, *CW*, 1:228–29.
40. AL to Stuart, February 3, 1841, *CWS*, 6.
41. AL to Stuart, February 3, 1841, *CWS*, 6.
42. AL to Stuart, January 23, 1841, *CW*, 1:229.
43. Holt, *American Whig Party*, 122–61.
44. AL to Henry Clay, August 29, 1842, *CW*, 1:297. Clay declined the invitation.
45. AL to Speed, March 27, 1842, *CW*, 1:282.
46. See Douglas L. Wilson, *Honor's Voice: The Transformation of Abraham Lincoln* (New York: Knopf, 1998), 265–92.
47. AL to Speed, October 5, 1842, *CW*, 1:302–3.

48. AL, Tabulation of Votes [September 9, 1842], *CW,* 1:297–98.
49. AL to Samuel Marshall, November 11, 1842, *CW,* 1:304–5.
50. David Herbert Donald, *Lincoln* (New York: Simon & Schuster, 1995), 97.
51. AL, Campaign Circular from Whig Committee, March 4, 1843, *CW,* 1:309–18.
52. AL, Campaign Circular from Whig Committee, March 4, 1843, *CW,* 1:314–15.
53. AL to John Bennett, March 7, 1843, *CW,* 1:318. The "house divided" line was adapted from various gospels: Matthew 12:25; Mark 3:25; and Luke 11:17.
54. AL to Martin Morris, March 26, 1843, *CW,* 1:320.
55. AL to Morris, March 26, 1843, *CW,* 1:320. See also AL, Second Reply to James Adams, October 19, 1837, *CW,* 1:106.
56. By contrast, the Democrats had a much wider field for their younger generation of leaders. The 1843 elections marked the first congressional victories for figures such as "Long John" Wentworth (age twenty-eight), Stephen A. Douglas (age thirty), and Robert Smith (age forty).
57. AL to Morris ("Dont show or speak of this letter"), March 26 and April 14, 1843, *CW,* 1:319–22. One of Lincoln's letters to Morris, an old friend from New Salem, refers explicitly to "insinuations" that Baker was attempting to undo the "instructions" from Menard County.
58. Resolution Adopted at Whig Convention at Pekin, Illinois, May 1, 1843, *CW,* 1:322. Lincoln's recollected account is in a letter to John Hardin, February 7, 1846, *CW,* 1:362–62.
59. Proposal of a Barbecue, May 11, 1843, *CW,* 1:322. AL to Hardin, May 11, 1843, *CW,* 1:322–23.
60. Benjamin P. Thomas, "Lincoln: Voter and Candidate, Part Two," *Bulletin of the Abraham Lincoln Association* 37 (December 1934): 7.
61. AL to Hardin, May 21, 1844, *CW,* 1:336.
62. Robert S. Wicks and Fred R. Foister, *Junius and Joseph: Presidential Politics and the Assassination of the First Mormon Prophet* (Logan: Utah State University Press, 2005), 62–69.
63. Mark R. Cheathem, *Who Is James K. Polk? The Presidential Election of 1844* (Lawrence: University Press of Kansas, 2021).
64. AL to Williamson Durley, October 3, 1845, *CW,* 1:347.
65. AL, Protest in Illinois Legislature on Slavery, March 3, 1837, *CW,* 1:74–75.
66. AL to Durley, October 3, 1845, *CW,* 1:347–48.
67. AL to Durley, October 3, 1845, *CW,* 1:348.
68. We know about these private meetings in autumn 1845 only because Hardin described them in a subsequent public airing of his grievances. Lincoln then responded by acknowledging some elements of truth in the accusations. The

narrative in the paragraph is based on Lincoln's version of these events. See AL to Hardin, February 7, 1846, *CW*, 1:361–62.

69. Martin Morris to Hardin, November 6, 1845, and P. H. Thompson to Hardin, January 12, 1846, both in John J. Hardin Papers, Chicago History Museum, Chicago.
70. This phrase appears in the following Lincoln letters: AL to Henry Dummer ("Let this be confidential") November 18, 1845, *CW*, 1:350; AL to Benjamin James ("confidential"), December 6, 1845, *CWS*, 8–9; AL to Robert Boal ("strictly confidential"), January 7, 1846, *CW*, 1:353; AL to N. J. Rockwell, January 21, 1846, *CW*, 1:359; and finally AL to Hardin, February 7, 1846, *CW*, 1:361.
71. AL to James, November 24, 1845, *CW*, 1:351.
72. AL to Boal, January 7, 1846, *CW*, 1:353; AL to James, January 14, 1846, *CW*, 1:354.
73. AL to James, January 16, 1846, *CW*, 1:355–56; AL to Hardin, January 19, 1846, *CW*, 1:356–57.
74. AL to Hardin, February 7, 1846, *CW*, 1:360–61.
75. AL to Hardin, February 7, 1846, *CW*, 1:362–64.
76. AL to Hardin, February 7, 1846, *CW*, 1:364–65.
77. AL to James ("show it to some of our friends"), February 9, 1846, *CW*, 1:365–66.
78. AL to Isaac Williams, April 24, 1846, *CW*, 1:379.
79. AL, Speech in the U.S. House of Representatives, January 12, 1848, *CW*, 1:442; AL, Speech at Lacon, July 18, 1848, *CW*, 1:381–82.
80. AL, Handbill Replying to Charges of Infidelity, July 31, 1846, *CW*, 1:382. The handbill was not rediscovered and made part of Lincoln's canon of writings until 1942.
81. Allen C. Guelzo, "Abraham Lincoln and the Doctrine of Necessity," *Journal of the Abraham Lincoln Association* 18 (Winter 1997): 57–81.
82. AL to Allen Ford ("give this letter . . . a place in your paper"), August 11, 1846, *CW*, 1:383–84.
83. AL to William Herndon, January 8, 1848, *CW*, 1:431.
84. AL to Joshua Speed, October 22, 1846, *CW*, 1:391.
85. For Lincoln's poems, see AL to Andrew Johnston, February 24, April 18, and September 6, 1846, all in *CW*, 1:366–70, 377–79, and 384–89.
86. Gibson Harris to George Williams, October 31, 1846, in Roger D. Bridges, ed., "Three Letters from a Lincoln Law Student," *Journal of the Illinois State Historical Society* 66 (Spring 1973): 87.
87. AL to Orville Browning, June 24, 1847, *CW*, 1:395.
88. Resolutions Adopted at John J. Hardin Memorial Meeting, April 5, 1847, *CW*, 1:392.

89. AL, Speech in U.S. House of Representatives on the Presidential Question, July 27, 1848, *CW*, 1:515.
90. AL, Eulogy on Zachary Taylor, July 25, 1850, *CW*, 2:86.
91. Buckingham, "Illinois," 112.
92. The only other Democratic member of the Illinois congressional delegation present at the convention besides Smith and Wentworth was Congressman-Elect Thomas J. Turner from Freeport, who later became an early organizer of the state's Republican party.
93. Holt, *American Whig Party*, 265–66.
94. "Thurlow Weed's Report," in Fergus, *Chicago River-and-Harbor Convention*, 152.
95. David Dudley Field to Thomas Kettell, August 20, 1847, in "Chicago Convention: Speech of David Dudley Field," *United States Magazine and Democratic Review* 21 (September 1847): 98.
96. For decades, scholars were under the impression that there had been no transcript of these remarks, only a few passing notices culled from what seemed to be an underwhelmed contemporary press. But A. B. Chambers, one of the convention's principal recording secretaries, took careful notes of Lincoln's statement, which he then published in the *Missouri Republican* (St. Louis) on July 12, 1847—a fact that had been overlooked until just a few years ago. See Papers of Abraham Lincoln Digital Library, Springfield, IL (hereafter cited as PAL).
97. Horace Greeley, "The Great River-and-Harbor Convention at Chicago," *New-York Tribune*, July 17, 1847, quoted in Fergus, *Chicago River-and-Harbor Convention*, 141.
98. "The River and Harbor Convention," *National Intelligencer* (Washington, DC), July 15, 1847, 2:2.
99. Fergus, *Chicago River-and-Harbor Convention*, 89.
100. David Davis to Sarah Davis, August 8, 1847, David Davis Family Papers, Abraham Lincoln Presidential Library and Museum (hereafter cited as ALPLM).
101. Davis to Davis, August 8, 1847, ALPLM.

CHAPTER 2: WHIG FUSIONIST

1. J. H. Buckingham, "Illinois as Lincoln Knew It: A Boston Reporter's Record of a Trip in 1847," ed. Harry Pratt, in *Papers in Illinois History and Transactions for the Year 1937* (Springfield, IL: Abraham Lincoln Association, 1938), 116, 118.
2. *Cong. Globe*, 30th Cong., 1st Sess., 62 (December 21, 1847).

3. AL, Debate at Ottawa, August 21, 1858, *CW*, 3:29.
4. See Alexander Keyssar, *The Right to Vote: The Contested History of Democracy in the United States* (New York: Basic Books, 2000).
5. For background and context on this period, see Daniel Walker Howe, *What Hath God Wrought: The Transformation of America, 1815–1848* (New York: Oxford University Press, 2007).
6. Michael F. Holt, *The Rise and Fall of the American Whig Party* (New York: Oxford University Press, 1999), 284–330.
7. *Illinois Gazette*, September 11, 1847, reported in entry for August 30, 1847, in *Lincoln Log: A Daily Chronology of the Life of Abraham Lincoln*, thelincolnlog.org; and AL to Taylor Committee, February 9, 1848, *CW*, 1:449.
8. Stephen Douglas invoked Singleton's claims during the 1858 Lincoln-Douglas debates at Alton, Illinois, October 15, 1858. See Rodney O. Davis and Douglas L. Wilson, eds., *The Lincoln-Douglas Debates* (Urbana: University of Illinois Press, 2008), 289. The charges also reappeared during the 1860 campaign: John Hill, *Opposing Principles of Henry Clay, and Abraham Lincoln* (St. Louis: George Knapp, 1860); AL to Archibald Williams, April 30, 1848, *CW*, 1:468; and diary entry for May 7, 1861, in John Hay, *Inside Lincoln's White House: The Complete Civil War Diary of John Hay*, ed. Michael Burlingame and John R. Turner Ettlinger (Carbondale: Southern Illinois University Press, 1997), 19.
9. During this period, Robert Todd was already providing the family with about $120 per year as a regular supplement; see Harry E. Pratt, *The Personal Finances of Abraham Lincoln* (Springfield, IL: Abraham Lincoln Association, 1943), 66.
10. Henry Clay, Speech in Lexington, Kentucky, November 13, 1847, in Clay, *The Papers of Henry Clay, Candidate, Compromiser, Elder Statesman: January 1, 1844–June 29, 1852*, ed. Melba Porter Hay, 10 vols. (Lexington: University Press of Kentucky, 1991), 10:361–76.
11. Clay to Horace Greeley, November 22, 1847, in *Papers of Henry Clay*, 10:377–78. See also Amy S. Greenberg, *A Wicked War: Polk, Clay, Lincoln, and the U.S. Invasion of Mexico* (New York: Knopf, 2012), 311n.
12. AL to Richard Yates, December 10, 1847, *CW*, 1:419; AL to Richard Thomas, January 1, 1848, *CW*, 1:422; Joshua Giddings to Charles Francis Adams, December 15, 1847, quoted in Holt, *American Whig Party*, 284; Washburne in *Reminiscences of Abraham Lincoln by Distinguished Men of His Time*, ed. Allen Thorndike Rice, rev. ed. (New York: North American Publishing, 1909), 94. Lincoln himself recalled Washburne as a "lobby member" in a letter to him on December 19, 1854, *CW*, 2:295. For "Abolition House" and background on Ann Sprigg, see Kenneth J. Winkle, *Lincoln's Citadel: The Civil War in Washington, DC* (New York: W. W. Norton, 2013), 3–13.

13. For the "Young Indian" movement, see Alexander Stephens, *Recollections of Alexander H. Stephens*, ed. Myrta Lockett Avary (New York: Doubleday, Page & Co., 1910), 21; Thomas E. Schott, *Alexander H. Stephens: A Biography* (Baton Rouge: Louisiana State University Press, 1988), 83; and Rachel A. Shelden, *Washington Brotherhood: Politics, Social Life, and the Coming of the Civil War* (Chapel Hill: University of North Carolina Press, 2013), 41–62.
14. For background on changing presidential campaign customs, see Gil Troy, *See How They Ran: The Changing Role of the Presidential Candidate* (New York: Free Press, 1991).
15. Holt, *American Whig Party*, 270–75.
16. AL, Speech at Peoria, October 16, 1854, *CW*, 2:252.
17. AL to William Herndon, February 1, 15, 1848, *CW*, 1:446–47 and 451–52; AL to Herndon, June 22, 1848, *CW*, 1:490–92.
18. AL, Speech on Internal Improvements, June 20, 1848, *CW*, 1:484. The *Tribune* is quoted in Paul Findley, *A. Lincoln: The Crucible of Congress* (New York: Crown, 1979), 160. Wentworth had introduced a memorial to the River and Harbor Convention the day before Lincoln's speech, on June 19, 1848; *Cong. Globe*, 30th Cong., 1st Sess., 852 (1848).
19. AL to Taylor Committee, February 9, 1848, *CW*, 1:449; AL to Thomas Flournoy, February 17, 1848, *CW*, 1:452.
20. AL to Taylor Committee, February 9, 1848, *CW*, 1:449–50; and AL to Flournoy, February 17, 1848, *CW*, 1:452.
21. Zachary Taylor to John Allison, April 22, 1848, reprinted in *Niles' National Register* 74 (July 5, 1848); AL, Fragment: What General Taylor Ought to Say [March 7], 1848, *CW*, 1:454.
22. AL to Mary Lincoln, June 12, 1848; and AL to Richard Thomas, June 13, 1848, both in *CW*, 1:477–48.
23. AL to Simeon Francis, June 9, 1848, *Illinois Journal*, June 15, 1848, 2:4, PAL.
24. AL to William Herndon, June 12, 1848, *CW*, 1:476–77.
25. AL to Mary Lincoln, April 16, June 12, and July 2, 1848, all in *CW*, 1:465–66, 477–78, and 495–96.
26. AL to Thaddeus Stevens, September 3, 1848, *CW*, 2:1.
27. Stevens to AL, September 7, 1848, in *The Selected Papers of Thaddeus Stevens*, ed. Beverly Wilson Palmer and Holly Byers Ochoa (Pittsburgh: University of Pittsburgh Press, 1997), 1:102–3.
28. Findley, *Crucible of Congress*, 189.
29. In historian Michael Holt's estimation, Truman Smith was "the party's shrewdest political strategist and manager" and "the Whigs' closest equivalent to a modern national party chairman." See Holt, *American Whig Party*, 236–37.

30. AL to William Schouler, August 8 and 28, 1848; and AL, Whig Circular Letter, August 17, 1848, all in *CW*, 1:516–18.
31. Mary Lincoln to AL, c. May 1848, in Lincoln, *Mary Todd Lincoln: Her Life and Letters*, ed. Justin G. Turner and Linda Levitt Turner (New York: Knopf, 1972), 38.
32. AL to Junius Hall, September 3, 1848, *CWS*, 11–12.
33. Mary Lincoln on "lake route," in Lincoln, *Life and Letters*, 38; AL, Speech on Presidential Question, July 27, 1848, *CW*, 1:505.
34. *Boston Courier*, September 23, 1848, quoted in Doris Kearns Goodwin, *Team of Rivals: The Political Genius of Abraham Lincoln* (New York: Simon & Schuster, 2005), 127. Joseph T. Buckingham, the father of the River and Harbor Convention correspondent and owner of the newspaper, had sold his interest earlier in 1848.
35. Years later Seward claimed that the two men spent the night together at a hotel in Worcester intently discussing the future of slavery, and that the New Yorker mentored the future president on the need to do more to confront the institution's evils. For a convincing demolition of this dubious anecdote, which has nonetheless been repeated by many historians, see Walter Stahr, *Seward: Lincoln's Indispensable Man* (New York: Simon & Schuster, 2012), 110.
36. AL to Herndon, June 22, 1848, *CW*, 1:491.
37. David Davis to W. P. Walker, May 16, 1848, quoted in David Herbert Donald, *Lincoln* (New York: Simon & Schuster, 1995), 132.
38. "T. L. Harris' Electioneering," *Illinois Journal*, August 16, 1848, 2:2; *Illinois Journal*, October 12, 1850, 2:1; and "Look-out for Lying Handbills," *Illinois Journal*, November 3, 1854, 2:1.
39. *Illinois State Register* quoted in entry for October 10, 1848, *Lincoln Log: A Daily Chronology of the Life of Abraham Lincoln*, thelincolnlog.org.
40. For the "Taylor Republican" movement, see Holt, *American Whig Party*, 406–8.
41. AL to William Schouler, February 2, 1849, *CW*, 2:25; AL to Zachary Taylor, February 27, 1849, *CW*, 2:30.
42. David Davis to Sarah Davis, June 25, 1847, quoted in Richard Lawrence Miller, *The Rise to National Prominence, 1843–1853*, vol. 3 of *Lincoln and His World* (Jefferson, NC: McFarland, 2011), 204; AL to Elihu Washburne, April 30, 1848, *CW*, 1:467.
43. Joshua Speed to AL, February 13, 1849, Lincoln Papers, LC; AL to Speed, February 20, 1849, *CW*, 2:28–29.
44. AL to David Davis, February 12, 1849, *CWS*, 14; Davis to AL, February 21, 1849, Lincoln Papers, LC; AL to Speed, February 20, 1849, *CW*, 2:28–29.
45. Cyrus Edwards to Justin Butterfield, June 11, 1849, quoted in Thomas Ewing,

"Lincoln and the General Land Office, 1849," *Journal of the Illinois State Historical Society* 25 (October 1932): 144. Lincoln and Edwards may have discussed the Land Office opening even earlier. See AL to William Warren and others, April 7, 1849, *CW*, 2:41.

46. Usher F. Linder, *Reminiscences of the Early Bench and Bar of Illinois* (Chicago: Chicago Legal News, 1879), 353–55.
47. For Lincoln's possible romance with Matilda Edwards, see Douglas L. Wilson, *Honor's Voice: The Transformation of Abraham Lincoln* (New York: Knopf, 1998), 221–31.
48. Edwards to Butterfield, June 11, 1849, quoted in Ewing, "Land Office," 143–45; Linder, *Reminiscences*, 366–70.
49. See Wayne C. Temple, *Lincoln's Connection with the Illinois & Michigan Canal, His Return from Congress in '48, and His Invention* (Springfield: Illinois Bell, 1986), 54–59; and AL to William Herndon, January 5, 1849, *CW*, 2:18–19. For the "skulking" charges against Harris, see Miller, *Rise to National Prominence*, 204.
50. AL to Walter Davis, January 5, 1849, *CW*, 2:18. When Herndon later passed a copy of this letter over to one of Lincoln's earliest biographers, he claimed it was "*thoroughly* Characteristic" of his former partner's broad-minded leadership qualities, even though it was probably even more revealing of Lincoln's long partisan memory. See William Herndon to Josiah Holland, May 26, 1865, in Allen C. Guelzo, "Holland's Informants: The Construction of Josiah Holland's 'Life of Abraham Lincoln,'" *Journal of the Abraham Lincoln Association* 23 (Winter 2002): 1–53.
51. AL to Josiah Herrick, January 19, 1849; and AL to John Murray, January 27, 1849, both in *CW*, 2:23–24.
52. AL to George Rives, May 7, 1849, *CW*, 2:46.
53. AL to John Clayton, March 8, 1849, *CW*, 2:31; AL to Thomas Ewing, March 12, 1849, PAL. This letter has been recently rediscovered and was not part of *CW*.
54. AL to William Meredith, March 9, 1849, *CW*, 2:32; AL to Meredith, March 10, 1849, PAL. This letter is also newly rediscovered and was not part of *CW*.
55. AL to George Crawford, March 11, 1849, *CWS*, 14. The letter to the War Department regarding the absence of Whig clerks from Illinois (with the exception, Lincoln noted, of Josiah Lucas in the General Land Office) was signed by Lincoln but not drafted in his own handwriting. Various editors have been unable to identify the person who produced the note for Lincoln, but it appears to be in the handwriting of John Morrison of Tremont. A version of the unidentified note is in the Lincoln Papers at LC, though it is misdated March 22, 1849.

56. AL to Thomas Ewing, March 11, 1849, *CWS*, 15. See also Paul I. Miller, "Lincoln and the Governorship of Oregon," *Mississippi Valley Historical Review* 23 (December 1936): 391.

57. Relying mainly on the impressions of Josiah Lucas, a clerk in the General Land Office, many Lincoln scholars have assumed that Butterfield came to his desire for the Land Office commissionership only later, in mid-April, but that seems like a mistake. Butterfield did present his petitions to the Interior Department in mid-April, but that meant he had started collecting signatures much earlier, and those petitions indicated support from Chicago attorneys for his appointment as *either* solicitor for the Treasury Department or commissioner of the General Land Office; Ewing, "Land Office," 146–47. See also Lucas to AL, April 12, 1849, Lincoln Papers, LC.

58. The story about Butterfield's alleged stroke is almost too funny to be true. It involved a "Dr. Duck" who turned out to be a quack. In his angry denial rushed off to "Secretary of the Treasury" [*sic*] Ewing on April 6, 1849, Butterfield blamed the whole story on "one Dr. Duck" who had bled him "most profusely" following a "rheumatic attack," then tried to cover his tracks by diagnosing "blood to the head" and thus leaving the false impression that he had apoplexy. Dr. Charles H. Duck was a real Chicago physician, with a mixed reputation, and Butterfield did produce the "certificates" from other leading Chicago physicians that did "flatly contradict" Duck's "subterfuge." See Butterfield to Ewing, April 6, 1849, in Ewing, "Land Office," 146–47; and Elihu Washburne to Caleb Smith, May 7, 1849, quoted in Donald W. Riddle, *Congressman Abraham Lincoln* (Urbana: University of Illinois Press, 1957), 219.

59. Lincoln recalled the Sunday evening encounter in a letter to Preston written two months later. He didn't remember the exact date, but there is only one Sunday possible—March 11; AL to William Preston, May 16, 1849, *CW*, 2:48–49. But the editors of *The Lincoln Log*, the online daily schedule of Lincoln's activities derived from the earlier Day-By-Day publication, have so far excluded this meeting from their records. *Lincoln Log: A Daily Chronology of the Life of Abraham Lincoln*, thelincolnlog.org.

60. AL to David Davis, February 12, 1849, *CWS*, 14.

61. John Morrison to AL, March 13, 1849, Lincoln Papers, LC. Information about Morrison's family is derived from the 1850 U.S. Census household records in Tazewell County. Morrison never received his appointment and never again lived on his own land. He spent his remaining years, according to various census records, living with his children.

62. For the chronology of Lincoln's journey home from Washington in March 1849, see Endorsement, Edward Baker to John M. Clayton (Louisville, KY),

March 20, 1849; AL to John Clayton (St. Louis), March 26, 1849, *CW*, 2:38; and AL to William Preston (Carrollton, IL), March 29, 1849, PAL. There is also a missing letter from Lincoln to Cyrus Edwards (Alton, IL), March 27, 1849, that concerned Edwards's claims on the Land Office; it is described by Edwards in a letter to Justin Butterfield, June 11, 1849, in Ewing, "Land Office," 144.

63. All the quotations from Lincoln's letter to Edwards come from Edwards's account of that now-missing letter, Edwards to Butterfield, June 11, 1849, in Ewing, "Land Office," 143–45.
64. Riddle, *Congressman Abraham Lincoln*, 198–221.
65. In his fortieth birthday letter to David Davis, Lincoln wrote that "Baker has just looked over my shoulder, and seen that I am writing to you." Since Congress was not in session that day, Lincoln was probably writing from his room at the boardinghouse where Baker was likely staying with him. AL to Davis, February 12, 1849, *CWS*, 14. Also, Lincoln's endorsement on Baker's March 20 letter to John Clayton was datelined Louisville, KY; see *CW*, 2:38.
66. AL to William Warren and others, April 7, 1849, *CW*, 2:41–42.
67. See Thomas F. Schwartz, "'An Egregious Political Blunder': Justin Butterfield, Lincoln, and Illinois Whiggery," *Papers of the Abraham Lincoln Association* 8 (1986): 9–19.
68. AL to Jacob Collamer, April 7, 1849; AL to Thomas Ewing, April 7, 1849; AL to Ewing, April 7, 1849; and AL to Ewing, April 7, 1849, all in *CW*, 2:39–41.
69. AL to William Briggs, April 21, 1849, PAL. This letter has been recently rediscovered and was not part of *CW*.
70. AL to Philo Thompson, April 25, 1849; AL to Ewing, April 26, 1849; and AL to Ewing, May 10, 1849, all in *CW*, 2:44–47. See also Thompson to AL, April 23, 1849, and Pekin Citizens to AL, May 1, 1849 [with 139 signatures], Lincoln Papers, LC.
71. AL to Caleb Smith, May 1, 1849; AL to George Rives, May 7, 1849; both in *CW*, 2:46.
72. Josiah Lucas to AL, April 12, 15, 25, and May 7, 9, 10, 1849, Lincoln Papers, LC. The quotations are from the April 15 letter. See also John Addison to AL, April 20, 1849, Lincoln Papers, LC.
73. AL to Lucas, April 25, 1849; AL to William Preston, May 16, 1849; both in *CW*, 2:42–43.
74. Butterfield to Ewing, April 6, 1849, in Ewing, "Land Office," 146.
75. AL to William Preston, May 16, 1849, *CW*, 2:42–43. Lucas had mentioned Lisle Smith in his April 15 letter, which Lincoln acknowledged in his reply dated April 25, 1849.

76. AL to Duff Green, May 18, 1849; AL to Joseph Gillespie, May 19, 1849 (regarding Crittenden); AL to Elisha Embree, May 25, 1849; AL to Richard Thompson, May 25, 1849; all in *CW*, 2:49–51.
77. John Johnston to AL, May 25, 1849; Augustus Chapman to AL, May 24 [*sic*], 1849; both in Lincoln Papers, LC.
78. Chapman to AL, May 28, 1849, Lincoln Papers, LC.
79. Anson Henry to AL [May 29, 1849], Lincoln Papers, LC. This document was misdated by the editors as May 24.
80. AL to Moses Hampton, June 1, 1849, in Lincoln, *Collected Works of Abraham Lincoln: Second Supplement, 1848–1865*, eds. Roy P. Basler and Christian O. Basler (New Brunswick, NJ: Rutgers University Press, 1990), 1–2 (hereafter cited as *CWSS*).
81. Hampton to AL, March 30, 1849, Lincoln Papers, LC.
82. Anson Henry described the contents of Preston's telegram in a letter to Joseph Gillespie, June 2, 1849; see *Lincoln Log: A Daily Chronology of the Life of Abraham Lincoln*, thelincolnlog.org. Lincoln's version of those events is in AL to Gillespie, July 13, 1849, *CW*, 2:58.
83. AL to William Seward, June 4, 1849, *CW*, 8:414; Form Letter to Duff Green, June 5, 1849, *CW*, 2:53. See Green's annotations on the letter in Lincoln Papers, LC. The editors of *CW* do not attempt to identify the handwriting on the form letter to Green, and the editors at the Library of Congress mistakenly believe it to be William Herndon's penmanship, but it was clearly Anson Henry who copied out this particular letter.
84. See Form Letter [to James McLean?], June 3, 1849, *CW*, 2:52.
85. Butterfield to David Hunter, June 4, 1849, in Ewing, "Land Office," 151–52.
86. Diary entry for August 12, 1863, in Hay, *Inside Lincoln's White House*, 73.
87. Ewing quoted in Josiah Lucas to AL, May 9, 1849, Lincoln Papers, LC. Comments from McLean (originally a Democrat but now aligning himself with Whigs) and Washburne appear in Ewing, "Land Office," 147–48.
88. Butterfield to J. J. Brown, June 7, 1849, and George Meeker to Thomas Ewing, June 9, 1894, both in Ewing, "Land Office," 140–42, 149.
89. Butterfield to Brown, June 7, 1849; Edwards to Butterfield, June 11, 1849; and James Morrison to Butterfield, June 9, 1849, all in Ewing, "Land Office," 140–42, 143–44, and 150.
90. Butterfield to AL, June 9, 1849, and Levi Davis to Butterfield, June 9, 1849, both in Ewing, "Land Office," 142–43; entry for June 10, 1849, *Lincoln Log: A Daily Chronology of the Life of Abraham Lincoln*, thelincolnlog.org.

CHAPTER 3: MAN OF CONSEQUENCE

1. AL to Jesse Fell (Enclosing Autobiography; "it must not appear to have been written by myself"), December 20, 1859, *CW*, 3:512. See also AL, Autobiography Written for John L. Scripps [c. June, 1860], *CW*, 4:67.
2. See Nathaniel G. Wilcox recollection, Abraham Lincoln Papers, University of Chicago (hereafter cited as UC); and Nathaniel Wilcox to AL, June 6, 1864, Lincoln Papers, LC. The Wilcox account from June 1864 was less dramatic than his recollection but more reliable because it was offered within a letter to Lincoln himself. Wilcox, then a former U.S. army paymaster, had been dismissed from service in 1863 and had appealed to the president for help, convincing him to rescind the orders so he could resign without any taint of scandal. But after complying, the president distanced himself from his old friend, refusing to see him anymore or to correspond, telling him roughly that he had "never been any account" to him. This reaction infuriated Wilcox, about whom Lincoln had once observed, "my confidence in him [is] unlimited." So the disgraced officer responded by detailing for the ungrateful president all the contributions that he had made in the past, such as hosting him at his Washington boardinghouse in June 1849.
3. Wilcox to AL, June 6, 1864, Lincoln Papers, LC. For Lincoln's endorsement of Wilcox (one of several), see Lincoln to Thomas Ewing, June 19, 1849, *CW*, 2:55. See also AL, Memorandum for Zachary Taylor, June [15?], 1849, *CW*, 2:54, but note that it has been misdated by the editors if Wilcox was being accurate in his 1864 claims to Lincoln.
4. Wilcox recollection, Lincoln Papers, UC.
5. AL to David Davis, July 6, 1849, *CWS*, 16.
6. AL to Ewing, July 9, 1849, *CWSS*, 3–4; Ewing to AL, July 18, 1849, PAL; and AL to Ewing, July 27, 1849, *CWSS*, 4–5.
7. AL to John Clayton, July 28, 1849, *CW*, 2:60.
8. For Clayton's role as Taylor's man, see Michael F. Holt, *The Rise and Fall of the American Whig Party* (New York: Oxford University Press, 1999), 421.
9. Turner King was now register of the Springfield Land Office, with Walter Davis as his receiver. Abner Ellis was the town's new postmaster, and Mary Lincoln's brother-in-law William Wallace was appointed as a federal pension agent.
10. AL to Ewing, October 13, 1849, *CWSS*, 5–6.
11. AL to the editor of *Chicago Journal*, November 21, 1849, *CW*, 2:68.
12. AL to Josiah Lucas, November 17, 1849, *CW*, 2:67.
13. AL to Lucas, November 17, 1849, *CW*, 2:67.
14. Holt, *American Whig Party*, 455.

15. "By Telegraph: 12 pm, 3pm, 8pm," *Illinois Journal*, January 30, 1850, 3:3.
16. Edward Lincoln died on Friday, February 1, 1850.
17. Zachary Taylor, Special Message, January 23, 1850, American Presidency Project, presidency.ucsb.edu.
18. *Cong. Globe*, 31st Cong., 1st Sess., 245 (January 29, 1850).
19. AL to John Clayton, March 20, 1849, *CW*, 2:38.
20. AL to William Seward, February 1, 1861, *CW*, 4:183.
21. Chase to E. S. Hamlin, February 2, 1850, in "Diary and Correspondence of Salmon P. Chase," *American Historical Association Annual Report* (Washington, DC: Government Printing Office, 1903), 200; "Washington, Jan. 29 –8pm," *Illinois Journal*, January 30, 1850.
22. AL, Concerning Abolition of Slavery in the District of Columbia, January 10, 1849, *CW*, 1:20–22.
23. AL to Joshua Speed, August 24, 1855, *CW*, 2:320.
24. AL to Speed, August 24, 1855, *CW*, 2:320.
25. For "slave stampede," see "We have received a communication," *Illinois Journal*, January 22, 1850, 2:1, and J. C. Goodhue to editors, *Illinois Journal*, January 23, 1850, 3:1. Lincoln also remained on good terms with Jameson Jenkins, who took him by carriage to the Springfield railroad depot on February 11, 1861, as the president-elect was preparing to leave for Washington. See Bonnie E. Paul and Richard E. Hart, *Lincoln's Springfield Neighborhood* (Charleston, SC: History Press, 2015), 94–96.
26. See Fergus M. Bordewich, *America's Great Debate: Henry Clay, Stephen A. Douglas, and the Compromise That Preserved the Union* (New York: Simon & Schuster, 2012).
27. James Oakes, *Freedom National: The Destruction of Slavery in the United States, 1861–1865* (New York: W. W. Norton, 2013), 29–34.
28. William Seward, "Freedom in the New Territories" speech, U.S. Senate, 31st Cong., 1st sess., March 11, 1850.
29. "Union Meeting," *Illinois State Register*, June 13, 1850; "Union Meeting," *Illinois Journal*, June 18, 1850.
30. AL, Eulogy on Zachary Taylor, July 25, 1850, *CW*, 2:89.
31. Historian David Potter once memorably labeled the so-called compromise as the "Armistice of 1850." See David M. Potter and Don E. Fehrenbacher, eds., *The Impending Crisis: 1848–1861* (New York: Harper & Row, 1976), chap. 5.
32. AL to the editors of *Illinois Journal*, June 5, 1850, *CW*, 2:79.
33. Mark E. Neely, Jr., was the first historian to identify the significance of this document; see *Lincoln Lore* no. 1683 (May 1978). Neely details how Robert Lincoln once verified the handwriting as his father's but explains that there is currently no manuscript version available. The document did not appear in the

1953 edition of *CW* and thus often gets overlooked in modern treatments of Lincoln. David Donald, however, does analyze it, calling Lincoln's advice "cautiously noncommittal." See David Herbert Donald, *Lincoln* (New York: Simon & Schuster, 1995), 162–63.

34. *Lincoln Lore* no. 1683.
35. Quoted in Richard Lawrence Miller, *The Rise to National Prominence, 1843–1853*, vol. 3 of *Lincoln and His World* (Jefferson, NC: McFarland, 2011), 272.
36. Robert W. Johannsen, *Stephen A. Douglas* (Urbana: University of Illinois Press, 1973), 304–38.
37. William D. Beard, "'I Have Labored Hard to Find the Law': Abraham Lincoln for the Alton and Sangamon Railroad," *Illinois Historical Journal* 85 (Winter 1992): 209–20.
38. AL to William Martin, February 19, 1851, *CW*, 2:98.
39. AL to John D. Johnston, January 12, 1851, *CW*, 2:96–97.
40. AL to Johnston, January 12, 1851, *CW*, 2:96.
41. AL et al., Call for Whig Convention, November 29, 1851, *CW*, 2:113; "Whig State Convention," *Illinois Journal*, November 29, 1851.
42. "The Whig Convention—A Failure," *Illinois State Register*, December 23, 1851; and "Whig State Convention," *Illinois State Register*, December 24, 1851.
43. Whig Party Platform, June 17, 1852.
44. The Whig platform intentionally echoed—but still modified—Fillmore's December 2, 1850, statement: "The series of measures to which I have alluded are regarded by me as a settlement in principle and substance—a final settlement of the dangerous and exciting subjects which they embraced."
45. Whig Party Platform, June 17, 1852, in American Presidency Project, presidency.ucsb.edu.
46. Holt, *American Whig Party*, 714, 719.
47. David Davis to Sarah Davis, March 23, 1851, quoted in Miller, *Rise to National Prominence*, 297. See also Nicole Etcheson, "Private Interest and Public Good: Upland Southerners and Antebellum Midwestern Political Culture," in *The Pursuit of Public Power: Political Culture in Ohio, 1787–1861*, ed. Jeffrey P. Brown and Andrew R. L. Cayton (Kent, OH: Kent State University Press, 1994), 83–98. See also "The Especial Election," *Illinois Journal*, June 7, 1852, 3:1. Edwards lost to Springfield mayor James Conkling, later the recipient of Lincoln's famous August 1863 public letter defending his emancipation policy.
48. Gustave Koerner, a Democrat from Belleville (near St. Louis) who won election as lieutenant governor of Illinois that year, later recalled Washburne as being thoroughly "uncouth." Koerner was a German immigrant originally from Frankfurt. Koerner, *Memoirs of Gustave Koerner, 1809–1896*, ed. Thomas J. McCormack (Cedar Rapids, IA: Torch Press, 1909), 2:489.

49. Yates to Fell, November 17, 1852 (transcript), in Jesse W. Fell Papers, Illinois Historical Survey, University of Illinois, Urbana.
50. Gideon Welles, a former Democrat, relayed the contents of this revealing and brutally frank conversation between Lincoln and Seward about Clay and the demise of the Whig party. Entry for January 8, 1864, in Gideon Welles, *The Civil War Diary of Gideon Welles, Lincoln's Secretary of the Navy*, ed. William E. Gienapp and Erica L. Gienapp (Urbana: University of Illinois Press, 2014), 343–44.
51. AL, Eulogy on Henry Clay, July 6, 1852, *CW*, 2:121–32.
52. AL, Eulogy on Henry Clay, July 6, 1852, *CW*, 2:130.
53. To be precise, there is no record of Lincoln's attendance at the Whig convention on July 7. Some scholars believe he was present anyway.
54. AL, Autobiography Written for John L. Scripps [c. June 1860], *CW*, 4:64. AL to Willie Mangum, August 19, 1852, *CWSS*, 23. Mangum was a prominent U.S. senator and Whig leader. Lincoln's strange reference to "Miss L.K." may have been an allusion to a popular story that Mangum had enjoyed telling in the late 1840s about a Whig activist who had tried to use his attractive sister as a sexual lure for help with obtaining a patronage appointment. See Rachel A. Shelden, *Washington Brotherhood: Politics, Social Life, and the Coming of the Civil War* (Chapel Hill: University of North Carolina Press, 2013), 135.
55. John Chesnut to Richard Yates, July 16, 1852, quoted in Miller, *Rise to National Prominence*, 309.
56. It has been a common error in Lincoln scholarship to describe him as a Scott elector in 1852, because he wrote in his 1860 autobiographical sketch for John Scripps that "he was upon the Scott electoral ticket." But he did not mean that he was an official presidential elector capable of casting votes in the Electoral College. The two at-large Whig spots in Illinois in 1852 were held by William Bebb and Joseph Gillespie, and the Scott elector from Lincoln's district was John A. Chesnut. AL, Speech to Springfield Scott Club, August 14, 26, 1852, *CW*, 2:135–57, esp. 135–36, 143–44.
57. AL, Speech to the Springfield Scott Club, *CW*, 2:136. One of the previous speakers was Ninian W. Edwards, who was trying to hold on to some element of his Whig identity by supporting Scott.
58. AL, Speech to the Springfield Scott Club, *CW*, 2:156–57.
59. See Matthew Pinsker, "After 1850: Reassessing the Impact of the Fugitive Slave Law," in *Fugitive Slaves and Spaces of Freedom in North America, 1775–1860*, ed. D. A. Pargas (Gainesville: University Press of Florida, 2018), 93–115.
60. AL, Speech to the Springfield Scott Club, *CW*, 2:138.
61. "The Account of the Democratic Doings," *Illinois Journal*, October 30, 1852, 2:1.

62. AL, Opinion on Election Laws, November 1, 1852, *CW*, 2:160. Prior to the adoption of the 1848 constitution, Illinois had actually allowed alien residents to vote without holding citizenship.
63. Seward to Washburne, September 22, 1852, quoted in William E. Gienapp, *The Origins of the Republican Party, 1852–1856* (New York: Oxford University Press, 1987), 24.
64. John Shaw to Richard Yates, August 22, 1850, Richard Yates Papers, ALPLM.
65. "The Democratic Nominees for Governor and Lieut. Governor," *Illinois State Register*, May 3, 1852, 2:3.
66. "Animadversions," *Illinois Journal*, March 1, 1853, 2:1. The full text of the law, "An act to prevent the emigration of free negroes into this State," with selections from the General Assembly debates, appeared in *Illinois Journal* on February 17, 1853, 2:4.
67. *Frederick Douglass' Paper*, March 18, 1853, quoted in Matthew Norman, "The Other Lincoln-Douglas Debate: The Race Issue in Comparative Context," *Journal of the Abraham Lincoln Association* 31 (Winter 2010): 5.
68. Donald, *Lincoln*, 622n.
69. AL to Thompson Webber, September 12, 1853, *CW*, 2:202. Income estimates based on Harry E. Pratt, *The Personal Finances of Abraham Lincoln* (Springfield, IL: Abraham Lincoln Association, 1943).
70. "Chicago and Mississippi Railroad," *Illinois State Register*, August 22, 1853.
71. John Stevens to Lawrence Stringer, April 30, 1926, quoted in Raymond N. Dooley and R. B. Latham, "Lincoln and His Namesake Town," *Journal of the Illinois State Historical Society* 52 (Spring 1959): 136.

CHAPTER 4: STANDING WITH ANYBODY

1. Robert W. Johannsen, *Stephen A. Douglas* (Urbana: University of Illinois Press, 1973), 401–18.
2. [Salmon P. Chase], Appeal of the Independent Democrats in Congress, to the People of the United States, January 24, 1854, in J. W. Schuckers, *The Life and Public Services of Salmon Portland Chase* (New York: D. Appleton, 1874), 147; John Niven, *Salmon P. Chase: A Biography* (New York: Oxford University Press, 1995).
3. Stephen Douglas, Speech on the Compromise Measures, U.S. Senate, December 23, 1851, LC.
4. Douglas made his comments about the Missouri Compromise during a speech at Springfield on October 23, 1849. Lincoln quoted the words back to Douglas in the fall of 1854 and beyond; see "Substance of Senator Douglas' Speech,"

Illinois State Register, November 2, 1849, 2:3–4; and AL, Speech at Peoria, October 16, 1854, *CW*, 2:252.

5. During contentious debates over the expensive 1852 river and harbor appropriations, Douglas had pushed unsuccessfully for using state tonnage duties to help finance the needed efforts. It was becoming one of his pet projects. The outlines of Douglas's grand strategic vision were apparent in a letter he sent to Illinois governor Joel Matteson in early January 1854, before the firestorm over popular sovereignty developed. See Paul F. Paskoff, *Troubled Waters: Steamboat Disasters, River Improvements, and American Public Policy, 1821–1860* (Baton Rouge: Louisiana State University Press, 2007), 88–101.
6. Stephen Douglas to Charles Lanphier, February 13, 1854, in Douglas, *Letters*, 283.
7. AL to Joshua Speed, August 24, 1855, *CW*, 2:321.
8. AL to Joseph Gillespie, February 11, 1854, *CW*, 2:211.
9. William H. Seward, Speech to the U.S. Senate, February 17, 1854, in *The Works of William H. Seward*, ed. George E. Baker, 5 vols. (Boston: Houghton Mifflin, 1884), 4:461–62; William Herndon to Seward, March 21, 1854, quoted in Walter Stahr, *Seward: Lincoln's Indispensable Man* (New York: Simon & Schuster, 2012), 143. Apparently Seward did not reply.
10. The *CW* editors identify only a single unsigned editorial from 1854 as being authored by Lincoln "beyond a reasonable doubt": September 11, 1854, *CW*, 2:229–30. Using a lower standard of evidence but still providing a thoughtful framework, Lincoln biographer Michael Burlingame suggests several more pieces from the spring and summer of 1854 as being "probably by Lincoln" or "in all likelihood by Lincoln." Michael Burlingame, *Abraham Lincoln: A Life*, 2 vols. (2008; Knox College online edition), 1:1076–77. Francis published a notice of his absence from work on multiple days, including *Illinois Journal*, March 25, 1854.
11. See Don E. Fehrenbacher, *Chicago Giant: A Biography of "Long John" Wentworth* (Madison, WI: American History Research Center, 1957), 124–35. Bissell went public with his opposition to the Nebraska bill but got ill and was unable to vote on the measure for final passage.
12. Jonathan Baldwin Turner to Richard Yates, April 8, 1854, quoted in Richard Lawrence Miller, *The Path to the Presidency, 1854–1860*, vol. 4 of *Lincoln and His World* (Jefferson, NC: McFarland, 2012), 32; Yates to Turner, April 14, 1854, Jonathan Baldwin Turner Papers, University of Illinois.
13. Douglas speech, May 25, 1854, quoted in Miller, *Path to the Presidency*, 32.
14. William Seward, Speech to U.S. Senate, May 26, 1854, in George E. Baker, ed., *The Life of William Seward with Selections from His Works* (New York: Redfield, 1855), 393; William Seward to Frances Seward, May 31, 1854, in Frederick W. Seward, *Seward at Washington: As Senator and Secretary of State:*

A Memoir of His Life with Selections from His Letters, 1846–1861 (New York: Derby & Miller, 1891), 231.

15. Charles Ray to Elihu Washburne, February 14, 1854, in Washburne Papers, LC.
16. Washburne to Zebina Eastman, July 5, 1854, Eastman Papers, Chicago History Museum.
17. Schneider's daughter later recalled that the photograph was "taken in the presence of my father, August 9th 1854." Clara Schneider Berger, statement attached to ambrotype by Polycarpus von Schneidau showing Lincoln in 1854, Chicago History Museum. Schneider also signed a post–Civil War era card featuring the 1854 image with this statement: "Taken in my presence Aug. 9th 1854." Abraham Lincoln O-6, Boudoir card of 1854 photograph, October 27, 1854 [common dating], currently held in private possession and sold by Heritage Auctions in 2016. Other versions of this image have been retouched to show "Press & Tribune" as the newspaper banner, not the *Chicago Democrat*, but see Schneider's recollection in Ezra M. Prince, ed., "Meeting of May 29, 1900, Commemorative of the Convention of May 29, 1856," *Transactions of the McLean County Historical Society* 3 (1900): 12.
18. AL to Richard Yates, August 18, 1854, *CW*, 2:226.
19. See Tyler G. Anbinder, *Nativism and Slavery: The Northern Know Nothings and the Politics of Slavery* (New York: Oxford University Press, 1992).
20. Quoted in Bruce M. Cole, "The Chicago Press and the Know Nothings" (MA thesis, University of Chicago, 1948), 28.
21. Benjamin Edwards to Yates, August 17, 1854, collection of R. Y. Henderson, Scotland, UK. Scattered issues of *Capital Enterprise* (Springfield) from 1854 are available at ALPLM.
22. AL to Richard Yates, August 18, 1854, *CW*, 2:226.
23. "Hon. Richard Yates," *Illinois Journal*, August 22, 1854, 2:1; "We are requested to announce," *Illinois Journal*, September 4, 1854, 2:1.
24. "Political Intelligence," *New-York Tribune*, September 23, 1854, 4:1–2.
25. "Are We Jolly, or Not?," *Illinois State Register*, September 28, 1854, 2:2.
26. See John S. Wright, *Lincoln and the Politics of Slavery* (Reno: University of Nevada Press, 1970).
27. AL, Speech at Winchester, August 26, 1854, *CW*, 2:226–27; *Illinois State Register* quoted in AL, Speech at Springfield, September 9, 1854, *CW*, 2:229.
28. AL to John Palmer ("Confidential"), September 7, 1854; and AL to Alexander Morean, September 7, 1854, *CW*, 2:227–29. Meanwhile other fusionists were trying to get Lincoln as Yates's chief surrogate; see Richard Yates to Thomas Harris, August 28, 1854, in "Stop That Silly Lie," *Illinois Journal*, September 1, 1854, 2:2.

29. AL to Richard Oglesby ("Confidential"), September 8, 1854, *CWS*, 24.
30. Mark A. Plummer, *Lincoln's Rail-Splitter: Governor Richard J. Oglesby* (Urbana: University of Illinois Press, 2001), 17. During the Andrew Johnson impeachment trial in 1868, Yates was forced to admit in a public letter that he had a "weakness" for alcohol and that he had "often yielded to temptation" during his long years of public service. Richard Yates to People of Illinois, April 21, 1868, Yates Papers, ALPLM.
31. AL to Oglesby, September 8, 1854, *CWS*, 24.
32. AL, Speech at Springfield, September 9, 1854, *CW*, 2:229.
33. AL, Speech at Springfield, September 9, 1854, *CW*, 2:229–30.
34. "The Fusion Congressional Convention," *Ottawa Free Trader*, September 16, 1854, 2:3. See also a recollection by Edwin S. Leland in U. J. Hoffman, *History of LaSalle County, Illinois* (Chicago: S. J. Clarke, 1906), 122–26.
35. "The Speeches Last Night," *Illinois State Register*, October 6, 1854, 2:1.
36. Abraham Jonas to AL, September 16, 1854, Lincoln Papers, LC.
37. AL, Speech at Bloomington, September 26, 1854, *CW*, 2:234–35.
38. "Illinois State Agricultural Fair," *Missouri Republican*, October 6, 1854, transcribed in Graham A. Peck, "New Records of the Lincoln-Douglas Debate at the 1854 Illinois State Fair: The Missouri Republican and the Missouri Democrat Report from Springfield," *Journal of the Abraham Lincoln Association* 30 (Summer 2009): 48.
39. "Grand Passage of Arms—Douglas and Lincoln," *Chicago Journal*, October 9, 1854, reprinted in Peck, "New Records," 75.
40. AL, Speech at Springfield, October 4, 1854, *CW*, 2:245.
41. AL, Speech at Peoria, October 16, 1854, *CW*, 2:275. The *Illinois Journal* provided summary coverage of Lincoln's Springfield speech on October 4 but offered a more complete version of his 1854 standard stump speech, presumably from Lincoln's own manuscript, following his address at Peoria on October 16. I have used passages from that version in describing Lincoln's comments here. The *Missouri Republican* did provide a more complete account of Lincoln's Springfield speech—one long overlooked by historians—but after a thorough comparison of the October 4 and October 16 texts, Graham Peck concludes they "were essentially the same"; Peck, "New Records," 36. See also Lewis E. Lehrman, *Lincoln at Peoria: The Turning Point* (Mechanicsburg, PA: Stackpole Books, 2008), for a deeper analysis of Lincoln's rhetorical strategies in the 1854 campaign.
42. "Illinois State Agricultural Fair," *Missouri Republican*, October 6, 1854, excerpted in Peck, "New Records," 67.
43. See Matthew Pinsker, "Not Always Such a Whig: Lincoln's Partisan Realignment in the 1850s," *Journal of the Abraham Lincoln Association* 29 (Summer 2008): 27–46. See also Mitchell Snay, "Abraham Lincoln, Owen Lovejoy, and

the Emergence of the Republican Party in Illinois," *Journal of the Abraham Lincoln Association* 22 (Winter 2001): 82–99; and Victor B. Howard, "The Illinois Republican Party: Part I, A Party Organizer for the Republicans in 1854," *Journal of the Illinois State Historical Society* 64 (Summer 1971): 125–60.

44. For firsthand accounts of the Republican convention, see Paul Selby, "Genesis of the Republican Party in Illinois," *Transactions of the Illinois State Historical Society* 11 (1906): 270–83; William H. Herndon and Jesse W. Weik, *Herndon's Life of Lincoln* (1889; reprint New York: Da Capo Press, 1983), 2:371–72; and Zebina Eastman in Rufus Blanchard, ed., *Discovery and Conquests of the Northwest with the History of Chicago*, 2 vols. (Chicago: R. Blanchard, 1900), 1:669. President Franklin Pierce vetoed yet another attempt at more river and harbor funding on December 30, 1854.

45. Years afterward William Herndon, then mayor of Springfield and as earnest an antislavery figure as anyone in the town, claimed credit for having "saved Lincoln" from these self-proclaimed Republicans by convincing his longtime law partner to leave town rather than reject the "Abolitionists" directly. What Herndon omitted from his self-aggrandizing version of that episode, however, was that Lincoln seemed relatively unconcerned about these radicals at the time. Herndon and Weik, *Herndon's Life of Lincoln*, 298–300.

46. "Lincoln Completely Fused—His Abolitionism Avowed," *Illinois State Register*, October 14, 1854, 2:3.

47. "Yates with the Abolitionists," *Illinois State Register*, October 16, 1854, 2:1. The *Register* had employed the "Black Republican" label on October 7, 1854. The fraudulent resolutions were largely drawn from the second district convention at Aurora, Illinois, adopted on September 20, 1854; "Republican Platform," *Chicago Daily Tribune*, September 28, 1854, 2.

48. AL, Speech at Peoria, October 16, 1854, *CW*, 2:273.

49. AL to Ichabod Codding ("Copy"), November 27, 1854, *CW*, 2:288. It was rare for Lincoln to retain a formal copy of a letter in this fashion.

50. *The Lincoln Log* indicates only one night spent in Springfield on October 19, 1854, and that claim is based on a recollection, not contemporary evidence. *The Lincoln Log: A Daily Chronology of the Life of Abraham Lincoln*, thelincolnlog.org.

51. Jane Martin Johns, "A Momentous Incident in Illinois History," *Journal of the Illinois State Historical Society* 10 (1918): 552.

52. *Springfield Capital Enterprise*, September 9, 1854, 1:5. Richard H. Ballinger, a local Sangamon County Know Nothing member, once recalled that Lincoln explicitly rejected their attempt at giving him an endorsement in the 1854 campaign. See Noah Levering, "Recollections of Abraham Lincoln," *Iowa Historical Record* 12 (July 1896): 495–97.

53. AL to Richard Yates, October 30 and 31, 1854, *CW*, 2:284–85; Douglas K.

Meyer, "Foreign Immigrants in Illinois," *Illinois History Teacher* 5 (1998): 15–21.

54. Yates to Isaac Arnold, June 17, 1869, *CW*, 2:284n; AL to Orville Browning, November 12, 1854, *CW*, 2:286–87. Lincoln also blamed Yates's defeat at least in part on a local controversy about the leadership of a state insane asylum in Jacksonville.
55. *A List of Members Composing the Nineteenth General Assembly of Illinois* (E. Rust, 1855), Illinois Digital Archives.
56. Stephen Douglas to Charles Lanphier, February 13, 1854, in *The Letters of Stephen A. Douglas*, ed. Robert W. Johannsen (Urbana: University of Illinois Press, 1961), 283.

CHAPTER 5: REPUBLICAN ORGANIZATION

1. "The Elections," *Illinois Journal*, November 10, 1854, 2:1. Lincoln wrote at least six letters on November 10, 1854, to recipients across the state's northern counties (Charles Hoyt, A. G. Jones, James Knox, Ward Hill Lamon, Elihu Powell, and Jonathan Scammon), although only two are extant (Hoyt and Scammon).
2. AL to Charles Hoyt ("confidential"), November 10, 1854, *CW*, 2:286.
3. Hoyt to AL, November 20 and 27, 1854, Lincoln Papers, LC.
4. James Shields to Charles Lanphier, November 23, 1854, Lanphier Papers, ALPLM. See Matthew Pinsker, "Senator Abraham Lincoln," *Journal of the Abraham Lincoln Association* 14 (Summer 1993): 1–21.
5. William H. Herndon and Jesse W. Weik, *Herndon's Life of Lincoln* (1889; reprint New York: Da Capo Press, 1983), 302, 304.
6. AL to Thomas Henderson ("confidential"), November 27, 1854; and AL to Hugh Lemaster ("confidential"), November 29, 1854, both in *CW*, 2:288–89.
7. Elihu Washburne to AL, November 14, 1854, Lincoln Papers, LC.
8. AL to Jonathan Scammon ("confidential"), November 10, 1854, *CWS*, 25; Scammon to AL, December 10, 1854, Lincoln Papers, LC.
9. *Free West* (Chicago) reprinted in *Freeman's Advocate* (Waukegan), December 21, 1854; James Morrison to Sidney Breese, December 27, 1854, Breese Papers, ALPLM; and Leonard Swett to AL, December 22, 1854, Lincoln Papers, LC.
10. AL to Elihu Powell, November 27, 1854, *CW*, 2:289.
11. *Free West*, November 30, 1854, 2:4.
12. AL to Elihu Washburne ("Don't let *any one* know I have written you this"), December 14, 1854, *CW*, 2:293; and Washburne to Zebina Eastman, December 19, 1854, Eastman Papers, Chicago History Museum.

13. *Boston Post* quoted in *Chicago Journal*, January 5, 1855, 2:3.
14. Charles Ray to Washburne, December 29, 1854, Washburne Papers, LC.
15. AL to Washburne, January 6, 1855, *CW*, 2:304.
16. List of Members of the Illinois Legislature [c. January 1, 1855], *CW*, 2:296–98.
17. AL to Richard Yates, January 14, 1855, *CWS*, 26.
18. Stephen Douglas to Charles Lanphier, December 18, 1854, in *The Letters of Stephen A. Douglas*, ed. Robert W. Johannsen (Urbana: University of Illinois Press, 1961), 331.
19. James Shields to Charles Lanphier, January 14, 1855, Lanphier Papers, ALPLM.
20. AL to Richard Yates, January 14, 1855, *CWS*, 25.
21. AL to Yates, January 14, 1855, *CWS*, 25.
22. Lincoln became a dues-paying member of the Illinois State Colonization Society only in 1856. Michael Burlingame, *The Black Man's President: Abraham Lincoln, African Americans, and the Pursuit of Racial Equality* (New York: Pegasus Books, 2021), 54.
23. I use the word *apparently* because we have only Lincoln's outline of the speech and not any kind of transcript. See "Outline for a Speech to the Colonization Society," c. January 4, 1855, and "Drafts of Resolutions," c. January 4, 1855, both of which the *CW* editors believe Lincoln produced at the same time for this colonization meeting, *CW*, 2:298–301.
24. *Democratic Press* (Chicago), January 8, 1855, 2:4; and "The editor of the Chicago Tribune," *Illinois State Register*, January 10, 1855, 2:3. See also *Telegraph* (Alton, IL), January 8, 1855, 2:1.
25. Elijah Haines quoted in Francis F. Browne, *The Every-Day Life of Abraham Lincoln* (New York: N. D. Thompson, 1886), 257.
26. AL to Elihu Washburne, January 6, 1855, *CW*, 2:304–5.
27. *Aurora Guardian*, January 10, 1855, 2:1.
28. Yates to AL, January 8, 1855, Lincoln Papers, LC; AL to Yates, January 15, 1855, *CWS*, 25–26.
29. See *Telegraph*, January 12, 1855, 2:3; *Democratic Press*, January 15, 1855, 2:2; and *Belleville (IL) Advocate*, January 17, 1855, 2:4–5.
30. AL to Washburne, February 9, 1855, *CW*, 2:304–6.
31. Mary Stuart to Elizabeth Stuart, January 28, 1855, Stuart-Hay Family Papers, ALPLM; *St. Louis Democrat* quoted in *Belleville Advocate*, February 7, 1855; *Telegraph*, February 7, 1855, 2:3; and John Palmer to Elizabeth Palmer, January 31, 1855, John M. Palmer II Papers, ALPLM. I rearranged the order of Palmer's comments slightly but kept his meaning intact.
32. AL to Jesse Norton ("confidential"), February 16, 1855, *CWSS*, 9.
33. "House of Representatives," *Illinois Journal*, February 8, 1855, 2:3; "House of Representatives," *Illinois State Register*, February 8, 1855, 2:4.

34. AL to Norton, February 16, 1855, *CWSS*, 9.
35. AL to Elihu Washburne, *CW*, 2:305.
36. *Missouri Democrat* (St. Louis) quoted in *Belleville Advocate*, February 7, 1855; *Telegraph*, February 7, 1855, 2:3; AL to Washburne, *CW*, 2:305.
37. "February 8, 1855," *Senate Journal* (Springfield, 1855), 242–55.
38. AL to Norton, February 16, 1855, *CWSS*, 9. Lincoln later described Dr. Johns as "a most worthy gentleman," who was "far more than an ordinarily capable and energetic business man." AL, Appointment of Harvey C. Johns, January 25, 1862, *CW*, 5:110.
39. AL to Norton, February 16, 1855, *CWSS*, 9–11.
40. "U.S. Senator," *Illinois Sentinel* (Jacksonville), February 16, 1855, 2:1.
41. John Palmer recollection, *Chicago Evening Post* (1892), vertical file clipping, ALPLM; Lyman Trumbull to AL, February 24, 1855, and January 3, 1858, Lincoln Papers, LC.
42. David Davis to Julius Rockwell, February 15, 1855, David Davis Family Papers, ALPLM; Albert J. Beveridge, *Abraham Lincoln, 1809–1865* (Boston: Houghton Mifflin, 1928), 2:286, 288.
43. AL to Washburne, January 6, 1855, *CW*, 2:304–5; AL to Norton, February 16, 1855, *CWSS*, 9; AL to William Henderson, February 21, 1855, *CW*, 2:307.
44. "Item Column," *Illinois Journal*, February 16, 1855, 3:1.
45. Lyman Trumbull to AL, February 24, 1855, Lincoln Papers, LC. Lincoln's letter to Trumbull has not been found, but Trumbull described Lincoln's lighthearted comments in his reply.
46. AL to Owen Lovejoy, August 11, 1855, *CW*, 2:317.
47. See Victor B. Howard, "The Illinois Republican Party: Part II, The Party Becomes Conservative, 1855–1856," *Journal of the Illinois State Historical Society* 64 (Autumn 1971): 285–311.
48. The Know Nothing mayor of Chicago was Levi Boone, a descendant of frontier legend Daniel Boone.
49. AL to Henry Dummer, March 19, 1855; and AL, B. S. Edwards, and John Stuart to Orville Browning, *CW*, 2:309–10.
50. Antislavery nativists were known as Jonathans. Hard-line nativists were called Sams. For more background and context, see William E. Gienapp, *The Origins of the Republican Party, 1852–1856* (New York: Oxford University Press, 1987), and Tyler Anbinder, *Nativism and Slavery: The Northern Know Nothings and the Politics of Slavery* (New York: Oxford University Press, 1992).
51. AL to Henry Clay Whitney, June 7, 1855, *CW*, 2:313.
52. Gienapp, *Origins of the Republican Party*, 287–88.
53. Simeon Francis to AL, December 26, 1859, Lincoln Papers, LC.
54. Lovejoy's letter to Lincoln has never been found, but there is a copy of his cor-

respondence with Archibald Williams from Quincy. That document, combined with some textual clues in Lincoln's and Trumbull's responses, suggests that Lovejoy was working from a common template in his outreach efforts that summer. See Owen Lovejoy to Archibald Williams, August 6, 1855, U.S. History Papers, Indiana University; AL to Lovejoy, August 11, 1855, *CW*, 2:316–17; Lyman Trumbull to Lovejoy, August 20, 1855, Trumbull Family Papers, ALPLM.

55. Lovejoy to Williams, August 6, 1855, U.S. History Papers, Indiana University.
56. Trumbull to Lovejoy, August 20, 1855, Trumbull Family Papers, ALPLM.
57. AL to Lovejoy, August 11, 1855, *CW*, 2:316–17.
58. AL to Lovejoy, August 11, 1855, *CW*, 2:317.
59. Lincoln and Williams spent a week together in Chicago, from July 11 to 14, 1855, trying a case against Quincy attorney (and fellow former Whig) Orville H. Browning. One of the judges overseeing that trial was the antislavery Whig jurist and associate Supreme Court justice John McLean. See entry for July 11, 1855, in Orville Browning, *The Diary of Orville Hickman Browning*, ed. Theodore Calvin Pease and James G. Randall, 2 vols. (Springfield: Illinois State Historical Library, 1925), 1:190–92.
60. See Matthew Pinsker, "Stampedes as Mobile Insurrections: An Introductory Essay," Slave Stampedes on the Southern Borderlands, stampedes.dickinson.edu, 2021.
61. "Republican Meeting at Quincy," *Monmouth (IL) Atlas*, August 10, 1855, 2:1. Williams appears to have been adapting his version of the so-called federal consensus about slavery from language in an 1840 speech by Daniel Webster in Richmond, Virginia: "I hold, by the Constitution of the United States, that congress is absolutely precluded from interfering in any manner, directly or indirectly, with the institution of slavery, or with any other state institution." Reported in G. W. F. Mellen, *An Argument on the Unconstitutionality of Slavery* (Boston: Saxton & Peirce, 1841), 136.
62. Sumner definitely met with Quincy attorney Orville Browning while he was in Chicago. Browning was opposing counsel in the case where Lincoln and Williams served as co-counsels. The phrasing at the 1855 Quincy fusionist meeting (freedom as the rule and slavery as the exception) originally came from Rep. Horace Mann of Massachusetts during the Compromise of 1850 debates, but Browning's diary makes clear that Sumner, who arrived in Chicago on Saturday, July 14, was being loquacious and engaging—and thus probably addressed this issue with them at some point. Entry for July 14, 1855, in Browning, *Diary*, 1:192.
63. "Letter from Ichabod Codding," *Chicago Tribune*, July 30, 1855, quoted in Howard, "Republican Party Part II," 291.

64. AL to George Robertson, August 15, 1855, *CW*, 2:317–18. Lincoln and Robertson knew each other because of legal work they had conducted together concerning the contested estate of Mary Lincoln's late father. For alternative views on Lincoln's positioning in his Robertson letter, see Daniel W. Crofts, *Lincoln and the Politics of Slavery: The Other Thirteenth Amendment and the Struggle to Save the Union* (Chapel Hill: University of North Carolina Press, 2016), 71; and Michael F. Holt, *The Election of 1860: "A Campaign Fraught with Consequences"* (Lawrence: University Press of Kansas, 2017), 161.
65. AL to George Robertson, August 15, 1855, *CW*, 2:318.
66. AL to Joshua Speed, August 24, 1855, *CW*, 2:321.
67. Lincoln also observed in the Speed letter that nobody had ever tried to "unwhig" him for supporting the Wilmot Proviso in the 1840s but he knew the difference between being an antislavery Whig and organizing a political movement on the basis of an antislavery principle.
68. AL to Speed, August 24, 1855, *CW*, 2:322–23.
69. AL to Speed, August 24, 1855, *CW*, 2:322–23.
70. AL to Isham Reavis, November 5, 1855, *CW*, 2:327.
71. Thomas Quick to Lyman Trumbull, January 24, 1856, Trumbull Papers, LC; Wright, *Lincoln and Politics*, 92–93; Ebenezer Peck to Trumbull, January 14, 1856, Trumbull Papers, LC.
72. Paul Selby to Richard Yates, February 14, 1856, quoted in Miller, *Path to the Presidency*, 122.
73. "The Fusion Editorial Convention," *Illinois State Register*, February 25, 1856, 2:1.
74. The editors supported the continuation of open naturalization laws and opposed any nativist restrictions on public officeholding.
75. Ezra M. Prince, ed., "The Bloomington Convention of 1856," *Transactions of the McLean County Historical Society* 3 (1900): 88–90. Appreciation for the Decatur meeting has evolved over the years. Herndon, in his biography of Lincoln, did not even mention the gathering, but according to Don E. Fehrenbacher, "In every way except formal use of the name, this Decatur 'editorial convention' marks the launching of the state Republican party." Fehrenbacher, *Prelude to Greatness: Abraham Lincoln in the 1850's* (Stanford, CA: Stanford University Press, 1962), 44. Robert W. Johannsen also calls Decatur the "real beginning" of the Republican party in Illinois, in Johannsen, *Lincoln, The South, and Slavery: The Political Dimension* (Baton Rouge: Louisiana State University Press, 1993), 53.
76. "Republican Convention," *New York Times*, February 26, 1856.

CHAPTER 6: UNDER HOT FIRE

1. Quoted in David S. Reynolds, *John Brown: Abolitionist* (New York: Knopf, 2005), 64–65.
2. Reynolds, *John Brown*, 137.
3. AL, Address Before the Young Men's Lyceum, January 27, 1838, *CW*, 1:112.
4. AL, "House Divided" Speech, June 16, 1858, *CW*, 2:468.
5. Joseph Gillespie to AL, June 6, 1856, Herndon-Weik Papers, LC. Note that this letter does not appear in the online database for Lincoln Papers, LC.
6. In mid-May, Archer claimed about his refusal, "If published, I will lose some six votes certain." William B. Archer to Robert L. Dulaney, May 19 and 24, 1856, Archer Papers, ALPLM.
7. Elihu Washburne to Richard Yates, April 3, 1856, quoted in "A Prelude to the Birth of the Republican Party," *Journal of the Illinois State Historical Society* 46 (Autumn 1953): 312–13.
8. William Herndon to Lyman Trumbull, May 20, 1856, in Herndon, *Herndon on Lincoln: Letters*, ed. Douglas L. Wilson and Rodney O. Davis (Urbana: University of Illinois Press, 2016), 4. Herndon did suggest that Lincoln had said "nigger driving gentlemen," but that ugly phrase was one the junior partner liked to use as a special insult for the slave power. Lincoln probably did not use the term himself.
9. About 250 delegates received credentials at Bloomington, representing most, but not all, of the state's counties. See Ezra M. Prince, ed., "Meeting of May 29, 1900, Commemorative of the Convention of May 29, 1856," *Transactions of the McLean County Historical Society* 3 (1900): 148–64.
10. The *Illinois Journal* masthead touted the "People's Ticket" in 1856. The *Quincy Whig* promoted the "Anti-Nebraska Ticket." Newspapers around Chicago were more likely to use the term *Republican*, but they also were not consistent in their party designations.
11. Entry for February 21, 1856, in Orville H. Browning, *The Diary of Orville Hickman Browning*, ed. Theodore Calvin Pease and James G. Randall, 2 vols. (Springfield: Illinois State Historical Library, 1925), 1:227; and Lyman Trumbull to John Palmer, January 24, 1856, in George Thomas Palmer, ed., "A Collection of Letters from Lyman Trumbull to John M. Palmer, 1854–1858," *Journal of the Illinois State Historical Society* 16 (April–July 1923): 28–29.
12. The Bloomington delegates nominated Bissell despite an illness that had left him partially paralyzed. Browning's platform draft departed from—and toned down—the language of the Quincy and Decatur platforms but essentially followed their model. Among the speakers at the convention was Andrew Reeder,

former Kansas territorial governor, who had broken dramatically with the Pierce administration and was now aligned with the Free State movement.

13. Herndon quoted in Francis F. Browne, *The Every-Day Life of Abraham Lincoln* (New York: N. D. Thompson, 1886), 261; AL, Speech at Bloomington, May 29, 1856, *CW*, 2:341; contemporary coverage from *Alton Weekly Courier*, June 5, 1856. Other recollected accounts of Lincoln's so-called Lost Speech at Bloomington, especially the one from Henry Clay Whitney, are not credible.
14. AL to Lyman Trumbull ("confidential"), June 7, 1856, *CW*, 2:342–43.
15. Nathaniel Wilcox recollection, in Lincoln Papers, UC; Horace Greeley, ed., *Proceedings of the First Three Republican National Conventions 1856, 1860 and 1864* (Minneapolis: Charles W. Johnson, 1893), 62.
16. Wilcox recollection, Lincoln Papers, UC.
17. Lincoln later estimated that he delivered over fifty speeches during the campaign. David Herbert Donald, *Lincoln* (New York: Simon & Schuster, 1995), 193–94.
18. AL to James Grimes, July 12, 1856, *CW*, 2:348; AL, Speech at Kalamazoo, Michigan, August 27, 1856, *CW*, 2:361–66.
19. AL to Davis, July 7, 1856, *CWS*, 27; and AL to Henry Clay Whitney, July 9, 1856, *CW*, 2:347.
20. AL to Trumbull, June 27, 1856, *CWSS*, 11. See also William E. Gienapp, "The Election of 1856: An Unpublished Lincoln Letter," *Journal of Illinois State Historical Society* 70 (February 1977): 18–21. The Americans eventually did find a gubernatorial candidate: Buckner S. Morris.
21. Thomas F. Schwartz, "Lincoln, Form Letters, and Fillmore Men," *Illinois Historical Journal* 78 (Spring 1985): 65–70.
22. AL, Form Letter to Fillmore Men ("Confidential"), September 8, 1858, *CW*, 2:374.
23. Richard Yates to AL, September 18, 1856, Lincoln Papers, LC. See also A. J. Brooks to Yates, September 18, 1856; and Gustave Koerner to Yates, October 25, 1856, Yates Papers, ALPLM.
24. Entry for September 3, 1856, in Browning, *Diary*, 1:252; *Rockford (IL) Register*, October 25, 1856; Thomas M. Keefe, "Chicago's Flirtation with Political Nativism, 1854–1856," *Records of the American Catholic Historical Society of Philadelphia* 82 (September 1971): 152. Herndon to Jesse W. Weik, February 21, 1891, in Herndon, *The Hidden Lincoln: From the Letters and Papers of William H. Herndon*, ed. Emanuel Hertz (New York: Viking, 1938), 264.
25. AL, Speech at a Republican Banquet [with Scammon toast], December 10, 1856, *CW*, 2:383–85.
26. AL, Speech at a Republican Banquet, December 10, 1856, *CW*, 2:385.
27. AL to Robert Boal, December 25, 1856, *CW*, 2:387; William Herndon to

Lyman Trumbull, February 17, 1857, excerpted in Harry E. Pratt, ed., *Concerning Mr. Lincoln: In Which Abraham Lincoln Is Pictured as He Appeared to Letter Writers of His Time* (Springfield, IL: Abraham Lincoln Association, 1944), 7–9.

28. Bissell to AL, January 2, 1857, PAL.
29. AL to Yates, September 20, 1857, *CW*, 2:424.
30. AL to Henry Clay Whitney, December 18, 1857, *CW*, 2:429.
31. The *CW* editors confess that they could find "little" detail about Johnson's career other than to confirm his residence in Springfield from 1857 to 1859. But additional letters from the Lincoln Papers at LC and the Ozias Hatch Papers at ALPLM make clear that Johnson had moved to New York City by 1860, got himself elected to the Republican central committee there, received a lucrative patronage appointment in the New York Custom House, and kept up occasional contact with President Lincoln throughout the war, culminating with a request (not granted) that he be named head of the Freedmen's Bureau. See John Johnson to Ozias Hatch, February 17, 1860, Hatch Papers, ALPLM; John Johnson to AL, May 18, 1860, and March 12, 1864, Lincoln Papers, LC. Apparently responding to pressure from Mrs. Lincoln, Hiram Barney, the collector of the port of New York, reported to President Lincoln in 1861: "Please inform Mrs. Lincoln that Mr. John O. Johnson has a pleasant situation in the custom House." Hiram Barney to AL, May 11, 1861, Lincoln Papers, LC.
32. Mary Lincoln to Emilie Todd Helm, November 23, 1856, in Lincoln, *Mary Todd Lincoln: Her Life and Letters*, ed. Justin G. Turner and Linda Levitt Turner (New York: Knopf, 1972), 46.
33. Mary Lincoln to Helm, September 20, [1857], in Lincoln, *Life and Letters*, 50–51.
34. Mary Lincoln to Helm, February 16, 1857, in Lincoln, *Life and Letters*, 48–49.
35. AL to James Steel and Charles Summers, February 12, 1857, *CW*, 2:389.
36. AL to John Rosette ("Private"), February 20, 1857, *CW*, 2:389.
37. AL to Ichabod Codding, November 27, 1854, *CW*, 2:288.
38. See Don E. Fehrenbacher, *The Dred Scott Case: Its Significance in Law and Politics* (New York: Oxford University Press, 1978).
39. Robert Grier to James Buchanan, February 23, 1857, in Buchanan, *The Works of James Buchanan, Comprising His Speeches, State Papers, and Private Correspondence*, ed. John Bassett Moore, 12 vols. (Philadelphia: J. B. Lippincott, 1908–11), 10:106. See also Fehrenbacher, *Dred Scott*, 308–14.
40. Fehrenbacher, *Dred Scott*, 314–21.
41. AL, Fragment of a Speech [c. December 1857], *CW*, 2:454; William Seward, Speech to the Senate, March 3, 1858, in *Seward at Washington: As Senator and*

Secretary of State: A Memoir of His Life with Selections from His Letters, 1846–1861, ed. Frederick W. Seward (New York: Derby & Miller, 1891), 337.

42. AL, "House Divided" Speech, June 16, 1858, *CW*, 2:465.
43. AL, "House Divided" Speech, June 16, 1858, *CW*, 2:465.
44. Entry for June 12, 1857, in Browning, *Diary*, 1:289.
45. "Remarks of Hon. Stephen A. Douglas," *Illinois State Register*, June 18, 1857, 2:2–5.
46. AL, Speech at Springfield, June 26, 1857, *CW*, 2:398–410.
47. AL, Speech at Springfield, June 26, 1857, *CW*, 2:408–9.
48. AL, Speech at Springfield, June 26, 1857, *CW*, 2:409.
49. Trumbull's speech was reported in two issues of *Illinois Journal*, July 1–2, 1857.
50. AL to B. Clarke Lundy, July 20, 1857, *CW*, 2:412.
51. Historian Manisha Sinha describes Lundy as "a John the Baptist to Garrison's Christ in the eyes of devout abolitionists." Sinha, *The Slave's Cause: A History of Abolition* (New Haven, CT: Yale University Press, 2016), 177.
52. AL to B. Clarke Lundy, August 5, 1857, *CW*, 2:412–13.
53. AL to Lundy and others, July 28, 1856, *CW*, 2:357.
54. William Herndon to Wendell Phillips, May 12, 1857, in Herndon, *Herndon on Lincoln*, 5.
55. Ebenezer Lane to W. H. Osborn, [August] 14, 1857, in Lincoln, *The Lincoln Reader*, ed. Paul M. Angle (1947: reprint New York: Da Capo Press, 1990), 182. Angle relied on a typescript that mistakenly listed this letter as May 14, 1857.
56. Harry E. Pratt, *The Personal Finances of Abraham Lincoln* (Springfield, IL: Abraham Lincoln Association, 1943), 54.
57. Agreement Regarding the *Missouri Democrat*, July 3, 1857, *CW*, 2:410.
58. John G. Nicolay, *With Lincoln in the White House: Letters, Memoranda, and Other Writings of John G. Nicolay, 1860–1865*, ed. Michael Burlingame (Carbondale: Southern Illinois University Press, 2000), xviii.
59. See Kenneth M. Stampp, *America in 1857: A Nation on the Brink* (New York: Oxford University Press, 1990). See also Emory R. Johnson, "River and Harbor Bills," *Annals of the American Academy of Political and Social Science* 2 (1892): 50–80.
60. AL, Call for Sangamon County Convention, October 8, 1857, *CW*, 2:424.
61. Reynolds, *John Brown*, 239–43.
62. Stampp, *America in 1857*, 144–81, 266–94. Notably, however, Stampp essentially ignores charges from the 1860 campaign that accused Douglas of orchestrating Calhoun's behavior at Lecompton (273).
63. "Astounding Disclosures," *Chicago Tribune*, November 12, 1857, 2:2. See also "Adjournment of the Convention," *Chicago Tribune*, November 16, 1857, 1:2.

64. Stephen Douglas to William Weer, November 23, 1857, quoted in Robert W. Johannsen, *Stephen A. Douglas* (Urbana: University of Illinois Press, 1973), 581.
65. Matthew Pinsker, "'General Jackson Is Dead': Dissecting a Popular Anecdote of Nineteenth-Century Party Leadership," in *The Worlds of James Buchanan and Thaddeus Stevens: Place, Personality, and Politics in the Civil War Era*, ed. Michael J. Birkner, Randall M. Miller, and John W. Quist (Baton Rouge: Louisiana State University Press, 2019), 82–108.
66. AL to Trumbull, November 30, 1857, *CW*, 2:427; "Douglas and Buchanan at Issue," *Chicago Tribune*, December 4, 1857, 1:1. See also "From Washington," *New-York Tribune*, December 4, 1857, 4:6.
67. "Affairs at Washington," *New York Herald*, December 5, 1857, 4.
68. James Buchanan, Annual Message, December 8, 1857, in American Presidency Project, presidency.ucsb.edu/; AL to Lyman Trumbull, December 18, 1857, *CW*, 2:428. Douglas biographer Robert Johannsen calls the Illinois senator's speech on December 9, 1857, "probably the most significant of his career"; Johannsen, *Douglas*, 592.
69. AL to Trumbull, December 28, 1857, *CW*, 2:430.
70. Trumbull to AL, January 3, 1858, Lincoln Papers, LC.

CHAPTER 7: AN ULTRA STRATEGY

1. This draft speech was misdated for many years. Nicolay and Hay originally put it in October 1858; John G. Nicolay and John Hay, eds., *Abraham Lincoln: Complete Works*, 2 vols. (New York: Century, 1894), 1:422–27; Roy Basler, in *CW*, moved the date back to May 1858, but Don Fehrenbacher has argued persuasively that Lincoln created at least the first part of the material in late December 1857 or early January 1858. Thus, the text (as currently transcribed in *CW*) really includes two separate parts written at different times—one draft from the winter immediately following the Buchanan-Douglas rupture, and then a second fragment from a later period (which includes a version of the "house divided" line) that has been mistakenly combined with it. See AL, Fragment of a Speech [c. May 18, 1858], *CW*, 2:448–54, and Don E. Fehrenbacher, *Prelude to Greatness: Abraham Lincoln in the 1850's* (Stanford, CA: Stanford University Press, 1962), 89–94. One way to illustrate the difference between the two fragments is to compare the image of the first part (via the Papers of Abraham Lincoln) with the second image (held by the Gilder Lehrman Institute). The margins and line spacing are different, as are the paper and pen markings.
2. AL to Henry Clay Whitney, December 18, 1857, *CW*, 2:428–29.
3. AL to Owen Lovejoy ("strictly confidential"), March 8, 1858, *CW*, 2:435–36.

4. AL to Charles Ray, June 6, 1858, PAL. This letter has only recently been rediscovered at Cantigny, the Col. Robert R. McCormick Research Center in Wheaton, IL.
5. AL to editors, *Chicago Tribune*, June 8, 1858, *CWS*, 31.
6. The original *Tribune* article, "Opposition to Lovejoy," appeared on June 4, 1858, 2:3. Davis replied to Lincoln thanking him for sending the letter, which he called "a manifestation of your friendship." Davis to AL, June 14, 1858, Lincoln Papers, LC.
7. The full breakdown of Bissell's signatures: 154 bills on February 14, another 43 on February 17, and finally 149 on February 18, 1857. Richard Lawrence Miller, *The Path to the Presidency, 1854–1860*, vol. 4 of *Lincoln and His World* (Jefferson, NC: McFarland, 2012), 193.
8. Lincoln had his eye on recruiting for the 1858 legislative contests as early as the fall of 1857. He reached out unsuccessfully to Richard Yates about a statehouse seat in Morgan County. "It will be something of a sacrifice to you," Lincoln wrote, "but can you not make it?" Of course, that was exactly what Lincoln had done for Yates in 1854 when he ran (and won) a legislative seat from Sangamon County. Yates declined. AL to Yates, September 30, 1857, *CW*, 2:424.
9. AL to Thomas Marshall, April 23, 1858, *CW*, 2:443.
10. AL to Yates, March 9, 1858, *CWS*, 29.
11. AL to Josiah Lucas, May 10, 1858, *CW*, 2:445.
12. H[enry] J. R[aymond], "The Kansas Question; Prospect in the House; Feeling in Kansas; The Future," *New York Times*, March 26, 1858.
13. R[aymond], "Kansas Question."
14. AL to Ozias Hatch, March 24, 1858, *CWS*, 29.
15. William Herndon to Theodore Parker, March 4, May 29, and September 20, 1858, quoted in David Herbert Donald, *Lincoln's Herndon: A Biography* (1948; reprint New York: Da Capo Press, 1989), 114.
16. AL to Hatch ("show to discreet friends"), March 24, 1858, *CWS*, 29–30.
17. *Weekly Register* (Rockford, IL), May 15, 1858, 2:1. See also Albert J. Beveridge, *Abraham Lincoln, 1809–1865* (Boston: Houghton Mifflin, 1928), 2:558–59.
18. Lincoln used the phrase "high spirits" in two separate letters: AL to Thomas Marshall, April 23, 1858, and AL to Elihu Washburne, April 26, 1858, both in *CW*, 2:443–44. The Republican state central committee, led by chairman Norman B. Judd, issued the formal call for the June 16 convention on April 22, 1858.
19. AL to Thomas Marshall, April 23, 1858, *CW*, 2:443.
20. AL to Washburne ("confidential"), May 27, 1858, *CW*, 2:455.
21. AL to Washburne, May 10, 1858, *CW*, 2:445.
22. Washburne to AL, May 6, 1858, Lincoln Papers, LC.

23. Charles Wilson to AL, May 31, 1858, Lincoln Papers, LC. AL to Wilson, June 1, 1858, *CW*, 2:456–57. Lincoln claimed to have had many "free conversations" with Wentworth, but not long after the assassination, the cagey Wentworth told Herndon almost exactly the opposite. "Personally I knew but little of Mr Lincoln," he wrote in 1866. "I have no remembrance of ever being in any room alone with him or of ever conversing with him upon any subject except politics." Wentworth to Herndon, February 4, 1866, in Douglas L. Wilson and Rodney O. Davis, eds., *Herndon's Informants: Letters, Interviews, and Statements About Abraham Lincoln* (Urbana: University of Illinois Press, 2020), 194–95.
24. AL to Wilson, June 1, 1858, *CW*, 2:457.
25. AL to Josiah Lucas, May 10, 1858, *CW*, 2:445.
26. John Johnson to Horace Greeley, May 6, 1858, quoted in Michael Burlingame, *Abraham Lincoln: A Life*, 2 vols. (2008; Knox College online edition), 1:446.
27. AL to Stephen Hurlbut, June 1, 1858, *CW*, 2:456. See also "Illinois Sends Her Answer," *Chicago Tribune*, June 14, 1858, 2:1; and David Phillips to AL, June 9, 1858, Lincoln Papers, LC.
28. *Proceedings of the Republican State Convention, June 16, 1858* (Springfield, IL, 1858).
29. *Proceedings of the Republican State Convention, June 16, 1858* (Springfield, IL, 1858).
30. AL, "House Divided" Speech, June 16, 1858, *CW*, 2:461–69.
31. AL, Campaign Circular from Whig Committee, March 4, 1843, *CW*, 1:315; AL to George Robertson, August 15, 1855, *CW*, 2:317–18; AL to Joshua Speed, August 24, 1855, *CW*, 2:320–23.
32. AL, "House Divided" Speech, June 16, 1858, *CW*, 2:461–69.
33. One audience member recalled that Lincoln "confined himself far more than he usually did to his notes." William Pitt Kellogg recollection, Lincoln Centennial Association Papers, ALPLM.
34. Norman Judd told John Hay during the Civil War that he had told Lincoln, "If we had seen the speech we would have cut that [House Divided section] out." "Would you," Lincoln had replied dismissively. See diary entry for December 9, 1863, in John Hay, *Inside Lincoln's White House: The Complete Civil War Diary of John Hay*, ed. Michael Burlingame and John R. Turner Ettlinger (Carbondale: Southern Illinois University Press, 1997), 122.
35. John Locke Scripps to AL, June 22, 1858, Lincoln Papers, LC; AL to Scripps ("do not intend this for publication"), June 23, 1858, *CW*, 2:471.
36. Scripps was editor of the formerly independent *Democratic Press* while Medill edited the *Tribune* with Dr. Charles Ray, but the two journals were in the pro-

cess of consolidating into what would become the city's premier Republican newspaper during the 1858 campaign, the *Press and Tribune* (before evolving again in 1860 to become—and remain—the *Chicago Tribune*). See Scripps's second letter to Lincoln in two days, June 23, 1858; Joseph Medill to AL, June 23, 1858; and Henry Clay Whitney to AL, June 23, 1858, all in Lincoln Papers, LC.

37. AL to Whitney ("Show this to whomever you please"), June 24, 1858; AL to Joseph Medill, June 25, 1858; both in *CW*, 2:472–73.
38. AL to Ray, June 27, 1858, PAL. This letter was originally kept out of the *Collected Works* by descendants of Col. Robert McCormick, who retained Lincoln correspondence to the *Tribune* editors. The document was held at McCormick's Cantigny estate. It has been available to scholars and the public only since about 2008, but it remains essentially unknown and rarely quoted. The clipping was "Indiana—John G. Davis Thrown Overboard," *Chicago Tribune*, June 26, 1858, 2:1.
39. Ray to AL, July 1858, Lincoln Papers, LC.
40. For Lincoln's disdain for those politicians who only seem to "take care of 'number one,'" see AL to John Hardin, February 7, 1846, *CW*, 1:365.
41. Ray and Medill to AL, June 29, 1858; and Ray to AL, July 1858, both in Lincoln Papers, LC.
42. AL to Trumbull, June 23, 1858, *CW*, 2:472.
43. AL to Trumbull, June 23, 1858, *CW*, 2:471–72. Herndon told Trumbull just the next month that Lincoln remained "gloomy" and "uncertain" about his own prospects. Herndon to Trumbull, July 8, 1858, in Herndon, *Herndon on Lincoln: Letters*, ed. Douglas L. Wilson and Rodney O. Davis (Urbana: University of Illinois Press, 2016), 7.
44. AL, 1858 Campaign Strategy [c. July 15, 1858], *CW*, 2:476–81.
45. On Crittenden, see Daniel W. Crofts, "The Southern Opposition and the Crisis of the Union," in *A Political Nation: New Directions in Mid-Nineteenth-Century American Political History*, ed. Gary W. Gallagher and Rachel A. Shelden (Charlottesville: University of Virginia Press, 2012), 85–111.
46. AL to Crittenden, July 7, 1858, *CW*, 2:483–84.
47. Crittenden to AL, July 29, 1858, Lincoln Papers, LC.
48. AL to Joseph Gillespie, July 16, 1858, *CW*, 2:503; Gillespie to AL, July 19, 1858, Lincoln Papers, LC; AL to Gillespie, July 25, 1858, *CW*, 2:523.
49. AL to Alexander Campbell, June 25, 1858, *CW*, 2:473.
50. AL to Henry Dummer, July 20, 1858, *CW*, 2:521.
51. AL to Gustave Koerner ("for your private eye"), July 15, 1858, *CW*, 2:502.
52. AL to Koerner, July 25, 1858, *CW*, 2:524.
53. Robert W. Johannsen, *Stephen A. Douglas* (Urbana: University of Illinois Press, 1973), 625–31.

54. AL to Trumbull, June 23, 1858, *CW*, 2:471–72; Herndon to Trumbull, June 24, 1858, in Herndon, *Herndon on Lincoln*, 6.
55. In July, Lincoln had met with John Dougherty, the Buchanan candidate for state treasurer. If Jesse Dubois had met with Dougherty, who was quite prominent, he would have identified him by name, instead of referring to him as "your man." See Jesse Dubois to AL, September 7, 1858, Lincoln Papers, LC.
56. A. Sherman to Ozias Hatch, September 27, 1858, Hatch Papers, ALPLM. See also Rodney O. Davis, "Dr. Charles Lieb: Lincoln's Mole?," *Journal of the American Lincoln Association* 24 (Summer 2003): 20–35.
57. Quoted in "The Republican Convention," *Illinois Journal*, June 24, 1858, 2:2.
58. Horace Greeley to Joseph Medill (copy), July 24, 1858, Lincoln Papers, LC.
59. "Senatorial Contest in Illinois—Speech of Mr. Lincoln," *New York Times*, July 16, 1858, 4.
60. John Mathers to AL, July 19, 1858, Lincoln Papers, LC; AL to Mathers, July 20, 1858, *CW*, 2:522.
61. AL to Stephen Douglas, July 24, 29, and 31, 1858, *CW*, 2:522, 528–30, 531; Douglas to AL, July 24, 1858, Lincoln Papers, LC.
62. Douglas in AL, First Debate with Douglas, August 21, 1858, *CW*, 3:1–12.
63. AL, First Debate with Douglas, August 21, 1858, *CW*, 3:29.
64. AL, Fragment [c. August 21, 1858], *CW*, 2:553. See also AL, First Debate with Douglas, August 21, 1858, *CW*, 3:27.
65. AL to Henry Dummer, August 5, 1858, *CW*, 2:536.
66. AL to Washburne ("burn this"), September 16, 1858, *CW*, 3:144–45. The original allegation came from the *Illinois State Register*, September 15, 1858, quoting from the *Galena Advertiser*, "the mouthpiece of Elihu B. Washburne." Once again, the allegation concerned a "platform" adopted in 1854, this time by Rockford County Republicans. Their resolutions did apparently call "to prohibit the admission of any more slave states into the Union."
67. Herndon to Theodore Parker, August 31, 1858, in Herndon, *Herndon on Lincoln*, 11–12.
68. AL to Judd, September 23, 1858, *CW*, 3:202. Michael Burlingame calls moving illegal voters into doubtful districts "a common electoral strategy of the 1850s" and identifies at least two illicit Republican voter colonization proposals, from Ozias Hatch in 1857 and David Davis in 1860. Burlingame, *Lincoln: A Life*, 1:545–46.
69. Henry Clay Whitney to AL, October 14, 1858, Lincoln Papers, LC.
70. AL to Judd, October 20, 1858, *CW*, 3:329–30. Lincoln also mentioned noticing "about a dozen Irishmen" in a speech he gave at Meredosia, a day after

encountering them in Naples. He suggested in public that "those Irishmen had been imported expressly to vote him down," according to the Democratic newspaper account of his remarks; AL, Speech at Meredosia, October 18, 1858, *CW*, 3:328.

71. AL to Judd, October 20, 1858, *CW*, 3:329–30; "Arrest of Distelberg, the Prussian Defaulter," *Chicago Tribune*, April 10, 1858, 1:2. For more on Pinkerton, see Frank Morn, *"The Eye That Never Sleeps": A History of the Pinkerton National Detective Agency* (Bloomington: Indiana University Press, 1982). "You know my confidence in Pinkerton and his men," Judd would write to the president in 1861. Judd to AL, April 21, 1861, Lincoln Papers, LC.
72. Herndon to Trumbull, June 24, 1858, in Herndon, *Herndon on Lincoln*, 6.
73. AL to Judd, October 20, 1858, *CW*, 3:330.
74. "Dickey's Speech at Decatur: Letter from John J. Crittenden!," *Illinois State Register*, October 23, 1858, 2:3. Following the reading of Crittenden's letter to Dickey, the *Missouri Republican*, a Democratic newspaper from St. Louis, also managed to report on the contents of Crittenden's previously unknown correspondence with Lincoln; see AL to Crittenden, November 4, 1858, *CW*, 3:335. But that was not the moment when the news actually broke in Illinois.
75. Davis to AL, November 7, 1858, Lincoln Papers, LC. Davis also used this note to apologize to Lincoln for not doing more on his behalf, claiming he should have resigned from his judgeship so that he would not have been so "Chained" by his responsibilities.
76. Judd, circular letter, October 22, 1858, Hatch Papers, ALPLM; AL, Opinion on Election Laws of Illinois [October 15, 1858?], *CW*, 3:325–26; L. H. Waters to Hatch, November 3, 1858, Hatch Papers, ALPLM.
77. Cyrus W. Vanderen of the fifteenth senatorial district around Morgan and Sangamon counties was the area's lone Republican holdover. He had been elected in 1856, though the *CW* editors mistakenly indicate that he was reelected in 1858. See their annotations on Lincoln's summer calculations, *CW*, 2:480n.
78. AL to Salmon Chase, April 11, 1861, *CW*, 4:327.
79. Don Fehrenbacher reports that a swing of 150 votes in three counties would have provided the Republicans with a 51–49 majority in the legislature. Fehrenbacher, *Prelude*, 186n.
80. AL, Fragment on the Struggle Against Slavery, c. July 1858, *CW*, 2:482. The dating on this passage is suspect. Robert Lincoln wrote in 1908 when he presented it to someone as a gift, "The MS. is a note made in preparing for one of the speeches in the joint-debate Campaign between Mr. Douglas & my father in 1858." *CW*, 2:482n. But the content of the fragment seems to match the

reports of Lincoln's closing campaign speeches, not those from July or from any of the individual debates.

81. The *CW* editors tentatively place this quotation about "the race of ambition" in December 1856, but they seem to be mistaken. In the undated fragment, Lincoln wrote that it had been exactly twenty-two years since he and Douglas "first became acquainted." Relying on an annotation that Lincoln had provided on the margin of a page from William Dean Howell's 1860 campaign biography indicating that he "first saw Douglas at Vandalia, Dec. 1834," the editors assume it meant the same thing as when he wrote "became acquainted" a few years earlier. However, Lincoln "saw" Douglas in late 1834, when he was a first-term legislator, but they were not "acquainted" until 1836, at the beginning of the next session of the state legislature. That would also explain why this fragment fits so much better with the various passages from Lincoln's closing speeches at the end of the 1858 campaign. See AL, Fragment on Stephen A. Douglas [December 1856?], *CW*, 2:382–83; and William Dean Howells, *Life of Abraham Lincoln* (1860; reprint Bloomington: Indiana University Press, 1960), facsimile 41.
82. AL, Fragment: Last Speech of the Campaign at Springfield, October 30, 1858, *CW*, 3:334–35. This fragment in particular seems to be a variant of the one about Douglas attributed (mistakenly in my opinion) to December 1856; AL to Bissell, Dubois, and Miller, May 28, 1859, *CW*, 2:382–83.
83. Lincoln was actually replying to a second note from Crittenden that the Kentuckian had sent on October 27, and that Herndon had opened and answered on his own while Lincoln was out campaigning. See AL to John Crittenden, November 4, 1858, *CW*, 3:335; and Herndon to Crittenden, November 1, 1858, in Herndon, *Herndon on Lincoln*, 12.
84. AL to Judd, November 15, 1858, *CW*, 3:336–37. In the letter declining to authorize $250 to help cover the central committee's debts, at least not until their "private matter" got "settled," Lincoln claimed, "I am the poorest hand living to get others to pay," and said he had "been on expenses so long" that he was "absolutely without money now for even household purposes." See AL to Judd, November 16, 1858, *CW*, 3:337.
85. AL to Anson Henry, November 19, 1858, *CW*, 3:339.
86. AL to Eleazar Paine, November 19, 1858, *CW*, 3:340.
87. AL to Henry, November 19, 1858, *CW*, 3:339.
88. AL to Judd, November 15, 1858, *CWS*, 34.
89. AL to Ray, November 20, 1858; and AL to Whitney, November 30, 1858, *CW*, 3:341, 343.
90. AL to Benjamin Clarke Lundy, November 26, 1858, *CW*, 3:342.
91. AL to Trumbull, December 11, 1858, *CW*, 3:344–45.
92. Josiah Lucas to Ozias Hatch, November 20, 1858, Hatch Papers, ALPLM.

CHAPTER 8: REPRESENTATIVE MAN

1. AL, Speech at Chicago, March 1, 1859, *CW*, 3:365–70.
2. AL to Henry Pierce and others, April 6, 1859, *CW*, 3:374–76.
3. The amendment to the Massachusetts Constitution, establishing a two-year waiting period for naturalized citizens to exercise their voting and officeholding rights, passed later in the year in a statewide referendum. See Christian G. Samito, *Becoming American Under Fire: Irish Americans, African Americans, and the Politics of Citizenship During the Civil War* (Ithaca, NY: Cornell University Press, 2009), 18.
4. Gustave Koerner to AL, April 4, 1859, Lincoln Papers, LC; AL to Koerner, April 11, 1859, *CW*, 3:376.
5. AL to Theodore Canisius, May 17, 1859, *CW*, 3:380.
6. Koerner to AL, April 4, 1859, Lincoln Papers, LC.
7. Norman Judd to AL, May 13, 1859, Lincoln Papers, LC. See also Harold Holzer, *Lincoln and the Power of the Press* (New York: Simon & Schuster, 2014), 186–94.
8. AL to Theodore Canisius, May 17, 1859, *CW*, 3:380.
9. AL to Mark Delahay, May 14, 1859, *CW*, 3:379.
10. AL to Nathan Sargent, June 23, 1859, *CW*, 3:387–88. Lincoln did hedge here to a degree, however, telling Sargent, perhaps disingenuously, "For my single self I would be willing to risk some Southern men without a platform; but I am satisfied that is not the case with the Republican party generally." Sargent had been a Whig journalist and House clerk when Lincoln was in Congress, and they had boarded together at Mrs. Sprigg's house. See Samuel C. Busey, *Personal Recollections and Reminiscences* (Washington, DC, 1895), 25–28. See also Josiah Lucas to AL, June 13, 1859, and Nathan Sargent to AL, June 13, 1859, Lincoln Papers, LC.
11. In his letter to Chase, Lincoln mistakenly identified that plank as one titled, "A repeal of the atrocious Fugitive Slave Law," a phrase repeated in several biographies but not actually based on the proceedings of the state convention, which met in Columbus on June 2, 1859. See "Republican State Convention: Official Report of Proceedings," *Wooster (OH) Republican*, June 9, 1859, 4:2–3. Lincoln had misunderstood how the Democratic newspaper in Springfield was quoting from another newspaper's coverage of the Ohio resolution. See "How Stands the Journal?," *Illinois State Register*, June 8, 1859, 2:1.
12. AL to Salmon Chase, June 9, 1859, *CW*, 3:384.
13. Chase to AL, June 13, 1859, Lincoln Papers, LC.
14. See Matthew Pinsker, "After 1850: Reassessing the Impact of the Fugitive Slave Law," in *Fugitive Slaves and Spaces of Freedom in North America, 1775–1860*, ed. D. A. Pargas (Gainesville: University Press of Florida, 2018), 93–115.

15. AL, Second Debate with Douglas at Freeport, August 21, 1858, *CW*, 3:41.
16. AL, Seventh Debate with Douglas at Alton, October 15, 1858, *CW*, 3:317.
17. Lincoln made the parsing over words (*a* versus *the*) explicit in a letter he sent to an Illinois abolitionist about six months after his exchange with Chase: AL to Alonzo Grover, January 15, 1860, *CW*, 3:514.
18. Salmon Chase to AL, June 13, 1859, Lincoln Papers, LC.
19. AL to Chase, June 30, 1859, *CW*, 3:386.
20. AL to Schuyler Colfax ("For your eye only"), July 6, 1859, *CW*, 3:390–91.
21. Colfax to AL, July 14, 1859, Lincoln Papers, LC.
22. AL to Thomas Pickett, April 16, 1859, *CW*, 3:377.
23. AL, Notes for Speeches at Columbus and Cincinnati [September 16, 17, 1859], *CW*, 3:435–36. See also AL, Speech at Cincinnati, September 17, 1859, *CW*, 3:460–61.
24. AL to Chase, September 21, 1859, *CW*, 3:471.
25. AL, Speech at Cincinnati, September 17, 1859, *CW*, 3:454.
26. AL, Speech at Leavenworth, Kansas, December 3, 1859, *CW*, 3:502.
27. AL to Tom Corwin ("Confidential"), October 9, 1859, PAL. This letter first became available to scholars in the early 2000s. As biographer Ronald White notes, this was the only time in Lincoln's writings that he employed the term *idiotic*. Ronald C. White, Jr., *A. Lincoln: A Biography* (New York: Random House, 2009), 302.
28. Republicans won important statewide victories in Indiana, Iowa, Minnesota, Ohio, and Pennsylvania. The results in the key state of New York were more mixed but still promising for Republican prospects in 1860, provided that they could find a way to neutralize the lingering influence of the American party.
29. AL to James Miller, July 11, 1859, *CWS*, 40; William Plato to Ozias Hatch, July 26, 1859, Hatch Papers, ALPLM. See Gabor S. Boritt, "Was Lincoln a Vulnerable Candidate in 1860?," *Civil War History* 27 (1981): 32–48.
30. Norman Judd to AL, December 1, 1859, Lincoln Papers, LC.
31. AL to Judd, December 14, 1859, *CW*, 3:509. For Judd's claim, see diary entry for November 22, 1863, in John Hay, *Inside Lincoln's White House: The Complete Civil War Diary of John Hay*, ed. Michael Burlingame and John R. Turner Ettlinger (Carbondale: Southern Illinois University Press, 1997), 116.
32. AL to Jesse Fell, December 20, 1859 (with autobiographical sketch), *CW*, 3:511–12.
33. John Wentworth to AL, February 7, 1860, Lincoln Papers, LC. Lincoln's letter to Wentworth on February 5 has not yet been recovered.
34. AL to Judd, February 9, 1860, *CW*, 3:517.
35. AL to Wentworth, February 9, 1860, *CWSS*, 18–19.
36. "The Presidency—Abraham Lincoln," *Chicago Tribune*, February 16, 1860, in

Abraham Lincoln: A Press Portrait, ed. Herbert Mitgang (Athens: University of Georgia Press, 1956), 153; Wentworth to AL, February 27, 1860, Lincoln Papers, LC.

37. "Our Presidential Candidates," New York *Evening Post*, February 1860.
38. Ralph Waldo Emerson, *Representative Men: Seven Lectures* (1850; reprint Cambridge, MA: Harvard University Press, 1996).
39. Mark Delahay to AL, November 14, 1859, Lincoln Papers, LC.
40. AL, Speech at Cooper Institute, February 27, 1860, *CW*, 3:522–50. See Harold Holzer, *Lincoln at Cooper Union: The Speech That Made Abraham Lincoln President* (New York: Simon & Schuster, 2004).
41. AL to Mary Lincoln, March 4, 1860, *CWS*, 49.
42. John Savage, *Our Living Representative Men: From Official and Original Sources* (Philadelphia: Childs & Peterson, 1860).
43. AL to Samuel Galloway, March 24, 1860, *CW*, 4:34.
44. "The Winning Man: Abraham Lincoln," *Chicago Press and Tribune*, May 15, 1860, in Mitgang, *Press Portrait*, 164–67.
45. Lyman Trumbull to AL, April 24, 1860, Lincoln Papers, LC.
46. AL to Trumbull, April 29, 1860, *CW*, 4:45.
47. AL to Richard Corwine, May 2, 1860, *CW*, 4:47.
48. David Herbert Donald, *Lincoln* (New York: Simon & Schuster, 1995), 244–46.
49. For "no offence" [*sic*], see AL to Mark Delahay, May 12, 1860, *CW*, 4:49. On "money basis," see AL to Delahay, March 16, 1860, *CW*, 4:32. On "fate of John Brown," see AL to E. Stafford, March 17, 1860, *CW*, 4:33.
50. Jesse Dubois to AL, May 13, 1860, Lincoln Papers, LC. AL to John Wentworth ("Show this letter to Judge Davis"), February 13, 1860, *CWS*, 48; David Davis to AL, April 23, 1860, Lincoln Papers, LC. See also Willard L. King, *Lincoln's Manager: David Davis* (Cambridge, MA: Harvard University Press, 1960).
51. Charles Ray to AL, May 14, 1860, Lincoln Papers, LC.
52. Diary entry for November 22, 1863, in Hay, *Inside Lincoln's White House*, 116.
53. Judd to AL, May 16, 1860, Lincoln Papers, LC.
54. Horace Greeley, ed., *Proceedings of the First Three Republican National Conventions 1856, 1860 and 1864* (Minneapolis: Charles W. Johnson, 1893); see also Michael Burlingame, *Abraham Lincoln: A Life*, 2 vols. (2008; Knox College online edition), 1:1642–716.
55. Judd to AL, January 4, 1864, Lincoln Papers, LC.
56. David Davis to Sarah Davis (Springfield), August 8, 1847, David Davis Family Papers, ALPLM.
57. See Michael F. Holt, *The Election of 1860: "A Campaign Fraught with Consequences"* (Lawrence: University Press of Kansas, 2017).

58. Speed to AL, May 19, 1860, Lincoln Papers, LC.
59. Speed had been one of those members of the Southern Opposition whom Lincoln had been warning the Republicans against fusing with in the months prior to the 1860 contest. Speed supported the Constitutional Unionists in the four-way presidential election.
60. William Cullen Bryant, editor of the *New York Evening Post*, was just one of many pundits and politicos who were warning Lincoln to keep quiet. See Bryant to AL, June 16, 1860, Lincoln Papers, LC; and AL to Bryant, June 28, 1860, *CW*, 4:81. See also Gil Troy, *See How They Ran: The Changing Role of the Presidential Candidate* (New York: Free Press, 1991), chap. 4.
61. Elihu Washburne in *Cong. Globe*, 36th Cong., 1st Sess., 377–80 (May 29, 1860). See also Thomas A. Horrocks, *Lincoln's Campaign Biographies* (Carbondale: Southern Illinois University Press, 2014), 50.
62. The bill was actually sent to Lincoln from Cincinnati, Ohio, for charges related to his speaking tour in late 1859—but clearly the proprietors were trying to take advantage of the Springfield attorney's newfound celebrity as a presidential candidate. See AL to William Dickson, June 7, 1860, *CW*, 4:72–73.
63. Lincoln was particularly adamant about the editing of his New York speech, claiming, "I do not wish the sense changed, or modified, to a hair's breadth," and demanding to see the "proof-sheets" before any publication. AL to Charles Nott, May 31, 1860, *CW*, 4:58–59; Autobiography Written for John L. Scripps [c. June 1860], *CW*, 4:60–68.
64. AL to Samuel Haycraft ("Private"), June 4, 1860, *CW*, 4:69–70; Haycraft to AL, October 26, 1860, Lincoln Papers, LC.
65. AL to George Fogg ("Private"), August 16 and 29, 1860, *CW*, 4:96–97, 102. Lincoln apologized to Haycraft for getting him mixed up in this matter, although the Kentuckian got concerned himself, because he thought Lincoln was trying to blame him for the leak. Haycraft revealed something about the norms of political communication by trying to confirm his understanding of the difference between a "private" letter and a "confidential" one, explaining that since Lincoln had only marked his letter as "private," Haycraft felt free to share it with others as long as he refrained from publishing it. See AL to Haycraft, August 16 and 23, 1860, *CW*, 4:97, 99, and Haycraft to AL, August 19, 1860, Lincoln Papers, LC.
66. John Nicolay, Form Letter to Applicants for Biographical Data [c. June 1860], *CW*, 4:60; AL, Autobiography Written for John L. Scripps [c. June 1860], *CW*, 4:60–68; and AL to Samuel Galloway ("Especially Confidential"), June 19, 1860, *CW*, 4:79–80. See also Horrocks, *Lincoln's Campaign Biographies*, 51–52.
67. William Herndon to Lyman Trumbull, June 19, 1860, in Herndon, *Herndon*

on Lincoln: Letters, ed. Douglas L. Wilson and Rodney O. Davis (Urbana: University of Illinois Press, 2016), 13.

68. AL to David Davis, May 26, 1860, *CWSS*, 20.

69. AL to Leonard Swett, May 30, 1860, *CW*, 4:57. AL [to Swett, June 1860], PAL. The identification of this brief note is described in a press release from PAL, March 8, 2014.

70. AL to Richard Thompson, July 10, 1860, *CW*, 4:82–83. Lincoln began the correspondence with Thompson in May 1860 after conferring with Indiana politician Schuyler Colfax. Thompson—unlike Lincoln—was a true conservative and utterly indifferent to the slavery question. Eric Foner quotes the Indiana politician, in *Free Soil, Free Labor, Free Men* (New York: Oxford University Press, 1971), as denying that slavery even presented "a *moral* question" (188–89). In their exchange, Lincoln also urged Thompson to consult with Henry Winter Davis of Maryland, a former Know Nothing and leader in the Southern Opposition who was a cousin of David Davis. AL to Colfax, May 26, 1860, *CW*, 4:54; Thompson to AL, June 12, 1860, AL to Thompson, June 18, 1860, and Thompson to AL, July 6, 1860, all in Lincoln Papers, LC. Lincoln's original contact with Thompson, dated May 26, 1860, has not yet been discovered and may well have been destroyed. When Nicolay recalled this episode in an undated essay, "Lincoln in the Campaign of 1860," he emphasized Lincoln's need to keep his contacts with former Know Nothings quiet. John Nicolay, *An Oral History of Abraham Lincoln: John G. Nicolay's Interviews and Essays*, ed. Michael Burlingame (Carbondale: Southern Illinois University Press, 1996), 93–95.

71. Thompson to AL, July 6, 1860; AL, Instructions for John G. Nicolay [c. July 16, 1860], *CW*, 4:83.

72. Carl Schurz to AL, May 22, 1860, Lincoln Papers, LC.

73. AL to Schurz, June 18, 1860, *CW*, 4:78.

74. Carl Schurz to Margarethe Schurz, July 25, 1860, reprinted in *Wisconsin Then and Now*, January 1963, with German-English translation available online from the Wisconsin Historical Society Archives. A slightly different translation appears in Carl Schurz, *Speeches, Correspondence, and Political Writings of Carl Schurz*, ed. Frederic Bancroft, 6 vols. (New York: G. P. Putnam's Sons, 1913), 1:120–21.

75. Schurz to Schurz, July 25, 1860. Lincoln had used the term *drones* previously in 1849 letters to William Preston and Duff Green; see *CW*, 2:49–50.

76. William Herndon to Sydney Howard Gay, August 10, 1860, in Herndon, *Herndon on Lincoln*, 14.

77. Philip S. Klein, *President James Buchanan: A Biography* (University Park: Penn State University Press, 1962), 347–48.

78. Stephen Douglas to Charles Lanphier, July 5, 1860, in Douglas, *Letters*, 498.

79. Douglas, Speech at Concord, NH, July 31, 1860, in "Movements of Senator Douglas," *New York Times*, August 3, 1860, 2:1–3.
80. Douglas, Speech at Concord, NH, July 31, 1860. See also "The President's Warfare upon Mr. Douglas," *Buffalo Daily Courier*, August 11, 1860, 2:1.
81. James Buchanan to Gerard Hallock, August 11, 1860, Dickinson College Archives and Special Collections, House Divided Project at Dickinson College.
82. Buchanan to William Smith, August 11, 1860, quoted in "The President's Warfare upon Mr. Douglas," *Buffalo Daily Courier*, August 11, 1860, 2:1. See also Matthew Pinsker, "'General Jackson Is Dead': Dissecting a Popular Anecdote of Nineteenth-Century Party Leadership," in *The Worlds of James Buchanan and Thaddeus Stevens: Place, Personality, and Politics in the Civil War Era*, ed. Michael J. Birkner, Randall M. Miller, and John W. Quist (Baton Rouge: Louisiana State University Press, 2019), 82–108.
83. AL to Thurlow Weed, August 17, 1860, *CW*, 4:97–98.
84. AL to Caleb Smith, May 26, 1860, Lyman Trumbull, May 26, 1860, and Elihu Washburne, May 26, 1860, all in *CW*, 4:55–56.
85. AL to Anson Henry, *CW*, 4:81–82.
86. AL to Simeon Francis, *CW*, 4:89–90.
87. AL to Thurlow Weed, *CW*, 4:98; AL to Abraham Jonas, July 21, 1860, *CW*, 4:85–86; and AL to John Hill [with fragments], September 1860, *CW*, 4:104–8.
88. AL to Alexander McClure, August 30, 1860, PAL. This note has only recently been rediscovered and was not included in any of the published volumes of *CW*.
89. AL to Hannibal Hamlin, July 18, 1860, *CW*, 4:84; AL to Hamlin, September 4, 1860, *CW*, 4:110.
90. AL to William Fithian, August 15, 1860, *CW*, 4:95. In this case, Lincoln's intervention was unsuccessful. The Democrats won the legislative seat from Vermilion—though Trumbull ultimately won reelection anyway.
91. Henry Wilson to AL, August 25, 1860, Lincoln Papers, LC; AL to Wilson, September 1, 1860, *CW*, 4:109.
92. AL to John Pettit, September 14, 1860, *CW*, 4:115. Pettit's original letter to Lincoln has not been discovered, but his follow-up to Lincoln's request is available; John Pettit to AL, September 29, 1860, PAL. Pettit was originally from New York and was friendly with Mark Delahay, Lincoln's conservative-minded political ally in the Kansas territory. In June Delahay had told Lincoln that Pettit was "a strange old Cock" but that they could count on him as a reliable "Union man." Delahay to AL, July 9, 1860, Lincoln Papers, LC. It appears that Lincoln had first met Pettit during his 1859 speaking tour in Kansas, one that Delahay had helped arrange. Senator Pettit made his infamous statement about the meaning of the Declaration's preamble during the

debates over the Kansas-Nebraska Act. *Cong. Globe*, 33rd Cong., 1st Sess., 214 (February 20, 1854). Sometime during Douglas's bitter feud with Buchanan, however, Pettit broke with him and subsequently received appointment as chief justice of the U.S. Courts in Kansas (1859–61). During the summer of 1860, newspapers across the country featured excerpts from a letter by Judge Pettit condemning Douglas and endorsing Breckinridge but also including this provocative opinion: "It is said that this policy will elect Lincoln. Let it be so, rather than Douglas should succeed. I believe that Lincoln is a more conservative and sounder national man than Douglas." "Pettit on the Presidency," *Freedom's Champion* (Atchison, KS), August 18, 1860. The significance of Lincoln's secret exchange with Pettit during the 1860 campaign seems to have escaped nearly all previous Lincoln scholars.

93. Seward to AL, October 8, 1860, Lincoln Papers, LC; AL to Seward, October 12, 1860, *CW*, 4:126–27. The written exchange between Lincoln and Seward does not actually identify the subject of Lincoln's concern. In his short note, Seward claimed that he had done better on the unnamed subject of Lincoln's "uneasiness" in a previous speech at Dubuque, Iowa. A comparison of Seward's speeches at Dubuque and Chicago suggests pretty clearly, however, that Lincoln had wanted a more definitive statement on the Republican position regarding noninterference with slavery in the existing slave states. See "The Republicans in Council," *Chicago Press and Tribune*, October 3, 1860; and "Mr. Seward in the West," *New York Times*, September 27, 1860. See also Michael Burlingame, *Abraham Lincoln: A Life* (2008; Knox College online edition), 1:1801–7.
94. AL to Seward, October 12, 1860, *CW*, 4:126–27. See also Holt, *Election of 1860*, 168–71.
95. Robert W. Johannsen, *Stephen A. Douglas* (Urbana: University of Illinois Press, 1973), 795. Douglas biographer Martin Quitt describes this period as "a strenuous stretch of constant movement." See Martin H. Quitt, *Stephen A. Douglas and Antebellum Democracy* (New York: Cambridge University Press, 2012), 162.
96. John W. Forney, Eulogy upon the Hon. Stephen A. Douglas, July 3, 1861 (Philadelphia: Ringwalt, 1861), 11; and Henry Wilson, *The Rise and Fall of the Slave Power in America*, 2 vols. (Boston: J. R. Osgood, 1872), 2:700.
97. "Mr. Douglas and the Lecompton Constitution," *New York Herald*, October 20, 1860, 4; "STARTLING DISCLOSURES: Douglas Responsible for the Lecompton Constitution; His Pledge to Support It; Violation of His Pledge and Treachery to His Friends; Read! Read! Read!," *Chicago Tribune*, October 12, 1860, 2:5–7. The story had first appeared on October 7 in the *New Orleans Delta*. For more details, see Pinsker, "'Jackson Is Dead.'"

98. "The Kansas Question as Between President Buchanan and Gov. Walker," *Daily Cleveland Herald*, December 3, 1857.
99. *Western Argus* quoted in "Judge Douglas and the Lecompton Constitution," *National Intelligencer*, October 31, 1860.
100. For the importance of the Lecompton crisis on the Democratic Party, see Kenneth M. Stampp, *America in 1857: A Nation on the Brink* (New York: Oxford University Press, 1990); "Speech of the Hon. S. A. Douglas," *Illinois State Register*, October 19, 1860, 2:2–4.
101. Mary Lincoln to Hannah Shearer, October 20, 1860, in Lincoln, *Mary Todd Lincoln: Her Life and Letters*, ed. Justin G. Turner and Linda Levitt Turner (New York: Knopf, 1972), 66.
102. Grace Bedell to "Hon. A.B. Lincoln," October 15, 1860, and AL to Bedell ("Private"), October 19, 1860, *CW*, 4:129–30.
103. AL to John Brockman, September 25, 1860, *CW*, 4:121.
104. AL to David Hunter ("Private & confidential"), October 26, 1860, *CW*, 4:132. Hunter had known Lincoln for years, though he had supported Justin Butterfield over Lincoln in 1849 for the Land Office position.
105. AL to George Prentice ("Private & confidential"), October 29, 1860, *CW*, 4:134–35; Truman Smith to AL, November 7, 1860, Lincoln Papers, LC; AL to Smith, November 10, 1860, *CW*, 4:138–39. Smith had sent another message urging conciliation prior to the election that has not yet been found. That was the one delivered by businessman Henry Sanford of Connecticut on election eve. John Nicolay wrote a contemporary memorandum of Sanford's conversation with Lincoln, including the quoted line about standing by the men who elected him. See Nicolay, Memorandum, November 5, 1860, in Nicolay, *With Lincoln in the White House: Letters, Memoranda, and Other Writings of John G. Nicolay, 1860–1865*, ed. Michael Burlingame (Carbondale: Southern Illinois University Press, 2000), 7–8.
106. In 1860 Black men were eligible to vote in five New England states: Connecticut, Maine, Massachusetts, Rhode Island, and Vermont. Some Black men were also voting in New York in 1860, but with restrictions based on property holdings.
107. There are competing reports about the totals for the results in Missouri, but regardless Douglas defeated Bell by mere hundreds of votes. See Holt, *Election of 1860*, chap. 8, "America Votes," and app. A, "Election Returns."
108. "Complimentary Serenade," *Charleston Mercury*, November 7, 1860. For Boyce's earlier campaign speech, see "Another Disunion Blast: Hon. W. W. Boyce, of South Carolina, in Favor of Dissolving the Union," *New York Times*, August 11, 1860.

CHAPTER 9: LINCOLN'S UNION

1. AL to Truman Smith ("Private & confidential"), November 10, 1860, *CW*, 4:138; AL to Nathaniel Paschall ("Private & confidential"), November 16, 1860, *CW*, 4:139; "Mr. Lincoln's Tact," *Illinois Journal*, November 26, 1860, 1:2.
2. Lincoln admitted his election night anxieties to Gideon Welles in the summer of 1862. Welles first recounted the story in his diary on August 15, 1862; see Welles, *The Civil War Diary of Gideon Welles, Lincoln's Secretary of the Navy*, ed. William E. Gienapp and Erica L. Gienapp (Urbana: University of Illinois Press, 2014), 7. The card where Lincoln compiled the two columns of his cabinet prospects is undated but appears in the Lincoln Papers, LC, along with a note from Zachariah Chandler and others from January 21, 1861. David Herbert Donald, however, argues convincingly that Lincoln prepared this card on November 6, 1860; see Donald, *Lincoln* (New York: Simon & Schuster, 1995), 261–62, though he interprets the episode differently.
3. AL to Joshua Speed, November 19, 1860, *CW*, 4:140–41; "Movements of Lincoln and Hamlin," *New York Times*, November 27, 1860, 5:2; and various daily entries for November 21–26, 1860, in *Lincoln Log: A Daily Chronology of the Life of Abraham Lincoln*, thelincolnlog.org.
4. The first public notice of this new beard had occurred just a few days earlier, in a Bloomington-area newspaper that suggested Lincoln "looks younger than usual" because of "a beautiful pair of whiskers." The correspondent was not really impressed, however, writing, "Still, there is no disguising the fact that he is homely." See *Lexington (IL) Weekly Globe*, November 22, 1860, quoted in *CW*, 4:144n.
5. See Harold Holzer, *Lincoln Seen and Heard* (Lawrence: University Press of Kansas, 2000). But for the cosmopolitan symbolism of Lincoln's new bearded image, see also Louise L. Stevenson, *Lincoln in the Atlantic World* (New York: Cambridge University Press, 2015), 96–103.
6. In his memoir, Henry Adams, grandson of a president (John Quincy Adams), described Seward as he appeared at this time, around December 1860, as "a wise macaw" with "a beaked nose . . . and perpetual cigar." Adams, *The Education of Henry Adams* (Boston: Houghton Mifflin, 1918), chap. 7.
7. It was characteristic of Lincoln that he sent, via Hamlin and Trumbull, two separate offer letters to Seward, one essentially public and another confidential one (to help explain the meaning of the other). AL to Hamlin ("Private"), December 8, 1860; AL to Seward, December 8, 1860; AL to Seward ("Private & confidential"), December 8, 1860; and AL to Trumbull ("Private"), December 8, 1860; all in *CW*, 4:147–49.

8. See also Michael Robinson, "William Henry Seward and the Onset of the Secession Crisis," *Civil War History* 59 (March 2013): 32–66.
9. AL, Memorandum on the Charges Against Simon Cameron [December 31, 1860], *CW*, 4:165. This document is undated and appears to be a copy in John Nicolay's hand of a missing original created by Lincoln as part of a series of notes he was constructing on the pros and cons of the Cameron appointment.
10. AL to William Bryant, December 29, 1860, *CW*, 4:163.
11. AL to William Seward ("Private"), January 12, 1861, *CW*, 4:173.
12. See Harold Holzer, *Lincoln President-Elect: Abraham Lincoln and the Great Secession Winter, 1860–1861* (New York: Simon & Schuster, 2008); and Russell A. McClintock, *Lincoln and the Decision for War: The Northern Response to Secession* (Chapel Hill: University of North Carolina Press, 2008).
13. AL to John Defrees, December 18, 1860, *CW*, 4:155. Lincoln also put a more refined version of these questions into the *Illinois Journal* on December 12, 1860, *CW*, 4:150.
14. AL to Seward, December 29, 1860, and January 12, 1861, *CW*, 4:164, 173. Gilmer declined Lincoln's request for a visit by claiming it would "not be useful." Gilmer to AL, December 29, 1860, Lincoln Papers, LC. But Lincoln's original invitation, dated December 21, apparently was not preserved, and there's some uncertainty about exactly what Gilmer understood the purpose of the meeting to be. Historian Michael Burlingame believes that Gilmer declined totally unaware that the visit was about cabinet selection; Burlingame, *Abraham Lincoln: A Life*, 2 vols. (2008; Knox College online edition), 1:724. However, Gilmer himself claimed right after the war that Lincoln was explicit about offering him a cabinet post as late as March 1861; "Letter from Hon. John A. Gilmer," *Raleigh (NC) Progress*, August 16, 1865.
15. AL, Passage Written for Lyman Trumbull's Speech at Springfield, November 20, 1860, *CW*, 4:141–42; AL to Henry Raymond, November 28, 1860, *CW*, 4:145–46.
16. AL to Alexander Stephens, November 30 and December 22, 1860, *CW*, 4:146, 160.
17. AL to Trumbull ("Private & confidential"), December 10, 1860; AL to William Kellogg ("Private & confidential"), December 11, 1860; AL to Elihu Washburne ("Private & Confidential"), December 13, 1860; AL to John Defrees ("Confidential"), December 18, 1860; AL to Trumbull ("Confidential"), December 17, 1860; all *CW*, 4:149–55.
18. AL to Kellogg ("Private & confidential"), December 11, 1860; John Gilmer to AL, December 10, 1860, Lincoln Papers, LC; and AL to Gilmer ("Strictly

confidential"), December 15, 1860, *CW*, 4:151–53. Lincoln would have encountered personal liberty statutes in 1847, for example, when he unsuccessfully represented a Kentucky slaveowner seeking his runaways. He was obviously playing coy and being intentionally nonresponsive with Gilmer.

19. AL, "House Divided" Speech, June 16, 1858, *CW*, 2:468; AL to Salmon Chase, June 9, 1859, *CW*, 3:384; AL to Chase, June 30, 1859, *CW*, 3:386.
20. AL, Resolutions Drawn Up for Republican Members of the Senate Committee of Thirteen [December 20, 1860], *CW*, 4:156–57; Seward to AL, December 26, 1860, Lincoln Papers, LC.
21. Chase to AL, January 28, 1861, Lincoln Papers, LC.
22. See Michael Robinson, "William Henry Seward and the Onset of the Secession Crisis," *Civil War History* 59 (March 2013): 32–66; and Robinson, *Union Indivisible: Secession and the Politics of Slavery in the Border South* (Chapel Hill: University of North Carolina Press, 2017).
23. AL to James Hale ("Confidential"), January 11, 1861, *CW*, 4:172. Lincoln added in this letter that he believed there was "but one compromise which would really settle the slavery question, and that would be a prohibition against acquiring any more territory."
24. William Herndon to Wendell Phillips, December 28, 1860, January 12 and February 1, 1861; Herndon to [Samuel E.?] Sewall, February 1, 1861; and Herndon to Edward L. Pierce, February 18, 1861, in Herndon, *Herndon on Lincoln: Letters*, ed. Douglas L. Wilson and Rodney O. Davis (Urbana: University of Illinois Press, 2016), 15–18.
25. For Herndon's escalating troubles, see David Herbert Donald, *Lincoln's Herndon: A Biography* (1948; reprint New York: Da Capo Press, 1989), but also Michael Burlingame, "Why a New Biography of William Herndon Is Needed," *Journal of the Abraham Lincoln Association* 35 (Summer 2014): 55–66.
26. Norman Judd to William Butler, January 12, 1860, Butler Papers, Chicago History Museum.
27. Elihu Washburne to Charles Ray, January 2, 1861, Ray Papers, Huntington Library, Pasadena, CA; Trumbull to Butler, January 9, 1861, Butler Papers, Chicago History Museum.
28. Joseph Casey to David Davis, January 22, 1861, David Davis Family Papers, ALPLM. Despite his growing worries about Cameron's place in the cabinet, Casey made no reference to any arrangements made at the Chicago convention. In an earlier letter to Leonard Swett, however, he did allude to the "conversations and understandings" that he thought he had secured from Davis and Swett and with which he believed Lincoln seemed less than "<u>fully acquainted</u>." Swett subsequently explained it this way to Lincoln: "The truth

is, at Chicago we thought the Cameron influence was the controlling element & tried to procure that rather than the factions. The negotiations we had with them, so far as I can judge was one of the reasons, which induced the Cameron leaders to throw the bulk of that force to you." Casey to Swett, November 27, 1860, and Swett to AL, November 30, 1860, both in Lincoln Papers, LC. The real point here is that nobody treated anything that happened at Chicago as fully binding on Lincoln, and the president-elect himself seemed totally prepared to ignore any alleged deals.

29. Lyman Trumbull to Jesse Dubois, March 22, 1861, Dubois Papers, ALPLM.
30. AL to Seward, February 1, 1861, *CW*, 4:183.
31. Chase wrote to Lincoln from Columbus, Ohio, on January 28, 1861, Lincoln Papers, LC. Lincoln surely had received his warning about New Mexico when he wrote Seward from Springfield on February 1, 1861.
32. AL, Farewell Address at Springfield, February 11, 1861, *CW*, 4:190–91.
33. William Herndon to Edward Pierce, February 18, 1861, in Herndon, *Herndon on Lincoln*, 17. Herndon claimed this was the "substance" of what Lincoln had told him in private just about a week earlier.
34. AL, Fragment of a Speech Intended for Kentuckians [c. February 12, 1861], *CW*, 4:200–1.
35. Grace Bedell to William Herndon, December 14, 1866, in Douglas L. Wilson and Rodney O. Davis, eds., *Herndon's Informants: Letters, Interviews, and Statements About Abraham Lincoln* (Urbana: University of Illinois Press, 2020), 517.
36. AL, Address to New Jersey Senate, February 21, 1861, *CW*, 4:235–36.
37. AL, Address to New Jersey Senate, February 21, 1861, *CW*, 4:235–36.
38. Apparently Lincoln was approached in Philadelphia on Thursday evening by both Allan Pinkerton and Frederick Seward, each relaying separate warnings about the Baltimore plot. These narrative details, however, come from a cascade of sometimes self-serving—and occasionally contradictory—recollections. The most provocative account comes from one attributed to Lincoln himself by author Benson J. Lossing, who claims that he interviewed the president on this subject in December 1864 at the White House along with Rep. Isaac N. Arnold. This is the main source for depicting Lincoln as being reluctant to appear to be sneaking into Washington late on Friday night. Lossing, *Pictorial History of the Civil War in the United States* (Philadelphia: George W. Childs, 1866), 1:279–80, and Arnold, *The History of Abraham Lincoln, and the Overthrow of Slavery* (Chicago: Clarke, 1866), 169–71.
39. There are also a variety of conflicting accounts about Lincoln's arrival in Washington on February 23, 1861. Some sources suggest that Seward was with Washburne at the railroad depot as they greeted the president-elect

together. Others, most notably Washburne himself, explain that Seward ended up meeting them at the hotel instead. See Walter Stahr, *Seward: Lincoln's Indispensable Man* (New York: Simon & Schuster, 2012), 601–2n. On Seward's announcement as secretary, see numerous newspaper articles such as "Mr. Lincoln's Secretary of State," *Albany Evening Journal*, reprinted in *Nashville Union and American*, January 18, 1861.

40. AL, First Inaugural Address—First Edition and Revisions, *CW*, 4:249–62; AL, Final Text, *CW*, 4:262–71.
41. Salmon Chase to AL, January 28, 1861, Lincoln Papers, LC.
42. Seward to AL, February 24, 1861, Special Collections, University of Rochester Library, Rochester, NY. This confidential cover letter from Seward is not part of the Lincoln Papers at LC, though several pages of Seward's corrections (including his famous alternate final paragraph) are there. Nicolay and Hay thanked Frederick Seward for sharing a copy of Seward's cover letter and other related documents with them; John Nicolay and John Hay, *Abraham Lincoln: A History*, 10 vols. (New York: Century, 1890), 3:319–21. They presumably kept the corrections in the collection but then returned the cover note, which now resides at the University of Rochester.
43. "Thirty-Sixth Congress, Second Session, Thursday, January 3, 1861," *National Republican* (Washington, DC), January 4, 1861. An edited and much more complete version of this speech appears in *Cong. Globe*, 36th Cong., 2nd Sess. (January 3 1861), appendix, "State of the Union, Speech of Hon. S.A. Douglas, pp. 35–41."
44. Seward to AL, February 24, 1861, Special Collections, University of Rochester Library.
45. The content of Campbell's memorandum did not appear until 1920, but according to the text, it was "made and preserved" by the justice in February 1861 sometime shortly after the dinner. Henry G. Connor, *John Archibald Campbell: Associate Justice of the United States Supreme Court, 1853–1861* (Boston: Houghton Mifflin, 1920), 116.
46. Martin Crawford to Robert Toombs, March 6, 1861; and Crawford, John Forsyth, and A. B. Roman to Toombs, March 8, 1861, both in Frederic Bancroft, *The Life of William H. Seward*, 2 vols. (New York: Harper & Brothers, 1900), 2:107–10. Crawford, Forsyth, and Roman were three Confederate agents sent to the nation's capital by Confederate secretary of state Toombs at the end of February to attempt to open negotiations with the federal government. Their contemporary descriptions of Seward's views appear based on a combination of firsthand interactions and secondhand reports; hence their qualification about conveying the "tenor" of his statements.
47. Seward to AL, April 1, 1861, *CW*, 4:317n. Seward's apparent transformation

from radical to "conservative" perplexed a number of his contemporaries and many historians ever since. See Mark J. Stegmaier, ed., *Henry Adams in the Secession Crisis: Dispatches to the Boston Daily Advertiser, December 1860–March 1861* (Baton Rouge: Louisiana State University Press, 2012).

48. "Letter from a National Union Man to Hon. William H. Seward," *New York Times*, February 28, 1861, 2:1–2. Francis Lieber later popularized the phrase "No Party Now" in his midwar pamphlet under the name "No Party Now but All for Our Country" (1863). See Adam I. P. Smith, *No Party Now: Politics in the Civil War North* (New York: Oxford University Press, 2006).

49. "One who loves his Country" to AL, Boston, March 5, 1861, Lincoln Papers, LC. The correspondent urged Lincoln to "dissolve your Cabinet and place in it Wm H. Seward, Chas. F. Adams, John Bell, J. C Breckenridge S. A. Douglass & Crittenden," promising that if he did so, "every union man woman & child from one extreme of the country to the other will rise up & call you blessed."

50. [Joseph Howard, Jr.], "Highly Important News: Secret Departure of the President from Harrisburgh," *New York Times*, February 25, 1861. Howard later freely admitted his fake news scoop in an 1884 interview: "I asked myself what possible disguise could Lincoln get in Harrisburg, and, as I wrote on, I imagined him in a Scotch cap, which would be about as marked an opposite to his high silk hat as one could conceive, and a military cloak, which I borrowed in my imagination, from the shapely shoulders of Col. Sumner, who was traveling with the president-elect." Quoted in *Lincoln Lore* No. 1424, October 1956. See also Harold Holzer, *Lincoln and the Power of the Press* (New York: Simon & Schuster, 2014), 286–87.

51. According to Ohio congressman Albert Riddle's recollection, Lincoln invited the prospective cabinet officers to a dinner without announcing that it was their debut as a cabinet: "A thing much talked of at the time in the Capital was that Mr. Lincoln, on Sunday the 3d, gave a dinner to seven gentlemen, and they happened to be those whose names were sent to the Senate the next day." Albert G. Riddle, *Recollections of War Times* (New York: G. P. Putnam's Sons, 1895), 12. Contemporary newspapers do not appear to describe this dinner, but they do at least corroborate that with the arrival in town of Gideon Welles on Sunday, March 3, 1861, all the future cabinet officers were in Washington by that Sunday evening; see *Baltimore Daily Exchange*, March 4, 1861.

52. AL to Seward, March 4, 1861, *CW*, 4:273.

53. Chase recalled these circumstances in a series of biographical letters to John T. Trowbridge written in late 1863 and early 1864, when he was attempting to launch a presidential campaign to succeed Lincoln. He claimed, somewhat improbably, that Lincoln had not secured his assent before sending his name forward as the Treasury nominee and that he only reluctantly agreed to serve

in order to save the president this initial "embarrassment." Jacob W. Schuckers, *The Life and Public Services of Salmon Portland Chase* (New York: Appleton, 1874), 207.

54. Entry for March 1861 in Adam Gurowski, *Diary from March 4, 1861 to November 12, 1862* (Boston: Lee & Shepard, 1862), 16. Charles Francis Adams, Sr., a Republican congressman from Massachusetts, dismissed the cabinet as a "motley mixture" in his diary, "containing one statesman, one politician, two jobber[s], one intriguer, and two respectable old gentlemen." Diary entry for March 5, 1861, Adams Sr. Papers, Massachusetts Historical Society, Boston.

55. AL, First Inaugural Address, March 4, 1861, *CW*, 4:262–71. Chapter 5 describes how Archibald Williams drafted a version of this sentence for an early Republican organizing effort in Quincy in July 1855, one that Williams had produced most likely after consulting with both Lincoln and Charles Sumner (who was in court at Chicago at that time) and also after reading an earlier iteration of similar language from an 1840 speech by Daniel Webster. Lincoln had pointedly endorsed this Quincy platform for Owen Lovejoy in a private letter from August 1855 and then had taken the document to one of the first statewide organizational meetings for the Illinois Republican party (at Decatur in February 1856), where he helped get the delegates to endorse it. Lincoln then repeated this sentence about Republicans disclaiming any intention of interfering with slavery in the existing slave states throughout the 1858 campaign against Stephen Douglas.

56. According to John Hay, Lincoln did claim after the war had begun that during the heart of the secession crisis, he had offered "Southern Pseudo Unionists" a cooling-off proposal—namely to withdraw from Fort Sumter in exchange for keeping states like Virginia out of the emerging Confederacy. But there is not much else to document that he was serious or persistent about such a potential deal. Diary entry for October 22, 1861, in John Hay, *Inside Lincoln's White House: The Complete Civil War Diary of John Hay*, ed. Michael Burlingame and John R. Turner Ettlinger (Carbondale: Southern Illinois University Press, 1997), 28.

57. The *New York Herald* commented sharply on Lincoln's "cunning" regarding compromise: "Not a single pledge or proposition, with regard to the future, is contained in the Inaugural Message, from beginning to end." March 5, 1861. Rep. Charles Francis Adams of Massachusetts and Seward had also laid claim to originating the idea behind the so-called Corwin Amendment. For a different view, see Daniel W. Crofts, *Lincoln and the Politics of Slavery: The Other Thirteenth Amendment and the Struggle to Save the Union* (Chapel Hill: University of North Carolina Press, 2016).

58. Lincoln said specifically, "In any law upon this subject ought not all the safeguards of liberty known in civilized and humane jurisprudence to be introduced, so that a free man be not in any case surrendered as a slave?" AL, First Inaugural Address, March 4, 1861, *CW*, 4:264. Most historians either ignore or discount the impact of Lincoln's formulation of this personal liberty idea in the inaugural address. They also tend to downplay his fine distinctions over the need to acquiesce to the fugitive slave clause versus making pledges of actual support for the Fugitive Slave Law. For a more complete explanation about why these nuances matter, see James Oakes, *The Crooked Path to Abolition: Abraham Lincoln and the Antislavery Constitution* (New York: W. W. Norton, 2021).
59. Douglas L. Wilson, *Lincoln's Sword: The Presidency and the Power of Words* (New York: Knopf, 2006), 42–70.
60. AL, First Inaugural Address, March 4, 1861, *CW*, 4:271.
61. The story of Douglas holding Lincoln's hat first appeared in Murat Halstead's *Cincinnati Commercial* in mid-March 1861 and then quickly got reprinted across the North. A Democratic newspaper from Iowa, however, had a particularly cynical take on the episode: "It is said that Douglas held Lincoln's hat while the Inaugural was being read. If appearances may be trusted, the 'Little Giant' is holding his hat now while 'Abe' is fighting the not-give-an-inch men of his party." *North Iowa Times* (McGregor), April 3, 1861.
62. AL, First Inaugural Address, March 4, 1861, *CW*, 4:268.

CHAPTER 10: MAKE HASTE SLOWLY

1. AL, Second Inaugural Address, March 4, 1865, *CW*, 8:332–23.
2. Entry for July 3, 1861, in Orville H. Browning, *The Diary of Orville Hickman Browning*, ed. Theodore Calvin Pease and James G. Randall, 2 vols. (Springfield: Illinois State Historical Library, 1925), 1:476.
3. Entry for July 3, 1861, in Browning, *Diary*, 1:476.
4. Robert Anderson and John G. Foster, reports, February 28, 1861; Winfield Scott to William Seward, March 5, 1861; AL to Scott, March 9, 1861; Scott to AL, March 11 and 12, 1861; all in Lincoln Papers, LC.
5. AL to Seward [and others], March 15, 1861; and replies from all seven cabinet officers dated March 15 or March 16; all in Lincoln Papers, LC. See also David Herbert Donald, *Lincoln* (New York: Simon & Schuster, 1995), 285–88, which makes a different judgment about Lincoln's leadership strategy in this moment.
6. Stephen Hurlbut to AL, March 27, 1861, Lincoln Papers, LC.
7. AL, Memorandum on Fort Sumter, March 18 [?], 1861, *CW*, 4:288–89. This

document (not in Lincoln's handwriting) was discovered in the Gideon Welles Papers at the Library of Congress, with the heading: "Some considerations in favor of withdrawing the Troops from Fort Sumpter, by President Lincoln."

8. "Senate Extra Session," *New York Times*, March 29, 1861; Donald, *Lincoln*, 285–91; and James M. McPherson, *Tried by War: Abraham Lincoln as Commander in Chief* (New York: Penguin Press, 2008), 9–25.
9. Phillip Shaw Paludan, *The Presidency of Abraham Lincoln* (Lawrence: University Press of Kansas, 1995), 35–36.
10. Historians dispute the exact figures concerning Republican replacements by the Lincoln administration. See Harry J. Carman and Reinhard H. Luthin, *Lincoln and the Patronage* (Gloucester, MA: Peter Smith, 1964), 331; and Mark E. Neely, *The Union Divided: Party Conflict in the Civil War North* (Cambridge, MA: Harvard University Press, 2002), 7–36. For Lincoln's comments on "lessons," see AL to John Clayton, July 28, 1849, *CW*, 2:60.
11. Seward quoted in diary entry for March 10, 1861, Charles Francis Adams, Sr., Papers, Massachusetts Historical Society. See also AL to Seward, March 18, 1860, *CW*, 4:292–93; and Carl Schurz to Margarethe Schurz, March 28, 1860, in Schurz, *Intimate Letters of Carl Schurz, 1841–1869*, ed. Joseph Schafer (Madison: State Historical Society of Wisconsin, 1929), 252–53.
12. Diary entry for March 10, 1861, Adams Sr. Papers, Massachusetts Historical Society. Some historians, such as David Herbert Donald, believe it was Charles Sumner who made those remarks about Lincoln in conversation and that Adams was merely paraphrasing Sumner in his diary. Donald, *Lincoln*, 285.
13. Edwin Stanton to John Dix, March 16 and 19, 1861, quoted in Michael Burlingame, *Abraham Lincoln: A Life*, 2 vols. (2008; Knox College online edition), 2:103.
14. Winfield Scott to Simon Cameron, March 28, 1861, in *The War of the Rebellion: Official Records of the Union and Confederate Armies* (1894), ser. 1, vol. 1, chap. 1, Operations in Charleston Harbor, 200–201 (hereafter cited as *OR*).
15. Seward to AL, February 24, 1861, Special Collections, University of Rochester Library, Rochester, NY.
16. Seward to AL, April 1, 1861, *CW*, 4:317n.
17. Seward to AL, April 1, 1861, *CW*, 4:317n.
18. AL to Seward, April 1, 1861, *CW*, 4:316–17.
19. "Wanted—A Policy," *New York Times*, April 3, 1861.
20. For a defense of Seward's behavior, see Walter Stahr, *Seward: Lincoln's Indispensable Man* (New York: Simon & Schuster, 2012), 274–81.
21. Entry for July 3, 1861, in Browning, *Diary*, 1:476.
22. See AL's executive proclamations on April 15, 19, and 27, 1861, *CW*, 4:331–32, 338–39, 347.

23. Entry for April 1861, in Gorowski, *Diary*, 23.
24. The narrative for this important April 15, 1861, meeting on New York patronage derives from a combination of sources: Salmon Chase to AL, April 15, 1865, Lincoln Papers, LC; Henry M. Field, *The Life of David Dudley Field* (New York: Charles Scribner's Sons, 1898), 165–66; and Charles A. Dana, *Recollections of the Civil War* (New York: D. Appleton, 1898), 2–3. The *CW* editors provide a tentative date of April 15, 1861, for Lincoln's notes about the Field meeting and offer slightly different suggestions for decoding Lincoln's party abbreviations than I provided. These notes from Lincoln were also available only as copies, provided to his former aides John Nicolay and John Hay by Frederick Seward as they were preparing their multivolume Lincoln biography in the 1880s. See AL, Memorandum: New York Appointments, April 15, 1861, *CW*, 4:334, and pencil annotations on the actual copy in Lincoln Papers, LC. Last, Michael Burlingame argues for a much different interpretation of the meeting, one that focuses on possible bribes paid to Mary Lincoln. Burlingame, *Lincoln: A Life*, 2:265–66. For additional background, see Carman and Luthin, *Lincoln and Patronage*, 62–64.
25. "For Government or Against It!!!," *Philadelphia Inquirer*, April 15, 1861.
26. "Patriots and Partisans," *New York Times*, April 5, 1861.
27. "Senator Douglas on the Union" and "Senator Douglas at Chicago," *New York Times*, May 5, 1861. For the May 1 speech at Chicago, see "Senator Douglas' Speech," *Chicago Post*, reprinted in *Rock Island Argus*, May 6, 1861.
28. On May 3, 1861, the president issued an important follow-up to his April 15 militia proclamation, calling for over 42,000 volunteers at three-year terms and an expansion of the regular army and naval forces. After Congress returned in July, it authorized the reorganization of the military, and on July 22, 1861, it approved up to an additional 500,000 three-year volunteers. More reorganizations and expansions in force size followed during the rest of the conflict, and by the end of 1865, over two million men had served in the Federal military to help secure the suppression of the rebellion.
29. AL to Scott ("Private"), June 5, 1861, *CW*, 4:394. On Seward lobbying for Meigs, see Stahr, *Seward*, 299. For the appointments of Hurlbut and Pope and the mention of "Rosencrantz," see AL to Simon Cameron, June 14, 1861, *CW*, 4:407.
30. "Senator Douglas's Successor," *Chambersburg (PA) Valley Spirit*, June 19, 1861; and Robert W. Johannsen, *Stephen A. Douglas* (Urbana: University of Illinois Press, 1973), 870–72.
31. Isaac N. Morris on Lincoln and Douglas's "understanding" in 1861, quoted in entry for August 2, 1864, in Browning, *Diary*, 1:678.
32. Douglas's quotation is from his April 25, 1861, speech in Springfield, *New*

York Times, May 5, 1861. For Lincoln's statement on fugitive slaves, see AL, First Inaugural Address—Final Text, March 4, 1851, *CW*, 4:269.

33. Stephen Douglas to Virgil Hickox, May 10, 1861, reprinted in "Senator Douglas' Last Letter," *Lancaster (OH) Gazette*, August 29, 1861.

34. The first public mention of the runaways at Fortress Monroe as "contraband of war" occurred in "Carrying the War into Africa Sure Enough," *New York Herald*, May 31, 1861. See Butler to Winfield Scott, May 24, 1861, and Simon Cameron's reply, May 30, 1861, in *OR*, ser. 2, vol. 1, "Prisoners of War, etc.: Military Treatment of Captured and Fugitive Slaves." For a discussion of how Butler applied the international laws of war to what had previously been considered a matter of domestic rendition policy, see James Oakes, *Freedom National: The Destruction of Slavery in the United States, 1861–1865* (New York: W. W. Norton, 2013), 84–105.

35. Charles Sumner to Joshua Giddings, April 28, 1861, and Giddings to Sumner, April 30, 1861, in George Julian, *Life of Joshua R. Giddings* (Chicago: A. C. McClurg, 1892), 385.

36. Browning sent Lincoln letters on April 18, 22, and 30, 1861, noting only that "if my letters are troublesome, you can easily throw them in the fire without reading." Lincoln Papers, LC.

37. Diary entry for May 7, 1861, in John Hay, *Inside Lincoln's White House: The Complete Civil War Diary of John Hay*, ed. Michael Burlingame and John R. Turner Ettlinger (Carbondale: Southern Illinois University Press, 1997), 19. Hamilton, who lived to the age of one hundred, read a paper to the president in early May, outlining how to win the war with Black support, which Lincoln reportedly received with "much interest." Hamilton, *Reminiscences of James A. Hamilton* (New York: Charles Scribner, 1869), 477–80.

38. Diary entry for May 7, 1861, in Hay, *Inside Lincoln's White House*, 20; and Nicolay memorandum, May 7, 1861, in John G. Nicolay, *With Lincoln in the White House: Letters, Memoranda, and Other Writings of John G. Nicolay, 1860–1865*, ed. Michael Burlingame (Carbondale: Southern Illinois University Press, 2000), 41. Lincoln was not soliciting input here so much as testing out his phrasing. Nicolay noted in his memo that the president said he "had about made up his mind, though he should still think further about it."

39. Lincoln used the phrase "disturbing element" to describe slavery on multiple occasions in the 1858 contest, such as during the debate at Quincy, October 13, *CW*, 3:256.

40. Diary entry for May 7, 1861, in Hay, *Inside Lincoln's White House*, 19–20; and Nicolay memorandum, May 7, 1861, in Nicolay, *With Lincoln*, 41. But Nicolay and Hay omitted the May 7 meeting from *Abraham Lincoln: A History*, 10 vols. (New York: Century, 1890). Most historians have since either down-

played or ignored the revealing episode. For more detail on the preparation of the special message, see Douglas L. Wilson, *Lincoln's Sword: The Presidency and the Power of Words* (New York: Knopf, 2006), 71–104.

41. Seward to Frances Seward, May 17 and June 5, 1861, in Frederick W. Seward, *Seward at Washington: As Senator and Secretary of State: A Memoir of His Life with Selections from His Letters, 1846–1861* (New York: Derby & Miller, 1891), 575, 590.
42. AL, Message to Congress, Second Printed Draft with Changes in Lincoln's Hand [June or July 1861], Lincoln Papers, LC.
43. AL, Message to Congress in Special Session, July 4, 1861, *CW*, 4:421–26. For Lincoln's original inaugural draft, see AL, First Inaugural Address—First Edition and Revisions, March 4, 1861, *CW*, 4:249–61.
44. For this critical section of the message, see AL, Message to Congress in Special Session, July 4, 1861, *CW*, 4:426–38. "Anecdote of the President," *Chicago Tribune*, July 15, 1861, reprinted Defrees's unsigned "Indiana" column from the *Cincinnati Commercial.* See also Burlingame, *Lincoln: A Life*, 2:2503n, and Wilson, *Lincoln's Sword*, 86–91.
45. AL, Message to Congress in Special Session, July 4, 1861, *CW*, 4:440; *Ex parte Merryman*, 17 F. Cas. 144 (C.C.D. Md. 1861).
46. AL, Message to Congress in Special Session, July 4, 1861, *CW*, 4:441.
47. AL, Reply to Baltimore Convention, April 22, 1861, *CW*, 4:341.
48. Diary entry for May 3, 1861, in Hay, *Inside Lincoln's White House*, 17.
49. Entry for July 8, 1861, in Browning, *Diary*, 1:478.
50. AL to Chase ("Private"), July 18, 1861, *CW*, 4:452; AL to Seward, August 20, 1861, *CW*, 4:494; AL to Cameron, July 16, 1861, *CWS*, 83.
51. Jesse Dubois to AL, April 6, 1861, Lincoln Papers, LC.
52. Nicolay to David Davis, January 5, 1862, in Nicolay, *With Lincoln*, 65–66. See also Henry Clay Whitney to William Herndon, June 23, 1887, in Douglas L. Wilson and Rodney O. Davis, eds., *Herndon's Informants: Letters, Interviews, and Statements About Abraham Lincoln* (Urbana: University of Illinois Press, 2020), 616–20.
53. Modern historians usually attribute this line about the troops being "green alike" to Lincoln, but that seems to be a mistake. The Lincoln attribution appears to have begun with T. Harry Williams, *Lincoln and His Generals* (New York: Knopf, 1952), 21. But McDowell's testimony before the Joint Committee on the Conduct of the War used the passive voice and never identified Lincoln as the source. From the context of the transcript, it appears clear that the speaker pressuring McDowell was Winfield Scott, during a conversation where the general-in-chief was reiterating the orders to the nervous field commander ("I wanted very much a little time; all of us wanted it. We did not have

a bit of it. The answer was: "You are green, it is true; but they are green, also; you are all green alike.") *Report of the Joint Committee on the Conduct of the War. Part II: Bull Run–Ball's Bluff* (Washington, DC: Government Printing Office, 1863), 38.

54. AL, Memorandum of Military Policy Suggested by the Bull Run Defeat, July 23–27, 1861, *CW*, 4:457–58.
55. Oakes, *Freedom National*, 128–31.
56. Oakes, *Freedom National*, 106–44.
57. Frank Blair's reports to his brother (which the cabinet officer dutifully shared with Lincoln) got increasingly agitated over August and September. Frank P. Blair, Jr., to Montgomery Blair, August 8, 15, and September 1, 1862, Lincoln Papers, LC; "Proclamation," *Missouri Democrat* (St. Louis), August 31, 1861, 2:2.
58. AL to John Frémont ("Private & confidential"), September 2, 1861, *CW*, 4:506.
59. Lincoln's version of the late-night meeting is recounted in diary entry for December 9, 1863, in Hay, *Inside Lincoln's White House*, 123. Jessie Benton Frémont's version from 1891 is in Frémont, *The Letters of Jessie Benton Frémont*, ed. Pamela Herr and Mary Lee Spence (Urbana: University of Illinois Press, 1993), 265–66.
60. Diary entry for December 9, 1863, in Hay, *Inside Lincoln's White House*, 123.
61. Burlingame, *Lincoln: A Life*, 2:2601–11.
62. Ward Hill Lamon to AL, August 17, 1861, Lincoln Papers, LC.
63. Orville Browning to AL, August 19, 1861, Lincoln Papers, LC.
64. Browning to AL, September 11, 17, 1861, Lincoln Papers, LC.
65. AL to Browning ("Private & confidential"), September 22, 1861, *CW*, 4:531–33; Browning to AL, September 30, 1861, Lincoln Papers, LC. Hurlbut did not end up resigning but continued to serve in the U.S. military (though not without controversy) until 1865.
66. Frederick Douglass, "Cast Off the Mill-Stone," *Douglass' Monthly*, September 1861; Carl Schurz to Frederick Althaus, October 11, 1861, in Schurz, *Intimate Letters of Carl Schurz*, 255.
67. Harry C. Blair and Rebecca Tarshis, *Colonel Edward D. Baker: Lincoln's Constant Ally* (Portland: Oregon Historical Society, 1960).
68. Herndon to Lyman Trumbull, November 20, 1861, in Herndon, *Herndon on Lincoln: Letters*, ed. Douglas L. Wilson and Rodney O. Davis (Urbana: University of Illinois Press, 2016), 19.
69. Entries for October 1 and 22, 1861, in Edward Bates, *The Diary of Edward Bates, 1859–1866*, ed. Howard K. Beale (Washington, DC: Government Printing Office, 1933), 196, 199.
70. AL to Oliver Morton, September 29, 1861, *CW*, 4:541.

71. AL to John McClernand, November 10, 1861, *CW*, 5:20.
72. Diary entry [c. November 1860], in Hay, *Inside Lincoln's White House*, 30.
73. Diary entry for November 13, 1861, in Hay, *Inside Lincoln's White House*, 32.
74. AL, Annual Message to Congress, December 3, 1861, *CW*, 5:51.
75. See Bruce Tap, *Over Lincoln's Shoulder: The Committee on the Conduct of the War* (Lawrence: University Press of Kansas, 1998).
76. AL to Ambrose Burnside, December 26, 1861, *CWSS*, 39.
77. George McClellan to Mary Ellen McClellan, November 17, 1861, in McClellan, *The Civil War Papers of George B. McClellan: Selected Correspondence, 1860–1865*, ed. Stephen W. Sears (New York: Ticknor & Fields, 1989), 135.
78. Entry for December 31, 1861, in Bates, *Diary*, 218–19.
79. David Hunter to AL, December 21, 1861, Lincoln Papers, LC; AL to Hunter, December 31, 1861, *CW*, 5:84–85. For Hunter's embittered assessment of Lincoln, see Chase's diary entry for October 11, 1862, in *Sixth Report of Historical Manuscripts Commission: With Diary and Correspondence of Salmon P. Chase*, vol. 2 of *Annual Report of the American Historical Association for the Year 1902* (Washington, DC: Government Printing Office, 1903), 105.
80. AL to George McClellan, January 1, 1862, *CW*, 5:88.
81. AL to Henry Halleck and Don Buell, December 31, 1862, *CW*, 5:84; AL to Halleck and Buell, January 7, 1862, *CW*, 5:92; Halleck to AL, *CW*, 5:92n; AL to McClellan, January 9, 1862, *CW*, 5:94; Irvin McDowell meeting notes, January 10, 1862, excerpted in William Swinton, *Campaigns of the Army of the Potomac* (New York: Richardson, 1866), 79–80.
82. McDowell meeting notes for January 10, 11, and 12, 1862, in Swinton, *Campaigns*, 79–84.
83. Quoted in Stahr, *Seward*, 325.
84. McDowell meeting notes for January 13, 1862, in Swinton, *Campaigns*, 84–85; AL to Buell, January 13, 1862, *CW*, 5:98–99.
85. Diary entry [c. March 1862], in Hay, *Inside Lincoln's White House*, 35; AL, President's General War Order No. 1, January 27, 1862, *CW*, 5:111–12.
86. Diary entry [c. March 1862], in Hay, *Inside Lincoln's White House*, 36.
87. Francis Pierpont to AL, March 14, 1861, Lincoln Papers, LC. The name is also spelled *Pierpoint* and sometimes *Peirpont*.
88. AL to Pierpoint, *CW*, 5:166.
89. The president met with General Irvin McDowell on April 20, 1862, at Aquia Creek, spent a full week at Fortress Monroe from May 5 to 12, 1862, and finally met again with McDowell, this time in Fredericksburg, on May 23, 1862. See Tom Wheeler, *Mr. Lincoln's T-Mails: How Abraham Lincoln Used the Telegraph to Win the Civil War* (New York: HarperCollins, 2006).

90. For a different view on Lincoln's motivations in seeking out Scott's counsel, see James M. McPherson, *Tried by War: Abraham Lincoln as Commander in Chief* (New York: Penguin, 2008), 97–98.
91. "The President at West Point," *New York Times*, June 26, 1862. See also Anthony J. Czarnecki, "Mr. Lincoln's Secret Visit to West Point: The Sesquicentennial of a Military Mission," *New York History* 93 (Winter 2012): 5–51.
92. Scott to AL, June 24, 1862, Lincoln Papers, LC.
93. Czarnecki, "Secret Visit," 16–35. See also "The President at West Point," *New York Times*, June 26, 1862, and the account from the *New York Express* reprinted in G. W. Richards, *Lives of Gens. Halleck and Pope* (Philadelphia: J. Magee, 1862), 30–31.
94. William Johnson was identified in newspapers only by first name, race, and job description. One of the telegrams from Stanton is now part of Lincoln's papers; see Edwin Stanton to Samuel Sloan, June 25, 1862, Lincoln Papers, LC.
95. The *CW* editors used the *New York Times* for the text of these remarks (which they uncharacteristically misdated), but a more accurate transcript seems available in the *New York Express*, as it was reprinted in Richards, *Lives of Halleck and Pope*, 30–31. See AL, Remarks at Jersey City, New Jersey, June 24 [*sic*], 1862, *CW*, 5:284. The *Express* also explicitly identified Joseph Howard as one of the correspondents who had rushed up from the city to travel with Lincoln on his return from West Point.
96. AL, Remarks at Jersey City, New Jersey, June 24 [*sic*], 1862, *CW*, 5:284.

CHAPTER 11: BRINK OF DESTRUCTION

1. "President Lincoln and Gen. Pope at West Point," *Detroit Free Press*, June 25, 1862.
2. John Pope, *The Military Memoirs of General John Pope*, ed. Peter Cozzens and Robert I. Girardi (Chapel Hill: University of North Carolina Press, 1998), 114–18.
3. Winfield Scott to AL, June 24, 1862, Lincoln Papers, LC.
4. George McClellan to Edwin Stanton, June 28, 1862, *CW*, 5:290n–291n.
5. AL to McClellan, June 28, 1862, *CW*, 5:289–90; AL to Seward, June 28, 1862, *CW*, 5:291–92. For more analysis of the underappreciated role of wartime governors, see Stephen D. Engle, *Gathering to Save a Nation: Lincoln and the Union's War Governors* (Chapel Hill: University of North Carolina Press, 2016).

6. AL, Call for Troops, June 30, 1862, *CW*, 5:294n. See also Engle, *Gathering*, 184–85.
7. See Matthew Pinsker, *Lincoln's Sanctuary: Abraham Lincoln and the Soldiers' Home* (New York: Oxford University Press, 2003).
8. Pinsker, *Lincoln's Sanctuary*, 34–35.
9. AL, Call for Troops, June 30, 1862, *CW*, 5:293–94; AL, Call for 300,000 Volunteers, July 1, 1862, *CW*, 5:296–97; AL to Edwin Morgan, July 2, 1862, *CW*, 5:302.
10. AL to Seward, June 28, 1862, *CW*, 5:292; entry for July 1, 1862, in Orville H. Browning, *The Diary of Orville Hickman Browning*, ed. Theodore Calvin Pease and James G. Randall, 2 vols. (Springfield: Illinois State Historical Library, 1925), 1:555.
11. Entry for July 1, 1862, in Browning, *Diary*, 1; 555.
12. See Leonard P. Curry, *Blueprint for Modern America: Non-Military Legislation of the First Civil War Congress* (Nashville: Vanderbilt University Press, 1968); Heather Cox Richardson, *The Greatest Nation on Earth: Republican Economic Policies During the Civil War* (Cambridge, MA: Harvard University Press, 1998); and Fergus M. Bordewich, *Congress at War: How Republican Reformers Fought the Civil War, Defied Lincoln, Ended Slavery, and Remade America* (New York: Penguin Random House, 2020).
13. AL to Union Governors, July 3, 1862, *CW*, 5:304; "The President and the Wounded," *New-York Tribune*, July 8, 1862.
14. Diary entry for July 5, 1862, in John Dahlgren, *Memoir of John A. Dahlgren, Rear-Admiral United States Navy*, ed. Madeleine Vinton Dahlgren (Boston: James R. Osgood, 1882), 375, quoted in Stephen W. Sears, *George B. McClellan: The Young Napoleon* (New York: Ticknor & Fields, 1988), 227; John G. Nicolay to Therena Bates, July 13, 1862, in Nicolay, *With Lincoln in the White House: Letters, Memoranda, and Other Writings of John G. Nicolay, 1860–1865*, ed. Michael Burlingame (Carbondale: Southern Illinois University Press, 2000), 85.
15. AL, Order Making Henry W. Halleck General-in-Chief, July 11, 1862, *CW*, 5:312–13; AL, Appeal to Border State Representatives, July 12, 1862, *CW*, 5:317–19.
16. Entry for July 1, 1862, in Browning, *Diary*, 1:555. See also James Oakes, *Freedom National: The Destruction of Slavery in the United States, 1861–1865* (New York: W. W. Norton, 2013), 224–55; and Eric Foner, *The Fiery Trial: Abraham Lincoln and American Slavery* (New York: W. W. Norton, 2011), 206–47.
17. Gideon Welles to Mary Ann Welles, July 13, 1862, Welles Papers, LC. Welles kept a diary, but after the outbreak of the war, he suspended his daily writing efforts, then restarted them in August 1862. Nonetheless, at some point much

later, he added a recollection of the July 13 carriage discussion where he claimed that Lincoln unveiled his emancipation plans. This has since become a popular story about the origins of emancipation, but it seems far likelier that on that date Lincoln was talking with Seward and Welles about confiscation. Gideon Welles, *The Civil War Diary of Gideon Welles, Lincoln's Secretary of the Navy*, ed. William E. Gienapp and Erica L. Gienapp (Urbana: University of Illinois Press, 2014), 3–4. For an analysis of other popular but dubious recollected accounts of the origins of Lincoln's emancipation policy, see Matthew Pinsker, "Lincoln's Summer of Emancipation," in *Lincoln and Freedom: Slavery, Emancipation, and the Thirteenth Amendment*, ed. Harold Holzer and Sarah Vaughn Gabbard (Carbondale: Southern Illinois University Press, 2007), 79–99.

18. AL to the Senate and House of Representatives, July 17, 1862, *CW*, 5:328.
19. Entry for July 15, 1862, in Browning, *Diary*, 1: 559-60; AL to the Senate and House of Representatives, July 17, 1862, *CW*, 5: 328–31; AL to Solomon Foot, July 15, 1862, *CW*, 5:326.
20. William Pitt Fessenden to Hamilton Fish, July 15, 1862, quoted in Michael Burlingame, *Abraham Lincoln: A Life*, 2 vols. (2008; Knox College online edition), 2:2986–87.
21. George W. Julian recollection, in *Reminiscences of Abraham Lincoln by Distinguished Men of His Time*, ed. Allen Thorndike Rice (New York: North American Publishing, 1886), 57–58.
22. *An Act to Suppress Insurrection, to Punish Treason and Rebellion, to Seize and Confiscate the Property of Rebels, and for Other Purposes*, U.S. Congress, July 17, 1862, 589–92. Lincoln's comment about motivating "misguided men" was part of his original draft veto message, though he edited it out of the final version. AL to the Senate and House of Representatives, July 17, 1862, *CW*, 5:330n.
23. During the previous week, Lincoln had signaled his plans for aiding gradual abolition in the border states by preparing a draft resolution for congressional consideration. AL to the Senate and House of Representatives, July 14, 1862, *CW*, 5:324–25; AL, Emancipation Proclamation—First Draft [July 22, 1862], *CW*, 5:336–37.
24. An Act to Suppress Insurrection, to Punish Treason and Rebellion, . . . July 17, 1862, usually identified as the Second Confiscation Act (the first having been adopted on August 6, 1861).
25. John Hay to Mary Jay, July 20, 1862, in Hay, *At Lincoln's Side: John Hay's Civil War Correspondence and Civil War Writings*, ed. Michael Burlingame (Carbondale: Southern Illinois University Press, 2000), 23; Pinsker, "Summer of Emancipation," 92–96.
26. Entry for July 21, 1862, in Salmon P. Chase, *Inside Lincoln's Cabinet: The Civil*

War Diaries of Salmon P. Chase*, ed. David Donald (New York: Longmans, Green, 1954), 95–97.

27. Diary entry for July 22, 1862, in Chase, *Inside Lincoln's Cabinet*, 97–100. See also Burlingame, *Lincoln: A Life*, 2:2995–3000.
28. The original source for the story that Seward's suggestion was the only one that "stuck" was painter Francis B. Carpenter, who claimed in his memoir that Lincoln had told him in 1864 that Seward's arguments were the reason that he delayed the emancipation announcement. F. B. Carpenter, *The Inner Life of Abraham Lincoln: Six Months at the White House* (1866; reprint Lincoln: University of Nebraska Press, 1995), 20–24.
29. AL, Proclamation of the Act to Suppress Insurrection, July 25, 1862, *CW*, 5:341–42.
30. Entry for July 21, 1862, in Browning, *Diary*, 1:561–62.
31. Entry for November 15, 1862, in Bemis diary, George Bemis Papers, Massachusetts Historical Society.
32. Entry for July 24, 1862, in Browning, *Diary*, 1:562–63.
33. The *CW* editors confused this antislavery General Phelps (John W., from Vermont), who was managing contrabands at a camp near New Orleans, with the proslavery General Phelps (John S., from Missouri), who was serving as the military governor of neighboring Arkansas (and later also Louisiana). See AL to Reverdy Johnson, July 26, 1862, *CW*, 5:343n.
34. Reverdy Johnson to AL, July 16, 1862, Lincoln Papers, LC. Lincoln made this copy in his own hand (with some pencil additions provided in brackets), apparently because Johnson's handwriting was so indecipherable.
35. AL to Johnson ("Private"), July 26, 1862, *CW*, 5:342–43; entry for July 26, 1862, in Browning, *Diary*, 1:564.
36. AL to Cuthbert Bullitt ("Private"), July 28, 1862, *CW*, 5:344–46.
37. AL to August Belmont, July 31, 1862, *CW*, 5:350–51.
38. James Sloan Gibbons, "We Are Coming, Father Abraham," *New York Evening Post*, August 16, 1862.
39. See Mark E. Neely, Jr., *The Fate of Liberty: Abraham Lincoln and Civil Liberties* (New York: Oxford University Press, 1991).
40. "News from Washington: A Great War Meeting Held at the Capitol," *New York Times*, August 7, 1862.
41. Diary entry for August 6, 1862, in Chase, *Inside Lincoln's Cabinet*, 110.
42. AL, Address to Union Meeting at Washington, August 6, 1862, *CW*, 5:358–59.
43. Entries for November 27, 1860, and August 10, 1862, in Benjamin Brown French, *Witness to the Young Republic: A Yankee's Journal, 1828–1870*, ed. Donald B. Cole and John J. McDonough (Hanover, NH: University Press of New England, 1989), 336–37 and 405.

44. See the example from John W. Forney, "Plans and Practices of the Breckinridge Democrats," *Philadelphia Press*, reprinted in *Buffalo Commercial*, August 1, 1862.
45. Lincoln's uncharacteristic comments about the "Eternal niggar" were reported by Sergeant Lucien Waters in a contemporary letter to his brother (which also included a memorable sketch of the president seated on the ground outside the White House); it is quoted in Elizabeth Brown Pryor, *Six Encounters with Lincoln: A President Confronts Democracy and Its Demons* (New York: Penguin, 2017), 119–52.
46. Leonard Swett to Laura Swett, August 10, 1862, in David Davis Family Papers, ALPLM. See also Leonard Swett to AL, August 9, 1862, PAL, for a good example of Swett's urgent lobbying over patronage during what turned out to be his final day in Washington that summer. Pennsylvania newspaperman Alexander K. McClure called Swett the one figure "most trusted by Abraham Lincoln." McClure, *Abraham Lincoln and Men of War-Times: Some Personal Recollections of War and Politics During the Lincoln Administration*, 4th ed. (Philadelphia: Times Publishing, 1892), 463.
47. Michael Burlingame, "A Tub to the Whale: Lincoln's 1862 Colonization Speech to African Americans & the 'Lullaby Thesis,'" *Lincoln Lore* no. 1940 (Winter 2023): 3–10. Burlingame is the first historian to identify James Clephane as the stenographer for Lincoln's colonization meeting.
48. AL, Address on Colonization, August 14, 1862, *CW*, 5:370–75. See also Kate Masur, "The African American Delegation to Abraham Lincoln: A Reappraisal," *Civil War History* 56 (June 2010): 117–44.
49. "The President and His Speeches," *Douglass' Monthly*, September 1862.
50. "The President and His Speeches," *Douglass' Monthly*, September 1862.
51. Horace Greeley, "The Prayer of the Twenty Millions," *New-York Tribune*, August 20, 1862.
52. "A Letter from the President," (Washington, DC) *National Intelligencer*, August 23, 1862. Editor James C. Welling also silently corrected Lincoln's misspelling of "Greely." That summer the *Tribune* and the *Intelligencer* had been engaged in a persistent argument over whether or how the president should "enforce" the revised confiscation statute. "The President at the Bar," *National Intelligencer*, August 22, 1862.
53. AL to Horace Greeley, August 22, 1862, *CW*, 5:388–89.
54. Clement Vallandigham, Address, May 8, 1862, in Vallandigham, *Speeches, Arguments, Addresses and Letters of Clement L. Vallandigham* (New York: J. Walter, 1864), 365; Adam I. P. Smith, *No Party Now: Politics in the Civil War North* (New York: Oxford University Press, 2006), 49–57.
55. James C. Welling in Rice, *Reminiscences*, 519–57.

56. AL to Horace Greeley, August 22, 1862, *CW*, 5:389.
57. Lincoln's public letter to Greeley had no real precedents in presidential campaign communication; only George Washington's 1796 Farewell Address (issued in October to help Vice President John Adams's campaign) and Buchanan's grumpy August 1860 blast against Stephen Douglas were somewhat comparable examples of such an innovative presidential use of partisan newspapers for electioneering purposes. Douglas L. Wilson, *Lincoln's Sword: The Presidency and the Power of Words* (New York: Knopf, 2006), 148–60.
58. Thurlow Weed to Seward, August 23, 1862, Lincoln Papers, LC.
59. Diary entries for September 1 and 5, 1862, in John Hay, *Inside Lincoln's White House: The Complete Civil War Diary of John Hay*, ed. Michael Burlingame and John R. Turner Ettlinger (Carbondale: Southern Illinois University Press, 1997), 38.
60. AL, Preliminary Emancipation Proclamation, September 22, 1862, *CW*, 5:433–36.
61. Entry for September 22, 1862, in Welles, *Civil War Diary*, 54.
62. AL, Proclamation Suspending the Writ of Habeas Corpus, September 24, 1862, *CW*, 5:436–37.
63. Diary entry for September 24, 1862, in Hay, *Inside Lincoln's White House*, 40–41.
64. Diary entry for September 24, 1862, in Hay, *Inside Lincoln's White House*, 41.
65. William Seward to Fanny Seward, September 24, 1862, quoted in Walter Stahr, *Seward: Lincoln's Indispensable Man* (New York: Simon & Schuster, 2012), 347.
66. AL, Reply to Serenade, September 24, 1862, *CW*, 5:438–39; AL to Hannibal Hamlin ("Strictly Private"), September 28, 1862, *CW*, 5:444.
67. Robert Smith to Richard Yates, October 13, 1862 [enclosed in Yates to AL, October 17, 1862], and David Davis to AL, October 14, 1862, Lincoln Papers, LC. For Yates's urgency, see Yates to AL, October 13, 1862, PAL (enclosing the Yates telegram to General [James] Tuttle, October 14, 1862), and Stanton to Tuttle, October 13, 1862, *OR* (1894), ser. 3, vol. 2, 663. See also Chandra Manning, *Troubled Refuge: Struggling for Freedom in the Civil War* (New York: Knopf, 2016), 112–13.
68. Carl Schurz to AL, November 8, 1862, Lincoln Papers, LC. According to John Hay, Schurz was "a wonderful man" and "eloquent Teuton," who was "bold, quick brilliant and reckless." Diary entry for April 25, 1861, in Hay, *Inside Lincoln's White House*, 13–14.
69. AL to Schurz, November 10, 1862, *CW*, 5:493–94; Hay to John Nicolay, October 28, 1862, in Hay, *At Lincoln's Side*, 27.
70. AL to William Morrison, November 5, 1862, *CW*, 5:486.

71. Quoted in James M. McPherson, *Tried by War: Abraham Lincoln as Commander in Chief* (New York: Penguin Press, 2008), 6–7.
72. Schurz to AL, November 20, 1862, Lincoln Papers, LC.
73. AL to Schurz, November 24, 1862, *CW*, 5:509–10.
74. AL to George Robertson, November 20, 1862, *CW*, 5:502.
75. AL to Robertson, November 26, 1862, *CW*, 5:512. See also Roy P. Basler, "'Beef! Beef! Beef!' Lincoln and Judge Robertson," *Abraham Lincoln Quarterly* 6 (1951): 400–7.
76. Browning dismissed Lincoln's package as a "hallucination" that "would require at least four years to have adopted as he proposes." Entry for December 1, 1862, in Browning, *Diary*, 1:591.
77. AL, Annual Message to Congress, December 1, 1862, *CW*, 5:530.
78. AL to Schurz, November 24, 1862, *CW*, 5:510.
79. Entry for December 16, 1862, in Browning, *Diary*, 1:596–98. See also David Herbert Donald, *Lincoln* (New York: Simon & Schuster, 1995), 401–6; and Doris Kearns Goodwin, *Team of Rivals: The Political Genius of Abraham Lincoln* (New York: Simon & Schuster, 2005), 486–95.
80. Entry for November 29, 1862, in Browning, *Diary*, 1:588–89.
81. Entry for December 16, 1862, in Browning, *Diary*, 1:597–98.
82. Entry for December 17, 1862, in Browning, *Diary*, 1:598–99; Republican Senators to AL, December 17, 1862, Lincoln Papers, LC.
83. Browning was ostensibly escorting a would-be biographer to meet with the president, but Lincoln was "in no mood" for such discussions. The editors of *The Lincoln Log* (formerly Lincoln Day-By-Day) mistakenly place the Browning session "late in the evening," but the diary makes clear that the Illinois senator met with Lincoln before he engaged at seven p.m. with the committee from the Republican senatorial caucus. Entry for December 18, 1862, in Browning, *Diary*, 1:599–600; and entry for December 18, 1862, in *Lincoln Log: A Daily Chronology of the Life of Abraham Lincoln*, thelincolnlog.org.
84. Entries for December 18 and 19, 1862, in Browning, *Diary*, 1:599–602.
85. [Henry] R[aymond], "The Cabinet Crisis," *New York Times*, December 22, 1862, 1:1–3.
86. Diary entry for October 30, 1863, in Hay, *Inside Lincoln's White House*, 104–5.
87. Quoted in entry for December 19, 1862, in Edward Bates, *The Diary of Edward Bates, 1859–1866*, ed. Howard K. Beale (Washington, DC: Government Printing Office, 1933), 269.
88. Quoted in Bates, *Diary*, 270.
89. Entry for December 22, 1862, in Browning, *Diary*, 1:602–3.
90. Entry for December 20, 1862, in Welles, *Civil War Diary*, 100–2; extract

dated December 22, 1862, in John A. Dahlgren diary, John G. Nicolay Papers, LC.

91. Entry for December 20, 1862, in Welles, *Civil War Diary*, 104; AL to Seward and Chase, December 20, 1862, *CW*, 6:12.
92. Entry for December 22, 1862, in Browning, *Diary*, 1:603–4. Browning was disappointed in Lincoln and added another harsh passage of criticism about him, including a phrase that read in part, "He is not equal to the . . . ," but most of the words have been crossed out by an unknown person, and the editors of Browning's diary were unable to reconstruct these critical fragments of the senator's closing critique of the cabinet crisis.
93. Entry for December 20, 1862, in Bates, *Diary*, 271.
94. Entry for December 22, 1862, in Dahlgren diary, Nicolay Papers, LC.
95. Entry for December 24, 1862, in Browning, *Diary*, 1:605.
96. Entry for December 20, 1862, in Bates, *Diary*, 270.
97. AL to Ambrose Burnside, December 30, 1862, *CW*, 6:22.
98. Entry for December 30, 1862, in Bates, *Diary*, 271–72.
99. AL to Halleck, January 1, 1863, *CW*, 6:31–33. See also McPherson, *Tried by War*, 147–49. The detail about the second meeting with Burnside comes directly from Browning, *Diary*, 1:608. The Lincoln-Halleck relationship never fully recovered from this revealing New Year's Day confrontation. The president had originally praised Halleck in private as "wholly for the service," his greatest form of compliment, but by 1864 he was dismissing the respected military leader to John Hay as having "nerve and pluck all gone" and offering little more service to him than that of "a first-rate clerk." Diary entries for September 1, 1862, and April 28, 1864, in Hay, *Inside Lincoln's White House*, 37, 191–92. By March 1864, the president had demoted Halleck to army chief of staff to make room for Grant as the Federal army's final general-in-chief of the war.
100. AL, Emancipation Proclamation, January 1, 1863, *CW*, 6:28–31. For the origins of the final sentence, see Burrus M. Carnahan, *Act of Justice: Lincoln's Emancipation Proclamation and the Law of War* (Lexington: University Press of Kentucky, 2007).
101. AL, Reply to Emancipation Memorial, September 13, 1862, *CW*, 5:420.
102. Entry for January 2, 1863, in Browning, *Diary*, 1:609.
103. For a good descriptive account of the Emancipation Day ceremonies at Beaufort, South Carolina, in 1863 (also called Port Royal), see Stephen V. Ash, *Firebrand of Liberty: The Story of Two Black Regiments That Changed the Course of the Civil War* (New York: W. W. Norton, 2008), 13–30. For background on the wartime occupation of the Sea Islands, see Willie Lee Rose, *Rehearsal for Reconstruction: The Port Royal Experiment* (Indianapolis: Bobbs-

Merrill, 1964). To understand how the diverse participants at Beaufort embodied the complex evolution of emancipation policy, see, especially, James Oakes, *Freedom National: The Destruction of Slavery in the United States, 1861–1865* (New York: W. W. Norton, 2013), and Manisha Sinha, *The Slave's Cause: A History of Abolition* (New Haven, CT: Yale University Press, 2016). Although neither Oakes nor Sinha includes the Beaufort ceremony in their magisterial studies, this story elegantly testifies to the power of their revisionist interpretations.

104. There are multiple eyewitness accounts of Emancipation Day 1863 in Beaufort. See "Emancipation Day in South Carolina," *Frank Leslie's Illustrated Newspaper*, January 24, 1863, 276; Thomas Wentworth Higginson, "Leaves from an Officer's Journal," *Atlantic Monthly*, December 1864; Charlotte L. Forten, "A Social Experiment: The Port Royal Journal of Charlotte L. Forten, 1862–1863," ed. Ray Allen Billington, *Journal of Negro History* 35 (July 1950): 233–64; and Elizabeth Ware Pearson, *Letters from Port Royal, 1862–1868* (Boston: W. B. Clarke, 1906), 131–32.

CHAPTER 12: PARTISAN IN CHIEF

1. Edward Rosewater letter, September 18, 1862, in Victor Rosewater, "Lincoln in Emancipation Days," *St. Nicholas* 65 (February 1937), 12.
2. [William Newman], "Lincoln's Dream; Or, There's a Good Time Coming," *Frank Leslie's Illustrated Newspaper*, February 14, 1863, 336. Rosewater did confuse some details from the image in his recollection of the scene; see Rosewater, "Lincoln in Emancipation Days," 13.
3. Entry for December 31, 1862, in Orville H. Browning, *The Diary of Orville Hickman Browning*, ed. Theodore Calvin Pease and James G. Randall, 2 vols. (Springfield: Illinois State Historical Library, 1925), 1:606–7.
4. Entry for January 19, 1863, in Browning, *Diary*, 1:616.
5. AL to John McClernand ("better not make this letter public"), January 8, 1863, *CW*, 6:48–49.
6. Entry for January 9, 1863, in Browning, *Diary*, 1:611–12.
7. Entry for January 10, 1863, in Gideon Welles, *The Civil War Diary of Gideon Welles, Lincoln's Secretary of the Navy*, ed. William E. Gienapp and Erica L. Gienapp (Urbana: University of Illinois Press, 2014), 121.
8. AL to John Dix ("Private & confidential"), January 14, 1863, *CW*, 6:56; John Dix to AL, January 15, 1863, Lincoln Papers, LC.
9. AL to McClernand, January 22, 1863, *CW*, 6:70.
10. AL to Samuel Curtis, January 2, 5, and 10, 1863, *CW*, 6:33, 36–37 and 52;

Curtis to AL, January 31, 1863, Lincoln Papers, LC. See also AL to Curtis, June 8, 1863, *CW*, 6:253; AL quoted by James Taussig in *Missouri Democrat*, June 9, 1863, in *Recollected Words of Abraham Lincoln*, ed. Don E. Fehrenbacher and Virginia Fehrenbacher (Stanford, CA: Stanford University Press, 1996), 443. See also Dennis K. Boman, *Lincoln's Resolute Unionist: Hamilton Gamble, Dred Scott Dissenter and Missouri's Civil War Governor* (Baton Rouge: Louisiana State University Press, 2006), 187–225.

11. Burnside quoted in "Extracts from the Journal of Henry J. Raymond," *Scribner's Monthly* 19 (March 1880): 707.
12. Raymond diary entry for January 24, 1863, in "Extracts," *Scribner's*, 705.
13. AL to Joseph Hooker [delivered in person], January 26, 1863, *CW*, 6:78–79; see also editorial note, 79n; and James M. McPherson, *Tried by War: Abraham Lincoln as Commander in Chief* (New York: Penguin Press, 2008), 162–65.
14. Sharpe's BMI operation essentially pioneered what is now called all-source intelligence. See Edwin C. Fishel, *The Secret War for the Union: The Untold Story of Military Intelligence in the Civil War* (Boston: Houghton Mifflin, 1996); and Peter G. Tsouras, *George H. Sharpe and the Creation of American Military Intelligence in the Civil War* (Philadelphia: Casemate, 2018).
15. For details on the schedule of the 1862–63 midterms, see Jamie L. Carson, Jeffery A. Jenkins, David W. Rohde, and Mark A. Souva, "The Impact of National Tides and District-Level Effects on Electoral Outcomes: The U.S. Congressional Elections of 1862–63," *American Journal of Political Science* 45 (October 2001): 887–98.
16. [John G. Nicolay], "Democratic War Pledges," *Washington Daily Morning Chronicle*, November 12, 1862, in Nicolay, *With Lincoln in the White House: Letters, Memoranda, and Other Writings of John G. Nicolay, 1860–1865*, ed. Michael Burlingame (Carbondale: Southern Illinois University Press, 2000), 91–92.
17. Entry for February 10, 1863, in Welles, *Civil War Diary*, 137; AL to Thurlow Weed, February 19, 1863, *CW*, 6:112. See also Thurlow Weed, *Life of Thurlow Weed*, ed. Harriet A. Weed (Boston, 1883–84), 2:434–35; and Weed to AL, March 8, 1863, Lincoln Papers, LC.
18. Weed to AL, March 8, 1863, Lincoln Papers, LC.
19. AL to Henry Winter Davis, March 18, 1863, *CW*, 6:140–41; Davis to AL, March 20, 1863, Lincoln Papers, LC.
20. Elihu Washburne to AL, April 9, 1863, Lincoln Papers, LC.
21. John Nicolay to Therena Bates, January 11, 1863, in Nicolay, *With Lincoln*, 102–3.
22. Nicolay, *With Lincoln*, 103.
23. Robert E. Lee to Mary Lee, April 19, 1863, Papers of the Lee Family, Stratford

Hall, VA. See also Stephen W. Sears, *Gettysburg* (Boston: Houghton Mifflin, 2004), 1–17.

24. AL to Joseph Hooker, "Cypher," June 10, 1863, *CW*, 6:257; AL to Hooker ("Private"), June 16, 1863, *CW*, 6:281.
25. "The Rebel Invasion: Our Harrisburg Correspondence," *New York Herald*, June 18, 1863; "The Democratic Convention" and "Movements of the Rebel Army," *Philadelphia Inquirer*, June 18, 1863. See also Allen C. Guelzo, *Gettysburg: The Last Invasion* (New York: Knopf, 2013), 99–114.
26. AL to Mary Lincoln, June 16, 1863, *CW*, 6:283; AL to Joel Parker, June 30, 1863, *CW*, 6:311.
27. [Samuel Wilkeson], "Details from Our Special Correspondent," *New York Times*, July 6, 1863, 1:4–6.
28. AL to Henry Halleck, July 6, 1863, *CW*, 6:318.
29. AL to Halleck [forwarded to George Meade], July 7, 1863, *CW*, 6:319; Halleck to Meade, July 8, 1863, *CW*, 6:319n.
30. AL, Response to a Serenade, July 7, 1863, *CW*, 6:319.
31. For more details on Hamlin's special mission to Meade's camp (which some scholars question), see Gabor S. Boritt, "'Unfinished Work': Lincoln, Meade, and Gettysburg," in *Lincoln's Generals*, ed. Gabor S. Boritt (New York: Oxford University Press, 1994), 81–120; and John Hay, *Inside Lincoln's White House: The Complete Civil War Diary of John Hay*, ed. Michael Burlingame and John R. Turner Ettlinger (Carbondale: Southern Illinois University Press, 1997), 303n–304n. For what he perceived as Hamlin's "strange" patronage request, see entry for July 8, 1863, in Welles, *Civil War Diary*, 244.
32. Halleck to Meade, July 14, 1863, and Meade to Halleck, July 14, 1863, both in Lincoln Papers, LC; AL to Meade ("never sent, or signed"), July 14, 1863, *CW*, 6:327–28.
33. Diary entry for July 14 and 15, 1863, in Hay, *Inside Lincoln's White House*, 62–63; entry for July 14, 1863, in Welles, *Civil War Diary*, 246–48; Oliver Otis Howard to AL ("Unofficial"), July 18, 1863, *CW*, 6:341n; AL to Howard, July 21, 1863, *CW*, 6:341.
34. See David M. Silver, *Lincoln's Supreme Court* (1956; reprint Urbana: University of Illinois Press, 1998); Brian McGinty, *Lincoln and the Court* (Cambridge, MA: Harvard University Press, 2008); and Mark E. Neely, Jr., *Lincoln and the Democrats: The Politics of Opposition in the Civil War* (New York: Cambridge University Press, 2017).
35. James M. McPherson, *Battle Cry of Freedom: The Civil War Era* (New York: Oxford University Press, 1988), 609–11.
36. "The Scourged Back," *Independent*, May 28, 1863; "The Dumb Witness" and "The Scourged Back," *Liberator*, June 12 and 19, 1863; [Vincent Colyer],

"A Typical Negro," *Harper's Weekly*, July 4, 1863. Note that the *Harper's* article contains errors, most notably calling the newly recruited Black soldier by the name Gordon. The *New-York Tribune* later interviewed the man and claimed his real name was Peter and that he was French speaking; see "Poor Peter," *New-York Tribune*, December 3, 1863. See also David Silkenat, "'A Typical Negro': Gordon, Peter, Vincent Colyer, and the Story Behind Slavery's Most Famous Photograph," *American Nineteenth Century History* 15 (2014): 169–86.

37. AL, Autobiography Written for John L. Scripps [c. June, 1860], *CW*, 4:62; entry for July 24, 1862, in Browning, *Diary*, 1:562.
38. AL to Ulysses S. Grant, August 9, 1863, *CW*, 6:374.
39. John Hay to John Nicolay, August 7, 1863, in Hay, *At Lincoln's Side: John Hay's Civil War Correspondence and Civil War Writings*, ed. Michael Burlingame (Carbondale: Southern Illinois University Press, 2000), 49. See also AL to Nathaniel Banks, August 5, 1863, *CW*, 6:364–66; AL to Horatio Seymour, August 7, 1863, *CW*, 6:369–70; and entry for August 7, 1863, in Edward Bates, *The Diary of Edward Bates, 1859–1866*, ed. Howard K. Beale (Washington, DC: Government Printing Office, 1933), 302.
40. Charles A. Dana, *Recollections of the Civil War: With the Leaders at Washington and in the Field in the Sixties* (New York: D. Appleton, 1913), 171, 174.
41. Frederick Douglass to George Stearns, August 12, 1863, Historical Society of Pennsylvania; and Douglass, "Our Work Is Not Done," Speech to American Anti-Slavery Society, December 30, 1863. Douglass told audiences shortly afterward that he was impressed by how Lincoln treated him. "I felt big there," he said. See also James Oakes, *The Radical and the Republican: Frederick Douglass, Abraham Lincoln, and the Triumph of Antislavery Politics* (New York: W. W. Norton, 2007), 209–19.
42. Diary entry for August 31, 1863, in Salmon P. Chase, *Inside Lincoln's Cabinet: The Civil War Diaries of Salmon P. Chase*, ed. David Donald (New York: Longmans, Green, 1954), 181; AL to Chase, September 2, 1863, *CW*, 6:428–29. This unfinished letter to Chase appears to have been drafted but not sent.
43. Entry for August 22, 1863, in Welles, *Civil War Diary*, 280–83.
44. James Conkling to AL, August 14 and 21, 1863, Lincoln Papers, LC; AL to Conkling, August 20, 1863, *CW*, 6:399; William Herndon to AL, August 29, 1863, Lincoln Papers, LC.
45. Robert Smith to Elihu Washburne, March 29, 1863, Lincoln Papers, LC. See also Arthur C. Cole, *The Era of the Civil War, 1848 to 1870* (Springfield: Illinois Centennial Commission, 1919), 296–307; Jennifer L. Weber, *Copperheads: The Rise and Fall of Lincoln's Opponents in the North* (New York: Oxford University Press, 2006).

46. Douglas L. Wilson, *Lincoln's Sword: The Presidency and the Power of Words* (New York: Knopf, 2006), 182–88.
47. Lincoln sent the letter to James Conkling but then updated it with a key passage on politics; AL to Conkling, August 26, 1863; and AL to Conkling, August 31, 1863, *CW*, 6:406–10, 423. For the special reading instructions, see AL to Conkling ("Private"), August 27, 1863, *CW*, 6:414. See also Allen C. Guelzo, "Defending Emancipation: Abraham Lincoln and the Conkling Letter, 1863," *Civil War History* 48 (December 2002): 313–37.
48. AL to Conkling, August 31, 1863, *CW*, 6:406–10. In a passage that he ultimately deleted, Lincoln also referred to slavery as the nation's great "disturbing element," the phraseology he had used with Nicolay and Hay in their private May 1861 meeting (see chapter 10). He also planned to emphasize how important it was to discourage political violence: "This war is an appeal, by you, from the ballot to the sword, and a great object with me has been to teach the futility of such appeal—to teach that what is decided by the ballot, can not be reversed by the sword—to teach that there can be no successful appeal from a fair election, but to the next election." This was a reference to his earlier Cooper Union speech in 1860 and a point that he returned to later after his reelection in 1864. AL, Fragment, *CW*, 6:440–41.
49. AL to Workingmen of Manchester, January 19, 1863, *CW*, 6:63–65; AL to Workingmen of London, February 2, 1863, *CW*, 6:88–89; AL to Erastus Corning and others, June 12, 1863, *CW*, 6:260–69; AL to Matthew Birchard and others, June 29, 1863, *CW*, 6:300–6.
50. "Mr. Lincoln's Letters," *Chicago Tribune*, September 3, 1863, 2:1.
51. "The Great Gathering at Springfield," *Chicago Tribune*, September 7, 1863; Richard Yates to editors, *Chicago Tribune*, September 10, 1863.
52. William Eliot to Charles Sumner, September 4, 1863, enclosed with Sumner to AL, September 8, 1863, Lincoln Papers, LC. AL to Henry Blow and others, May 15, 1863, *CW*, 6:218; Hay memorandum, September 30, 1863, in Hay, *At Lincoln's Side*, 60.
53. Diary entry for September 29, 1863, in Hay, *Inside Lincoln's White House*, 88–89.
54. Hay memorandum, September 30, 1863, in Hay, *At Lincoln's Side*, 60; diary entry for September 30, 1863, in Hay, *Inside Lincoln's White House*, 89–90.
55. Entries for May 10 and 30, 1863, in Bates, *Diary*, 291, 294.
56. "Judge Blair's Speech," *New York Times*, October 17, 1863.
57. Thaddeus Stevens to Salmon Chase, October 8, 1863, in Chase, *Correspondence, April 1863–1864*, vol. 4 of *The Salmon P. Chase Papers*, ed. John Niven (Kent, OH: Kent State University Press, 1997), 166n; Chase to Edward Mans-

field, October 18, 1863, in Chase, *Correspondence*, 154; entry for October 20, 1863, in Bates, *Diary*, 311; Chase to Horace Greeley, October 31, 1863, in Chase, *Correspondence*, 162.

58. Diary entries for August 13 and November 22, 1863, in Hay, *Inside Lincoln's White House*, 73, 116.

59. Jonathan W. White, *Emancipation, the Union Army, and the Reelection of Abraham Lincoln* (Baton Rouge: Louisiana State University Press, 2014), 13–37. See also diary entry for October 12, 1863, in Adam Gurowski, *Diary from November 18, 1862, to October 18, 1863* (New York: Carleton, 1864), 343–44.

60. Elihu Washburne to AL, October 12, 1863, Lincoln Papers; and AL to Washburne ("Private & Confidential"), October 26, 1863, *CW*, 6:541.

61. Herman Belz, "The Etheridge Conspiracy of 1863: A Projected Conservative Coup," *Journal of Southern History* 36 (November 1970): 549–67; AL to James Grimes, October 29, 1863; AL to Hannibal Hamlin ("Let it [all] be done quietly"), October 29, 1863; AL to Zachariah Chandler, October 30, 1863; AL to Jacob Collamer, October 30, 1863; and AL to Frederick F. Low ("Cypher"), October 30, 1863, all in *CW*, 6:546–50. See also Hay's description of Emerson Etheridge, the House clerk ("This crazy Tennessean"), and his plan for the attempted political coup, diary entry for October 29, 1863, in Hay, *Inside Lincoln's White House*, 102.

62. Diary entries for October 29 and November 12, 1863, in Hay, *Inside Lincoln's White House*, 103, 111.

63. Quoted in "From Washington," *Missouri Democrat* (St. Louis), November 26, 1863, 2:4. See also Martin P. Johnson, *Writing the Gettysburg Address* (Lawrence: University Press of Kansas, 2013), 68.

64. AL to Stanton, November 17, 1863, *CW*, 7:16.

65. Diary entry for November 18, 1863, in Hay, *Inside Lincoln's White House*, 111; "The Gettysburg Ceremonies," *Philadelphia Inquirer*, November 20, 1863.

66. Diary entry for November 18, 1863, in Hay, *Inside Lincoln's White House*, 111.

67. Diary entry for November 19, 1863, in Hay, *Inside Lincoln's White House*, 113; "Gettysburg 'Celebration': Our Great National Cemetery," *Philadelphia Inquirer*, November 20, 1863.

68. Diary entry for November 19, 1863, in Hay, *Inside Lincoln's White House*, 113; AL, Gettysburg Address [5 versions], November 17–19, 1863, *CW*, 7:17–23.

69. [Samuel Wilkeson], "Details from Our Special Correspondent," *New York Times*, July 6, 1863, 1:5. On July 4, 1861, Lincoln referred to the United States as "a constitutional republic, or a democracy—a government of the people, by the same people"; *CW*, 4:426. On January 26, 1830, in his "Second Reply to Hayne" speech, Daniel Webster said on the Senate floor: "It is, Sir, the people's Constitution, the people's government, made for the people, made by the peo-

ple, and answerable to the people." And on May 29, 1850, Theodore Parker first defined *democracy* at the New England Anti-Slavery Convention as "a government of all the people, by all the people, for all the people." Parker, *The Collected Works of Theodore Parker*, ed. Francis Power Cobbe (London: Trübner, 1863–71), 105. Parker later reiterated that definition in an 1858 sermon that Herndon claimed to have brought back for Lincoln to read after his trip to the East. See Garry Wills, *Lincoln at Gettysburg: The Words That Remade America* (New York: Simon & Schuster, 1992).

70. Samuel Wilkeson to Sydney Howard Gay, March 7, 1863, quoted in Chuck Raasch, *Imperfect Union: A Father's Search for His Son in the Aftermath of the Battle of Gettysburg* (Lanham, MD: Stackpole Books, 2016), 138.
71. Diary entry for November 2, 1863, in Hay, *Inside Lincoln's White House*, 107. But Wilkeson also told Hay that "a necessary condition" for Lincoln's reelection was "a reorganization of the cabinet." That did not sit well with the president's aide, who mocked Wilkeson for resembling "an elderly owl."
72. Zachariah Chandler to AL, November 15, 1863, Lincoln Papers, LC.
73. AL to Chandler, November 20, 1863, *CW*, 7:23–24; diary entry for November 20, 1863, in Hay, *Inside Lincoln's White House*, 114.
74. Diary entries for November 21 and December 9, 1863, in Hay, *Inside Lincoln's White House*, 115, 120–21.
75. Diary entry for December 9, 1863, in Hay, *Inside Lincoln's White House*, 121; Nicolay Memorandum, December 6, 1863, in Nicolay, *With Lincoln*, 120–21.
76. "Scenes at the Organization of the New House of Representatives," reprinted in *Xenia Sentinel*, December 22, 1863. See also Belz, "Etheridge Conspiracy," 549–67. Lovejoy died a just few months later from kidney disease in March 1864.
77. For an extended discussion of this point, see Elizabeth R. Varon, *Armies of Deliverance: A New History of the Civil War* (New York: Oxford University Press, 2019).
78. Diary entry for December 9, 1864, in Hay, *Inside Lincoln's White House*, 121–22.
79. Diary entry for December 9, 1864, in Hay, *Inside Lincoln's White House*, 121–24. See also Adam I. P. Smith, *No Party Now: Politics in the Civil War North* (New York: Oxford University Press, 2006), 67–84.
80. Diary entries for October 22, November 28, and December 9, 10, in Hay, *Inside Lincoln's White House*, 97, 119, 124, 126.
81. "Address of Miss Anna Dickinson," *National Republican*, January 18, 1864; Nicolay to Hay, January 18, 1864, in Nicolay, *With Lincoln*, 125. See also J. Matthew Gallman, *America's Joan of Arc: The Life of Anna Elizabeth Dickinson* (New York: Oxford University Press, 2006). The same week Lincoln earned

his endorsement from twenty-one-year-old Anna Dickinson, he also received a patronage request from fourteen-year-old Grace Bedell of New York, the girl who had written him during the 1860 campaign urging him to "let your whiskers grow." Claiming that the war had been challenging for her father's business, Bedell asked for a job as what people called then a "treasury girl," someone, usually a single woman, who copied official documents in Chase's department. Bedell's letter was apparently lost in government files and was not rediscovered until 2007 by researcher Karen Needles. See Grace Bedell to AL, January 14, 1864, National Archives, Washington, DC.

82. "The Mission of the War," *New-York Tribune*, January 14, 1864. Cooper Union, the experimental college in Manhattan, was also called Cooper Institute. Stanton's sister Catherine was Bayard Wilkeson's mother.
83. David Herbert Donald, *Lincoln* (New York: Simon & Schuster, 1995), 481–83.
84. On the Clay brothers, see James Larry Hood, "The Union and Slavery: Congressman Brutus J. Clay of the Bluegrass," *Register of the Kentucky Historical Society* 75 (1977): 214–21; and John Kuhn Bliemaier, "Cassius Marcellus Clay in St. Petersburg," *Register of the Kentucky Historical Society* 73 (1975): 263–87.
85. For background on the kidnapping ring at Cairo, see Chandra Manning, *Troubled Refuge: Struggling for Freedom in the Civil War* (New York: Knopf, 2016), 123–32. For Lincoln's comments, see AL, Endorsement, January 22, 1864, *CW*, 7:144.
86. AL, Endorsement, January 22, 1864, *CW*, 7:144. See also Discharges for Nine Soldiers and William Yocum signed by Brutus J. Clay, January 22, 1864, Gilder Lehrman Collection, New York, which includes Stanton's annotation "Yocum's card countermanded / EMS" and which is not in *CW*. Other exchanges are in *CW*, 7:167, 187, 254–57, and 389.
87. Bates to Seward, Seward to Stanton, and Stanton to Seward, all on March 24, 1864, Lincoln Papers, LC; AL to Stanton, March 18, 1864, *CW*, 7:254–57; Stanton to AL, March 19, 1864, Lincoln Papers, LC; AL to Stanton, April 8, 1864, *CWS*, 235; "Arrest of William Yocum," *National Intelligencer*, April 19, 1864, 2:6; AL to Senate, June 13, 1864, *CW*, 7:389.
88. Entry for March 28, 1864, in Bates, *Diary*, 352; Entry for April 3, 1864, in Browning, *Diary*, 1:665; AL to Albert Hodges, April 4, 1864, *CW*, 7:281–83.
89. AL to Hodges, April 4, 1864, *CW*, 7:281–83.
90. AL to Joseph Barrett, April 3, 1864, *CW*, 7:279–80; Joseph H. Barrett, *Life of Abraham Lincoln (of Illinois)* (Cincinnati: Moore, Wilstach, Keys, 1860); "The Presidential Canvass: Postponement Suggested," and "The Presidency," *New-York Tribune*, April 1, 1864, 2 and 4; Nicolay to Hay, April 1, 1864, in Nicolay, *With Lincoln*, 134.

91. "Lincoln to Hodges," *New-York Tribune*, April 29, 1864.
92. Nicolay to AL, March 30, 1864, Lincoln Papers, LC.
93. D. F. Murphy, *Proceedings of the National Union Convention Held in Baltimore, Md., June 7–8, 1864* (New York: Baker & Godwin, 1864), 7.
94. Murphy, *Proceedings*, 26.
95. Hay to Nicolay, June 6, 1864, in Hay, *At Lincoln's Side*, 84. Ever since, participants in their memoirs and scholars have debated how to interpret Lincoln's behavior in the ultimately catastrophic decision to dump Hannibal Hamlin for Andrew Johnson as the Unionist vice-presidential nominee. See Don E. Fehrenbacher, "The Making of a Myth: Lincoln and the Vice-Presidential Nomination of 1864," *Civil War History* 41 (1995): 273–90.
96. AL to Andrew Johnson ("Private"), September 11, 1863, *CW*, 6:446; Johnson to AL, September 17, 1864, Lincoln Papers, LC; Hans L. Trefousse, *Andrew Johnson: A Biography* (New York: W. W. Norton, 1989).
97. Ironically, modern scholars have been more inclined to follow the Democratic agenda than the Unionist example when it comes to using the term *Republican* during the wartime period. Conflating *Republican* and *Unionist*—or even sometimes leaving out *Unionist* from biographies or political narratives altogether—has been fairly common across historical scholarship for this period. For an important exception to this trend that grapples explicitly (albeit briefly) with Lincoln's role in building a Union party, see Michael F. Holt, *Political Parties and American Political Development from the Age of Jackson to the Age of Lincoln* (Baton Rouge: Louisiana State University Press, 1992), 323–54.

EPILOGUE

1. AL, Reply to Committee Notifying Lincoln of His Renomination, June 9, 1864, *CW*, 7:380; and AL, Reply to Delegation from National Union League, June 9, 1864, *CW*, 7:383–84.
2. AL, Reply to Committee, June 9, 1864, *CW*, 7:380; AL, Response to a Serenade by Ohio Delegation, June 9, 1864, *CW*, 7:384.
3. The dust-up between the president and the secretary concerned Chase's plans for filling a vacancy for assistant U.S. treasurer in New York over the objections of the state's U.S. senator, E. D. Morgan, who was also chairman of the National Union Committee. See diary entries for June 24–30, 1864, in Salmon P. Chase, *Inside Lincoln's Cabinet: The Civil War Diaries of Salmon P. Chase*, ed. David Donald (New York: Longmans, Green, 1954), 212–26. See also entry for June 30, 1864, in John Hay, *Inside Lincoln's White House: The Complete Civil War*

Diary of John Hay, ed. Michael Burlingame and John R. Turner Ettlinger (Carbondale: Southern Illinois University Press, 1997), 212–17.

4. Diary entry for June 30, 1864, in Hay, *Inside Lincoln's White House*, 217.
5. AL, Proclamation Concerning Reconstruction, July 8, 1864, *CW*, 7:433–34.
6. "Extracts from the Journal of Henry J. Raymond," *Scribner's Monthly* 19 (1880): 705.
7. AL to Whom It May Concern, July 18, 1864, *CW*, 7:451; Gregory A. Borchard, *Abraham Lincoln and Horace Greeley* (Carbondale: Southern Illinois University Press, 2011), 83–89.
8. AL to Abram Wakeman, July 25, 1864, *CW*, 7:461.
9. Diary entry [for June 17, 1864], in Hay, *Inside Lincoln's White House*, 208.
10. Frank Wolford to AL, July 30, 1864, Lincoln Papers, LC. Wolford in his letter did not mention the late Stephen Douglas by name, but his invocation of Douglas's famous quotation was revealing. See also AL, Parole and Discharge for Frank L. Wolford, July 17, 1864, *CW*, 7:446–47, 480. By that point, Wolford had been arrested and released multiple times since his original discharge in March 1864. See also Dan Lee, *Wolford's Cavalry: The Colonel, the War in the West, and the Emancipation Question in Kentucky* (Lincoln: University of Nebraska Press, 2016).
11. Wolford and another Democratic officer got arrested on Election Day, accused of promoting armed resistance at the polling places. In late November the reelected president wrote to Governor Thomas Bramlette of Kentucky confessing that he hoped to finally dispense with the Wolford problem "now that the *passion-exciting* subject of the election is past." AL to Bramlette, November 22, 1864, *CW*, 8:120. For Lincoln under enemy fire and the burning of Blair's home, see Matthew Pinsker, *Lincoln's Sanctuary: Abraham Lincoln and the Soldiers' Home* (New York: Oxford University Press, 2003), 127–45.
12. Entry for July 13, 1864, in Orville H. Browning, *The Diary of Orville Hickman Browning*, ed. Theodore Calvin Pease and James G. Randall, 2 vols. (Springfield: Illinois State Historical Library, 1925), 1:676. But in that same conversation, Bates admitted that he "still did not know how we were to do better than support Lincoln." Orville H. Browning to Edgar Cowan, September 6, 1864, quoted in Michael Burlingame, *The Inner World of Abraham Lincoln* (Champaign: University of Illinois Press, 1997), 351n.
13. Weed quoted in J. K. Herbert to Benjamin F. Butler, August 6, 1864, in Butler, *Private and Official Correspondence of Gen. Benjamin F. Butler: During the Period of the Civil War*, ed. Jessie Ames Marshall, 5 vols. (Privately published, 1917), 5:9.
14. AL to Ulysses S. Grant ("Cypher"), August 3, 1864, *CW*, 7:476. Grant's tough-sounding order about Sheridan went through Henry Halleck; see *CW*, 7:476n.

15. AL to William Rosecrans, August 10, 1863, *CW*, 6:377–78.
16. "President Lincoln Denounced by His Party—A Congressional Manifesto Against Him," *New York Herald*, August 6, 1864.
17. The critical August 18 meeting in New York, hosted by Mayor George Opdyke, included over two dozen radicals and party power brokers, including Benjamin Wade, Henry Winter Davis, Horace Greeley, David Dudley Field, Massachusetts governor John Andrew, and Senator Charles Sumner. See letters from J. K. Herbert to Benjamin F. Butler, August 4, August 6 (twice), August 11, August 27, and September 3, 1864, in Butler, *Correspondence*, 5:9–123. See Henry Winter Davis to Samuel F. DuPont, August 25, 1864, in DuPont, *Samuel Francis DuPont: A Selection from His Civil War Letters*, ed. John D. Hayes, 3 vols. (Ithaca, NY: Cornell University Press, 1969), 3:372–75. See also William Frank Zornow, *Lincoln and the Party Divided* (Norman: University of Oklahoma Press, 1954); and David E. Long, *The Jewel of Liberty: Abraham Lincoln's Re-Election and the End of Slavery* (1994; reprint New York: Da Capo Press, 1997).
18. Charles Robinson to AL, August 7, 1864, Lincoln Papers, LC; AL to Robinson [pencil draft], August 17, 1864, Lincoln Papers, LC; AL to Robinson [second draft], August 17, 1864, *CW*, 7:499–501. See also Alexander W. Randall to AL, August 22, 1864, Lincoln Papers, LC.
19. For alternative views on this episode, see David W. Blight, *Frederick Douglass: Prophet of Freedom* (New York: Simon & Schuster, 2018), 435–39; and James Oakes, *The Radical and the Republican: Frederick Douglass, Abraham Lincoln, and the Triumph of Antislavery Politics* (New York: W. W. Norton, 2007), 229–37.
20. Historians disagree over how to interpret Lincoln's unsent reply to Charles Robinson, but it is worth noting that the president received the original Robinson letter by hand delivery from Alexander Randall on August 16 and began his pencil draft the next day. On that day, August 17, he also sent one of his coded dispatches to General Grant, making clear that he was in a fighting mood: "I have seen your despatch expressing your unwillingness to break your hold where you are. Neither am I willing. Hold on with a bull-dog gripe, and chew & choke, as much as possible." AL to Grant ("Cypher"), August 17, 1864, *CW*, 7:499.
21. Frederick Douglass to Theodore Tilton, October 15, 1864, in Douglass, *The Life and Writings of Frederick Douglass*, ed. Philip S. Foner, 5 vols. (New York: International Publishers, 1952), 3:423–24; AL, Interview by Alexander W. Randall and Joseph T. Mills, August 19, 1864, *CW*, 7:506–8. See also Pinsker, *Lincoln's Sanctuary*, 157–62.
22. Thurlow Weed to William Seward, August 20, 1864 Lincoln Papers, LC; and

David Davis (Herndon interview), September 19, 1866; in Douglas L. Wilson and Rodney O. Davis, eds., *Herndon's Informants: Letters, Interviews, and Statements About Abraham Lincoln* (Urbana: University of Illinois Press, 2020), 346. Davis had been complaining about Lincoln for months. "Mr. Lincoln annoys me more than I can express," he had written in March, referring to the challenge from Salmon Chase, "by his persistence in letting things take their course, without effort or organization when a combined organization in the Treasury Dept. is in antagonism." Davis to William Orme, March 30, 1864, David Davis Papers, ALPLM; Henry Raymond to AL, August 22, 1864, Lincoln Papers, LC; and John Nicolay to Therena Bates, August 28, 1864, in Nicolay, *With Lincoln in the White House: Letters, Memoranda, and Other Writings of John G. Nicolay, 1860–1865*, ed. Michael Burlingame (Carbondale: Southern Illinois University Press, 2000), 153. See also Robert S. Eckley, *Lincoln's Forgotten Friend: Leonard Swett* (Carbondale: Southern Illinois University Press, 2012).

23. AL, Speech to 166th Ohio Regiment, August 22, 1864, *CW*, 7:512.
24. The original document in Lincoln's handwriting is [Memorandum on Probable Failure of Reelection], August 23, 1864, Lincoln Papers, LC. There is also a copy of the same document in John Hay's handwriting. See also AL, "Memorandum Concerning His Probable Failure of Reelection," August 23, 1864, *CW*, 7:514–15.
25. AL, Memorandum, August 23, 1864, Lincoln Papers, LC; entry for November 11, 1864, in Hay, *Inside Lincoln's White House*, 247–48.
26. Most historians interpret this document—usually called the "Blind Memorandum" or "Blind Memo"—differently than I do, emphasizing Lincoln's anxieties about his reelection and his cabinet's implicit support for his secret plan of cooperation with the president-elect. See James M. McPherson, *Battle Cry of Freedom: The Civil War Era* (New York: Oxford University Press, 1988), 770–71; and Doris Kearns Goodwin, *Team of Rivals: The Political Genius of Abraham Lincoln* (New York: Simon & Schuster, 2005), 647–48, as examples. For more detail on the challenges of interpreting this document, see Matthew Pinsker, "Seeing Lincoln's Blind Memorandum," in *Lincoln and Leadership: Military, Political and Religious Decision Making*, ed. Randall Miller (New York: Fordham University Press, 2012), 60–77.
27. AL to Raymond, August 24, 1864, *CW*, 7:517; Nicolay to Hay, August 25, 1864, in Nicolay, *With Lincoln*, 152.
28. Nicolay to Hay, August 25, 1864, and Nicolay to Therena Bates, August 28, 1864, both in Nicolay, *With Lincoln*, 152–53.
29. Remark about "real condition of affairs" quoted in "The President and the Wounded," *New-York Tribune*, July 8, 1862.

30. Stephen W. Sears, *George B. McClellan: The Young Napoleon* (New York: Ticknor & Fields, 1988), 371–86.
31. Lincoln considered breaking political custom by writing a public letter for a Union meeting in Buffalo, New York, but changed his mind. See AL to Isaac Schermerhorn, September 12, 1864, *CW*, 8:2. On McClellan's problems with his acceptance letter, see Sears, *McClellan*, 374–78.
32. Mary Lincoln to Abram Wakeman, September 23, [1864], in Todd Lincoln, *Mary Todd Lincoln: Her Life and Letters*, ed. Justin G. Turner and Linda Levitt Turner (New York: Knopf, 1972), 180–81. While discussing the various patronage issues, Todd Lincoln also blithely assured Wakeman that her husband was "almost a monomaniac on the subject of honesty." David Herbert Donald, *Lincoln* (New York: Simon & Schuster, 1995), 532–33.
33. Frederick Douglass to AL, August 29, 1864, Lincoln Papers, LC; Blight, *Frederick Douglass*, 422–23.
34. Douglass to Tilton, October 15, 1864, in Douglass, *Life and Writings*, 3:423–24; AL to Montgomery Blair, September 23, 1864, *CW*, 8:18; Long, *Jewel of Liberty*, 239–43.
35. J. K. Herbert to Benjamin Butler, September 26, 1864, in Butler, *Correspondence*, 5:167–68. Lincoln had earlier floated the idea of Chase replacing Taney when he pushed Chase out of the cabinet in June; diary entry for June 30, 1864, in Chase, *Inside Lincoln's Cabinet*, 224.
36. Nicolay sent the president a series of letters (October 10, 12, and 18, 1864) detailing the problems in Missouri and his mostly successful efforts to overcome them. Lincoln Papers, LC.
37. On polling 1860s style, see George Tuthill Borett, *Letters from Canada and the United States* (London: J. E. Adlard, 1865), 182. On Maryland abolition, see AL, Response to Serenade, October 19, 1864, *CW*, 8:52–53. For Lincoln's electoral card (which omitted the new state of Nevada by mistake), see AL, Estimated Electoral Vote, October 13, 1864, *CW*, 8:46.
38. Diary entry for November 8, 1864, in Hay, *Inside Lincoln's White House*, 243–46.
39. Diary entry for November 8, 1864, in Hay, *Inside Lincoln's White House*, 243–46.
40. Diary entry for November 8, 1864, in Hay, *Inside Lincoln's White House*, 245; diary entry for November 11, 1864, in Hay, *Inside Lincoln's White House*, 249.
41. AL, Response to a Serenade, November 8, 1864, *CW*, 8:96.
42. Diary entry for November 8, 1864, in Hay, *Inside Lincoln's White House*, 243–46.
43. Some occupied southern states, such as Louisiana and Tennessee, participated in the elections but their votes did not count. Analyzing the 1864 soldier vote

is also complicated; see Jonathan W. White, *Emancipation, the Union Army, and the Reelection of Abraham Lincoln* (Baton Rouge: Louisiana State University Press, 2014), 112–28. For the John Phillips story, see "Interesting Incident of Election Day," *Lancaster Evening Express*, November 12, 1864; F. W. Emmons to AL, November 9, 1864, Lincoln Papers, LC; and AL to John Phillips, November 21, 1864, *CW*, 8:118. Michael Burlingame notes that John Hay actually wrote Lincoln's thank-you note to Phillips.

44. AL, Response to a Serenade, November 10, 1864, *CW*, 8:100–101.
45. AL, Response to a Serenade, November 10, 1864, *CW*, 8:100–101.
46. AL, Response to a Serenade, November 10, 1864, *CW*, 8:101.
47. Diary entry for November 11, 1864, in Hay, *Inside Lincoln's White House*, 247–48.
48. Diary entry for November 11, 1864, in Hay, *Inside Lincoln's White House*, 247–48.
49. AL to Reverdy Johnson, July 26, 1862, *CW*, 5:342–43; diary entry for November 11, 1864, in Hay, *Inside Lincoln's White House*, 247–48. Edward Bates resigned from the administration the next month, but before he left Washington, he asked Hay for a copy of the August 23 memo. The existence of the document did not become public until 1878, when Gideon Welles mentioned it briefly in an article for *The Atlantic Monthly* that largely blamed the radicals for nearly losing the 1864 election. Hay was furious about that leak, concerned that he and Nicolay were getting scooped. "Do you understand Mr. Welles' reference to a 'Memorandum,' written by Lincoln in 1864 in anticipation of defeat, in [the] Atlantic?" he asked Nicolay sharply afterward. Eventually, Nicolay and Hay were the first to publish the text of the August 23 document in their multivolume biography of Lincoln that appeared in 1890. But it seems that Mark E. Neely, Jr., was the first historian to label Lincoln's mysterious action as the "Blind Memorandum," which he did in 1979 and 1982 in an important journal article and a popular encyclopedia entry. The term is slightly miscast—in bureaucratic parlance, a "blind" memo is one unsigned, not one unseen. Gideon Welles, "The Opposition to Lincoln in 1864," *Atlantic Monthly* 41 (March 1878): 367; John Hay to John Nicolay, February 27, 1878, in William Roscoe Thayer, *John Hay: American Statesman*, 2 vols. (New York: Harper & Bros., 1915), 2:21–22; John Nicolay and John Hay, *Abraham Lincoln: A History*, 10 vols. (New York: Century, 1890), 9:249–51; Mark E. Neely, Jr., "The Lincoln Theme Since Randall's Call: The Promises and Perils of Professionalism," *Journal of the Abraham Lincoln Association* 1 (1979): 18–19; and *The Abraham Lincoln Encyclopedia* (New York: McGraw-Hill, 1982), 32.
50. AL, Annual Message to Congress, December 6, 1864, *CW*, 8:138–53; and Horace Greeley to AL, July 7, 1864, Lincoln Papers, LC.

51. AL, Annual Message to Congress, December 6, 1864, *CW,* 8:148–49; and AL to William Sherman, December 26, 1864, *CW,* 8:181.
52. The recollection by House clerk Edward Barber, published in 1900, has been overlooked by other scholars. It has the usual challenges of any recollection, but it contains several assertions that can be corroborated. The actual tally sheet that Barber remembers as the key to the lobbying operation, however, apparently has never located. See Edward W. Barber, "The Story of Emancipation," *Historical Collections, Michigan Pioneer and Historical Society* 29 (1901): 583–84; and "Tells How Slaves of America Were Freed," *Tampa Tribune*, February 13, 1918.
53. Elizabeth Peabody to Horace Mann, Jr., [c. February 1865], in Arlin Turner, ed., "Elizabeth Peabody Visits Lincoln, February 1865," *New England Quarterly* 48 (March 1975): 119. See also Michael Vorenberg, *Final Freedom: The Civil War, the Abolition of Slavery, and the Thirteenth Amendment* (Cambridge: Cambridge University Press, 2001); and Leonard L. Richards, *Who Freed the Slaves? The Fight over the Thirteenth Amendment* (Chicago: University of Chicago Press, 2015).
54. John Forney to Andrew Johnson, January 27, 1865, in Johnson, *The Papers of Andrew Johnson*, ed. Leroy P. Graf (Knoxville: University of Tennessee Press, 1986), 7:439.
55. AL, Second Inaugural Address, March 4, 1865, *CW,* 8:332–33.
56. AL to Ulysses Grant ("Cypher"), April 7, 1865, *CW,* 8:392.
57. *Evening Star* (Washington, DC), April 11, 1865, 2:4.
58. AL, Last Public Address, April 11, 1865, *CW,* 8:399–405.
59. AL, Last Public Address, April 11, 1865, *CW,* 8:400–1.
60. AL, Last Public Address, April 11, 1865, *CW,* 8:402–3.
61. Diary entry for July 4, 1864, in Hay, *Inside Lincoln's White House*, 218.
62. AL, Last Public Address, April 11, 1865, *CW,* 8:404–5. I slightly rearranged these closing phrases while leaving Lincoln's meaning intact. For Lincoln's remarks from the River and Harbor Convention, see *St. Louis Missouri Republican*, July 12, 1847, PAL.
63. AL, Last Public Address, April 11, 1865, *CW,* 8:400, 402–4.
64. Salmon Chase to AL, April 12, 1865, in Chase, *Correspondence, 1865–1873*, vol. 5 of *The Salmon P. Chase Papers*, ed. John Niven (Kent, OH: Kent State University Press, 1998), 17–19.
65. Tradition holds that John Wilkes Booth was not only present outside the White House during the April 11, 1865, speech but allegedly said afterward, "That means nigger citizenship," and then began the final stages of his assassination conspiracy. But this widely repeated story came thirdhand in a historical novel published twenty years after the assassination by an author who claimed he had

heard it from attorney Frederick Stone, who had himself reportedly heard it from his client David Herrold, one of Booth's co-conspirators. See George Alfred Townsend, *Katy of Catoctin* (New York: D. Appleton, 1886), 490. A different version of Booth's reaction to Lincoln's April speech appeared in the testimony of Thomas T. Eckert during the Andrew Johnson House impeachment investigation in 1867; see *Impeachment of the President*, Report No. 7, 40th Cong., 1st Sess., 674 (1868). Eckert claimed that Booth wanted Lincoln shot that very night without mentioning the details of Black citizenship. Eckert said he got this information from Lewis Powell in 1865.

66. This revealing interview from February 16, 1864, transcribed by one of John Forney's reporters, has never been made part of *CW*, though it should be. See Joseph George, Jr., "Long-Neglected Lincoln Speech: An 1864 Preliminary," *Journal of the Abraham Lincoln Association* 16 (Summer 1995): 23–28.

INDEX

Page numbers beginning with 451 refer to notes.